USAGE AND ABUSAGE

A Guide to Good English

Some Works by Eric Partridge
Published in the United States

———

THREE MEN'S WAR
(*with R. H. Mottram and John Easton*)

SLANG TODAY AND YESTERDAY:
A History and a Study
(*Third edition, revised and enlarged*)

A DICTIONARY OF SLANG AND
UNCONVENTIONAL ENGLISH
(*Third edition, revised and enlarged*)

NAME THIS CHILD:
A Pleasant Dictionary of Christian Names
(*Third edition, revised and enlarged*)

THE WORLD OF WORDS:
An Introduction to Language in General and to
English and American in Particular
(*Third edition, revised*)

SHAKESPEARE'S BAWDY
A Study and a Glossary

JOURNEY TO THE EDGE OF MORNING
Books, Love, Life

USAGE AND ABUSAGE

A Guide to Good English

by

ERIC PARTRIDGE

Abusus non tollit usum

HARPER & BROTHERS PUBLISHERS

NEW YORK AND LONDON

USAGE AND ABUSAGE

B-Y

Personal book shop
2.49
11-2-49 h

PUBLISHER'S NOTE

Without attempting in any way to change the author's ideas or alter his standard of usage, both of which are those of an English student of the English language, an American editor, Professor W. Cabell Greet, has annotated this work with such comment on American usage as seemed useful for the reader.

Professor Greet's comments are set off by brackets [[thus]].

ACKNOWLEDGMENTS

Grateful acknowledgment is made to the following publishers for the courtesy of quoting from the works listed below:

D. Appleton-Century Company, Inc.
  ENGLISH COMPOSITION AND RHETORIC, by Alexander Bain
  MODERN ENGLISH IN THE MAKING, by G. H. McKnight and Bert Emsley
  ENGLISH WORDS AND THEIR BACKGROUND, by G. H. McKnight
  GROWTH AND STRUCTURE OF THE ENGLISH LANGUAGE, by Otto Jespersen

Jonathon Cape Ltd.:
  AMERICAN SPEECHES, by James Ramsay MacDonald

The Clarendon Press:
  DICTIONARY OF MODERN ENGLISH USAGE and THE SOCIETY FOR PURE ENGLISH TRACT, NUMBER XIV, by H. W. Fowler.
  LOGIC AND GRAMMAR and ON SOME DISPUTED POINTS IN ENGLISH GRAMMAR, by Otto Jespersen
  OXFORD BOOK OF ENGLISH PROSE, edited by Arthur Quiller-Couch
  ENGLISH IDIOMS, by Logan Pearsall Smith
  PREFACE TO THE OXFORD ENGLISH DICTIONARY, by Sir James Murray

The Thomas Y. Crowell Company:
  WORDS CONFUSED AND MISUSED, by Maurice H. Weseen

Doubleday, Doran & Company, Inc.:
  WHAT A WORD! by A. P. Herbert, copyright 1935, 1936, by Doubleday, Doran & Company, Inc.

E. P. Dutton & Co., Inc.:
  THE GROWTH OF ENGLISH, SHORT HISTORY OF ENGLISH and HISTORY OF MODERN COLLOQUIAL ENGLISH, by H. C. K. Wyld

Harcourt, Brace and Company, Inc.:
  SEVEN TYPES OF AMBIGUITY, by William Empson
  THE TYRANNY OF WORDS, by Stuart Chase

Harper & Brothers:
  SLINGS AND ARROWS, by David Lloyd George

Harvard University Press:
  ADDRESSES ON INTERNATIONAL SUBJECTS, by Elihu Root, reprinted by permission of the President and Fellows of Harvard College

D. C. Heath & Company:
  A GRAMMAR OF THE ENGLISH LANGUAGE and SYNTAX, by George O. Curme

Houghton Mifflin Company:
  MEIN KAMPF, by Adolf Hitler
  WORDS AND IDIOMS, by Logan Pearsall Smith

The Macmillan Company:
  PLEA FOR THE QUEEN'S ENGLISH, by Henry Alford
  MIND THE STOP, by G. V. Carey
  WORDS AND THEIR WAYS IN ENGLISH SPEECH, by James B. Greenaugh and George L. Kittredge
  PROGRESS IN LANGUAGE, by Otto Jespersen
  ELEMENTS OF LOGIC, by W. S. Jevons and D. J. Hill
  DICTIONARY OF CLICHES, by Eric Partridge

G. & C. Merriam Company:
  WEBSTER'S NEW INTERNATIONAL DICTIONARY OF THE ENGLISH LANGUAGE, Second Edition, 1934

Acknowledgments   x

Oxford University Press, N. Y.:
  THE PHILOSOPHY OF RHETORIC, by I. A. Richards
  CONCISE OXFORD DICTIONARY OF CURRENT ENGLISH, Third Edition, edited by
    H. W. Fowler and F. G. Fowler

Rand McNally & Company:
  A COMPREHENSIVE GUIDE TO GOOD ENGLISH, by George Phillip Krapp

Scott, Foresman and Company:
  AN INDEX TO ENGLISH, by P. G. Perrin

USAGE AND ABUSAGE

A Guide to Good English

ABBREVIATIONS USED IN THIS BOOK

adj., adjective
adv., adverb
ca. (*circa*), about
cf. (*confer*), compare
Con. O.D., The Concise Oxford Dictionary
e. g. (*exempli gratia*), for instance
esp., especially
fig., figuratively
ibid. (*ibidem*). the same
i.e. (*id est*), that is
lit., literally
n., noun
N.B. (*nota bene*) note well
O.E.D., The Oxford English Dictionary
op. cit. (*opus citatum*), the work cited
opp., opposed; opposite
q.v. (quod vide), which see
R.C., Roman Catholic
S.E., Standard English
S.P.E. Tract, Society for Pure English Tract
Times Lit. Sup., The Times (London) Literary Supplement
v., verb
v.i., verb intransitive
v.t., verb transitive
Webster's, Webster's New International Dictionary (2nd ed.)

USAGE AND ABUSAGE

A

a, 'a. The indefinite article is often introduced, though quite superfluously, in such sentences as: 'No more signal a defeat was ever inflicted' (quoted by Fowler). In 'He's the party as had a done it,' its use is merely illiterate and may be due to the difficulty of pronouncing the two d's. It may represent *have* in 'I would 'a done it' and in *had 'ave (q.v.)*. It occurs also in illiterate speech such as Cockney 'I arst you wot you was a-doin' of' (D. Sayers, 1933), and American Southern Mountain 'He's a-singin' a love song' (ballad). Cf. 'Father's gone a-hunting.' It can hardly be condemned when used for lyrical euphony in 'all ablowing and agrowing'.

a-, an- for 'not' or 'without' should be prefixed only to Greek stems, e.g. *anarchic.* 'Amoral' (says Fowler) 'being literary is inexcusable, and *non-moral* should be used instead.'

a for *an.* See AN.

A in titles. See TITLES OF BOOKS AND PERIODICALS.

a + noun + or two takes a plural verb. The formula merely obeys the general rule governing an example such as 'Either the head or the legs *are* injured'; thus: 'Another good yarn or two [i.e. two good yarns] *are* to be found in "The Moon Endureth".' Regarded in another way, *a good yarn or two* is synonymous with and tantamount to *several good yarns,* which obviously takes a verb in the plural.

Note that *a* + noun + *or so* must not be used as synonymous with *a* + noun + *or two. A pint or so = a pint or thereabouts = a pint (approximately).* It would take a singular verb. If, however, you permit yourself to murder a woman or so, you must write *a woman or so are nothing to me:* jocular, maybe; bad writing, certainly!

abdomen. See BELLY.

aberration is not a synonym of *absentmindedness,* as John G. Brandon makes it in *The Mail-Van Mystery* (ca. 1937), 'Once, in a moment of temporary aberration, Mr Dorgan drew a huge, hookbladed knife from a hidden sheath, felt its razor-like edge carefully with a black and calloused thumb, then returned it with every sign of satisfaction.'

abide ('can't abide him') is not strictly incorrect, but a low-class colloquialism. ⟦In American usage it may have homely or half-humorous quality.⟧

ability and **capacity.** *Ability* is a power to do something, or skill in doing it, whether the something be physical or intellectual. 'Here, promotion is by ability, not by birth'; 'He has outstanding ability as a surgeon—a writer—a pugilist . . .'. *Capacity,* apart from its physical sense ('power to receive or to contain': capacity of 1,000 gallons), means either 'power to absorb or learn knowledge as opposed to power-in-doing' or 'innate or native power as opposed to acquired power'. 'My capacity for mathematics is negligible.'

abjure, 'to renounce an oath', is very easily confused with *adjure,* 'to request earnestly, to charge a person under oath'. (*The Con. O.D.*)

-able and **-ible.** See '-IBLE and -ABLE'.

ablution is now intolerably pedantic for 'the act of washing one's hands and/or face'; and *perform one's ablutions* is but a sorry jest. *Ablution* should be reserved for its religious senses:

1. (General.) 'The washing of the body as a religious rite.'
2. (Anglican; Roman Catholic.) 'The washing of the chalice and paten after the celebration.'
3. (Roman Catholic.) 'The washing of the priest's hands before assuming the sacred vestments, and during the celebration.'
4. (R.C.) 'The wine and water used to rinse the chalice, and wash the fingers of the celebrant after communion.'
(Definitions: *The O.E.D.*)

abnormal; subnormal; supra-normal. Any departure from the *normal* (or usual or standard) is *abnormal.* To distinguish further: Any such departure

1

that is *below* the normal is *subnormal*; *above* the normal, *supra-normal*.

about should be avoided in such phrases as these: 'It is about 9 or 10 o'clock'; 'The boy is about 9 or 10 years old'; 'It happened about the 9th or 10th of October, 1939'. Correct thus:—'It is 9 or 10 o'clock' or 'It is about 9.30'; 'The boy is 9 or 10 years old' or 'The boy must be somewhere near 10 years old'; 'It happened on either the 9th or the 10th of October' or, less precisely, 'It happened about the 9th of June'. These examples might have been listed at WOOLLINESS.

above (adj.), common in business writing and reference works. Avoid it! 'The above facts' should be 'The preceding (or, foregoing) facts' or, better still, 'These (or, Those) facts'. 'The above statement' should be 'The foregoing statement' or 'The last statement' or 'This (or That) statement'. Especially to be condemned is 'The above subject': read 'This (or That) subject' or 'The matter already mentioned (or, referred to)'. *Above* (adv.), as in 'The matter mentioned above', has been grievously overworked.

above, misused for *more than*. 'Above a yard' and 'above three months, a year, etc.' are loose for 'more than a yard, three months, a year, etc.'

above and **over**; **below** and **beneath** and **under**. (Prepositions.) *Above* is 'vertically up from; on the top of, upon', as in 'Hell opens, and the heavens in vengeance crack above his head'; *over* is now more usual in this sense.—'Higher up a slope, nearer the summit of a mountain or the source of a river' (also, of time, 'earlier than'), as in 'Behind and above it the vale head rises into grandeur'.—'Literally higher than; rising beyond (the level or reach of)', as in 'The citadel of Corinth towering high above all the land'; hence of sounds, as in 'His voice was audible above the din'.— Figuratively, 'superior to', as in 'He is above mere mundane considerations'.— 'Higher in rank or position than; (set) in authority over', as in 'The conscience looks to a law above it'.—'In excess of, beyond; more than', as in 'But above all things, my brethren, swear not'.—'Surpassing in quality, amount, number; more than', as in 'Above a sixth part of the nation is crowded into provincial towns'.—'Besides', occurring in *over and*

above, as in 'Over and above his salary, he receives commission'. (*The O.E.D.*)

Over is 'higher up than', either of position or of motion within the space above, as in 'Flitting about like a petrel over those stormy isles'; hence (after *hang, lean, jut, project*, etc.) in relation to something beneath, as in 'The upper story projects over the street'. Also, fig., as in 'His speech was over the heads of his audience'. 'The spatial sense "above" passes into other notions: the literal notion is (*a*) combined with that of purpose or occupation, as in [to sit] *over the fire*, [to talk *over*] *a bowl, a glass*; (*b*) sunk in that of having something under treatment, observation, or consideration, as in *to watch* or *talk over*, and in *make merry over*.—In sense *on* or *upon*:—'On the upper or outer surface of', sometimes implying the notion of 'covering the surface of'; as in 'Over one arm is the lusty courser's rein', 'Sitting with his hat low down over his eyes', 'She had a net over her hair'. 'Upon', with verbs of motion, as in 'He threw a dressing gown over the recumbent man' and 'Let us draw a veil over this dismal spectacle'. 'Upon', or 'down upon', as an influence, as in 'A great change came over him at this point of his life'. 'Everywhere on' or 'here and there upon', as in 'Cottages scattered over the moor' and 'Over (or, all over) his face there spread a seraphic smile'; cf. the sense 'to and fro upon; all about; throughout', with reference to motion, as in 'The hunter crew wide straggling o'er the plain', 'We may range over Europe, from shore to shore', 'They travel all over the country', and the sense 'through every part of', occasionally with a connotation of examination or consideration, as in 'He went over my proofs for me'.—In sense 'above in amount, number, degree, authority, preference', as in 'This court has no jurisdiction over unnaturalized foreigners', 'It cost him over £50', 'A distance of over 500 yards', 'The preference given to him over English captains', 'He has no command over himself'.—The general sense of 'across', whether 'indicating motion that passes over (something) on the way to the other side; or sometimes expressing only the latter part of this, as in *falling* or *jumping over a precipice*',—e.g., 'The sun is peering over the roofs', 'She turned and spoke to him over her shoulder', 'The room looking over Nightingale Lane'; or indicating 'from side to side of' (a surface, a space), 'across; to the other side of' (a sea, a river), 'from end to end of; along', as in 'He fled over the plains', 'A free pass over this company's lines of railways', 'He passed over the Channel'; or (of position) 'on the other side of; across', as in 'The king over the water', 'Our neighbours over the way'.—Of time: 'during; all through', as in 'Extending over a century'; or 'repayment over a series of years'; or 'till the end of; for a period that includes', as in 'If we only live over to-day', 'If you stay over Wednesday'. (*The O.É.D.*)

'*Over* and *above* differ in that *over* implies vertically, while *above* may or may not. Thus, the entire second story of a building is *above*, but only a small part of it is directly *over*, one who stands *on* (*upon*) the ground floor. . . . *Over* and *above* agree in the idea of superiority but differ in the immediacy of reference. Thus, the rank of ambassador is *above* that of minister, but the British ambassador is not *over* the Chinese minister; he stands in that relation to his subordinates only. Similarly, *above* and *over* agree in the idea of excess, which *beyond* heightens by carrying with it the suggestion that the thing exceeded, itself goes far; as "One there is *above* all others well deserves the name of friend; His is love *beyond* a brother's"' (*Webster's*).

In general, *over* is opposed to *under*; *above* to *below* (or *beneath*).

Below, beneath; under:—*Beneath* covers a narrower field than *below*; it has the following senses:—(*a*) 'Directly down from, overhung or surmounted by; under', as in 'To sleep beneath the same roof', 'To walk beneath the moon', 'The boat lay beneath a tall cliff'; (*b*) 'immediately under, in contact with the under side of; covered by', as in 'The dust beneath your feet', 'to sit with one's hand beneath one's head', 'No wise man kicks the ladder from beneath him'; (*c*) 'farther from (the surface); concealed by; inside of or behind' (now usually *under*), as in 'His musical art lay beneath the surface', 'A woollen vest which sometimes had beneath it another fitting close to the skin'; (*d*) 'under, as overborne or overwhelmed by some pressure', fig. 'subject to; under the action, influence, control of', as in 'Bending beneath a heavy weight', 'Brisk goes the work beneath each busy hand', now generally *under*; (*e*) 'lower than, in rank, dignity, excellence, etc.' (now usually *below*), as in 'Beings above and

beneath us probably have no opinions at all'; (*f*) 'unbefitting the dignity of, undeserving of, lowering to', as in 'Beneath the attention of serious critics', 'It's beneath his notice', hence 'lower than (a standard of quantity or quality)', as in 'Copies always fall beneath their original', *below* being preferable. *The O.E.D.* thus summarizes the status and usefulness of *beneath*:—'In ordinary spoken English, *under* and *below* now cover the whole field (*below* tending naturally to overlap the territory of *under*), leaving *beneath* more or less as a literary and slightly archaic equivalent of both (in some senses), but especially of *under*. The only senses in which *beneath* is preferred' are (*f*) as in 'beneath contempt', and the fig. use of (*d*) as in 'to fall beneath the assaults of temptation'.

What then of *below*? Primarily it = (*a*) 'at a less elevation than, i.e. lower than', as in 'below the level of the ocean', 'He hit his opponent below the knee', *below stairs*, fig. in 'It is possible to be below flattery as well as above it'; hence (*b*) 'lower on a slope than, farther down a valley or a stream than', also 'nearer the (actual or considered) bottom of a room than',—as in 'Below the village, the valley opens into a broad flat meadow', *below-bridge, below the gangway* (in the House of Commons); (*c*) 'deeper than' (lit. and fig.), as in 'Water was found about three feet below the surface', 'Language has to be studied both below the surface and superficially'; (*d*) 'Directly beneath; under the canopy or covering of; underneath', in which sense *under* (or *beneath*) is preferable,—'Books lay on tables and below tables'; (*e*) of position in a graduated scale, e.g., that of a barometer, hence 'lower in amount, weight, degree, value, price, than', as in 'a rainfall below the average', also 'lower in quality or excellence than, i.e., inferior to in either of these respects', as in 'Well I know how far my performance is below excellence', 'One places Marlowe below Shakespeare', also fig. ('Lower in rank, station, dignity than') as in 'A man far below them in station', 'Unless he is sunk below a beast'; (*f*) 'Unbefitting, unworthy of, lowering to' (better *beneath*), as in 'Too far below contempt to be worth castigating'. (*The O.E.D.*)

To give, here, every sense of *under* would be to fall into inappropriate excess. Its senses fall into four main groups:—(I) 'Senses denoting position beneath or below something, so as to have it above or overhead, or to be covered by it', as in 'Under a broiling sun, they toiled manfully', 'under the waves', *under ground* (dead; *above ground*, alive), 'Under a friend's roof one feels safe', 'He put his head under the tap', 'Under the veil was a lovely face', 'under the American flag', *under water* (flooded), 'a letter addressed under cover to a third party', 'Under the rock where the fowls build they row their boat', 'Chance led him under an appletree'; (II) 'senses denoting subordination or subjection', as in 'Under the major was a captain', 'He thanked me that had, under God, given him and so many miserable creatures their lives', 'an office under government', 'The great communistic uprising under Wat Tyler in 1381', 'He would have lost his head under Caligula', 'Under the direction of amateurish clerks', 'He is under medical treatment', *under the plough* (arable), *under steam*, 'Sent under a strong guard to the Tower', *under an obligation*, 'The glass vessels intended to retain gases under pressure', 'Under the ban of Rome', 'He is under the impression that . . .'; (III) 'senses implying that one thing is covered by, or included in, another', as in 'The several types under which our Ladye was represented in England', 'Extreme vanity sometimes hides under the garb of ultra modesty', *under the name of* (by the name of), 'Many matters that would come under this head are trivial', 'The word is explained under *house*' (i.e., at *house*, not in a separate entry of its own), 'under the auspices of a great name', 'All things here are under a perpetual vicissitude and alteration', *under my hand and seal*, *under the provisions of the Act*; (IV) 'senses which imply falling below a certain standard or level', as in 'It is under his majesty', 'It was too great an honour for any man under a duke', 'The weight proved to be under 114,000 ounces', *under age* or *under 21*, 'Wheat was under three shillings a bushel', 'Barbarous orders to sink every ship under 100 tons', (of spirit) *under proof*, *under one's breath* (in a whisper, in a very low voice). (*The O.E.D.*)

Of the relationship of *below* to *under*, *Webster's New International* writes thus: '*Below* (opposed to *above*) applies to that which is anywhere in a lower plane than the object of reference; *under* (opposed to *over*), to that which is below in a rela-

tively vertical line; *under* sometimes implies actual covering; as, *below* sea level, the valley far below us; *under* a tree, *under* the bed; the Whirlpool Rapids are *below*, the Cave of the Winds is *under*, Niagara Falls; the whole visible landscape is *below*, but only a small portion of it *under*, an observer in a balloon. . . . In their figurative senses, *below* and *under* agree in expressing inferiority, but differ (like *above* and *over*) in the immediacy of the relation expressed; thus, one officer may be *below* another in rank, without being *under* him in immediate subordination. Similarly, in reference to deficiency, *below* is commonly used in general, *under* in more specific, relations; as, a gold dollar weighing *under* 25.8 grains is *below* the standard; *under* six years of age, *below* the average.'

abridgement. See Précis writing, par. 2.

abroad is sometimes misused adjectively for *apart*. 'Please, 'm,' said the maid after a breakage, 'it come abroad in me 'and.' [[Not current in the U.S.A.]]

abrogate. See arrogate.

absence, misused for *abstinence,* as in 'Many schools allow absence from games to those who dislike them', essay script, in an examination, June, 1939. [[This sentence with *absence* or with *abstinence* would not occur in American English. The idea might be expressed thus: 'Many schools excuse from sports students who don't like athletics.' Of course, 'Absences are not allowed immediately before or after holidays' is school jargon.]]

absolute. See Comparatives, false.

absolutely and **positively.** [[Currently misused in flashy American speech to mean very or indeed nothing at all. 'He is absolutely (*or* positively) grand.' In slang their meaning is *yes* (popularized by a famous vaudeville duet between 'Mr. Gallagher and Mr. Sheehan'). Portmanteau *absotively* and *posolutely*.]]

abysmal; abyssal. Both = 'of the abyss', but whereas the former is figurative, as in 'abysmal ignorance' and 'abysmal despair', the latter is literal, with the specific sense, 'belonging to that belt of the ocean which is more than 300 fathoms down', as in 'abyssal zone', 'abyssal animals', 'abyssal mud'.

Acadia. See Arcadia.

accelerate and **exhilarate** are more often confused, especially in the noun forms (*acceleration; exhilaration*) than one might expect. To *accelerate* is to quicken, speed up, hasten, increase, advance, dispatch, and expedite. To *exhilarate* is to enliven, cheer, make gay, arouse to mirth, and raise to high spirits. 'An exhilarating conversation accelerates the mental faculties.'

accept. See EXCEPT.

acceptance; acceptation. The former is used in all senses denoting or connoting the act of accepting and the state (or condition) of being received, as in 'the acceptance of a gift or an offer'; *acceptation* is, in general usage, reserved for 'the current sense of a word', the prevailing sense of a word', as in 'The acceptation of *imply* differs from that of *infer*'.

access is an occasional error for excess, chiefly by phonetic confusion. There is, however, a psychological cause for the confusion: an *access* of rage is undeniably an *excess* of temper.

accessary and **accessory.** A minor participant in a crime is an *accessory*; the corresponding adjective is also *accessary*. [[In American usage *accessory* is usual as noun and adjective.]]

In the sense 'an adjunct, an accompaniment', *accessory* is now more general than *accessary*; as the corresponding adjective ('subordinate', 'accompanying', 'non-essential', 'adventitious'), *accessory* is correct, *accessary* catachrestic, for in good English *accessary* has, in these nuances, been obsolete since ca. 1700. (*The O.E.D.*)

accident is a mishap, a disaster. A fall from a horse is an accident; a broken leg, the result. Thus, 'He is suffering from an accident' is infelicitous for '. . . from the results of an accident'.

accidently for *accidentally*: a solecism occasionally met with both in spelling and in pronunciation.

accompanied by. See PREPOSITIONS WRONGLY USED.

accompanist, not *accompanyist*, is now the usual term for 'an accompanying musician'.

accomplish. See ATTAIN.

accountable should be confined to persons. 'This wretched nib is accountable for my scrawl' is catachrestic.

accounted for; in consequence of. See PREPOSITIONS WRONGLY USED.

accredit(ed). See CREDIT(ED).

accuse. See CHARGE.

ACCUSATIVE AND INFINITIVE. There is no difficulty with such sentences as 'I saw him fall' and 'Command the boy to appear'; or even with 'It is good for us to amuse ourselves sometimes'. 'I do not know where to go' and 'He is at a loss what to think' are simple enough. But 'Whom do men declare me to be?' is less obvious: it is the infinitive form of 'Who do men declare that I am?' (Onions.) Cf. 'WHO and WHOM', at end of article.

acknowledge, misused. 'His immediate departure had acknowledged the truth of that!', Cecil Freeman Gregg, *Tragedy at Wembley*, 1936. Things do not acknowledge, they constitute a proof of things, they prove.

acquirement; acquisition. The former denotes the power or faculty of acquiring; the latter, the thing acquired. 'His acquirements in music are greater than his acquisition of riches.'

act. See FUNCTION.

act on, misused for *react on*. 'The fear of losing his job acted on him in the performance of his duties and finally caused him to lose his precious job.'

activeness is to be avoided; *activity* is the word to use.

actual and **actually** are generally unnecessary, in precisely the same way as *real* and *really* are, for the most part, excessive; *actual* is especially uncalled-for in collocation with *fact*, as in 'He is said to have died on a Monday; the actual fact is that he died on a Tuesday'.

actually. See ACTUAL and REALLY. There is, however, a psychological difference between 'Is it true?' and 'Is it actually true?', for the *actually* connotes incredulity.

adapt and **adopt** are often confused. To *adapt* a thing is to change it for one's own purpose; to *adopt* it is to accept it unchanged and then use it. Moreover, *adopt* must be distinguished from *assume*: one adopts a child, a religion, but one assumes a pose, an attitude—a debt, a task, a duty.

adapted for *suitable* is infelicitous. 'Ordinary language is not adapted to describe processes within the atom', Stuart Chase, *The Tyranny of Words*, 1938.

add. See ANNEX.

addict, 'one who is addicted' (*to*: generally, a vice). This word is no longer objectionable. Cf. FIEND.

addict. See SUBJECT TO.

addicted (to) is a pejorative. Do not, for instance, say, 'Addicted to benevolent action'—unless you're being facetious.

address should not be synonymized with *speech*, but reserved for 'a formal speech', 'a set discourse', a speech to celebrate an important occasion; thus 'The King's inaugural speech' is inferior to '. . . inaugural address'. An *address* in church is less systematic and less formal than a *sermon*.

adduce is applied only to arguments, speeches, statements, or to persons, animals, objects as illustrations or samples, the sense being 'to bring forward (verbally) for consideration; to cite; to allege', but especially the first of these nuances. 'In proof of this they adduced many arguments', historian Robertson, 1765.—'He adduced Tilden as the supreme example of the value of physical fitness in lawn tennis.'—'She adduced some absurd reasons for her very odd preference.'

ADEQUACY of style to matter. See SUITABILITY.

adequate enough is incorrect for 'sufficient' or 'suitable', and tautological for 'adequate'. The idea of 'enough' is contained within that of 'adequate'.

adherence; adhesion. In general, the former is figurative ('He was noted for his adherence to the principles of free thought'); the latter, literal ('The adhesion of this stamp to that envelope is in itself sufficiently remarkable'). It must, however, be borne in mind that in politics, *adhesion* = 'being a supporter or a partisan of a movement, a party', and that, in botany, *adhesion* is the opposite of *cohesion*.

adjacent; contiguous. The latter = 'touching', as in 'France and Spain are contiguous', 'France is contiguous to Belgium'; loosely, 'neighbouring; near but not touching'—a sense to be avoided. But *adjacent* has, in correct usage, both of these senses.

The application of *contiguous* to relations of time is obsolescent.

ADJECTIVE FOR ADVERB. This is an illiteracy; but even a tolerably educated person may, in a slovenly moment, fall into such an error as this:—'The home team pressed *stronger* [for *more strongly*] towards the close of the game' (cited by Harold Herd in *Watch Your English*, 1925). Some adverbs, however, may occur with or without the suffix '-ly'; e.g. *slow(ly)*, *quick(ly)*, *cheap(ly)*. The *-ly* forms are more polite, the root forms are more vigorous. Sometimes there is a difference in meaning: 'The

ball went as *high* as the steeple'; 'I value it *highly*'.

adjectivally and **adjectively.** Both are correct, but the former is to be preferred, for the corresponding adjective is now *adjectival*, *adjective* being, as an adjective, obsolescent.

ADJECTIVES, POSITION OF. Make sure that the adjective immediately precedes the noun it qualifies; look out for group-words (*q.v.*) like *children's language*, *woman's college*, *men's shoes*. Harold Herd points out the absurdity of *stylish gentlemen's suits* for *gentlemen's stylish suits*. Is *an excellent woman's college* as clear as *an excellent college for women*?

ADJECTIVES, UNCOMPARABLE. See COMPARATIVES, FALSE.

administer (a blow) is not incorrect, but it is certainly infelicitous; one *gives* or, better, *delivers* a blow. *Administer*, as Weseen aptly remarks, 'is properly applied to that which gives relief, acts as a remedy, or promotes justice. It is not in good use as applied to a blow, reproof, or criticism'.

admissible. See ADMITTABLE.

admission. See ADMITTANCE.

admit, admit of; permit of; allow of. *Admit of* is a rather literary variation of one of the senses of *admit*, viz. 'to allow of the presence, or the coexistence, of; to be capable of; be compatible with', as in 'Sublimity admits not of mediocrity' and 'It hardly admits of the possibility of error'.

Permit of is rather rare, and rather literary, for *permit* in the sense, 'to give leave or opportunity to; to allow', as in 'Religion is reluctant to permit of idolatry', and is thus synonymous with *admit of* and *allow of*. (*The O.E.D.*)

admittable is rare and odd-sounding for *admissible*, except in the sense 'capable of being admitted to a place, a club, a society', as in 'Such a man is admittable to any society in London'.

admittance and **admission.** The former is physical ('No admittance here', as a sign or a notice); the latter, figurative and applied especially to 'reception or initiation into rights and/or privileges', as in 'His admission to the Athenaeum Club was duly noted' and 'The admission of immigrants into the United States of America has been much restricted of late years'; the latter example leads us to the fact that 'when physical entrance and access to privileges are combined, *admission* is the preferred form, as "admission to a concert, a play, a game"' (Weseen); cf. 'The charge for admission was one shilling'.

adopt. See ADAPT.

advantage and **vantage.** The latter is 'the position or a condition that is above another, either literally or figuratively', as in 'He viewed the struggle from the *vantage* (or, the vantage point) of a safe job' and 'He viewed the valley from the *vantage* (point) of the hill': *advantage* is here admissible. But 'He has an *advantage* over me, for he knows something about the subject'.

advent and **arrival.** The former connotes importance, deep significance, fate, the operation of natural law: 'The advent of summer had been preceded by the return to summer time'; 'The advent of peace on November 11, 1918, brought surcease from anxiety to many millions of people'; 'The advent of death is of supreme importance to at least one person'. But 'His arrival at Marseilles took place on the first of June': *arrival* is neutral and it connotes comparative unimportance.

adventure; venture. 'In present use *venture* applies chiefly to business undertakings, especially such as involve chance, hazard, and speculation. *Adventure* applies chiefly to bold and daring experiences in the meeting of danger. Both words are used as verbs, but *venture* more commonly. It means to risk, hazard, take a chance, speculate, expose, and dare.' (Weseen.)

ADVERB, POSITION OF THE. See ORDER, second half (*B*).

adverse to; averse to (or **from**). Respectively 'opposed to' and 'strongly disinclined to' or 'having a (strong) distaste for'. *Averse from*, though etymologically correct, is perhaps slightly pedantic.

advert; avert. Lit., these respectively mean 'to turn to (something)' and 'to turn (something) away, or 'to prevent': 'He adverted to the plan that had been suggested'; 'He said that, at all costs, the danger had to be averted'.

advice is the noun, **advise** the verb. (I should not have thought to include this possibility of error had not Mr Harold Herd given it space in his admirable short section, 'A Dictionary of Popular Errors', in *Watch Your English*.)

advisedly; intentionally. *Advisedly* = 'done judiciously, without haste, and after careful planning or consideration', whereas *intentionally* is much weaker, for it merely = 'done not by accident but *purposely*'. As Professor Weseen has shrewdly remarked, 'Many intentional acts are not carried out advisedly'.

aeriated, aeroplane, and **aerial.** See AIRIAL . . .

aeroplane. See AIRPLANE.

aesthetic; beautiful. Weseen has been luckier (?) than I, for I have never heard or seen them confused.

affect and **effect** as verbs are frequently confused, both in pronunciation and in spelling. *Effect* is 'to bring about', 'to accomplish'; *affect* is 'to produce an effect on'; 'to attack, move, touch'. (*S.O.E.D.*) An example occurs in *The Sessions Papers of the Old Bailey*, January, 1737: 'Mr. Bell, Surgeon, deposed, that upon his examining the Body of the Deceased, he found several Bruises and Wounds upon it, but not of consequence enough to effect her life'. Possibly the surgeon had, when he commenced his disposition, intended to say 'effect her death'. Even the nouns are occasionally confused, though only *effect* is in common usage.

AFFECTATION. Affectation is a putting-on of literary airs and graces: artificiality of style, of phrasing, of words. It may go so far that it becomes 'hollow or false display' (*The O.E.D.*). 'The essence of affectation', said Carlyle, 'is that it be assumed.'

Some critics synonymize it with PRECIOUSNESS, but the two terms are not coextensive. Preciousness might perhaps be considered as a special kind of affectation; that this, however, is too sweeping a statement may be perceived from the fact that whereas a good writer may fall into preciousness, he will not fall into affectation.

'The man who writes good English', we are told by Mr Harold Herd in his valuable little book, *Watch Your English*, 1925, 'avoids frills and verbal tricks. Gone are the virtues of polysyllabic words and lumbering sentences. To load a composition with inflated phrases and far-fetched words is now a gross literary vice.

'If you would write plainly, beware of affected words and phrases. Do not write *eventuate* when you mean *happen*, *conversed* for *talked*, *demise* for *death*, a member of the sterner sex for *man*, *organ of vision* for *eye*, *voiced the opinion* for *said*.

These are a few examples of tinsel expressions that try to usurp the place of simple words.'

Mr Herd then picks on the device known as 'elegant variation'. 'If', he says, 'the mayor has been mentioned, he makes further appearance as "the civic chief", "the leader of our official life", "our official head", "the town's chief representative"—and so on. Variation of this kind should be employed only when it is absolutely necessary',—in my opinion, it is never necessary. 'In most cases it is better to use a pronoun'—and when you can't, say 'the mayor' and have done with it.

affirm. See ASSERT.

affirmative, reply in the. See CLICHÉ.

Africander (better than *Afrikander*) is not to be synonymized with *African* (n. and adj.). An *African* belongs to the African race, whereas an *Africander* is a white native of South Africa. (*The O.E.D.*)

after. The senses 'on the analogy of' and 'according to', are Standard English, but they must be used with care, for they often lead to ambiguity, as in 'This word (*exist*), after *be*, has come to possess many nuances' and 'This statement is after Darwin'.

To be after, 'to pursue', is not, as some purists have asserted, a colloquialism; at lowest, it is familiar English, with a parallel in French usage.

aggravate, -tion. Already, in 1896, John Davidson, in *Baptist Lake*, remarked that the use of *aggravate* was beyond cure. It is incorrectly used in the sense *to annoy* (a person); properly it means *to intensify*, usually for the worse. On the misuse of this word see especially *The King's English*, by H. W. and F. C. Fowler. Stylists avoid *aggravate* in the sense 'to annoy, to exasperate, to provoke'; but humdrum writers and hurried journalists may, if they wish, take heart of disgrace from the fact that *aggravate* has been used in these nuances since early in the 17th Century,—for instance, it is enshrined in Cotgrave's famous French-English dictionary, 1611. *Aggravation* is likewise avoided by stylists, but pedants must cease from stigmatizing the word as bad English; it can no longer be classified as anything worse than an infelicity.

aggregate, 'to amount to a total of' (say 10 dollars or £2), is a colloquialism perhaps less frowned-on in the U.S.A. than in England.

agnostic and **atheist.** Whereas the latter denies the existence of God, the former merely says that His existence cannot be proved; a liberal agnostic admits that His existence cannot be disproved. (With *agnostic*, cf. SCEPTIC.)

agrarian for *agricultural* 'is still rather bookish'; in the main, it is confined to the *Agrarian Reforms* of Ancient Rome and the *agrarian policies* of political parties. As a noun, *agricultur(al)ist* is loose for 'a farmer', but it is justifiable when used as the opposite of *pastoralist* (a farmer of live stock); an *agrarian* is 'one who recommends an equitable division of land'.

AGREEMENT, FALSE. False Agreement* affects two groups of grammar; constitutes two pitfalls of writing.

A. NUMBER. Particularly verb with subject, as in 'He and I am going to Town'; but also in such phenomena as 'those kind of books'. Contrast 'that breed of horses', which, theoretically correct, is unidiomatic; as, idiomatically, we say 'that kind of book' (*not* 'that kind of books'), so, idiomatically we say 'that breed of horse'. See KIND OF, ALL. Note that the verb *to be* agrees with its subject, not with its complement: thus, not 'A man *are* thousands of different persons' but 'A man is thousands of different persons' is correct. Charles Robert Fanshawe, *Memoires of Lady F.*, 1829, has 'All which'—we should say 'all that'—'is required in compositions of that nature *are*, that the writer should record what he saw and heard': for *are* substitute *is*: Fanshawe seems to have been led astray by *compositions*. In 'The vividness of these delightful images *were* intensified by the desperateness of my own affairs' (C. H. B. Kitchen, *Birthday Party*, 1938), the subject is *vividness*, not *images*. In 'The rapidity of Lord Roberts's movements *are* deserving of the highest praise' (*The Daily Express*, May 14, 1900: cited by J. C. Nesfield in *Errors in English Composition*, 1903), the journalist has lost sight of the fact that it was the *rapidity* which deserved praise. See 'ONE, use of plural in v. after', for a very common type of false agreement between subject and verb; here I give two further examples:—'Sorel's "Reflections on Violence" is one of the few works upon Socialism that can be, or *deserves* to be, read

* For the beginner, there is a useful introduction in Harold Herd, *Watch Your English*, 1925, at pp. 12 (foot)–15 (top).

by the non-professional student' (A. R. Orage, ca. 1937); 'Mr Yeats has written one of the simplest accounts of poetical composition that *has* ever appeared' (Michael Roberts, in *The Spectator*, Nov. 19, 1937). *What* sometimes causes confusion, as in the following sentence from one of Agatha Christie's novels, 'I don't really see what my personal relationships *has* to do with the matter in hand, M. Poirot'.

B. POSITION. Theoretically, this kind of false agreement could be taken to include all wrong positions, whether of words in a phrase, or of words or phrases in a clause, or, indeed, of words, phrases, clauses in a sentence. And practically, it is most convenient to treat first of (I) relative clauses (subordinate clauses beginning with *who, which, that, when, where,* and such rarities as *wherever, whereof, wherefore, whenever*) that have slipped their moorings, got out of position, departed from apposition, departed therefore from positional agreement; and then consider (II) phrases and words (e.g. adjectives) that are out of position —that are, in other terms, in false agreement; and, finally, (III) several examples of pronominal falsity in agreement.

N.B. The position of adverbs, however, is discussed in ORDER, Section B, and confused or misrelated participles will be found at CONFUSED PARTICIPLES.

I. Relative Clauses out of position. Relevant to this section is the use or misuse of the relative pronouns, *who* and *that, which* and *that*: see 'WHICH and THAT; WHO and THAT'. The importance of the correct use of the relatives may be gauged by such a sentence as, 'It is the question of the house that Jack built which is important in architecture'.

The danger of separating the relative from its antecedent should be obvious: that it isn't obvious may be guessed from the following examples (selected from an astounding abundance of infelicities):

'I had in the County of Northampton deposited my Heart in a Virgin's Breast, who failed in Credit and Sincerity', *The Life of Benjamin Stratford,* 1766: the writer's sense of position was as defective stylistically as it was cardially. A rearrangement is necessary; thus, 'I had . . . deposited my heart in the breast of a virgin, who failed . . .'.

'He stripped off the drunkard's covering (who never stirred)', Richard Hughes, 'Poor Man's Inn', in *A Moment of Time,*

1929. Correct to: 'He stripped off the covering of the drunkard, who never stirred' (i.e., did not stir).

In 'There is room for a persistent, systematic, detailed inquiry into how words work that will take the place of the discredited subject which goes by the name of Rhetoric' (I. A. Richards, *The Philosophy of Rhetoric,* 1936), the very acute and intelligent author has the excuse that if he attaches to 'words' its relative clause 'that will take the place of . . . Rhetoric', he thrusts 'work' to the end of the sentence; true, but why not recast the sentence, thus, 'There is room for a persistent . . . inquiry into the workability (or activities or operations or potentialities) of words that will take the place of . . . Rhetoric'? One is not always obliged to knock down a brick wall; often it is easier—and occasionally it is much more effective—to go through the gate or to walk to the end of the wall or to scale the wall.

'The modes of causal recurrence on which meaning depends are peculiar through that delegated efficacy I have been talking about' (*ibid.*). The uninstructed reader would probably suppose that *which* referred to 'causal recurrence'; it refers to 'the modes'. The ambiguity would not have arisen if the anticipatory *those* had been used; 'Those modes of causal recurrence on which meaning depends are . . .' is unambiguous.

'The operational approach makes knowledge about the world outside no longer absolute, but relative. The operation is performed relative'—i.e., in relation to—'some standard, say the gauge or the meter stick. Concepts emerge from these operations which are definite and verifiable' (Stuart Chase, *The Tyranny of Words,* 1938). Does 'which' refer to 'operations' or to 'concepts'? If to 'operations', should there not be a comma after 'operations'? But does not 'which' refer to 'concepts'? Perhaps rewrite, thus:—'Such concepts emerge from these operations as are definite and verifiable.'

'The latest major engagement [struggle between science and theology] was over Darwin, which lingered on to the Scopes trial in Tennessee' (*ibid.*): no ambiguity here; merely slovenliness.

'C. E. M. Joad wrote a book to drive home the message of Radhakishnan, in which he states flatly that his hero has attained to truth about the universe which is "from its nature incommunicable"' (*ibid.*): 'such truth about the universe as is "from its nature incommunicable"'?

'Many factors affect judicial decisions, of which the rules of law constitute but one' (*ibid.*): 'of which' refers to 'many factors', not—as one might think—to 'judicial decisions'.

'The girl, furious, goes to Mr Frost's club to complain *who*, at first, thinks her visit is one of the practical jokes of his inventive friend. (And the heavens forbid that I should mar that choice sentence with any bracket of mine!) But eventually he agrees to carry out his forgetful wife's undertaking' (James Agate, in *The Tatler*, Dec. 15, 1937). The omission of the comma after 'complain' increases the clumsiness of the sentence. And what does Mr Agate mean by bracket? See BRACKET.

II. *In the agreement of words other than antecedent and relative*, we find that the implication of incorrect or foolish order is as strong as in the foregoing examples. Witness the following:—

'What is the ultimate nature of matter? The question we know by now is meaningless' (Stuart Chase, *The Tyranny of Words*, 1938). Here the false agreement is flagrant. The writer means, 'By now, we know that this question is meaningless'.

'He arranges a meeting of his suspects to find out whether anyone reacts in any way peculiar 'to the sight of the body' (C. McCabe, *The Face on the Cutting-Room Floor*, 1937). Obviously the author does not intend us to understand a 'way peculiar to the sight of the body'; he does mean, 'react to the sight of the body'. Therefore he should have written '. . . reacts in any peculiar way to the sight of the body'.

'They sat at ease in the boat, which lay moored in a tiny creek of the island, canopied by an overhanging willow' (Gerald Bullett, *The Snare of the Fowler*, 1936). What was canopied? The island (as grammatically it should be)? The creek (as is possible though improbable)? Or the persons? Apparently the persons, for the spread of a willow's branches is not very large. Therefore the sentence should read, 'Canopied by an overhanging willow, they sat at ease in the boat, which lay moored in a tiny creek of the island'. (This sentence might have been included in the entry, CONFUSED PARTICIPLES.)

'But, unlike North, it was not necessary for him to surrender his own judgment to that of George III' (J. R. Green, *A Short History of the English People*, 1874: cited by Nesfield in *Errors in English Composition*, 1903). Read, 'But it was not necessary for him, as it was necessary for North, to surrender his own judgment to that of George III'.

'"You'll like the Ole Man. . . . Treats you as if you was a human being—not a machine."—Ten minutes later Meredith endorsed this opinion for himself. Alert, efficient, quiet both in manner and speech, he found the head of the borough police not only ready to condone his presence on the scene but to thank him for his co-operation.' John Bude, *The Cheltenham Square Murder*, 1937. 'Alert, efficient, quiet both in manner and speech' does not, as it should, refer to Meredith but to the head of the borough police ('the Ole Man').

'When they were gone, still carrying me, she sat down on a great smooth stone that was beside the well' (Wilfranc Hubbard, 'The Road to Eleusis' in his *Tanagra Figures*, 1927). Who was carrying 'me'—'they' or 'she'? Presumably 'they'. The sentence should be rewritten in some such manner as this:—'When, still carrying me, they were gone [better: they went], she sat down on a great smooth stone.'

III. *Pronominal agreement, or lack of agreement*, has, in part, been exemplified in the section on relative pronouns. Here are several examples where other pronouns are involved:—

'Left without a father at the age of three-and-a-half, her mother was her only guide.' It was not her mother who had, at the age of 3½, been left without a father; it was the little girl. Recast thus: —'To the girl left without a father at the age of 3½, the mother was the only guide.' Cf. this: 'An only son, his mother had died when he was a child' (W. H. Lane Crauford, *Murder to Music*, 1936): his mother was not an only son; *he* was: therefore read, 'He was an only son, and his mother had died when he was a child', or, less happily, 'He was an only son, whose mother had died when he was a child'.

'A sensation would be something that just was *so*, on its own, a datum; as such we have none' (I. A. Richards, *The Philosophy of Rhetoric*, 1936): ? '. . .; we have no sensations—no data—as such'.

'It is well known that once a man or woman has become a town councillor, they are never quite the same again' (a letter in *Time and Tide*, Nov. 13, 1937). By the advocates of expedience, 'they' may be defended on the ground that it avoids the clumsiness of 'he or she'; but why not 'It is well known that once a person has become a town councillor, he is never quite the same again'? '"Neither Emilienne nor I really understand pictures"', Naomi Royde-Smith, *The Younger Venus*, 1938. 'I', being the nearer, governs: therefore, 'understand'.

agricultural; agricultur(al)ist. See AGRARIAN. *Agriculturist* is gradually displacing the longer form.

ain't for *isn't* (colloquial) or *is not* (Standard English) is an error so illiterate that I blush to record it. As for *ain't* for *hasn't* (*has not*) or *haven't* (*have not*) . . .! More is to be said for *ain't* = *am not*, but it is now—and long has been—adjudged to be illiterate. [To Americans, G. P. Krapp's comment is of interest (*A Comprehensive Guide to Good English*, 1927): 'Although students of English and critical speakers would probably agree that *ain't* is low colloquial, it is true nevertheless that many educated persons permit themselves this habit, even though they reprehend it as careless. Only the enforcement of a strong academic authority prevents *ain't* from becoming universal colloquial use.']

airial, airiated and **airioplane** (phonetically spelt) are the frequent mispronunciations of persons (not necessarily ill-educated) that are unable to enunciate *aërial*, *aërated* and *aëroplane*. The same originally applied to *aereal*, *aerated*, *aeroplane*; but usage now permits *aerial* and *aeroplane* as trisyllabic,—indeed it is considered pedantic to pronounce these two words as having four syllables. [Among American engineers *aerated* has commonly three syllables. *Webster's* allows for *aery* three syllables or two syllables.]

airplane is the usual American, **aeroplane** the usual English form.

airship is a dirigible balloon.

akin with for *akin to*. A not uncommon error. Eric Partridge falls into it in his *Eighteenth Century English Romantic Poetry*, 1924. *Akin* is a contraction of *of kin*, that form being occasionally found in literary English.

alarum is archaic for *alarm* (n).

albumen; albumin. Respectively, 'the white of an egg' and 'a member of a class of proteins rich in sulphur and nitrogenous substance'; the former is a general scientific term, the latter a chemical technicality.

alias is sometimes—though less now than formerly—misused for a disguise, a concealment. 'He dressed up as a costermonger; *that* was his alias.'

alibi is sometimes used, esp. in U.S.A., for an *excuse* or *pretext* of almost any kind, whereas, properly, it is only 'the plea that when an alleged act took place one was elsewhere' (*The Con. O.D.*). '"I was too ill to write." "That's no alibi for failing to let me know—somebody could have 'phoned that information."'

alienate; allineate. The former = 'to estrange'; the latter is pedantic for 'to align'.

alike, misplaced. 'For the moment it appeared quite convenient to regard myself as an executioner about to terminate a life alike forfeit to the laws of God and man', for 'a life forfeit to the laws of God and man alike', Eden Phillpotts, *Physician, Heal Thyself*, 1935.

alike . . . or for **alike . . . and.** '. . . He was taking, in colonial parlance, *a dry smoke*—that is, it was alike destitute of fire or tobacco', Parker Gilmore, *Days and Nights in the Desert*, 1888.

all, ambiguous. 'We have not always . . . sufficient means of distinguishing conveniently between the general and collective use of terms. In Latin [we have] *omnes* meaning *all* distributively, and *cuncti* [contracted from *coniuncti*, joined together] meaning all taken together. In English *all men* may mean *any man* or *all men together*. Even the more exact word *every* is sometimes misused, as in the old proverb, "Every mickle makes a muckle", where it is obvious that every little portion cannot by itself make much, [and that it can make much] only when joined to other little portions', Jevons & Hill, *The Elements of Logic*, 1883.

all, colloquially used with the genitive (e.g., *all their sakes* instead of (*for*) *the sake(s) of all of them*). See GENITIVE, VAGARIES OF THE, the last paragraph but one.

all alone is tautological for *alone*, but can be excused when 'all' is a genuine intensive.

all kind. Walking in London, W.C.2, on April 7, 1937, I saw a horse-driven cart bearing the legend, *All kind of old iron wanted*. Though 'all' should be followed by the plural 'kinds', it must be admitted that Swinburne, seldom at fault, has 'all kind of flowers', presumably to avoid the sibilant.

all-powerful, like **omnipotent,** is incomparable. See COMPARATIVES, FALSE. The same restriction holds for the other *all*-compounds—e.g., *all-seeing.*

all right. See ALRIGHT.

all the lot. See LOT and WHOLE, THE.

allege commonly means 'to declare or assert on insufficient grounds' and it must not be made synonymous with *affirm, assert, declare.*

allegiance and **alliance** may be confused. The former is the loyalty (theoretical and practical) that one owes to a person (e.g., one's king, one's overlord), whereas the latter is a pact between two nations or states.

ALLEGORY. 'When a comparison is protracted and sustained through numerous details, it is named an Allegory.

'Allegories on the grand scale are exemplified by Spenser's *Faery Queen,* Bunyan's *Pilgrim's Progress,* and Swift's *Tale of a Tub* and *Gulliver.* In these a whole series of adventures is sustained with a double meaning.

'. . . The short Allegory is frequent in literature. In *The Spectator,* we have the Vision of Mirza, No. 159; Luxury and Avarice, 55; Truth, Falsehood and Fiction, 460.'

A lengthily developed simile constitutes the shortest form of allegory, as in Sir Arthur Helps's 'picture' of the course of history:—

'The course of history is like that of a great river wandering through various countries; now, in the infancy of its current, collecting its waters from obscure small springs in plashy meadows, and from unconsidered rivulets which the neighbouring rustics do not know the names of; now, in its boisterous youth, forcing its way through mountains; now, in middle life, flowing with equable currents busily by great towns, its waters sullied, yet enriched with commerce; and, now, in its burdened old age, making its slow and difficult way with an ever-widening expanse of waters, over which the declining sun looms grandly, to the sea.' (Alexander Bain, *English Composition and Rhetoric,* enlarged edition, 1887–88.) As a literary device, allegory is outmoded: and when it is used nowadays, we demand a virtuosity far beyond that displayed by Sir Arthur.

alleluia (h) and **allelujah** are, in general usage, inferior to *hallelujah;* as a representation of the term in the Septuagint, *alleluia* is to be preferred.

allineate. See ALIENATE.

ALLITERATION. Apt alliteration's artful aid. Charles Churchill, *The Prophecy of Famine,* 1763.

In his *English Composition and Rhetoric,* enlarged edition, Part II, 1888, Alexander Bain has the following short section, which may serve as an introduction.

'The term *Alliteration* is employed to signify the commencing of successive words with the same letter or syllable [as in *u-, ewe, yew, you*]. Unless'—read *except*—'when carried out on a set purpose, it offends the ear: as *long live Lewis, come conqueror, convenient contrivance.*' Several other examples (likewise from Bain):—'That is *al*so *al*tered'; 'He *im*itated it *at* once'; 'To *per*manently im*pair* the *pow*er of the *Peers*'.

Alliteration is employed either stylistically (that is, to obtain emphasis, effectiveness, pointedness, humour, euphony) or as a mnemonic device. It is frequent in advertisements: *beautiful Bournemouth, Guinness is good for you, pink pills for pale people, the sunny South.*

The poets have made a happy use of it: for instance, Keats's 'the winnowing wind'; Swinburne's 'welling water's winsome word' and

    Even the weariest river
Winds somewhere safe to sea,—

but then, of all poets writing the English language, Swinburne is the most frequent, versatile and felicitous alliterator.

But alliteration can be, and has been, employed no less felicitously by the prose writers. The two great masters, in the present century, are G. K. Chesterton and Frank Binder.

Chesterton is the more impressive and at the same time the more pointed and epigrammatic manipulator of alliteration; Binder the more rhythmical and euphonious, the more sophisticated and yet the more profound: but, in their different ways, they 'know their job'.

Of Chesterton's works I choose one of the less famous, *The Paradoxes of Mr Pond,* 1936. It opens thus:—'The curious and sometimes creepy effect which Mr Pond produced upon me, despite his commonplace courtesy and dapper decorum, was possibly connected with some memories of childhood; and the

vague verbal association of his name.'
And here are a few other examples:—
'At this moment could be seen, striding
across the sun-chequered lawn, the large
and swaggering figure of Captain Ga-
hagan'; 'The Asa-Smith school of drama,
in which every sentence stops as soon as
it starts'; 'Paradox has been defended
on the ground that so many fashionable
fallacies still stand firmly on their feet,
because they have no heads to stand on.
But it must be admitted that writers,
like other mendicants and mountebanks,
frequently do try to attract attention';
(concerning Shakespeare's clowns and
fools) 'The Fool is like a fantastic dancing flame lighting up the features and
furniture of the dark house of death';
'Nobody who looked at the baldish,
rather corrugated brow that bulged between the streaks of black hair, and the
anxious, though angry eyes, could doubt
that he was in fanatical good faith'; 'the
trail of official fussing that crossed the
track of the tragedy'.

Mr Frank Binder has, I believe, published only two books: *A Journey in
England*, 1931, and *Dialectic; or, the
Tactics of Thinking*, 1932. From the
former:—'It may be . . ., a craving for
echoes that never come, but I still lose
myself in the solemn and insinuating
stillness of the North German Plain, in
its long, quiet, contemplative stretches
of wistful woodland, in its calm and grey
religious skies.' (Of Ely) 'I had stepped
into a lofty sepulchre of stone, a mausoleum of mediaeval memory, one of the
stately desolations of Isaiah which served
as proof of the failing frailty of humanity,
and as a wrecking rebuke to perspiring
ambition and pride. . . . All was empty,
dark, and still. Not a breath, not a foot-
fall! Nothing to move the emotion, nothing to dispel the deadening dread of
death, but all shrouded in shadow, grey
as a forgotten grave, built up and barri-
caded above like a tomb, and all below,
in the sombre seclusion of the aisles, the
hard flags of unremembered burials,
tablets to long-since nameless names,
mural memorials to the well-noted un-
knowns of past time. Never have my
thoughts been so reduced to the down-
trodden dust of human destiny and of
human despair as in the nave and in the
aisles of Ely Church . . . I am a poor
pagan, but as I beheld the work of our
own Alan of Walsingham I was prepared
to believe in inspiration, to believe in a

benevolent breathing from the beyond,
and in courteous communications from
some superior spirit who takes our
favoured ones by the hand, and who
leads them with a studied certainty of
step to the sure summits of art.'

And from *Dialectic*:—'The debates of
to-day are not, as the wrangles of the
Middle Ages, the battles of brain against
brain, but a duet of defiances hurled from
behind the fortifications, a banging of the
big drums and a deciding of the issue in
favour of the bigger din.'

'The opinions of most people rarely
spring from a principle by which their
knowledge is selected and their thoughts
arranged, but may be referred to little
forts of fact and to blockhouses of bias
where the defender lies entrenched for
life, deeply enough as a rule to assure
himself of safety and safely enough to
bring any besieger to despair. A prejudice
is early acquired, and as we are doubly
attentive to those who agree with us and
deaf to all we do not wish to hear, not a
day goes without our piling Ossas of absolute assent on Pelions of dubious belief.'

'The peddlers of practicability . . . the
criers-up of so-called common sense.'

'The perennial personality of God.'

'. . . The seers and astrologers of long
ago who, looking at nature as we look at
a printed page, saw in fact phenomena,
events, and beings, symbols of celestial
significance and emblems of immanent
meaning, types and figures in the splendid speech of all things where, from the
quaint contingency of eclipses and calam-
ities, comets and the comings of greater
kings, planetary aspects and the collapse
of kingdoms, the mystical mind might
come to read the alliteration of life, the
assonance of the soul, the far-off arpeg-
gios in the concords of God.'

'Life in this embracing sense is not a
fact but a faculty of nature, not a thing
unique, discrete, and segregated with a
poor and temporary place in our provincial bosoms, but a power both absolute
and universal, a lasting possibility to
which each atom has some trend and
latent inclination. Each has a bias or
bent to the spirit, a final predisposition,
and allowing this, how shall we speak of
men as being apart or as moving in a
mystic remove from the world which
holds us at one with itself? But not only
are we so held, and not only the fabric
of earth and sky is seen to fall into the

bigger form and . . . personality of being, but all our aery estate of thoughts and dreams, of virtue and vice, of blessings and blasphemies, of purity and filth, of beauty and abomination, has, whether good or bad, its palpable part in the plan of things. For the world is an irrespective place, full, plenteous, and cosmopolitan, so free from prohibitions that he who seeks will find, who hopes will be sustained, who despairs will be left to despondency; a place so infinite in the forms of fact and fancy that men appear as everything and nothing, as the elect of heaven, as items of nature, or as poor parochial pawns in the one imperial purpose of God.'

allow. See ADMIT; ADMIT OF.

allude, vaguer than *refer*, is applied to a mention either incidental (or casual) or indirect, whereas *refer* is specific and direct. 'She often alludes to her early life'; 'He refers to Clemenceau on page 89'.

allure (n.), 'attractiveness', seems, to those of us who know French, to be an unhappy word: for in that language it means 'pace' or 'gait'. Its use in English hardly antedates the 20th Century.

allure (v.) is 'to attract' (a person), favourably or neutrally; **lure** is 'to attract' (a person) to his disadvantage. 'Allured by the prospect of fame, he was lured into indiscretion by the purveyors of publicity.'

allusion. See ILLUDE.

almost for *virtual*, esp. in *almost certainty* for *virtual certainty* or *near certainty*. 'The almost certainty that the woman was by this time far away', Mrs Belloc Lowndes, *The House by the Sea*, 1937. *Webster's* cites from Hawthorne: 'The almost insanity of the moment'. *Almost*, I believe, should not be used to qualify a *thing*, abstract or concrete; correct uses are, 'he was almost certain', 'he almost succeeded'. Nesfield quotes from *The Review of Reviews*, April, 1900— 'The almost impossibility of frontal attacks, &c', which he corrects to 'the practical impossibility'. (But see PRACTICAL.) *Almost* for *virtual* has probably arisen on the analogy of *then* in, e.g., 'the then king'; but 'the then king' may be justified as a convenient brevity for 'the then reigning king' or as a shortened reversal of 'the king then reigning'.

almost never is feeble—so feeble as to be incorrect—for *hardly ever* or *very seldom*. 'He almost never visits me any more' = 'He rarely visits me (nowadays)'.

alone (adj.) is sometimes misused for the adv. *only*, as in 'It [the seizure of Kiaochau] was undertaken not alone without the knowledge of the Chancellor, but directly against his will', quoted by Nesfield from Wolf von Schiebrand, 'Germany as a World-Power' (*The Daily Telegraph*, April, 1903), and in 'The roads, in these days of wireless and wireless-carrying cars, were not the proposition in a get-away that they had been in the era which depended alone upon telephonic communication' (John G. Brandon, *The Mail-Van Mystery*, 1937); in the latter quotation, 'alone' could be changed to 'only' or retained and placed after 'communication'. See also LONELY.

along about. Samuel Putnam, *Marguerite of Navarre*, 1936, 'But along about 1517, Lefèvre and his teaching were quite the talk of the court'. This use of *along* is an American colloquialism. It seems to me ugly and useless.

along of for (1) *owing to* and (2) *with* is used only by the uneducated.

along with, in the sense of *beside* or *in company with*, is admissible.

already is an adverb; **all ready,** an adjective. 'Are they already all ready?' illustrates the usage.

already sometimes requires a progressive tense (*am doing, was doing, has been doing*, etc.) instead of a simple one (*do, did, shall do*, etc.). One cannot draw up a rule: here, as so often in the finer points of idiom, literary tact or grammatical intuition or, indeed, both are required. 'If the legacy gave him a motive' [in the past: complete], 'it's too late now to remove that motive. It operated, or it did operate[,] already' (Vernon Loder, *The Button in the Plate*, 1938). Here I should, for 'operated . . . already', substitute, according to the precise time point required (only the author could tell us that), either 'was operating already' or, less probably (I feel), 'had been operating already'. (Already is badly placed.)

alright is an incorrect spelling of *all right* and an illogical form thereof. *All right* is an amplified form of *right* (correct; just, equitable; safe), as in 'He's all right: the fall did him no harm'. The exclamatory form (= Yes, I shall) is therefore *all right!*, not *alright!*, as in '"Will you attend to that little matter for me?" "All right!"' *The Observer* of Jan. 23, 1938, quotes the following letter.

'Students of languages are familiar with the fact that in every language there is a constant fusion of words going on which has the effect that frequently a combination which consisted originally of two words comes to be recognised as one word with a different meaning from the original pair out of which it was formed.

'Sometimes it happens that in this process the original pair of words in that combination disappears, with the result that the new compound ceases to be recognisable as such. Thus, no one but the etymologist is conscious nowadays that *lord* represents an original combination of *loaf* and *ward*. But often the original combination continues to exist side by side with the new compound, and then people have sooner or later to make up their minds whether the new compound is to be recognised as such by writing it as one word.

'There are a great many instances in which a compound is recognised and written as such to distinguish it from the pair from which it is formed: thus we distinguish between *a black cap* and *a blackcap*. But when the fusion is of recent occurrence we often hesitate for long to recognise it in writing. *Alright* is a case in point.

'We recognise *almost* and *already* as compound words which are different in meaning from *all most* and *all ready*. That is worth while, because it at least enables us in writing to distinguish between such pairs of sentences as *That is all most interesting*, and *That is almost interesting. They are all ready there*, and *They are already there*. Obviously, if *alright* represents a compound word which actually exists, it has a certain justification. But is there such a compound? I believe there is.

'The key to the problem of whether two words have fused in one is the accent with which they are spoken. When two words fuse they are pronounced with a different accent from the original pair. This is easily perceived if we compare *a black cap* with *a blackcap*. Let us take a sentence like *They are all right* and ask ourselves whether the accent of the last two words can be so varied that the sentence means two quite different things. We find that this can actually take place. If we pronounce the last two words so that they are equal in stress, we find that the sentence means *All of them are right*; if we pronounce them so that *right* is more strongly accented than *all*, it means *They are not in danger, they are safe*, or more generally, *You needn't worry about them*. It is easy to see that this second meaning of *all right* represents a fusion of the original elements.

'I have personally no doubt that there is a single word *alright*, with a somewhat fluid meaning, but distinct from that of *all right*. This word, however, is a colloquialism, very convenient in everyday intercouse, but of no importance whatever in literary composition. I find that I use it regularly in ordinary conversation, but never have occasion to write it except in familiar correspondence. When I do write it, I spell it as two words!'

altercation and **fight.** The former is verbal; the latter, physical. An *altercation* is a wrangle, a quarrelsome dispute, a heated controversy: 'Their altercation developed into a fight'.

alternate, alternately. See par. 2 of the next entry.

alternative and **choice.** The latter can be applied to any number, whereas *alternative* may be applied only to two courses of action—two possible decisions. 'The alternatives are death with honour and exile with dishonour'; 'He had the choice between fighting, running away, and capture'; 'The alternative is to . . .'; 'If you don't do that, you don't necessarily have to do this, for there are several choices'. Strictly, therefore, 'the *only* alternative' is tautological; equally tautological is 'the *only* alternative course (plan, method, etc. etc.) is . . .'.

The adverb of *alternative* is *alternatively*, 'in a way that offers a choice between *two*'; in this sense, *alternately* is obsolete. The adjective *alternate* = 'arranged by terms', 1 and 2 being alternate numbers in 1,2,1,2, 1,2 1,2, . . . In ordinary speech, 'He and I did the work on alternate days'—i.e., 'by turns of one day each', he one day, I the next; but 'The alternative days on which the work can be done are Monday and Wednesday'. In mathematics and botany, alternate has certain technical senses.

although is more dignified, more literary than *though*, except in *as though*, where *although* could not be substituted for *though*. Also see THOUGH.

although . . . yet. To use both in a short sentence ('Although he returned only yesterday, yet he left again to-day') is unnecessary, but to imply that *al-*

though ... *yet* is always redundant is wrong, as can be seen from almost any long sentence. In long sentences, as also in short, (*al*)*though* posits a handicap, an obstacle, or an advantage, and *yet* emphasizes the result—the victory or the defeat. Of the two, *yet* is, in any sentence, the more safely omitted, for the omission of (*al*)*though* leaves the sense unresolved for too long, as in 'He came only yesterday, yet he departed this morning'.

altogether and **all together** are often confused: the former = 'entirely, on the whole'; the latter implies collocation or coincidence or unanimity of individuals. The misuse can lead to strange ambiguities; 'The house party came altogether' (Anthony Wynne, *The Holbein Mystery*, 1935) should read: '... came all together'.

alumnus has plural *alumni*. A former pupil of any school or college or, whether graduate or not, of any university. Properly, a male pupil or student; but the pl. *alumni* is used generically of both sexes, unless it is scientifically opposed to *alumnae* (sing. *alumna*, a girl pupil or student); the feminine is rarely used in Great Britain. [In American usage, *alumnus* is a graduate or former student of a university or a college; less commonly of a school, *former student* or *old student* being more usual except in phrases like *alumni association*. The feminine *alumna, alumnae* is a cause of confusion at our colleges for women, especially because the 'English' pronunciation of *alumni* and *alumnae* are similar to the 'Roman' pronunciations of *alumnae* and *alumni*.]

always can hardly be confused with *all ways*, short for *all the ways*: and yet I have seen it more than an inconclusive once.

always, improperly employed. 'I have been a militant Communist and a constitutional Socialist and a Pacifist, and always there have been moments when I see all people . . . as frightened children', article 'Under Thirty' in *The Spectator*, Dec. 17, 1937. Existence only in 'moments' is contradictory of 'always'.

a.m. = in the morning, **p.m.** in the afternoon and up to midnight. Avoid such phrases as '11 a.m. in the morning', '11 p.m. at night'.

am. Except in telegrams, diaries and in letters to intimate friends, *am* for *I am* should be avoided. Recast the sentence if necessary.

amatory and **amorous.** In current usage, *amorous* connotes concupiscence, the favourable adjective being *loving* (contrast 'a *loving* look' with 'an *amorous* look'). One speaks of *amatory* or *love-poems*; an *amorous* poem would be a love-poem that is sexually frank or ardent.

amazement is 'overwhelming wonder, whether due to mere surprise or to admiration'; in the sense 'mental stupefaction', it is obsolete. It must not be confused with the *surprise* (or the *wonder*) itself.

amazing means 'astounding'—capable of amazing a person. It should not be debased to mean *unusual* or *good* (or even *very good*) or *bad* (or even *very bad*). Many journalists and many popular novelists and almost innumerable careless speakers have combined to make it a verbal counter—a 'rubber-stamp word', as Mr Frank Whitaker has called it along with *ban, bid* (as noun), *chief* (as noun), *coup, drama, dream* (as adjective), *gang, gem, girl-wife, haul, pact, rail* (noun), *revelation, riddle, rush, trek, thrill* (both noun, especially, and verb), *trek, wonder* (as adjective). Mr Whitaker's witty and trenchant address, delivered on Dec. 13, 1938, to the Institute of Journalists, was reproduced in the Institute's *Journal*, January, 1939. [In the U.S.A., *amazing* is said to be especially frequent in the speech of Southerners.]

AMBIGUITY

'I have often been apprehensive, that the manner in which I express myself, may lead you into some mistakes of my meaning, the signification of words, in the language of men, being so unsettled, that it is scarce possible to convey a determinate sense . . .; for where different, or perhaps contrary meanings are signified by the same word, how easy is it for a mind, prone to error, to take the wrong one?' C. Johnston, *Chrysal*, 1768.

Ambiguity springs from woolly and muddled thinking; from a hasty fitting of words to the thought; from ignorance of the right uses of words; from the wrong order of words; from defective punctuation; and from a multiplicity of minor causes.

That ambiguity which springs from vague and muddled thinking—general ambiguity rather than particular ambiguities—is treated at WOOLLINESS, which is ambiguity on a large scale and is especially to be found in political speeches, in the words of publicists, and in the writings of such numerous vulgarizers as have failed to understand the views and thoughts of those whom they seek to vulgarize.

Obscurity is treated at OBSCURITY, where clarity is also dealt with. Ambiguity arising from defective punctuation is briefly treated at PUNCTUATION. Ambiguity arising from misuses of single terms is touched-on in the ensuing paragraphs based on Jevons; but see also CATACHRESIS.

The relation of ambiguity to logic is so close that a chapter on ambiguity is to be found in every reputable treatise on logic. Instead of utilizing such works as Wm. Ernest Johnson's *Logic*, 3 vols., 1921 (the Cambridge school of thought) and H. W. B. Joseph's *An Introduction to Logic*, 2nd edition, 1916 (the Oxford school of thought), which are excellent for dons and dons-to-be but a trifle difficult for the ordinary man and woman, I shall draw—and draw copiously—on a mid-Victorian logician (and economist), Wm. Stanley Jevons, whose *Elementary Lessons in Logic* was recast as *The Elements of Logic*, 1883, by an American professor well known in the 1870's and 1880's—David J. Hill. What follows is in parts an adoption, in parts an adaptation of the revised work.

Of Logic, the most general practical part is that which treats of the ambiguity of terms—of the uncertainty and the variety of meaning possessed by words. Nothing can be of more importance to the attainment of correct habits of thinking and reasoning than a thorough acquaintance with the imperfections of language. Comparatively few terms have one single clear meaning and one meaning only; and whenever two or more meanings are confused, we inevitably commit a logical fallacy, darken counsel, render hazardous the way of communication. If, for instance, a person should argue that 'Punishment is an evil', and that, according to the principles of morality, 'No evil is to be allowed even with the purpose of doing good', we might not immediately see how to avoid the conclusion that 'No punishments should be allowed', because punishments cause evil. A little reflection will show that the word *evil* is here used in two totally different senses: in the first case it means 'physical evil', 'pain'; in the second, 'moral evil'. Because moral evil is never to be committed, it does not follow that physical evils are never to be inflicted.—The more a person studies the subtle variations in the meaning of common words, the more he will be convinced of the dangerous nature of the tools he has to use in all communications and arguments; the more careful should he therefore be in his use of words and the more critical he will be of propagandic writings.

In Logic, terms are said to be *univocal* when they can suggest no more than one definite meaning; to be *equivocal* (or *ambiguous*) when they have two or more different meanings. The word *cathedral* is probably univocal or of one logical meaning only. *Church*, on the other hand, sometimes means the building in which religious worship is performed; sometimes the body of persons who belong to one sect and assemble in churches; and *the church* means the body of the clergy as distinguished from the laity. *Equivocal* itself is ambiguous: its meaning in logic, as in philology, has been defined above; but in common life, *equivocal* is applied to the statements or the terms of one who uses words consciously and deceitfully in a manner designed to produce a confusion of the true and apparent meanings; in the moral sphere, it means 'questionable', 'of suspect or dubious character or reputation'.

Equivocal words fall into three classes, according as they are equivocal

in sound only;
in spelling only;
in both sound and spelling.

Words equivocal in sound only or in spelling only give rise to trivial mistakes. When we hear them, we may confuse *right, rite, wright, write*; *rain, reign; might* and *mite*; but the context usually precludes misapprehension. Compare, too, *air* and *heir, hair* and *hare*. Words equivocal in spelling but not in pronunciation are a *tear*-(drop) and a *tear*, or rent, in cloth; *lead*, the metal, and the *lead* given by a person.

Much more important are the words equivocal in both spelling and pronunciation. These in their turn may be divided into three groups according as they arise:

(i) from the *accidental confusion* of different words;
(ii) from that *transference of meaning which is caused by an association of ideas*; and
(iii) from the *logical transference of meaning to analogous objects*.

(i) *Accidental Confusion.* In this class we have those odd and interesting, though comparatively unimportant, cases in which ambiguity has arisen from the confusion of entirely different words (whether from different languages or from different roots of the same language) that have in the course of—and from the rough usage by—time, come to have the same sound and the same spelling. Thus *mean* signifies either 'medium', 'mediocre', from the Mediaeval French *moien* (Modern Fr. *moyen*), and 'base', 'vulgar', from Old English *gemæne*, 'belonging to the many'. The verb *mean* can hardly be confused with either of the adjectives *mean*, and it has, of course, a distinct root.

(ii) *Transference of Meaning by Association of Ideas.* By far the largest proportion of equivocal words have become so by a transference of the meaning from the thing originally denoted by the word to some other thing so habitually connected with it as to be closely associated in thought. We have already seen the equivocality of *church.* In Parliamentary language, *the House* means either the chamber in which the members meet or the body of members that happen to be assembled in it at any time. Consider *foot*: the *foot* of a man; a *foot* measure; the *foot* (or base) of a mountain; those soldiers who fight on *foot*. Take *post*: that which is *posited* or *posted* firmly in the ground; a military *post*, the *post* of danger; *posts*, or horse-stages; the *post(s)*, or conveyance of news. *Man* is a male person, but it is also man or woman (*man* = mankind).

(iii) *Transference of Meaning by Analogy or by Real Resemblance.* A good example is afforded by *sweet*: a sweet taste, a sweet face, a sweet tune, a sweet poem. For *brilliant*, we have the original sense 'sparkling' or 'glittering'; a person who 'shines' is brilliant, perhaps because he has a brilliant or sparkling wit. It must, however, be admitted that in this group, there is little chance of confusion.

Related to Logic is Rhetoric; and in this connexion we may recall I. A. Richards's dictum (*The Philosophy of Rhetoric*, 1936), that '[Whereas] the old Rhetoric treated ambiguity as a fault in language, the new Rhetoric sees it as an inevitable consequence of the powers of language and as the indispensable means of most of our most important utter-ances—especially in Poetry and Religion'.

Ambiguity, however, is found not merely in single words but also and especially in phrases, clauses, and sentences (whether single or compound; simple or complex). On ambiguity in general, the *locus classicus* is William Empson's *Seven Types of Ambiguity*, 1930: whence the following paragraph (direct borrowings being within quotation marks).

'There are three possible scales or dimensions [that] seem of reliable importance, along which ambiguities may be spread out; the degree of logical or grammatical disorder, the degree to which the apprehension of the ambiguity must be conscious, and the degree of psychological complexity concerned. Of these, the first seems to be the one about which there is least danger of talking nonsense, the one it is most important to be clear about . . . My seven types, so far as they are not merely a convenient framework, are intended as stages of advancing logical disorder.' For us, there is, however, an obstacle in Empson's seven types: some of them constitute, not actual errors but mere potentialities of error or ambiguity; they are theoretic rather than practical. From his book, therefore, I select a few passages illustrative of such ambiguities as the ordinary reader—and, for that matter, the ordinary writer—is likely to encounter.

There is, for instance, that type of ambiguity in which ambiguity—in word or syntax, or in both word and syntax—'occurs when two or more meanings all add to the single meaning of the author'. In

Cupid is winged and doth range;
Her country so my love doth change.
But change she earth, or change she sky
Yet I will love her till I die

'*change* may mean "move to another" or "alter the one you have got", and earth may be the lady's private world, or the poet's, or that of mankind at large'; the third verse shows that in the second verse the subject of *doth change* is *my love*, not *her country*,—a fact that in the second verse is still a doubt; also, does *yet* = the second member of an *although . . . yet* antithesis, or does it = *still* (in time)? A moment's thought shows that *yet* is the concomitant of *although* understood after *But.* 'All meanings to be extracted from these [terms] are the immediate meanings insisted upon by the words, and yet the whole charm of the poem is its extravagant, its unreasonable simplicity.'

'However, as a rule, complexity of meaning is produced by complexity of thought, even where . . . there is only one main meaning as a resultant.' In

If th' Assassination
Could trammel up the Consequence, and catch
With his surcease, success . .

'Consequence means casual result. . . . *Trammel* was a technical term used about netting birds, hobbling horses . . . *Surcease* means completion, stopping proceedings in the middle of a lawsuit, or the overruling of a judgment. . . . *His* may apply to Duncan, *assassination* or *consequence*. *Success* means fortunate result, result whether fortunate or not, and succession to the throne. . . . The meanings cannot be remembered all at once.'

'It is clear that ambiguity . . . of grammar, though common enough in poetry, cannot be brought to this pitch without chaos. . . . Sometimes the [ambiguity resides in] a relative clause, with "that" omitted, which is able to appear for a moment as an independent sentence on its own, before it is fitted into the grammar', as in *Their images* [which] *I lov'd* in

Their images I lov'd, I view in thee,
And thou (all they) hast all the all of thee.

'There is some suggestion that the first clause may be wholly independent, and that *I view in thee* means "I look for them in you"; but on the whole the device merely puts "which I loved" into special prominence.'

After subjecting Shakespeare's 16th Sonnet, 'But wherefore do not you a mightier way', to a searching analysis of the equivocal words, the slightly ambiguous grammar, and the danger of inserting more punctuation-marks with a view to simplification, Empson draws this conclusion:—'Ambiguities of this sort may profitably be divided into those which, once understood, remain an intelligible unit in the mind; those in which the pleasure belongs to the act of working out and understanding, which must at each reading, though with less labour, be repeated; and those in which the ambiguity works best if it is never discovered.'

Another type of ambiguity 'occurs when two ideas, which are connected only by being both relevant in the context, can be given in one word simultaneously. This is often done by reference to derivation; thus Delilah is

That specious monster, my accomplished snare.

Specious, "beautiful and deceitful"; *monster*, "something unnatural and something striking shown as a sign of disaster"; *accomplished*, "skilled in the arts of blandishment and successful in undoing her husband". The point here is the sharpness of distinction between the two meanings [of each of these three words], of which the reader is forced to be aware; they are two pieces of information, two parts of the narrative; if ingenuity had not used an accident, they would [each of them] have required two words.' Note, however, that the Classical reader feels no ambiguity, for he perceives the pairs of meanings, and that the modern non-Classical reader feels none, for he becomes aware of only *one* sense in each pair. Yet (Empson adds) 'it must seem trivial to use one word with an effort when there is time enough to say two more simply; even if time is short it seems only twice as useful, in a sort of numerical way'.

Another type of ambiguity 'occurs when two or more meanings of a statement do not agree among themselves but combine to make clear a more complicated state of mind in the author. . . . One is [primarily] conscious of the most important aspect of a thing, not the most complicated; the subsidiary complexities, once they have been understood, merely leave an impression in the mind that they were to such-and-such an effect and they are within reach if you wish to examine them.' This being a matter rather of psychological ambiguity and of a cumulative atmosphere and meaning arising from that psychological complexity than of verbal ambiguity, I shall refrain from examples and merely refer the inquirer to the subtle Fourth Chapter of Empson's book.

Germane to our article, however, is the type in which ambiguity 'occurs when the author is discovering his idea in the act of writing, or [is] not holding it all in his mind at once, so that, for instance, there is a simile which applies to nothing exactly, but lies half-way between two things when the author is moving from one to the other. Shakespeare continually does it:—

Our natures do pursue
Like rats that raven down their proper
bane
A thirsty evil, and when we drink we die.

Evidently the first idea was that lust itself was the poison; but the word *proper*, introduced as meaning "suitable for rats", but also having an irrelevant suggestion of "right and natural", and more exact memory of those . . . poisons which are designed to prevent rats from dying in the wainscot, produced the grander and less usual image, in which the eating of the poison corresponds to the Fall of Man, and it is [the] drinking [of] water, a healthful and natural human function, which it is intolerable to avoid, and which brings death. By reflection, then, *proper bane* becomes ambiguous, since it is now water as well as poison.'

Another interesting type 'occurs when a statement says nothing, by tautology, by contradiction, or by irrelevant statements, if any; so that the reader is forced to invent statements of his own and they are liable to conflict with one another'. This type is perceived the most clearly when a joke is implied, for the reader is meant to be conscious of the joke—the intelligent reader, of the mean also. Take Max Beerbohm's remark that 'Zuleika [Dobson] was not strictly beautiful'. Empson tackles it thus:—'"Do not suppose that she was anything so commonplace as [merely beautiful]; do not suppose that you can easily imagine what she was like, or that she was, probably, the rather out-of-the-way type that you particularly admire"; in this way (or rather, in the gambit of which this is a parody) jealousy is placated, imagination is set free, and nothing has been said (what is this strict [i.e., particular] type of beauty, anyway?) which can be used against the author afterwards.'

In 'Let me not love thee, if I love thee not' (Herbert) there is 'an ambiguity by tautology'.

Empson's seventh type, 'the most ambiguous that can be conceived, occurs when the two meanings of the word, the two values of the ambiguity [or equivocality], are the two opposite meanings defined by the context, so that the total effect is to show a fundamental division in the writer's mind . . . A contradiction

of this kind may be meaningless, but can never be a blank; it has at least stated the subject which is under discussion . . .; it is at once an indecision and a structure. . . . It seems likely . . . that words uniting two opposites are seldom or never actually formed in a language to express the conflict between them; such words come to exist for more sensible reasons, and may then be used to express conflict . . . People much more often need to mention the noticeable than the usual, so that a word which defines a scale comes to be narrowed down more and more to its two ends; the English "temper" is an example of this. Another reason is that, of relational opposites one cannot be known without the other; to know what a ruled person is you must know whether the ruler is a general or an archbishop. Thus a word which names both parts of a relation may be more precise than a word which only names half of it. . . . In so far, in short, as you know that two things are opposites, you know a relation which connects them. . . . [This] type of ambiguity involves both the anthropological idea of opposite and the psychological idea of context, so that it must be approached warily.' Empson is wary, in that he begins 'by listing some very moderate and sensible examples'. Of the numerous excellent examples, this seems to me to be one of the best:—
'Macbeth, faced suddenly with the Thaneship of Cawdor and the foreknowledge of the witches, is drowned for a moment in the fearful anticipation of crime and in intolerable doubts as to the nature of foreknowledge. Then throwing the problem away for a moment (he must speak to the messengers, he need not decide anything till he has seen his wife)—

Come what may,
Time, and the hour, runs through the
roughest day.'

Two interpretations lie open to us. 'Either, if he wants it to happen: "Opportunity for crime, or the accomplished fact* of crime, the crisis of action or decision, will arrive whatever happens; however much, swamped in the horrors of the imagination one feels as if one could never make up one's mind. I need

---

* Obviously Mr Empson would have avoided *fact* if he had remembered that, in Latin, *factum* = 'a fact' and 'a crime' and that, in legal terminology, *fact* = 'a crime' (as in 'to confess the fact').

not, therefore, worry about this at the moment"; or, if he does not want it to happen: "This condition of horror has only lasted a few minutes; the clock has gone on ticking all this time; I have not yet killed him; there is nothing, therefore, for me to worry about yet". These opposites may be paired with predestination and free will: "The hour will come, whatever I do, when I am fated to kill him [less ambiguously, "Whatever I do, that hour will come in which I am fated to kill him"], so I may as well keep quiet; and yet if I keep quiet and feel detached and philosophical, all these horrors will have passed over me and nothing can [? rather "will"] have happened". And in any case (remembering the martial suggestion of *roughest day*), "Whatever I do, even if and when I kill him, the sensible [= tangible and visible] world will go on, it [the murder] will not really be as fearful as I am now thinking it, it is just an ordinary killing like the ones in the battle".'

In the course of summing up, Empson says that 'Of the increasing vagueness, compactness, and lack of logical distinctions in English, the most obvious example is the newspaper headline. I remember a very fine one that went

ITALIAN ASSASSIN BOMB PLOT DISASTER.'

He notes that the assassin was not an Italian and that therefore *Italian* must qualify the rest of the headline; that the dominant noun is *disaster*; hints that the adjective qualifying *disaster* is *bomb-plot*, that *assassin* should be *assassin's* and that *Italian* should be *in Italy*; and concludes that 'the main rhythm conveys: "This is a particularly exciting sort of disaster, the assassin-bomb-plot type they have in Italy"'. I suggest that the following rearrangement explains the headline:

ITALIAN DISASTER

ASSASSIN'S BOMB-PLOT,

which = 'There has been in Italy a disaster caused by a bomb in an assassin's plot'. Empson's comment is delightful: 'Evidently this is a very effective piece of writing . . . It conveys [its point] with a compactness which gives the mind several notions at one glance of the eye, with a unity like that of metaphor, with

a force like that of its own favourite *bombs*: and he gently refrains from pointing out that it has one slight drawback, in that its meaning—even after an exasperating amount of cogitation by the reader—is far from clear.

It was this example and an ensuing pronouncement of Empson's which caused Mr Frank Whitaker, in an address delivered to practising journalists on Dec. 13, 1938, and reproduced in *The J. I. J.*, January, 1939, to speak as follows:—

'Headlines are a good starting point, not only because they offer the greatest temptation to the debaser owing to the stress under which they are often written, but also because they have created an important problem of another kind. They remind us every day, particularly in our more popular newspapers, that the grammatical sentence is no longer the only way of expressing a thought in modern English. We are, indeed, rapidly evolving a distinct headline language which bears little relation to everyday speech. That cannot be a good thing, because it means that we are approaching a stage, if we have not already reached it, at which a word will mean one thing when it is written and another when it is spoken.

ANTI-POSSESSIVE CRAZE

'In this headline language logical distinctions in the meaning of words are being ruthlessly flattened out. It is a counterfeit language within a language, in which nouns are habitually made to do the work of adjectives, commas the work of heaven knows what, and from which the possessive case has almost disappeared. "Beware of the possessive", I read in one Fleet Street style sheet which in many respects is admirable—"beware of the possessive; it shows up a headline".

'What does that mean? I can quite understand the desire for action in headlines—the preference for lively, vigorous words—and there are no doubt many contexts in which the possessive case can be avoided without creating ambiguity. But this anti-possessive craze should be carefully watched. For example, I read in the "Star" last week the headline, "Question on Earl de la Warr speech", from which it was impossible to tell whether the speech was by Earl de la Warr or about Earl de la Warr. The distinction might be important, and it should be jealously preserved. Ambiguity is the enemy we have to watch, and our new headline language is full of it.'

After the felicities of Mr Empson and Mr Whitaker, it is a sad decline to pass to some particular examples collected by myself; but they may serve as warnings. They fall roughly into five unequal and fortuitous groups of horrible examples: Wrong Adjective; Wrong Pronoun; *when* and *where*; Wrong Order; and Miscellaneous.

A good instance of wrong adjective occurs in Froude's *Henry the Eighth*: 'The Reformation . . . in the sixteenth century would have been left to fight its independent way unsupported by *the* moral corruption of the church from which it received the most powerful impetus': the *impetus* comes from corruption, not from *church*: if *that* had been written for *the*, there would have been no ambiguity. A very different example is this of double-pointedness (where only one point was intended) in a mid-Victorian's commencement of an article: 'We are all born idiots'.

Pronouns have to be handled with care; their misuse engenders some queer ambiguities, as in:—

'He put his feet upon the stove as *it* was cold' (examination question). Was the stove cold?—This example illustrates the potential ambiguity of the impersonal (or *it*) verbs—*it rains, it is raining*, etc.

'Such preparation may occupy six or seven stages. First of all *it* may be necessary to bleach the object, though *it* is by no means universal' (Nigel Morland, *The Conquest of Crime*, 1937). The first *it* at first sight appears to refer to *preparation*; reflection shows that *it* is part of the verbal phrase *it may be necessary*. The second *it* should refer to *object*, but it obviously doesn't: this *it* = 'this practice'.

'He succeeded in dominating large meetings of operatives and in them causing them to think' (E. P., *A Critical Medley*, 1926). The first *them* is condonable, although *at them* would have been preferable; but the second *them* is unforgivable, and should be *those men*.

'Although it [an estate] was not then specially laid out for shooting, a century and a half has, in fact, made it a very attractive *one*' (*Country Life*, Jan. 15, 1938). *One* refers to *shooting*, but in a sense not yet mentioned: 'a tract of country over which one has the exclusive right to shoot'.

'Overtopping all was the knoll planted with cedars *that* always served as assembly point; as watch-tower before sunrise shot golden darts into the mists that flounced on the hills; as platform for a parting chant or chorus at night' (an article in *The Times*, January, 1938). Not the cedars but the knoll constituted the assembly point: change either to 'the cedar-planted knoll that always served' or to 'that knoll which, planted with cedars, always served' or 'the knoll that, planted with cedars, always served'. Nor is the repetition of *as* without a shade of ambiguity.

'Jack and Florence met George and Lily at *his* place. I had told *them* to arrange something, but *they* thought if *he* asked one of *them* to lunch *she* wouldn't come—*they* never quite hit it, perhaps *they* told you': a monstrous mass of ambiguity, cited by C. C. Boyd in his useful little book, *Grammar for Great and Small*.

When and *where* look innocent enough, but they are very far from being so innocent as they look. 'When did you arrange to meet him on Saturday night?' is a question that, when I read it, I took to mean 'On what date did you arrange that you should meet him on the Saturday night?'; I was mildly annoyed when I saw that the reply was 'Somewhere about 7 o'clock, I think'. During the War of 1914–18, the constantly recurring 'Where were you wounded?' obviously admitted of two answers—locality (e.g., 'On the Somme'); part of the body ('In the arm'). Experienced men soon learnt to reply, 'In the arm; on the Somme'.

Often the ambiguity springs from a careless arrangement of words. 'Smart men's suiting' and 'Stylish gentlemen's suits' are likely to be misunderstood.

'The flames . . . destroyed almost the last vestiges of past eras . . . vestiges which the ruthlessness of Henry VIII failed entirely to erase' (J. A. Froude): the context shows that 'failed to erase entirely' or 'failed to entirely erase', not 'entirely failed to erase', is intended.

'Europe desires to see weakened the non-warlike influence of China over Russia, which has increased enormously of late' (*The Daily Telegraph*, October, 1900—cited by Nesfield). Preferably: 'Europe desires the weakening of China's non-warlike influence over Russia, for that influence has enormously increased of late'.

'*Paradise Lost* is the name of Milton's great epic poem on the loss of Paradise divided into twelve separate parts' is cited by Nesfield, who proposes: '*Paradise Lost*, divided into twelve separate parts, is the name of Milton's great epic poem', which is a poor improvement. Read: '*Paradise Lost* is the name of Milton's great epic poem on the loss of Paradise; the poem is divided into twelve parts.'

'I shall begin by listing some very moderate and sensible examples', Wm. Empson, *Seven Types of Ambiguity*, 1930. This author, as modest as he is subtle, does not mean that his examples are 'very moderate and very sensible': he would have avoided this ambiguity of intention if he had written 'some sensible and very moderate [i.e., unexaggerated or simple] examples'.

'I was speaking to Miss Worsley of Holly Tye' (Adrian Bell, *By Road*, 1937). He was not speaking to a Miss Worsley that lived at Holly Tye, but of Holly Tye to Miss Worsley.

And here is a miscellaneous lot, of which the first five are drawn from Charles Boyd's *Grammar for Grown-Ups*:—

'I am not going out because it is warm'; a comma after 'out' would remove the ambiguity.

'I do not write for that reason': does the costive fellow mean that he doesn't write at all? Or that, although he writes, it is not for *that* reason (e.g., praise)?

'Miss B. will probably never give another performance as the result of a motor smash': this example might have been included in the preceding group, for ambiguity disappears if we change the order, thus: 'As the result of a motor smash, Miss B. will probably never give another performance.'

'I shall hope to see you next week' should be 'I hope to see you next week', for the meaning is not 'Next week, I shall be hoping to see you'.

'Complaints are made of the system of forwarding permits for the removal of cattle to Ireland by post' (quoted by *Punch* from an Irish newspaper).

'Jewels of unimpeachable genuineness gleamed upon white arms and necks of a value enough [i.e., sufficient] to make up a king's ransom', John G. Brandon, *The Dragnet*.

'One remarks it as a defect only when judging the plan of the book apart from the contents,—a practice that leads one into illogical statements concerning things that are illogical only in appearance', E. P., *Eighteenth Century English Romantic Poetry*, 1924: for *a practice* read *the practice of thus judging books*.

'"You won't catch the flu germs walking in the open air"', states a health enthusiast' (*Punch*, Feb. 16, 1938): ambiguity would have been removed if the statement had been written in the form, "You won't catch flu germs while you are walking"—or "Walking in the open air, you won't catch flu germs".

'The railway will be long before it approaches paying' (cited by Nesfield).

'Removers of distinction' is the proud slogan of a firm of carriers. Many of us would refrain from so cynically philistine a boast.

ameliorate, misused for *appease.* '"How about taking advantage of Mrs Burleigh's invitation [to lunch] and ameliorating the more animal wants?"', Ellery Queen, *The Spanish Cape Mystery* (English edition), 1935.

amend, amendment; emend, emendation. To *amend* is 'to better; to improve' (something imperfect); politically, 'to make professed improvements in (a measure before Parliament)'; in the sense 'to emendate', it is archaic. In present use, *emend = emendate*, 'to remove errors from the text of (a document, a book)'. (*The O.E.D.*)

America or **the States** for **the United States of America.** The former is commonly used, but obviously it is illogical, for it ignores the existence of Canada, Mexico, and the other nations of North and South America. There is, however, no other convenient adjective for *U.S.A.* The English language is not rich in proper adjectives. *The States* is not incorrect, but it is colloquial; in Australia, *the States* would, to a native-born Australian, refer rather to the various *States* of Australia than to the *States* of the U.S.A.

AMERICANISMS. See ENGLISH AND AMERICAN USAGE.

am finished for **have finished.** 'Je suis fini', said an Englishman in a French hotel when offered a second helping by the waiter, who looked at the 'finished' customer with sympathetic concern. *Be done with* is occasionally used!

amiable and **amicable.** *Amiable*, 'agreeable and good-natured', is applied to persons and their disposition: 'He was an amiable fellow', 'His was a most amiable nature'. *Amicable*, 'friendly', 'peaceable and pleasant', refers to relationships, attitudes (towards other persons), arrangements, settlements, conferences,—in short, to the manner or process of doing: 'Amiable people generally have amicable relationships'; in law, an *amicable* suit is a pre-arranged test case between friendly parties.

amid, amidst. See 'AMONG and AMONGST'.

amity and **enmity** must be carefully enunciated or the most absurd misunderstanding may arise.

amn't. See A'N'T.

amok. See AMUCK.

among and **amongst; amid, amidst; while, whilst.** The *st* forms are falling into disuse, partly because they are less easy to pronounce; partly because, when pronounced, they are less euphonious than their alternatives.

among other reasons; among other things. 'I am not . . . going to take you far into technical depths, because, among other reasons, I do not know enough', Stuart Chase, *The Tyranny of Words*, 1938. If Mr Chase intends *along with other reasons*, why does he not say so? If *aside* (anglice *apart*) *from*, why not say so? If *in addition to*, then why not *in addition to*? *Among other things* is generally excused as an idiom: but even if it is an idiom, it is so blatantly self-contradictory and absurd that careful writers avoid it. To extend the absurdity and thus to propagate the contradiction is—well, careless, to say the least of it.

amongst is obsolescent for *among*, than which nothing is less euphonious.

among(st) is occasionally misused for *amid*(st), as in '. . . Reveille, the voice of Western order amongst the babble of the East', Humfrey Jordan, *The Commander Shall . . .*, 1933. *Among* is used with separable objects and is usually followed by the plural; *amidst* means in the middle of, and 'that which surrounds may or may not consist of distinct and separable objects'. (*Webster's*.)

among(st) **others** or *other things* is incorrectly used for 'along with', 'besides' or 'in addition to, other things'.

amoral = non-moral, not connected with morality; *immoral* = wicked; corrupt, licentious. 'A physiological textbook is amoral, but immoral persons may use such a text for immoral purposes';

'A person ignorant of morality may easily become immoral because of his amoral training'; 'The bright amoral virtue of courage' (Rachel Taylor: *The O.E.D.*).

amorous. See AMATORY.

amount applies to mass or bulk, not to number. 'A large amount of animals' is absurd; 'a large amount of books' becomes ludicrous when juxtaposed to 'a large amount of paper'.

amphibian; amphibion. The latter is obsolete for the noun, incorrect for the adjective. In post-War usage, *amphibian* is, in the main, a noun, with adj. *amphibious*. In aeronautics, an *amphibian* is a seaplane. (*The O.E.D.*)]

ample for *enough* (absolutely) is a colloquialism to be avoided in all self-respecting writing. 'Have you enough?'—'Yes, ample.' Probably short for the pretentious *an ample sufficiency*.

amuck is now more usual than **amok** in *run amok* or *amuck*. Originally, *amuck* was, in this phrase, an adjective, from *amok* '(a Malay) in a frenzy'. (*The O.E.D.*)

an; a. Before vowels and silent *h*, *an*; before consonants (other than silent *h*) and before *u* sounded *yoo*, *a*. Thus 'an airy room', 'a bad boy', 'a use not known before'; 'a horse'; 'an hour ago'; 'an honest fellow'; 'a unique signature', 'a eulogy as unexpected as it was flattering', 'a union of two countries', 'an hotel'. [[Usually in America, 'a hotel', 'a historian'. (*After Webster's*.)]]

an before nouns and adjectives beginning with the *u* that is pronounced *yew*. This is incorrect now, whatever it may have been in the 17th Century. 'Traffrail', *The Sub*, 1917, 'An uniform tin case'. This English *u* at the beginning of a noun or adjective consists phonetically of a consonant and a vowel (yōō). On the other hand, *an* is correct before a mute *h*: *an honorable man* but *a humorous writer*.

anachronism is catachrestically employed for *anomaly* more often than you might think. 'I myself [disguised as a gypsy] went off to buy a car! An anachronism for a gypsy?', Bernard Newman, *Death under Gibraltar*, 1938.

analogous and **similar.** See 'SIMILAR and ANALOGOUS'.

analyst (one who analyzes); **annalist** (a writer of annals). These should not cause confusion, except in such a statement as 'He's an analyst (annalist)'.

ancient is opposed to *modern*; it refers to the remote past, especially to primitive languages and civilizations and to very early buildings, statues, writings, etc. Something that is no longer used—no longer in the style or the fashion, no longer handwrought or manufactured—is *antiquated*; but unless it is some hundreds of years old, it is not *ancient*. Words and phrases no longer used are *obsolete*; words used only in poetry or by very old people are *archaic, historical, obsolescent*,—but the obsolescence of a word that has not long been in use cannot properly be called archaism.

and. In general, avoid beginning a sentence with *and*: its use is justified only when a very effective addition is desired or when an arresting accumulation is to be concluded.

and is unnecessary and incorrect in such a sentence as the following, from the Introduction to *Tom Thumb's Diary and Proverb Book*, 1893, 'But of all dwarfs none has bulked as largely in the public imagination . . . as "General Tom Thumb", and with whom all successors have had to stand invidious comparison'. Here 'and' should be omitted or 'and with him' substituted for 'and with whom'.

and (or an') **all**, meaninglessly tacked on to the end of a statement, esp. N.W. England, as when I heard a Westmorland boy say: 'I got my 'an stung wi' a bee an' all'.

and etc. is a vulgarism for *and so forth, and so on, and other things, and the rest*.

and me with . . . This formula exemplifies the illiterate use of the accusative (or object) word where there is no governing word. 'How could the room be cleaned, and me with my rheumatism?' (Onions, *An Advanced English Syntax*) is the illiterate equivalent of the standard nominative absolute used in

How can ye chant, ye little birds,
And I sae fu' o' care (Burns: cited by Onions).

and moreover may occasionally be justified as an emphasized *and*—or an emphatic *moreover*. Generally, however, it is a tautological form of *and*, as in 'And, moreover, when Big Tito had started a vicious fight, certainly for liberty if not for life . . .' (John G. Brandon, *The Mail-Van Mystery*, ca. 1937).

and nor is occasionally found; all it can mean is 'nor', and literally ('and not . . . not') it is nonsense. 'But he did not

move and nor did Julia', Margery Sharp, *The Nutmeg Tree*, 1937.

and which is permissible only when there is a preceding *which* clause, as in 'The house, which was empty and which was likely to remain empty, stood on the hill'. 'The house, situated on the hill and which was empty, was destroyed by fire' is inadmissible in English. The adjective + *and which* construction is a Gallicism. The following occurs in Hazlitt's *A Journey through France and Italy*, 1826, 'He had leisure to look back to the town as we proceeded, and which, with its church . . ., shrunk into a miniature model of itself'.

and who is merely the personal counterpart of **and which**, *q.v.*

and whose. See WHOSE, AND.

and yet which is extremely clumsy for *which yet* or *and which yet*. In 'They were countryman's hands, which could break a rabbit's neck as scientifically as possible; and yet which could set a dog's leg . . . with as much kindness as any woman would show' (Robert Eton, *The Journey*, 1938), change *and yet which could* to *which could, however, set*.

anenemy or **anenome** for **anemone.** Universal among street flower-sellers and too frequent among those who ought to know better.

anent, 'about, concerning', is archaic and pretentious.

angle. See STANDPOINT.

angle, 'point of view', is an Americanism (as is the slangy synonym, *slant*); not objectionable, but to be used sparingly.

angry at; angry with. The former of things and events; the latter of persons. 'He was angry *at* this incident—and *with* the policeman for having been too slow to prevent it.'

animalculae is incorrect for *animalcula*, which is plural, the singular being *animalculum*. See also PLURALS, UN-ENGLISH.

annex. In British usage this is the verb, the noun being either *annexe* (of a building) or *annexation* (acquisition—esp., political acquisition of territory). [[In American usage *annexe* is a Gallicism, *annex* serving as verb and noun.]]

Do not misuse *annex* for *add*, or vice versa, for *annex* is not equivalent to *add*: *annex* is 'to add as an additional part to existing possessions', as in Wellington's 'The whole country is permanently annexed to the British Empire' (the prevailing sense), and 'to attach as a consequence', as in Matthew Arnold's 'Salvation is not annexed to a right knowledge of geometry', a literary sense. (*The O.E.D.*)

annunciation, 'announcement', is not to be confused with *enunciation*, 'manner of, or degree of distinctness in, pronouncing one's words'. (Weseen is rather confusing on this point.)

another . . . also is excessive for *another*, as in 'There was another idea also at the back of his mind' (John G. Brandon, *The Mail-Van Mystery*).

another, misused for *other*. Weseen gives the following examples of this misuse:—'Some kind or another'; 'one kind or another'; 'some way or another'.

another must not be used for *one other*. 'There is only another stile to cross before we reach the wood'; 'Talking of stiles, there's only another to cross before we reach the wood'.

another to is misused when made synonymous with *different from*. 'He wore another cap to mine.'

answer for, misused for *answer to*. In the following example, *answer for* is not wrong; it is merely feeble:—'It is possible to substitute yards or . . . kilometres to apply to oblongs anywhere . . . and get an answer for what you want to know', Stuart Chase, *The Tyranny of Words*, 1938.

a'n't, in my opinion, is the phonetically natural and the philologically logical shortening of *am not*, esp. in *a'n't I?*; *aren't*, though very common in print is both illogical and illiterate, the more so as the *r* is not pronounced; *amn't* is ugly; *ain't* is illiterate and, on other grounds, inferior to *a'n't*.

Note that *a'n't I* offers only two different stresses (of emphasis), whereas *am I not* affords three.

See esp. Jackdaw's 'column' in *John o' London's Weekly*, April 21, 1939.

antagonist; opponent. An *opponent* is one who is on the opposite side, or one who opposes an idea, a measure; it is neutral—one's opponents in games are merely the other competitors or the opposing team. *Antagonist* is stronger; it connotes personal opposition in combat —duel, battle, war.

antagonize. 'To *antagonize*' is much stronger than 'to *oppose*'. To *oppose* is simply 'to be on the opposite side to', hence 'to resist'; to *antagonize* is to cause a strongly inimical reaction in another

person by active opposition or by unfriendly behaviour, as in 'She antagonizes him by her personal remarks.'

ante = 'before' (in place or in time); *anti* = 'against; in opposition to'. See any good dictionary for examples. One of the commonest errors is *antichamber* for *antechamber*. Cf. *antedate* and *antidote*. But, exceptionally, in *anticipate*, *ante* has been changed into *anti*.

anthracite coal. *Anthracite* is sufficient.

anticipate and **expect.** The former is incorrect both for the latter and for *await*, and its prevailing sense is 'to forestall' an action or a person. Weseen is wrong in saying that 'it is questionable in the sense of to foresee or foretaste experiences either pleasant or unpleasant as "He anticipates a pleasant vacation"': *The O.E.D.* registers, as blameless English, the senses, 'to take into consideration before the appropriate or due time' (e.g., 'to anticipate consequences and provide for the future')—'to realize beforehand (a certain future event)', as in 'Some real lives . . . actually anticipate the happiness of heaven' (C. Brontë)— 'to look forward to, look for (an uncertain event) as certain', as in 'Those, not in the secret, anticipated an acquittal'.

antimony; antinomy. The former, 'a hard white element used chiefly in alloys' (chemistry); the latter, 'an opposition or contradiction between two laws or principles' (philosophy).

ANTI-POSSESSIVE CRAZE, THE. See AMBIGUITY.

antiquated; antique. The former = 'grown old', 'inveterate', as in 'antiquated jealousy',—a sense that is obsolescent; 'out of use by reason of age; obsolete'; 'so old as to be unworthy to survive', as in 'the antiquated delusion of a papal supremacy'; 'old-fashioned, whether as survival or as imitation', as in 'antiquated phraseology'; 'advanced in and/or incapacitated by age', as in 'His antiquated aunt was a sore trial to him'. (*The O.E.D.*)

Antique = 'of the "good old times"'; antiquated; no longer extant', as in 'an antique courtesy'; 'of or after the manner of the ancients, esp. of Greece and Rome', as in Byron's

And thus they form a group that's quite
    antique,
Half naked, loving, natural and Greek;

and 'archaic', as in 'the antique mystery

of the Sphinx'. (*The O.E.D.*) Cf. the entry at ANCIENT.

ANTIQUES. See ARCHAISMS.

anxious is not to be used as a synonym of *eager* ('He is anxious to go on this journey') or *desirous* ('She is rather anxious to paint'); but it is permissible for *solicitous* or *earnestly desirous*.

anxious of. 'I am not hopeless of our future. But I am profoundly anxious of it', Beverley Nichols, *News of England*, 1938: which makes us profoundly anxious *for* (or *about*)—not *of*—Mr Nichols's literary future.

any, in a blended genitive. See GENITIVE, VAGARIES OF THE, last paragraph.

any, incorrectly used for *every*, *all*, etc. '*Best of any*' for '*best of all*'. 'James is the best schoolmaster of psychological manners of any novelist that has ever written', A. R. Orage, *The Art of Reading*.

any, misused for **any other.** Examples:—'That winter was colder than any he had experienced' for '... any other'; better change to 'That winter was the coldest he had experienced'.—'It is a longer book than any he has yet written'.

any, misused for *at all*. 'It did not hurt him any.' A colloquialism, more common in the U.S.A. than elsewhere.

any, superfluous. *Any* is not needed in 'Such is indeed the fact, but it is a fact that does not help this Opus any, and so we disregard it in the argument', Don Marquis, *The Almost Perfect State*, 1927. This use of 'any' is an Americanism which has not yet been admitted into good English.

anybody's (or **anyone's**)**else; anybody's else's.** See ELSE'S.

any case, in. See CASE, IN ANY.

anyday; anyrate; anytime. Incorrect for *any day*, *any rate*, *any time*.

any more. See at **almost never.** As a synonym for *now*, it is, I believe, to be avoided. For 'I do not see him any more' read 'I do not see him now(adays)' or 'I no longer see him'.

any one; anyone. *Anyone* is synonymous with *anybody*; *any one* occurs, e.g., in 'He can beat any one of you'. The pronunciation is: '*any'one*; *any one*".

anyone is incorrect for either *any one* (*of*..) or *any* (pronoun); e.g., 'Mr. Huitt ... did not ... summon anyone of the clients who were waiting to see him', E. P. Oppenheim, *The Bank Manager*, 1934.

anyone, anybody or **nobody (no one)** or **somebody (someone) ... they.** The pronoun following these pronouns is *he* or *him* or *his* or *himself*, not *they* or *them* or *theirs* or *their own*; the same applies to the possessive adjectives, *anybody* (etc.) requiring *his*, not *their*. Thus, in Ruskin's 'Anyone may be a companion of St. George who sincerely does what they can to make themselves useful', *they* should be *he*, and *themselves* should be *himself* (Onions); in 'Somebody came into the restaurant, ordered their meal, eat (American *ate*) it; and then hurriedly they departed with a friend of theirs', *their* should be *his*, *they* should be *he*, and *theirs* should be *his*; 'Nobody cares what they do on holiday' is not only incorrect; it is ambiguous.

any place (anywhere); **anyways; anywheres.** Illiteracies.

any thing is justifiable when there is an opposition (whether explicit or implicit) to *any person*. Thus, 'He'll believe anything', but 'He is a fool to believe that any thing will ensure happiness'.

any way. See ANYWAY.

anyway, not *any way*, is correct for 'in any case'.

apart from ('in addition to'; 'without counting or considering') is English, the American equivalent being *aside from*.

apathetic and **epithetic** are noted by Weseen. But the person that knows *epithetic* is unlikely to confuse it with *apathetic*. Still, they are words that require very careful enunciation.

apiary (a place for bee-hives) and **aviary** (a place for captive birds) are occasionally confused.

apiece; a piece. The latter is a noun ('a portion'); the former is an adverb ('singly', 'each by itself'). 'Their pork pies cost sixpence apiece; a piece [i.e., the half of a pie] costs threepence.'

apologetic(s). [['Systematic argumentative tactics ... in defense ...'; 'that branch of theology which formally defends, on the grounds of reason, the divine origin and authority of Christianity' (*Webster's*).]]

apology is too important to be used as a synonym of *excuse*. Nowadays an apology connotes recognition that one is in the wrong, whereas an *excuse* is a plea offered in extenuation or justification of a minor fault or neglect, or an explanation of such a fault or oversight. Further, *excuse* can be extended to the impersonal, as in 'The derailing of the train was the doctor's excuse for failing to attend his extremely important patient'. But do not, from that example, fall into the error of synonymizing *excuse* with *reason*.

appliable, applyable,—on the analogy of *reliable*, no doubt,—are incorrect for *applicable*.

appreciate is incorrectly used in 'Do you appreciate that something terrible may happen?' The correct uses of *appreciate* are these: To form (or make) an estimate of the worth, price, quality or quantity of (a person or thing); to estimate correctly, or perceive the full force or significance of; to esteem adequately, esp. to esteem highly; to recognize the value or excellence of or in; (commercially) to raise the value of (opp. *depreciate*), or, v.i., to rise in value; to be aware of or sensitive to (a delicate impression, a nice distinction).

apprehensive. See TIMID.

apprise; apprize. *Apprise* = to inform, to notify; *apprize* is to appraise, evaluate, estimate—and is obsolescent except in Scottish Law.

approaches, 'preliminary efforts to obtain or effect something', is depreciative in tendency, and, in my opinion, it is best to avoid it in favourable contexts.

appropriate (v.); **take.** These are not synonymous. To *appropriate* is 'to take to oneself, for oneself alone', but the prevailing sense is 'to set apart or to assign a sum of money for a specific purpose, especially by formal action'.

approximate (v.) for *resemble* is incorrect. 'Her murder was . . . skilfully arranged to approximate a suicide', Robert G. Dean, *The Sutton Place Murders*, 1936.

approximately, misused for *almost* or *comparatively*. 'With . . . everything open it would be cool, or approximately cool, in the tropics', Humfrey Jordan, *The Commander Shall . . .*, 1933.

apt (to do something) = fit, suitable, or inclined to do it. Not to be identified with *likely*, as it is in 'He is not apt to gain that distinguished honour' when all that is meant is that he is unlikely to gain it. But *be apt to* (*do*) is good English in the following nuances:—

(Of things) to be habitually liable, to be ready, to (do); (of persons) to be given, inclined, or prone to (do); to tend to (do).

arbiter; arbitrator. The former is general; the latter specific for one who has been chosen or appointed to adjudge and settle a specific question.

arbour is sometimes confused with *harbour* and thought to be of the same derivation, but *arbour* is a shelter under trees (Fr. *arbres*), and *harbour* (akin to German 'Herberge', French 'auberge', and Italian 'albergo', is otherwise derived. [[American spellings are *arbor*, *harbor*.]]

Arcadia; Acadia. The latter is the old name for Nova Scotia and the name for a parish in S.W. Louisiana; the former, of a rural district in Southern Greece—the district that has become generic for the land of rural contentment, a kind of pastoral paradise. *Arcady* is poetic and somewhat archaic for *Arcadia*. (*Et ego in Arcadia vixi*; *Arcades ambo*; and all that.)

archaic. See ANCIENT.

ARCHAISMS or **ANTIQUES.** Archaisms are of two kinds: actual and potential. The potential antiques will be found at CLICHÉ and at SIMILES, BATTERED. Actual antiques—not, of course, all of them!—are listed here.

The modern word (or phrase) is given in the second column; and when the antique is, in some special context, not an antique but a technicality, e.g. *whereas* in law and *morn* and *eve* in poetry, an indication is made parenthetically.

ANTIQUE	MODERN EQUIVALENT
abed (becoming an archaism)	in bed
abide (becoming an archaism)	
aforetime	formerly, previously
albeit	although
amid(*st*)	among
an one	a one
anent	about, or concerning (preposition)

ANTIQUE	MODERN EQUIVALENT
annoy (noun: poetic)	annoyance
Araby	Arabia
Arcady (poetic)	Arcadia
aright (only slightly archaic)	correctly
astonied	astonished
aught	anything
aye, for ever and	for all time; for ever
bale	evil; woe
behest; hest	an order
behoove or *behove* (vv.); *behoof; it behoves me*	to be an obligation on; an obligation; I ought . . .
benison	a blessing
betide	to happen to
betimes	early
betrothal; betrothed	engagement (to be married); engaged. 〖*Betrothal* and *betrothed* are current in American newspaper-English.〗
betwixt	between
bewray	to expose, reveal, indicate
bootless (adv.)	bootlessly
bounden	bound (except in *bounden duty*)
bridal	a wedding. 〖*Bridal* is American newspa- perese.〗
burgess	a citizen
burthen	burden
caitiff	a coward
castor	a beaver
chiefer; chiefest	more important; most important
Christmastide	Christmas time
citizenry	a body of citizens; citizens collectively
clang (preterite and past participle of cling)	clung
clime (poetic)	climate
clomb	climbed
clyster	an enema; a suppository
coal oil	kerosene. 〖*Coal oil* is still common in the U.S.A., though it will probably give place to *kerosene*.〗
coolth	coolness
cruse	an earthenware pot or jar
damosel (or *-zel*)	damsel (see Elegancies), girl
date	limit, term, end
deceptious	deceptive
deem	to think or believe. 〖*Deem* in this sense is in American usage a false elegance.〗
delicate (n.)	a delicacy or dainty
delve (not obsolete but obsolescent)	to dig
demesne; demesnes	domain; estates
despiteful	spiteful
destrier or *destrer*	war-horse
dight (ppl. adj.: poetic)	clad, clothed
doughty	brave; formidable
doxy	mistress; sweetheart; whore
drear (poetic)	dreary
drouth (poetic)	dryness; drought. 〖*Drouth* is current in parts of the U.S.A.〗

ANTIQUE	MODERN EQUIVALENT
durst	dared
dwell	to live (at a place)
eke	also
eld (poetic)	age
emprise	enterprise
engraven	engraved
ensample	an example, a sample
ere (poetic)	before
eremite	hermit
errant (adj.)	wandering
erst (poetic)	formerly; once upon a time
erstwhile (poetic)	formerly [improperly: former]; some while ago
essay	to attempt
eve (poetic)	evening
exceeding	exceedingly
fain (poetic adj. and adv.)	glad, gladly; ready, readily
fair, the (poetic)	beautiful, lovely or merely pretty woman
fare	to travel
fealty	fidelity, loyalty
foison	abundance
forgat (preterite)	forgot
forgot (past participle)	forgotten
forsooth!	truly!
fraught (poetic)	filled; laden
froward	haughty
gentle	well-born
glad (v.); *glad oneself*	to make glad; to rejoice
goodly	good; attractive
gotten	(in England) got; [[in the U.S.A. often *gotten*]]; see entry at GOTTEN
grammatic	grammatical
habit; habits	clothing
haply (poetic)	by chance or accident
helpmeet	helpmate
hereof (legal)	of this
heretofore (legal)	before this; up to this time
hereunto (legal)	unto this
hest (poetic)	see *behest*
hight (ppl. adj.)	called, named
hindermost	hindmost
howbeit	nevertheless
I wis	I know
illume	illuminate
ken	knowledge
kin	relatives; one's family. [[Old-fashioned but current in American usage.]]
kine	cows
leman (Romance)	sweetheart (either sex); lover or mistress
lief; I'd as lief	willing, glad; I'd gladly or willingly
liefer was to me, him, etc.	I (or he or . . .) had rather (do . . .)
liege	liege lord or liege man
mart	a market
maugre	despite (preposition)
meet	fitting, proper, seemly
meseems	it seems to me

ANTIQUE	MODERN EQUIVALENT
methinks	I think
minion	a male favourite
moon	a month
monstrous	exceedingly
morn (poetic)	morning
natheless	nevertheless
nether; nethermost (poetic)	lower; lowest
nigh	near
oft; ofttimes (both poetic)	often
olden (*times*)	the past, the distant past
Orient (adj. poetic)	Oriental
orison (poetic)	prayer
otherwhile(s)	at times; at another time
pantaloon (whether as garment or as actor)	
pard	leopard
parlous	perilous, dangerous. [[Dialectal in the U.S.A.]]
pecunious	wealthy
perchance (poetic; facetious); *peradventure* (facetious)	perhaps
plaint	a weeping; a complaint
plight	to pledge
price of	precious; (of persons) excellent
proven (except in the legal *not proven*)	proved. [[According to *Webster's*, dialectal; nevertheless *proven* is common in general American usage.]]
quick (except in 'the quick and the dead')	living; alive
quoth; quotha	said; said he
rufous	red
saith	says
sate	sat
save (poetic)	except
scarce (adv.)	scarcely
seigneur	lord
selfsame	(very) same
sideling	oblique(ly); sidelong
silvern	of silver; silvery
silly	simple; innocent
simples	herbs, or medicines therefrom
sire	father
something (adv.)	somewhat
spake	(he) spoke
span	(he) spun
speed (v.)	to thrive
spilth	a spilling; something spilled
stoup (poetic; ecclesiastic)	a tankard; holy-water vessel
subtile	subtle
swoon (n. and v.: poetic)	faint
talesman (legal)	juror
tarry	linger
teen (poetic)	grief
tend (poetic)	attend to
testimony (legal)	an open attestation; a confession
thenceforth	from that time on(wards)
thereafter (legal)	after that time

ANTIQUE	MODERN EQUIVALENT
thereof (")	of that
theretofore (")	up to that time
thrall	a slave
tilth	tillage
troth (also the verb)	truth; faith
troublous	troublesome, tiresome
trow	to believe
trusty (e.g., one's trusty sword)	trustworthy
tryst (poetic)	a meeting; esp. a lovers' meeting
twain	two
umbrage, take	to take offence
unhand (v.), as in *unhand me, villain!*	to take one's hands off (a person)
unwitting	unknowing; ignorant
vagrom (adj.)	vagrant, vagabond; hence, erratic
varlet	a groom, a menial; a rogue
verily	truly
vicinage (legal)	neighbourhood, vicinity
void	empty
wax (v.i.)	to grow or increase
weal	welfare; the general good
ween	to think
whereas (legal)	since or because
whereat	at which
wherefore (legal)	for which reason
whereof (")	of which
whereon	on (or upon) which; immediately after which
whilom	once upon a time; some time before
whomso; whoso	whomever; whoever
whosesoever	of whatever person's
wight	a human being; gen. a man
wit, in *to wit*	namely
withal (except as an elegancy)	in addition, as well; nevertheless therewith
wondrous (adv.)	wonderfully
wont	custom, habit
wot	know
woundy	extremely; excessively
writ (past participle)	written
yare	ready, alert, nimble
yclept	named; known by the name of
yon	yonder
yore, of	in ancient times; in the past
Yule; Yuletide	Christmas; Christmas-time
zany	a clown; a fool

aren't. See A'N'T.

are to + infinitive + preposition. See IS TO + infinitive + preposition.

Argentina; Argentine. It is best to retain *Argentina* as the name (based on the Spanish *la Republica Argentina*) of the South American Republic, *Argentine* (or *Argentinean*, preferably *-ian*) as that of a native of Argentina. *Argentine* is also the adjective, 'of or relating to Argentina', as in 'Argentine trade' and 'the Argentine republic is wealthy'. The modern tendency to speak of *the Argentine* instead of *Argentina* is to be resisted.

argot is misused when it is made an equivalent of *jargon* (technical vocabulary or language; technicalities). 'Mathematics has been called the language of science. This is not quite accurate. Each branch of science has also an argot of its own', Stuart Chase, *The Tyranny of Words*, 1938.

arm for *sleeve* is sometimes condemned, but as this sense (a natural one, after all) is passed as blameless by *The O.E.D.*, it certainly is good English.

arise is now, in ordinary speech, used in preference to *rise* only in the transferred sense of a discussion (controversy, argument), a quarrel, a war arising. In formal writing, however, we may still *arise* from a sick bed or from a seat.

around for *about* is incorrect in 'I'll visit you around Easter' and 'He wandered around the city'. So too for *round*.

arresting for *striking* or *impressive* is correct—but, as Weseen remarks, overworked.

arrogate and **abrogate.** To *abrogate* a law is to repeal it; to *abrogate* a custom is to discontinue it; the sense, 'to do away with, put an end to' is obsolescent. To *arrogate to oneself* (the simple verb is falling rapidly into disuse) is to claim or assume that to which one is not entitled, or to claim or assume unreasonably or arrogantly, as in 'They arrogated to themselves the right of approving or rejecting all that was done' (Brougham) and 'She arrogated to herself a certain importance' (Wm. Black). (*The O.E.D.*)

artifice is usually derogatory.

artist; artiste. The latter has been introduced into English 'in consequence of the modern tendency to restrict *artist* to those engaged in the fine arts, and especially painting', *The O.E.D.*, 1888; an *artiste* being there defined as 'a public performer who appeals to the aesthetic faculties, as a professional singer, dancer, etc.' This derivative sense, 'one who makes a "fine art" of his employment, as an artistic cook, hairdresser', etc., is moribund,—and soon, I hope, it will be dead.

artless; ignorant. The former is favourable (with a connotation of ingenuousness); the latter unfavourable.

as for *because* is heavily taxed—grossly overworked—by many writers, who are apparently enamoured of its brevity; often *as* is ambiguous ('He could not work as he was ill in bed'). It is difficult to lay down rules for the use and discrimination of *as, because, for, since*, their correct employment being a matter of idiom. *As* is colloquial both for the objective, logical *because* and for the subjective *for*, either of which is to be preferred to *as* in good writing and dig-

nified speech. In *since* there is a connotation of time: as a causal conjunction it derives from the temporal *since* (= after).

as for *that* (conjunction) is a solecism. 'He did not say as he liked it'; 'Not as I've heard or know of'. Read: 'He did not say that he liked it'; 'Not that I know of'—or 'Not so far as I know'.

as, unnecessary in such a sentence as: 'He expressed himself as anxious to do everything in his power to help', F. W. Crofts, *The Loss of the Jane Vosper*, 1936.

as, wrongly omitted, esp. after *such*. 'The only thing that spurred (annoyed) me was me being such a flat [as] to buy the home', 'Autobiography of a Thief' in *Macmillan's Magazine*, October, 1879. And it is better to retain the *as* introducing a simile; thus 'as dry as a bone' is preferable to 'dry as a bone'.

as, equally. 'It was accompanied by a hissing inbreath from Ferradi which was equally as vicious', John G. Brandon, *The Dragnet*, 1936, for 'equally vicious' or 'as vicious'.

as, such. See SUCH AS.

as a consequence of. See CONSEQUENCE OF.

as a rule . . . always. 'As a rule he was always in the drawing-room before the first gong sounded.' This is no less excessive and unnecessary than *generally . . . always*.

as . . . as. The second *as* should not be abandoned in such a sentence as 'The younger Pitt was as great and even greater than his father': read, 'The younger Pitt was as great as and even greater than his father', or 'The younger Pitt was as great as his father or even greater'.

as . . . as and so . . . as. The former is neutral, colourless; the latter, emphatic. 'As soon as they were ready, they departed'; 'So soon as you are ready, we shall depart'. Where *to* + an infinitive follows, the formula is *so . . . as* (e.g., 'They were so clumsy as to be dangerous to their companions'), not because there is *to* + an infinitive but because there is considerable emphasis: here, there is—in addition to the idea of comparison—an unmistakable connotation of degree, so that *so . . . as* + infinitive has a different psychological origin from that of *as . . . as*. 'In negative assertions and questions implying a negative answer, *so . . . as* and *as . . . as* are now generally used interchangeably, but *so . . . as* is preferred by many writers and authorities . . .; as, he is not *so* cruel *as* the average boy.' (*Webster's*.)

as far as and **so far as**. In literal statements concerning distance, *as far as* is used in positive sentences ('I ran as far as I could and then walked'), *so far as* in negative sentences ('It was not so far as I expected'). In figurative statements, *so far as* is usual, as in 'So far as I can see, your idea is admirable'.

as follow is wrong for *as follows*. 'There were many articles in the room, as follow: a large table and a small one, a bookcase, six chairs, twelve maps, etc.' *As follows* is short for *as it follows* and, because it is impersonal, it is of the same order as the italicized words in 'I shall act *as seems* best', 'So far *as* in me *lies*'. (Onions.)

as if and **as though** are often synony mous, but should they not be differenti ated? To define the difference is not easy: to exemplify is easy enough. 'Could you drive a ball four hundred yards?' 'As if I could!'—'Jack X. is an exponent of personal publicity, you know.' 'Oh yes, as though he lived aloud!' In short, *as though* connotes comparison, whereas *as if* stresses possibility or potentiality—or their opposite, impossibility.

as is (or **was** or **will be**) **the case with** is an intolerable tautology for *like*: 'As was the case with Bonnor, Bartlett is a mighty hitter'. Sometimes it is misused for *as for* or *as with*: 'As will be the case with the future, the past has been falsi fied by historians'; 'As is the case with you, I fear the unknown less than I do the known'.

as many as is loose—indeed, it is incorrect—for *such persons as* or *those who* (or all those who) in 'As many as require the book should order it before the edition (strictly limited) is exhausted'.

as per, 'in accordance with', is such horrible commercialese that even merchant princes are less than riotously happy when their secretaries wish it on them.

as to for *of* or *with* or *for*. 'A brief indication as to the English [influence] . . . affords a useful comment . . .' (E. Partridge, *French Romantics' Knowledge of English Literature*, 1924), where *of* was the right word to use.

as to is sometimes introduced quite unnecessarily, as in: 'One can only guess as to how Mr Jaggers knew . . .' (Cecil Freeman Gregg, *Tragedy at Wembley*,

1936). One would not insert *as to* before a 'why', so why insert it before a 'how'? A less reprehensible example is this, cited by Dr C. T. Onions in *An Advanced English Syntax*: 'They could not agree as to whom they should elect', concerning which Onions comments: '"As to" may be omitted. It is not at all necessary, and is inserted in such cases probably in imitation of "They could not agree as to that".' *As to* in such senses is well described by Mr Whitten (*Good and Bad English*, 1938) as 'fog-English'. It is defensible when it synonymizes *in respect of* or *in the matter of*; it is defensible, too, though unnecessary as a synonym of *about* or *concerning*.

as to whether is unnecessary for **whether.**

as too. In the following, from J. A. Froude, *English Seamen in the Sixteenth Century*, 'As often happens with irresolute men, when they have once been fixed to a decision they are as too hasty as before they were too slow', *as too* is a very awkward construction, though perhaps not demonstrably ungrammatical; 'as much too hasty' or 'as over-hasty' would be better.

as well as is often ambiguous, as in 'The captain, as well as the sailors, suffered this bitter reverse', which may convey the fact that both the captain and his crew suffered them—or the different fact that the captain's power of endurance was equal to the crew's.

as what. See WHAT, AS.

as yet is unnecessary for *yet*. 'His mind . . . was not as yet completely ossified', Francis Brett Young, *Dr Bradley Remembers*, 1938.

ascend up is absurd for 'to *ascend*'.

ascribe and **attribute**. To *ascribe* something is to enter it in an account, to reckon or count it; to consider or allege as belonging *to*, to claim *for*. To *attribute* is to consider or regard (something) as belonging *to* ('To attribute to a word a sense it does not possess'); to declare or impute as a quality belonging or proper *to*, or inherent in ('A mystical character is apt to be attributed to the idea of moral obligation'); to reckon as a consequence of ('His shrivelled arm was attributed to witchcraft'); to consider as belonging *to*, declare to belong *to* an author ('A play attributed to Shakespeare'); to assign to its proper place or time ('This manuscript may be attributed to the 4th Century, A.D.'). (*The O.E.D.*)

aside from. See APART FROM.

aspen, frequently applied as a name to the branching poplar tree, is actually only an adj. derived from the obsolete designation of that tree, 'asp', and means *quivering, tremulous*, like the leaf of the poplar.

assemble together (v.i. or v.t.) is excessive, and wrong, for *assemble*. For 'The people assembled together' read 'The people assembled'; for 'He assembled the people together', read 'He assembled the people'.

assert is a strong word: do not debase it to equivalence with *say*.

assert, like *affirm* and *declare*, cannot be used with the infinitive unless a noun or a pronoun is put with that infinitive. 'I assert [or affirm or declare] you [or her or him or John or that fellow] to be a thief' is correct, though less idiomatic than 'I assert [etc.] that you [etc.] are [or is] a thief'. But one cannot say 'I affirm [etc.] to be a thief' instead of 'I declare [idiomatically; *not* 'affirm', nor 'assert'] myself to be a thief'. (Note that the first person requires, not *me* or *us* but *myself* or, after 'we', *ourselves*.) In C. McCabe's *The Face on the Cutting-Room Floor*, 1937, we find this example of 'the infinitive in the air':—'The reader, knowing, just as McCabe does, that Robertson's telephone was engaged between 6.30 and 6.35 . . ., more than two hours after the time at which Robertson now asserts to have left the room, . . .'

asset for *amenity* (of a place), or *valuable feature* or *factor*, is incorrect and shows a misunderstanding. *Assets* are the property of a person (or business) available for the discharge of his debts. Used 'loosely', says *The Con. O.D.* for *any possession*; and 'improperly' for any useful quality, as in *The Evening News*, Feb. 10, 1938, 'Nearly everyone has graduated either through Surrey schoolboys' teams or the Surrey Wanderers, an asset which has played no small part in improving the county spirit, etc.'

assist to (do something) is incorrect for *assist in* (doing). We help a person to do, we *assist* in the action. Nesfield gives an example from that fruitful source of error in his time, *The Daily Telegraph* (Aug. 8, 1900). 'He is looked upon as a great authority on these questions, and will assist to examine scientifically a

number of these questions.' The first meaning of *assist* is *to be present at*; to *help* or *give aid* is subsidiary, and the word *help* is generally better.

assoil, 'to absolve', has been erroneously used for 'to *soil* or *stain*'.

assume. See 'ADAPT and ADOPT'.

assume and **presume.** *Presume* (v.i.), 'to be presumptuous', and *presume (up)on*, 'to take for granted', offer no difficulty: *assume* can never be substituted, here, for *presume*. As v.t., *presume* has the following extant senses: 'to take upon oneself, to undertake without permission or adequate authority', as in 'To presume to sit in judgment on the actions of kings'; 'to take for granted', especially in Law, as in 'to presume the death of the man that disappeared eight years before' or 'to presume that he who disappeared so long ago is dead'. To *assume* is 'to take unto oneself; to adopt', as in 'to assume a partner'; 'to take upon oneself, to put on', as in 'Habits are soon assumed' (obsolescent), 'The Netherland revolt had . . . assumed world-wide proportions' (Motley); 'to take to oneself formally' (insignia of office; symbol of a vocation) and 'to undertake' (an office, a duty), as in 'The community which he had assumed the spiritual charge of' (Mrs Oliphant), 'He assumed the monastic habit' (Freeman); 'to take as being one's own, to claim, to take for granted', as in 'That disposition . . . to assume . . . jurisdiction over other men's conduct'; 'to simulate or feign', as in 'scepticism, assumed or real'; 'to take for granted as the basis of an argument, a negotiation', as in 'William assumes the willingness of the assembly', 'To assume that we have the most accurate possible translation', 'The entire length of our farm is assumed to be about thirty-two miles'. In Logic, *assume* = 'to add the minor premise to a syllogism'. (*The O.E.D.*)

assumption and **presumption** correspond exactly to *assume* and *presume*.

assurance and **insurance.** In *life assurance* and *l. insurance*, *marine assurance* and *m. insurance*, etc., *assurance* is falling into disuse. [[It is obsolescent in the U.S.A.]]

astonish, astonishment are stronger, than *surprise* (n. and v.); *astound* and *astoundment* are even stronger.

astray and **estray.** The former is adjective and adverb, as in 'The animal is astray' or, usually, 'The animal has gone astray'. *Estray* is a noun, as in 'That cow is an estray' (it is lost or has gone astray) and a legal verb, 'to roam, to wander, to stray'. And whereas *estray* is used only literally, *astray* has also a figurative sense.

at about (six o'clock; half way) is incorrect for *about* (six o'clock; halfway).

at all is misapplied by a writer of a letter quoted by *The New Statesman and Nation*, who wonders 'if it is at all possible for us to be warned if there is likely to be a return of the aurora borealis'. A thing is either 'possible' or not. See COMPARATIVES, FALSE.

at and in. See IN and AT.

at is bad, if not absolutely ungrammatical, for *against*, in the following from a newspaper placard, *The Daily Worker*, Feb. 6, 1938,—

40,000 PROTEST AT FOOD PRICES.

at last. See LAST.

at length = *at last* but it also = 'fully' or 'in detail'.

ate, past tense of *eat* (q.v.).

atheist. See AGNOSTIC.

attach together. Read *attach*.

attached hereto. Read *attached*.

attain; accomplish; attain to. To *attain* is 'to reach, to gain, to achieve'; to *accomplish* is 'to perform (a task), to succeed in (an undertaking)'. Weseen gives a useful example:—'He who wishes to attain success must accomplish something every day'. *Attain to* connotes either effort or a lofty ambition, as in 'He attained to fame only when he had been striving for thirty years'. Note also that *attain* in the sense 'to obtain, to acquire' is archaic. (*The O.E.D.*)

attended by. See PREPOSITIONS WRONGLY USED.

attitude. See REACTION.

attorney. See LAWYER.

attorney-general. The preferable plural is *attorney-generals*.

attribute (v.) is misused in the following: 'Mr. Collier, remembering that this (1593) was the very year *Venus and Adonis* was published, attributes some great gift of the Earl of Southampton to Shakespeare to have immediately followed', Thornbury, *Old and New London*, 1880. The latter half of the sentence is awkwardly constructed and would be better expressed, '*assumes that some great gift was made by the Earl to Shakespeare immediately afterwards*'. See also ASCRIBE

and ATTRIBUTE. Note, too, the different pronunciation of the noun and the verb.

attributed is misplaced and misunderstood in this deplorable sentence set for correction in a school examination paper. 'Though Shakespeare had a fair education, it was not acquired knowledge that can be attributed to his brilliance'; the second clause should read, 'his brilliance can not be attributed to acquired knowledge'.

audience is properly a gathering of hearers or listeners. Otherwise, *spectators*, i.e. 'onlookers', is required.

aught, 'anything', is incorrectly used for the cypher, *nought*, which represents 'nothing'. 'For aught I know, he may be there' is correct, though slightly archaic; 'Put an *aught* (or *ought*) after 7 and you have 70' is incorrect—indeed, illiterate.

aura. 'McCarthy . . . lit his cigarette, holding the lighter so that it etched an aura upon its owner's face', John G. Brandon, *The Dragnet*, 1936, exemplifies a not infrequent misconception, for the *aura* of person or thing is an *emanation from* him or it, *not shed* by something outside.

Aura is occasionally misused for figurative *air* (or *atmosphere*), as in 'In view of Lord Northcliffe's famous maxim, "When a dog bites a man, that's not news; but when a man bites a dog, that is news", it appears as if every happening of importance should be given an aura of drama' (examination essay script, June, 1939).

aural, 'of the ear', hence 'of hearing'; *oral*, 'of the mouth', hence 'spoken'.

Aurora Borealis. 'All over England last night the Aurora Borealis gave a magnificent display of their beauty', *The Evening News*, leaderette, Jan. 26, 1938. —The writer, thinking perhaps unconsciously of the *northern lights*, and ignorant of Latin, supposed *Aurora Borealis* to be a plural formation.

AUSTRALIAN ENGLISH. See STANDARD ENGLISH, Section iv.

author. See MAN OF LETTERS.

authoress. Authoresses generally prefer to be called *authors*.

authoritive is wrong for *authoritative*. *Authoritarian* (n. and adj.) means '(one who is) favourable to the principle of authority as opposed to that of individual freedom'. (*The O.E.D.*)

auto for *automobile* is a colloquialism —hence, to be avoided in formal speech and writing. [In the U.S.A., *automobile* is now usually limited to attributive and adjectival uses, such as *the automobile business*. The noun is commonly *car*.]]

autocracy and **autonomy** are occasionally confused; e.g. George Ryley Scott in *The History of Corporal Punishment*, 1938, twice misuses the latter for the former. The meaning of *autocracy* is 'absolute government (by an individual or a paramount authority'); of *autonomy*, 'the right of a state or institution to govern itself' (or the condition of a state possessing such right). According to *The O.E.D.* there was formerly a use, 'now obsolete', of the former for the latter, but not *vice versa*.

autography for *autobiography* (as, e.g., in C. McCabe, *The Face on the Cutting-Room Floor*, 1937) is dead—despite misguided efforts to keep it alive. The surviving senses are: the action of writing with one's own hand; an author's own handwriting; autographs collectively (a rare sense); and especially a lithographic process 'by which a writing or drawing is transferred from paper to stone' (*The O.E.D.*).

AUXILIARY VERB (have, had, etc.), omission of. 'The preparation of a history of . . . reactionary movements which contributed towards shaping the course of political events for the past one hundred and fifty years' (for 'which have contributed'), *Guggenheim Fellowship prospectus*, for 1938, New York.—'I been to see', low colloquialism; in other words, an illiteracy, a solecism. [[The substitution of the preterite and of *did* + inf. for the perfect is a distressing tendency in American speech.]]

avail for *afford, provide.* 'Behind all variants and shades, there stands the absolute certainty that fingers are not the fonts of knowledge, and sucking them will avail no information' (Julian Franklyn). *Avail* is here misused; a correct construction would be 'such action will not avail (or, be of value to) them'.

avenge and **revenge** (vv.); **vengeance** and **revenge** (nn.). The noun that corresponds to *avenge* is *vengeance*; that which pairs with *revenge* is—*revenge*. One *avenges* another or, less commonly, the wrong done to another, but one *revenges* oneself or the wrong done to oneself; *vengeance* is the exaction of justice ('"Vengeance is mine", saith the Lord') or, for oneself, what one considers justice (a 'getting even'), whereas *revenge* is satisfaction accorded to personal resent-

ment ('He shall have his revenge the next time we meet'). The nn. are less often confused than the vv., and it is particularly to be noted that, in idiomatic English, one does not say 'I shall avenge —or, revenge—the person that does the wrong'. In short, *revenge* (n. and v.) is the more subjective or personal, *avenge* and *vengeance* the more objective and impersonal. See also Fowler's *Modern English Usage.*

avenue, explore every. See EXPLORE EVERY AVENUE. Other strange uses of the word *avenue* have been noticed by A. P. Herbert, who quotes Mr J. H. Thomas's reported statement, '. . . I certainly did not shut the door to any avenue of peace'.

average = 'estimated by average' or 'equal to what would be the result of taking an average', hence 'of the prevalent (or, the usual) standard', as in 'A modern drawing of average merit' (Ruskin); 'the average man'—despite there being no such animal—is permissible; but it is slovenly English to equate it with 'common' or 'typical'. (*The O.E.D.*)

averse to (or **from**). See ADVERSE TO.

avert. See ADVERT.

aviatress; aviatrix. Avoid these insults to women.

avocation and **vocation.** One's *vocation* is one's occupation, one's work or employment; an *avocation* is that which calls one away from one's *vocation*— hence, a minor or subsidiary occupation, a by-work (or *parergon*), hence even a hobby. 'But as, in many cases, the business which called away was one of equal or greater importance . . . , the new meaning was improperly foisted upon the word: Ordinary employment, usual occupation . . .' (*The O.E.D.*). Prudent and scrupulous writers observe the etymological and proper distinction, which, after all, makes both for the enrichment of the language and for clarity, economy, nicety.

avoiding for *excepting* or *except.* 'I have found Guinness . . . the only thing— avoiding drugs—to give me . . . natural sleep', an advertisement in *The Evening News*, Oct. 8, 1937. Though it implies deliberate exception, it is too much to expect *avoiding* to= 'except if, and as, I avoid'.

avoirdupois as a synonym for 'a person's weight' is permissible only as a jocular colloquialism.

await and **wait.** *Await* is used, (*a*) of persons, 'to wait for' (a coming event or person), as in 'King Brindi awaited them at the head of the Picts' (J. R. Green) and 'I shall await your answer with the greatest eagerness' (Seeley); and (*b*) of events, fate, honours, offices, duties, 'to be in store—or to reserve for', as in 'Honours and rewards which he little deserved awaited him' (Macaulay) and 'What fates await the Duke of Suffolk?' (Shakespeare). To *wait* is intransitive (with occasional transitive uses) and has a transitive form *wait for*: to *wait for* a person is to *await* him. (*The O.E.D.*)— See also WAIT.

awake; awaken. The past tenses are *awoke* and *awakened*; the past participles *awaked* (or *awoke*) and *awakened*. As past tense of *awake*, *awaked* is archaic; as past participle of either *awake* or *awaken*, *awoken* is incorrect. 'I was awoken by that rather flashy young woman', Agatha Christie, *Death on the Nile*, 1937. Moreover, the past tense of *wake* is *woke*; the past participle is *woken*. Of *waken*, both the past tense and the past participle are *wakened*.

award and **reward.** The latter is either a recompense or a recognition of merit; the former is 'a judicial sentence, esp. that of an arbitrator or umpire', hence 'that which is . . . assigned, as payment, penalty, etc., by the terms of the judge's sentence or arbitrator's decision' (*The O.E.D.*). So, too, for the verbs.

awful, 'inspiring awe'; **aweful,** 'full of awe'. Do not use the former in good speech or writing (where, moreover, *awfully* is equally to be avoided).

awhile for **a while** is catachrestic when *while* is a noun. 'I shall stay here for awhile' is incorrect for '. . . for a while'. Such a sentence as 'They followed it [an inlet] for awhile along the edge of the bank' (Hulbert Footner, *The Dark Ships*, 1937) brings one up with a jerk; *for a while* or, simply, *awhile* would have been correct.

AWKWARD PHRASING. The worst awkwardnesses are so idiosyncratic and so obvious that they require no comment; of the others, the majority will be found under such headings as False Agreement (*q.v.* at AGREEMENT, FALSE) and Order.

One cannot prescribe against awkward phrasing except in a general way: re-read everything you write, and do it as externally as you can by putting yourself in the place of the reader; any awkwardness will then manifest itself to you, and it will, indeed, hit you in the eye. Awkwardness is, if you like, the opposite of elegance; I prefer to call it the opposite of economy of words on the one hand, and on the other, the opposite of clarity.

Here is an example from a writer in whom such awkwardness is a rarity: '[There] stood, a slight, white-clad figure, in the bright circle of light cast by one of the lamps which was still alight, of the car from which she had been flung' (Mrs Belloc Lowndes, *The House by the Sea*, 1937).

awoke; awoken. See AWAKE.

ay and **aye.** In the sense 'ever', *ay* is to be preferred; in that of 'yes', *aye* is to be preferred, though *ay* is etymologically as correct as *aye*. *Ay(e)*, 'ever', is pronounced like the *ay* of *hay*; *ay(e)*, 'yes', is pronounced either 'eye' or like the 'ever' *ay(e)*. (*The O.E.D.*)

B

baby. See INFANT.

Bacchic, misused for *gastronomic*. 'Ellery engulfed the last mouthful, put aside his serviette, and sighed with Bacchic repletion', Ellery Queen, *The Spanish Cape Mystery* (English edition), 1935.

back again is superfluous for *back* ('He gave me the coat back again'); also for *returned* ('I see you're back again').

back of for *behind* is a colloquialism; *in back of* for *behind* is an illiteracy *In front of* is good English. So is *at the back of*, as in 'At the back of all this lay the conviction . . . ' (Krapp). [[Note: *Webster's* lists *in back of* = *behind* without a qualification such as *obs.* or *vulgar*. It is certainly common in American usage.]]

bacterial is the usual adjective for 'of or pertaining to bacteria'; *bacteric* and *bacterical* are rare—not, as Weseen states, incorrect.

bad (for *ill*), as in 'she was taken bad in the street', is a low colloquialism—a solecism. *Bad* is an adjective and correct in 'She feels bad'.

bad friends is absurd for *enemies*.

balance for *remainder* is catachrestic. 'The considerable balance of this list will be found in *Modern Criminal Investigation* . . . from which the above extract is taken' (Nigel Morland, *The Conquest of Crime*, 1937). Its use for *the* *rest* or *remainder* is described by *The O.E.D.* as 'commercial slang': it may have come from America. I remember hearing, fifty years ago, of an Irishwoman at Killarney offering bog-oak ornaments to American tourists and saying 'Sure, I'm the Belle of Killarney!' To which one of the Americans replied, 'Are you the Belle? Then I wouldn't give much for the balance!' (W.B.)

baleful and **baneful.** *Baleful* is 'pernicious; destructive', also 'malignant'; as 'unhappy; distressed' it is an archaism. *Baneful* is 'life-destroying; poisonous', also 'pernicious, injurious'. The points to note are that *baneful* does not mean 'malignant' and that *baleful* does not mean 'poisonous'. (*The O.E.D.*)

balk. See BAULK.

baluster and **banister.** Weseen is misleading on this point. The facts are these:—A *baluster* is a short, circular-sectioned, double-curved pillar or column, slender above and larger, pear-shaped below, 'usually applied in a series called a *balustrade*'; hence, 'a slender upright post or pillar of any shape supporting a rail; in pl. a railing or balustrade'; hence, usually in plural, 'the upright posts or rails which support the handrail, and guard the side, of a staircase; often applied to the whole structure of uprights and handrail. Now more usually banister(s)', *The O.E.D.*

balustrade. See the preceding.

baptismal name. See CHRISTIAN NAME.

ban (v.) has since ca. 1930 been grossly overworked and foully misused by journalists and by approximatists among writers. In current Standard English, it = 'to prohibit' (a thing) or 'to interdict or proscribe' (a person). The two chief journalistic senses are 'to dismiss' (a person), 'to deny the right of entry to' (either a person or a thing): which, to put it bluntly, are as incorrect as they are unnecessary. Deplored by Mr Frank Whitaker in *The J.I.J.*, January, 1939.

banister(s). See BALUSTER . . .

bank (n.). See SHORE.

Barbadoes is correct; but *Barbados* is now more usual for the British island in the West Indies. The river in Brazil is always *Barbados*.

barbarian (adj.) = 'non-Hellenic' or 'non-Roman' (with reference to Classical times); as a synonym of *barbarous* (uncivilized), it is best avoided, and *bar-*

barous used in its place; *barbarous* also = 'cruelly harsh' and (of speech) 'harsh-sounding'. **Barbaric** = 'uncivilized', 'illiterate', 'non-Latin', 'outlandish'; it is well to reserve it for 'in the characteristic style of barbarians, as opposed to that of civilized countries or ages' as in 'Barbaric pearl and gold' (Milton), 'Each maiden's short barbaric vest', 'Barbaric splendour of decoration' (Wm. Black), and 'barbaric art'.

To all of these adjectives, the corresponding agential noun is *barbarian*. (*The O.E.D.*)

barely (or **hardly** or **scarcely**) **than** is catachrestic for *barely* (etc.) . . . *when*. 'Barely had her spirits fallen, leaving her to brood over the sea, than the pinch was repeated', Louis Bromfield, *The Strange Case of Miss Annie Spragg*, 1928. See also the entry at HARDLY . . . THAN.

barrage. A barrage (of gunfire) is a military term, defined by *The Con. O.D.* as 'gunfire so directed as to make a given line impassable': it is, therefore, synonymous with *curtain(-)fire*. The term falls within our scope on two counts.

1. It is often misused for *fusillade*, as I noticed in a School Certificate candidate's précis—July, 1938—of Macaulay's *Defence of Arcot*.

2. Soldiers often, though decreasingly, use it in the slang sense, 'an excessive number or quantity', as in 'I received a barrage of invitations'.

barring. See CONJUNCTIONS, DISGUISED.

barrister. See LAWYER.

base or **basis.** In brief, *base* is literal for 'the lowest or supporting part', with various derivative technical senses, and *basis* is figurative, 'the main constituent, fundamental ingredient', 'foundation; groundwork', 'a principle, or a set of principles', as in 'Society rested on the basis of the family' (J. R. Green), and 'a basis of legislation'. (*The O.E.D.*) The plural of *base* is *bases*. The plural of *basis* is *bases*.

basketfuls and **baskets full.** A *basketful* is a quantity that will fill a basket, whereas a *basket full* is a basket full of (e.g. potatoes).

bathos and **pathos.** (Adjectives **bathetic** and **pathetic**.) The former is a 'ludicrous descent from the elevated to the commonplace' (in Rhetoric); the latter is that artistic, musical or literary quality—hence, that quality in life—which excites either pity or sadness. (*The O.E.D.*)

BATTERED SIMILES. See SIMILES, BATTERED.

baulk and **balk.** '*Balk* is the analogous spelling: cf. *stalk, talk, walk,* etc.; but *baulk* is frequent, and in Billiards . . . the prevailing spelling' (*The O.E.D.*).

bay-window; bow-window. The latter is segmentally *curved;* the former, rectangular or polygonal, though some writers make the term include curved windows, *bay* thus becoming generic and *bow* specific. (*The O.E.D.*)

be (or **become**) + a single active verb. Ambiguity or awkwardness often results, as in 'They were not uncreative in their work, had to tackle new problems all the time, and so they were interested and worked with zest', J. B. Priestley, *They Walk in the City*, 1936.

beau ideal, as *The Con. O.D.* usefully points out, does not mean 'a beautiful ideal' but 'the ideal beauty', one's idea of the highest type of beauty.

be being + past participle. The progressive or expanded infinitive.

'He will not *be being* wounded every day but perhaps only once—possibly not at all—in the fighting.'

On asking one friend what he thought of this, I received the answer, 'There is no such construction'. Another friend said 'Yes, I've heard it, but it's obviously wrong'. I first wondered about it when I heard myself saying, 'I should not be being disturbed all the time by rushed jobs if I had independent means'. If I can say 'I am being disturbed all the time', why not 'I shall (or should or may or might) be being disturbed'? Is there a difference between 'I should not be disturbed all the time' and 'I should not be being disturbed all the time'? There is. In the former (and in all sensible variations of the same formula), the past participle has much the same force and function as an adjective (with *disturbed,* cf. *perturbed*): all past participles have become, or are in process of becoming, adjectives ('*Heard* melodies are sweet'): there we have the idea of *continuous* state. But in the latter—'I should not be being disturbed all the time'—we have the idea of a *continual* act or a recurring state of things.

Contrast 'He will be seen every day of the week' with 'He will *be being* seen every day of the week': in the former

seen is virtually synonymous with *visible.*

Set 'He was not to be wounded in the War of 1914–18' over against 'He was not to *be being* wounded in the War'. In the former, the sense is 'He was not'—i.e., was not destined—'to receive a wound', whereas in the latter it is 'He was not (destined) to be wounded on numerous occasions'.

Now take the three forms of gerund (the verbal noun, the *-ing* noun): the active (*receiving wounds*), the neutral or intransitive (*becoming a casualty*), and the passive (*being wounded*). Put them within the frame of a sentence and we get:

'Receiving wounds is no fun';
'Becoming a casualty is no fun';
'Being wounded is no fun'.

Turn those sentences into *to be* equivalents:

'To receive wounds is no fun';
'To become a casualty is no fun';
'To be wounded is no fun':

crisp, clear-cut, single-action, time-limited connotations, as also are the gerundial variants. The continual, plural-action, time-extended (or expanded) forms corresponding to those gerunds and infinitival nouns are:

'To be (continually) receiving wounds is no fun';
'To be (continually) becoming a casualty is no fun';
To *be* (continually) *being* wounded is no fun'.

In short, I firmly uphold the *be being* (*wounded*) construction because it expresses a shade of meaning not otherwise expressible: 'to be continually wounded or disturbed or perturbed or visited or captured or imprisoned or pursued or . . .' is ambiguous; but 'to be being constantly wounded or disturbed or perturbed or . . .' is unambiguous—and expressive.

P.S. Having written the above, I thought, 'Perhaps I had better obtain outside opinion—the opinions of experts'. So I wrote to Professor Otto Jespersen, Dr C. T. Onions, and 'Jackdaw' of *John o' London's Weekly*. Professor Jespersen referred me to his four-volumed *A Modern English Grammar on Historical Principles*, where the construction is given as a variety of the expanded tense; he cites 'There's no wedding. Who could be being married?' (Barrie, *Barbara's Wedding*) and 'I shall always be being pushed away' (Galsworthy). 'The difficulty is evaded in . . . "'Nothing seemed to be getting done," he complained" [H. G. Wells]' (He goes on to say, 'I have no examples of the perfect and pluperfect: *has (had) been being —d*'.) He adduces the comparable construction *being to be*, as in 'He had to think of everything familiar to him as being to be parted with'.

Dr Onions replied thus: 'There is no doubt that *be being —ed* is current and has a meaning. Thus, if one were not in the habit of shaving oneself, one might say, "This is the time I ought to be being shaved". It is, as you imply, usual with the modal· or so called auxiliary verbs; I suppose some people include even *ought* among these!'

And 'John o' London' thus:—'I can but suggest that while—? *whereas*—[this form is] logical and grammatical, [it is] awkward. Why not "I have no wish to be wounded every day", or "At least I shall not be wounded every day"?' But those suggestions do not cope with the ambiguity treated above. 'There are,' continues that writer, 'many like cruxes of speech that are best avoided by the back door.' Not very helpful, I fear.

It was odd that, as I was rounding off this entry, I saw Professor Stephen Leacock's 'How Much Does Language Change?' in *John o' London's Weekly*, Jan. 20, 1939. In it occur the words, 'We can even say, without taking a fit, "I will be being praised"—a usage that would have made Addison or Gibbon feel faint'.

became + past participle. This construction is often ambiguous and always awkward or, at the least, infelicitous, as in 'Alan Kent became roused from sleep by the rattle of distant thunder' (Henry Holt, *Wanted for Murder*, 1938). That this construction is to be avoided will be the more readily perceived when we add another example: 'Her eyes became filled with tears'. Certain persons would suggest: 'Kent was roused from sleep by . . . distant thunder' and 'Her eyes were filled with tears': but both those sentences are time-ambiguous. I think that, in all such instances, the simple *active* tense is the best: 'Her eyes filled with tears'; 'The rattle of distant thunder roused Alan Kent from sleep'.

because is sometimes misused for *that*, as in David Garnett's review of Dr. Lin Yutang's *The Importance of Living* in *The New Statesman and Nation* of June 18, 1938: 'The value of the book to civilised Europeans is because it is an anthology of Chinese ideas and anecdotes'; cf. 'Because terms are muzzy . . . does not mean that nothing can be accomplished on the economic front' (Stuart Chase, *The Tyranny of Words*, 1938). [[See Fannye Cherry, 'The Reason Is Because' (*American Speech*, February, 1933) for an arresting list of examples of this misuse.]]

because and **for.** See FOR and BECAUSE and AS for BECAUSE.

become to be for *become*. In 'He became to be known as a most reliable person' there is confusion between *became known* and *came to be known*.

befall has a pejorative connotation; *happen to* is neutral and, occasionally, favourable; *fall out for* is favourable ('It might so fall out for anyone'). For the wrong use of *befall*, see the quotation at '*ones* for *those*'.

before for *until*. 'Not *until* I have passed that examination, shall I be able to go out to parties' is correct; 'Not *before* I have . . .' is catachrestic. Perhaps the reason is that *until* connotes inclusion in the following act or event, whereas *before* emphasizes not so much the ensuing act or event as the time or events preceding it.

begin. See COMMENCE.

beg leave (to say, etc.); **beg permission** (to differ, etc.). These forms are preferable to 'I beg to say' and 'I beg permission to depart'. Especially nauseating is 'I beg to advise you', and 'I beg to remain Yours faithfully, ——' is insufferable.

begrudge and **grudge** are virtually synonymous: 'To give, grant, allow unwillingly; to be unwilling to give, grant or allow; to envy (a person) the possession of': but *begrudge* is the stronger—also the more formal—word.

behalf of, in and **on.** Confusion leads to the loss of a very useful distinction. *On behalf of* = 'on the part of (another), in the name of, as the agent or representative of, on account of, instead of a person', often with the connotation of official agency, as in 'An application was made on behalf of the prosecutor for a remand' (Sir J. Mathers). *In behalf of* = 'in the interest of, as a friend or defender of, for the benefit of (a person)': 'Speak in my behalf, please' is 'Put in a good word for me, please'. (*The O.E.D.*)

behind is the most serviceable of all the words for that portion of the anatomy on which one sits. See my *Slang To-Day and Yesterday*, at the section on Vulgarisms. So late as 1882, it was a low colloquialism.

beholding is obsolete for *beholden*, 'obliged (*to* a person)', 'under a personal obligation for services or favours'. (*The O.E.D.*)

being to be. See BE BEING . . .

belief of. See PREPOSITIONS WRONGLY USED.

believable. See UNBELIEVABLE.

belittle; belittling (the game). This verb was formerly frowned on by purists and is still deprecated occasionally by inveterate pedants—for the terrible reason that it was American. Nothing can be said against it; much for it.

bellicose; belligerent. Respectively 'warlike' and 'engaged in waging war'.

belly is 'that part of the body which receives food', i.e., the stomach with its adjuncts; *stomach* is now more general than *belly* in this sense. The prevailing current sense of belly is 'that part of the human body which lies between the breast and the thighs, and contains the bowels', the medical term being abdomen, which, by the euphemistic and the mealy-mouthed, is used in preference to the good English word (a doublet, by the way, of *bellows*).

below and **beneath.** See 'ABOVE and OVER'.

beneath for **under.** This misuse occurs especially in 'This (that, etc.) fell beneath my notice (or observation)'; *beneath* = 'lower than'.

Benedick, benedict. An incorrect spelling of *benedick*, which means a newly married man, esp. one who has escaped matrimony until late in life. Ackermann quotes Brewer, *Phrase and Fable*: 'Benedick. A sworn bachelor caught in the wiles of matrimony.—Benedict. A bachelor, not necessarily one pledged to celibacy, but a man of marriageable age, not married.' St. Benedict was a most uncompromising stickler for celibacy. [[*Webster's* does not recognize this distinction between *benedict* and *benedick*.]]

benefaction, misused for *benefit*. 'Gypsies were such a nuisance, they would say, that whoever had killed this man had probably conferred some benefaction

upon the community at large', Bernard Newman, *Death under Gibraltar*, 1938.

beneficence is occasionally misused for *benevolence*, as *maleficence* is for *malevolence*; and vice versa. *Beneficence* and *maleficence* are the doing of good and harm respectively; *benevolence* and *malevolence* are the corresponding sentiments. An instance of *beneficence* misused for *benevolence* occurs in the following quotation from Vernon Loder's detective novel, *The Button in the Plate*, 1938:— 'Floating on a serene plane of airy beneficence, he suddenly discovered that people were not looking up to him among the stars, but somewhere on the ground near their feet.'

benzene; benzine. The former 'is now generally used by chemists, but *benzine* is in common use for the commercial product'; *benzol* (same sense), 'less correctly *benzole*', has been obsolescent since ca. 1880. (*The O.E.D.*)

beside, as used by Coleridge in

> The moving moon went up the sky
> And nowhere did abide,
> Softly she was going up,
> And a star or two beside,

is incorrect if he meant *as well, in addition*; he chose to avoid sibilance and to get the rhyme he wanted. He is, perhaps not to be censured, for, according to *The Con. O.D.*, *beside*, the preposition, was 'formerly also adverb' and equivalent to *besides*.

Mr Harold Herd, in *Watch Your English*, rightly insists on the distinction, giving examples of correct use: 'I first saw him beside the main entrance', and 'Have you any money besides this?', also 'Besides, the season will not be over, etc.'

besides means 'in addition to', not *other than*. Clearly, then, it is misused in '"Otherwise the wound must have been on the right side of his face—unless it was made by something besides the handle of the gear-lever"' (Lee Thayer, *Death in the Gorge*, English ed., 1937).

best two (or **three** or . . .) and **two** (or **three** or . . .) **best.** Usage has tended to justify *two best*, probably on the ground that if we can say 'The most popular writers are X. and Y.', we can also say 'The two most popular writers are X. and Y.'—as we do. Contrast *first two* (etc.) which is correct, and *two first*, which is incorrect.

bête noir is a very frequent error for *bête noire*. Even *bête noire* is to be used with caution, for it is a cliché. What is wrong with *bugbear* that it should be supplanted by a Gallicism?

betide, meaning *happen* or *come to pass,* is sometimes misused to mean *betoken* or *bode,* as in 'His slipping as he crossed the threshold betided a misfortune'.

betray for *exhibit* or *disclose* is sometimes ambiguous. 'Only once . . . did I see J. W. H. T. Douglas betray his punishing powers [as a batsman]': cricketers know that the younger Douglas was a dour bat and that, here, *betray* must = 'exhibit'; but the uninformed might be pardoned for thinking that, on this occasion, he failed to do justice to an ability and habit of smiting the ball.

better. Than what?—"Better buy Capstan, they're blended better"—a Tobacco advertisement.

better and **bettor,** as the noun-agent of *bet* (v.). *The O.E.D.* admits the two forms. Despite one's first feeling of prejudice against it, the *-or* form has much to be said for it.

better for *longer.* See BETTER THAN . . .

better for *rather.* 'On a May morning where should an Englishman be better than on Wenlock Edge?', Robert Eton, *The Journey,* 1938. The context shows that *better* does not signify 'morally better'; the reference is to choice.

better than for *more than* is not Standard English but dialect. 'Better than a mile' is a frequent example. *Better* in the sense of *longer* (in time)—'"When did he marry his mistress?" "about four weeks ago, or better"' (*The Sessions Papers of the Old Bailey,* 1759)—is obsolete in Standard English.

between, misused. 'The Trades Union' as nickname of the 1st Dragoon Guards is derived, according to Frazer & Gibbons, 'from the K.D.G's being constantly employed in suppressing Trade Union disturbances in Lancashire and the Midlands between 1825–34'. It should be 'from 1825 to '34' or 'between 1825 and 1834.' The same error occurs in 'I got between five or six foont [sovereigns]', in 'Autobiography of a Thief' in *Macmillan's Magazine,* October, 1879. *Between* is also misused for *among, amongst,* where more than two objects are referred to. 'Between her hair' was written by a poet who ought to have known better. Note too the error in 'In 1926 [Louis

Bromfield] returned to France, and since then has lived between there and the U.S.A.' (biographical note in the Penguin edition of that author's *The Strange Case of Miss Annie Spragg*).

between and **among.** One divides money, goods, property *between* two persons, but *among* three or more.

between each. See EACH, BETWEEN.

between [noun] **to** [noun] is incorrect —and silly—for *between . . . and . . . .* as in 'Between London to Manchester, there are several large cities'; 'Between 9 a.m. to 6 p.m., I saw a battle'. Foolish, too, is 'Between 7 B.C.–21 A.D., there were several wars'.

between you and I. *Between,* being a preposition, takes the accusative case equally with all other prepositions (*after me, after him and me, for you and me*): therefore, between *you and me. Between* and *betwixt* are, however, not, in function, parallel to *after, for, in, to,* where the preposition is governing single units: *for you and me* is *for you and for me; in him and me* (there is ambition) is *in him and in me . . .* But *between him and me, between you and me* do not equal *between him and between me, between you and between me,* the latter pair being nonsense. *He and I, you and I* may be regarded in phrasal units, of which only the first member (*he* and *you*) take the accusative, thus: *between him and I, between you and I.* Also, there are persons that, immediately detecting the grammatical error in *between him and I,* are blind to that in *between you and I,* for the reason that *you* is the same in the accusative (*for you*) as in the nominative (*you are here*), whereas it is *for him* and *he is here. Between you and I,* though indefensible grammatically, may be considered as a sense construction, and is often used by those who would never dream of saying *between he and I.*

For an excellent account of *between you and I,* see the article by Professor Robert J. Menner in *American Speech,* October, 1937.

betwixt is now archaic for *between,* except in poetry.

bevy, misused. 'A bevy of men's voices reached them from the hall', G. Pleydell Bancroft, *The Ware Case,* 1913.

biannual should be reserved for 'half-yearly'; **biennial** for 'two-yearly'. I myself, however, prefer *half-yearly* to *biannual.*

biased or **biassed.** *The O.E.D.* sanctifies usage: and permits either form.

bibliography must not now be used—as before ca. 1925 it could be used—of a *list of authorities and/or sources, a list of books (and documents) read (or consulted),* a *list of books to read and study* (or a *reading list);* nor of a *catalogue raisonné,* which is a list of works, authorities, sources, with the addition of descriptive and/or critical details (e.g., 'Esp. valuable for the French influence on English drama'). A *bibliography* is properly, in general 'the' and in particular 'a', 'systematic description and history of books, their authorship, printing, publication, editions, etc.' *(The O.E.D.);* that 'etc.' includes format, number of pages (e.g. viii plus 288), type-fount (or *font*), number and kind of illustrations. The list of books by or on an author, or on a subject, becomes a bibliography only when the preceding particulars are noted against each book-title.

bi-cennoctury for *bi-centennial* is both incorrect and absurd.

biennial. See BIANNUAL.

bid—preterite *bid* (archaic: *bad, bade*) —past participle *bid* (archaic: *bidden*).

bid. In an address delivered at the Hall of the Institute of Journalists on Dec. 13, 1938, Mr Frank Whitaker, the editor of *John o' London's Weekly,* uttered these moving words (published in *The J.I.J.,* January, 1939):—'The sub-editor's worst crime is that he either takes a word with a simple meaning, and makes it stand for a vague, illogical mass of other meanings, or . . . applies strong, colourful words to unworthy ends, and so ruins their effectiveness when their use is appropriate.—To take a single instance, let me return to *bid,* which sub-editors have made me hate more than any other word in the language. According to my dictionary the verb *to bid* means to command, order, invite, announce, proclaim, or make an offer at a sale. The noun means an offer of a price. Now usage often leaves a dictionary behind, and for my part I am quite prepared to accept a new meaning of a word if there is anything to be gained by it. But the slavish way in which our sub-editors use *bid* to mean an attempt to do anything under the sun arouses my lowest instincts. "New bid for Europe pact", "Navy bid", "boxing bid", "desperate bid", "legitimisation bid",—I take them all from last week's papers.'

big for *important* or *leading* is a loose colloquialism, as in 'The big man in that firm is Smith'.

biggest share for the *majority* or *most* is incorrect, as in 'The biggest share of the students were in uniform'.

billion is, in England, a million millions; in the U.S.A. (and France and Germany), it is a thousand millions. Cf. MILLIARD.

bi-monthly; by-weekly. See following entry.

bimonthly; and **semi-monthly** respectively = 'once every two months' and '(happening) twice a month'. **Biweekly** and **semi-weekly** = 'occurring every two weeks' and 'twice a week'. The spellings *bi-monthly* and *bi-weekly* are preferable.

birth date, or **date of birth; birthday.** Respectively 'date on which one was born' and 'anniversary of one's birth'.

bison. See BUFFALO.

black (v.) is literal (e.g., to black one's shoes); **blacken** (v.t.) is figurative, as in 'She blackened his character in the most unscrupulous manner'. But as an intransitive, *blacken* is used both lit. and fig.— as in 'I . . . believe that rain will fall when the air blackens' (Johnson) and 'It may blacken into cynicism' (Morley). *(The O.E.D.)*

blame (something) **on** (a person) is colloquial—and unnecessary—for *blame* (a person) *for* (something).

blank cheque (or, in U.S.A., **check**) is needlessly and wrongly stigmatized by Weseen.

blatant for *flagrant.* Anthony Eden, in a speech delivered in December, 1936, said 'a blatant breach of good faith'.

-ble. This is a defective series: we have *double* and *treble,* but there it stops.—For the difference between *treble* and *triple,* see TREBLE . . .

blend into is incorrect for *blend with* and for the preferable *merge into* or *with.* 'Professional gardeners blend into their surroundings, and it is often possible to miss them completely in a walk around the garden' (L.C.C. Major Establishment examination, 1938: an essay script).

blend together is a foolish, redundant variation of *blend* (v.).

BLENDED GENITIVE. See GENITIVE, VAGARIES OF THE, last paragraph.

BLENDS. See PORTMANTEAU WORDS.

block ought not to be used for a political *bloc,* a political group formed for a special purpose. [[*Webster's* approves *block* in the sense of *bloc* in American usage.]]

bloody 'is entirely without improper significance in America' (the U.S.A.), as H. L. Mencken has remarked in *The American Language*. But Americans writing for an English public and American visitors to Britain should remember that, in Great Britain, this word, despite its growing popularity there and its consequent weakening, is still regarded as unsuitable for, and in, respectable circles and dignified writing. (For a full account, see 'The Word *Bloody*' in my *Words, Words, Words!*, 1933.)

bluff, misused for *simulate*. 'To bluff intelligence is the easiest thing possible'; a crass Philistine once remarked: to simulate stupidity (or even to be stupid) is much easier.

bogey; bogie; bogy. These three spellings are interchangeable for the three meanings, 'the number of strokes a good golfer may be assumed to need for a hole or a course'—'an open railway freight-car' or 'a revolving undercarriage'—'a bogle, a goblin'. Writers would do well to attach the first meaning to *bogey*, the second to *bogie*, the third to *bogy*, as Weseen recommends. See also *The O.E.D.*

Bohemian is 'a native of Bohemia', hence 'a Gypsy'; **bohemian,** a transferred use, is 'a Gypsy of society', esp. 'a writer, artist, musician, actor that leads a vagabond or a free and irregular life'. (*The O.E.D.*)

bona fide is occasionally misused for *bona fides*. In a manuscript I read on March 9, 1939, I came upon the curious information that 'Mussolini's *bona fide* has never been questioned'. *Bona fide* is a Latin ablative; it = 'with good faith'. In English *bona fide* is an adverb, and it = 'in good faith; sincerely; genuinely'; hence it is used as an adjective = 'acting, or done in good faith; sincere; genuine'. *Bona fides* is the Latin nominative, and in English it can be used both as nominative and as accusative. Properly it is a Law term = 'good faith; freedom from intent to deceive' (*The O.E.D.*). *Bona fides* is singular, not plural as in '. . . As though Kingdom's *bona fides* were not accepted', R. Philmore, *No Mourning in the Family*, 1937.

book for *magazine, periodical*, etc. A book is a complete volume, not a single issue of a serial publication.

book-learned and **bookish** are now uncomplimentary. The corresponding complimentaries are *erudite, learned, scholarly*. *Book-learned* and *bookish* connote 'ignorant of life, however much book-learning one may possess'.

born, borne. Correct uses are 'He was born on the first day of the New Year' and 'He was borne by his mother after three hours of labour'. Also, 'The body was borne (not *born*) into the house'.

borrow (money) **of** (a person) is correct but slightly obsolescent; *borrow from* is now the usual construction.

boss (n.) is restricted by good writers to its political sense, 'a manager or dictator of a party organization in the U.S.A.'

both for *alike*. *Both* refers to two persons, things, groups, classes, kinds, etc., not to three or more thereof. '. . . A shrewd common sense, which kept her safe . . . from all the larger follies, whilst still permitting her to give full run to minor eccentricities, both in speech, deed and dress' (R. B. Cunninghame Graham, 'Aunt Eleanor', in *Scottish Stories*, 1914). Cf. *both alike*, redundant for *alike*, in 'Both of the suits are alike' and 'The sisters are both alike'.

both for *each*. 'There is a garage on both sides of the street' should be 'There is a garage on each side of the street' unless the author means that a garage is partly on one, partly on the other side of the street.

both, the. This is catachrestic for *the two* ('The both bowlers were unsuccessful') and also for *both* (" "Good for the both of you", grinned Punch', Robert Eton, *The Journey*, 1938).

both + noun, misused for *the* + noun + *together*. 'Then *x* plus 650 is her share. Both shares equal $5,000' (read 'The shares together equal $5,000'), Stuart Chase, *The Tyranny of Words*, 1938.

both . . . as well as is incorrect for *both . . . and*. See quotation at PERSONNEL.

both of us—you—them are correct; *we both* and *us both—you both* (whether nominative or accusative)—*they both* and *them both*—these are incorrect, though one often hears all of them except *they both*. That *they both* lags behind the others appears from the queer effect it produces in 'Estella threatening to kill herself—Jensen gripping her—they both struggling for the knife' (C. McCabe, *The Face on the Cutting-Room Floor*, 1937). See also GENITIVE, VAGARIES OF THE, penultimate paragraph (Unclear Genitives). [[To an American this distinction may well seem pedantic and unreal. 'This said, they both betook them several ways' (Milton).]]

both our fathers, both your husbands, both their books. These are the colloquial forms that correspond to Standard English *the fathers of both of us, the husbands of both of you, the books of both of them.* 'The need for a compact expression of this kind is often felt. We may sympathize with the little girl who, wishing to state that a certain pet was the common property of herself and her brother, said "It's both of our donkey"!' (Onions.) The day may arrive when these colloquialisms will become good English: if they do, they will merely revert to Middle English practice. But although one can say *both our fathers,* what happens when the reference is to the father of two children? *Both our father* is (at present, anyway) impossible. *Both your husbands* is clear enough, at first sight; but it may refer to a young film star's two husbands (the present one and the divorced one). *Both their books* may, to the unthinking, appear innocuous: but there may be two persons, who have one book apiece, and therefore the reference could as well be to the entire book-stock of these two book-lovers ('*Both* their books are at the bindery') as to the thousands of books owned by a pair of bibliophiles. All in all, it looks as though we had better remain faithful to the accepted usage of the literate.

both the last is catachrestic for *the last two.* 'He could not have received both her last letters and not answered them' (Sheila Kaye-Smith, *Joanna Godden Married*, 1936). *Both of her last two letters* and *her last two letters* are equally correct; the latter, the more idiomatic.

bounden. See ARCHAISMS.

bow-window. See BAY-WINDOW.

bracket, singular, is not to be used for *brackets* (plural), a pair of brackets, properly *square brackets*: [ ]. *Round brackets,* an absurdity now happily obsolete, are properly called *parentheses*: ( ); and one of these round signs is a *parenthesis,* as also is the word, phrase or

sentence within the pair of parentheses. To employ *bracket* for the *brace* used in coupling two lines of writing or printing, thus

$$\left\{ \begin{array}{l} \text{L. } vinculum \\ \text{Eng. } bond, \end{array} \right.$$

is a catachresis.

brand, a trademark, or the make of goods distinguished by such mark, can also be metaphorically applied when the intention is humorous; but it is highly inappropriate in the following: 'The Queen had her own brand of services in her own private chapel', Samuel Putnam, *Marguerite of Navarre*, 1937.

bran-new; brand-new; brank-new. The third is incorrect, except in Scottish; the second is the original and best form; the first is etymologically senseless, and unnecessary, but—on the score of usage —is uncensoriously admitted by *The O.E.D.*

bravado and **bravery.** The former is never synonymous with the latter. *Bravado* is defined by *The O.E.D.* as 'boastful or threatening behaviour', an archaic nuance; 'ostentatious display of courage or boldness; bold or daring action intended to intimidate or to express defiance; often, an assumption of courage or hardihood to conceal felt timidity, or to carry one out of a doubtful or difficult position'.

breach and **breech** are synonymous in none of their senses.

breadth; broadness. *Breadth* is the physical noun. It is also used in the transferred senses, *breadth of mind* (never *width of mind*), an extensive display of a quality ('breadth and accuracy of vision', Morley), and, in art, a broad effect. *Broadness* was, from the 14th to early 18th Centuries, employed for 'breadth' (physical—as a measure, etc.): long disused and to be avoided. But as the abstract noun corresponding to *broad,* 'coarse, indelicate', *broadness* (never *breadth*) is the correct term.

breath (*brĕth*) is the noun; **breathe** (*brēthe*) is the verb.

breezy (of persons: 'lively or brisk') is familiar Standard English—not a colloquialism.

brethren is archaic for *brothers* except 'in reference to spiritual, ecclesiastical, or professional relationship' (*The O.E.D.*); for certain technical and/or highly specialized senses, consult *The O.E.D.*

BREVITY.

Since brevity is the soul of wit . . .
I will be brief.—Shakespeare.

I labour to be brief and become obscure.
—Horace

'On the principle of attaining ends at the smallest cost, it is a virtue of language to be brief. If a thought can be properly expressed in five words, there is a waste of strength in employing ten', as Bain remarks (*English Composition and Rhetoric*, 1887–88, at I, 27).

In one sense, brevity is the enemy of tautology (see TAUTOLOGY) and the opposite of verbosity (see VERBOSITY). But to avoid tautology and verbosity 'is not all; there are direct means of attaining Brevity by the help of various devices of style' (Bain).

I. *The Choice of Words.* 'The extension of our vocabulary by classical and other foreign words has greatly enhanced the power of brief yet adequate expression. Many of the words thus acquired have in themselves a great fulness of meaning, the consequence of their being employed in the higher kinds of knowledge, and in the complicated operations of society. Such are—strategy, census, codification, autonomy, altruism, hedonism, correlation.' To which we may add such words as *adaptability, complex* (in the psychological sense), flair.

'Take', continues Bain, 'a few quotations to illustrate this point:—

Man is described by Pope as—

The *glory, jest,* and *riddle* of the world;

the words summing up very happily the substance of a preceding paragraph, which expatiates on the greatness of man's powers, the frequent absurdity of his conduct, and the mysteries of his nature. Again:—

And he, who now to sense, now nonsense
       leaning,
Means not, *but blunders round about a
       meaning.*

Thomson has the following, in reference to birds teaching their young to fly:—

                The *surging* air receives
Its plumy burden; and their self-taught
       wings
Winnow the waving element.

The expressions here used bring before us in a few words the fan-like stroke of the wings on the one hand and the corresponding motion of the air, like that of waves, on the other.

But as along the river's edge
They went, and brown birds in the sedge
Twittered their *sweet* and *formless* tune.
                    (William Morris.)

Here, *twittered* describes the short, tremulous notes characteristic of the songs of the birds; *sweet* conveys the mental impression of the listener; while *formless* gives in one word the idea that the song is not shaped after any fixed standard but is poured forth in endless variety.

"Governments are not *made*, but *grow.*"

'"The progress of civilisation has been from *status* to *contract.*" (Maine.) A large amount of meaning is at once conveyed by each of the two contrasted words.'

II. *Grammatical Forms and Syntactical Usages.*

(1) *Abstract Nouns.* 'His *refusal* justified my *adherence* to my plan' = 'The fact that he refused justified me *in adhering* (or, when I adhered) to my plan'. Still more condensed is 'The passionate confidence of interested falsehood' (Adam Smith).

(2) *The attributive use of nouns,* i.e. *nouns used as adjectives* or as elements of compound nouns. E.g. 'a *bosom* friend', 'table talk', 'an *earth* worm', 'a *birthday* present'.

(3) *Adjectives* are rather obviously short-cuts, as in—

Goodness and wit
In *seldom-meeting* harmony combined,

'The *mazy-running* soul of melody', 'The *astonished* mother finds a *vacant* nest'. So too the *adverb*, or the adverb and adjective, or the adverb and adjective and abstract noun, as in—

See nations *slowly wise* and *meanly just*
To *buried merit* raise the *tardy* bust.

(4) *Participial phrases for clauses.* 'Enraged and mortified, he soon returned to his mansion' = 'Because he was enraged and mortified, he soon returned to his mansion'. 'The Romans, *having* now *set foot* in Sicily, determined to declare war against Carthage' = 'The Romans had now set foot in Sicily, and therefore they

determined to declare war against Carthage'.

An excellent example—

Vanished every fear, and every power
Roused into life and action, light in air
The *acquitted* parents see their *soaring*
  race,
And once *rejoicing* never know them
  more.

(5) *Prefixes and Suffixes; and Compounds.*
Consider '*re*turn', '*re*unite', '*re*fund'; '*ab*-
sentee*ism*' and '*admissibility*'; 'forcible-
feeble', 'semi-popish', 'little-minded'.

III. *Rhetorical Devices.* To go adequately
into these, I should require inordinate
space. But perhaps a hint may be conveyed by the following examples:—

'He lives to build, not boast, a generous
  race.'

'And read their history in a nation's eyes.'

'Leave to the nightingale her woods;
A privacy of glorious light is thine.'

'A hand-to-mouth liar.'

'Murder will out.'

A great—perhaps the greatest—master
of brevity is Shakespeare. Here are two
examples:—

My thought, whose murder yet is but
  fantastical,
Shakes so my single state of man, that
  function
Is smothered in surmise.

                    If th' assassination
Could trammel up the consequence, and
  catch,
With his surcease, success; that but this
  blow
Might be the be-all and the end-all here,
But here, upon this bank and shoal of
  time,
We'd jump the life to come.

Both of these passages come, of course,
from *Macbeth*; the latter passage occurs
in a speech that I once set to be paraphrased; the whole speech (I, vii) would
repay study, for it is of the essence of
forceful brevity. Pope is another master
of brevity: neater than Shakespeare, but
less connotation-suggestive. 'Of the following four lines on the origin of Society'
(as Bain says), 'Mark Pattison observes
that they are "expressed with a con-

densed energy which it would be difficult
to improve upon"':—

Heaven forming each on other to depend,
A master, or a servant, or a friend,
Bids each on other for assistance call
Till one man's weakness grow the
  strength of all.

BREVITY, leading to OBSCURITY. See
OBSCURITY.

brief and **short.** *Brief* = 'of short duration, quickly passing away or ending',
hence (of speeches, writings) 'concise or
short'; it is virtually obsolete in reference
to extent in space. *Short*, on the other
hand, refers to either time or space; but
when it refers to the latter, it often has a
connotation of curtailment or incom-
pleteness, or sudden cessation, as in 'a
short nap', 'a short description'. (*The
O.E.D.*)

briefness is now rare for *brevity.*

bring is confused with *take* only by the
illiterate or the unthinking. See esp. the
introductory note (to I) in *The O.E.D.*

BRITICISMS are such English words
as are used in Great Britain and the
British Empire (except Americanized
Canada) but not, in the relevant senses,
in the United States of America. See
ENGLISH AND AMERICAN USAGE.

Mr Allen Walker Read is now preparing an authoritative study of Briticisms.

British Empire, the. See GREAT
BRITAIN.

Brittania is a frequent misspelling of
Britannia (as *Britany* is of *Brittany*).

broadcast, to; he **broadcasted;** the
news was **broadcast** or **broadcasted.**
This is the ruling of *The O.E.D.*

broadness. See BREADTH.

Brobdignag, -ian are incorrect for
Brobdingnag, -ian. The incorrect adjective occurs in no less a writer on English
than Alexander Bain:—'Brobdignagian is
purposely made hard to pronounce'
(*English Composition and Rhetoric*, enlarged edition, Part II, 1888).

Brussel sprouts for *Brussels sprouts* is
an astonishingly frequent error. I have
seen it on bills of fare in restaurants that
ought to know better and even in the
work of so good a novelist as G. S. Marlowe.

Bruxelles, Gand, Lyon, Marseille for
Brussels, Ghent, Lyons, Marseilles are af-
fectations in any English or American
author writing for the English or American public. It is equally affected to pro-

nounce *Lyons* or *Marseilles* or *Paris* as
the French pronounce them. 'Dr Edmond
Locard, of the Police Laboratory of Lyon'
(Nigel Morland, *The Conquest of Crime*,
1937) is a good example of the error.

bucket full; bucketful. Cf. the entry
at BASKETFULS.

buffalo and **bison.** *Bison* originally was
'a species of Wild Ox . . . formerly prevalent in Europe' but now the term is
applied properly to the North American
species, which, therefore, is improperly
called *buffalo. Buffalo* is that species of ox
which was 'originally a native of India'
(*The O.E.D.*). [[Nevertheless, in the
U.S.A., the North American bison is
generally known as the buffalo and under this name figures in the national
stock of stories. 'The bison nickel' would
be unintelligible to young America and
a British boner to their elders.]]

Buhl (as in *Buhl table*) should be *Boule.
Buhl*, says *The O.E.D.*, 'seems to be a
modern Germanized spelling' and *Boule*
is 'the more correct form of the word
commonly spelt *Buhl*': but this is a far
too lenient comment, for *Buhl* has no
justification—not even that of universal
error, *Boule* being, among the educated,
an equally common spelling. 'Boule
(André Charles) célèbre ébéniste, né à
Paris en 1642, mort en 1732. Il éléva
l'ébénisterie à la hauteur d'un art, et
acquit une grande réputation.' (Larousse,
*Grand dictionnaire universel du xix^e
siècle*.)

build a building is, at the lowest estimate, ugly in sound and redundant in
sense.

bulk, the (never *a*). *Bulk* should be
reserved for 'volume' or 'mass'. It is incorrect both for *the majority*, as in 'The
bulk of slow bowlers prefer the eight-ball
over, but the bulk of fast bowlers prefer
the six-ball over', and for *the greater part*
as in 'the bulk of the book'.

BULLS. A *bull* is 'an expression containing a manifest contradiction in terms
or involving a ludicrous inconsistency
unperceived by the speaker' (*TheO.E.D.*).
Often called *Irish bulls*: but *bull* was
used in this sense long before it came to
be associated with that people which has
given us the best examples of felicitous
incongruities.

See Maria and Richard Edgeworth's
Essay on Irish Bulls, 1802, and Walter
Jerrold's *Bulls, Blunders and Howlers*,
1928.

Here are two bulls, said to be of Irish
perpetration:

the entrance out.

'If there was twelve cows lyin' down in a
field and one of them was shtandin' up,
that would be a bull.'

bumble-bee. See HUMBLE-BEE.

bunch. 'Good usage does not sanction
the indiscriminate use of *bunch* for any
and every group, and certainly not for
groups of people.' (Weseen).

bungalow. A bungalow is a (generally
lightly built) one-storeyed house; hence
Arnold Bennett's 'two-storeyed bungalow' in *The City of Pleasure*, 1907, is
absurd.

burglarize is at all times inferior to
rob (a house). In Great Britain it is regarded as journalese. *Burgle* is a facetious
synonym. (*The O.E.D.*)

burn down and **burn up** are excessive,
unnecessary for *burn*—unless an intensive
force is required. A house 'burnt *down*'
connotes total destruction, a burning
right to the ground; a letter 'burnt *up*'
connotes total destruction, not a mere
scorching.

burthen. See ARCHAISMS.

bus (not '*bus*) is now Standard English
for *omnibus.* The plural is *buses.*

BUSINESS ENGLISH. See 'OFFICIAL-
ESE, JOURNALESE, COMMERCIALESE'.

busyness, the state of being busy, is,
according to *TheO.E.D.*, a modern formation, made to distinguish it from *business*, which has come to have another
meaning. It is a necessary word, and is
found also in the new *Webster's*, but not
in many other dictionaries.

but (adv.) (= *only*) is tautological in
such sentences as this: 'There was but
very little room for him in the small over-
crowded cottage', Hugh Walpole, *John
Cornelius*, 1937.

Like the adv. *only*, the adv. *but* sometimes gets into a foolish or illogical position—as in 'A semantic analysis of economic theory would fill a book . . . Here
we have space but for a few examples'
(read: 'space for but a few examples'),
Stuart Chase, *The Tyranny of Words*,
1938. Also it can be ambiguous when it
is used for *only*, as in 'Yes, but a portion
of my tribe is with me, yet I cannot say
that anyone is missing', Bernard Newman, *Death under Gibraltar*, 1938. And
'We splashed out on to the lane . . . its
mud was but less fathomless than the

yard's', Adrian Bell, *By Road*, 1937, is very awkward if not entirely incorrect.

but is wrongly used in the following quoted by C. C. Boyd (*Grammar for Grown-Ups*) from a newspaper: 'A gale swept the roads, and his (Mr Cobham's) machine was unprotected. At midnight he attached a second anchor, *but* the machine weathered the gale undamaged.' This is what is called a *non sequitur*. *But* must be used instead of *and*; the sentence should read: '. . . his machine was unprotected, but weathered the gale . . . because he had attached a second anchor'.

but (conjunction) is also incorrect in the following: 'He will certainly say of Mallet that as a detective he was remarkable not so much for the questions he put but for those he avoided putting' (John Ferguson, *Death of Mr Dodsley*, 1937); *not so much . . . as* is correct, but the sentence might also read: 'not for the questions he put, but for those, etc.'

J. B. Priestley, in *English Humour*, 1929, falls into the same error: 'He (Munden) was not so much a comic actor, consciously presenting an amusing part, but a real comedian . . .': here *but* should be *as*.

but (preposition). The clearest exposition I have seen is the following, from Dr Onions's *An Advanced English Syntax* (6th ed., 1932):—'But is a Preposition meaning "except", and, like other Prepositions, governs the Accusative [or Objective]:

'"No one would have thought of it *but him*."

'If, however, a sentence like this is otherwise arranged, the Nominative is very commonly put instead of the Accusative:

'"No one *but he* would have thought of it."

The Accusative, in fact, is felt to be inelegant. *But* thus becomes a Conjunction, and the sentence must be regarded as equivalent to "No one would have thought of it, *but* he thought of it".

'Compare:

The boy stood on the burning deck,
Whence all *but he* had fled.'

but (preposition) does not equal *more than*. '"I won't go into the house yet. Just give it the once over. Won't take me but a few minutes."' (See Thayer,

Death in the Gorge, English ed., 1937.) The negative misled him. Equally bad is: 'It is not possible in a short article to mention but a few of the, etc.' (Edward C. Ash in *Country Life*, Nov. 27, 1937).

but, misused for *than*. 'The choice of war or peace is now in other hands but ours', Arthur Bryant, July 15, 1939.

but in *help but* and *cannot help but* (do something) is awkward and to be deprecated. 'Millions of hearts could not help but thrill in response.' Why not 'could not help thrilling', or simply 'thrilled'? How does 'help' help? In the Scottish Leaving Certificate examination (in English) in March, 1938, an example of this error was set for correction: 'We cannot help but admire him for his loyalty': but the mistake is common enough among adults as well as adolescents. Here is an example from *Murder at the Polls* by Milton Propper, 1936: 'The detectives could not help but accept his statement about the brawlers' should read '. . . help accepting his statement', or 'could not but accept . . .'.

but . . . however, used where either *but* or *however* (or *notwithstanding*) is needed, is incorrect; e.g., 'After judgment [in court], she pleaded her belly, and a jury of matrons being impanelled, they found her not quick with child; but, however, she was afterwards reprieved'. Trial of Mary Roberts in July, 1728, sentenced to death for stealing (The Rev. John Villette, Ordinary of Newgate, *The Annals of Newgate*, 1776).

Gerard Manley Hopkins, in *The Bugler's First Commission*, wrote thus:

Recorded only, I have put my lips on pleas
Would brandle adamantine heaven with ride and jar, did Prayer go disregarded:
Forward-like, but however, and like favourable heaven heard these.

but that after *doubt*. See DOUBT.

but that used, unnecessarily, for *that . . . not*. 'Brington was not yet so overgrown but that the unspoilt country was within easy reach of it', Archibald Marshall, *Two Families*, 1931.

but what, in, e.g., 'I don't know but what . . .', is a clumsy alternative to *but that*.

but yet (cf. BUT . . . HOWEVER) is, at the least, infelicitous; *but* is strong, *yet* is mild, and *but yet* rings oddly. It is rather surprising to find it in so good a writer as R. B. Cunninghame Graham: 'Born when the echoes of the '45 were ringing (though faintly) through the land, he held the Stuarts in abhorrence, but yet hated the Hanoverians, whom he termed German Boors' ('The Colonel', in *Scottish Stories*, 1914).

by. I regret that *by* is being used more and more in place of the merely instrumental *with*. E.g., 'She moved him rather by her tears than by her appeal to his chivalry'. The Romans set, in this matter, an example that we should do well to follow.

by for *beside* can be dangerously (and indeed ridiculously) ambiguous. 'Two bottles which contained poison were found by the deceased', *The Daily Chronicle*, 1899, quoted by Nesfield in his admirable chapter, 'Errors in Prepositions'.

by a long way is a verbose way of saying *far* or *much*. 'The starlings are by a long way the greediest' (examination candidate's script, March, 1938).

by the name of and **of the name of** are intolerably wordy for *named* (or *called*). And **go by the name of** is ambiguous in that it implies—usually or often implies—that the name is an assumed one.

C

cacao, coca, cocoa, coco(nut). Confusion is common between these. *Cacao* is a tropical American tree from the seed of which the beverages *cocoa* and chocolate are made; *coca* is a Bolivian shrub the leaves of which are chewed as a stimulant; the *coco* or *coker* is a tropical palm-tree bearing the *coconut* or *cokernut*, the usual spelling in commerce being *coker*, to avoid ambiguity. (*The Con. O.D.*)

cache, for any hiding place, is loose, and *cache* for 'to hide' anything anywhere is catachrestic. To *cache* is 'to put in a cache', 'to store (provisions) underground'. (*The O.E.D.*)

cachuca is incorrect for *cachucha*, 'a lively Spanish dance'. (*The O.E.D.*)

cacography is the opposite of *calligraphy*, q.v., and is catachrestic when used as a synonym of *penmanship*. Its secondary meaning is 'incorrect spelling'—the opposite of *orthography*.

calculate is an Americanism—and, even as an Americanism, it is colloquial

—for 'to think, opine, suppose . . . ; to intend, purpose' (*The O.E.D.*).

calendar; calender. The latter is 'a rolling machine used in glazing paper or in smoothing cloth'. (Weseen.)

caliber (American), **calibre** (English). Don't use it indiscriminately to = *order of merit, class, kind* and *type*. 'A poem of high calibre' and 'an artist of low calibre' are not absolutely wrong: they are merely ludicrous.

calix, calyx. *Calix*, a cup-like cavity or organ, is often confused with the botanical *calyx* (either *ā* or *ă*), the whorl of leaves forming outer case of bud. (*The Con. O.D.*)

calk. See CAULK.

calligraphy is frequently misused; i.e., it is a catachresis for 'handwriting'. David Frome, *Mr Simpson Finds a Body*, 1933, 'The calligraphy expert'. Its correct sense is 'beautiful handwriting'.

calvary. See CAVALRY.

camelia for *camellia*: common misspelling and mispronunciation.

CANADIAN ENGLISH. See STANDARD ENGLISH, Section iv.

can and **may.** On Sept. 10, 1665, Pepys joined a party at Greenwich, where Sir John Minnes and Evelyn were the life of the company and full of mirth. 'Among other humours, Evelyn's repeating of some verses made up of nothing but the various acceptations of *may* and *can*, and doing it so aptly upon occasion of something of that nature, and so fast, did make us all die almost with laughing, and did so stop the mouth of Sir J. Minnes in the middle of all his mirth (and in a thing agreeing with his own manner of genius), that I never saw any man so outdone in all my life; and Sir J. Minnes' mirth too to see himself out-done, was the crown of all our mirth.' Unfortunately, Pepys does not quote the verses on *may* and *can*.

Briefly, *can* is used of ability (or capacity) to do something; *may* of permission or sanction to do it. 'He who will not when he may, may not when he will' (wishes—and is able—to do so).

can for **may.** Child at table: 'Please, can I get down?' Mother: 'Yes, and you *may*.'—Admirer to pretty maiden: 'Phyllis, you can come and kiss me.' Phyllis: 'Oh, can I?'

⟦Many American teachers and writers will agree with Mr Perrin's statements on the use of *can* and *may* (*Index to Usage*,

p. 108). After setting forth the usual distinctions as a guide for 'formal English', he boldly adds: 'In less formal usage *may* occurs rather rarely except in the sense of possibility: *It may be all right for her, but not for me. Can* is generally used for both permission and ability: *Can I go now? You can if you want to . . . .* This is in such general usage that it should be regarded as good English in speaking and in informal writing. *Can't* almost universally takes the place of the awkward *mayn't: Can't I go now? We can't have lights after twelve o'clock.'*]]

candelabra, plural **candelabras**. These are the modern forms of *candelabrum*, plural *candelabra*.

candidacy; candidateship; candidature. The first = 'the position or status of a candidate'; *candidateship*, 'the position of a candidate'; *candidature* is the most 'active' of the three terms, for it = 'standing as a candidate'. (*The O.E.D.*) [[Only the first of these words is commonly found in American usage.]]

cannot help but. See BUT in *but*

cannot seem to is misplacement of words = 'seem not to be able to'. Kathleen Norris in *The Passing Show*, Dec. 6, 1933, 'I must be nervous this afternoon. I can't seem to settle down to anything'. Change to '. . . I seem unable to settle down . . .'. [[American usage accepts *cannot seem to* as a useful colloquial idiom. *I seem unable to settle down* is, in comparison, awkward though logical.]]

canon (ecclesiastic and textual), **cañon** (a chasm or ravine), **cannon** (warfare and billiards), **canyon** (the anglicized form of *cañon*).

CANT. The everyday sense of *cant* is 'an affected or unreal use of religious or pietistic phraseology; language implying the pretended assumption of goodness or piety', as in 'He had a horror of cant' and 'The whole spiritual atmosphere was saturated with cant'. (*The O.E.D.*)

But in philology, *cant* is the technical term for the vocabulary peculiar to the underworld (criminals; tramps and beggars; prostitutes and 'ponces'; and such hangers on as 'fences'). It is to be hoped that the use of this short, convenient term will become more general.

Cant, in this sense, is often called 'thieves' (or underworld) slang. It is true that the underworld employs a great deal of slang, whether general or Cockney, or provincial; nevertheless, when—as often

it does—the underworld wishes to converse, or to communicate, in a manner incomprehensible to more respectable citizens (lumped together, by the English underworld, in the generic term, *mugs*), it employs what cannot accurately be designated as slang, for it is a 'secret language': but even 'secret language' is slightly misleading, for only the key-words, the significant words, are 'secret'. The words for departure, escape, flight; for dying and killing; for thief, cheat, swindler, confidence man, professional tough, receiver of stolen property, prostitute, pathic; for policeman, detective, prison warder; for arrest and imprisonment; for begging, and professional tramping; for the victims of criminals and beggars; for means of conveyance (ship, train, motorcar, aeroplane); for money, whether money in general or money in particular denominations; for food and drink in general and for certain specific drinks and foods; for such buildings as banks and houses, hospitals, barns and casual wards; for doors, windows, stairs; for certain household effects (linen, plate); for jewellery and gems; for telephones and other means of communication; for such animals as dogs and horses; for certain geographical and topographical features (e.g. roads); for the tools and devices used by criminals (a jemmy; dynamite); for such weapons as a cudgel, a life-preserver, a revolver, a machine-gun, mustard (or other offensive) gas; for such verbs as 'do' or 'make', 'unmake', 'destroy', 'hide', 'discover', 'place', 'forge', 'look', 'examine', 'handle', 'bungle'; for 'man', 'woman', 'child', 'father', 'mother', 'wife', 'husband'; for 'marriage'; for the sexual act and its preliminaries; for unnatural sexual acts; for physical functions; and so on, and so on.

With regard to the secrecy and vocationalism of cant, it must, however, be remembered that, as Henri Bauche has pointed out, 'Il faut reconnaître que l'argot des malfaiteurs, l'argot des prisons, entre pour une part importante dans la formation du langage populaire. La cause en est évidente: le crime naît plus souvent du besoin et de la misère des classes inférieures . . . parmi les gens qui ne manquent de rien'. In the staple as in the slangy portion of the speech of the lower classes there is, therefore, a considerable number of terms that are found also in cant: 'It's the poor as 'elps the poor': from the poor around them, criminals do not wish, do not even think, to hide their secret vocabulary: and often it is to the advantage of criminals that parts of their specialist vocabulary should be known by their non-criminal relatives and friends. (This holds equally for beggars and tramps.) Cant terms leak out from time to time, with the result that many of them are ultimately included in some dictionary or other; nor always only there. As Bauche has said, 'Les divers argots des prisons, des différentes catégories de malfaiteurs, de la prostitution ont . . . laissé des traces nombreuses dans le bas peuple, sans distinction de métier: de là ces termes spéciaux sont montés dans le people et parfois jusqu'aux classes cultivées'. Here are a few examples of such promotion or elevation in British English:—*Beak*, a magistrate; *bilk*, to cheat; *booze*, noun and verb, and *boozer* (drunkard and public-house); *cove* and *cull* (or *cully*); *doxy*; *duds* (clothes); *filch*; *hick* (a rustic); *jemmy*; *moll* (a woman); *nab*, to take, steal, arrest; *nob*, the head; *ponce*, a prostitute's bully; *prig*, to steal; *queer* and *rum* (odd, 'shady'); *ready* and *rhino*; *rig*, a swindle, to swindle; *scamp* (noun) and *scamper* (verb); *shicer*; *stow it!*; *tanner*, a sixpence, and *bob*, a shilling; *tip*, to give; *tout*, noun and verb; (to) *work* (a district, a street); *yokel*.

Strictly, then, cant is neither slang nor a secret language, but both; in its essence, however, it is a secret language, more precisely a secret vocabulary (the freemasonry of the underworld). John Farmer's opinion is here of great importance, for one of the most authoritative pronouncements on the relation of cant to slang is that of the operative editor of the seven-volumed *Slang and Its Analogues*. In the Preface to *Musa Pedestris*, 1896, he wrote thus: 'As to the distinction to be drawn between Slang and Cant it is somewhat difficult to speak. Cant we know; its limits and place in the world of philology are well defined. In Slang, however, we have a veritable Proteus, ever shifting . . . . Few, save scholars and suchlike folk, even distinguish between the two . . . . Slang is universal, whilst Cant is restricted in usage . . . . Slang boasts a quasi-respectability denied to Cant, though Cant is frequently more enduring, its use con-

tinuing without variation of meaning for many generations.'*

Many writers of 'thrillers' and, especially, 'deteccers' sprinkle their pages—chiefly their low-life dialogue—with cant words and phrases. Most of them, however, have but a slight knowledge of cant, and of the few words they know, some are obsolete; in one of the most popular crime-plays of recent years, a character was made to say *crack a crib*. Now, since 1918, to 'burgle a house (flat, etc.)' is not *crack a crib* but *screw a joint*. Among the most reliable cant-users are (to confine ourselves to the 20th Century) Edgar Wallace, Josiah Flynt, Bart Kennedy, Edwin Pugh, O. Henry, W. H. Davies, Stanley Scott, Jim Tully, Charles F. Coe, George Dilnot, Fred D. Pasley, E. D. Sullivan, Jack Bilbo, James Spenser, John G. Brandon, David Hume, Nigel Morland, James Curtis, Damon Runyan, Robert Westerby, Courtney R. Cooper, and Don Castle. The only trustworthy and comprehensive glossary of American cant is Godfrey Irwin's *American Tramp and Underworld Slang* (Oxford University Press, London; Sears, New York)—a most valuable work of reference. For English cant, there is no separate glossary, though many cant words and phrases are scattered about the pages of my *A Dictionary of Slang and Unconventional English* (revised and enlarged ed., 1938). [Mr. D. W. Maurer is compiling a dictionary of American criminal argots. He has published a number of articles in *American Speech*, for example, 'The Argot of Confidence Men' in the issue of April, 1940.]

can't seem to. See CANNOT SEEM TO.

canvas is a cloth material; **canvass** is 'to examine, discuss, solicit', as in 'to canvass votes'. As n., *canvass* = 'a solicitation of support [esp. at an election], custom, etc.' (Harold Herd: *The O.E.D.*)

canyon. See at CANON.

CAPITALS IN TITLES. See TITLES OF BOOKS.

capacious in the sense of *spacious* is now so little used that it rings almost oddly enough to be designated a misuse, though admittedly it isn't one. ('Chewing hay in Don Angel's capacious stable', Bernard Newman, *Death under Gibraltar*, 1938.)

* The preceding paragraphs are taken (and modified) from my *Slang To-Day and Yesterday*, revised ed., 1935.

capacity. See ABILITY

caption is often misused to mean a legend underneath (instead of above, as it should be) an illustration. [[In the U.S.A., this usage to signify the letter-press accompanying an illustration is probably established.]]

capturer is a 19th century variant of *captor*, which has successfully resisted the rivalry of the longer word.

car and **carload.** If you intend the latter, do not say (or write) the former. [[Car for Carload is American business slang.]]

carbolic acid; carbonic acid. The former is 'a substance more systematically called *Phenol* or *Phenyl alcohol*'; the latter, 'a name originally given to the gas now more systematically called *Carbon(ic) Dioxide* or *Carbonic anhydride* . . . . This is still popularly called *carbonic acid gas*, but the name *Carbonic acid* is applied in Chemistry to the hydrate or compound CH_2O_3'; **carbonic oxide** is now *carbon monoxide*. (*The O.E.D.*)

care-free; careless. The former (also written as one word) = 'free from care or anxiety'. So does *careless*, which also = (of persons) 'inattentive, negligent, thoughtless', hence 'inaccurate', and (of things) 'artless', 'unstudied', 'done, caused, or said heedlessly, thoughtlessly, negligently'. (*The O.E.D.*)

careful for; careful of (erroneously **with**). One is *careful* for (a person or thing) when one is full of care or concern for him or it; but one is *careful of* (a person or thing) when one is attentive to his or her interests, or when one takes good care of him or it. (*The O.E.D.*) [[In American usage *careful with* is as common as *careful of* in regard to things.]]

cargo and **shipment.** The former is a ship-load, a lading, a freight; the latter has the same sense, but with the nuance 'a consignment of goods', and the active sense, 'an act of shipping (goods)'. On trains, *freight* or *load*; on lorries, in motor-cars, and in trucks (U.S.A.), generally *load*.

carousal (v.: *carouse*) is a carouse, a drinking bout, a drunken revelry; *carousel* (or carrousel) is a special kind of chivalric tournament, and it has no corresponding verb. Historians and historical novelists confuse these two terms. [[In American usage, *carrousel* is a merry-go-round.]]

carping has occasionally been misused for *carking*, the former meaning 'fault-finding', the latter 'oppressive'.

case, in any, when used in the sense of *however you look at it*, is colloquial and rather ambiguous.

case (of), in the, is frequently misused for *in this* (or *that*) *connection*; also it is often quite unnecessarily used, as in 'There was a greater scarcity of crabs than is the case of herrings', which we owe to Mr. A. P. Herbert (from a newspaper). Despite Sir Arthur Quiller-Couch's furious and witty onslaught, *case* is still used with nauseating frequency.

caseine is incorrect for *casein* (*kay-seein*).

cast = *dramatis personae*—the list, hence the personnel, of actors and actresses performing a play, whereas **caste** is an exclusive class (of persons); the term having originally been, as in India it still is, used of hereditary classes; hence *caste* is applied to a rigid system of class-distinctions within a community.

caster; castor. The former is one who casts, e.g., a (metal-)founder; a certain type of wheel (formerly also *castor*); a variant (and indeed the original form) of *castor*, 'a vial', 'a cruet,' for either of which it is the more sensible form. A *castor* is an archaism for a beaver; the unctuous substance also named castoreum; a hat; a heavy broadcloth; the mineral also known as castorite; and *castor* (*oil*). (*The O.E.D.*)

casualty, 'a fatal or serious accident or event' (*The O.E.D.*), is often misapplied to the person to whom the accident happens; this misuse, 'to be or become a casualty', is rightly pilloried by A. P. Herbert. *Casuality* is an obsolete variant, now held to be an illiteracy. *Causality* is 'the principle of causal relationship'. [[*Webster's*: military and naval usage—'. . . a soldier unavailable for service, because of death, wounds, . . . or any cause' This usage, for sailors as well as soldiers, is established in U.S.]]

CATACHRESIS. A catachresis is a word misused (e.g., *anachronism* for *anomaly*, to *subject* for to *subordinate*); catachresis, as a fault in writing, is 'an improper use of words' (*The O.E.D.*); etymologically, 'contrary-to-usage-ness'. The adjective is *catachrestic*.

This book deals with the commonest catachreses of the English language: to write at length on the nature of cat-achresis is therefore unnecessary.

cataclasm and **cataclysm.** *Cataclasm*, lit. 'a breakage' (Gr. *kata* 'down'), means 'a break or disruption', as in 'The cata-clasms of the moral and social world' (Southey) and 'Any cataclasm, any violent disruption of what is the usual course of nature' (Bowen); hence, in Geology, 'a breaking down or crushing into fragments, of rocks', with adjective *cataclastic*. A *cataclysm* is 'a great and general flood of water', esp. the Noachian deluge, 'the Flood'; 'hence used vaguely for a sudden convulsion or alteration of physical conditions'; fig., 'a political or social upheaval that sweeps away the old order of things', e.g. the French Revolution of 1789, the Russian Revolu-tion of 1917. (*The O.E.D.*)

catastrophic is occasionally misused by violent and/or journalistic writers, for *severe* or *drastic*; it affords an excellent example of 'sending a man on a boy's errand'. Nigel Morland, *The Conquest of Crime*, 1937, chapter on finger-prints: 'The permanence of the prints against damage from wounding or burning was demonstrated painfully but conclusively by Dr Locard and Dr Witkowski of Lyon, who subjected their fingers to the action of boiling water, hot oil and to the pressure of hot plates. It was proved that while these catastrophic measures did destroy the marks on the epidermis, or outer skin, the patterns impressed on the corium, or underlying true skin, were unaffected, and that as soon as the wounds or the burns were healed, the original pattern returned in all its detail.'

catch afire is unnecessary for *catch fire*.

catch up, 'to overtake' (a person), is despite Weseen, impeccable English; it is, however, familiar rather than literary.

catchup or **catsup.** See KETCHUP.

catholic, Catholic, Roman Catholic. See ROMAN CATHOLIC.

caulk is to be preferred to *calk*.

causality. See CASUALTY.

cause and reason. A *cause* is that which produces an effect; that which gives rise to any action, phenomenon, or condition. '*Cause* and *effect* are correla-tive terms' (*The O.E.D.*). A *reason* is that which is advanced in order to explain the effect or result, or to justify it; the reason may or may not correspond to the facts; the reason one gives oneself may not be the true motive. 'The reason of

(or for) the seasons is physical' affords an obvious example of *reason* misused for *cause*.

cause why? is an illiterate colloqui-alism for *why?*

cavalcade; procession. To use the former for the latter is not incorrect, but it is unnecessary and loose. Properly, *cavalcade* is 'a procession on horseback, esp. on a festive or solemn occasion'; hence 'a company of riders on the march or in procession' (*The O.E.D.*). The recent theatrical and cinematic use of *cavalcade* for *pageant*, or for *march of events* (or *history*), is to be deprecated.

cavalry and **calvary** are occasionally confused by the ignorant. The less ignorant, however, tend to lose sight of the fact that whereas *Calvary* is 'the place where Christ was crucified', *calvary* is 'a life-sized representation of the Crucifixion', properly on a raised ground in the open air', and in Roman Cathol-icism it is also 'a series of representations, in a church or [a] chapel, of the scenes of the Passion' (*The O.E.D.*).

celebrity, 'fame', 'famousness', 'no-toriety', is correct; correct, too, is the derivative sense, 'a celebrated (or dis-tinguished) person', 'a famous person',—but it is grossly overworked.

Celt and **celt.** Ackermann, *Popular Fallacies*, very concisely points out that '*Celt*, pronounced *kelt*, means the race (early inhabitants of parts of Britain); *celt*, pronounced *selt*, means a stone or bronze-age implement of flint, stone or metal' [[In American usage, *Celt* and *Celtic* may be pronounced with *k*- or *s*-. The implement is pronounced 'selt'.]]

cement and **concrete** are not synony-mous. The latter is 'a composition of stone chippings, sand, gravel, pebbles, etc., formed into a mass with cement; used for building under water, for foundations, pavements, walls, etc.' *Cement* is a substance—esp., a strong mortar—'used to bind the stones or bricks of a building firmly together, to cover floors, etc.'; hence, almost any cohesive, as, e.g., for stopping (or [[American]] filling) teeth. (*The O.E.D.*)

censer (a vessel in which incense is or may be burnt) is not to be confused with censor.

censor (v.) and **censure** (v.). To *censor* is 'to act as censor to or of', 'to examine rigorously for moral or political fault, or for the untimely disclosure of official or military or other state secrets', applied esp. to news, letters, plays, films. To *censure* is 'to criticize harshly or unfavorably; to condemn; find fault with; blame'. The corresponding nouns are *censure* and, to *censor*, the agential *censor* and the abstract *censorship*.

centenary (noun and adj.) should be employed as a noun only, for the more usual adjective is *centennial*.

centre (American **center**) and **middle**. *Centre* is applied properly to a circle, a (literal) revolution, and centripetal attraction; in Geometry, it is the middle point of figures other than circles; it is the point of equilibrium; and in general use, it is 'the middle point or part, the middle or midst of anything', as in 'Full in the center of the grove' (Addison), 'The puniness of man in the centre of a cruel and frowning universe'. But one would not say 'in the centre of the road'. *Middle* applies to time, whereas *centre* does not; and spatially, *middle* 'applies to mere linear extension . . . but *centre* does not. *Centre* . . . is more precise than *middle*. The *centre* of the floor is a definite point; the middle of the floor is the indefinite space around or near the centre'; in May, 1938, a certain newspaper, with unconscious humour related that 'Colonel Woodhouse sat in the centre of a long table and on either side of him were officials of the Board'. In military phraseology, however, *centre* is 'the main body of troops occupying the space between the two wings'; cf. the political use of *centre*. (Mostly: *The O.E.D.*)

centre round for 'to gather, or to be arranged, around a centre' is ungrammatical, though sometimes used by statesmen and others. To *centre on* is correct, as will appear in the following incorrect sentence:—'The scenes of the Waverley Novels are centered round the Borders' (set for correction in the Scottish Leaving Certificate examination, March, 1938). So are *centre in*, *be centred in*, but these imply an exact position or precise point. Also one can say that a thing is 'centered at' such and such a place, when the thing's *centre* is situated or has been placed in that locality. But one cannot with grammatical propriety (or, for that matter, with good sense) speak of *centre about* or *(a)round*, *be centred about* or *(a)round*.

centuary. In England a frequent mispronunciation and misspelling of *century*.

century is not always synonymous

with *hundred years*, as is seen in 'The connection between the law and medicine, although it has reached its fullest development only during the past century, is by no means new' (Nigel Morland, *Conquest of Crime*, 1937). Here obviously, 'past hundred years' would be better.

cerebellum and **cerebrum** are ignorantly confused. *Cerebrum* is, loosely, the whole brain, 'the chief organ of mind'; *cerebellum* is 'the mass of nervous matter forming the posterior part of the brain, and looked upon as the centre of the higher order of combined actions' (*The O.E.D.*).

ceremonial (adj.); **ceremonious**. The former corresponds to the noun *ceremonial*, as in 'ceremonial dress'; it also = 'of the nature of a ceremony or rite; ritual, formal'; hence, 'relating to or involving the formalities of social intercourse'. *Ceremonious* is obsolete in the sense 'ritual, formal'; of sacrifices, shows, displays, it means 'full of ceremony; showy'; as a synonym of *ceremonial*, 'relating to the formalities of social intercourse', it is obsolescent; its prevailing current sense is '(of persons) given to ceremony; punctilious'. *Ceremonial*, therefore, is now applied only to things; *ceremonious* to both persons and things. (*The O.E.D.*)

certain. *A certain* is sometimes employed uselessly, as in 'Upon the other hand, the Inspector's feeling for "The Wallflower" was, perhaps, more than anything a certain admiration for an adversary who combined keen brain with utter fearlessness' (John G. Brandon, *The Mail-Van Mystery*, ca. 1937).

See also COMPARATIVES, FALSE; and also MORE OR LESS CERTAIN.

cession (yielding, surrender) and **cessation** (end, ending) are occasionally confused. Do not confuse *cession* with *session*.

champagne is the drink; **champaign** is a plain or level field; a clearing. Without a plural and without *a* or *the*, it is 'a species of land or landscape: Flat open country, without hills, woods, or other impediments' (*The O.E.D.*). These words are doublets, from L. *campania*, 'plain, level country', from *campus*, 'a level field'.

change from and **change to** are often confused. 'A pleasant change *from* something *to* something else' is correct;

'Comfort is a pleasant change *to* discomfort' is incorrect.

chaperon is correct, **chaperone** is correct. The careless are misled by the pronunciation (-*ōn*). [[*Webster's*: 'The form *chaperone* is often used for a woman chaperon'.]]

character is much wider than **reputation**; the former includes the latter term and may be used as a synonym for it, as in 'His character for sanctity' (Freeman). (*The O.E.D.*)

character of. See PREPOSITIONS WRONGLY USED.

charge. To *charge* a person *with* (a crime or even a fault) is to *accuse* him of it; *charge*, though synonymous with *accuse*, is more formal. Only the former can be used absolutely, as in 'It has been charged that Coleridge appropriated the ideas of Lessing'. (*The O.E.D.*)

chart is obsolete in the general sense 'map'. In current use, it is short for *sea-chart*; it is used in certain technical senses, as in *magnetic chart, temperature chart, barometric chart*; where there is not a map but a graph, *graph* is displacing *chart*; hence it may be used for 'a sheet bearing information of any kind arranged in a tabular form'. (*The O.E.D.*)

Charta, Magna. See MAGNA CHARTA.

cheap price; dear price. Use *low price* and *high price*. To buy goods at a low price is to *buy* them *cheap*; *buy cheaply* is to do business at a low cost of buying.

check is the American form of *cheque*.

cheery is rather trivial colloquialism for *cheerful*.

cheirognomy, etc. See CHIROGNOMY.

chica is incorrect for *chicha* (occ. *chichi* or *chichia*) a South American fermented liquor. (*The O.E.D.*)

chief. See COMPARATIVES, FALSE; *chiefest* is a literary antique.

child. See INFANT.

childbed and **childbirth.** The former, which is slightly obsolescent, stresses 'confinement' (the state of a woman in labour); the latter stresses 'parturition' (the action of bringing forth—or of being delivered of—young). *Parturition* is a technical term. (*The O.E.D.*)

childish; childlike. *Childlike* is 'like a child'; (of qualities, actions) 'characteristic of a child', as in 'To place a childlike trust in Providence' (Southey), 'childlike simplicity'; it is sometimes a neutral, sometimes (indeed, generally) a favourable adjective, whereas *childish* is either neutral, as 'in childish curls' (an obsolescent sense, this of 'infantile' or 'juvenile'), or unfavourable, as usually, with sense 'puerile', *too* childlike', e.g.

What cannot be avoided,
Twere childish weakness to lament
(Shakespeare),

'He's becoming childish', 'Don't be so childish!' Based on *The O.E.D.*

Chinese. See JAP.

chirognomy; chirology; chiromancy. (Also *cheiro-* in all three terms.) *Chirology* is the generic term for both character-reading and fortune-telling by the hand; *chirognomy* refers to the character-reading only; *chiromancy* to the fortune-telling only. The agents are *chirognomist chirologist, chiromancer*.

Chirology is obviously preferable to *palmistry*, which, relating to the *palm* of the hand, ignores the fact that the whole of the hand is examined.

chiropody; chiropractic. The former is 'the art of treating corns, warts, defective nails, etc., on feet or hands'; now, generally restricted to the feet. The practitioner is a *chiropodist*.

Chiropractic is 'manipulation of the spinal column as a method of curing disease'; the art is now generally called *chiropractics* (a singular noun); the practitioner is a *chiropractor*.

In these words, *chiro* (pronounced *keiro*) is a combining-element = 'manual', 'of the hand'.

choice (n). See ALTERNATIVE.—Adj.: avoid *choice* as an adjective, for it is commercialese.

choose, 'to want, to wish to have', is an illiteracy; but *not to choose* (to do something) is 'to forbear to do it',—from *choose*, 'to think fit' (to do it),—and excellent English, which seems to have alarmed certain Americans when, in 1927, Coolidge said, 'I do not choose to run for President in 1928'. (*The O.E.D.*)

chord for the string (or *cord*) of a musical instrument, allowed by *The O.E.D.* (but "now only poetic"), may create confusion by its use in this sense, as in Tennyson, *Locksley Hall*—

Love took up the harp of Life, and smote
on all its chords with might,
Smote the chord of Self, which, trembling, passed in music out of sight.

If 'chords' in the first line are the harp-strings, what is 'chord' in the second? The *string* cannot "pass . . . out of sight'.

Yet if we are to understand 'chords' as harmonious combinations of notes (as in 'I struck one chord of music like the sound of a great Amen', *The Lost Chord*, famous song by Sullivan), it is obvious that one does not strike *on* them; nor even in this sense can the chord be said to 'pass out of sight': it is the 'Self' of which the chord is the expression that does so.

It is likely that the confusion in this case was purely due to Tennyson's ignorance of music. (W.B.)

Christian name is inferior to *given name*, for what are non-Christians to make of *Christian*? FONT-NAME and BAPTISMAL NAME are synonyms.

Christmas is now generally used in England instead of *Christmastide* or *Christmas-time* (24th–26th December); December 25th is *Christmas Day*, but formerly it was simply *Christmas*. [[In American usage, *Christmas Holidays*, *Christmas Season*, *Christmas Day* are current. *Christmas* alone may mean December 25th or the week or ten days of the 'holidays' or 'season'. Only December 25th is a legal holiday (the 26th if Christmas Day falls on a Sunday).]]

The abbreviation *Xmas* should not be used in formal contexts, and the pronunciation *Exmas* is an abomination.

chronic. As applied to diseases, *chronic* = 'lingering', 'inveterate', and is the opposite of *acute*; derivatively, then it = 'continuous, constant'. The sense 'severe' or 'bad' is slangy.—The variant *chronical* is obsolescent and unnecessary.

cicada and **cicala.** The former is the usual, the English form; *cicala* is the Italian form and it has not been Anglicized. [[The term *locust* is common in the U.S.A. for the cicada.]]

Cilician and **Sicilian** are still often confused, as they have been since ca. 1600, *Cilicia* being a province of Asia Minor and *Sicily* the island divided from Italy by the Straits of Messina.

circumference. See RADIUS.

circumfluous, surrounded by water, can easily be confused with *circumfluent*, flowing round.

CIRCUMLOCUTION. See TAUTOLOGY.

circumlocution. See LOCUTION.

circumstances, in the and **under the.** Certain newspaper editors, in their style sheets (see Mr Frank Whitaker's animadversion in *The J.I.J.*, January, 1939),

recommend the one and forbid the use of the other (*under the circumstances*). If one turns to *The O.E.D.*, one finds that both phrases are correct but that they have different functions: '*In the circumstances* is the phrase to use when mere situation is to be expressed; *under the circumstances* when one's action is affected by the circumstances'—and that is usually the sense to be conveyed.

cirrhous, cirrhus are incorrect for *cirrous* (adj.), *cirrus* (n.), usually descriptive of 'a form of cloud with diverging filaments' (*The Con. O.D.*), the *h* being incorrectly introduced by confusion with a word of very different application: *cirrhosis*, a disease of the liver.

cite and **quote.** One may *cite* or *quote* a passage, a book, an author; for book and author, if only the title or the name is mentioned, it is better to use *efer to* or *mention* or *adduce*. It would be a convenience if *quote* were restricted to 'repeating the actual words', and *cite* to 'referring to the words (i.e., to the passage), the book, or the author': but usage has, so far, refused to yield to the need for precision. (Weseen's treatment of these two words is arbitrary: he transforms desirability into accomplished fact.)

citizeness is unnecessary: cf. AUTHORESS.

city and **town.** *City* is correctly applied only to a town which has been created a city by charter; the presence of a cathedral does not, as often supposed, make a city, nor has every city a cathedral. In general, a *city* is larger, more important than a town; but usage differs in different countries. Idiom decrees that 'we go to town, but we go to *the* city. We live in town or live in *the* city. We leave town but leave *the* city' (Weseen). In England, *Town* = London, and *the City* (short for *the City of London*) is 'that part of London which is situated within the ancient boundaries' and esp. 'the business part . . . in the neighbourhood of the Exchange and Bank of England, the centre of financial and commercial activity' (*The O.E.D.*, q.v. for admirable historical accounts of *city* and *town*).

claim is catachrestic when used for *assert*, *contend*, or *maintain*, constructed with *that* . . . , as in 'He claims that it is true', 'He claims that he was absent', 'He claims that it would be better to

...'. *Claim to be* is not wrong, but it is to be used with care; 'This book claims to be superior to the other' would read less oddly in the form, 'The author of this book contends that it is superior to the other'. (*The O.E.D.*)

clang—*clanged*—*clanged*; **cling**—*clung* (obsoletely *clang*)—*clung*.

CLARITY. The opposite of OBSCURITY, *q.v.*

class, as in 'He's no class', is an invidious colloquialism. [[The phrase *no class*, when it occurs in American usage, is a vulgarism or 'illiteracy'.]]

classic for 'important—or, the most important—event' is overdone by writers in sports and games.

Classical and **classic.** The former refers to the Greek and Latin Classics; the latter to the accepted literary works in other languages; or to the qualities thereof.

Classified into classes. See TAUTOLOGY.

cleanly = 'habitually clean' and (of things) 'habitually kept clean'; *clean*, therefore, is not to be used in these senses, the only ones now possessed by *cleanly*. The same applies to *cleanliness* and *cleanness*. (*The O.E.D.*)

cleanse should be reserved for moral, spiritual, religious, ceremonial (or ritual) cleaning.

cleave. (1) 'to hew asunder, to split': preterite *cleaved*, (archaic *clave*, *cleft*, *clove*): past ppl., *cleaved* (archaic, *cleft*, *clove*, *cloven*): ppl. adj., *cleft* ('a cleft stick') and *cloven* ('the cloven hoof').

(2) 'To adhere *to*': preterite, *cleaved* (archaic *clave*, *clove*): past ppl., *cleaved*.

clench and **clinch.** *Clench* is 'to fix securely, make fast', but in reference to nails, *clinch* is more usual, as in 'The girder which was clinched into the plaintiff's party wall' and 'to clinch the nails'. One either *clenches* or *clinches* a matter, affair, argument, bargain, but one *clenches* one's fist, fingers, jaw, lips, or, fig., one's nerves. In the sense 'to grip, to grasp firmly, to hold firmly in one's grasp', *clench* is used, as in 'Men who clench with one hand what they have grasped with the other' (Coleridge). *Clinch* is a latter variant of *clench*. (*The O.E.D.*)

CLERGYMAN'S DICTION IN THE CHURCH OF ENGLAND. The following passage, caustically true of many clerics, occurs in Ernest Raymond's *Mary Leith*, 1931. (Part I, ch. iii): '"All", when Mr

Broadley was in high emotional state, showed a strange tendency to become "ull"'—"Brethren, we shall ull now rise and sing a hymn"; the holy Apostles, on the crest of the wave of very strong feeling, changed most distinctly into "The holy Aparcels, O Lord"; and at times—at really stirring times—"Lord" enriched and strengthened itself into something very like "Lorder".' This passage is preceded by an equally pertinent one on cleric clichés. [[It is often difficult for Americans to appreciate an Englishman's respelling to indicate peculiarities of pronunciation. In British Standard English, *r* is not pronounced after vowels; therefore 'Aparcels' = '*a* p ä s'l' and 'Lorder' = 'l ô d *e*' (i.e., there is a perceptible vowel sound after the *d*, or at least there is perceptible plosion).]]

clever, 'good-natured, amiable', is an American colloquialism; as 'well, fit in health', it is Australian slang, from English dialect.

clew and **clue.** As 'an indication, a "key" to a puzzle or a problem', *clew*, formerly common in English, is now an American spelling. This sense derives from *clew*, 'a ball of thread'—esp. as used in the legend of the Cretan Labyrinth. The nautical term is *clew*.

CLICHÉ. As to clichés, I daresay we are all in agreement. Haste encourages them, but more often they spring from mental laziness. I have, however, heard their use in football reports defended on the ground that the public expects them, and would feel lost without them. I may be wrong, but I don't believe it. Can anything be said in favour of this specimen, which I found in a Yorkshire sports edition:—

'Stung by this reverse, the speedy left-winger propelled the sphere straight into the home custodian's hands. He found it a rare handful and was glad to let go.'

'It was wonderful . . . And most wonderful of all are words, and how they make friends with one another, being oft associated, until not even obituary notices do them part.'—O. Henry, *Whirligigs*, 1910.

'There is no bigger peril either to thinking or to education than the popular phrase.'—Frank Binder, *Dialectic*, 1932.

A cliché is an outworn commonplace; a phrase (or virtual phrase) that has become so hackneyed that scrupulous speakers and writers shrink from it because they feel that its use is an insult to the intelligence of their auditor or audience, reader or public. 'A coin so battered by use as to be defaced' (George Baker). They range from fly-blown phrases (*explore every avenue*), through sobriquets that have lost all point and freshness (*the Iron Duke*), to quotations that have become debased currency (*cups that cheer but not inebriate*), metaphors that are now pointless, and formulas that have become mere counters (*far be it from me to* . . .).

Here follows an alphabetical list* of most of the clichés still current. A query (?) after a phrase indicates rather that it is in danger of becoming a cliché than that it is already an indubitable cliché.

For clichés that are battered similes, see SIMILES, BATTERED. Proverbs and catch phrases (tell that to the marines) are omitted.

a

Admirable Crichton, an
à l'outrance [*French*]
Al at Lloyd's
abject apology, an
abject terror
able to make heads or tails of, not
abomination of desolation, the
absit omen! [*Latin*]
accidents *do* (or *will*) happen
Achilles heel, the [*obsolescent*]
aching void, an
according to Cocker
ace up one's sleeve, an; *esp.*, have an . . .
acid test, the
act in cold blood, to
acute agony *or* shock
ad infinitum [*Latin*]
ad libitum [*Latin*]
ad nauseam [*Latin*]
add(ing) insult to injury
admit . . . ; *see* soft impeachment
affront to national honour, an
after (*e.g.*, my) own heart, it is *or* was
again and again
age before beauty

* Compiled by Professor A. W. Stewart, Mr Wilson Benington, and myself. With thanks also to Frank Sullivan's article, 'The Cliché Expert Tells All', in *The New Yorker*, June 20, 1936: a source I owe to the kindness of Mr Allen Walker Read. Those who desire to know the origins and sources of these phrases and quotations should consult my *A Dictionary of Clichés*. A list, however, cannot be omitted from *Usage and Abusage*, especially as the subject has hitherto been ignored.

agree to differ [*U.S.A.*: agree to disagree] to
airy nothings; *esp.*, to whisper airy nothings
al fresco [*Italian*]
alarums and excursions
alas, poor Yorick!
alive and kicking
all alive
all and sundry
all hope abandon ye who enter here
all in a lifetime
all in the day's work, it is (*or* was)
all is fish that comes to (*e.g.*, his) net
all sorts and conditions of men
all that in one lies, to do
all the good in the world; *esp.*, do someone . . .
all the relevant considerations
all the world and his wife
all things considered
all things to all men
all through the ages
all to the good, it is (was, will be)
almighty dollar, the
almost incredible (?)
am I my brother's keeper?
ambulance responds (*generally*, responded), the [*American*]
amende honorable [*French*]
amiable qualities
ample opportunity
ample sufficiency, an
ancestral acres
and how! [*American*]
and so to bed!
. . . and something to spare
angry passions
animated scene, an (the, that, this)
another Richmond in the field
answer: *see* in the affirmative
answer a fool according to his folly, to
any port in a storm
apostle of culture
appeal from Philip drunk to Philip sober, to [*obsolescent literary*]
appear on the scene, to
appears to be without foundation, it [*legal*]
apple of discord, the [*obsolescent literary*]
apple of one's eye, the
approximately correct
aqua pura [*Latin*; *properly it* = '*pure water*', *not merely* '*water*']
arbiter elegantiarum [*Latin*]
Arcades ambo [*Latin*]
Argus-eyed [*obsolescent*]
armed to the teeth
arrangements (*or* suitable a.) have been made

arrive on the scene, to
artful deceiver, an
as a matter of fact, . . .
as a matter of form (?)
as every schoolboy knows [*slightly obsolescent*]
as (*or* so) far as in one lies
as good (*or* well) as can (*or* could) be expected
as good luck would have it
as one man (?)
as the crow flies
ashes to ashes, dust to dust
ask for bread and receive a stone, to
assume as proved, we must [*legal*]
at a loose end; *e.g.*, I was at . . . [or *American*, 'at loose ends']
at a tender age
at (a person's) beck and call
at daggers drawn
at death's door, be (*or* lie); bring to death's door
at long last
at one fell swoop
at one's last gasp
at one's own sweet will
at one's wit's end
at sixes and sevens (?)
at the cross-roads
at the end of one's tether
at the first blush
at the psychological moment
at this juncture
atmosphere of doubt, an
Attic salt [*obsolescent*]
au courant [*French*]
auspicious occasion; *esp.*, on this a.o.
average ability
avoid: *see* plague
awkward alternative, an
awkward fix [*colloquial*]
awkward predicament, an
axe to grind; *e.g.*, to have an

b

back the wrong horse, to
back to the wall; *esp.*, to have one's . . . , *or* to stand with one's back to the wall
bag and baggage
baker's dozen, a
balm in Gilead; *esp.*, is there no balm in Gilead? [*obsolescent*]
balmy weather
baptism of fire; *esp.*, to receive one's
Barkis is willin'
Barmecide feast, a [*obsolescent journalistic*]
battle royal, a
be-all and end-all, the

be in good hands, to
be in the same boat with, to
be that as it may
beard the lion in his den, to; *hence*, to beard a person in his den
bear a charmed life, to
beat a retreat, to
beat about the bush, to
beat swords into ploughshares, to [*obsolescent*]
beaten at the post
beaten track, the
bed and board; *esp.*, at b. and b.
bed of roses, a
bee in one's bonnet, a; *esp.*, to have . . .
beer and skittles, it is (*or* was *or* will be) not
before: *see* born or . . .
beg and petition, to [*obsolescent*]
beggars (*or* beggared) description, it
beginning of a new era, the
beginning of the end, the
behind the scenes
believe (*or* can't believe) one's own eyes
believe it or not [*introduction formula*]
belong to a world apart, to; *also*, to live in . . .
belted earl, a
beneath contempt
benefit of the doubt, (to give) the
best is yet to be, the
best-laid schemes of mice and men gang aft agley, the
best of all possible worlds, the
bête noire [*French*]
better and better
better half, one's
better left unsaid
better or . . . : *see* for better
between Scylla . . . : *see* Scylla . . .
between the Devil and the deep (blue) sea
between two fires
between wind and water [*figurative*]
between you and me and the bedpost
beyond a (*or* any) shadow of doubt
beyond belief
beyond the ken of mortal man
beyond the pale
big fleas have little fleas
bird has flown, the
bird of ill omen, a
bird of passage, a
birds of a feather
bite off more than one can chew, to
bitter complaint, a; bitter complaints
bitter end, the; *esp.*, to the . . .
bitter irony
blank amazement
blank despair

blaze a trail, to
blessing in disguise, a
bless one's (lucky) stars, to
blind leading the blind, the
blissful ignorance
bloated armaments (?)
bloated plutocrat, a
blood and iron
blood and treasure: see expense of
blood-curdling yell, a
bloody but unbowed
bloody Mary
blot on the landscape, a
blow off steam, to
blow one's own trumpet, to
blow hot and cold, to
blown to smithereens
blue Mediterranean, the
blunt instrument, a [detective-story writers']
blushing honours thick upon him; gen-
    erally, he bears his . . . ; occasionally,
    with his . . .
bolt from the blue, a
bone of contention, a
boon companion, a
boot is on the other leg, the
booted and spurred
bored to death (or tears)
born and bred (in . . .)
born or thought of, before you were
born under a lucky star
born with a silver spoon in one's mouth
borrowed plumes
bottom of the deep blue sea, esp., at
    the . . .
bounden duty, one's
bowels of the earth, the; esp., in the . . .
bowing and scraping
Box and Cox
brand of Cain, the
brave and the fair, the
brave men and fair women
break the ice, to
breath of heaven (or Spring), a; generally
    as a simile, like a . . .
breath of one's nostrils, to [obsolescent]
breathe freely, to [figurative]
breathe one's last (breath), to
bred in the bone
bright and early
(bright) orb of the day, the
bring grist to the (or one's) mill, to
bring home to, to
bring someone to his knees, to [obsoles-
    cent]
broke to the wide world
broken reed, a
brown study, a; esp., in a . . .
bruit about, to
brutal atrocity, a

brute force
buffeting (or buffets) of fate, the; buffeted
    by fate
built upon sand
bulwark of the state, a
bundle of nerves; esp., to be a . . .
burden and (the) heat of the day, the
burden of proof, the
burden of (the) years, the
burn one's boats, to
burn one's fingers, to
burn the candle at both ends, to
burn the midnight oil, to
(of lights) burning far into the night
burning question, a
burnt to a cinder
bury the hatchet, to [obsolescent]
business, go about one's; send (a person)
    about his business
business as usual (?)
but me no buts
butchered to make a Roman holiday
butter wouldn't melt in her mouth
butterfly (broken) on the wheel, a
buxom wench, a
buy a pig in a poke, to
buy for an old song, to
by a long chalk, not [[or American, 'not by
    a long chance or shot']]
by all means, do!
by fits and starts (?)
by hook or by crook
by leaps and bounds; esp., go ahead
    by . . .
by no manner of means
by no means certain, it is
by rule of thumb
by the same token
by the sweat of one's brow
by word of mouth

c

cacoëthes scribendi [Latin]
cakes and ale
call a halt, to
call a spade a spade, to
call in question
call of the wild, the
call (esp., not to be able to call) one's
    soul one's own
call the tune, to
calm (or lull) before the storm, the
came (the), as in, esp., came the dawn,
    but also, e.g., came the French Revolu-
    tion, came the War of 1914–1918, or
    even came Lenin
can safely say (that . . .), I or you
captain of one's soul, the
captains of industry

card up one's sleeve, a; *esp.*, to have a . . .
care a pin for; *e.g.*, he does not . . .
care a rap, not to
cart before the horse, the; *esp.*, to put
   the cart . . .
carte blanche [*French*]; *esp.*, to give a person carte blanche
cast in one's lot with, to [*obsolescent*]
cast in the teeth of, to [*obsolescent*]
cast into the outer darkness, to (*or* to be)
cast one's bread upon the waters, to
cast pearls: *see* pearls . . .
cast the first stone, to
castle in Spain, a; *or* castles in Spain
castle in the air, a; *or* castles . . .
casual encounter, a
casual remark, a
caviare to the general
certain lewd fellows of the baser sort
ceteris paribus [*Latin*]
chacun à son goût [*French*]
change of heart, a
change of scene, a
chapter of accidents, a
chasing the rainbow
cheek by jowl
cheer to the echo, to
cherchez la femme! [*French*]
cherished belief(s)
chew the cud, to
chick or child, have no; have neither
   chick nor child; without chick or child
child of nature, a
children of this world, the [*obsolescent*]
chilled to the marrow
chip of the old block, a
chop and change, to
chosen people, the
chronicle small beer, to [*obsolescent*]
circumstances over which I have (*or* one
   has) no control
citizen of no mean city, a
City: *see* magnate
city swelters in record heat-wave [*American journalese*]
civis Romanus sum [*Latin*]
classes and the masses, the (?)
clean sheet, a [*figurative*]
cleanse one's bosom of such (*or* this)
   perilous stuff, to [*from a quotation*]
cleanse the Augean stables, to [*obsolescent*]
clear the decks, to [*figurative*]
clears the air, that
clerk of the weather, the
cloistered virtue
close finish, a (?)
close on the heels of
close (*or* near) thing, a
clothed and in one's right mind

cloud of witnesses, a [*obsolescent*]
cloven hoof, the
clumsy lout, a
coals of fire on a person's head, to heap
coast is clear, the
cock of the walk; *esp.*, to be . . .
coign of vantage, a
cold douche, a [*figurative*]
cold light of reason, the; *esp.*, in the . . .
cold wave spells suffering to thousands
   [*American journalese*]
colorful scene, a [*American*]
colossal undertakings
colourable imitation, a
comb, to go through with a fine (*or* a
   fine-tooth)
come home to roost, to
come into a person's life, to
come on the scene, to
come to grief, to
come to light, to
come to the ear(s) of, to
come to the end of one's tether, to; *or*, to
   have come . . .
come together again, to
comes to the same thing (in the end), it
comme il faut [*French*]
common herd, the
common or garden [*adjectival*]
common understanding (?)
comparisons are odious
completely gutted by fire [*American*]
con amore [*Italian*]
condemn (a person) out of his own
   mouth, to
confusion worse confounded (?)
conservative estimate [*American*]
considered opinion that, it is my (*or* his
   or . . .)
consigned to oblivion
conspicuous by its (*or* their) absence
constant communication, in
consummation devoutly to be wish'd, a
contract a chill, to
controlling factor, the [*American*]
controversial question, a (*etc.*)
cook someone's goose for him, to
cool, calm and collected
cost a pretty penny, to
counsel of perfection, a
country cousin, a
country mouse, a
coup de grâce [*French*]
crack of doom, the
cradled in luxury
crass stupidity
cribbed, cabined and confined [*see* MIS-
   QUOTATIONS]
cricket, *as in* it's not cricket *and* is it
   cricket?

crocodile tears [*originally* a crocodile's tears]
cross the Rubicon, to
cross the Styx, to [*obsolescent*]
crown of glory, a
crowning mercy, a
crumbs from the rich man's table
cry for the moon, to
cry is Still they come, the
cry over spilt milk, to
cry wolf too often, to
crystal-clear
cudgel one's brains, to
cui bono? [*Latin*]
cum grano salis [*Latin; obsolescent*]
cups that cheer but not inebriate
curious to relate
curiously enough
curtain lecture, a; to give a curtain lecture
cut a long story short, to
cut and run, to
cut and thrust
cut off one's nose to spite one's face, to
cut off with a shilling, to
cut one's coat according to one's cloth, to
cut the painter, to
cut to the quick, to
cynosure of all eyes, the; *or*, as quotation, '. . . of neighbouring eyes'

d

dabble in the occult, to
damn with faint praise, to
damned Yankee [*American*]
dance attendance on, to [*obsolescent*]
Daniel come to judgement, a
Dark Continent, the
dark horse, a
darken counsel, to
darken one's doors (*or* threshold); darken the door of, to
dastardly crime, a
dawn suddenly (up)on *or* dawn (up)on suddenly; *e.g.*, it suddenly dawned upon him
day after the fair, to be a
day of wrath, the
days are numbered, one's
days that are gone, the
de gustibus (non est disputandum) [*Latin*]
de mortuis nil nisi bonum [*Latin*]
dead and done with
dead and gone
dead certainty, a
dead letter, a [*figurative*]
dead men's shoes; *esp.*, to wait for . . .

dead of night, at; *or* in the . . .
Dead Sea fruit
deadly earnest; *esp.*, in d.e.
deadly menace, a
deadly precision (?)
dear departed, the [*pulpit*]
death and destruction
death's door: *see* at . . .
decent, honest, (and) God-fearing (?)
decisive effect, a (?)
deep calling unto deep
definite step, a [*American*]
deliberate falsehood, a
delicate negotiations
deliver the goods, to [*figurative*]
demon rum, the
deny . . .: *see* soft impeachment
Deo volente; *or* D.v. [*Latin*]
depart this life, to
depths of bathos, the
deserving poor, the
desire someone's better acquaintance, to
desperate position *or* situation, a
deus ex machina [*Latin*]
devil incarnate, a
Devil's own: *see* luck
devoted solely to [*American*]
devouring element, the [i.e., fire]
devoutly hope; *e.g.*, I devoutly hope; *also* it is devoutly to be hoped
diabolical rage, a
diabolical skill
dictates of one's feelings (*or* heart), the
dictatorship of the proletariat, the
die a natural death, to
die in harness, to
die in the last ditch, to
die in the odour of sanctity, to
die is cast, the
dim and distant past, from (*or* in) the
dim religious light, a
ding-dong battle, a
discard precedent, to [*American*]
discerning reader, the
disjecta membra [*Latin*]
disrupt train schedules, to; *e.g.*, snow disrupts t.s. [*American*]
distance has been annihilated
distinction without a difference, a
disturbance of mind
Divine order of things, the
divinity that shapes . . .: *see* there's a . . .
do a good turn to (a person)
do one's heart good, to
do or die, to
dog's chance, a; *esp.*, not to have . . .
dog in the manger, a
dolce far niente [*Italian*]
done to a turn
doom is sealed, one's

dose of his own medicine, a; *esp.*, give someone a . . .
dot one's I's and cross one's T's, to
double-dyed traitor, a
double harness; *esp.*, in d.h.
doubt one (*or* we *or* you, *etc.*), cannot justly
doubtful advantage, a
doubtful cause, a
down and out (?)
down at (the) heel
down to the last detail
drag into the mire (*or* through the dirt), to
draw a bow at a venture, to
draw a veil over, to [*obsolescent*]
draw in one's horns, to
draw the line at, to
draw the long bow, to
draw to a close, to
dree one's weird, to
drenched to the skin (?)
dressed up to the nines (*or* to kill)
drift apart, to
drop the pilot, to [*figurative; obsolescent*]
drown one's sorrows in drink, to
due consideration, on (*or* upon)
durance vile; *esp.*, in d.v.
dust and ashes
dust to dust: *see* ashes . . .
Dutch courage
Dutch treat [*American*]
dyed in the wool

e

each and every (one)
eager . . .: *see* ready for . . .
eagle eye, an *or* one's
earnest consideration
earnest desire to make the world a better place in which to live, an *or* one's
earth has not anything to show more fair
Earth, the Great Mother [*obsolescent literary*]
East is East, and West is West (and never the twain shall meet)
eat from (*or* out of) a person's hand, to
eat humble pie, to
eat one's heart out, to
eat out of house and home, to
Eclipse first and the rest nowhere
economic factor, the
elegant sufficiency, an [*obsolescent*]
eleventh hour; *esp.*, at the e.h.
eloquent silence
embarras de richesses [*French*]
Emerald Isle, the
eminently successful
emotion overcame him (*etc.*), his (*etc.*)

endowed with this world's goods; *esp.*, well endowed . . .
ends of the earth, the; *e.g.*, to *or* from the ends of the earth
enemy at the gate, an *or* the
enemy in our midst, an *or* the
engage in conversation, to
enter the lists, to
entertain an angel unawares, to
entertain high hopes, to
entre nous [*French*]
errand of mercy, an
error in taste, an
escape by the skin of one's teeth, to
escape unscathed, to [*American*]
et in Arcadia ego [*Latin*]
et hoc genus omne [*Latin*]
et tu, Brute [*Latin*]
eternal feminine, the
eternal triangle, the
eternal verities, the [*literary*]
eve of great events, the; *esp.*, on the . . .
even if the worst happens (*or* happened)
even tenor of one's way, the; *esp.*, pursue the . . .
event: *see* more than
ever and anon [*adolescent*]
every canon on international law [*political and journalistic*]
every effort is (*or* was) being (*or* will be) made
every inch a king
every man has his price
every mother's son
every principle of decency and humanity [*journalistic*]
ex pede Herculem [*Latin; adolescent*]
existing conditions; *esp.*, under . . .
expense of blood and treasure, an (?)
experto crede [*Latin; cosmopolitan literary*]
explore every avenue, to [*mostly political*]
express concern, to
express one's appreciation, to
extra precautions, to take [*American*]
eye for an eye, an
eye to (*now often* on) the main chance, an; *esp.*, to have . . .
eyes of faith, the

f

face the music, to
facilis descensus Averni [*Latin*]
fair and square
fair, fat and forty
fair sex, the
fair women and brave men
fait accompli [*French*]
fall between two stools, to

fall from grace, to
fall on deaf ears, to
fall on stony ground, to
fall to with a will, to
far and away (*e.g.*, the best)
far and wide
far as in me lies: *see* as far . . .
far be it from me to . . .
far cry, a; *esp.*, it is a far cry from . . .
far-flung Empire, our [*British*]
far from accurate
far from the madding crowd
far-reaching effects
far-reaching policy, a
fast and furious
fasten the blame on, to
fatal deed, a *or* the
fatal scene, the
fate worse than death, a; *esp.*, suffer a
    fate . . .
Father Time
fatted calf: *see* kill the . . .
faute de mieux [*French*]
feather, to show the; to show the white
    feather
feather in one's cap, (that is) a
feather one's nest, to
feel a different person, to
feel in one's bones that . . ., to
feel one's age, to (?)
feet of clay
feline amenities
female of the species, the
festive board, the
festive occasion, a
few and far between
fiat justitia, ruat caelum [*Latin*]
fiddle while Rome burns, to
fierce light which beats upon a throne,
    that
fight tooth and nail, to
filthy lucre
fin de siècle [*French; literary*]
final and unalterable (?)
find—*generally*, be unable to find—it in
    one's heart to do something, to
find (*or* get) one's bearings, to
fine feather; *esp.*, to be in fine feather
finishing touch, the
fingers (*esp.*, my fingers) itch to
firm footing, a
first and foremost
first and last [= *all the time*]
first fine careless rapture, the
first robin, the [[*American*, cf. English
    '*the first cuckoo*', in reference to Spring]]
first saw the light of day
fish in troubled waters, to
fish out of water, a; *esp.*, like . . .
fit for a king

fit to hold a candle to, not
flash in the pan, a
flashed into (*e.g.*, his) mind, it
flat denial, a
flat, stale and improfitable (*or* unprofit-
    able) [*see* Misquotations]
flatter only (*or* but) to deceive, to
flesh and blood; *esp.*, one's own
flesh-pots of Egypt, the
flight of fancy, a (?)
flood-gates of (affection, grief, *etc.*), to
    open (*or* loose) the
flotsam and jetsam
flourish like the green bay-tree, to
flowers of speech
flowing bowl, the
fly in the face of Providence, to
fly in the ointment, a
fly off at a tangent, to
foam at the mouth
foeman worthy of one's steel, a [*obsoles-
    cent*]
follow in the footsteps of (a person, *esp.*,
    a great man)
fons et origo [*Latin*]
fool (a person) to the top of his bent
    [*obsolescent*]
fool's paradise, a; *esp.*, to live in . . .
for auld lang syne *and* for old time's sake
for better or (for) worse
for good and all
for love or money
for the life of me, I cannot . . .
for this relief, much thanks
for very shame; *esp.*, not to (be able to)
    do something for v.s.
forbidden fruit
force to be reckoned with, a
foregone conclusion, a
foreign devil, a [trans. of *Chinese*]
forgotten man, the [*American, political*]
forlorn hope, a
formulate a plan, to [*American*]
foul one's own nest, to
founding fathers, the *or* our [*American*]
four corners of the earth (*or* world), the
Fourth Estate, the
frame an excuse, to
fraught with danger (*or* peril)
free and easy
free, gratis and for nothing
fresh fields and pastures new [*see* Mis-
    quotations]
fret and fume, to
friend at court, (to have) a
friend in need, a
friend of man, the [*a dog*]
from *A* to *Z*
from bad to worse
from Dan to Beersheba

from head to heels
from pillar to post
from start to finish (?)
from the bottom of one's heart
from the cradle to the grave
from the functional point of view [*American educational jargon*] (?)
from time immemorial
from top to toe (?)
from whose bourne no traveller returns [*obsolescent*]
frozen to the marrow
full and hearty coöperation, a *or* one's
full of sound and fury
fulsome compliments; fulsome flattery
further the interests of someone, to

g

gain ground, to (?)
gala occasion, a [*American*]
gall and wormwood
gay Lothario, a
general exodus, a
generous to a fault
gentle reader (*vocative*); the gentle reader
germane to the matter
get down to bed-rock, to; *slangily,* to get down to brass tacks [*rhyming on 'hard facts'*]
get more than one bargained for, to
get one's second wind, to
get one's teeth into, to
get to the bottom of, to
get up on the wrong side of the bed, to
giddy vortex, the [*obsolescent*]
gift from the gods, a
gift of tongues, the
gild the pill, to
gilded youth [*obsolescent*]
gilding refinèd gold; *or* gilding (*properly*: painting) the lily
gird up one's loins, to
give a bad mark to, to
give a dog a bad name, to
give a wide berth to, to
give and take
give chapter and verse, to
give oneself airs, to
give pause to, to
give short shrift to, to [*obsolescent*]
give the cold shoulder to, to
give the Devil his due, to
give thanks to
glorious uncertainty (*e.g.,* of cricket), the
glorious victory, a
go about . . .: *see* business
go at it hammer and tongs, to
go by the board, to
go from strength to strength, to

go further and fare worse, to
go hat in hand, to
go in one ear and out of the other, to
go off with one's tail between one's legs, to
go on the war-path, to
go the whole hog, to
go through fire and water for (a person), to
go to one's account, to
go to the dogs, to
go to the other extreme
God and Mammon
goes without saying, it *or* that
golden age, the [*literary*]
golden mean, the
Golden West, the
gone (*or* gone before) but not forgotten
gone with the wind (?)
good, bad, and (*or* or) indifferent
good cheer, to be of
good clean fun
good for nothing
good general education, a
good in parts; *or, as a battered simile,* good in parts, like the curate's egg
good Indian, a [*American*]
good men and true; (*of a jury*) twelve good men and true
good Queen Bess
good Samaritan, a
good time was had by all, a [*literary*]
good woman's love, a; the love of a good woman
goods and chattels
Gordian knot; *esp.,* to cut the . . .
gorgeous East, the
gorge rises at, (*e.g.*) my
grain or chaff; to separate the grain from the chaff
grand finale, the
Grand Old Man (*e.g.,* of English politics), the
grapes of wrath, the [*obsolescent*]
graphic description, a; graphic descriptions
grasp the nettle, to [*obsolescent*]
grateful acknowledgements
grave concern; *esp.,* it occasioned grave concern
grave international situation, the
great majority, the; *esp.,* to join the . . .
great open spaces, the
great ovation, a *or* the
great strapping girl, a
great unwashed, the [*obsolescent*]
greater love hath no man than this
Greek kalends, the; *esp.,* to put off to the . . .
green-eyed monster, the

grievous error, a

grim death [and *see* SIMILES, BATTERED, at '*hang*' and '*look*')

grin and bear it, to

grind the faces of the poor, to

gross exaggeration, a; a gross overstatement

ground floor: *see* in on the . . .

grow no younger, to; *esp.*, to be growing no younger

guide, philosopher and friend, a

guiding light, a *or* one's

h

hair, *as in* without turning a hair *and* he did not turn a hair

hair of (*or* like) spun gold (?)

halcyon days

hale and hearty

half the battle; *esp.*, it's . .

hall-mark(s) of truth (*or* sincerity), the

hammer and tongs; *esp.*, to go at it hammer and tongs

hand and foot; *esp.*, bound (*or* tied) hand and foot

hand has lost its cunning, one's

hand in glove with

hand on the torch, to

hand-to-mouth (*adjective*); live from hand to mouth, to

handle without (*or* with [*American*]) gloves, to (?)

hands across the sea

hang by a thread, to

hang on: *see* grim death

hang on by one's eyelids, to [*obsolescent*]

hanging in the balance (?)

happy couple, a *or* the

happy despatch [*obsolescent*]

happy ending, a (?)

happy event, a *or* the

happy ever after

happy hunting-ground, one's; the Happy Hunting Grounds

happy pair, the [a *bridal couple*]

happy solution, a

happy termination, a (?)

hard and fast line; *esp.*, to draw a . . .

hard facts

hastily summoned

have a bone to pick with (someone), to

have a finger in the (*or* in every) pie, to

have a great mind to, to

have a shot at something, to

have and to hold to, to

have one's cake and eat it (too) (*or* eat one's cake and have it), to

have other fish to fry, to

have no truck with, to

have the whip hand of (someone), to

have too many irons in the fire, to

head and front of it, the

head and shoulders above

heap: *see* coals of fire

heard a pin drop, one (*or* you) could have

heart and soul

heart bleeds for, one's

heart in one's mouth, to have one's

heart in the right place; *esp.*, have one's . . . *or* one's heart is in . . .

heart of gold, one has *or* had a

heart of hearts, in one's

heart of stone, a

heart of the matter, the

heart to heart talk, a

hearts of oak [*obsolescent*]

hearty applause

hearty British cheer, a

hearty congratulations

heated argument, a

heated retort, a; *esp.*, make a . . .

heathen Chinee, the [*obsolescent*]

heave a sigh of relief, to

heaven on earth, a

heavy responsibilities; *esp.*, to assume h.r.

height of absurdity, the

hell for leather

Hell is paved with good intentions

Hell knows (*or* has) no fury like a woman scorned [a *misquotation*]

help a lame dog over a stile, to

helping hand, a

here and there (?)

here is God's plenty

here to-day and gone to-morrow

hewers of wood and drawers of water

hide one's light under a bushel, to

high and dry

high days and holidays

high hopes

high in the heavens; *esp.*, the sun was . . .

high moral tone, a

highly confidential information

highly improbable

highly respected; a highly respected member of the community

historic occasion; *esp.*, that h.o. *or* on this h.o.

hit below the belt, to

hit or miss

hit the nail on the head, to

hitch one's waggon to a star, to

hither and thither

hive of industry, a

Hobson's choice

hoi polloi, the [*tautological*]

hoist on (*or* with) one's own petard, to be

hold forth, to (?)

hold (a person) in suspense, to
hold no brief for, to
hold one's head high, to (?)
holding one's own
hole and corner [adjective]
holiday exodus, a [American]
hollow tones (?)
holy matrimony
holy of holies, the [obsolescent]
home comforts (?)
home of the lost causes, the
home of one's own, a
Homeric laughter
honest penny, an; esp., to turn an h.p.
honest truth, the
honourable mention
hope against hope, to
hope deferred ... [thus; in full, it is
    merely a proverb]
hope springs eternal (in the human
    breast)
hopeless despair
horny-handed: see son of the soil
horse of another colour; esp., that's a
    horse ...
host of friends, a; esp., to have a ...
hotly contested
hour of need, one's
how the world wags
howling wilderness, a [obsolescent]
hub of the universe, the
hue and cry, a
hum and haw, to
human—all too human
human interest [journalistic]
hundred-to-one chance, a [non-literally]

i

I am no orator, as Brutus is
I could hardly believe my eyes
I hate to mention it, but ...
I have no hesitation in saying
I mean to say
I shall not die happy unless (or until) ...
I should be the last to say
I think I ought to tell you
I would not touch (e.g., it) with a barge-
    pole
idle rich, the
if the mountain won't come to Mahomet,
    Mahomet must go to the mountain
if the truth were known
if the worst comes (occasionally came) to
    the worst
ignominious retreat, an; esp., to beat an
    ignominious retreat
ilk: see of that ilk
ill-gotten gains

ills that flesh is heir to, the [see also
    MISQUOTATIONS]
illustrious dead, our or the
imagination runs riot, one's
immaculate attire
immeasurably superior
'immemorial elms' (?)
impenetrable darkness
implicit confidence; esp., to have (or
    place) i.c. in
important inside information
improve the shining hour, to [obsolescent]
in a certain condition
in a cleft stick
in a nutshell
in a Pickwickian sense
in a trice [obsolescent]
in all conscience
in apple-pie order
in at the death
in black and white
in character; esp., not to be ...
in flagrante delicto [Latin]
in full cry
in good set terms
in hot water
in less than no time
in medias res [Latin]
in my opinion
in no uncertain manner (or terms or
    voice)
in on the ground floor
in round numbers
in some mysterious way
in the affirmative (or the negative); esp.,
    the answer is ...
in the arms of Morpheus
in the event of (an) emergency
... in the extreme; e.g., difficult in the
    extreme
in the flesh
in the fulness of time
in the heat of the moment
in the land of the living
in the last analysis
in the last resort
in the light of recent (or subsequent)
    events
in the mind's eye
in the nick of time
in the public eye
in the same boat
in the toils; esp., taken in the toils
in the twinkling of an eye
in the whole wide world; in the wide, wide
    world
in the world (of) to-day
in the wrong box
in this year of grace
in vino veritas [Latin]

incident is (or was) closed, the
incident passed without further comment, the [journalistic]
incontrovertible fact, an
indistinguishably mixed
ineffable contempt (or scorn); esp., with
   a look of . . .
inevitable conclusion is, the
inevitable consequences, the
inevitable surrender, an or one's
inferno, a blazing or raging
infinite capacity for taking pains, an
initial steps have been taken; or the initial steps . . .
inner man, the
ins and outs; e.g., the ins and outs of the
   case
instant destruction
intents: see to all . . .
insubstantial pageant, an or the [obsoles-
   cent]
Iron Duke, the
irons in the fire; e.g., to have too many . . .
iron hand in the velvet glove, the
irreducible minimum, an
irreparable loss, an
islands (or isles) of the blest, the
it all came out
it gives furiously to think [obsolescent]
it hurts me more than it does you
it is a far, far better thing that I do
   (now) than I have (ever) done before
it is better to have loved and lost than
   never to have loved at all
it is notorious that . . .
it may interest (generally you) to hear
   that . . .
it may well be that . . .
it might be worse
it stands to reason that . . .
it was not to be (generally), but it was . . .
it would ill become me to . . .
itching palm, an

j

Je ne sais quoi [literary]
Job's comforter, a; Job's comforters
John Bull (with or without his other
   island)
Johnny Reb [American]
join issue, to
jot or tittle
joy and a delight, a [obsolescent]
joy cometh in the morning
jump from the frying pan into the fire, to
Jupiter Pluvius [also an Elegancy]
justly famous (?)

k

keep a civil tongue in one's head [origi-
   nally: mouth]
keep a stiff upper lip, to
keep at arm's length, to
keep body and soul together, to
keep in watertight compartments, to
keep one's head above water, to [figura-
   tive]
keep (one's own or someone's) nose to the
   grindstone, to
keep one's mouth shut, to
keep one's weather eye open, to
keep the ball rolling, to [obsolescent]
keep the pot boiling, to
keep to oneself, to (?)
keep watch and ward, to
key of the mystery, the
kick against the pricks, to
kick one's heels, to
kill or cure; esp., it's kill or cure
kill the fatted calf, to
kill the goose that lays the golden eggs,
   to
kill two birds with one stone, to
kindred spirit, a; kindred spirits
King Charles's head
king is dead, long live the king, the
kiss the Blarney stone, to
kith and kin
knit one's brows, to [obsolescent]
knock the bottom out of, to
knotty point, a (?)
know for a fact, to
know from Adam, not to (She did not
   know him from Adam)
know enough to come in out of the rain,
   not to
know full well, to
know on which side one's bread is but-
   tered, to
know the ropes, to
know where one stands, to (?)
know where the shoe pinches, to [obsoles-
   cent]
know whether one is standing on one's
   head or one's heels, not to

l

labour of love, a
labourer is worthy of his hire, the
lady of the house, the
Lafayette, we are here [American, obsolete?]
land of milk and honey, a
lap of luxury, the; often, living in the . . .
lapse from virtue, a or one's
Lares and Penates [obsolescent]

last but not least
last extremity, the
last gasp, at one's (or the)
last legs; esp., to be on one's . . .
last straw, the
late in the day; esp., rather . . .
latest intelligence, the
laudator temporis acti [Latin]
laugh in (now often up) one's sleeve, to
laugh on the wrong side of one's mouth, to
laugh out of court, to [obsolescent]
laugh to scorn, to
law-abiding citizens
law and order
law is an ass, the
law to [obsolescent: unto] oneself, to be a
lawful occasions; esp., to go about one's
laws: see Medes and Persians
lay down the law, to
lay it on with a trowel, to
lay on, Macduff!
lay one's cards on the table, to
lay the flattering unction to one's soul [obsolescent]
lead a cat-and-dog life, to
lead (someone) a dance, to
lead a dog's life, to
lean and hungry look, a
learn something to one's advantage, to
leather and prunella [obsolescent]
leave a door open, to [politicians]
leave (or leaves) much to be desired; esp., it leaves much . . .
leave (a person) no option, to
leave no stone unturned, to
leave out in the cold, to (?)
leave severely alone, to
leeway to make up
left-handed compliment, a
left in the lurch, to be
left to one's own devices
leg to stand on, not to have a
legal light (or luminary), a
legible hand, a
lend a (helping) hand, to
lend an ear, to
lend me your ears
length and breadth of the land, through (occasionally throughout) the
leonine locks
let loose—or let slip—the dogs of war, to [obsolescent]
let slip through one's fingers, to
let the cat out of the bag, to
let the grass grow under one's feet, (not) to
let the sun go down on one's wrath, (not) to
lethal weapon, a

letting 'I dare not' wait upon 'I would' (?)
lick into shape, to
lick one's chops, to
life and soul of the party; to be the . . .
life-blood of industry, the
life in the raw
life is (or was) not worth living without her (or him); generally, . . . simply not worth . . .
light and leading [obsolescent]
light fantastic (toe), (to trip) the
light on the subject; esp., to shed (more or a little) light on the subject
light that never was on sea or land, the
lighten one's darkness, to
like a giant refreshed
like the curate's egg: see good in parts
lilies and languors [obsolescent]
limpid glance, a or her
link in the chain of progress, a
lion shall lie down with the lamb, (and) the
lion's share, the
lips are (or were) sealed, one's
Little Corporal, the [obsolescent]
little dreaming (or thinking) that . . .
little (properly, small) Latin and less Greek
little stranger, a
live from hand to mouth, to
live in . . .: see belong to . . .
live in clover, to (?)
live in the past, to
livery of shame, the [obsolescent]
living rock, the; esp., sculptured in the . . .
loaves and fishes [obsolescent]
local habitation and a name, a
lock, stock and barrel
lock the stable door after the horse is stolen, to
lone wolf, a [mostly American]
lonely furrow, the [obsolescent]
long and (the) short of it, the
long arm of coincidence, the
long arm of the law, the
long-drawn sigh, a
long-felt want, a; esp., to fulfil . . .
long pull and a strong pull, a
longo intervallo [Latin]
look facts in the face, to
look for a needle in a haystack, to
look daggers, to
look on the wine when it's red, to
lords of Creation, the
lose the thread of one's discourse, to
lost to view
loud enough to waken the dead
love in a cottage
love of . . .: see good woman

luck of the Devil, the; *or* the Devil's own luck
Lucullan banquet, a [*obsolescent*]
lucus a non lucendo [*Latin*]
lull: *see* calm
lulled to a false sense of security

m

magnate: *in* a City magnate *and* a newspaper magnate
magnitude: *see* of the first . . .
mailed fist, the
maintain the *status quo*, to [*journalistic and political*]
major phenomenon, a
make a clean breast of it, to
make assurance doubly sure, to
make a mountain out of a mole-hill, to
make bricks without straw, to
make ends meet, to
make glad the heart of man, to
make good, to
make hay while the sun shines, to
make no bones about it, to
make on the swings what one loses on the roundabouts, to
make one's blood boil, to
make one's hair stand on end, to
make one's mouth water, to
make or mar, to; *now often* to make or break
make the best of a bad bargain (*or* job), to
make (*properly*, let) the punishment fit the crime, to
make the welkin ring, to
make the world a better place: *see* earnest desire
make the world safe for democracy, to [*American, obsolete*]
make the worse appear the better cause (*properly*, reason), to (?)
malignant fate, a
Mammon of unrighteousness, the
man after my own heart, a
man and a brother, a
man at the top, the [*American*]
man in the street, the
man of parts, a
man of straw, a
man of substance, a
manner: *see* to the manner
manners makyth man
many are called; *or, as a quotation*, 'many are called, but few are chosen'
many times and oft [*obsolescent*]
march of time, the
mare's nest, a
mark of recognition, a; *esp.*, as a . . .

mark of the beast (*or* Beast), the
mark time, to (?)
maroon thousands, to; *as in* snow maroons thousands of commuters [*American journalese*]
marriage terminated in divorce, the [*American journalese*]
martial tread
marvels of Science, the
master mind, the
master of one's fate, the
material interests
matter is receiving the closest attention, the
matter of life and death, a
means well, he *or* she
meat and drink to (somebody), something is
Medes and Persians, the; *esp.*, according to the laws of the . . .
meet with an untimely end, to
melancholy intelligence (= *news*), the [*obsolescent*]
mention in this connexion; *esp.*, I may mention . . .
mercury continues to soar, the [*American journalese*]
merest conjecture, the
Merry Monarch, the
meum et tuum [*Latin*]
midsummer madness
might and main; *esp.*, with (all) one's might and main
mighty hunter before the Lord, a
milk and water [*noun or adjective*, when *figurative*]
milk of human kindness, the
mills of God, the [*The mills of God grind slowly, yet they grind exceeding small*]
mince matters, not to
mind one's P's and Q's
mine host
minion of fortune, a; a minion of the moon [*both obsolescent*]
minions of the law
minister to a mind diseased, to
minor matters
mint of money, a [*obsolescent*]
miraculous escape, a *or* one's
miscarriage of justice, a; *generally*, a grave . . .
missing link, the
modern classic, a [*journalistic*]
moment of victory, the; *esp.*, in the
momentary aberration, a
momentous decision, a *or* the *or* one's
monarch of all one surveys [*obsolescent*]
monumental effort, a; a monumental work
monumentum aere perennius [*Latin*]

moot point, a
moral victory, a
more and more (?)
more anon: *see* of which . . .
more dead than alive
more frightened than hurt
more in sorrow than in anger
more or less
more sinned against than sinning
more than a languid interest
more than meets the eye
more than ordinary importance; *esp.*, an
  event of more . . .
more than pleased
more (*or* perhaps more) than you realize
  or may realize
more the merrier, the
Mother Earth
Mother of Parliaments, the
move and have one's being, to
move heaven and earth, to
much ado about nothing
much as I hate to say it (*or* . . . say so)
much in evidence
much of a muchness
much water has flowed (*or* flown) under
  the bridge(s) since then (*or* that time)
muffled report, a [*detective-story writers'*]
multum in parvo [*Latin*]
murder most foul
must of necessity; *e.g.*, it must of necessity be discovered
mutatis mutandis [*Latin*]
mutual attraction of opposites, the
my opinion, for what it is worth, is
  that . . .

n

nail one's flag to the mast, to
nail to the counter, to (?)
naked truth, the [*obsolescent*]
name is Legion, their
Napoleon of finance, a
nasty spill, a
nation speaks to nation; *or* (and) nation
  shall speak to nation
naughty Nineties, the
ne: *see* nec
near: *see* close
nec plus ultra; ne plus ultra [*Latin*]
neck and crop
neck and neck (?)
neck or nothing
needle in a haystack, a
needs no introduction, *as in* Mr X. needs
  no introduction (to you)
neither fish, flesh, nor good red herring
neither here nor there; *generally*, it's . . .
neither rhyme nor reason

Nemesis pursues him, a
nethermost pit, the; *esp.*, condemn to
  the . . .
never the time and the place and the
  loved one all together
nevertheless and notwithstanding
new broom, a
new lease on life, a
new wine in old bottles
newspaper: *see* magnate
nice distinction, a; nice distinctions
night out, a; *esp.*, to have a . . .
nihil tetigit quod non ornavit [*modern
  Latin*]
nine days' wonder, a
nip it in the bud, to
no balm: *see* balm
no better than she should be; *esp.*, she's
  (*or* she was) . . .
no love lost between them, there is (*or*
  was)
no mean (*e.g.*, city)
no respecter of persons
no sinecure, it (*or* this) is (*or* was)
no small (value, *etc.*)
no uncertain: *see* in no . . .
noble red man [*American*]
noblesse oblige [*French*]
nodding acquaintance, a
noised abroad
non compos mentis [*Latin*]
not a shadow of doubt
not a whit [*obsolescent*]
not all beer . . .: *see* beer and skittles
not by a long chalk (*or* chance): *see* by a
  long chalk . . .
not enough room to swing a cat (?)
not for me to say, it's *or* that's
not impossible (?)
not impossibly
not in our stars [*obsolescent*]
not lost but gone before
not the only pebble on the beach
not theirs to reason why
not to put too fine a point upon it
not wisely but too well
not without reason
not worth powder and shot (to blow him
  up with)
not worth the paper it's written on
nothing in his life became him like the
  leaving it
nothing in it; *esp.*, there's . . . [[In U.S.A.,
  means there is no importance or no
  profit]]
nothing to boast about
nous avons changé tout cela [*French*]
now and then (?)
now or never (?)

null and void
nuptial knot, the [obsolescent]

o

O tempora! O mores! [Latin]
observed of all observers, the [obsolescent]
obvious to even the meanest intelligence
ocean greyhound, an
ocular proof
odds and ends (?)
of course
of no avail
of no value to anyone but the owner
of one flesh; esp., to be . . .
of pith and moment [obsolescent]
of that ilk [when used incorrectly]
of the earth, earthy
of the first magnitude
of the first water
of the same kidney
of which (or whom), more anon
off and on
off the beaten track
officer and a gentleman, an
official capacity; esp., in one's . . .
Oh! to be in England, now that April's
    there
oil and water
old Adam, the
old head on young shoulders, an
old order changeth, the
old school tie, the
oldest inhabitant, the
Olympian calm or indifference or pride
    or scorn
on . . . there can be no two opinions
on bended knee
on his own head be it!
on one's mettle
on one's native heath
on more than one occasion
on pins and needles
on pleasure bent
on speaking terms
on tenterhooks, e.g., I was on tenterhooks
on the fence; esp., to sit . . .
on the horns of a dilemma
on the knees (or lap) of the gods
on the qui vive
on the right side of the law
on the rocks (?)
on the side of the angels
on the spot
on the spur of the moment
on the threshold of life
on the tip of one's tongue; esp., to have
    or it is . . .
on unimpeachable authority

once and for all
once upon a time
one and all
one crowded hour of glorious life
one foot in the grave; esp., to have . . .
one in a thousand
one knows very well
one touch of nature makes the whole
    world kin
onerous duties of public office, the
only too glad (or happy or pleased) to
    (do something)
only too well did he (or she) know . . .
open-mouthed surprise (?)
open road, the
open secret, an
or I'll know the reason why
orb . . . : see bright orb . . .
organ of the press, an
other things being equal
our rough island story (?)
our withers are unwrung
out and about
out at elbows (?)
out-Herod Herod, to
out of one's depth
out of the blue
out of the wood, (not) to be
outbreak of hostilities, the; esp., on
    the . . .
outstanding features; esp., one of the . . .
outstanding figure, an
over and above
over and done with
over and over again
over head and ears
overcome by emotion
overwhelming force
overwhelming odds
own flesh and blood; esp., to be . . .
own master; esp., to be one's . . .
own worst enemy, to be one's . . .

p

pageant of history, the
paid on the nail
pains and penalties
pales into insignificance
palpable lie (or untruth), a
Pandora's box [literary]
parlous state, esp., in a parlous state
part and parcel
parting of the ways, the; esp., come to
    the . . .
parting shot, a [properly, a Parthian shot]
passing belief
passing fair
past and gone
patience of Job, the

pay (someone) back in his own coin, to
pay on the nail, to
pay the piper (and call the tune), to
pay up and look pleasant, to
peace be on his (*or* her) ashes—
peace in our time (?)
peace that passeth all understanding, a
(*or* the)
peace with honour
pearls before swine; *esp.*, to cast . . .
peg to hang something on, a
penny plain, twopence (*or* tuppence)
coloured
per ardua ad astra [*Latin*]
perfidious Albion
perform yeoman service, to
persistent rumour, a; persistent rumours
persona grata [*Latin*]
personal affront, a
personal attack, a
personal factor(s)
pick and choose, to
pick of the bunch, the (?)
pick up the threads, to
picture of health, a
pile Pelion on Ossa [*literary*]
pillar of the church, a
pinch hitter, a [*American*]
pious fraud, a
piping times of peace, the
pity of it!, the
place in the sun, a
plague, to avoid like the; *or* to shun as
the plague
play fast and loose (with), to
play the game, to [*figurative*]
play to the gallery, to
play with edged tools, to [*obsolescent*]
play with fire, to
plot thickens, the
plough the sands, to [*obsolescent*]
pluck out the heart of the mystery, to
[*obsolescent*]
plunge heavily, to
plus ça change, plus ça reste la même
chose [*French*]
point-blank refusal, a
police have the matter well in hand, the
pomp(s) and vanity
pool our (*or* their *or* your) resources, to
poor but honest [*when used facetiously*]
popular member(s) of the younger set
[*American*]
possess one's soul in patience, to
possible sympathy, all (*or, loosely*, every)
postpone the evil hour, to; *often*, to put
off . . .
pound of flesh, the (*or* one's)
pour oil on troubled waters, to
power behind the throne, the

powers that be, the
praise to the skies, to
prancing steed(s)
preconcerted arrangement, a
prepared to say (*or* state), to be
pretty kettle of fish, a
prey on one's mind, to (?)
prick up one's ears, to (?)
pride of place
prime of life, the; *esp.*, in the . . .
primrose path, the
principalities and powers [*literary*]
pro bono publico [*Latin*]
proclaim from the housetops, to
progressive and enlightened policy, a
prolonged absence, a *or* one's
prominent citizen, a; prominent citizens
prophet without honour (in his own
country), a
proud parents, the
psychological data
psychological moment: *see* at the . . .
public-school spirit, the
pukka sahib, a
pull the chestnuts out of the fire, to
pull one's weight, to
pull (the) strings, to
pulvis et umbra [*Latin*]
pure and simple; purely and simply
purple, in the; or, born in (*or* to) the
purple
pursuit of happiness, the
push and go [*noun phrase*]
put a good face (up)on, to
put a spoke in someone's wheel, to
put all one's eggs in one basket, to
put back the clock, to
put down one's foot, to
put in good heart, to (?)
put on one's thinking cap, to
put one's best foot forward, to
put one's pride in one's pocket, to
[*obsolescent*]
put one's shoulder to the wheel [*obsolescent*]
put pen to paper, to
put the cart . . . : *see* cart . . .
put through the mill, to
put too fine . . . : *see* not to put . . .
put words into the mouth of, to
pyrrhic victory, a

q

Q.E.D. [*in non-geometrical contexts*]
quality of mercy is not strained, the
quarrel with one's bread and butter, to
queer fish, a
queer the pitch, to

quem deus vult perdere, prius dementat [*Latin*]
quis custodiet ipsos custodes? [*Latin*]
quite frankly I should [*or* shouldn't] . . .
quite providential; *esp.*, it is (*or* was) . . .
quite the opposite
quorum pars magna fui [*Latin*]
quoth the raven [*obsolescent*]

r

Rabelaisian humour [*literary*]
race is (not) to the swift, the
rack and ruin; *esp.*, to go to rack and ruin
rack one's brains, to
rack one's memory, to (?)
radiantly happy
rags and tatters
rain cats and dogs, to; *esp.*, it's raining . . .
rain (*or* heavy rain) interrupted the festivities [*American journalese*]
rain or shine
rake's progress, the
rank and file, the [*figurative*]
rank treason
rap on the knuckles, a
rapid stream of time, the (?)
rara avis [*Latin*]
rash act, a
rattling good yarn, a
raze to the ground, to
read between the lines, to
read, mark, learn and inwardly digest, to
read the riot act to, to (?)
ready (*properly*, eager) for the fray
ready response, a *or* one's
really and truly
receive every consideration, to
record for all time, a
red-letter day, a
red rag to a bull, a
red ruin
reduced to a skeleton
refined irony [*literary*]
regrettable incident (*or* affair), a
reliable source, a; *esp.*, from a . . .
reply in the affirmative (*or* the negative), to
representations are being (*or* have been) made
resist to the death, to
resplendent uniform, a
rest in peace, to
rest in silence, the
rest upon one's laurels, to
resume one's customary avocations, to [*obsolescent*]
retort courteous, the
return to one's vomit, to

return to the charge, to
return to the fold, to
revenons à nos moutons [*French*]
rich beyond the dreams of avarice
rich in . . . : *see* this world's goods
ride rough-shod over, to
rift within the lute, a *or* the [*obsolescent*]
right and proper
right royal
right side: *see* on the right side . . .
rigour of the game, the
ring down the curtain, to
riotous living
rise as one man, to
rise with the lark, to
risk life and limb, to
road to perdition (*or* ruin), the
roar a welcome, to [*American*]
roast beef of old England, the
rob Peter to pay Paul, to
rod in pickle, to; *esp.*, to have a . . .
Roland for an Oliver, a
rolling wave, the [*for 'the sea': obsolescent*]
Roman matron
Roman virtue [*literary*]
root and branch
root of all evil, the
root of the matter, the (?)
rooted in dishonour [*obsolescent*]
rose between two thorns, a
roses and raptures [*obsolescent*]
rotten to the core
rough and ready
rough and tumble (?)
rough diamond, a
rough idea, a
round dozen, a
round oath, a
rousing cheers
royal road, the (?); a *or* the royal road to success [*obsolescent*]
rub the wrong way, to
ruin stared him in the face
rule the roost, to
ruling precedent, a
rumour hath it (that . . .)
run amuck, to [*figurative*]
run one's head against a stone wall, to
run to earth, to (?)
run to seed, to
run with the hare and hunt with the hounds, to
runs in the blood, *e.g.*, it

s

sackcloth and ashes
sacred edifice, a *or* the
sadder and wiser man, a

sadly at fault
saeva indignatio [*Latin*]
safe and sound
safety first (?)
sail near the wind, to
sailor's yarn, a
salad days
salt of the earth, the
sanctity of the home, the
saunter to and fro, to
save another's (*or* one's own) good name, to
saving for a rainy day
saving grace
say (*e.g.*, me) nay, (there is) no one to
say the least . . . : *see* to say the least
scales of Justice, the
scantily clad
scapegoat
Scarlet Woman, the
scathing sarcasm; scathingly sarcastic
scotch, not kill a snake, to [*obsolescent*]
scrap of paper, a [*figurative*]
screw one's courage to the sticking-point, to [*obsolescent*]; to screw up one's courage
sculptured: *see* living rock
Scylla and Charybdis; *esp.*, between S. and C.
sea-change, a; *esp.*, to suffer a . . .
seamy side of life, the
second to none
sedulous ape, the; *esp.*, to play the . . .
see eye to eye; *usually*, not to see eye to eye (with a person)
see how the cat jumps, to
see how the land lies, to
see it through, to
see no further than one's nose, to [*slightly obsolescent*]
see red, to
see the finger of God in (something or other), to
see the wood for the trees, not to be able to *or* to be unable to *or* cannot . . .
see with half an eye, to (?)
see with one's own eyes, to
see one's virtuous couch, to [*obsolescent*]
seething masses of humanity
select few, a *or* the
sell like hot cakes, to
sell one's soul, to
sell the pass, to [*obsolescent*]
send about: *see* business
send to Coventry, to
separate: *see* grain
sere and yellow leaf, the
sermons in stones
serve . . . : *see* wait on . . .
serve one's turn, to

set by the ears, to
set one's face against, to
set one's hand to the plough, to
set one's heart on, to
set one's house in order, to
set one's teeth, to
set one's teeth on edge, to
set the Thames on fire, to
set to (*or* work) with a will, to
seven-leagued boots
seventh heaven of delight, (in) the
shadow and the dust, the [*obsolescent literary*]
shadow of death, the
shadow of one's former self, to be but the
shake in one's shoes, to
shake off the dust from (*originally of*) one's feet, to
shaken to its (*or* their) foundations
shape: *see* things to come
shape or form; *esp.*, in any . . .
share and share about, to (?)
shattering effect, a; with (a) shattering effect
she is—*usually* she's—no chicken
shed light: *see* light on . . .
sheer physical exhaustion (*or* inability)
shining armour [*obsolescent*]
ship of state, the
ship stood out to sea, the
ships that pass in the night
shipshape and Bristol fashion [*obsolescent*]
shoot one's bolt; *generally* to have shot one's bolt
short and sweet
short life and a merry one, a
short shrift; *esp.*, to give . . .
shoulder the burden, to
show a bold front, to
show a clean pair of heels, to
show one's cards, to
show the cloven hoof, to [*obsolescent*]
show the: *see* feather
shreds and patches
shuffle off one's mortal coils, to
shun: *see* plague
si jeunesse savait, si vieillesse pouvait [*French*]
sic transit gloria mundi [*Latin*]
sick at heart
Sick Man of Europe, the [*obsolescent*]
sickening thud, a
sight for sore eyes, a
signed, sealed, and delivered
silence reigns (*or* reigned) supreme
silver lining, a
silver sea, the
simple truth, the
sin against the light, to

sinews of war, the
single blessedness
single iota, a; *esp.*, not (by) a . . .
sink or swim, to
sit on the fence, to
six of one and half a dozen of the other
skate on thin ice, to
skeleton at the feast, the
skeleton in the cupboard, a
skin and bones; *esp.*, to be all . . . *or*
  nothing but . . .
sleep the sleep of the just, to
slings and arrows of outrageous fortune,
  the
slippery slope (?)
slipshod reasoning
Slough of Despond, the
slow but sure; slowly but surely
slow to anger
smack of the soil, to
smell a rat, to
smell of the lamp, to [*obsolescent literary*]
smell to heaven, to (?)
smiling hypocrite, a
smite hip and thigh, to
smoke the pipe of peace, to [*obsolescent*]
snake in the grass, a
snapper-up of unconsidered trifles, a
snatch a hasty meal, to
snow blankets (*or* blanketed) the city
  (*or* country) [*American journalese*]
so far as that goes . . .
so shines a good deed in a naughty world
so to say (*or* speak)
social amenities
social whirl, the
Society butterflies
soft impeachment, the; *esp.*, to deny the
  . . . *or* to admit the . . .
soft place in one's heart, a; *esp.*, have a
  . . . for someone
sold one's birthright for a mess of
  pottage, to have
solvitur ambulando [*Latin*]
something in the wind; *esp.*, there's . . .
something must be done (about it)
son of the soil, a; *esp.*, a horny-handed
  son . . .
sooner or later
sop to Cerberus, a [*literary*]
sorry jest, a
sort of day that makes one glad to be
  alive, the
sotto voce [*Italian*]
soul of honour, the
sound and fury
sound in wind and limb [*esp. when not
  used literally*]
sound policy, a
sounding brass (and tinkling cymbals)

sour grapes
sovereign remedy, a
sow one's wild oats, to
sow the wind and reap the whirlwind, to
spacious times of good Queen Bess (*or*
  Queen Elizabeth), (in) the
speak by the book, to [*obsolescent*]
speak volumes for; *esp.*, it *or* that speaks
  . . .
. . . spectators line (*or* lined) the streets
speed the parting guest, to
spend money like water, to
spent rocket, a [*obsolescent*]
spick and span
spicy breezes
spike someone's guns, to [*obsolescent*]
spirit is willing, but the flesh is weak, the
spirit of the troops (*or* men) is excellent,
  the
spiritual home, one's
splendid isolation
spoil the Egyptians, to
Springtime of life, (in) the
square meal, a
square peg in a round hole, a
square the circle, to
stab in the back, a; to stab . . .
stab to the heart, to
staff of life, the
stage whisper, a
stagger humanity, to
stamped on every link
stand or fall, to
stand not upon the order of one's going,
  to [*ex Lady Macbeth's 'Stand not upon
  the order of your going, but go at once'*]
stand on one's own legs (*or* feet), to
stand (*or* stay) the pace, to
stand with . . . : *see* back to the wall
star has set, one's
starry heavens, the
stars in their courses, the
stately homes of (old) England, the
stay one's hand, to [*obsolescent*]
stay the course, to
steady improvement, a
steal a march on, to
steal someone's thunder, to
steer clear of, to
step by step
step in the right direction, a
stem the tide, to
step into someone's shoes, to
stepping-stones of their dead selves
stern reality
stew in one's own juice, to
stitch in time, a
stick in one's throat, to [*obsolescent*]
stick to one's guns, to
still, small voice, a *or* the

stink in the nostrils of, to [*obsolescent*]
stir up strife, to (?)
stolen fruit
stone dead
storm brewing, a
storm in a tea-cup, a
straight (*or* strait) and narrow path, the
straight deal, a
straight from the horse's mouth
straight from the shoulder
straight off the reel
strain at a gnat, to
strain every nerve, to
straitened circumstances; *esp.*, in . . .
strange but true
stranger in a strange land, a
stranger than fiction
stranger within their gates, the
stress and strain
stretch one's legs, to
strictly accurate
strike while the iron is hot, to
striking example, a
strong silent man, a
strong support
struck all of a heap
struck dumb with surprise
stuff and nonsense; *e.g.*, it's all . . .
stung to the quick
stunned with surprise
stupendous success, a
sturdy independence
Sturm and Drang [*German; literary*]
sub rosa [*Latin*]
submerged tenth, the
substantial agreement; *esp.*, to be in . . .
subterranean manoeuvres
such stuff as dreams are made on
suck someone's brains, to
suffer: *see* fate worse than death
suffer fools gladly, (not) to
suffer in silence, to
sui generis [*Latin*]
suit all tastes, to
suit one's book, to
suitably inscribed
sum and substance, the [*obsolescent*]
sumptuous repast
sunnier climes
sunny South, the
superhuman effort, a
supply and demand
supreme importance; *esp.*, of s.i.
supreme moment, the
supreme sacrifice, the
sure and certain hope; *esp.*, in the . . .
survival of the fittest, the
swallow a camel, to
Swan of Avon, the
swan-song, a *or* one's

swear by all the gods, to
swear that black is white, to
sweat of one's brow, the; *esp.*, by the . . .
sweep the board, to
sweeping statement, a
sweetness and light
swim into one's ken, to
swing of the pendulum, the
sword of Damocles, the

t

tablets of memory, the
take a hand in the game, to
take a leaf out of someone's book, to
take away one's breath, to
take by storm, to
take French leave, to
take heart of grace, to
take immediate steps, to
take into due account, to
take it as read, I'll *or* we'll . . .
take it or leave it!
take one's Bible oath, to
take one's courage in both hands, to
take one's life in one's hands, to
take one's name in vain, to
take one's pleasures sadly, to
take pot-luck, to
take the bit in one's teeth, to
take the bread out of a person's mouth, to
take the bull by the horns, to
take the gilt off the gingerbread, to
take the rough with the smooth, to
take the wind out of a person's sails, to
take the wrong turning, to
take time by the forelock, to
take (*e.g.*, a wife) to one's bosom, to
take to one's heels, to
take up the cudgels, to
take with a grain of salt, to
taken: *see* in the toils
taken aback
talk double Dutch, to
talk of the Devil!
talk through one's hat, to
Tapers and Tadpoles [*obsolescent*]
tar with the same brush, to
task confronts (*or* confronted) one; *esp.*, a difficult task . . .
tastefully arranged [*esp.*, *of flowers or a table*]
taxed to its utmost capacity [*American*]
teach one's grandmother, to
teach the young idea how to shoot, to
team spirit, the
tear one's hair, to [*figurative*]
teeming earth, the
teeming millions (?)

tell it not in Gath!
tell tales out of school, to
telling effect; *esp.*, with telling effect
temper the wind to the shorn lamb, to
tempus fugit [*Latin*]
tender a testimonial dinner, to [*American*]
tender one's thanks, to
tender susceptibilities
terminated fatally, it *or* the affair
terminated the proceedings
terra firma [*Latin*]
Terrible Turk, the [*obsolescent*]
thank God on one's bended knees, to (?)
thankful for small mercies
thanking you in anticipation
that way madness lies
that will be all for the present
that's flat; *often* and that's flat
their name: *see* name is . . .
then and there
there are more things in heaven and earth, Horatio, than are dreamt of in your philosophy
there, but for the grace of God, goes . . . (*or* go I)
there is (*or* was) not a breath of air
thereby hangs a tale
there's a divinity that shapes our ends, rough-hew them how we will
there's something rotten in the state of Denmark
there's the rub
these little things are sent to try us
thin end of the wedge, the
thin (*or* a little thin) on the top, to be
thing of beauty is a joy for ever, a
thing of the past, to be *or* become
things to come; *esp.*, the shape of things to come
think no small beer of (*esp.*, oneself), to
thirst for someone's blood, to
this being the case (?)
this is a bloody business [*jocular in England*]
this is the happiest moment of my life
this is not the case; *generally either* but this . . . *or* this, however, is . . .
this vale of tears
this world of ours
this world's goods; *e.g.*, rich in this world's goods
thorn in one's (*or* the) flesh (*or* side), a
though I say it as shouldn't
thousands flock to beaches to seek relief [*American journalese*]
threadbare excuse, a
threescore and ten (years); threescore years and ten
through and through (?)

through (*or* throughout) the ages
through thick and thin
throw a veil over, to
throw down the glove, to
throw dust in a person's eyes, to (?)
throw off the scent, to
throw oneself on another's generosity, to
thrust and parry
thrust down someone's throat, to (?)
thus far—and no farther
tied hand and foot
tied to someone's apron-strings
tighten one's belt, to
tilt at windmills, to
time and time again
time immemorial; *generally*, from t.i.
time is not far distant when . . . , the
time is (*or* was) ripe, the
time marches on
time out of mind [*obsolescent*]
time (*or* Time) stood still
Time, the great healer
Time with his sickle (*or* hour-glass)
timeo Danaos et dona ferentes [*Latin*]
times are out of joint, the
tinkling cymbal, a
tip from the stables, a
tit for tat (?)
. . . to a fault; *e.g.*, good-natured to a fault
to all intents and purposes
to be or not to be, that is the question
to say the least of it
to sleep or not to sleep, that is the question
to tell someone a few home-truths
to tell the truth, . . .
to the end of the chapter
to the finger-tips
to the manner born; *generally*, as to the manner born
to the tune of
to thine own self be true
toe the mark, to
toiling millions *or* multitudes
token of one's esteem, a [*American*]
tongue in one's cheek; *esp.*, have one's . . . *or* with one's . . .
tongues of rumour, the (?)
too (*e.g.*, thrilling) for words
too numerous to mention
tooth and nail
top of one's bent: *see* fool
torn asunder
tortures of the damned; *esp.*, suffer the . . .
touch and go; *esp.*, it is (*or* was *or* will be) touch and go
touch with a pair of tongs, not to (?)
touched on the raw

touched to finer issues
toujours la politesse! [*French*]
tower of strength, a
towering passion, a
town mouse, a
traffic is (*or* was) at a virtual standstill [*American*]
trail one's cloak (*or* coat), to [*obsolescent*]
trailing clouds of glory
trashy fiction (?)
trials and tribulations
tried and found wanting
trifles light as air
Triton among minnows, a
trouble brewing; *esp.*, there is (*or* was) . . .
true blue
true inwardness [*literary*]
true to one's colours
truly representative(?)
trusty sword, one's [*obsolescent*]
truth is beauty, beauty truth
truth to tell
tug of war, the [*figurative; obsolescent*]
turn a blind eye to, to
turn a deaf ear, to
turn a hair, not to
turn an honest penny, to
turn of the tide, the
turn out en masse; *e.g.*, Society turned out en masse [*American, obsolescent*]
turn over a new leaf, to
turn tail, to
turn the other cheek, to
turn the tables on, to [*obsolescent*]
turn up like a bad penny, to
turn up one's nose at, to
turn up trumps, to
twelve: *see* good men and true
Twelve Tribes, the [*jocular for Jews*]
twist round one's little finger, to
two of a kind (*or* a trade)
two strings to one's bow; *esp.*, to have . . .
tycoon (from the magazines *Fortune, Time,* and *Life*)

u

unavoidable increase, an
ugly duckling, a *or* one's
unalloyed pleasure
unbridled licence [*obsolescent*]
Uncle Sam
unconfirmed rumour, an (?)
unconsidered trifles: *see* snapper-up
uncrowned king of . . . , the
und so weiter [*German*]
under a cloud, to be
under a rough exterior
under one's breath

under the aegis of
under the rose [*cf.* sub rosa]
under the Southern Cross
under the sun; *e.g.*, the richest country under the sun
under the thumb of
undetermined origin [*American*]
uneasy lies the head that wears a crown
unfathomable designs; unfathomable secret, an
unfortunate pedestrian(s)
unfortunate woman, an
unkindest cut of all, the (most)
unleash the dogs (*or* hounds) of war, to [*cf.* let loose . . .]
unmistakable symptom, an
unprecedented situation, an
unshakable alibi, an
unsolved mystery, an
unspeakable Turk, the [*obsolescent*]
unsubstantiated report, an (?)
until death do them (*or* us) part
untimely end, an; *esp.*, come to an u.e.
untold advantages
untold wealth
unwept, unhonoured, and unsung
unwritten law, the
up and doing, to be
up in arms
up like a rocket and down like a stick [*obsolescent*]
up to one's eyes in work
up to scratch *or* up to the scratch
up to the hilt
ups and downs (?)
upset the apple-cart, to
use and wont
utter darkness

v

vae victis [*Latin*]
vagaries of the English climate, the
valley of the shadow of death, the [*or* with capitals]
valued guest of honour, a [*American*]
vanish into thin air, to
vast difference, a (?)
venerable pile, a *or* the
venture a guess (*or* an opinion), to
verray parfit, gentil knyght, a
very much the reverse
very present help in time of trouble, a
very right and proper
vested interests (?)
via dolorosa [*Latin: a literary cliché when used figuratively*]
vicious circle, a
view the prospect with complacence, to
Ville-Lumière, la (?)

violation of sacred principles, a [*American political*]
virgin page, a
voice an opinion, to
voice in the wilderness, a
vox et praeterea nihil [*Latin*]
vox populi, vox Dei [*Latin*]

w

wages of sin, the; the wages of sin is death
waifs and strays
wait on (*or* serve) hand and foot, to
walk on air, to
walking encyclopaedia, a
wallow in the mire, to
war and rumours of war
war impends, *or* war is impending
war to end war, a
war to the knife
warm the cockles of one's (*or* the) heart, to; *esp.*, it warms . . .
warm to one's work, to
was not to be; it *or* this *or* that . . .
wash one's dirty linen in public, to
wash one's hands of, to
waste one's breath, to
water, water everywhere, and not a drop to drink [*see* MISQUOTATIONS]
wave of optimism, a
wave the bloody shirt, to [*American*]
way of all flesh, the; to go the way of all flesh
way of the trangressor is hard, the
ways and means
we are not amused
we shall not look upon his like again
weaker sex, the
weaker vessel, the
weal and woe
wealth of meanings, a; *esp.*, with a . . .
wear and tear
wear one's heart on one's sleeve, to
wear the trousers, to
weariness of the flesh, a
(good, bad, etc.) weather (has) occurred over widespread areas [*American journalese*]
weather the storm, to
wedded bliss
weigh in the balance, to
weighed in the balance and found wanting
weighty reasons
welcome with open arms, to
well and good
well and truly
well-earned rest

well he (*or* she *or* they . . .) know(s)— or knew—it
well-known resident, a [*American*]
Welsh Wizard, the
wend one's way, to
wet to the skin
what a wonderful place the world would be if (*or* if only) . . .
what with one thing and another
wheels within wheels
when all is said and done
when Greek meets Greek (*see* MISQUOTATIONS)
when one's ship comes home
where every prospect pleases, and only man is vile
where (*e.g.* money) is (*or* was) concerned
whip-hand; *esp.*, to have the whip-hand of [*obsolescent*]
whirligig of time, the [*obsolescent*]
white blackbird, a [*obsolescent*]
white cliffs of Dover, the
white flower of a blameless life, the
white man, a
white man's burden, the
whited sepulchres
. . . who shall be nameless
who shall minister to a mind diseased?
wholesome respect, a; to have a wholesome respect for
why and (the) wherefore, the
wide open spaces, the
widow's mite, the
wild horses could not drag (*originally*, draw) it from me
wings of the wind, the; *esp.*, on the . . . [*obsolescent*]
win golden opinions, to
win hands down, to
win one's spurs, to [*obsolescent*]
win someone's heart, to
winter holds (*e.g.*, the entire Eastern seaboard) in its icy grip [*American journalese*]
wise after the event, to be
wise saws and modern instances
wish is father to the thought, the
wishful thinking
witching hour of night, the
with a grain of salt
with all one's heart (and soul)
with an eye to the main chance
with bated breath
with flying colours
with his blushing honours: *see* blushing honours
with one's tail . . . : *see* go off . . .
with might and main; *generally*, with all one's . . .
within limits

without counting the cost
without let or hindrance
without rhyme or reason
without turning a hair
Wizard of the North, the
woe betide . . .
wolf in sheep's clothing, a
woman of a certain age, a
woman's glory, a [obsolescent, as is the glory]
woman's intuition
woman's wiles
won in a canter
word from our sponsor, a [American radio]
word has been received that . . .
word in season, a
word in your ear, a
words cannot describe
words fail me
words of wisdom
work one's fingers to the bone, to
work with: see set to
worked to death
world has ever seen, that the
world of good, a; esp., something does (or did) somebody a (or the) . . .
world of truth in it, a; there's a world . . .
world of waters, the [obsolescent]
world, the flesh and the devil, the
world well lost for love, the; esp., to believe or think the world . . .
world-wide conflagration, a
world will not willingly let die, such as (or that) the
worldly wisdom
world's a stage, the; . . . , and all the men and women merely players
world's mine oyster and I will open it, the
worn threadbare
worn to a shadow (or to a shred)
worth makes a man, and want of it the fellow
worth one's weight in gold
worthy of a better cause; with an ability (or a courage) worthy . . .
would give the world to . . . , I or you or he, etc.
would not do (something) for anything in the world, I or he or they
wring one's withers, to
writing on the wall, the (originally—in the Bible—handwriting)
wry jest, a (?)

y

year in, year out
yield to no man in (my) admiration of; esp., I . . .

yield(ing) inch by inch
you could have knocked me down with a feather
you know what I mean
you know what I think
you may (or might or will or would) not believe it, but (e.g., it's true)
you took the (very) word(s) out of my mouth
young in heart, the (?)
young man's fancy; or in the spring a young man's fancy lightly turns to thoughts of love
young no matter what their age, the; the young of all ages
your earliest convenience, at

client and **customer.** As 'a dependant', client is obsolescent; it now = 'he who goes to a lawyer; he who has an advocate'; hence, 'he who employs the services of a professional man'. In relation to tradesmen, the correct term is customer: and what's wrong with customer, anyway? (The O.E.D., q.v. for several highly specialized senses.) See also PATRON.

climactic and **climatic; climacteric(al).** Climactic = 'of or pertaining to or resembling a climax' (an ascending series or scale); climatic = 'of or pertaining to climate'. Climacteric, less generally -al, is 'constituting or pertaining to a climacter or a critical period in human life', as in 'climacteric period', 'a . . . year'; hence, 'constituting a crisis or an important epoch', as in 'This age is as climacteric as that in which he lived' (Southey). (The O.E.D.)

climate, clime and **weather.** Clime is archaic and poetic for climate. Climate has two senses: 'a region considered in relation to its weather or to its atmospheric conditions' (obsolescent); 'a country's or region's weather and atmospheric conditions, esp. as these affect life—human, animal, vegetable'. Climate has been neatly defined as 'the sum and average of weather', weather as 'the atmospheric condition of a particular time and place'. Thus, 'In such a climate as that of Britain, there is no weather—only specimens of weather'. Based on The O.E.D.

climb down is manifestly absurd: but equally manifestly, it has been consecrated by usage. Purists tend to use descend.

climb up. (Climb—climbed—climbed. Archaic preterite: clomb; incorrect preterite: *clumb*.) In general, *climb up* is tautological for *climb* if *climb* is transitive; if it is intransitive, *up* is obviously necessary when the verb is not used absolutely.

clime. See CLIMATE.

clinch. See CLENCH.

clomb. See CLIMB UP.

close and **conclude.** See CONCLUDE, and CLOSE.

close and **shut.** *Close* is the more general verb, '*shut* being properly only a way of closing; hence the former is generally used when the notion is that of the resulting state, rather than the process', the process demanding rather *shut* than *close*. Although one either *closes* or *shuts* a door, an eyelid, the distinction just made holds good: properly, therefore, one *shuts* the door and then it is *closed*; one *shuts* one's eyelids and then one's eyes are *closed*. To say that 'The British Museum library is shut up in the first week of May every year' is loose and colloquial for *is closed* (*to the public*). (*The O.E.D.*) [['To *close* . . . (as compared with *shut*) is strictly to stop an opening; to *shut* is to close, esp. in such a way as to bar ingress or egress. *Close* is the more general, *shut*, the more direct, emphatic, and, often, strongly visualizing word.' (*Webster's*.)]]

close down (a shop, a business); 'His shop closed down'. *Close* (*closed*) is sufficient, except nautically (of hatches). The same applies to *close up*, except in certain technical contexts—military, architectural, geographical. In short, make sure that *down* or *up* is necessary before you use it. (*The O.E.D.*)

close proximity is tautological for *proximity*. For *in close proximity to*, say *close to* or *near*, according to the context.

clôture. The English *closure* is much to be preferred, even in the parliamentary sense.

clue. See CLEW.

clumb. See CLIMB UP.

co-respondent. See CORRESPONDENT.

cocoa-nut, coco(nut). See CACAO . . .

cognomen is incorrect when it is used for 'given (or Christian) name', for 'full name', or for 'nickname'. For 'surname' it is not incorrect, but it is an objectionable Latinism. Correctly and impeccably it means 'the last of the three names by which a Roman of good family was designated' (*Nuttall's Standard Dictionary*).

coker. See CACAO . . .

cold glass of water is incorrect for a glass of cold water.

collect together is tautological for *collect* (or *put together*), for *collect* means 'gather together'. To apply *collect* to a single object is loose—though pardonable when it is intended facetiously. (*The O.E.D.*)

COLLECTIVE NOUNS: when singular and when plural. Such collective nouns as can be used either in the singular or in the plural (*family, clergy, committee, Parliament*), are singular when unity (a unit) is intended; plural, when the idea of plurality is predominant. Thus, 'As the clergy are or are not what they ought to be, so are the rest of the nation' (Jane Austen), where *clergy = members of the clergy*; 'Is the family at home?', i.e. the family as a whole, a unit, but 'The family are stricken with grief at father's death', where the various members (other than father) are affected; 'The committee of public safety is to deal with this matter', but 'The Committee of Public Safety quarrel as to who its next chairman should be'; 'Parliament rises (*or*, goes into recess) at the beginning of August', where M.P.'s are viewed as one body, but 'Parliament differ over the question of war', where the differences of opinion are emphasized; set 'The club is to be closed down at the end of the year' over against 'The club all know that he is a disappointed man' (De Quincey); 'Our army was in a sad plight' but 'The military were called out'; 'The majority is thus resolved' but 'The majority are going home'.

Bain, in *A Companion to the Higher English Grammar*, draws attention to the 'convenience of a neutral number' and refers to the facilities there are in English 'for avoiding awkwardness and the committing oneself definitely to singular or plural in the use we can make of the forms common to both numbers, e.g., past tenses [except of *to be*], and the verbs *can, must, would, might*, and the like' (Onions); Bain illustrates his point thus:—

'But an *aggregate* [collective noun] of contemporary individuals of the same species *cannot* [good evasion of number] be properly said to form a generation, except by assuming that *they* and *their children are* all born, respectively at the same time' (*are* is especially wanted, there being an emphasis upon the separateness of the individuals).

(Based on Jespersen, *Growth and Structure of the English Language*, §16, and C. T. Onions, *An Advanced English Syntax*, §18.)

⟦Perrin's notes are valuable for American students: 'There is often a temptation to use a collective noun and to keep it singular when the meaning really calls for a plural construction. . . . Obviously a collective should not be treated as *both* singular and plural in the same context'. *The family is well and send their regards* is clearly colloquial.⟧

COLLOQUIALISMS. 'The colloquial' —'Colloquialisms'—is the name applied to that large tract of English which lies between Standard English and slang; it is of a status higher than that of slang, and, at its highest, it is scarcely distinguishable from Familiar English (informal Standard English). 'Every educated person has at least two ways of speaking his mother tongue. The first is that which he employs in his family, among his familiar friends, and on ordinary occasions. The second is that which he uses in discoursing on more complicated subjects, and in addressing persons with whom he is less intimately acquainted. . . . The difference between these two forms consists, in great measure, in a difference of vocabulary' (Greenough & Kittredge, *Words and Their Ways in English Speech*, 1902). Other and frequent features are a syntax so flexible as to become at times ungrammatical, a fondness for sentences with a single verb, the omission of *I* at the beginning of a sentence or a clause. A rapid leaping from one subject to another, and the use of words and phrases that, unintelligible or at best obscure in print, are made both clear and sometimes arresting by a tone or a gesture, a pause or an emphasis. 'The basis of familiar words must be the same in Standard as in colloquial English, but the vocabulary appropriate to the more formal occasion will include many terms which will be stilted or affected in ordinary talk. There is also considerable difference between familiar and dignified language in the manner of utterance'— in pronunciation and enunciation. 'In conversation, we habitually employ such contractions as *I'll, don't, won't, it's, we'd, he'd* . . . which we should never use in public speaking, unless with set purpose, to give a marked colloquial tinge to what one has to say' (Greenough & Kittredge, *op. cit.*).

Colloquialisms, like familiar and spoken English in general (of which it is the more lowly and racy part), vary tremendously from class to class, set to set, group to group, family to family, individual to individual, and even, according to the individual's mood or aspiration, from one *alter ego* to another. 'His social experience, traditions and general background, his ordinary tastes and pursuits, his intellectual and moral cultivation are all reflected in each man's conversation. . . . But the individual speaker is also affected by the character of those to whom he speaks. . . . There is naturally a large body of colloquial expressions which is common to all classes . . . but each class and interest has its own special way of expressing itself. The average colloquial speech of any age is . . . a compromise between a variety of [vocabularies]' (H. C. K. Wyld's *History of Modern Colloquial English*).

The colloquial is difficult to confine within practicable limits: and that difficulty is made none the easier by the fact that, as Henry Bradley once remarked, 'at no period . . . has the colloquial vocabulary and idiom of the English language been completely preserved in the literature' or even in the dictionaries. 'The homely expressions of everyday intercourse . . . have been but very imperfectly recorded in the writings of any age'; in the 20th Century, however, they have been far more fully and trustworthily recorded than in any earlier period. In the United States of America, the border-line between colloquialism and slang, like that between slang and cant, is less clearly marked than in England: but the general principles of differentiation remain the same.

⟦In American studies of usage, the term *colloquial* may include much of what Mr Partridge calls 'Familiar English (informal Standard English)'. Krapp defines *colloquial* as 'cultivated spoken English', *low-colloquial* as uses 'characteristic of the speech of persons who may be broadly described as uncultivated'. *Webster's*: '*colloquial*. . . . Of a word or a sense or use of a word or expression, acceptable and appropriate in ordinary conversational context, as in intimate speech among cultivated people, in familiar letters, in informal speeches or writings, but not in formal written discourse.' Cf. *The O.E.D.*: '*Colloquial* . . . Of words, phrases, etc.: Belonging to common speech; characteristic of or proper to ordinary conversation, as distinguished from formal or elevated language.']

collusion should not be used of favourable or neutral association or co-operation, for it implies a secret understanding, a preconcerted plan, for an illicit, illegal, or evil purpose. Do not, therefore, employ *collusion* as a synonym of *co-operation*.—Only the semi-literate confuse it with *collision*, 'a violent encounter of a moving body with another body, whether moving or stationary'.

COLONIAL ENGLISH. See STANDARD ENGLISH, Section iv.

Colonies, the. British overseas "possessions" were at one period called Colonies and were governed from the Colonial Office. Canada, Australia, New Zealand, India, are now *Dominions* acknowledging the British King (-Emperor); it is offensive to their citizens to call their countries *Colonies* or them *Colonials*.

colossal is an adjective that is overdone by indiscriminating writers (and speakers). Even so good a writer as Louis Bromfield falls into this error in *The Strange Case of Miss Annie Spragg*, 1928.

combat and **contest.** A *combat* is a fight, a struggle between enemies; a *contest* may be merely a competition, and is often between neutrals or friends.

combine (n.) is a specific kind of commercial combination and must not be used for any other sort.

combine (v.) for *co-ordinate* is careless, for the former does not comport the quite unmistakable and very particular senses of the latter: 'to place or class in the same order, rank, or division'; 'to place or arrange (things) in proper position relatively to one another and to the system of which they form parts'; 'to bring into proper combined order in accordance with a stated law, rule, or arrangement'; v.i., 'to act in combined order to ensure a specific result' (*The O.E.D.*). *Combine together* is a manifest tautology, far too often used by the unreflecting.

come and **go.** Of their use, Alford writes: 'We say of a wrecked ship that she *went* to pieces; but of a broken jug that it *came* to pieces. Plants *come up*, *come* into flower, but *go* to seed . . . The sun *goes* in behind a cloud and *comes* out from behind it. But we are not consistent in speaking of the sun. He is said to *go down* in the evening; but never to *come up*

in the morning.' But what about Coleridge's

The sun came up upon the right,
Out of the sea came he?

Idiom is paramount, as we see in *come loose* (cf. the slang *come unstuck*) and *go to pieces* (of a person); (of events) *come about*, but *so it went* (happened).

come in contact (with) should be *come into contact (with)*.

come in (correctly **into**) **touch with** should be *get into touch with*.

comic; comical. In current usage, only *comic* = 'belonging, or proper, to comedy' (opposite to tragedy, in the dramatic sense); but *comical* is more usual in the nuances 'mirth-provoking, humorous, funny; laughable, ludicrous'. *Comical* alone has the colloquial sense, 'odd, strange; queer'; and *comic* that of 'comic actor', which in Standard English is *comedian*. (*The O.E.D.*) [[In the U.S.A., *the comics*, or *the funnies*, is replacing *the funny paper* as a name for the infantile stories told in consecutive cartoons, which appear as a separate section of the Sunday newspapers. Of recent years blood-and-thunder adventure stories of the Buck Rogers and Dick Tracy sorts have become as characteristic of the so-called Comic Section as the older 'funny' sequences.]]

commander-in-chiefs is incorrect for *commanders-in-chief*.

commence, in its ordinary meaning of *begin*, is a wholly unnecessary word and its use is to be discouraged. *Commence* is more formal, and it should be reserved as a continuation of Anglo-French use: in association with law, official procedure, ceremonial, church service, (grave) combat. See esp. *The O.E.D.* [[*Commence* in circumstances where *begin* or *start* would be more suitable is not uncommon in American usage, especially in the South and West. Perhaps it was once a genteelism but it is idiomatic today.]]

COMMERCIALESE. See at OFFICIALESE.

common, basically 'belonging equally to more than one', 'possessed or shared alike by both or all (the persons or things in question)', as in 'The common ruin of king and people' (Burke), 'two triangles with a common base'; hence, 'belonging to all mankind alike', as in 'The higher attributes of our common humanity' (Nettleship); arising from or closely connected with those two senses are these others—'belonging to the community at large, or to a specific community; public', 'free to be used by all alike; public', 'of general application; general', as in 'common notions', and 'belonging to more than one as a result or sign of co-operation or agreement; joint, united', esp. *to make common cause with*:—All these are excellent English. Good English also are the following senses; but, as they are apt to cause ambiguity, they should be displaced by: 'ordinary'; 'frequent'; 'undistinguished'; 'of low degree'; 'mean, of little value'; (of persons or their qualities) 'unrefined, vulgar'. (*The O.E.D.*)

COMMONPLACES. See Cliché.

companionate is used only in *companionate marriage*, which may—or may not—be *companionable*, 'sociable', 'fitted for companionship'.

company, 'guests collectively; one or more persons invited or entertained' (*The O.E.D.*), is not a colloquialism, but familiar S.E., as in 'We do not often have company'.

COMPANY terms or names (e.g., a *flock* of sheep, a *herd* of cattle). See Sports technicalities.

comparative should not be used for *relative*. 'The argument that truth is comparative and not absolute is not valid' (an essay script in the L.C.C. Major Establishment examination, 1938).

COMPARATIVE CLAUSES present few difficulties. There is often an ellipsis, as in 'You do not play cricket so (*or*, as) well as he', i.e., 'as he does'; 'It concerns you as much as me', i.e., 'as much as it does me'; 'He is shorter than I', i.e., 'than I am'. But, as Dr Onions points out in *An Advanced English Syntax*, a relative pronoun after *than* is always in the accusative.

'And then there is Woolley, than whom I have never seen a more gracious batsman';

'Beelzebub . . . than whom none higher sat' (Milton).

Note:—'He is as tall as me', 'She is as wise as him', and all other such *as* sentences are colloquial, not Standard English. [[As C. C. Fries says, speakers of English have a feeling that when a verb does not follow a pronoun, the pronoun is probably in an objective relationship.]]

COMPARATIVES, FALSE, and False Superlatives. There are certain adjectives which are uncomparable: which do not admit of *more* or *most* before them, *-er*

or *-est* tacked on to them. They are absolute and, in this respect, unmodifiable. One can speak of *nearly* or *almost* or *not quite* 'infinite' or 'perfect' or 'simultaneous' or 'unique', but not of 'more infinite', 'more perfect', 'most simultaneous', 'most unique'.

Here is a short list of these uncomparable intransigents:

absolute
akin
all-powerful (see separate entry)
basic
certain (sure, convinced)
chief
city
comparative
complete
contemporary
country
crystal-clear
devoid
empty
entire
essential
eternal
everlasting
excellent (see separate entry)
fatal
final
full
fundamental
harmless
ideal (see separate entry)
immaculate
immortal
impossible
incessant
incomparable
indestructible   } There are many such
inevitable   }   adjectives in *in-*
inferior
infinite
innocuous
invaluable
invulnerable
irrefragable
main
major and *minor*
manifest
meaningless
mortal (see separate entry)
obvious
omnipotent
omniscient
pellucid
perdurable
perfect
possible (see Impossible)

preliminary
primary
primordial
principal
pure
replete
rife
sacrosanct
senior and *junior*
simultaneous
sufficient
superior
supreme
superlative
sure (convinced)
town
ultimate
unanimous
uncomparable (see separate entry)
unendurable
uninhabitable
unique (see separate entry)
universal
untouchable
   and other *un-* adjectives
utter, uttermost, utmost (*q.v.* at UTMOST)
void
vital
whole
worthless

Note, too, that the corresponding nouns are likewise uncomparable: it is folly to speak of 'the utmost absolute', 'absolute perfection', 'complete indestructibility', 'partial universality', and so forth. The same restriction applies to such nouns as *acme*. 'The acme of comfort' is permissible, but 'the utter acme of comfort' is not merely absurd but weak; 'the omnipotence of God' is dignified, but 'the omnipotence of Hitler' is demonstrably false.

So too of the adverbs corresponding to the adjectives listed above. 'Utterly exhausted' may be a fact, whereas 'too utterly done up' is a slangy misstatement.

[[Many of the best American grammarians are more tolerant than Mr Partridge of 'false comparatives and superlatives'. Some of these are illogical, some are not; almost all of them occur occasionally in the writings of the wise and judicious.]]

compare and **contrast**. See 'CONTRAST and COMPARE'.

compare for **liken**. *Compare* is commonly used in this sense, though comparison implies difference as well as similarity. When *compare* = *liken*, it is followed by *to*. Thus, in Shakespeare's 'Shall I compare thee to a summer's day', meaning 'to state or observe a likeness', the substitution of *with* for *to* would change the sense to 'to set up a comparison'.

compare to; compare with. See the preceding entry.

For other senses and nuances, the rulings of *The O.E.D.* are these:—'To mark or point out the similarities and differences of; to collocate or juxtapose, in order to note the differences and similarities': *with*, as in 'Property, compared with personal ability, stands for more in England than elsewhere': but *to* is not wrong, though it should be avoided: moreover, one can *compare* two or more things *together*. Intransitively, *compare*—'to bear comparison, to vie or rival', and always takes *with*, as in 'As athletes, men cannot . . . compare with . . . monkeys' (Jevons).

compendious may be applied to something that is *briefly* comprehensive, for its meaning is 'compact', 'concise', 'summary', 'succinct'; but *comprehensive* is obsolete in Standard English—and now regarded as catachrestic when careless writers, ignorant of the history of the word, use it—in the sense 'containing much in small compass'. Properly employed, *comprehensive* = 'extensive', 'embracing many things', 'widely sympathetic'.

competence is a fairly high degree of ability (in performance), but it falls short of *talent*, far short of *genius*: the following, therefore, rings oddly:—'He showed . . . extraordinary military competence', John Gunther, *Inside Asia*, 1939. [[*Competence*, to the American reader, is more suggestive of performance and may therefore be a stronger word than *talent* for Mr Gunther's purpose.]]

compilation is occasionally misused for *symposium* and for *collection* (of essays or articles). It is used properly of a (literary) work 'built up of materials from various sources' (*The O.E.D.*) and not of original compositions.

complacence and **complaisance** are easily confused; the former is *self-satisfaction*, the latter *obligingness, politeness* (*The Con. O.D.*). The adjectives are *complacent, complaisant*.

complement, -ary. See COMPLIMENT . . .

complement and **supplement**. See at SUPPLEMENT.

complete. See COMPARATIVES, FALSE. See following entry.

complete; entire; whole. The need to distinguish these terms was brought sharply to my notice when, in so competent a writer as Inez Irwin, I came upon this instance of *whole* misused for *entire*: 'The whole investigations of this murder case rests [*sic*] on my shoulders' (*The Poison Cross Mystery*, 1936); as Mr Wilson Benington has remarked to me, *whole* is now 'a singular adjective', i.e., it is used only with a singular noun, except in certain technical contexts.

complete:—'Having all its parts or members' ('The preface is complete in itself', Ruskin); (of a period) 'whole'; (of an action) 'concluded'; 'realized in its full extent' ('A complete historical cycle'), 'thorough'; 'without defect'; (of a person) 'fully equipped, endowed or trained' ('a complete horseman').

entire:—'With no part excepted'; 'constituting a whole'; (of a quality, state of feeling, condition; fact, action); 'realized in its full extent, thorough' ('Entire sincerity is a virtue'), 'thoroughly of the character described' ('An entire believer in Christianity'); 'unbroken, unimpaired, intact, undiminished' ('Even after this ordeal, his faith remained entire'); (in science) 'wholly of one piece, continuous throughout, undivided ('The calyx is entire'), of unbroken outline'; (in law) 'unshared' (*entire tenancy*).

whole:—(of man or animal) 'uninjured, unwounded'; (of inanimate objects) 'unbroken, intact, untainted'; 'having all its parts or elements'—cf. *complete* and *entire*—'full, perfect'; 'all, all of', the prevailing current sense, used only attributively and preceding the noun ('The whole Anglican priesthood', Macaulay); with rhetorical emphasis ('Whole libraries are filled with records of this quest'); 'undivided' ('apples baked whole'); (in mathematics) 'integral, not fractional'; 'unmixed, pure', as in *whole blood* and *whole holiday* (a full day's freedom from work). (With full thanks to *The O.E.D.*)

complex; especially inferiority complex.

In psycho-analysis, a *complex* is 'a group of ideas of a spontaneous and emotional character associated by the individual with a particular subject, often'—but not necessarily—'indicating a kind of mental abnormality arising from repressed instincts or the like' (*The O.E.D., Supplement*). It might, therefore, be defined as one's ideas and sentiments (not necessarily morbid) of and about any subject whatsoever; we, all of us, have numerous complexes, without our being necessarily morbid, neurotic, or abnormal.

Hence, incorrectly, in vague use: a fixed mental tendency, an obsession; esp. *inferiority complex*, a deep-rooted conviction that one is inferior to one's fellows.

A 'forbidding complex' is an *inhibition* (*q.v.* at INHIBIT).

[[*Webster's:* 'Complex . . . A system of desires and memories, esp. a repressed and unconscious system which in disguised form exerts a dominating influence upon the personality.' The word has been overused in loose senses, but its popularity seems to be waning.]]

compliment, -ary (flattering) is often confused with *complement, -ary* (in completion of).

COMPOSITION. To schoolboys and freshmen, the word means an essay or a literary exercise in literary self-expression. A very common definition is—with slight variations—that of *The O.E.D.*: 'The mode or style in which words and sentences are put together': but composition is, I think, best regarded as the mode of putting together not merely words in a sentence, and sentences in a paragraph, but also paragraphs in an essay or a chapter, and chapters in a book; it comprises, therefore, arrangement and ordonnance.

This work of mine, however, is not a manual of composition. But I should perhaps be shirking a duty—certainly I should be missing an opportunity—if I did not give a short list of at least some of the basically important or practically useful works.

A. Bain: *English Composition and Rhetoric*, 1887–1888; old-fashioned, but, to the mature student, still useful and suggestive.

J. C. Nesfield: *Senior Course of English Composition*, 1903; like Leonard's book, it is less advanced than Canby's and Krapp's; but very sound.

J. C. Nesfield: *Errors in English Composition*, 1903.

H. W. & F. G. Fowler: *The King's English*, 1906 (but use latest edition).

*Joseph M. Thomas and others: *Composition for College Students*, 1922; an excellent formal presentation of the subject.

H. W. Fowler: *A Dictionary of Modern English Usage*, 1926; at the risk of appearing impertinent, I must emphasize the inestimable value and usefulness of this work.

*H. S. Canby: *Better Writing*, 1927.

*G. P. Krapp: *A Comprehensive Guide to Good English*, 1927.

*Sterling Leonard: *Juniors' Own Composition Book*, 1928.

*J. R. & V. P. Hulbert: *Effective English*, 1929.

[[C. S. Baldwin, *Oral & Written Composition*, and Scott & Denny are old stand-bys in America. Perrin's *Index to English* is the best book now on *usage*—followed by Krapp, 1927, as a close second. See also the volumes of Albert H. Marckwardt.]]

See also the entries at GRAMMAR and STYLE; indeed, Bonamy Dobrée's *English Prose Style* (1928) should be read as an introduction to the study of composition.

But remember this: theory is very useful, both for the check and brake it applies and also for the suggestions it offers; nevertheless, the only way in which to learn to write is—to write. With the proviso that you cease from writing so soon as you become mentally stale or physically tired, write as much as you can on all sorts of subjects. Revise what you write; revise it carefully, but do not pace the floor in an agonized search for the right word, for in that stylistic agony, you may lose the inspiration and you probably will lose the thread of your discourse. There is no merit in costiveness: meagreness is a sour-grapers' preoccupation, the ideal of one-bookers. While you have the inspiration, the energy, the verve, the gusto: write! The letter is important; but let it wait on the spirit, and, above all, do not allow it to parch up the springs and wells of the spirit.

I do not mean that a writer should think everything he writes to be God-inspired and heaven-sent. It isn't. By all means let a writer prepare himself to write; let him study Canby and Fowler and Krapp (they will benefit him enormously), but he must not be dis-

*indicates American works (and how good they are!)

couraged by their advice; from theory one must pass to practice. Having passed to practice, he should write, full steam ahead: revision should come after, not in the course of, composition. Any writer worth the name thinks out his theme beforehand in its broad outlines and in its order of development; he knows, or should know, the goal towards which he is working, and how he will arrive there: but he does not 'stay the genial current of his soul' *while* he is writing.

Having written and having perhaps been, severely criticized for his composition, his style, a writer (whether potential as a student or apprentice, or actual) should take advantage of the surcease from writing to examine carefully his writing and to look again at Fowler and Hulbert and Thomas. Where formerly he thought of them as talking pedantically or professionally in the air, as being merely impractical, he will, if he is modest, come to recognize that what they say is thoroughly sound and extremely useful.

comprehensible to, understandable to; comprehensible by, understandable by. The following examples taken from *The O.E.D.* indicate the correct usage: Donne, 1631, 'It is apprehensible by sense, and not comprehensible by reason'.—*Scribblemania*, 1815, 'To render the subject comprehensible to the meanest capacity'.—*Southey*, 1799, 'I suffer a good deal from illness, and in a way hardly understandable by those in health'.—*Ruskin*, 1875, 'There are two of the Puritans, whose work if I can succeed in making clearly understandable to you . . . it is all I need care to do'. —A thing is therefore *comprehensible* (or *understandable*) *by* me or you, but one of us may 'make' or 'render' it *comprehensible* (or *understandable*) *to* the other.

comprehensive. See COMPENDIOUS.

comprehensive(ly), misused for *comprehensible*, (-*bly*); **incomprehensive(ly)** for *incomprehensible*, (-*bly*). 'All jabbering incomprehensively at the top of their powerful voices', E. C. R. Lorac, *A Pall for a Painter*, 1936.

comprise and **constitute.** *Comprise*, 'to constitute, to compose', is rare and, I think, to be avoided, as in 'Ten dogs comprise the pack'. Whereas *constitute* = 'to form, to make up', as in 'Reading, writing, and arithmetic . . . do not in themselves constitute an education'

(Lubbock), *comprise* = 'to include', esp. in a treatise; 'to sum up' (e.g., 'to comprise much in a short speech'); 'to comprehend or include *under* or *in* a class or denomination'; (of a thing) 'to contain, as parts forming the whole; to consist of (certain specified parts)', as in 'The house comprises box-room, nine bedrooms, bath-room, etc.'; and 'to embrace as its contents, matter, or subject', as in 'The word politics . . . comprises in itself, a difficult study' (Dickens). (*The O.E.D.*)

comptroller is archaic for *controller* except in a few official designations; for a list, see *Whitaker's Almanac.* The joke is that *controller* is the older word, *comptroller* being an erroneous spelling introduced ca. 1500. (*The O.E.D.*) Both spellings should be pronounced alike (-'nt'-), the pronunciation with '-mp-' being an error.

concensus. See CONSENSUS.

concerned about; concerned with. Respectively: anxious about; having an interest in or business with. Careless writers confuse them.

CONCESSIVE CLAUSES. Usually, the verb in concessive clauses is in the indicative; always, when the concessive verb implies a fact, as in '*Although you are poor*, you are happy'—or, where there is less emphasis on the concession, 'You are happy, *although you are poor*'; '*Though he talks so much*, he never says anything worth saying'; '*Young as he looked*, he was no fool'; '*Small though their army was*, the French fought bravely'.

In such concessive clauses as refer to future time and in such others as show an action in prospect or under consideration, it is usual to employ the subjunctive mood (or its equivalent—*may* or *should* + infinitive); present-day writers, it is true, often use the indicative, which is not incorrect but either crude or too matter-of-fact (brutal). 'Though everyone *deserts* you, I shall (or, will) not' seems youthful, approximate, secondrate, beside 'Though everyone *desert* (or, *should desert*) you, I shall (or, will) not'; and 'Though your faults may be many, he loves you' is preferable to 'Though your faults are many . . .'; and '(Al)though he die (or, should die) now, his name will live' is far superior to 'Though he dies now, his name will live',—indeed, there is a marked difference of nuance here.

In certain concessive clauses—'*Cost what it may . . .*', '*Be he* (or, *she*) *who he* (or, *she*) *may*, he must see me'—the verb comes at the beginning: but, these clauses being in the nature of formulas, there is less danger of one's going wrong in them than of one's using them too much.

Here, as in comparative clauses, the concession may be elliptical: 'Though no player, he appreciated the finer points of lawn tennis' is merely 'Though he was no player . . .'; cf. 'Though [they are] outnumbered, they are fighting to the death'. See especially C. T. Onions, *An Advanced English Syntax.*

conclude and **close** (a speech). To *close it* may connote merely to end it, esp. if one has nothing more to say; to *conclude it* (a more formal phrase) is to bring it to a predetermined and/or rhetorical end.

conclude, misused for *decide,* as in 'The matter must wait, and Stone concluded to go to bed', Carolyn Wells, *The Clue of the Eyelash, 1933. To conclude,* to make a considered judgment, is followed by a clause: 'He concluded that resistance was futile'.

CONCORD, WRONG. See AGREEMENT, FALSE.

concrete. See CEMENT.

condemn and **contemn.** In ordinary usage, *condemn* is the right word except in literary (formal, lofty) Standard English and in the following, very precise senses of *contemn:*—I, (as applied to persons and personal feelings or characteristics) 'to despise, disdain, scorn, slight', as in 'I have done penance for contemning love' (Shakespeare), 'Not that your father's mildness I contemn' (Dryden), 'It lay in Deronda's nature usually to contemn the feeble' (George Eliot).—II, 'To treat (law, orders, pacts, customs; advice) with contemptuous disregard', as in 'Mr Cooper contemned my lord's order, and would not obey it' (Mrs Hutchinson, ca. 1665), 'They . . . contemned and violated the engagement of treaties' (James Mill). (*The O.E.D.*)

CONDITIONAL CLAUSES have always caused trouble to the semi-educated and the demi-reflective; to the illiterate they give no trouble at all. Most well-educated or well-speaking persons have little difficulty.

The whole subject has been treated with the utmost clarity and an illuminating virtuosity of arrangement by Dr C. T. Onions in *An Advanced English*

Syntax: on his much fuller exposition and from his far more numerous examples the following cursory presentation is based, the following instances drawn.

The vast majority of conditional sentences fall into one or two classes, these being determined by the form (and meaning) of the principal clause, thus:—

Group I: Those sentences in which the principal clause speaks of what is, or was, or will certainly be (i.e., *not* of what would be or would have been), and in which the *if*-clause states, or implies, no fact and/or no fulfilment. This is what grammarians call Open Condition, as in 'If you are right, I am wrong', which does not imply that you actually are right. It does not matter whether the tenses are present or past ('If you did that, you were wrong') or future ('If you do this, you will be wrong')—or mixed, as in 'If he did it, he is a fool', 'If you have forged a cheque, you will be ruined'. Nor does it matter what the mood of the principal clause: 'If I did that, forgive me!'; 'If I do that, may I die!'

Group II: Those sentences in which the principal clause speaks of what would be or would have been, and in which the *if*-clause states, or implies, a negative. Grammarians call this: Rejected Condition, as in 'If wishes were horses, beggars would ride' (but wishes are not horses—'much virtue in an *if*').

In this group, there is a special conditional form, as in 'If you were right, I should be wrong', to connote the remoteness of the supposition.

But most sentences in this group belong to two kinds:

(a) When the time referred to is the same in both clauses, we have:—
Present. 'If he did this, he would sin' or 'If he were doing this, he would be sinning'.
Past. 'If he had done this (or 'Had he done this'), he would have sinned'; 'Had we done this, we should have let you know'.
Future. 'If he did this (or 'If he were to do this'), he would sin'.

(b) When the time is not the same in both clauses, we get the sentence-types, 'If he had not done this, he would be happier now' (or 'If I had not done this, I should be

. . .') or 'I should (or 'He would) be happier now, if I (or, he) had not done this'; and 'If I were doing that now, I should not have been wounded' (or 'If he were doing that now, he would not . . .') or 'I should not (or 'He would not') have been wounded, if I were (or 'If he were') doing that now'.

It is worth observing that in this group, the *if*-clause has its action thrown back in time and has its grammatical mood readjusted (subjunctive for indicative).

There is also a not unimportant

Group III: Here, there are conditional sentences in which, as in Group I, the principal clause does not state, nor imply, what would be or would have been, but in which the *if*-clause not only indicates an action that is contemplated (under consideration) or planned but also connotes some degree of reserve on the part of—some reservation hinted by—the speaker. 'If this be true, we are all wrong' (but it is neither stated nor implied that the fact *is* known or even said to be true); 'If this were true, we were all wrong') or, more clearly, 'If this were true, he was entirely wrong' (but it is neither stated nor known that this *was* true); 'Should this be true, we shall all be wrong' (but so far as our knowledge goes, we may be right).

In such sentences as '*Tell me a liar*, and I'll tell you a thief', '*Bid me discourse*, I will enchant thy ear' (Shakespeare), the italicized portions are virtual *if*-clauses, i.e., they are disguised conditionals; but conditional clauses are generally introduced by *if* or *unless* (i.e., if not): of the former, many examples have already been given; an example of the latter is 'I shall do as you ask, unless you countermand your instructions'.

Other disguised conditionals are those in which *were I* is used instead of *if I were*, and *had I* instead of *if I had*, and *should it* for *if it should*: 'Should it be wet, you had better remain in London'; 'Had I gone, I should have regretted it'; 'Were it possible, he would gladly do it'.

Semi-disguised conditionals are of the following kinds: '*Provided (that)* he leaves immediately, I agree to the plan'; '*Supposing (that)* it does not turn out as you say, what compensation—if any—shall

I get?'; 'Supposing it happened, what should you do?'; 'They were always prepared for the worst in case the worst should happen'; 'So long as you hold fast to me, you'll be all right', where so long as is merely a rather colloquial synonym of if only.

Not disguised but elliptical are such conditional sentences as 'If inevitable, why complain?' = 'If it is (or, be) inevitable, why do you complain?'; 'If necessary, we'll take drastic steps to prevent it' = ('If it is (or, be) necessary ...'; 'Whether safe or unsafe, the bridge will have to be crossed' = 'Whether it is (or, be) safe or unsafe ...'

The last example illustrates the rule that alternative clauses of condition are ushered-in by 'whether ... or'. This 'whether ... or' formula is simply a syntactical synonym of 'if ... or if': 'If the bridge is safe or if it is unsafe, it'll have to be crossed' is less convenient, and unidiomatic, for 'Whether the bridge is safe or unsafe ...'

conducive of. See PREPOSITIONS WRONGLY USED. See also CONDUCTIVE.

conduct. See DECORUM.

conductive and conducive. Conductive is extant in only one sense, that (in Physics) of 'having the property of conducting heat, etc.; of or pertaining to conducting: esp. used of conductors of electricity'. Conducive (constructed with to, not with of) = 'having the property of conducting or tending to (a specified end, purpose, or result); fitted to promote or subserve', as in 'A treaty conducive to American interests'; also a noun, as in 'Walking is a great conducive to health'. The verb is conduce to. (The O.E.D.)

conduit is pronounced 'kŭn'dit' or 'kŏn'dit' (less fashionable); so is Conduit (Street). [In the U.S., the usual pronunciations are 'kŏn'dĭt' and 'kŏn'dŏo-ĭt', the latter the pronunciation of the engineers and electricians who install conduits.]

confidant(e); confident. The latter is the adjective ('assured', 'trusting or trustful', 'bold'), the former the noun (feminine in -e)—'a person either trusted or being habitually or professionally trusted with secrets'.

CONFUSED METAPHORS. See METAPHOR, Part II.

CONFUSED PARTICIPLES. See also FUSED PARTICIPLES. Here will be treated what are variously known as disconnected or misrelated or suspended participles, 'misrelated participles' being the commonest of the three designations. (Compare the misrelated gerund, q.v. at GERUND, last paragraph.)

On this matter, as on all that he treats in An Advanced English Syntax, Dr C. T. Onions is both explicit and helpful. 'Avoid the error of using a Participle which has no subject of reference in the sentence, or which, if referred to its grammatical subject, makes nonsense. This mistake is not uncommonly made when a writer intends to use the Absolute construction [as in "This done, we went home" and "The signal being given"—or "having been given"—"we set off"]. ... A sentence like the following is incorrect because the word to which the Participle refers grammatically is not that with which it is meant to be connected in sense: "Born in 1850, a part of his education was received at Eton". Correct thus: "Born in 1850, he received part of his education at Eton".'

Dr Onions cites the following additional examples:—

Calling upon him last summer, he kindly offered to give me his copy. [Say: When I called.]

Being stolen, the Bank of England refused to honour the note. [Say: It being stolen; or better: The note being stolen, the Bank of England refused to honour it.]

Having left daughters only, the property was sold for the immense sum of £135,000.—Boswell, 1765. [Say: He or she having left ...]

Looking out for a theme, several crossed his mind. [Who was looking out? Not "several".]

Being a long-headed gentlewoman, I am apt to imagine she has some further designs than you have yet penetrated.— The Spectator, 1711.

Compare the following error in Addison's 'Tory Fox-Hunter' essay, 'His heart misgave him that there were so many meeting-houses; but upon communicating his suspicions to me, I soon made him easy in that particular'.

Another example not from Dr Onions's book:—'Completely surrounded by a deep wide moat, access to it was only possible by a brick bridge', R. H. Mottram, The Spanish Farm, 1924.

As Dr Onions points out, this sort of error is easy to fall into when one has such ellipses as 'while fighting' (while they were fighting), 'though fighting' (though he was fighting), where a conjunction (e.g., *while*, *though*) is coupled with a participle: 'While fighting, a mist rendered the combatants indistinguishable'; 'Though fighting bravely, his defeat was imminent'.

The error, however, will be avoided by all those who bear in mind the simple rule posited by that grammarian:— 'The only case in which it is permissible to omit the subject in an Absolute Clause [or phrase], is when the unexpressed subject is indefinite (= one, people, French *on*).' Here are two of his examples:—

Taking everything into consideration, our lot is not a happy one. [*Taking* = one taking, i.e., if one takes] Cf. CONJUNCTIONS, DISGUISED.

These prayers are to be said *kneeling* [= the people kneeling].

CONFUSION. See such headings as AMBIGUITY and CARELESSNESS.

confute. See 'REFUTE and DENY'.

congener — word imperfectly understood by many—is 'a member (person, animal, thing) of the same kind or class with another, or nearly allied to another in character', as in 'Some Alpine buttercups are snowy-white, while [*sic*] most of their lowland congeners are simply yellow' and fig., 'The American shopkeeper . . . has not the obsequiousness of his British congener' (Bryce). The adjective is *congener* or, now more usually *congeneric* (constructed with *with*); if the nuance is 'akin (to)', *congener*(*ic*) may take *to*.

congenial, 'to one's taste or liking' (as in 'controversies congenial to his temperament', 'a congenial task'),— 'suited to (the nature of a thing)', as in 'transplanted to a congenial soil, the hitherto sickly plant thrived wonderfully',—'kindred, sympathetic', as in 'We are congenial spirits', 'He had a character congenial with mine', 'Poetry and music are congenial', it is not to be confused with *genial*, 'affable', 'cordial', 'kindly and easily accessible'. (*The O.E.D.*)

conjugal and **connubial**. The former = 'of, belonging to, appropriate to marriage, the married state, married persons', as in Milton's 'conjugal rights' and the Law's 'conjugal rights'. (*Webster's*.) *Connubial* is eruditely facetious in the sense 'pertaining to a husband or a wife', as in Barham's 'Provoking from connubial toes a hint'. Reserve it for the senses 'nuptial', 'matrimonial', as in 'connubial rites', 'the connubial state', 'connubial contracts' (Johnson). (*The O.E.D.*)

CONJUNCTIONS, DISGUISED. These are *barring* ('Barring his weak heart, he was a healthy man'), *considering* ('Considering his opportunities, he was a failure'), *excepting*, *excluding* and *including*, *owing to* ('Owing to the flood, the bridge was impassable'), *regarding*, *respecting* (synonymous with *in respect of*), *seeing* ('Seeing [that] he is ill, he had better stay here'), *touching*. These were originally participles, as one perceives immediately one considers such alternatives as, 'If one bars his weak heart . . .' and 'When you consider his opportunities . . .'. See especially C. T. Onions, *An Advanced English Syntax*, §61c. Cf. DUE TO.

connection and **connexion**. See '-ECTION and -EXION'.

connotation, connote are sometimes confused with *denotation*, *denote*. Make quite sure that you know the difference in meaning between these two pairs.

consciously, used loosely for *deliberately* or *purposely*. 'He was no conceited actor, consciously seeking applause even when he was off stage.'

conscious of does, in certain contexts, mean *aware of*.

consensus (not *concensus*) is 'agreement in opinion', · esp. 'the collective unanimous opinion of a number of persons'; therefore *consensus of opinion* is, at the best, loose. One can, however, speak of a *consensus of MSS*, or a *consensus of evidence, testimony, authority*: but with care. (*The O.E.D.*)

consecutive for *successive*. 'Very few men have been in consecutive cabinets.'

consequence of, in; as a consequence of. These two phrases are occasionally misused for *by means of*. 'In consequence of their [certain swindlers'] address and conversation, they gain the esteem and confidence of some of the most opulent and respectable of their companions', Anon., *The Swindler Detected*, revised ed., 1781.

consequent and **consequential**. The former adjective = 'resulting', 'as a result', 'in the result', as in 'He made a seditious speech in that stronghold of Toryism; the consequent uproar was tremendous, the subsequent proceedings, lively'. (*Subsequent* = 'after', 'following', 'ensuing'.) *Consequential* is obsolescent—

and to be avoided—as a synonym of *consequent*; in Law, it = 'eventual', as in *consequential damages*; in general usage, it = 'self-important', as in 'Pampered and consequential freedmen' (Farrar) and the colloquial 'He's a cocky and consequential little blighter'. (*The O.E.D.*)

conservative estimate, 'a cautiously low estimate', is condemned by Weseen, passed as *S.E.* by *The O.E.D.*: up, conservative estimators, and at 'em! [[In the U.S.A., *conservative estimate* is worn-out phrase, a cliché.]]

consider for to *think, believe, hold the opinion* is not strictly incorrect, but, in these senses, it loses its proper meanings of *think over, ponder, meditate*. Thus Eric Partridge, *The French Romantics' Knowledge of English Literature*, 1924: 'He (Chateaubriand) always bore a grudge against Byron, whom he considered to have plagiarised, etc.'

considering. See CONJUNCTIONS, DISGUISED.

consistently and **persistently**. The former = 'uniformly'; 'without incongruity or absurdity', as in 'To act consistently, you must either admit Matter or reject Spirit' (Berkley); 'compatibly', as in 'consistently with my aims'.

Persistently = 'perseveringly', 'enduringly' (esp. of physical and natural processes and phenomena); 'with continuously repeated action', as in 'My frequent applications have been persistently ignored'. (*The O.E.D.*)

Confusion between the adjectives is much less common.

consist in and **consist of**. *Consist in* is, in general, 'to have its being in'; specifically, 'to be comprised or contained in (actions, conditions, qualities', or other things non-material); 'to be constituted of', as in 'Moral government consists . . . in rewarding the righteous, and punishing the wicked' (Butler, 1736), 'Not every one can tell in what the beauty of a figure consists' (Jowett). *Consist of* is 'to be made up—or, composed—of; to have as its constituent parts, or as its substance', as in 'Newton considered light to consist of particles darted out from luminous bodies' (Tyndall), 'An ordinary fence, consisting of a ditch and a bank' (Edge). (*The O.E.D.*)

consist of and **constitute**. 'A whole consists of parts; the parts constitute the whole', as Weseen has concisely and shrewdly noted.

constant, as applied to actions, processes, conditions, = 'perpetual, incessant, continuous; continual, but with only such intermissions as do not break the continuity': 'The supply of water may be either intermittent or constant', 'In a state of constant flux', 'The constant ticking of a watch', 'Constant repetition of a phrase renders it nauseating'. (*The O.E.D.*)

constitute. See COMPRISE and CONSIST OF.

constrain and **restrain**. To *constrain* a person is to compel or oblige him (to do it); it may be used with a simple object, as in 'The love of Christ constraineth us'; as 'to enforce (an action)', which is an obsolescent sense; 'to confine forcibly, to imprison', now only literary.—To *restrain* is 'to hold back' (oneself or another), 'to impose a deterrent influence on', 'I restrained the madman from throwing himself in the river', 'Only fear restrained him'. Based on *The O.E.D.*

consume is to *use up*, not to *use*. The basic sense of *consume* is 'to destroy'. As Weseen has put it, 'A fire consumes a house, but does not use it; a man uses air, but without consuming it [unless he is in a hermetically sealed chamber]; a man both uses and consumes food'.

contact (v.). If you feel that without this American synonym for 'to establish contact with' or, more idiomatically, 'get in(to) touch with' [a person], life would be too unutterably drear and bleak and 'grim', do at least say or write 'to contact a person', not *contact with*, as in John G. Brandon's *The Mail-Van Mystery*, ca. 1937, 'I've questioned every C.I.D. man I've contacted with'. [[Many Americans of the interbelligerent period felt that *contact* supplied a lively and energetic metaphor, as indeed it does, and the word was grossly overused. Extremes of fashion bring their own corrective, and *contact*, the great word of the era of sales, promotion and consolidation is retiring to its rightful place, as the salesmen themselves, poor fellows, turn to other occupations. One may question whether peace and prosperity will return with or without this word, once magical, the 'Sesame' of *le temps perdu*.]]

contagious. See INFECTIOUS.

contemn. See CONDEMN.

contemporaneous and **contemporary** (erroneously *contempory*, both n. and adj.). Both = 'belonging to the same time or period; living, existing, or occurring at the same time', but the former is now applied mostly to things, the latter mostly to persons. There is, however, a further distinction that may—other things being equal—be held to overrule the preceding distinction: *contemporaneous* tends to refer to the past, *contemporary* to the present. Thus, 'Chatham and Johnson were contemporaneous, Baldwin and Churchill are contemporary'; as a noun, *contemporary* has to do duty for both of these adjectives. In other words *contemporary* and *contemporaneous* might profitably be made, not synonyms but distinctions: it would help the cause of clarity if *contemporary* were confined to the actual present, *contemporaneous* to past periods that are under consideration as present times in those past periods, as in 'The novels contemporaneous with Fielding are more leisurely than contemporary novels (are)'. For *contemporary*, see also COMPARATIVES, FALSE.

contemptible, properly 'despicable' is, in educated use, obsolete as a synonym of *contemptuous*, 'full of contempt; disdainful, scornful'.

contempt of and **contempt for** are, in general, synonymous; but the phrases *in contempt of* and *contempt of court* are invariable. With persons, however, we now prefer *for*, as in 'His contempt for John was immeasurable'.

contest. See COMBAT.

context of situation is a fairly new term, listed here because it puzzles many the first time they meet with it. It = 'the state of things at a given time and place'—as you see, little more than 'circumstances': but it looks so learned ...

contiguous. See ADJACENT.

continual and **continuous** must not be confused. The former is defined as 'always going on', the latter as 'connected, unbroken; uninterrupted in time or sequence' (*The Con. O.D.*). Cf. CONSTANT.

continuance; continuation; continuity. *Continuance* is obsolete in the senses 'continuity' and 'continuation'; properly it is the noun both of *continue* (v.t.), i.e., 'prolonging' or 'maintaining', as in 'The continuance of the unending task of human improvement' (John Morley) and as an American Law term, and of *continue* (v.i.), esp. as 'the going on (of an action or process), the lasting of duration (of a condition or state)', as in 'The sole cause of the continuance of the quarrel' (Froude). *Continuity* is lit. and fig. 'connectedness, unbrokenness, uninterruptedness'; hence, also, 'a continuous whole'. *Continuation* is 'continued maintenance; resumption', also, 'that by which or in which anything is maintained or prolonged': 'A continuation of fine weather' combines these two ideas. (*The O.E.D.*)

continue to say is ambiguous for *continue by saying*. 'Smith asserted that the world was always square, and he continued to say, "If not square, at least oblong".' He did not continue the latter statement; he went on to make it: it was the statement about squareness which he continued.

continuum is a scientific and philosophic term, defined by *The O.E.D.* as 'a continuous thing, quantity, or substance', as in 'The human body is an admirable continuum'; hence, 'a continuous series of elements passing into each other', as in 'The external world is, to a man with eyesight, a continuum of sights'. Its post-War use is mostly in Physics: in the phrase *the space-time continuum* (or *manifold*), a continuum (or manifold) that results from the fusion of time with three-dimensional space, in Einstein's theory of relativity. The plural is *continua*. (*The O.E.D.*)

contradictious and **contradictory.** *Contradictious* is extant only of persons, or their dispositions, that are 'inclined to contradict, addicted to contradicting; given to cavil; disputatious', a sense in which *contradictory* also is used, although it is generally applied to things that are diametrically opposed, or inconsistent in themselves, and although it has two technical nuances in Logic—*contradictory opposition* and *contradictory terms*. The latter is worth noting, for it is to be distinguished from the sense of *contrary;* '"Contradictory terms", such as white and not-white ... are terms which admit of no medium' (Fowler, *Deductive Logic*, 1887); cf. *living* and *non* (or *not*)-*living, possible* and *not-possible* (i.e., *impossible*). Contrary terms, on the other hand, are 'those which are extreme opposites within the same class, as *black* and *white*', the *contradictory* of *black* being *not-black*. (*The O.E.D.*)

contrary. See 'CONTRADICTIOUS and CONTRADICTORY', and following entry.

contrary and **opposite.** *Opposite* is stronger than *contrary*, and in Rhetoric, Dialectics, and Logic, there is a distinction. To adapt Fowler's admirable exposition (in *Modern English Usage*), we notice that *All humans are mortal* has as its contrary *Not all humans are mortal* (which is untrue); as its opposite, *No humans are mortal* (also untrue). The converse, by the way, is *All mortals are humans.* Likewise, *I hit him* has no opposite; but its contrary is *I did not hit him* and its converse is *He hit me.* See CONVERSE.

contrast and **compare.** To *compare* is to align the two (or more) sets of similarities and identities; to *contrast* is to align the two sets of differences and distinctions. In doing either, one is conscious of the other; whence that favourite type of examination question, 'Compare and contrast (e.g., Caesar and Napoleon)'.

conversation. See DIALOGUE.

conversationalist; conversationist. The latter is obsolescent.

converse, inverse, obverse, reverse. By far the most general of these terms is *reverse*, 'the opposite or contrary of something', as in 'His speech was the reverse of cheerful'; in coinage, *reverse* is the back of a coin, whereas *obverse* is the front (that side which bears the head or other principal design).

Except the last, these terms are technicalities of Logic and Dialectics: venturesome journalists and dare-all writers should employ them with care and discretion. The corresponding abstract nouns are *conversion, inversion, obversion*; the verbs are *convert, invert, obvert.*

In general a *converse* is 'a thing or action that is the exact opposite of another'; in Rhetoric it is 'a phrase or sentence derived from another by the turning about or transposition of two important antithetical members', thus the converse of 'the possession of courage without discretion' is 'the possession of discretion without courage'; in Logic, *converse* is 'the transposition of the subject and predicate of a proposition . . . to form a new proposition by immediate inference', thus the converse of 'No A is B' is 'No B is A'.—For the relation of *converse* to *contrary* and *opposite*, see CONTRARY.

Inverse:—In general, it is 'an inverted state or condition; that which is in order or direction the direct opposite of something else': the inverse of ABC is CBA. In Logic, it is that form of immediate inference in which there is formed a new proposition whose subject is the negative of that of the original proposition.

Obverse:—In general, it is 'the counterpart of any fact or truth'; in Logic, 'that form of immediate inference in which, by changing the quality, from one proposition another is inferred, having a contradictory predicate'.

These definitions come, either verbatim or slightly changed, from *The O.E.D.*

co-operation. See COLLUSION.

coppice and **copse** are synonymous, both collectively for 'underwood' or '*coppice* (or *copse*)-*wood*', and as 'a small wood or thicket consisting of underwood and small trees grown for the purpose of periodical cutting'. *Copse* is a syncopated form of *coppice.* (*The O.E.D.*) [[In American English, *copse* is rare and *coppice* unknown.]]

copyright (v.). The past tense and past participle are *copyrighted.*

corporal and **corporeal** are no longer interchangeable. *Corporal* = 'of or belonging to the human body', as in 'A favourite topic of ancient raillery was corporal defects' (Gibbon); in legal language, 'personal', as in 'corporal possession of a benefice'; *Corporal punishment* is punishment inflicted on the body, esp. flogging. *Corporeal* is 'of the nature of the animal body as opposed to the spirit; physical, mortal', as in 'That which is corporeal dies at our death' and 'the corporeal frame of every human being'; hence 'of the nature of matter as opposed to mind and spirit; material', as in 'The Devil is punished by a corporeal fire'; in Law, 'tangible; consisting of material objects', esp. in *corporeal hereditament.* (*The O.E.D.*)

corrective (n.) like *corrective* (adj.) takes *of*, not *for.* 'Mathematics is a powerful corrective for the spook-making of ordinary language', Stuart Chase, *The World of Words*, 1938. [[In American usage, *corrective for* instead of *corrective of* is not uncommon.]]

CORRECTNESS or **CORRECTITUDE.** See STANDARD ENGLISH, Section iii.

correspond to and **with.** The question is often asked whether *to* or *with* is correct: both are correct, but their senses must be carefully distinguished. *Correspond to* = answer to in character or function, answer or agree in regard to position, amount, etc.; *correspond with* = communicate by interchange of letters. (*The O.E.D.*) In the latter the sense-stress is on the 'with' implied in the Latin derivation of the first syllable; in the former, it is on the 'response' or 'answering to'.

correspondent is one who corresponds (writes letters); a **co-respondent** (or *corespondent*) is the external offending party in a divorce case.

coruscate must not be spelt *corruscate*.

cosmopolitan (n.) and **cosmopolite** are synonymous; the latter, obsolescent. [[For American usage, *cosmopolite* has been revived by the 'sophisticated press'.]]

costly and **dear** are not so sharply distinguished as Weseen makes out. Both = 'expensive' or 'too expensive'; but *costly* is preferred when the sense is 'of great price or value; sumptuous', as in 'a costly gown or jewel', 'a costly shrub', 'a costly palace', and in such transferred nuances as 'a costly emotion', 'a costly sacrifice'. Based on *The O.E.D.*

cotemporaneous and **cotemporary** are obsolete.

could for *can*. See PAST SUBJUNCTIVE . . .

could, misused for *might*. 'If there's no more need to sew your shirt on'—the reference is to the taking of risks—'you could just as well jump in [properly, 'into'] the lake' (a detective novel, 1937).

council and **counsel** are often misused one for the other, the former being 'an advisory or deliberative assembly or body of persons', the latter meaning 'advice and opinion given or offered' (*The O.E.D.*); *counsel* is also the correct spelling for a counsellor-at-law, a barrister, an advocate.

counterpart has, in legal and musical phraseology, senses unproductive of confusion. In ordinary English, however, it bears two senses almost startlingly different: i, one of two persons or things that are complementary to each other ('Popular fury finds its counterpart in courtly servility', Hazlitt); ii, 'a person or thing so answering to another as to appear a duplicate or exact copy of it', as in 'A portrait, the counterpart of her visitor'. (With thanks to *The O.E.D.*)

countless for *many*. 'The cellars of Fitzwaren Towers were reached by a fine spiral stair, the steps of which had been worn into deep ruts by the tread of countless generations' (perhaps twenty-five), Warner Allen, *The Uncounted Hour*, 1936.

country man (or **woman**) and **countryman** (or **countrywoman**). Reserve the former for 'one who lives in the country and follows a rural occupation'; the latter is 'a native, an inhabitant', as in 'a North-Countryman', 'a fellow-country-man', and also 'a compatriot'. 'The English avoid their countrymen when they are abroad', frequent in the form 'a countryman of mine'; i.e., a *fellow-countryman*, a form later than the single word. (*The O.E.D.*)

coup is correct English (and well established by the end of the 18th Century) in the sense, 'a successful move (that one makes); a "hit"', but journalists are overworking it. See, e.g., the article by Mr Frank Whitaker in *The J.I.J.*, January, 1939.

couple, a. Avoid as a mere synonym of *two*; still more as = *two or three*. See esp. *The O.E.D.*

course. *Of course* is to be used sparingly. (I say this with much feeling, for I myself tend to use it far too often.)

courtesy. See CURTESY.

courts-martial is the correct plural of *court-martial*. [[The plural *court-martials* has wide currency in the U.S.A., though *Webster's* allows only *courts-martial*.]]

crape. See CRÊPE.

crawfish is American for *crayfish*, 'a fresh-water crustacean'. In England it is also used for the spiny lobster. (*The O.E.D.*)

credible; creditable; credulous. (Negatives: *incredible; uncreditable* or, more generally, *discreditable; incredulous*.) *Credible* = believable; worthy of belief; susceptible of belief. *Creditable* = worthy of praise or credit; redounding to one's credit or reputation. *Credulous* = gullible; showing—or given to—excessive readiness or willingness to believe.

credit and **accredit**. In no sense are these two terms interchangeable. The latter = 'to invest with authority', 'to vouch for'.

creole is a descendant of European (chiefly Spanish and French) settlers in West Indies, Louisiana, Mauritius, etc.; not, as is often supposed, a half-breed of white and native races in those colonized countries. According to *Webster's*, *Creole* (with capital) has the first sense. It also means 'the French patois spoken in Louisiana'. Not capitalized it may mean 'a Negro born in America; a person of mixed Creole and Negro blood speaking a French or Spanish dialect; a half-breed.' There is also an Alaskan usage, meaning 'a person of mixed Russian and Eskimo or Indian descent'.

crêpe should be confined to *crêpe de chine* and *crêpe lisse*. In general use, *crape* is to be preferred.

crevasse and **crevice**. A *crevice* is, in general, a cleft or rift, a small fissure, and in mining a crevice is 'a fissure in which a deposit of ore or metal is found', whereas a *crevasse* is a fissure, usually of great depth and sometimes very wide, in the ice of a glacier, and in the U.S.A., 'a breach in the bank of a river, canal, etc.; esp. a breach in the levée (or artificial bank) of the lower Mississippi' (*The O.E.D.*). Do not use *crevice* for *crevasse*, nor, except of extensive breaches, *crevasse* of ordinary chasms or deep cracks in the earth.

crime should not, except in jest, be debased to = 'an error, a minor fault or offence'.

critical. Weseen is wrong in his assertion that '*Critical* is not in good use as a general substitute for *serious* or *dangerous*, as "The invalid is in a critical condition", "He is critically ill"'. It certainly is not a general substitute for *dangerous*: obviously one wouldn't speak of 'a critical animal'. But following from the medical sense, 'relating to the crisis or turning-point of a disease' (as in pneumonia), are the closely related nuances, 'of decisive importance in relation to the issue', as in 'Socrates taught that on great and critical occasions he was often directed by a mysterious voice' (J. B. Blackie, 1871) and 'involving suspense or grave fear as to the issue; attended with uncertainty or risk', as in 'Relations . . . were . . . in a critical state; in fact, the two countries were on the eve of a war' (Washington Irving) and 'His throat had been cut; his condition was critical'. *Critical* also = 'crucial'. (*The O.E.D.*)

crossway, crossways, crosswise. *Crossway* is a noun ('by-way' or 'cross-road') and an adjective, 'placed, made, executed crossways', i.e., *crosswise*, which is only an adverb, with which, by the way, *The O.E.D.* makes *crossways* (only an adverb) exactly synonymous. *Cross-*

wise = 'in the form of a cross' ('A church built crosswise', Johnson) or 'so as to intersect' ('Four of these streets are built cross-wise', Nugent, 1754); 'across, athwart, transversely' ('A frame of logs placed cross-wise', Jowett); hence figuratively, 'perversely, wrongly.' ('He seeks pleasure cross-wise').

crowd for *group* is extremely colloquial.

crumby; crummy. Both = 'like, or of the nature of, the crumb of bread', but only the former = 'full of, or strewed with, crumbs' and only the latter is used in the slang senses. (*The O.E.D.*) [[The two are pronounced alike, i.e., without *b*; and in American English *crumby* may carry the slang senses (*Webster's*).]]

crystallized. We are tempted to borrow from Mr A. P. Herbert (*What a Word!*) the following: "'A Daily Mail reporter who made inquiries in London learned that among Church leaders there is no *crystallized viewpoint* towards spiritual healing." Note.—The *crystallized viewpoint* is not to be confused with the Standard *Glacé* or Frosted Angle.' Crystallized is here used metaphorically: for the dangers of this practice see METAPHOR.

ct and **x** as variants (*connection, connexion*). See '-ECTION and -EXION'.

CUMULATIVE NEGATION. See NEGATION, Section *C*, *a* from third paragraph to end; also sub-section *b*.

cunning, 'amusing' or 'attractive' is an Americanism.

cupfuls and **cups full.** Cf. 'BASKETFULS and BASKETS FULL' for sense.

curb and **kerb.** The latter is the usual spelling (in England but not in the U.S.A.) for the protective margin of a sidewalk.

curious. Subjectively it = 'desirous of seeing or knowing; eager to learn'; hence 'inquisitive', hence derogatory 'prying'. Hence objectively, 'deserving—or arousing—attention on account of novelty, peculiarity, oddity; exciting curiosity', hence 'rather surprising, strange, singular, or odd; queer'. (*The O.E.D.*)

curtesy, courtesy; curts(e)y. *Curts(e)y* is an obeisance; *curtesy*, an obsolete form of *courtesy* in all its senses. *Courtesy*, 'an obeisance', is obsolete. In current usage, *courtesy* is limited to 'graceful politeness or considerateness in intercourse with others'; 'a courteous disposition'; 'a courteous act or expression'; a form of legal tenure, and an American political custom. *Of* (or *by*) *courtesy* = 'by favour or indulgence; by gracious permission'. A *courtesy title* is 'one that, without legal validity, is accorded by courtesy or social custom'; cf. *courtesy rank*. (*The O.E.D.*)

customer. See CLIENT and cf. PATRON.

cute for *acute* is a colloquialism; for 'amusing' or 'attractive', an American colloquialism. Cf. CUNNING and CLEVER.

cyclone, tornado, typhoon and **hurricane.** It is best to confine these terms to their meteorological senses. A *cyclone* is 'a general name for a low-area storm [with] high winds rotating about a centre of low atmospheric pressure. *Tornado* is the name of a specific type of storm characterized by rapidly falling barometric pressure, a funnel-shaped cloud, vertical motion of the air, and a narrow path' (Weseen). A *typhoon* is (*a*) 'a violent storm or tempest occurring in India'; (*b*) the prevalent sense, 'a violent cyclonic storm or hurricane occurring in the China seas and adjacent regions, chiefly from July to October' (*The O.E.D.*). *Hurricane* should be reserved for storms originating in the neighborhood of the West Indies: a violent windstorm, with a diameter of 500–1000 miles, wherein the air moves at 80–130 m.p.h. round a central calm space that advances with the rest of the system in either a straight or a curved track. (*The O.E.D.*)

cyclopede (obsolete for *cyclopaedia*) is occasionally confused with *velocipede*, a superseded form of bicycle (or tricycle).

Cymric, 'Welsh'. The *c* is hard, i.e., pronounced as *k*. [[For American English, the initial *c* may be pronounced *s* or *k*. (*Webster's*.)]]

D

daily and **diurnal.** *Daily* is 'of or belonging to each day; occurring or done every day; issued or published every day (or every week-day)', as in 'A daily paper comes out call'd The Spectator' (Hearne) and 'The daily labour to gain their daily bread' (Brougham).

In current usage, *diurnal* is the opposite of *nocturnal*, and (of the motion of the heavenly bodies) it = 'performed in or occupying one day', as in 'the planet's diurnal rotation'. (*The O.E.D.*)

dam is incorrect for *damn* (n., v., and interjection); and *damn* ('It's damn

cold') is incorrect for *damn'*, short for *damned* = *damnably*.

damaged is used of things (or, jocularly, of persons); *injured*, of persons and animal life. One should not, for instance, speak of one's teeth as being (or getting) *injured*.

'd and **'ld.** At present, *'d* is used both for *had* ('If I'd only known!') and for *would* ('If he'd only do it!'). Would it not be better to reserve *'d* for *had* and set *'ld* aside for *would*? The adoption of this recommendation (already observed by F. E. Brett Young, who has a sense of style) would at least serve to prevent an occasional ambiguity. According to certain authorities *should* has no shortened form. [[American authorities regard *'d* as a colloquial contraction of *had*, *would* and *should*.]]

dangerous. See CRITICAL.

dare, misused for *dared*. "'Did you touch the body?'' ''Oh, no, sir—I daren't''', John Bude, *The Cheltenham Square Murder*, 1937.

data is wrong when it is used for the correct singular, *datum*. 'For this data, much of it routine, it would be sensible to enlist the local authorities', Milton Propper, *Murder at the Polls*, 1936. [[In American English, *data* may be singular or plural. *Webster's*, Krapp, Perrin.]]

date back to and **date back from.** Certain newspaper editors, on their style sheets, forbid the former and recommend the latter: actually, both usage and good sense tell us to prefer *date back to* to *date back from*. Style, prompted by economy of words, suggests that *date from* is preferable to either of the phrases under discussion.

daughters-in-law is the correct plural; so *sons-in-law, mothers-in-law, fathers-in-law*, etc.

Day of Rest, the. See SABBATH.

deadly and **deathly.** Both = 'causing death, fatal, mortal', but *deathly* is obsolescent in this sense; as = 'of or pertaining to death', *deathly* is poetical; indeed, the only general extant sense of *deathly* is 'death-like; as gloomy or still or silent or pale as death', as in 'Poor fellow, he looks deathly; can't last much longer, I fear', 'a deathly silence, stillness, pallor'.

Deadly is a more general word. In addition to the sense noted above, it = (of things) 'poisonous, venomous, pestilential, esp. if to a fatal degree'; in Theology, 'mortal' as opposite to 'venial', as in 'the seven deadly sins'; 'aiming at (or involving an aim) to kill or destroy; implacable; to the death', as in 'The contest . . . becomes sharp and deadly' (Mark Pattison); and 'death-like' ('a deadly faintness'), though in this nuance *deathly* is more usual. (*The O.E.D.*)

deaf and dumb is the adjective; **deaf-mute** the noun.

deal, a, like **a good** (or **great**) **deal**, 'a large quantity or number', is a colloquialism, to be avoided in formal literary language.

deal in; deal with. Weseen neatly epitomizes the distinctions: 'In business we deal *in* commodities and *with* persons, as "They deal chiefly *in* iron products and deal *with* contractors in many cities." In discussion we deal *with* a subject, as "He dealt with all phases of the matter".'

dean and **doyen** are dignified words; therefore do not, as certain journalists use, speak of 'the dean (or doyen) of the caddies', 'the dean (or doyen) of polo-players', and so forth; as applied to a diplomatic corps, they are in place, though *doyen* is here the better term.

dear. See EXPENSIVE.

dear price. See CHEAP PRICE.

deathless, immortal, undying. 'We have not only *immortal*, but also *undying* and *deathless*, expressing different shades of meaning, e.g., we would not speak of *immortal* admiration or affection' (Weekley, *Something about Words*, 1935). Cf. the following examples of correct use from *The O.E.D.*: 'The faith that animals have immaterial and deathless souls', Tyler, *Prim Cult*, 1871. 'The deathless name of Godwina', Freeman, *Norman Conquest*, 1876. 'Our deathlessness is in what we do, not in what we are', G. Meredith, *Rhoda Fleming*, 1865. 'The world itself probably is not immortal', Hume, 1752. 'The undying interest ever felt by kindly women in a question of love or marriage', Mrs. Alexander, *Valerie's Fate*, 1885. For *deathless*, see also 'DEADLY and DEATHLY'.

deathlike. See DEADLY.

debar; disbar. The latter is used in only one sense, 'to expel from the bar'; *debar* ('to exclude, prevent, prohibit') is not so used.

debate is misused when it is made synonymous with *doubt, pondering, question,* or *cogitation.* 'He wasted no debates on what had happened, but concentrated on how it had happened, and attempted

to guess how his own investigation might be involved', Robert George Dean, *The Sutton Place Murders*, 1936.

decease is the legal synonym of *to die,* which is preferable in every context other than the legal. The same applies to the noun.

decern. See DESCRY.

decimate means only 'to take or destroy one in ten', but is loosely used for 'cut up, wipe out entirely, destroy'.

decisive(ly) for *decided(ly)*; the reverse is rare. A good example of this misuse is found in Philip MacDonald's excellent thriller, *The Nursemaid Who Disappeared*, 1938: 'It being clear that the play was going to be a success, the party given after the show by Brooks-Carew was a decisively alcoholic affair.'

declare. See ASSERT.

decorum and **conduct.** The latter is neutral and it requires an adjective to determine it. *Decorum* is 'propriety of behaviour'; in plural it = 'proprieties', as in 'Hedged round by formalities and decorums' (Merivale). (*The O.E.D.*)

decrease over; decrease under. 'A 15% decrease over (or, under) the takings of last year': the former is absurd, the latter clumsy. Read 'A 15% decrease in the takings as compared with those of last year'. So too for *increase over.*

decumbent. See RECUMBENT.

definite and **definitive.** The difference is neatly given by Harold Herd, in *Watch Your English: Definite* implies that a thing is *precise; definitive* means that it is *final* (beyond criticism or refutation).

definitely. See REALLY.

deflection and **deflexion.** See '-ECTION and -EXION'.

degrade as v.i. ('to deteriorate', 'to degenerate') is moribund. It creates an odd impression in the following sentence from a detective novel of 1937, 'If men have nothing to do they degrade to monkeys'.—See also DEMEAN.

deign for *see fit* or *consider fit* is infelicitous—not to say catachrestic. 'Dinah Lee testified that she saw a lady leave my house . . . at four o'clock [in the morning], when she [Dinah Lee] claims to have found the film which the prosecution deigns to hold as evidence of my guilt' (a detective novel, 1937).

delightful. See at GLORIOUS.

deliver. See ADMINISTER.

deliverance need not be confused with *delivery*, the former now being used only for 'liberation or rescue', in several legal technicalities, 'A formal utterance or pronouncement', and 'a verdict' (obsolescent except in Law). (*The O.E.D.*)

Delphos. Incorrect for *Delphi*.

delude and **illude; delusion, illusion.** To *illude* is 'to trick', 'to deceive with false hopes', whereas *delude* is 'to befool the mind or judgment of (a person), so as to cause what is false to be accepted as true'. *Delusion* is 'believing—or causing another to believe—that the false is true'; 'a fixed false opinion', e.g., as a form of mental derangement. An *illusion* is 'a false conception or idea; a deceptive belief, statement, or appearance'. (*The O.E.D.*) [[Fortunately *illude* is rare in speech, for *elude* is commonly its homonym.]]

demand is not 'to *order*', but to ask authoritatively or peremptorily for (a thing); or that something be done, as in 'Assent was categorically demanded', 'He demanded to be allowed to enter' or 'that he should be allowed . . .'; and 'to ask formally or authoritatively to know or be told', as in 'He demanded the cause' and 'All the members demanded who it was'. (*The O.E.D.*)

demean is, by the prudent, used only in the v., *demean oneself*, 'to bear oneself', 'to comfort oneself', 'to behave'. The v. *demean*, 'to lower', 'to make mean', shows signs of obsolescence, even in the once-stock 'I would not so demean myself'. The following strikes one as being—well, infelicitous:—'Osaki had moved to a secluded position aft, where she sat rigidly aloof, as might some great lady who felt herself demeaned by contact . . . with her fellow beings' (John G. Brandon, *The Mail-Van Mystery*, ca. 1937). To *demean oneself* is, commonly, to behave, or to comport oneself, in a manner that is specified, as in 'He demeaned himself with courage'. *Demeanour* is 'bearing, (outward) behaviour'. (*The O.E.D.*)

demi and **semi.** Both literally mean '(a) half'; the former, direct from French, the latter direct from Latin. In Heraldry, the term is *demi*; in armoury, *demi* = half-sized or smaller,—so too in artillery, fortification, and military tactics; in weights and measures, music, geometry, *demi* = 'half'; in the names of fabrics and stuffs, it = 'inferior'; with class-nouns ('man', 'doctor', 'lady', etc.), it often = 'of equivocal character', as in 'demi-pagan', 'demi-priest'; with nouns of

action or condition, it = 'partial', as in 'demi-toilet'.

Semi follows the same tendencies: in technicalities, it = 'half' (or, less generally, 'on a reduced scale'); with class-nouns and nouns of action, it = 'partial'. In correlative pairs, only *semi* is used; as in 'semi-chemical, semi-mechanical'.

Word-coiners will, if they respect others as much as they respect themselves, reserve *demi* for words of French origin, *hemi* for words of Greek origin, *semi* for words of Latin origin, and *half* for those of Teutonic origin. See *The O.E.D.* for a very much fuller treatment.

demise is a legal term, to be employed only in specific contexts; as a synonym of *death*, it is infelicitous and unnecessary, and as a euphemism it is deplorable.

democrat and **Democrat.** The former is an advocate of or an adherent to democracy; a *Democrat* is a member of the Democratic party in American politics.

demolish, less general than *destroy*, should, literally, be applied only to structures (e.g., buildings), and, figuratively, be used only in the nuance 'put an end to', as in 'to demolish the Church, the Law, Medicine, etc.; an argument, an objection, a doctrine, a theory; an etymology'. Humorously, *demolish* = to consume (food), as in 'He demolished a leg of lamb all by himself'. (*The O.E.D.*)

denominate and **name** and **nominate.** To *denominate* is 'to name, to call by name, to give a name or appellation to', as in 'From him [Guelpho] they . . . were denominated Guelphs' (Fuller, 1639), 'This is what the world . . . denominates an itch for writing' (Cowper). It is, in current usage, constructed usually with a complement, i.e., as = 'to call' (witness the example from Cowper). In this, the only sense of *denominate*, *nominate* is a synonym—but obsolescent and, for the sake of clarity, to be avoided. *Nominate* obsolescent also in the two senses, 'to specify by name' and 'to specify, appoint, fix' ('The woman has the privilege of nominating the day of her marriage'). The prevalent—indeed, the only general current sense—is, 'to appoint (a person) by name to discharge some duty or to hold some office', as in 'The House of Commons was crowded with members nominated by the Royal Council' (J. R. Green), with the derivative sense, 'to propose, or formally enter, (a person) as a candidate for election', as in 'Any one may challenge the person nominated and start another candidate' (Jowett). (*The O.E.D.*)

denote, misused for *show.* 'His turned-up shirt-sleeves and bare neck . . . denoted him to be one of the stage hands', W. H. Lane Crauford, *Murder to Music,* 1936.—See also the entry at CONNOTATION.

dent and **dint.** In the literary sense, 'an indentation (in a material object)', *dent* is usual; in the figurative sense, 'an impairment, a shock or blow', almost 'a blemish', *dint* is usual, as in 'a dint in a character—a reputation'. But whereas *dent* is never used figuratively, *dint* is often used literally. (*The O.E.D.*)

deny, misused for *contradict.* 'I said that there were 101; he denied me and said there were 102.' See also REFUTE.

deny and **refute.** See 'REFUTE and DENY'.

dependant; dependent. As also for *pendant, pendent,* the *-ant* form is preferred for the noun, the *-ent* for the adjective. [In American English, the final syllable of the adjective is *-ent,* of the noun, *-ent* or *-ant.* (*Webster's.*)]

deplete and **reduce.** The former is not synonymous with the latter, though almost so in the nuance 'to reduce the fulness of', as in 'to deplete a garrison'; even here, however, one speaks of a garrison's 'being depleted' as the result of, e.g., an attack, whereas 'to reduce a garrison' implies deliberation by its officers. In general usage, to *deplete* = 'to empty out, to exhaust', as in 'to deplete one's strength'.

deplore governs a thing or a quality, not a person. Thus the correct form of 'We may deplore him for his conceit' (set, for correction, in the Scottish Leaving Certificate examination, March, 1938) is either 'We may deplore his conceit' or 'We may condemn him for his conceit'.

depositary and **depository.** The former is 'a trustee' or, in Law, 'a bailee'; the latter is 'a receptacle', a storehouse or repository', but is also used (though not in Law) of a person to whom something (lit. or fig.) is entrusted. (*The O.E.D.*) [In American English, *depositary* may mean a storehouse.]

depravation and **depravity.** In current usage, *depravation* is '(the act or fact of) making depraved or corrupt', whereas *depravity* is '(the process or fact of) becoming, or esp. having become, de-praved, bad, corrupt': 'depravation of instincts and morals'; 'an unspeakable depravity caused him to be shunned by all decent people'. (*The O.E.D.*)

deprecate for *depreciate* (and vice-versa). *Depreciating, -ly,* are often misused for *deprecating, -ly; depreciation* is much less commonly misused for *depre-cation.* (To) *depreciate* is the opposite of *appreciate* and is synonymous with *belittle*; to *deprecate* is to plead earnestly against, to express an earnest wish against or earnest disapproval of.

des- and **dis-.** For the history of these prefixes, see *The O.E.D.*

describe for *indicate* or *designate* or *denote* is catachrestic, slovenly, feeble, as in 'This blue print describes how the machine has been made'; 'The nickname "The Croucher" describes that famous cricketer, Jessop'; 'The term *accuracy* describes the result of accuracy'. As = 'to represent, picture, or portray', de-scribe is obsolete, and should be avoided. As = 'to descry', it is a catachresis; so discriminating a writer as Gibbon fell into this error: 'The smallest blemish has not been described by . . . jealous . . . eyes' (*The O.E.D.*). [The second sentence does not offend American usage, though *describes* might well be *characterizes*. *Designate* in this sense is not usual, although one would say, 'The insignia on his shoulder designate his rank'.]

description (or **descriptive**) **about** is incorrect for *description* (or *descriptive*) of. The former is exemplified in 'Instead of a long description about studies into human communication and the meaning of language, we fill the gap with a new symbol—*semantics*', Stuart Chase, *The Tyranny of Words,* 1938. Perhaps by confusion with *a discourse about* (something).

descry and **discern.** *Descry* is 'to catch sight of, esp. from a distance; to espy', as in 'To meet Albert, whom I descried coming towards us' (Queen Victoria, 1868) and 'At intervals we descried a maple'. Hence, 'to discover by observation; to detect; to perceive', and even—though this is a weakening of the sense—merely 'to see': 'To descry new lands, rivers or mountains in her spotty globe' (Milton); 'The bounds which separated that school from Romanism were very difficult to descry' (Brougham).

To *discern* (not to be confused with *decern,* 'to decree by judicial sentence' or, obsolescently, 'to see distinctly with eyes or mind') is, in current usage, 'to recognize or perceive distinctly' ('to discern the truth' or 'to discern that the truth is . . .'); 'to distinguish (an object) with the eyes', i.e. 'to descry', as in 'We could discern no trace of rupture [in the ice]' (Tyndall), 'Good sight is necessary for one to be able to discern minute objects'. (*The O.E.D.*)

desertion is dangerously ambiguous in the following: 'Pedro de Valdez was universally loved and honoured, and his desertion in the face of an enemy so inferior in numbers was regarded as scandalous poltroonery', J. A. Froude, *English Seamen in the Sixteenth Century*. The context shows that Valdez did not desert his friends but was deserted by them.

déshabillé should, as a French word, be *déshabillé*, e.g. *en déshabillé* (in undress). The English form carries no accent and should be *dishabille* (less correctly *deshabille*); the English phrase is *in dishabille*—not those hybrids, *en dishabille* (or *deshabille*) or *in déshabille* (or *déshabillé*).

designate should not be used as absolutely synonymous with *describe*, as in the butler's 'A suit which I should designate as on the loud side' (Georgette Heyer, *A Blunt Instrument*, 1938). There is confusion here with the sense 'to point out by a name or by a descriptive appellation'.

desirable is 'worthy to be desired', 'to be wished for', whereas *desirous* is 'full of, or characterized by desire' and is always constructed with *of* ('desirous of doing something') or the infinitive ('desirous to learn all he could') or, obsolescently, *that* ('He was desirous that nothing should be said about it').

despatch. See DISPATCH.

despite, 'notwithstanding (an opponent, an obstacle)', is a shortening of *despite of*, itself a shortening of *in despite of*. The usual current form is *in spite of*; *spite of* is colloquial. *Despite of* is obsolescent, as also—except in lofty or poetical style—is *in despite of*.

determinately and **determinedly** are occasionally confused. The latter = 'in a determined (i.e., resolute) manner', in which sense *determinately* is literary—but slightly obsolescent. As 'conclusively, inally', *determinately* is now rare; and as definitely, exactly, precisely' ('It was

determinately discovered that . . .') it seems to be going out of use.

determine is, in Law, 'to put an end to (in time)' or 'to come to an end'; in general, it is 'to bring to an end (a dispute, controversy, or doubtful matter)', as in 'This ambiguity should be determined in one direction or in the other' (Mark Pattison); 'to decide upon (one of several)', as in 'It is the will which determines what is to be preferred or rejected' (McCosh); 'to ascertain definitely, to fix or know', as in 'Let us determine our route before we start on our journey'; 'to direct to some end or conclusion, or to come to a conclusion', as in 'It only determines or facilitates the action of chemical force' (Grove), '[She] took credit to herself for having determined Shelley to travel abroad' (Dowden).

To *be determined* is 'to be firmly (and finally) resolved', as in 'He is determined' and 'He is determined to go, whatever the danger'. (*The O.E.D.*)

deterrent influence is an unnecessary elaboration of *deterrent* (which is noun as well as adjective), as in 'There cannot be too many methods of identification; the more certain a man is that he will be identified, the greater the deterrent influence to crime', Nigel Morland, *The Conquest of Crime*, 1937.

detract and **distract** are sometimes confused. In current usage, *detract* is common only in *detract from*, as in 'Nothing detracts from one's virtue so much as too much boasting about it'; *distract* is 'to divert the attention of', hence 'to perplex, to agitate, perturb', as in 'Love distracts the student'. See also at SUBSTRACT.

develop (preferable, by the way, to *develope*) is often used catachrestically for 'to arise', as in 'The totalitarian states, which have developed since the Great War [1914–1918], are opposed to the doctrines of democracy', examination essay script, June, 1939. See also ENVELOP.

device; devise. As a noun, *devise* occurs only in Law. In general usage, *device* is only a noun, *devise* only a verb ('to plan, arrange, contrive'); *device* is a means whereby one is assisted in achieving one's purpose.—*Deviser* is general; *devisor*, legal.

devices should be used with caution as a synonym of *plans* or *activities*. 'Left to his own devices' is a stock phrase—a commonplace (or cliché); but escape from that cliché and you fall into the pitfall of the unidiomatic, as in 'It was some hours later that the two men met, . . . because the Chief-Inspector [—why the hyphen?—] had been busy on his own devices' (E. R. Lorac, *Death of an Author*, 1935).

devilry; deviltry. The former is the Standard English word; *deviltry* is English dialect and an American variant. *Deviltry*, moreover, is less devilish and has a connotation of mischievousness and spiritedness.

deviser; devisor. See DEVICE.

dexterous is usual, though **dextrous** is the sounder formation.

DIALECT. 'Dialect is essentially local; a dialect is [that] variety of a language which prevails in a district, with local peculiarities of vocabulary, pronunciation, and phrase' (H. W. Fowler); dialects, therefore, are languages *within* a language.

The peculiarities, especially if they are picturesque or forcible, are constantly being incorporated into general colloquial speech or into slang. At ordinary times, the incorporation is slow and inconsiderable, but on special occasions and during intense periods, as in a war (when countrymen mingle at close quarters with townsmen), numerous dialectal terms become part of the common stock and some few of them pass into formal speech and into the language of literature, whether prose or poetry. 'Burn's *croon* was . . . a dialect term, but it almost immediately commended itself to the poets, and is now in good use' (Greenough & Kittredge, 1902). [Radio *crooners* in America have brought the word into disrepute.]

More fully than slang, much more fully and accurately than that hardly definable region of informal speech which we call 'colloquial and familiar', dialect has been charted and mapped. In 'Popular Speech' (see his *Words and Idioms*), Dr Logan Pearsall Smith has written:— 'Of all the various forms of non-literary English, the local dialects* have been most carefully documented and studied; glossaries of all, and grammars of some of them, have been published, and the material in these has been put together, with that collected by the Dialect So-

ciety, in . . . Dr [Joseph] Wright's immense *Dialect Dictionary*, which is . . . a work for the lover of words of inexhaustible fascination, enabling him as it does, to explore at ease the wild regions of English which lie around the streets and suburbs of our polite vernacular.'

Dialect has already contributed to Standard English and to colloquialisms, as we have seen: what we should like to see is a larger, more effectual contribution, for many effetenesses of Standard English would profitably be displaced by the picturesque and pithy words and phrases of much dialect. Those writers who deplore the outworn and senile-senseless character of many Standard English words and phrases and metaphors, would be better employed in rejuvenating the literary (and indeed the normal cultured) language by substituting dialectal freshness, force, pithiness, for Standard exhaustion, feebleness, long-windedness than in attempting to rejuvenate it with Gallicisms, Germanicisms, Grecisms, and Latinisms: and this holds for American Standard hardly less than for English Standard. There is, in English dialects and in American dialects,* a 'wealth of expressive words . . . , seemingly crude because of their unfamiliarity . . . , which have not been admitted to standard literary use' (G. H. McKnight): a fact that has been borne in on me with particular vividness in the last two or three years by the objectivity, the immediacy, the direct and simple force, and the correspondence of sound to sense that characterize the dialect in Eden Phillpotts's and Paul Horgan's novels.

It is to be hoped that dialect-speakers will not be shamed out of their words, phrases, and pronunciations by 'cultured' visitors, by near-visioned teachers, by B.B.C. 'experts'. The influence of 'education' is already visible in the weakening of the local pronunciations of *Cirencester* (*Sissiter*), *Bodiam* (*Bodjum*), *Daventry* (*Danetree*), *Yealm* (*Yam*): it is time that the curb and snaffle of good sense should put a check to the nefarious teachings of the unimaginatively genteel. Country people are too modest. They must sturdily resist the insidious ap-

---

* On dialect in general, there is an excellent account at pp. 1–16 of H. C. K. Wyld's *History of Modern Colloquial English*.

* The New England sections of the *Dialect Atlas of the United States and Canada* have recently been published. It is noteworthy that the American dialects are not so distinct as the British.

proaches of their 'betters'. They should boldly preserve the traditional pronunciations.

dialectal and **dialectical** are often confused; the former refers to *dialect*, the second to *dialectics* (the art of argument).

dialogue, duologue, monologue; conversation. In their speech senses, *dialogue* is a conversation (between two or more persons), a colloquy, a talk together; *duologue* is a conversation (esp. in a dramatic piece) between two persons; *monologue* is not a *soliloquy* (spoken by a person when he is alone), but a speech (or harangue) delivered by one person when he is with others. *Conversation* is rather more dignified than *talk*, but it cannot be used, as *talk* is, for an informal address or short, familiar speech or discourse. [[In American usage, monologue is often a synonym of soliloquy.]]

dicta, '(noteworthy) sayings', is the plural of L. *dictum* and therefore it must not be used as a singular as in '"After all, speed is everything in our game!" With which dicta "Freddie the Fly" agreed. "Yes", he said, "it's all fast work"' (John G. Brandon, *The Regent Street Raid*).

didn't ought. See OUGHT, DIDN'T . . .

dietician (or **dietitian**) is now much more common than the original *dietist*; *dietetic* is the adjective corresponding to *diet*, and *dietetics* is 'that part of medicine which relates to the regulation of diet' (*The O.E.D.*).

differ from; differ with. To *differ from* is 'to be not the same as; to hold an opinion different from that of another person', as in 'Milk differs from water', 'I differ from you in that matter'; the second sense ('to be at variance') may also be construed with *with* ('I differed with him in that matter'). (*The O.E.D.*)

different is incorrectly followed by singular instead of plural in the following (from *Swift or the egotist*, M. M. Rossi and J. M. Hone, 1934), 'Temple's basic mistake lay in failing to realise that the question had a completely different nature in France and in England', which should read 'had . . . different natures', or, more cumbrously, 'had a . . . different nature in France from that which it had in England'.

different should not be used for *several* or *various*, as in 'Different actors performed for the occasion'; nor unnecessarily, as in 'Three different statesmen came to dinner'.

different to; different than. See THAN, DIFFERENT.

differently than is incorrect for *otherwise than*, as in 'I felt about it differently than I had ever felt about it before', Frank Tilsley, *I'd Hate to Be Dead*, 1938.

DIFFUSENESS. See TAUTOLOGY.

dig; past tense and past participle, *digged* or, now usually, *dug*.

digraph. See DIPHTHONGS.

dilemma, as 'a choice between more than two things or decisions' hence 'a predicament or "fix"', is loose English.

dine is more formal—but also more economical—than *have dinner*.

dinner Parisienne, from a bill of fare in an Italian restaurant in Soho is doubly wrong, (a) in confusion of two languages, (b) in feminine gender of adjective. 'Parisian dinner' would be English; 'dîner parisien', French.

dint. See DENT.

dipthong is incorrect for *diphthong*; **diptheria** for *diphtheria*. [[*Webster's* lists *dipthong* as a variant of *diphthong*. The dissimilation whereby *-fth* becomes *-pth* in *diphthong* and *diphtheria* is very common in American speech. The spelling and the learned character of the words restrain but do not extirpate the tendency to dissimilate. In turn, the popular pronunciation creates a popular though erroneous spelling.]]

DIPHTHONGS. A diphthong is 'a union of two vowels pronounced in one syllable' (as in *out, boil, boy*). The term is 'often applied to a combination of two vowel characters, more properly called a *digraph*. When the two characters represent a simple sound, as *ea, ou*, in *head* (hed), *soup* (sup), they have been termed an *improper diphthong*: properly speaking, these are *monophthongs* [single vowel sounds] written by *digraphs*.—In popular use, [diphthong is] applied to the ligatures *æ, œ*, of the Latin alphabet. As pronounced . . . in modern use, these are no longer diphthongs, but monophthongs; the O.E. ligatures *æ* and *œ* always represented monophthongs.' (*The O.E.D.*)

dipsomania. See INEBRIETY.

direction, misused for *quarter*. '"It's our duty to act". "Oh, very well", said West wearily. "I'll mention the matter in the right direction and see what can be done about it"', John Bude, *The Cheltenham Square Murder*, 1937.

directly for *directly that* or *directly when*, i.e., for *immediately when*, is a colloquialism, as in 'The book was suppressed directly it appeared'. (*The O.E.D.*)

disagree from is incorrect for *disagree with*; or at least, *disagree from* is obsolete.

disassemble is to break up an assembly, or to take (esp. a machine) apart; *dissemble* is to hide one's feelings or purpose.

disassociate. See DISSOCIATE.

disaster is a grave word: do not use it lightly. No more than *tragedy* is it to be made a synonym of a mere *misfortune*.

disbeliever is active, positive; *unbeliever* is neutral. 'He attacks *dis*believers, but has very little to say to mere *un*believers' (Whewell). (*The O.E.D.*)

disc is a mere variant of *disk*, 'the earlier and better spelling' (*The O.E.D.*). (Zoology and, in some senses, Botany employ the spelling 'disc'.)

discern. See DESCRY.

disclose (v.t.) is 'to reveal, declare'; *expose* is 'to unmask' or 'to place in a dangerous situation'.

discomfit; discomfort (v.). The latter is 'to make uncomfortable physically or uneasy mentally'; *discomfit* is both stronger and more general, for it = 'to defeat; to rout', 'to thwart, to foil'; 'to throw into dejection, perplexity, confusion; to disconcert'. The noun is *discomfort*, but only in the senses, 'lack of physical comfort', 'uneasiness whether physical or mental', and 'a hardship'. Its adjective is *discomfortable*. (*The O.E.D.*)

discountenance is misused for *discount* or *counterbalance* by F. R. Burrow, *The Centre Court*, 1937, in 'Barrett and Dixon kept their title. The challengers were Rahé and Kleinschroth; but the English pair discountenanced all the Continental brilliance by adopting safety tactics throughout, and won by three sets to one.' The true sense of *discountenance* is 'to show disapprobation of, to disfavour, a person or action'.

discourteous (noun: *discourtesy*) is 'rude', therefore stronger than *uncourteous* (noun: *uncourteousness*), 'wanting in courtesy'. Cf. the difference between *disbeliever* and *unbeliever*.

discover is archaic in the sense 'to reveal, make known'. Its prevailing current sense is 'to find out' (something already there). Cf. DISCLOSE, *q.v.*, and

UNCOVER, 'to remove the cover of'. And contrast INVENT, 'to originate or devise'.

discreet and **discrete.** The former is applied to sage or, at the least, prudent persons and circumspect behaviour; the latter is rare except among the philosophic-minded and those who possess a knowledge of logic, and it means 'individually distinct', 'belonging to or consisting of distinct or individual parts', 'discontinuous'. It is a learned term, to be used with caution. The negatives are formed with *in*.

disenfranchise is inferior to *disfranchise*.

DISGUISED CONJUNCTIONS. See CONJUNCTIONS, DISGUISED.

DISGUISED PREPOSITIONS. These are *during, pending,* and *notwithstanding,* as in 'during the week', 'pending these operations', 'notwithstanding his speeches'. For an excellent account, see Onions, *An Advanced English Syntax,* p. 69, or Curme, *Syntax,* pp. 562–66.

disillusionize. Now pedantic for 'to *disillusion*'.

disinterested is incorrectly used for *uninterested* or *not interested*; its meaning is 'impartial; not studying one's own advantage'. I have seen it used also for *apathetic* (—a usage given by *Webster's*).

disk. See DISC.

dislike to is incorrect for *dislike of*. 'It may be just a dislike to getting mixed up in such things', E. R. Punshon, *The Dusky Hour*, 1937. [[In American English, *dislike for* is probably more common than *dislike of*.]]

dislogistic is incorrect for *dyslogistic*, (of speech, words) unfavourable, opprobrious; *dyslogistic* is the opposite of *eulogistic*, as *dyslogism* is the opposite of *euphemism*.

dispatch and **despatch** (n. and v.). '*Dispatch* is to be preferred, as at once historical, and in accordance with English analogy' (*The O.E.D.*).

dispense with is erroneously used for *dispose of*. 'The moment he had dispensed with all the formalities . . ., he was not long in starting', writes an able young novelist in 1935.

displace. See REPLACE.

dispose and **depose** are ignorantly confused.

dissemble. See DISASSEMBLE.

dissimulate and **simulate.** One *dissimulates*—pretends not to have or be—that which one has or is; one *simulates*—pretends to have or be—that which one has not or is not. 'He dissimulated his cowardice, envy, suspicion, etc.'; 'He simulated drunkenness, interest, disinterest, etc.'

dissociate is now preferred to *disassociate*, no matter what the context.

distinctive is often misused for *distinct* and *distinguished*. *Distinguished*, 'now almost always of persons', = 'remarkable, eminent, of high standing, famous'. *Distinctive* = 'characteristic; distinguishing'; it is very rare in the sense 'distinct'. *Distinct* = 'separate' ('Absolute as distinct from relative knowledge'); 'individual' (not identical); 'different in quality or kind' ('A distinct species of composition'); 'individually peculiar'; 'clear, plain, definite' (to the senses or to the mind); 'unmistakable, pronounced, positive, decided' ('A distinct change').

distract. See DETRACT.

diurnal. See DAILY.

divers and **diverse**, originally the same word and still frequently confused, now mean, (the former) *several* or *a certain number of*, (the latter) *of different natures or aspects*.

divolve for *devolve* is an infrequent error. But it merits inclusion, because it is committed by persons of some education.

divorcee is generic English for French *divorcé* (a divorced man) and *divorcée* (a divorced woman). But the distinction in the French terms is not to be lightly dismissed in deference to the snortings of Gallophobes. To use *divorcée* of a man is, however, indefensible. Based on *The O.E.D.*

do. As a makeshift, the verb *do* is colloquial rather than literary, except where it is obviously the best word to use. But be sure to put it in the same tense as the verb it represents. Obvious? Maybe! Yet I have seen and heard instances of the wrong tense. The present tense can be represented only by *do*; the progressive present by *am, is, are doing*, not by *do*; the preterite (simple past), only by *did*; the progressive past (or imperfect) by *was* or *were doing*, not by *did*, as in C. McCabe, *The Face on the Cutting-Room Floor*, 1937, 'Another company was making almost the same triangle story as you did'—properly, 'as you *were* [*making*, or *doing*]'; the simple future, by *shall* (or *will*) *do*; the progressive future by *shall* (or *will*) *be doing*.

The same applies to the perfect tenses (whether present, past, or future).

dock is not to be synonymized with *pier* or *wharf*.

doctress is to be used only where sex is heavily (or humorously) emphasized; but even then—except when facetiousness is intended—*woman doctor* (or *lady doctor*) is preferred. (*The O.E.D.*)

domicile is in place as a legal term and as = 'the dwelling-place of an animal': otherwise, it is an affectation or, at best, an elegancy.

dominated with is incorrect in such a sentence as, 'They were enthusiasts dominated with one idea, but domination by one idea is often, if not usually, the equivalent of monomania', *Church Times*, 1899, quoted by Nesfield, who points out that 'domination by' in the second clause is correct, since 'idea' is here the agent which dominates.

dominating, misused for *predominant*. The former = 'masterful'; the latter, 'principal' or 'outstanding'. Distinguish also *dominating* from *domineering* ('bullying', 'actively arrogant').

DOMINIONS, ENGLISH. See STANDARD ENGLISH, Section iv.

domino (cloak and mask; a piece in the game) has plural *dominoes*; Weseen's differentiation of plural is baseless.

done with, be for *have done with*. See AM FINISHED.

don't is now a solecism for *doesn't, does not.*

double entendre for *double entente* is a frequent curiosity, presented—e.g., by Robert G. Dean in *The Sutton Place Murders*, 1936. The French phrase is *d. entente*; the French language knowing not *d. entendre*—a figment of the English imagination.

DOUBLE GENITIVE. See 'OF HER—OF HERS' and GENITIVE, VAGARIES OF THE.

DOUBLE NEGATIVE. See NEGATION, Section *C*.

DOUBLE SINGULAR. This device is at its most obvious in the hyphenated form, e.g., 'The you-and-I that forms the dominant chord in youthful love is not wholly selfish'. The less obvious, though more general form is that which sets two disparate things (or actions) in a combination, as in 'The din and smell was overpowering'. Apparently a modification of the latter is 'The coming and going of passengers is variable'; but actually it is a mere typographical variant of the former, because one might equally well write 'the coming-and-going' (cf. the French *le va-et-vient*). Occasionally we find the double singular either misused or, at best, confused, as in 'The heat and the jam'—i.e., crowd—'was so oppressive that Iris was actually glad to reach her own compartment' (Ethel Lina White, *The Wheel Spins*, 1936).

doubt (if, that, whether, etc.). *Doubt*, verb, may be transitive or intransitive; no difficulty arises in its transitive use ('I doubt the man's honesty'), though J. R. Green, 1874, writes 'who never doubted of the final triumph of freedom and law', in which 'of' is unnecessary. In its intransitive use, the sentence following 'doubt' begins with a conjunction, which in nearly every case should be *that* or *whether*, in spite of the employment by many writers of *if*, *but*, *but that*, and even (in the 16th Century) of *at* and *lest*. In the two following examples *that* would be better than *but* and *but that*: Steele, 1711, 'I do not doubt but England is at present as polite a nation as any in the world'; W. Selwyn, 1817, 'It never was doubted but that one partner might bind the rest'. It is, however, to be noted that in negative and interrogative sentences, doubt 'may take *but that* or (simply) *but*, with the same meaning as the ordinary *that*:

I do not doubt *but that you are surprised*.

Who doubted *but* [or *but that*] the catastrophe *was over?*',

as Dr Onions writes in *An Advanced English Syntax* (6th ed., 1932). But the following sentence in Crosbie Garstin's *The Owl's House*, 1923, 'Had not Carveth goods enough in this world but that he must have Tregors' as well', is an illicit extension of the *doubt but that* sentence-type: 'but that he must have' should be changed to 'without his having'. In the two following, *whether* would be more correct than *that* and *if*: Bayard Taylor, 1871, 'Schiller doubted that a poetic measure would be formed capable of holding Goethe's plan'; *The Law Times*, 1891, 'The master doubted if all remedies were not barred'.—Hawthorne, 1858, 'I doubt whether English cookery is not better', is correct. Some ambiguity arises when 'doubt' is used in the sense of *suspect* or *fear* (*that*). Trollope's (1879) 'I doubt that Thackeray did not write

the Latin epitaph', and Shelley's (1820) 'I doubt that they will not contain the latest news', would have been more clearly expressed, 'I doubt whether Thackeray wrote—' and 'I doubt whether they will contain—'. Pepys's (1665) 'Doubting that all will break in pieces in the kingdom' is an expression not of dubiety but of fear. (The above examples are from *The O.E.D.*) [[American textbooks note that *doubt* (v.) is followed by *that* when there is little or no doubt, and by *whether* (formal usage) or *if* (informal usage) when there is uncertainty. In a sentence such as 'I doubt *whether* he will come or not', *if* would be loose and incorrect, because of the presence of *or not*.]]

doubtless being both an adjective and an adverb, the adverb *doubtlessly* is unnecessary.

dove for *dived* (past tense) is dialectal in Great Britain, colloquial in America.

dower and **dowry** should be kept distinct. *Dower* is that 'portion of a deceased husband's estate which the law allows to his widow for her life'; avoid it both in the legal sense of *dowry* ('that money or property which the wife brings her husband') and in the derivative sense of *dowry* ('gift or talent bestowed by nature or by fortune'). (*The O.E.D.*)

downward is adjective and adverb; *downwards* is adverb only, exactly synonymous with *downward*: euphony is the criterion.

Dr, I believe, is preferable to *Dr.*; if you wish to be pedantic, you will write 'D'r': but who does so write it?

draft is in America preferred to *draught*, whether noun, verb, or adjective; in Great Britain, *draught* is preferred for a plan or sketch (hence *draughtsman*), a ship's displacement, a draught horse, and other senses. See esp. *The O.E.D.* [[*Webster's*, q.v., cites six senses in which *draught* is more usual than *draft*.]]

drama. Do not use this powerful word in trivial contexts, as in 'Drama in the monkey's compound'.

dramatic for *drastic*. L. Seccombe, broadcasting on Jan. 19, 1937, 'Lynch will have to do something dramatic in the last round if he is to win the fight.' To lose it might have been equally 'dramatic'.

DRAMATIC IRONY. See IRONY, fourth paragraph.

drank is the past tense; **drunk** the past participle, of *drink*.

drastic means 'vigorous', 'vigorously effective', 'violent', (of a medicine) 'acting strongly', or (of a person) 'acting severely'; it is incorrect to speak of 'a drastic result'.

dream, as an adjective, is journalese; e.g., 'his dream girl', 'my dream home'. (With acknowledgements to an address given by Mr Frank Whitaker on Dec. 13, 1938.)

drinker. See TOPER.

drop out for *omit* or *exclude* or *ignore* is feeble; in fact, it's so feeble that it drops into the catachrestic mire, as the following example from Stuart Chase's *The Tyranny of Words*, 1938, may help to show:—'Marx went off the deep end by making this verifiable *tendency* into an *absolute*. He *dropped out* many characteristics—as moralists *drop* them in the case of the "bad" girl.'

drunk (v.). See DRANK.

drunk (adj.); **drunken.** The former is predicative ('The man is drunk'); the latter, attributive ('The drunken man'). *Drunken*, however, is preferred in the nuance 'given to drink, habitually drunk', whereas 'drunk on a given occasion' is *intoxicated*. A person habitually drunk is a *drunkard*; one ungovernably given to drink is a *dipsomaniac* (the same form as the adjective).—See also TOPER.

due to rings false in such a sentence as this: 'Their masts, due to the sloping effect given by the after legs of the tripod, always looked from a distance to be falling in towards each other' ('Taffrail', *The Sub*, 1917, of a battleship). We have the authority of *The Con. O. D.* for saying that 'the adverbial use for *owing*, as *I came late due to an accident*, is incorrect'. *Owing to*, used absolutely, like *considering*, is equivalent, by usage to a preposition; *due to* is not acceptable —and it may easily lead to ambiguity. [[For another opinion, founded upon numerous and impressive quotations, see J. S. Kenyon's article on *due to* in *American Speech*, vol. 6 (1930), pp. 61–70; also Perrin, pp. 221–22.]]

duologue. See DIALOGUE.

DUPLICATED POSSESSIVE. See POSSESSIVE, DUPLICATED.

Dutch must not be used for *German*, nor *Dutchman* for *a German*.

dyeing from to *dye*; **dying** from to *die*.

dynamic, misused for *tense*. 'He was cognizant of the state of affairs behind [the stage], and these were so dynamic, that it seemed an explosion might occur at any moment', W. H. Lane Crauford, *Murder to Music*, 1936.

E

e, intrusive, as in *musheroom, umberella, atheletic*; examples of the habit, frequent among the illiterate, of introducing a vowel sound to ease their way among the clotted consonants. [Compare *ellum* and *fillum* for *elm* and *film*.]

-e- for *æ* or *œ* (*oe* or *ae*) is becoming fairly general. In *eternal* and *coeval* (in early Modern English, *æternal* and *cœval*), *e* is the rule; *medieval* is now the usual—the fully anglicized—form of the formerly (even in the 19th Century) general *mediaeval* (or, before the 19th Century, *mediæval*). The *æ* form is now rare; still rarer is *œ*. In scientific and technical terms, however, *ae* is retained, as in *palaeontology*, although *archeology* is fast gaining ground at the expense of *archaeology*. When the English word comes from Greek (as *palaeontology* does) the *ae* represents Greek *ai*—though this is as true of *archaeology* as of *palaeontology*. But whether the origin is Greek *ai* or Latin *ae* (or *œ*), the pronunciation of the English *œ* or *ae* or *e* is always *ee*: hence the general trend towards the spelling in *e*.

each as a plural. John Farmer, in Forewords to *Musa Pedestris*, 1896, says, in speaking of slang and cant: 'One thing, indeed, both have in common, each are derived from a correct normal use of language.' 'Both' *are* and *have* but 'each' *is* and *has*. Mr James Agate, giving in *The Sunday Times*, Nov. 23, 1937, a recipe for the production of *The School for Scandal*, says: 'You find out when the play was written, build one room each in the houses of Lady Teazle, Sir Peter Teazle, Charles Surface, etc.' One room in each house,—but the sentence must be recast. Mr Wilfrid Whitten, in *Good and Bad English*, p. 70, justifies the plural verb in the sentence, 'Brown, Jones and Robinson each have their plans', on the ground that the writer 'refers to B., J. and R. as being of one mind'. With due respect to Mr Whitten, is it clear that the plans of the trio are not separate and different plans? Is it not clear that *each has his own plan*? [[Professors Krapp and Perrin, and general American practice, agree with Mr Whitten.]]

each, between. 'The crack way of running over hurdles, in which just three strides are taken mechanically between each hurdle' is loose. *And the next,* following *hurdle,* is required.

each and **every** are constantly used with a plural pronoun in spite of the obvious inaccuracy; famous writers are guilty of this error, as in the following examples cited by Nesfield (*Errors in English Composition,* 1903). 'Each of them was busy in arranging their particular concerns' (Jane Austen).—'Everyone must judge of their own feelings' (Byron).—'Let each esteem other better than themselves' (*Phil.,* ii, 3).

Usually *each* or *every* can be changed to *all* or *both* without injuring the sense.

each other. 'We know what each other are doing' is cited by Henry Bradley, as instance of wrong use as a nominative; it also illustrates the confusion of singular and plural so often caused by the word 'each'. 'We know each what the other is doing', is correct but stilted; 'Each of us knows what the other is doing' overcomes all difficulties.

each other and **one another.** 'Even the atmospheres of Italy and Spain are quite distinct from one another—or from each other; I leave this point for grammarians to decide; it leaves your humble preface-writer gravelled', R. B. Cunninghame Graham, Introduction to Wilfranc Hubbard, *Orvieto Dust,* 1925.

There is a rule,—a very simple rule:— *each other* applies to two persons, animals, or things; *one another* to three or more. This constitutes, not a mere grammarians' *ex cathedra* but a practical utility; for instance, if the rule is observed, one can be in no doubt that 'They hit each other' refers to two persons, whereas 'They hit one another' refers to three or more. Obviously, to follow the rule is to ensure economy of words.

It is odd to find so fine a writer as Paul Horgan saying, 'The train and the town were moving towards one another; the train, across distance; the town, across time' (*A Lamp on the Plains,* English ed., 1937). [[*Webster's*: 'Some have sought to restrict *each other* to two, as opp. to *one another,* but the distinction is disregarded by writers.']]

each other's, misused for *each other.* '"We're both biassed . . . but perhaps your bias and mine will correct each other's"'—i.e., 'will correct each other' or, better, 'will cancel each other'. (E. R. Lorac, *Death of an Author,* 1935.)

each, them, and **they each; we each** and **us each; you each.** Here, the case of *each* is parallel to that of *both* in *they* (or *them*) *both, we* (or *us*) *both,* and *you both.*

'They each did something' should be 'Each of them did something'; 'You hit them each' should be 'You hit each of them' (or, better, 'both of them' if it's two,—'all of them', if it's more than two). *We each* and *us each* should be *each of us*: thus 'We each ate too much' should be 'Each of us ate too much'; and 'The bullet frightened us each' should be '. . . frightened each of us' (but why not 'the bullet frightened both of us' or '. . . all of us'?).

You each (whether nominative or accusative) should be *each of you.* Thus, 'You each knew your lessons' should be 'Each of you knew your lessons' or, more clearly, 'Both of you'—or 'all of you'—'knew your lessons'; 'I taught you each' should be 'I taught each of you' (or, to make it clearer, 'both of you' or 'all of you').

Heaven knows why the late Professor George O. Curme should have permitted himself the following laxity: 'In the case of *each* we may say: "She kissed *them each*" (or *each of them*)': and I gravely doubt the Professor's saying it himself.

early date, at an. If it = 'soon', use *soon;* otherwise it is too vague to be useful.

earth; globe; world. *The O.E.D.* defines the relevant senses thus: *Earth,* 'the world on which we dwell' (land and/or sea), hence 'the present abode of man' (often contrasted with heaven or hell).

Globe, a synonym for *earth* (first sense); also, 'One of the planetary or celestial bodies', the earth being itself a planet.

World, 'the earth', also 'the universe or a part of it'; *the world's end* (generic), 'the farthest limit of the earth'. A *world* is also 'a planet or other heavenly body, esp. one viewed as inhabited'.

earthly is opposed to 'heavenly'; **earthy** is 'of earth or soil; like earth', and it is used in *of the earth, earthy* for 'frail, human'.

easier or **more easy,** adjective; **more easily,** adverb. Hence, *easier* is not an adverb, although it is permissible in American speech.

easterly and **eastern**. In current use, *easterly* is used mostly of winds, *eastern* being the general adjective; *easterly*, however, is not incorrect in the sense 'situated towards the east'. (*The O.E.D.*)

eastern (or **E.**) and **oriental** (or **O.**). See 'ORIENTAL and EASTERN'.

eat has, in the past tense, either *ate* or *eat*; both are correct, but the pronunciation of the past *eat* is *ĕt*.

eatable; edible. Whether as noun or as adjective, these two words are correct; they are synonymous, but *edible* is the more formal, esp. as the noun. As nouns, they are mostly used in the plural.

ebriety (obsolescent) is 'drunkenness'; **inebriety** (*q.v.*) is 'habitual drunkenness'.

echoism and **onomatopœia; echoic** and **onomatopœic; echo-words** and **echoic-words.** *Onomatopœia* is the old name (still used by some grammarians) for 'the formation of names or words from sounds associated with the object or action to be named, or that seem naturally suggestive of its qualities' (*The Con. O.D.*); Jespersen, the great Danish philologist and grammarian, proposes *echoism* for this formation. Collectively, such words are now called *echo-words* (or *echoic words*), a better term than *onomatopœia*, or *onomatopœic words* (*onomatopœia* means, literally, 'word-making'). *Echoism* is preferable to *onomatopœia*, but rings a trifle pedantically; diffidently I propose to substitute *word-echo* (or *word-echoing*). And naturally one says, 'That word is echoic', whereas one may say either '*Cuckoo* is an echoic word' or 'It is an echo-word'.

eclectic is occasionally misused, perhaps more frequently misunderstood, in the sense of *fastidious in choice of the best*, but has the opposite meaning (*The Con. O.D.*), 'borrowing freely from various sources, *not exclusive* in opinion, taste, etc.'

economic corresponds to Political Economy, as in 'the economic factor'; *economical* is 'thrifty' or, of a thing, 'inexpensive'. See also '-IC and -ICAL'.

ecstacy, a frequent misspelling of *ecstasy.*

-ection and **-exion.** In the nouns: *connection, connexion; deflection, -exion; inflection, -exion; reflection, -exion*: the etymological spelling, (with *x*), is preferred by *The O.E.D.*, which, however,

allows that *reflection* is much commoner than *reflexion* in non-scientific terms, and implies that the same holds for *deflection* and *inflection*. The earliest spellings in English are in the *x* mode.

In non-scientific, non-technical senses, then, the *ct* form is the more usual but the less logical; *connexion*, however, is fast becoming predominant in all senses. [[In American usage, *connexion, reflexion*, etc. are rare.]]

-ed, termination of past participle. On the pronunciation of this we may quote *The O.E.D.*: 'The pronunciation *-èd* regularly occurs in ordinary speech only in the endings *-ted, -ded*; but it is frequently required by the metre of verse, and is still often used in the public reading of the Bible and the Liturgy. A few words such as *blessèd, cursèd*, [*accursèd*], *belovèd*, which are familiar chiefly in religious use, have escaped the general tendency to contraction when used as adjectives; and the adjectival use of *learnèd* is distinguished by its pronunciation from its use as simple participle (*learn'd*).'

edible. See EATABLE.

edifice = 'a building, a structure' or, derivatively, 'a large and/or imposing building'. Do not, for the love of architecture, call a *house* an edifice.

edition; impression; reprint; state. A book in its first printing is inevitably an edition; but it may—as also may any later edition—have two or several *states*. For instance, if after a certain number of copies have been machined, a correction or a change is made, or even if a different paper is used, the copies containing the change or correction or the different paper comprise a later (second, third . . .) *state*, the original being the *first state*. When an edition is reprinted without correction, the resulting copies form an *impression*: an edition may have one, two or more impressions. The first uncorrected reprint of the first edition is the *second* impression of the book; the second uncorrected reprint thereof, is the *third* impression. But the several uncorrected impressions of the second or any later edition are numbered anew: *2nd edition, 1st impression; 2nd edition, 2nd impression;* and so on. The term *reprint* is sometimes used loosely for an impression; so too is *reprinting*, which properly applies to the process, not to the result. Nowadays, *reprint* is generally reserved for a new edition (or a new impression) brought out some or many years after the issue of the preceding edition or impression, especially if the type has to be reset or the photographic process employed.

editress. Avoid unless there is an all-compelling reason for its being used.

educational; educative; eductive. The first is the general adjective corresponding to *education*. The second can be used in much the same way, but its specific sense is 'that has the power of educating, i.e., potentially educational; conducive to education'. The third corresponds to *eduction* and it = 'having the function of eliciting or developing', as in 'An eductive method of education'. (*The O.E.D.*)

e'er and **ere** (both pronounced *air*), constantly met with in poetry, are sometimes misunderstood. The former is a contraction of *ever*, the latter is an old word meaning *before* (as in '*ere* long').

effect, effection, effective. See AFFECT.

effective; effectual. See EFFICIENT.

effeminate is not 'womanly', but 'womanish', 'unmanly', applied to men, their character, tendencies, habits, actions.

efficiency, misused for *proficiency*; **efficient** for *proficient*. 'If an amateur, through specialising, reaches a certain state [? stage] of efficiency and becomes a professional player [of games], his motive for playing often changes with his status', examination essay script, June, 1939.

efficient, effectual, effective, and **efficacious** are often confused. The *efficient* man (capable, *knowing his job*) is *effective* in action, and his action is *effectual* in achieving its purpose. An efficient doctor prescribes only such medicines as are *efficacious*.

effort for 'any kind of achievement', 'any result of activity', is trivial and it should be used only where the jocular is permissible. 'That drawing was a particularly good effort of the child's' is trivial; 'His greatest effort was to pull a cork out of a bottle' is—presumably—jocular.

ego and **id.** In French, these conjoint terms are translated *le moi et le cela* ('the *I* and the *that*').

Ego is Latin *ego*, 'I'; in psychology, the *ego* is 'the conscious thinking subject, as opposed to the *non-ego* or object'; *id* is Latin for 'it', and in psycho-analysis, it represents 'the inherited instinctive

impulses of the individual'. These two definitions, which are those of *The O.E.D.*, serve to indicate why the two terms are so often contrasted in psychology, esp. in psycho-analysis.

egoism and **egotism.** The former is 'the habit of looking upon all questions chiefly in their relations to oneself', also, 'excessive exaltation of one's own opinion; self-opinionatedness': as in 'The egoism of man . . . can . . . read in the planets only prophecies of himself' (Robertson, 1852).

Egotism is 'too much *I* in conversation', 'the practice of talking about oneself or one's doings', as in 'the egotism of personal narrative'. Hence 'boastfulness' and 'selfishness', as in 'Without egotism, I can safely say . . .'

An egoistic man is not necessarily selfish; an egotistic one is. (*The O.E.D.*)

Eiré. See GREAT BRITAIN.

either, often incorrectly used for *any* or *any one*. 'Did you notice anything peculiar about the manner of either of these three?' Henry Holt, *Murder at the Bookstall*, 1934. 'There have been three famous talkers in Great Britain, either of whom would illustrate what I say', Holmes, *Poet at the Breakfast Table* (quoted by Nesfield).

either for *each.* Letter signed J. M. S., *The Observer*, Jan. 9, 1938:—'When I was a child at an elementary school I was taught that it was incorrect to say "There are trees on either side of the road", as "either" means on one side or the other, but not both. Yet I find nearly all novelists, a famous thriller writer, and the daily Press making this mistake.' Cf. 'They never spoke about it: Edward would not, and she could not; but either knew what was in the other's thoughts' (Guy Pocock, *Somebody Must*, 1931).

either or **either of,** (*neither* or *neither of*) + n. with a pl. v.: these are incorrect; e.g. 'This was not to say that during those wearing days either of them were idle', Freeman Wills Crofts, *Mystery on Southampton Water*, 1934. A similar error is made with *either . . . or*; e.g., 'Religious rites by which either Thebes or Eleusis were afterwards distinguished', Thirlwall, 1833, quoted by *The O.E.D.*—'Both poets are on the verge of mystical vision; neither actually seem to express it', Charles Williams, *Introduction to Poems of G. M. Hopkins*, 1930. Dean Alford, one of our best authorities (*The*

Queen's English, 1870), himself commits this error, when he speaks of 'the requirements of parenthesis, neither of which are taken into account in the ordinary rule'. [[When the whole thought has a plural character, such sentences 'have a natural if not a correct grammatical ring'. (Krapp.)]]

either . . . nor for **either . . . or** is, one might say, the fantastic dream of a fanatical heresy-hunter: and yet it occurs, not rarely but—if one allows for the enormity of the error—fairly often. Mr Philip MacDonald is not in the habit of doing this sort of thing; sometimes, however, the excitement of his stories carries him away (he has an excellent excuse), and he falls into an example of the pilloried error: 'Its small and neat exterior gives to the unsuspecting client who tries it for the first time no indication either of the excellence of Mons. Laplanche's food, wines and cooking, nor of the preposterous charges made by Monsieur Laplanche' (*The Rynox Mystery*, 1930).

either of their sakes. See GENITIVE, VAGARIES OF THE, penultimate paragraph.

either . . . or, misused for *both . . . and.* 'Until then, I must ask you to preserve an open mind in your opinions, either of me or of what happened last night', Seamark, *The Man They Couldn't Arrest*, 1927.

either . . . or, wrongly positioned. This is a frequent error. The only rule is that the division must be made with logical precision.

eke. Cowper, in *John Gilpin*, has 'and eke with all his might'. Some other child may be puzzled as I was by knowing the verb *to eke out* and being ignorant of the old adverb *eke*, meaning 'also'.

elapse and **lapse** (vv.). Time *elapses* or slips away, passes, expires; *lapse* is (of men) 'to err', (of things) 'to fail, fall into disuse, become invalid', as when a life-policy lapses because the insurance premiums have not been paid. [For all senses, the usual noun is *lapse*, *elapse* being obsolete or rare.]

elder and **older.** The former is used only in family relationships or in reference to two specified persons: 'the elder brother', 'the elder partner'; in the sense—'pertaining to an earlier period, or to ancient times' ('A writer in the elder, more formal style'), it is obsolescent. *Older* is 'of greater age', 'longer

established', as in 'an older custom', 'He looks much older'. (*The O.E.D.*)

electric; electrical. The former is now much the commoner. *Electrical* = 'connected with, dealing with electricity', as in 'There are very few electrical books in that library'; also *an electrical machine*. (*The O.E.D.*) Figuratively, *electric* is now obligatory.

ELEGANCIES. Here is a short list of those words and phrases which the semi-literate and far too many of the literate believe to be more elegant than the terms they displace. Some are genteel; some euphemistic; some plain catachrestic. If in doubt, consult also ARCHAISMS and LITERARISMS.

ablutions, perform one's
abode (home)
al fresco
albeit (also an archaism)
anent
anno domini (age; old age)
anon
aroma
assemblage (collection; assortment)
assignation
at this juncture
au courant and *au fait*
bairn (except in Scotland)
bard
beauteous (except in poetry)
boon (noun)
bosom
broidered
cachet (figuratively)
can but (can only)
charger (any horse)
charlady
City fathers
collation
connubial rites
consume (to eat)
converse (as exactly synonymous with talk, v.i.)
corpulent
countenance (n.)
crave (to beg; to ask)
cull (v.)
Cupid
damsel (except in verse or jocularity)
deboshed
deem
demise
denizen
develop (v.i. = to happen)
devotions, at one's
distrait(e)
divers (several, sundry)

divulge

dolorous (permissible in poetry and lofty prose)

domicile (noun, non-legally, non-scientifically)

éclat

effluvium (smell); *effluvia* (scents)

elegant sufficiency, an

emanate (incorrectly used)

emolument

employ of, in the

emporium (shop)

epistle (any letter)

ere (also an archaism)

espousal

evince

expectorate

fain (also an archaism)

festive board, the (also a cliché)

floral tribute(s)

fraught

function (noun; used trivially)

garb (n.), *garbed*

garments

genus homo

goodly

gratis

habiliments

helpmeet

histrionic art

Hymen (marriage, wedding)

imbibe

impecunious

implement (verb)

individual

instanter

interred; interment

Jehu (a coachman)

Jupiter Pluvius

lapsus calami

Leo (a lion)

liaison

libation (any potation)

liquid refreshment

lonely couch

luminary (e.g.; a legal luminary)

magnum opus

menial (a servant)

mentor

mine host

misalliance

modicum

monarch

(to) *moot*

my Lady Nicotine

myrmidons

natal day

neophyte

non compos mentis

nuptials; nuptial couch

obsequies

of late (recently)

orb (sun, moon)

orient (or *O.*) *pearl*

ozone

panegyric (of any praise however trivial)

partake of (to eat)

paterfamilias

patronize (shop at; go to, visit)

peruse (to read)

petite

plight one's troth

post-prandial

posterior (backside) and *posteriors* (buttocks)

prevaricate

purloin

raiment

redolent

remuneration

repast

repose (n. and v. in the senses: rest; sleep)

reside at

retire (go to bed)

Sabbath, the (as used by Gentiles as merely Sunday)

sanctum (a study, a 'den')

satellite (a follower)

save (preposition; also an archaism)

soirée

sotto voce

spirituelle

spouse

steed

strand (shore)

sumptuous repast

swain

swoon (n. and v.)

tender one's apologies, condolences, congratulations, etc.

terra firma

Thespian

thrice (except in poetry or lofty prose)

tiro (or *tyro*)

to the full (e.g., appreciate to the full)

transpire (to happen)

truly (as in 'truly great')

tryst (also an archaism)

twain (also an archaism)

umbrage (offence)

verily

veritable

verve

very (*heart-strings, life,* etc.)

viands (food)

victuals

visage

weal (also an archaism)

welkin

well nigh

wend one's way
withal
wont (custom; habit)
Yuletide (also an archaism)

elegant is not good English (nor yet good American) as a synonym for 'excellent' ('an elegant party') or 'first-rate' ('an elegant lawn-tennis player').

elemental, elementary. The former = 'of, connected with, like one or more of the four "elements" (earth, air, fire, water)'; 'pertaining to the powers, forces, agencies of the physical world', as in 'elemental gods or spirits', 'elemental religion', or 'like those powers' ('elemental grandeur'); 'of the nature of an ultimate constituent of physical substances' ('the elemental operations of Nature—of thought—of passion'); hence, 'constituent', as in 'elemental ingredients'.

Elementary has a technical sense in chemistry; in general usage, its prevailing sense is 'rudimentary', as in 'an elementary book' or one that deals (simply) with first principles, 'elementary school' (one in which primary instruction or lessons are given). (*The O.E.D.*)

elements, misused. See OFFICIALESE.

elicit and **illicit** are often confused in careless speech.

eliminate and **isolate.** Confusion seems to have arisen from the fact that to *eliminate* is to *remove* (get rid of) something from something, *isolate* is to *separate* something from other things.

elliptic is a technical term in mathematics and botany, 'of or like an ellipse'; *elliptical* is in general use for 'shaped like, or as, an ellipse', as in the pun 'A kiss is elliptical', and in grammar it means 'lacking in a word or words necessary to the complete sense', hence applied to style in which (numerous) sentences are thus defective (*The O.E.D.*).

eloquent. See at GRANDILOQUENT.

else but is still worse than the following entry.

else than is unfortunate; the sense should be rendered by *but* or *other than*. The editor himself was guilty of this error in his *The French Romantics' Knowledge of English Literature*, 1924, 'Swift was rarely [known as] anything else than the author of "Gulliver's Travels"'. Nesfield, too, in his *Errors in English Composition*, commits it by saying 'The omission [of the Relative] can

hardly be considered as anything else than a defect'.

else's. The following are correct although once they were colloquial and even now they are familiar S.E., and not full Standard:—

> *anybody* (or *anyone*) *else's*
> *everybody* (or *everyone*) *else's*
> *nobody* (or *no one*) *else's*
> *somebody* (or *someone*) *else's*
> *who* (or *whoever* or *whosoever*) *else's*.

What has happened is this: the *else* has, in essence, become incorporated with the pronoun (*anybody, someone, who,* etc.): although we do not write *anybodyelse, whoelse,* etc., yet we think of the combination as a unit. Therefore it is only *else* which takes the genitive form, *else's*.

Of the following sets, the first—regarded in England as incorrect—is acceptable in America, though only in a predicate position; the second set is wrong everywhere and in any position.

> *anybody's* (or *anyone's*) *else*
> *everybody's* (or *everyone's*) *else*
> *nobody's* (or *no one's*) *else*
> *somebody's* (or *someone's*) *else*
> *whose* (or *whosever* or *whosoever*) *else*.

> *anybody's* (or *anyone's*) *else's*
> *everybody's* (or *everyone's*) *else's*
> *nobody's* (or *no one's*) *else's*
> *somebody's* (or *someone's*) *else's*
> *whose* (or *whosever* or *whosoever*) *else's*.

elude, delude, illude are often erroneously used one for another; their precise meanings are defined in dictionaries. See also ILLUDE.

emanate, misused. 'The crime has astonished me. It's not the kind of thing I could ever imagine emanating from that house', Margery Allingham, *Dancers in Mourning*, 1937. The writer means 'happening in that house'. *Emanating* is *flowing from*, immaterially.

emend. See AMEND.

emerge and **immerge.** See 'IMMERGE and EMERGE', as well as the following entry.

emerge and **issue.** To *emerge* is 'to come forth into view from an enclosed and obscure place', as in 'The stream emerges from the lake, the moon from the clouds'; 'to rise into notice' and esp. 'to issue (come forth) from suffering, subjection, danger, embarrassment, etc.', as in 'France emerged triumphant from the great Revolution'; (of a fact, a principle) 'to come out as the result of investigation, cogitation, discussion', as in 'At last there emerged Einstein's Theory of Relativity'.

To *issue*:—There is no difficulty about the transitive use. The v.i. is 'to go out or come out; come forth; flow out, sally out', as in 'A band of brigands issued from the stronghold', 'The river issued into the sea at a desolate point of the coast'; figuratively it is used in much the same way as *emerge*, i.e., 'to go out, or come out, of a state or a condition', as in 'He issued scatheless from that peril', 'She will issue dazed from the coma'; legally, 'to be born or descended' (cf. *'bodily issue'*) and, of revenue, income, etc., 'to accrue'; compare the more general sense, 'to take (its) origin; to spring; be derived', as in 'Can malevolence and misery issue from the bosom of infinite goodness?'; hence, 'to result', as in 'Excitement issuing from a stimulus'; hence, to *issue* (or end or result) *in*; 'to be published', as in 'Far too many books are issued nowadays'. *(The O.E.D.)*

emigrant and **immigrant.** The same person may be both, but not at the same time: leaving his own for another country, he is an *emigrant*; arriving from another country, an *immigrant*.

emit and **inmit.** The former is to put or send forth, to utter; the latter, to put or send in, to insert or introduce.

employ is obsolescent for *employment*, even in *in the employ of*.

employée is incorrect for *employee* or, as a masculine, for (French) *employé*, which latter should be avoided. English *employee* is used for either gender.

empty and **vacant.** Empty = 'containing nothing' (a jug without water, a room without furniture); 'carrying nothing' (*empty ship, empty hands*); of persons, 'frivolous'; of things, 'vain' (*empty pleasures*). But a *vacant* room or house is a room or house in which there are no people, i.e., 'unoccupied', as also in *a vacant post* (or *position*), *office, benefice*; as 'devoid of' (*vacant of generosity*), it is obsolescent; (of time) 'free, leisure(d)', as in 'a hobby for one's vacant hours'; 'idle' (*a vacant life*); 'meaningless, expressionless, inane' (*vacant stare* or *look* or *smile*). *(The O.E.D.)*

en- and **in-** in verbs. In new verb formations, *en-* (*em-* before *b* and *p*, always; before *m*, occasionally) may well be confined to derivatives from French, for *en-* was originally a French prefix, corresponding to the Latin *in-*. Likewise, in new verb formations, *in-* should be used in words from Latin.

enclose, enclosure are, by usage, preferred to *inclose, inclosure*.

end by. See PREPOSITIONS WRONGLY USED.

ended is 'that *has* come to an end'; **ending** is 'that is ending' or, loosely, 'that is about to end'. In other words, *ended* refers to the past, *ending* to the present or the future. Actually, the future is often implied in the present, the present in the past; nevertheless this philosophical subtlety does not justify the use of *ended* for *ending*, as in 'We shall dismiss him in the year ended in four days' time'. But *ending* can, as an historic present, convey a past, as in 'We are sending a report for the quarter ending (on) March 31st, 19—'. Weseen is too dogmatic on this point, for even in reference to an event (or a period) already passed, *ending* is usual.

endless is 'without actual or readily discernible end'; it does not, in sober prose, = *innumerable*, as it is made to do in 'endless platitudes', 'endless examples', but it is hyperbolical, not incorrect English.

endorse; indorse. See INDORSE.

endways and **endwise** are given by *The O.E.D.* as interchangeable.

enervate is to weaken (a person or an animal) physically or mentally or morally; the rare *innervate* is to nerve or invigorate (a person).

engender for *cause* should be used with care. (An an intransitive, *engender* is obsolete.) Primarily (esp. of the male), it = 'to produce (a child)'; its transferred senses are 'to give rise to, produce (a state of things), a disease, force, quality, feeling, etc.' *(The O.E.D.)*. 'Hate engenders strife' and 'Heat engendered by friction' are correct, whereas 'Coal is engendered by buried forests' is incorrect.

ENGLISH, STANDARD. See STANDARD ENGLISH.

ENGLISH AND AMERICAN USAGE. For those who wish to compare Americanisms and Briticisms, I list the five most important authorities on the subject:

H. W. Horwill: *A Dictionary of American English on Historical Principles*, 1936.
A Dictionary of American Usage, 1935.
G. P. Krapp: *The English Language in America*, 1925.
G. H. McKnight: *English Words and Their Background*, 1933.
H. L. Mencken: *The American Language*, 4th edition, 1936.
A. W. Read: *Briticisms* (now in preparation).

English cholera. 'Epidemic diarrhoea . . . was sometimes ignorantly known as "English cholera", and was by no means always fatal', Anthony Berkeley, *Not to Be Taken*, 1938.

enigmae is an incorrect plural of *enigma*, as though of Latin origin (*Notes and Queries*, Apr. 24, 1937). *Enigma* is Greek, but, having become an English word, it takes the ordinary plural in -*s*.

enjoy; enjoyed. 'Fortunately the Wages Tribunal disallowed this claim, although it virtually invited the applicants to make an application for some further improvement in the terms enjoyed'—i.e., to be had—'in the near future', Stockholders' Union circular. Another common misuse is the expression, 'he enjoys very poor health', and (almost as bad) 'does not enjoy good health', where there is no question of 'enjoyment', but of *having* good or bad health, or even of *suffering* from some complaint.

enlarge and **enlarge(ment).** C. C. Boyd (*Grammar for Grown-Ups*) quotes from a newspaper: 'For the enlargement of the activity of his Department Mr N. Chamberlain etc.', and points out that 'you do not *enlarge* activity: you *increase* it'.

enlargen. 'There ain't no sech animal.'

enormity; enormousness. The former is used of extreme wickedness, a gross offence; the latter only of great size.

enough, following an adjective, is equivalent to *sufficiently* preceding that adjective. Thus, *strange enough = sufficiently strange*, except that the former emphasizes *strange*, whereas the latter throws the emphasis on the adverb. (One does not say *enough strange*: usage forbids it.) But if we separate *strange* from *enough* by inserting a noun, we create at best a strangeness, at worst an ambiguity, as in 'Nature, that moves in us by strange courses enough if need be, . . .' (Michael Innes, *Lament for a Maker*, 1938), where usage demands 'Nature, that moves in us by courses strange enough . . .'

enough that, enough so that. Incorrect for *enough to* (+ infinitive).

enough and **sufficient.** See SUFFICIENT.

enquire is superseding **inquire; enquiry, inquiry.** See also the entry 'QUERY and INQUIRY'. [But *Webster's* maintains the opposite: "*Inquire*, etc., have for the most part superseded *enquire*, etc."]

ensure is to make sure or make sure of (a thing, or that . . .); **insure** is the more usual word in the field of *life-insurance* and similar contracts.

enthuse is to be avoided, though it has its apologists.

enthusiastic, misused for *excited*. 'The children are wildly enthusiastic as they push forward into the big tent (of the circus).'

entire. See COMPARATIVES, FALSE, also 'COMPLETE, ENTIRE, WHOLE'.

entirely. A witness in a notorious lawcase was reported in *The Evening News* on Jan. 26, 1938, as saying: 'I was put entirely in a rather awkward position'. —'Entirely' and 'rather' are mutually contradictory,—but a witness under cross-examination cannot always make cool choice of his words.

entirely without being is very clumsy for *being without* or *being far from* or *although not at all*, as in 'Entirely without being distinguished, Meade had a brisk business-like way', Carolyn Wells, *The Clue of the Eyelash*, 1933.

entity, misused. 'The medical profession, as a distinct entity, was afforded official recognition' (Nigel Morland, *The Conquest of Crime*, 1937). *Entity*, in its concrete sense, is 'something that has a real existence as opposed to a mere function' (*The O.E.D.*). Now a 'profession' has no concrete existence, but exists only by its 'function'.

entrance; entry. Both = 'the action of coming or going in', but *entrance* connotes the action, *entry* the result. *Entrance = right of entry* in 'Free entrance and safe egress' (Lytton). Both nouns are used of 'that (whether open or closed) by which one enters', as a door or gate or passage; but only *entrance* is used attributively (*entrance-hall*). In seamanship and book-keeping, only *entry*. (*The O.E.D.*) *Entry* is loose for *entrant* (in a competition or contest).

entrust. See INTRUST.

enumerable. See INNUMERABLE.

enunciation. See ANNUNCIATION.

envelop and **envelope** (vv.). The shorter form is preferable—as for *develop(e)*.

envelope (n.). Pronounce *enn-*, I say, not *on-*; the latter being French. *On-* is the more absurd in that the French noun is *enveloppe*.

enviable, worthy of envy; **envious,** (of a person) feeling envy.

epigraph and **epitaph.** The latter, an inscription only on a tomb; the former, on any building, but now rarely on a tomb. *Epigraph* is also a legend on a coin; a motto or key-quotation on a title-page or under a chapter number or heading.

epistle and **letter.** Do not use the former as an exact synonym of the latter: an *epistle* is a formal or didactic or literary or elegant letter.

equal should not be used (as it is once used early in R. H. Mottram's *You Can't Have It Back*, 1939) for *equable* as applied to mind or temper. One says 'an *equable* or tranquil mind' and 'an *equable* or even or unruffled temper': to employ *equal* for *equable* is, at best, an archaism.

equal as. See PREPOSITIONS WRONGLY USED.

equally as. See AS, EQUALLY.

equate. One *equates* one thing either *to* or *with* another.

EQUIVOCAL WORDS. See AMBIGUITY.

ere. See E'ER.

eruption is a bursting out, **irruption** a bursting in.

escape is not synonymous with *not to be present in* (or *be absent from*). 'This word has in Australia a derogatory tang that escapes the English usage' rings oddly.

especial and **special.** As the opposite to *general*, *special* is preferred. But for 'pre-eminent, very distinguished', 'pertaining to one particular case' and also in the obsolescent phrase *in especial* (*for your especial benefit*), *especial* is used. The same applies to *especially* and *specially*. But in colloquial speech, *special(ly)* is displacing *especial(ly)*. (*The O.E.D.*)

essential ('absolutely necessary') should not be debased to mean merely *necessary* or *needful*.

essential . . . must. 'It is essential that pageant must play its part', for *should* play its part.

estray. See ASTRAY.

esurient, meaning 'hungry' or 'impecunious and greedy' (*The O.E.D.*) is erroneously used to = *gastronomic*.

et cetera, etc., meaning 'and other things' (Latin plural neuter), is insulting when applied to persons. Publishers sometimes put *etc.* at the end of an incomplete list of authors. In December, 1937, there appeared a Christmas number with this inset on the front page:

Contributions by:

Hugh
WALPOLE

Stephen
LEACOCK

Laurence
HOUSMAN

etc.

8-Page Supplement
CURIOSITIES ROUND
THE WORLD

In formal writing, *etc.* should be avoided: use either *et cetera* or, better, an English equivalent.

eternal. See COMPARATIVES, FALSE.

ethic and **ethical,** adjectives. Except occasionally in grammar (e.g., *ethic dative*), *ethical* is now the usual adjective corresponding to *ethics*.

ethic and **ethics,** nouns, are occasionally confused by those who should know better, for *ethic* is a word unknown, or at the least, unused by the great majority. *The O.E.D.* defines *ethics* as 'the science of morals', but a man's (or institution's) particular system of moral science may be called his *ethic*; e.g., 'The drab discipline of his days was beginning to suggest that one may purchase too dearly the satisfaction of sticking to a private and unpopular ethic' (Richard Aldington, *Very Heaven*, 1937). The adjective *ethic*, now usually *ethical*, is defined as 'of or pertaining to morality or the science of ethics' (*The O.E.D.*).

ethnic and **ethnical** are now limited to the senses, 'pertaining to race'; hence 'peculiar to a given race or nation'; hence 'pertaining to the science of races' (i.e., *ethnological*), to which the noun is *ethnology*. The careless have been known to confuse *ethnic(al)* with *ethic(al)*, *q.v.*

euphemism, confused with *euphuism*. A *euphemism* is a prudish evasion (*to go to his eternal rest* = to die); a *euphuism* is a literary, a stylistic excess (e.g., of antitheses) exemplified in and fathered by Lyly's *Euphues*, 1579, and *Euphues and His England*, 1580. (For a common misapprehension of the precise meaning of euphuism, see my *The World of Words*.)

EUPHEMISMS. *Euphemism* comes from a Greek word meaning 'to speak favourably', and Greek provides what is perhaps the most famous of all euphemisms: *Eumenides*, 'the Kindly Ones', for the Furies, the Avenging Gods.

In *The King's English*, the Fowlers define euphemism as the 'substitution of mild or vague expression for harsh or blunt one.' In *The Romance of Words*, Professor Ernest Weekley speaks of euphemism as 'that form of speech which avoids calling things by their names' and observes that it results from 'various human instincts which range from religious reverence down to common decency'. Often, I fear, it springs from nothing so decent as either reverence or decency: too often it is an indication of prudery or an exaggerated genteelism.

Perhaps I may here interpolate my belief that if there were no synonyms, there would be no euphemisms—and no obscenity. If it were made compulsory to use one word and one word only for 'to defecate', 'to urinate', 'to die', 'to kill', 'to copulate', and their nouns, as well as for certain bodily parts (especially the genitals), the squeamish would be reduced to using gestures and then, by force of public opinion and by a growing shamefacedness, to employing the sole terms. The same thing would apply to obscenities, which, after all, represent merely the polar counterparts of euphemisms.

But let us pass from speculation to fact. Three writers* have written pertinently and clearly and suggestively on the subject: Professor G. H. McKnight, M. Henri Bauche, and Professor Albert Carnoy.

* On certain specific points and words, Mr Allen Walker Read has contributed invaluable information and views.

In 1933, McKnight, in *English Words and Their Background*, pointed out that, contrary to a rather general impression, 'one of the most distinctive features of sophisticated speech, as distinguished from unsophisticated speech in our time, is the absence of squeamishness and the ready courage to name things directly'. Since the War of 1914–18, indeed, it is only the semi-educated and the uneducated who have persisted in constant euphemism, and, since civilization began, it has always been the 'half-baked' who practise euphemism the most.

Bauche has contributed to the subject chiefly by pointing out that the distinction between the harsh or the gross word and the word not thought to be either harsh or gross is somewhat arbitrary in all languages; that the harshness or the grossness does not correspond exactly to the picture evoked by the word; that different peoples and different social classes vary considerably not only at different but at the same periods with regard to which things, which acts, and which words, are to be treated as objectionable; and that, in one restricted but important group (physical intimacy and the sexual parts), the euphemisms are to some extent accountable by the fact that the anatomical terms would, with perhaps one exception (the male generative organ), be out of place and pompous, whereas the 'old Roman words' have become too gross to be used by the respectable—except among intimates.

In *La science du mot* (a wholly admirable book), Carnoy has a very important chapter on euphemism and its opposite, dysphemism. Euphemism he neatly defines as discretion in speech. He shrewdly notes that euphemism is employed, not to hide the truth—the fact—the thing (silence were best for that), but merely to minimize the painful impression on the listener or the perhaps unpleasant results for the speaker; related to the latter purpose is the speaker's desire to make a favourable impression. Carnoy has classified the direct causes of euphemism and the particular reasons for its use. Here is that classification, which I have taken the liberty of slightly modifying.

1. *The desire to adapt oneself to the general sentiment suitable to, or the general atmosphere of, the time, the place, the company.* In an elevated form: anxiety

to preserve a lofty or a beautiful style in poetry, oratory, etc., where unseemly trivial words or metaphors would jar on one. In addressing children, or in lowly or very friendly circles: avoidance of medical (or otherwise technical) or literary words by the employment of euphemistic terms; in addressing children, a euphemism is frequently due to a modesty that would be ludicrous or misplaced among adults, or to a wish to spare them painful knowledge.

2. *The desire to enhance the value of what one possesses or of what one wishes to give.* (A form of hyperbole.) As in *saloon* for a bar, *university* for a technical school, *engineer* for a mechanic, and *professor* for a teacher or simply an exponent.

3. *Respect for the person addressed (or referred to); or desire to impress or please or merely not offend the person addressed.* Titles; the stereotyped politenesses of the professions and of commerce; *Hebrew* for Jew, *coloured man* or *coloured gentleman* for Negro, and *dark gentleman* for an Indian of India; *lady* for any woman, and especially *charlady* for charwoman.

4. *The need to diminish, to tone down a painful evocation or to soften tragic or painful news.* This, among civilized peoples and especially in refined circles, is the most frequent of all reasons. Death above all, but also madness (or idiocy), disease, ruin. *To pass away, be no more, leave this world, go to a better world, go west, pass over, expire, breathe one's last, fall asleep in the Lord, join the great majority,* and many other phrases, instead of the simple and infinitely dignified 'to die'; and this tendency has spread to undertakers and their functions: *mortician, funeral director, obsequies,* and other atrocities.

5. *Social and moral taboos.* There are actions and objects that are either blameworthy or very intimate: and therefore not, as a rule, mentioned directly in good company. A mild example is drunkenness, which gives rise to many euphemisms: *half-seas over, elevated, happy, lively.* The 'inferior' physical processes and functions afford a stronger and better example: for these, delicacy, reticence and politeness devise euphemisms as discreet as *retire* or *pay a visit* or (among women) *powder one's nose* or (among men) *wash one's hands.* All that relates to sex is heavily veiled:

a pregnant woman is *in an interesting condition;* a person lacking in restraint is *fast,* whereas one that constantly exercises self-restraint is *slow* and *dumb;* a lover of either sex is a *friend;* the intimacy of marriage becomes *conjugal relations;* obscene (in the sense of rich in sexual detail) becomes *blue* or *hot* or even *frank.*

6. *Superstitious taboos and religious interdictions.* The word is God; speech has a mysterious power; the name evokes the thing.* These three points of view—these three facets of the one idea—explain many ancient and modern euphemisms; and the same emotion or attitude, at different stages, is represented by the philosophic concept of the *Logos* and the popular belief implicit in *speak of the devil.* The latter is seen in the old superstition that one must be particularly careful in speaking of God, the gods, important persons, the dead; with regard to the Deity and Jesus Christ, this belief survives in such mild oaths as *by gad!, by golly!, drat it!, gee-whizz!* Superstition may, however, become pure reverence, and reverence of another kind is felt by those who are profoundly in love, for, to them, reverence dictates a euphemistic vocabulary of intimacy.

Frequently, euphemism causes successive synonyms to be suspect, displeasing, indelicate, immoral, even blasphemous. This we see in such words as *lover* and *mistress, simple* and *silly,* and French *fille.* As Weekley has said, 'a euphemism is doomed from its birth'; Carnoy has said much the same: 'La vertu adoucissante des termes euphémistiques n'est naturellement pas de très longue durée. Dès que les gens se sont pour de bon habitués à comprendre *B* quand on dit *A, A* exprime aussi clairement *B* que le symbole propre à ce dernier. Il faut donc recommencer et aller chercher un nouveau mot qui puisse voiler *B* sans l'obscurcir tout à fait. Dans l'entretemps, *A* s'est définitivement infecté du sens défavorable de *B* et s'est donc dégradé.' (Et ainsi de suite.) An excellent example is afforded by *mad,* which became *crazy,* which became *insane,* which became *lunatic,* which became *mentally deranged,* which became

---

* *Numen et nomen,* essence and name (or manifestation). In the Scriptural 'the Word is God', the Latin is *verbum.* The taboo springs from the primitive notion: the name = the potence or reality of the god, person, or thing. (See my *Name This Child,* p. 2, n. 3.)

deranged and a little later and in slang, *mental*.

Euphemism may be obtained by directing the thought in the desired direction, as in *honorarium* or *convey* (to plagiarize); by using an extremely vague phrase, as in *commit a nuisance*; by mentioning a significantly concomitant circumstance, as in *remove* (to murder); by being enigmatical or elusive, as in *lose the number of one's mess* (to die); by understatement, as in *have had a glass* (to be tipsy), or the negative litotes (*it's not too safe*); by irony, by employing another language (e.g., the Latin found in translations of *Daphnis and Chloe*); by reticence, as in *you know where to go* (to hell!); and by abbreviation as in *w.c.* (itself euphemized to *w.*) and T.B. (more properly, *Tb.*: tuberculosis).

(This represents an adaptation and reduction of 'Euphemism and Euphemisms' in my *Words, Words, Words!*.)

euphuism. See EUPHEMISM.

European requires *a* not *an*.

evacuate the wounded is a horrible variation of the dignified *remove the wounded*. Beginning as military officialese, it has become journalese—and far too general. I won't swear that I haven't used it myself.

even (like *actually, definitely,* and *really*) is often used where there is no need for it, with the result that, instead of the desired emphasis, there is weakness, as in 'That thoughtful, appraising look turned all the time upon himself, worried Granadi, rather; even hardbitten as he was, and plausible, specious liar that he knew himself to be at a moment's pinch' (John G. Brandon, *The Mail-Van Mystery*, ca. 1937); 'hardbitten though he was' would have served, with 'as' for 'that' as a further improvement.

This adverb requires to be watched for punctuation; often a comma will prevent its being apprehended as an adjective.

event should not be made to do duty for *great event* or *important event*, for this use sometimes leads to ambiguity or obscurity.

eventuate. This bad, ugly and wholly unnecessary word usually means no more than *to happen, to come to pass*. A. P. Herbert (*What a Word!*) gets good fun out of it and quotes a misuse supplied to him by a curate in the East End:

—'If more people do not eventuate, the meeting will not be held.'

ever is often used unnecessarily, as in 'It remains doubtful whether any evidence against McCabe could ever have been collected by any methods other than those which Smith used' (a detective novel, 1937).

ever expect, ever hope, illogically used for *expect ever, hope ever*. 'Do you *ever* expect to see him again?' is a loose substitute for 'Do you *expect ever* to see . . . ?' This appears even more clearly in 'Do you ever hope to see. . . .' where *hope ever* is intended.

ever, seldom or. See SELDOM OR EVER.

everlasting. See COMPARATIVES, FALSE.

every. See ALL.

every, misused, e.g., by Mr Gerald Balfour, speaking in February, 1898, and quoted by Nesfield: 'We already possess four times as great a trade with China as every other nation put together' (*all other nations*).—Cf. '"We've got to have every possible information concerning him that we can get"' (John G. Brandon, *The Regent Street Raid*) where *every* should be *all*, though *every piece of information* would also be correct.

every for ALL POSSIBLE. Weseen cites 'The court exercised every leniency' and asks, 'Does the writer mean each of various kinds of leniency?' [If he did, he should have written *every kind of leniency*.] No, he means all possible leniency in the fullest possible measure!

Analogous are *every* for *ample* or *sufficient*, as in 'There is every reason for doing this', and *every* for *much* or *great*, as in 'He is deserving of every praise'; cf. also, *every* for *complete, entire* or *perfect*, as in 'We have every confidence in him'.

every, tautological use of. See TAUTOLOGY.—Ambiguous: see 'ALL, ambiguous'.

every takes the singular. 'Every man must be at *their* desk' is incorrect. Cf. EACH.

every, misused for *everyone*. 'It [Stacy Aumonier's *Ups and Downs*] is for all and every', John Galsworthy's Preface, 1929.

every place for *everywhere* is loose, as in 'I looked every place for his book'.

every time for *always*. The former refers to separate occasions, *on each occasion*; the latter means *at all times*, or *all the time*.

everybody or **everyone** followed by *they*, etc. See THEIR.

everyone, misused for *every one*; e.g., 'Everyone of the things was in its right place'. *Everyone* is of persons, *every one* of things; the former is self-contained, the latter sometimes not. So too *everything* for *every thing*.

everyone's (or **everybody's**) **else.** See ELSE'S.

everywhere means '*in every place*', not *every place*, as is intended in 'Everywhere would be desolate' (examination script, March, 1938).

evidence and **testimony.** If you are in doubt on this point, consult *Webster's New International* or *The Shorter Oxford Dictionary. Evidence* is 'an appearance from which inferences may be drawn; an indication'; hence, 'ground for belief', as in 'The weight of evidence appears strongly in favour of the claims of Cavendish' (T. H. Huxley); whence the legal senses, 'information given in a legal investigation, to establish the fact or point in question', as in *to bear*, or *give*, or *give in evidence; the evidence* is 'the testimony which in any particular cause has been received by the court and entered on its records'; cf. *to turn King's* (or *Queen's*) or *State's evidence*.

In current usage, it is best to reserve *testimony* for its set scriptural senses; one may, however, still speak of 'the *testimony* of the physical senses', though 'the *evidence* . . .' is now the general term. (*The O.E.D.*)

evidence (v.). *To be evidenced*, for *to be shown* (or *indicated*), is ugly—and overworked.

evince, originally meaning, to *overcome, subdue*, but now obsolete in that sense, is used for *to show, exhibit, make manifest*, but it is a bad word and unnecessary. Mr Whitten (*Good and Bad English*) rightly says, 'it is still a favourite with callow journalists who like to write "he evinced a desire" instead of "showed, expressed", etc.'

ex-. See 'LATE and EX-'.

exactly for *precisely* is a loose colloquialism, not reprehensible in *exactly!*, 'quite so!', but to be avoided in such a sentence as 'He had not been exactly intimate with Sutton, but he had . . . developed a genuine liking and respect for him', Freeman Wills Crofts, *The Loss of the Jane Vosper*, 1936.

exactly similar. See SIMILAR, EXACTLY.

EXAGGERATION. See HYPERBOLE.

exalt for *exult* is an amusing malapropism.

examination paper for *script* is ambiguous, an 'exam. paper' being strictly the paper of questions set for examination, not the candidate's written answers (his *script*). [[In American English, *script* is not current in this sense. Commonly, 'examination questions' are passed to the students, who write their '(examination) papers' or 'books'.]]

example and **instance.** An example is a typical *instance*; but we can say either *for instance* or *for example*. Whereas *by way of example* is idiomatic, the phrase, *ancient saws and modern instances*, cannot be varied to . . . *modern examples*. We make an *example*, not an instance, of a person when, deterrently, we punish him; we set a good *example*; '*example* is better than precept'.

Note too the difference between *example* and *sample*, the latter now being virtually confined to commerce. (*The O.E.D.*)

example where is incorrect for *example in which*, as in 'This is an example where great care must be exercised'.

exampler is incorrect for *exemplar*.

exceeding. See EXCESSIVE.

excellent. See COMPARATIVES, FALSE. It is true that there are degrees of excellence, but *excellent = excelling*. There is connoted a dichotomy comparable with that of *major* and *minor*: things that excel are *excellent*, things that do not excel are not excellent. 'Jones is an excellent chap, but Smith is more excellent still—and Robinson? Why! Robinson is the most excellent of these truly excellent fellows' rings oddly: such a sentence should be avoided. As for *the king's most excellent Majesty*, there are two significant points: it is an official formula, therefore inviolate; and originally the comparison may have been subjective. Whereas *a most excellent fellow* is defensible, *the most excellent fellow of them all* is—well, infelicitous.

except and **accept** are often confused by the semi-literate: *except* is 'to make an exception of', *accept* is 'to take (a present, a dismissal, etc.)'.

except as a conjunction (= *unless*) is in the present century to be avoided: idiom has left it behind; it is now a barbarism. 'He said he saw nobody with her [*except she had somebody under the cloak*]', *The Sessions Papers of the Old Bailey*, 1754, was all very well in the

18th Century, but 'I won't go except you do' is indefensible nowadays.

except for *instead of* is a catachresis, as in 'There seem to be dozens now, except about three as there used to be in my time' (based on a query in *John o' London's Weekly*, Jan. 6, 1939).

excepting. See CONJUNCTIONS, DISGUISED.

excepting and **except** as prepositions. In 20th Century usage, *excepting* is not an exact synonym of *except*: Mary Howitt's 'Nothing to be seen . . . excepting some blocks of marble' (1863) would now be '. . . except . . .'. It is obsolete in the sense 'unless'. Indeed, it is now virtually restricted to the phrase *not excepting*, as in John Morley's 'Of all societies . . . not even excepting the Roman Republic, England has been the most emphatically political'. (*The O.E.D.*)

exceptionable and **exceptional** are frequently confused. *Exceptionable* is that to which exception may be taken. *Exceptional* is that which is an exception.

excerpt and **extract** (nn.). *Excerpt* is a literary word, synonymous with *extract* in the sense, 'a passage taken out of a manuscript or a printed book or periodical; a selection; a quotation'. As a synonym for *off-print*, *excerpt* is not in general use.

excess, misused. See ACCESS. See also IN EXCESS OF.

excessive means 'beyond arrangement, beyond reason', as in 'excessive flattery', 'excessive expense'; *exceeding* means 'very, great', as in 'We are grateful for your exceeding generosity'.

excluding. See CONJUNCTIONS, DISGUISED.

excuse me! is less strong and less formal than *pardon me!*

excuse me . . . ; *excuse my doing* (something). '*Excuse my (me) doing* is sometimes used in the positive sense "forgive me for doing", but not infrequently in the negative sense "forgive me for not doing". Examples of the latter . . . : Hazlitt, She said she hoped I should excuse Sarah's coming up . . . ; Dickens, You must excuse my telling you . . . ; Kingsley, Excuse my rising, gentlemen, but I am very weak . . . ; Philips, You must excuse my saying anything more on the subject at the present moment' (Jespersen, *Negation*, 1917). The former is the logical usage; it is also the sensible one, for the second

(the negative) usage—unless the intonation or the context precludes doubt—is ambiguous, as the Hazlitt and Dickens examples show. 'She hoped I would excuse Sarah's not coming up' and 'You must excuse my not telling you' would have been unambiguous.

Idiomatically, the *excuse me doing* form is generally understood to be positive; but it is much rarer than the *excuse my doing* form, especially since ca. 1920, when the fused-participle doctrine began to ravage the land.

executor, executer; executioner. Only the illiterate confuse *executioner* (headsman, hangman) with either of the other two words. An *executor* is a legal term for 'a person appointed by a testator to execute (or carry into effect) his will after the testator's decease'; but an *executer* is a general term for one who, not in Law, executes or carries out a plan, an arrangement, an order, a promise,—it is, however, slightly obsolescent. The latter is stressed on the third syllable, the former on the second syllable (except in one uncommon sense). (*The O.E.D.*)

exemplary is not to be loosely used as a synonym of *excellent*. *Exemplary* = 'archetypal' and, as applied to persons or their attributes, 'fit to serve as an example or pattern for imitation', as in *exemplary conduct, exemplary morals, an exemplary clergyman*; the latter sense is linked with that of 'serving as a specimen, a type', as in *exemplary drawings* (for pupils or students). (*The O.E.D.*)

exert for *exercise* is a very common error—and a wholly useless synonym, productive also, at times, of ambiguity. 'This failure to identify exerted a depressing effect on the Chief of the Criminal Investigation Department which was not lessened by the garbled accounts published in the evening papers' (Anthony Wynne, *The Holbein Mystery*, 1935). Why not 'had'? (Moreover, it is a deplorable sentence in other ways.)

exhausting; exhaustive. *Exhaustive* (or very full; complete) instructions or information may, by the listeners, be found *exhausting*.

exhilarate. See at ACCELERATE.

exist, 'to be', 'to have being', 'to possess reality', 'to live (on a low plane, or barely)', is a weak word when used for *subsist*, 'to support life', 'to find sustenance'; but not an error, for *subsist* can signify merely 'to remain in being', i.e., 'to exist', although this neutral sense is much less used now than formerly. Thus, in the following passage from a School certificate candidate's précis, July, 1938, of Macaulay's *Defence of Arcot* (1751), *subsist* would be an improvement on *exist*: 'The sepoys told Clive that they would give their share of rice to the Europeans; saying that they [the sepoys] could exist on the gruel drained from it.'

exotic. Don't overdo this word, and make sure that you are using it correctly.

EXPANDED TENSES. See PROGRESSIVE ...

expect. See ANTICIPATE.

expectible for *expectable* is a senseless spelling.

expensive is not to be used as exactly synonymous with *dear* or *costly*, for its connotation is either 'excessively dear (or costly)', as in 'an expensive lawsuit', or 'deliberately or intentionally costly', as in 'an expensive education'; moreover a thing 'comes *expensive*' when the expense is unexpectedly great. An experiment may be, or turn out, either costly or expensive.

experience is incorrect for *firm opinion* and for *knowledge*. 'The *modus operandi* [of crime]—which it is the police experience all the world over very few criminals ever vary', E. R. Punshon, *The Dusky Hour*, 1937.

expertise, 'skill', should be used with caution, for it comes from French, where it means 'a survey', 'a valuation' (*The Observer*, Sept. 18, 1938), 'an expert's assessment or report' (Chevalley).

explain does not mean 'show', nor 'indicate', nor 'prove'. 'In this glossary I have reached only *E*. This explains my rate of progress'.

expletive for *term* or *appellation* is incorrect.

explicit. See IMPLICIT.

explore every avenue, one of the common clichés of politicians, is a feeble and even contradictory expression; to *explore* is to *search out* (where ways are difficult and unknown), but an *avenue* is a clear road made on purpose to lead directly to its object. One would 'explore' a by-path or a jungle, not an avenue. 'He'—an M.P.—'was tired of all the figures of speech about exploring every avenue, and leaving no stone unturned, and ploughing the sands, and so on' (John Ferguson, *Death of Mr Dodsley*, 1937).

expose. See DISCLOSE.

exposé for *exposition* (formal explanation; orderly précis; etc.) is a Gallicism—and unnecessary.

expressed is occasionally confused with *express* (adj.). *Expressed* is not a true adjective at all.

extant. See EXTENT.

extempore. See IMPROMPTU.

extemporize. See TEMPORIZE.

extempory is obsolete for *extempore*; illiterate for *extemporary*.

extend has been overworked in the sense of *offer* or *send*, as in 'I extended my deepest sympathy to him in his sorrow'.

extent is a noun; *extant* (surviving, still existing) is an adjective.

extra is colloquial when it is employed for *unusually*, as in 'extra good'; it is also cheap.

extra, misused for *especial*. '[The new hands], naturally, were the ones to be watched with extra vigour', Frank Shaw, *Atlantic Murder*, 1932.

EXTREME READINESS. See FACILITY.

exultance, a favourite word with a certain writer of thrillers, has no authentic existence; *exultation* is correct.

F

-f, plural of nouns in. The reason for the plural in *-fs* is a desire to ensure regularity—to make all nouns in *f* have their plural in *fs*. Admirable; yet the *-ves* plural is much more euphonious, I think, and easier to pronounce. (*Hoof*—*hoofs, roof*—*roofs;* but *loaf*—*loaves*.)

fabulous, 'fabled, mythical, of the nature of a fable, belonging to a fable', hence 'astonishing, incredible' (*The O.E.D.*). This word is being grossly overworked. Use it with care.

face up to for *face* or *look in the face*. A needless expression, the result of the tendency to add false props to words that can stand by themselves.

facetiae is a booksellers' euphemism for 'pornography' or 'a book with a certain amount of sexual interest' and should be avoided by anyone who is not a bookseller, for this is an absurd distortion of the correct sense of *facetiae*: 'Refined witticisms conceived in a spirit of pleasantry' (*Nuttall's Standard Dictionary*). One does not much like to see a bookseller so bend to the exigencies of his precarious trade as to fall into this ineptitude: 'FACETIAE. UNEXPUR-

GATED EDITION. *The Confessions* of Jean Jacques Rousseau . . .'

FACILITY, or Extreme Readiness. In speech, the man that has 'the gift of the gab' usually elucidates his loosenesses by gesture and by emphasis or intonation. But in writing there is no equivalent to gestures unless it be emphasis (with its concomitant risk of over-emphasis); none to intonation.

'Easy writing is hard reading' is true of everything but the most elementary and unsubtle writing.

I do not mean that, in writing, one should lose the thread and the verve by pacing the floor in search for the right word, the inevitable phrase: but all writing should be very carefully revised: at the back of one's mind should be the constant admonition, 'This may be clear in *my* mind, but it may not be clear to the reader'.

facility is often misused for *faculty*. Thus, 'He had a remarkable facility for flying'. The mistake seems to be caused by confusing such locutions as 'There were, he found, excellent facilities for flying' and 'He had a remarkable faculty in flying'; cf., too, such a possibility as 'He had a facile faculty for flying', and the implications of the French *arrêt facultatif*, which is one of the municipal facilities. In 'Then Haskins pulled himself up to consciousness again . . .; and when he did, it was as though he lifted his facilities from a great depth' (*The Revels Are Ended*, 1937), we may be sure that *facilities* is a printer's error, for Robert Carson is a fine writer.

fact, misused for *factor* (*q.v.*) is frequent in crime-novels since ca. 1922. E.g., A. Fielding, *Death of John Tait*, 1932, 'Altogether she was a strange fact of the case'.—Cf. the entry at FACTOR.

fact, in. *In fact* for *in brief* would seem an impossible error, but it is not rare. It generally comes after a list of objects or incidents, '*a* plus *b* plus *c* plus *d* . . . In fact . . .'

factitious and **fictitious** are occasionally confused. The former = artificial, not natural; not spontaneous; made up for a particular occasion. The latter = not genuine; arbitrarily—not rationally—devised; (of a name) not real; (of a character) deceptively assumed, simulated; imaginary, unreal; belonging to or characteristic of fiction. (*The O.E.D.*)

factor is often grossly misused to mean anything from *fact* to *feature* or from *causation* to *cause*; a 'factor' being correctly a contributory element in causation or the composition of anything. A. P. Herbert quotes Mr R. Davies, M.P., as reported in Hansard,—'I am assured that the greatest income from any single factor in Switzerland is in connection with the League of Nations'. Especially frequent is the misuse of *factor* for *occurrence*, as in 'Sunburn and sand in the food are usual factors of beach parties'. Frequent, too, is its misuse for *element* or *constituent*, as in 'If we did not have some other factor [than fat, starch, glycerine] in our make-up, we should all remain alike', examination essay script, June, 1939.

faëry; fairy. *Faërie* or *faëry* (with or without the diaeresis) is fairyland; hence an adjective (always attributive, as in 'the faëry world'), 'of or belonging to fairyland', hence 'beautiful and unsubstantial', hence, 'visionary, unreal' but with a connotation of beauty. *Fairy* is a fay, a supernatural being that lives in fairyland; hence an adjective (always attributive), 'of or pertaining to fairies', hence 'fairy-like'; also it = 'enchanted, illusory'. (*The O.E.D.*)

faker; fakir. The former (one who 'fakes', a swindler, an impostor) is incorrect for *fakir*, a Mohammedan religious mendicant, naked ascetic, wonderworker. For the latter word, see especially Yule & Burnell's *Hobson-Jobson*.

fall (U.S.A.) is the English *autumn*; *fall* is the more Saxon, the more poetical word ('the fall of the leaf, the fall of the year').

FALSE AGREEMENT. See AGREEMENT, FALSE.

FALSE COMPARATIVES and **SUPERLATIVES.** See COMPARATIVES, FALSE.

FALSE ILLITERACIES—false because the pronunciations are standard. E.g., *iz* for *is*, *duz* for *does*, and in England *wot* for *what*.

falseness; falsity. Both = 'contrariety to fact; want of truth'; both = 'duplicity, deceitfulness'; only *falseness* now = 'faithlessness, treachery', or an instance thereof; only *falsity* = 'error in general or a particular error, untrue proposition, statement, doctrine'. (*The O.E.D.*)

familiar to. See PREPOSITIONS WRONGLY USED.

family. See FOLKS.

famous. See 'NOTORIOUS and FAMOUS'.
—Also see CELEBRITY.

fantasy and phantasy. 'In modern use *fantasy* and *phantasy*, in spite of their identity in sound and in ultimate etymology, tend to be apprehended as separate words, the predominant sense of the former being "caprice, whim, fanciful invention", . . . that of the latter is "imagination, visionary notion"' (*The O.E.D.*).

far ago for *remote*. Sir Edwin Arnold in *The Daily Telegraph*, June, 1900, wrote, 'Between the far ago dates of these deposits, the layers of conglomerate rock had to be rolled and spread, and vast intervals of time were wasted for it all'. Nesfield, quoting this, thinks it sufficient to suggest *remote*, which can be applied to both time and space, but 'far off', 'far away', 'long ago'—all are better than 'far ago'.

farther, farthest; further, furthest. 'Thus far and no farther' is a quotation-become-formula; it is invariable. A rough distinction is this: *farther, farthest*, are applied to distance and nothing else; *further, furthest*, either to distance or to addition ('a *further* question').

farther to, misused for *farther from* or *opposite to*. 'On the farther side to that by which they entered', Ann Bridge, *Peking Picnic*, 1932.

fascination of—for—by—with. Something has a fascination for a person, i.e., it fascinates him. 'The fascination of Elaine by Lancelot' is clear; but 'the fascination of Elaine' without a modifying 'by Lancelot' might have meant 'Elaine's fascinating qualities, or power of fascinating'. One is fascinated *by a person*, but *with a thing* (or a happening).

fashion is, in my opinion, obsolescent for *manner* or *mode* of doing something, obsolescent for *method*. 'She has a strange fashion of speaking'.

fatal, 'deadly, mortal, resulting in death', should not be debased to mean *grave* or *serious*, as in the instance:— 'He had a fatal motor accident last month, but has completely recovered now.' To debase it to synonymity with *unfortunate* is still worse.

fatherhood is the quality of being a father; not, as sometimes, of having a father.

father-in-law is occasionally used for *step-father*; The *O.E.D.* quotes examples of this from Goldsmith, Dickens and George Eliot, but this use is both confusing and incorrect.

FAULTY PRECISION. 'If the burglar had chosen Vanderlyn's room, it would almost certainly be he [Vanderlyn] and not the English maid, who would be lying dead at Bella-colline', Mrs Belloc Lowndes, *The House by the Sea*, 1937. The correct form would be, 'it would almost certainly be Vanderlyn, and not the English maid, lying dead'.

favour, 'to regard with favour, to show favour to', even 'to have a liking or preference for' ('He favours Roman Catholicism'), should not be used as a synonym of *prefer*. A good example of its misuse is, 'He favours a dog to a cat'.

favourable reception with. See PREPOSITIONS WRONGLY USED.

fearful; fearsome. In current English, both of these terms = 'causing or inspiring fear'; *fearsome* is slightly obsolescent and rather literary.

feature for *achievement* is catachrestic. 'Until his retirement at 46, he retained his pace and accuracy in the field, a feature without parallel.'

feel (n.), 'feeling', is obsolescent for a mental sensation, as 'a feel of excitement'. (*The O.E.D.*)

female as 'a mere synonym for "woman"' is 'now commonly avoided by good writers, except with contemptuous implication' (*The O.E.D.*) or with a facetious one.

femineity and femininity. The former is 'the quality or nature of the female sex', hence 'womanliness', hence 'womanishness'; for 'the nature of the female sex', *femininity* is obsolete, although it is used for 'womanliness' and also for 'womanishness'. Concretely, *femininity* is 'womankind'; and it has two applied senses, 'the *fact* of being a female' and 'a feminine peculiarity, especially in form'. (*The O.E.D.*)

ferocious for *very great* is slang, as in 'a ferocious risk'.

festal; festive. Both = 'of or pertaining to a feast or festivity', though the former is now more usual, as it also is in the senses (of a person) 'keeping holiday' and (of a place) 'given up to feasting or festivity'. Both = 'befitting a feast; hence, joyous, gay', but *festive* is now preferred in these nuances. *Festive occasion* and *festive season* are now set phrases. (*The O.E.D.*)

fetch and **bring.** Weseen excellently distinguishes them. '*Fetch* implies that the [person] spoken to is some distance from the thing to be brought, . . . *bring* . . . that he is already near it. "Please bring me that paper you have"; "Please fetch my book from the library"'. *Go* is redundant with *fetch*, 'as "Go and fetch the paper". *Fetch* means go to something, get it, and bring it here.' [[For many Americans *fetch* is, unfortunately, a homely and obsolescent word.]]

few and **a few.** (Cf. the entry at GOOD FEW, A; GOOD MANY, A.

The difference has been admirably determined by *The O.E.D.*:—'Without prefixed word, *few* usually implies antithesis with "many" [whereas] in *a few*, *some few* the antithesis is with "none at all". Cf. "few, or perhaps none", "a few, or perhaps many".'

The few now generally = 'the minority' and is opposed to *the many*, i.e., 'the majority'.

fictional, fictitious, fictive. *Fictional* is 'of, pertaining to, or of the nature of fiction', as in 'fictional literature', 'It is a fictional work', 'His fictional friends give him more pleasure than he gets from his real ones'. Both *fictitious* and *fictive* = 'counterfeit, feigned, not genuine', but the latter is obsolescent; *fictitious* in the sense 'of, in, or like fiction (literature)' is now less common than *fictional*; both *fictitious* and (the now rare) *fictive* are applied to assumed names; both of these adjectives, though the latter now rarely, = 'existing in or created by the imagination'. But *fictive* is the correct term for 'imaginatively creative', as in 'Having a . . . great fictive faculty' (J. M. Robertson); *fictitious* alone is correct in the legal sense, 'a fictitious son', i.e., an adopted one, and in the general sense, 'arbitrarily devised; not founded on rational grounds', as in 'a fictitious measure of values'. (*The O.E.D.*)

fiddle for *violin* is 'now only in familiar or contemptuous use' (*The O.E.D.*). Unfortunately, the verb *fiddle* has gone the same way: we have to say, *play the violin*, and *violinist* rather than *fiddler*.

fiend is, in jocular usage, permissible for 'a person or agency causing mischief or annoyance', as in 'an autograph fiend', but in the sense 'addict' or 'devotee'—'fresh-air fiend', 'coffee fiend' —it is slang. (*The O.E.D.*)

figure is not synonymous with *number*, but only with 'a number expressed in figures', i.e., in numerical symbols. A *number* is expressed in *figures*; figures represent a number or numbers. (*The O.E.D.*)

FIGURES OF SPEECH, as part of the equipment of prose style, are outmoded; felt to be artificial. If we use them, we use them, for the most part, subconsciously. For an admirable set of definitions and examples, see Fowler's *Modern English Usage*, at 'Technical Terms'.

fill in; fill out. These two phrases are not interchangeable, as certain people seem to think. *Fill in* is to complete (an outline); to insert (into speech or writing) something that will occupy a vacancy, as in 'He left the date blank for me to fill in'. *Fill out* is to enlarge or extend to the desired size or limit; it can be used of a cheque, but *fill in* (or in England *fill up*) is perhaps better. (*The O.E.D.*)

final (adj.). See COMPARATIVES, FALSE.

final (n.). See FINALE.

FINAL CLAUSES (clauses of purpose). Final or purposive clauses form one of the eight types of adverbial clause. They are introduced either by *that* (generally preceded by *in order* or *so* or—now only in literary language—*to the* (*end*) or by *lest* (equivalent to *that . . . not*). The rule for the right use of final clauses has nowhere been more clearly stated than in Dr C. T. Onions's *An Advanced English Syntax.*

'Final Clauses introduced by *that* take *may* with the Infinite in present and future time, *might* in past time.'

'I eat that I *may* live' is the literary form of 'I eat in order that I may live' or the idiomatic 'I eat in order to live'.

'I shall eat well in order that I *may* keep fit.'

'They climbed higher that'—or *so that* —'they *might* get a better view.'

'Conspirators are always secretive to the end that their secrets *may* not be divulged.'

'The conspirators were secretive to the end that their secret *might* not be divulged.'

Negative final clauses may be couched in the *that . . . not* mode; so far as the verbs are concerned, the sentences follow the *that* mode.

'I eat that I may not die' or '. . . in order that I may not die'.

'They climbed higher (in order) that they *might* not fall.' But even now in formal or literary language, as formerly in nearly all cultured or educated speech, *that . . . not* is less usual than *lest* in negative final clauses. *Lest* takes *should* (or, after the present or the future, *may*) with the infinitive.

'I eat lest I *should* (or *may*) die'
'I *shall eat* lest I *should* (or *may*) die' } (*may* being obsolescent)
'I *ate* lest I *should* die'.

A good example of the wrong verb after *lest* occurs in E. R. Lorac's *Death of an Author*, 1935:—'He hastened his steps a little, lest he were left in the lurch again', *were* being incorrect for *should be*.

The true subjunctive (*may* + infinitive, *might* + infinitive, and *should* + infinitive being subjunctive-equivalents) is now rare, except in poetry, poetic prose, and prose that is either archaic or, without being poetic, is lofty or dignified or vatic.

'He forgets not his viaticum lest he *fail* to reach the happy shore.'

To act that each to-morrow
Find us farther than to-day,

where *to-morrow* is a noun.
'Relative Clauses with Final or Consecutive meaning sometimes take *shall* (*should*), equivalent to the Latin Subjunctive.'

Build me straight a goodly vessel
That *shall* laugh at all disaster.
—Longfellow.

'An act might be passed which *should* not entirely condemn the practice.' In this latter sentence, *did* would have been less formal than *should*.

final upshot, like **final completion** and **final ending**, is a tautological absurdity.

finale and **final** (n.). The latter in athletics and (also as *finals*) in examinations; the former in music, in drama or variety, and figuratively as 'the conclusion; the final catastrophe'. (*The O.E.D.*)

finalize is not recognized by *The O.E.D.*; *Webster's* admits it, but only by the back door. As a synonym for *to complete* or *to conclude* it is superfluous and ugly.

fine as an adverb ('He's doing fine') is dialectal and colloquial.

first for *at first* can lead only to ambiguity or to that momentary check which is more irritating though less dangerous. 'The murder might not be as commonplace in its occasion, nor its solution as simple as he had first been inclined to think', Sidney Fowler, *Four Callers in Razor Street*, 1938.

first for *just* (*after*) may be ambiguous, as in 'When they were first married they took several trips': better, 'Just after they married, they . . .'.

first, two; first, three; first, four, etc., are incorrect for *first two, first three*, etc. For 'the two first chapters in the book' read 'the first two chapters . . .'. This is the English idiom; French has 'les deux premiers chapitres . . .'.

firstly is inferior to *first*, even when *secondly, thirdly* . . . follow it.

fist for '*unclenched hand*' is now permissible only as a jocularity. (*The O.E.D.*)

flair. Don't overdo this noun (which properly = 'instinctive discernment', 'unusually keen perceptiveness') in such senses as 'inborn ability' ('He has a flair for cricket') and—much worse—'liking' ('She has a flair for gimcracks'). (*The O.E.D.*) [[For an informative discussion of the word, see Joseph E. Gillet, 'Flair', *American Speech*, vol. 12 (1937), pp. 247–257.]]

flaunt for *flout* seems to be a strange error—and, some would say, a rare one. It may be strange, but it is not rare. I fell into it in the 1st edition of *Slang To-Day and Yesterday*: and saw it with horror. Reading *The Owl's House*, 1923, by Crosbie Garstin, who could write well, I came on this, 'He achieved strong local popularity, a priceless asset to a man who lives by flaunting the law'.

flee and **fly.** The former has become literary; the latter, obsolescent, except in its literal sense, 'to move through the air on wings'. (*The O.E.D.*)

fleshly is now used only in the senses (1) 'carnal', (2) 'lascivious, sensual': in which senses *fleshy* is catachrestic.

flexibility is occasionally misused for *adaptability*. 'We can employ the pragmatic method; we can appreciate the flexibility of would-be absolutes' (a writer on philosophy).

flier; flyer. Both are correct, the latter (esp. for 'an aviator') being the more common. (*The O.E.D.*)

floor and **stor(e)y.** Usage prefers *stor(e)y* in relation to height, *floor* in relation to part of building; thus, 'The apartment is on the tenth floor of a fifteen-storey building', 'It's a ten-storey building, and only two floors are empty'.

flow—*flowed*—*flowed*; **fly**—*flew*—*flown*: —These are the correct forms.

flowery plants (or **shrubs**) is incorrect for *flowering plants* (or *shrubs*).

fluidly for *fluently*. 'The tea-lounge was full. Guests continued to arrive; all were greeted fluidly by the manager' (a typescript read on Jan. 12, 1939).

flustrated; flustration. Avoid in formal speech, lofty or technical writing. They are permissible as jocularities.

fly. See FLEE.

flyer. See FLIER.

-fold, as in *twofold, threefold, fourfold, fivefold,* etc., and in *manifold* (*q.v.*, separately), originally represents 'folded in 2, 3, 4, etc.' or 'plaited of 2, 3, 4, etc. strands' ('a *threefold* cord'); hence it serves as an arithmetical multiplicative. The multiplicative sense, once very common, is now employed chiefly with reference to largish numbers ('He has repaid me tenfold') or large numbers ('That is a thousandfold worse'), where the force of *-fold* is adverbial. The adjectives express 'rather a plurality of things more or less different than mere quantitative multiplication: cf. "a double charm" with "a twofold charm"' (*The O.E.D.*); the hyphenated form is now rare.

folks for *folk*. 'The old folks at home.' *Folk* is already plural, but the added *s*, though colloquial, modifies its meaning from the group or collective sense to that of the individuals composing the group, as in the above quotation.

follow. See SUCCEED.

follow behind is unnecessary for *follow*. 'I found certain men who had penetrated boldly into the heart of the subject . . . I follow behind them here' (Stuart Chase, *The Tyranny of Words*, 1938). If the gap is to be emphasized, why not 'follow from afar'? So too for *follow after*.

following, misused for *after*. 'For "following" . . . there is . . . a perfectly good substitute, the simple preposition "after". What the luckless "after" has done to merit being quietly cold-shouldered out of the language I cannot conceive . . .

'"Following dinner, the band of the Guards played a selection of music in the blue drawing-room."

'One hopes that the band managed to overtake their dinner before the evening was out.

'"Following a chase half across Europe, a beautiful spy was captured at Bucarest." The lady was apparently following the chase that was following her. It sounds like a vicious circle.' (G. V. Carey, *Mind the Stop*, 1939.)

Following, common journalese for *after,* is rightly ridiculed by A. P. Herbert in *What a Word!* It is often ambiguous; as it is (though only slightly) in '"To resume"—his tone had grown less abrupt following West-Drew's decision to talk freely—"I imagine . . ."', Anthony Webb, *Mr Pendlebury's Second Case*, 1938. Cf. too the following example:—'Not all cases in which chemistry is used can be so sub-classified, and following will be found two examples of special interest. Both are quoted from *Forensic Chemistry* by A. Lucas' (Nigel Morland, *The Conquest of Crime*, 1937).

font-name. See CHRISTIAN NAME.

footpath. See PAVEMENT.

for. '*For* does not mean *against*' sounds like a fatuous truism, yet I have seen this sentence, 'The sentry was on guard for parachute troops,' where the context made it clear that he was on guard *against* them.

for and **because.** The former is subjective ('Don't swear, for I dislike swearing'), the latter objective ('They did that, because events compelled them'); the former may represent the writer's own view, the latter the immediate and explicit cause. 'Hirst swerved somewhat more than any other bowler . . . But he was not the first swerver, because'—read *for*—'Rawlin and Walter Wright swerved occasionally before he was ever seen.'

for = *as understood by* is admirably brief; so brief as to lead to obscurity, as perhaps in '*Meaning for Scientists*'—one of the chapter headings in Mr Stuart Chase's *The Tyranny of Words*, 1938.

for certainty is incorrect for *for a certainty* or *for certain,* as in 'He did not know how much I knew. Nor could I tell for certainty how much he knew', Daphne du Maurier, *Rebecca*, 1938. (Here it may be a printer's error; I have, however, seen the mistake elsewhere.)

for ever means 'for eternity', 'for one's lifetime'; **forever** means 'constantly or continually', as in 'He's forever singing that song'.

for what? See WHAT . . . FOR?

for why, as in 'I'll tell you for why', is illiterate and verbose. It should not replace *for what*.

forbear is, I believe, more usual though less logical than *forebear* for 'an ancestor'. [The preferred spelling in Webster's is *forebear*.]

forceful; forcible. A *forceful* (not *forcible*) person is vigorous or strong or powerful; 'acting with force, impetuous, violent' is *forceful*; a writer, a painter, an orator that produces a powerful effect is *forcible*; a cogent, impressive or effective speech or style is either *forceful* or *forcible*; a weapon drawn with force or violence is a *forceful* weapon; something done by force, or involving the use of force or violence, is *forcible* (e.g., 'a *forcible* expulsion', '*forcible* means'), esp. in Law, as in *forcible detainer*, *forcible entry*, *forcible abduction*, *forcible dissolution* (of, e.g., Parliament). (*The O.E.D.*)

forecast—preterite *forecast* or *forecasted*—past participle *forecast* or *forecasted*.

forego and **forgo** should be distinguished, I believe; the former meaning *to precede in time or place* (i.e., to go before), the latter meaning *to relinquish*, *to go without*.

foregoing. See ABOVE.

foreign should not be used as synonym for *outside*: it means 'belonging to or coming from another *country*'—not merely from another town or district.

Forensic Medicine, although found in the calendars and syllabuses of many universities, is less correct than *Medical Jurisprudence*; Nigel Morland, *The Conquest of Crime*, 1937, 'Forensic Medicine —or, to use the correct title, Medical Jurisprudence . . .'. Later in the same book, however, it appears that there are the two sciences of Medical Jurisprudence and Forensic Chemistry (not, please note, Forensic Medicine).

forgo. See FOREGO.

form. See SHAPE.

former for *first*. 'Jeffrey, Alexander and Sutton met in the former's office to discuss the situation', Freeman Wills Crofts, *The Loss of the Jane Vosper*, 1936. 'In Jeffrey's office' would be the best phrase, but if there is a wish to avoid repetition of the name, 'in the office of the first-named'.

Former and *latter* are used only when there are two persons or things.—See also SUPERLATIVE DEGREE.

formerly and **formally** are often confused by slovenly speakers; occasionally by criminal writers. (I had forgotten this fact until I consulted Harold Herd's *Watch Your English*.)

fort; fortress. Only the latter is now used figuratively. As military terms, both = 'a fortified place', but the latter is specifically one that is capable of receiving a large force. In Canada and U.S.A., a fortified trading place is a *fort* (now only historical).

forte is, in Music, dissyllabic; elsewhere it has only one syllable. A *forte* is a person's strong point—that in which he excels; in fencing, it is the strongest part of a sword-blade.

fortress. See FORT.

forward and **forwards.** *Forwards* is an adverb only; *forward*, both an adverb and an adjective. In Great Britain, the adverbs *forward* and *forwards* are used as in the following masterly verdict of *The O.E.D.*:—'The . . . distinction . . . is that the latter expresses a definite direction viewed in contrast with other directions. In some contexts either form may be used without perceptible difference of meaning; the following are examples in which only one of them can be used: "The ratchet-wheel can move only *forwards*"; "the right side of the paper has the maker's name reading *forwards*"; "if you move at all it must be *forwards*"; "my companion has gone *forward*"; "to bring a matter *forward*"; "from this time *forward*".' [[Of American usage, *Webster's* says: 'In general, *forward* tends to displace *forwards* in most or all contexts, although the latter is still often used to express the actual direction, as of a movement.' The military order is '(forward,) march'.]]

fraction is infelicitous for *portion*; incorrect for *proportion*. 'A large fraction of what passes for human folly is failure of communication', Stuart Chase, *The Tyranny of* Words, 1938.

frank. Do not overdo this word in its euphemistic sense of 'sexually outspoken', 'indelicate'.

free, gratis, and for nothing is a cliché, excusable only as a jocularity; **free gratis** and **free for nothing** are ludicrous tautologies.

free-thinker (freethinker) is, in thought, an independent, but this usage is obsolescent;. a *free-thinker* refuses to allow authority to over-rule his reason in religious matters—not to be confused with an *agnostic*, nor yet with an *atheist*.

freedman, an emancipated slave; **freeman,** one who is politically free, also one to whom the freedom of a city (or a borough or a company) has been granted.

freight. See CARGO.

FRENCH TAGS. See CLICHÉ.

frequent is now, except in archaic or very literary writing, used only in the senses, 'happening at short intervals; often recurring; happening (or coming) in close succession; (of a pulse) faster than is normal', as in 'The crops suffered from frequent blights' and 'The snow was deep . . . and our immersions in unseen holes very frequent' (Tyndall); and (of an agent), 'constant or habitual', as in 'He was a frequent guest at the villa, a frequent patient at the hospital'. I myself often speak of 'a frequent error': this is a permissible sense, unfortunately obsolescent. (*The O.E.D.*)

friendlily is less frowned upon than it used to be: and when we become accustomed to the sound, we shall no longer find *friendlily* inferior to *in a friendly manner*, than which, obviously, it is much more economical. *Friendly* as an adverb ('He talked friendly to me') is an illiteracy.

friends with. 'I am friends with Bill' is as correct as 'We are friends of theirs'. As Dr Onions has remarked (*An Advanced English Syntax*, §24, last paragraph), this 'interesting case . . . is not so startling an anomaly as it seems; it is easy to see how (e.g.) "He and the Prime Minister are great friends", by assimilation to "He is very friendly with the Prime Minister", could give rise to "He is great friends with the Prime Minister"'. On the analogy of *friends with* is *shipmates with*: 'Captain Bolton of the *Caligula*, who tells me he was shipmates with you in the old *Indefatigable*' (C. S. Forester, *A Ship of the Line*, 1938).

frighten is not intransitive ('That horse frightens easily'); and *frightened of* is a colloquialism for *afraid of*. [[*Webster's* lists intransitive uses for both *frighten* and *scare*.]]

Frisco for *San Francisco* is a colloquialism contemned by the cultured.

from hence is unnecessary; *hence* = from here, from this. The same applies to *from thence* and *from whence*.

from how, incorrect for *in comparison with* (*what*). 'I followed him into the room, which seemed oddly small, somehow, from how I had remembered it' (Frank Tilsley, *I'd Hate to Be Dead*,

1938). Better: 'small in comparison with what I remembered of it' (slightly ambiguous); still better: 'in comparison with the room as I remembered it'.

front does not = *beginning*, as in 'the front of the book'; *at the front of the book*, however, is permissible in opposition to *at the back of the book* (Weseen).

froze, preterite; *frozen*, past participle. It is, therefore, an illiteracy to say 'I am nearly froze to death'.

fructicose and **fructiculose,** mentioned by *The O.E.D.* as 'erroneous' and 'spurious' words in some modern dictionaries, are errors for *fruticose*, which occurs in botanical descriptions and gardeners' catalogues and signifies 'of shrubby growth'.

-fs. See -F.

fumitory, now the correct spelling for the common wild plant *fumaria officinalis*, is sometimes confused with *fumatory*, a place for fumigation. Both words are derived from the root *fum-* ('smoke'), and both are to be found, in 17th and 18th Century books, spelt in many different and confusing ways.

function (v.) for *to act, to work* should be used only of machinery or of an organ that works like a machine. As a noun it is pretentious when used of an *informal* social gathering or festive meeting.

funds is permissible for one's pecuniary resources, money at one's disposal (see *The O.E.D.*); but do not use it indiscriminately for *money* or *cash*.

funeral and **funereal.** Only the latter is used figuratively ('gloomy, dark, dismal, melancholy, mournful'), as in 'We marched at a funereal pace' (Leslie Stephen), 'funereal shades of night'. As 'of or pertaining to or appropriate to a funeral', *funereal* is now rare except in poetry, and in archaeology (e.g., *funereal papyri*), precisely as *funeral* is archaic in figurative usage. *Funeral*, therefore, is the correct current term for 'of or pertaining to the ceremonial burial (or cremation) of the dead; used, observed, delivered, etc., at a burial' (*The O.E.D.*), as in *funeral rites, funeral urn, funeral pall, funeral pile* or *pyre, funeral column*.

fungous is the adjective of *fungus*; the adjective *fungoid* is a botanical and a pathological technicality.

funny for *odd* or *strange* is a colloquialism. Also it tends to produce ambiguity.

furnish, misused for *constitute*. 'It was the old once-valued concept of

length which furnished the confusion.'
Stuart Chase, *The Tyranny of Words*,
1938 (in a paragraph about the modern
physicists' experiments in and conclusions concerning length).

further, furthest. See FARTHER.

further to that is a commercialized
and verbose elaboration of *further* or
furthermore.

furtivity for *furtiveness* is an error that
occurs twice in John G. Brandon's *The
Mail-Van Mystery*—and elsewhere.

fuschia, a very frequent error for
fuchsia. (The plant is named after
Leonard *Fuchs*, a 16th Century German
botanist.)

FUSED PARTICIPLES. (For other
misuses of the participle, see CONFUSED
PARTICIPLES.)

'Fused Participle', says H. W. Fowler,
at the beginning of his spirited article
thereon in *A Dictionary of Modern
English Usage*, 'is a name given to the
construction exemplified in its simplest
form by "I like you pleading poverty",
and in its higher development by "The
collision was owing to *the signalling instructions* laid down by the international
regulations for use by ships at anchor in
a fog *not having been properly followed*"';
it was, by the way, Fowler who invented
the name. An example midway between
the two extremes is this, 'Y.Y's distillation of fun . . . has done much to make
up for *that paper having spoiled* other
Christmas dinners besides his and the
Professor's' (from a letter in *The New
Statesman and Nation*, early in 1938).

The fused participle has caused much
heartburning. There are two main schools
of thought: The Fowlerites, who consider it the abomination of abomina-
tions; the Onions men and the Jespersen-
ites, who, on certain points, oppose the
Fowlerites with a most English sturdi-
ness.

Let us consider the pronouncements of
the judicious Dr C. T. Onions in *An
Advanced English Syntax*; the much
lamented and inadequately appreciated
H. T. Fowler; the luminously sensible
Professor Otto Jespersen. In that order.

'Notice', says Dr Onions, 'the following alternative constructions, the first
involving the use of the Gerund, the
second that of the Verb Adjective in
-ing (Active Participle) [*being* or *having
been*]:

What is the use of *his coming*?—of
him coming?

He spoke of *its being* cold—*it being*
cold.

We hear every day of *the Emperor's
dying—the Emperor dying*.

Forts were erected to prevent *their
landing—them landing*.' To which I
should like to add:

What is the use of *his having come*—
of *him having come*?

He spoke of *its having been* cold—*it
having been* cold, &c., &c.

'Some people', continues Dr Onions,
'insist that the first of these constructions should always be used.' 'If', he
remarks in a footnote, 'this rule were
pressed, we should have to say: "His
premature death prevented *anything's
coming* of the scheme"—which can
hardly be called English', i.e., it is unidiomatic. 'But the second is the older
use, and, moreover, involves nothing
illogical or inconsistent with other uses
of the Participle, which may generally
be paraphrased by "in the act of -ing".
We find a good instance in Clarendon of
the Gerund qualified by a possessive:
"Sunday passed without *any man's taking* notice of *the keeper's being* absent".'
It is interesting to note that in the 18th
Century the apostrophized construction
(possessive adjective + gerund) was common enough, e.g., in the *The Sessions
Papers of the Old Bailey*, one example
(among many there) being, 'There was
no indictment for the first fact [i.e.,
crime], which was the reason of *Hayes's
being acquitted*' (April 4, 1744).

H. W. Fowler considered the fused
participle to be 'a usage . . . rapidly
corrupting modern style': but Dr Onions's positing of the historical facts has
shown that the fused participle was
formerly the general usage; the inference is that the apostrophized form (*his
coming*) is a modern improvement,—
for Dr Onions, Professor Jespersen and
other authorities fully admit that, in
many instances, the apostrophized (or
possessive adjective + gerund) form is
an improvement, a very useful distinction, but do not enforce its application so widely, nor so rigidly, as does
the tonic author of *Modern English
Usage*. Fowler takes three sentences—
(1) 'Women having the vote share political power with men', (2) 'Women's
having the vote reduces men's political
power', and (3) 'Women having the
vote reduces men's political power'. He
proceeds thus:—'In the first, the subject

of the sentence is *women*, and *having (the vote)* is a true participle attached to women [? *women*].' Agreed!, but would not the construction and the sense have been clearer if the sentence had been written either 'Women, having the vote, share political power with men' or (stylistically preferable) 'Having the vote, women share political power with men'? For if there is much virtue in an *if*, there is much value in a comma. In this matter, my advice is: Before you decide on a possessive + gerund construction or, if you are not sure of your ground, a fused participle, examine whether a participle construction, *duly punctuated*, does not make a more elegant as well as a more logical sentence. And I submit for your consideration, two sentences; I admit that possibly I err in my interpretation of both of these sentences:—

'All of you shouting at once confuse me': if the emphasis indicates, and the context connotes, that the sense is 'Shouting all at once, you confuse me', then *shouting* is an ordinary participle and the sentence is correct. But is not the sense 'Your (collective) shouting confuses me', with the emphasis on the noise of the shouting? The proposed alteration, however, is drastic. Let us, then, see what happens if we apply the possessive + gerund construction: 'All of your' or 'all your'—'shouting at once confuses me'. But 'all of your shouting at once' makes *all* the subject—and that is not the sense intended; 'all your shouting at once' provides the right sense, but strikes one as being unidiomatic. The general opinion is that in 'all of you shouting at once confuse me', *shouting* is a true participle, and that the sentence is therefore correct; and Fowler would have added, 'Well, anyway, "All of you shouting at once *confuses* me" is an example of the fused participle and the sentence is wrong'. But both forms ('all of you shouting at once confuse me' and '. . . confuses me') are heard, and *in both there is, I think, a fused participle*. And, assuming that the writer or speaker is using the form that conveys his meaning the better, are not both forms correct? In 'All of you shouting at once confuse me', there is a sense construction; in 'All of you shouting at once confuses me' one may postulate an ellipsis. In the latter, you may supply 'the fact of' before 'all of you . . .'; the subject would be 'the fact' and the verb,

therefore, singular. In the former there is, subconsciously, the apposition: 'all of you', which naturally will take a plural verb, and 'shouting at once' (i.e., simultaneously),—or, in other words, there are, according as one regards the sentence subjectively or objectively, two ideas, cumulative ideas, or two facts, cumulative facts: 'all of you' (i.e., 'your plurality', connoting 'mere weight of numbers') and 'shouting at once' (i.e., 'collective shouting', hence 'the din you make'): psychologically, the speaker is confused not only by the noise but also by the fact that he realizes that the noise is made, not by one person (who may be a lunatic) but by many (some of whom may be sensible men): considered together but *not* identified, the noise and his numerical inferiority confuse him. 'All of you shouting at once confuse me' I defend as containing, in grammar, an apposition of two subjects and as being, in reality, a juxtaposition (hence, a cumulation) of two facts.—This, however, is not to defend either form of the sentence stylistically ('By shouting all at once, you confuse me' would be preferable), but merely to defend my opinion that both forms of the sentence are idiomatic and psychologically coherent.

The second example is:

'In the moments of that reflection, George telling the story of Brenda quite obliterated the picture of George done in the eye and foaming at the mouth' (Richard Blaker, *But Beauty Vanishes* [ch. xiv], 1936). Concerning this sentence two preliminary observations may be made:—We can safely omit 'in the moments of that reflection'; we must take 'George telling the story of Brenda' as equivalent to 'the picture [i.e., the visual memory] of George telling the story of Brenda'. We may go further and reduce the sentence to a terser form, 'George telling the story of Brenda obliterated George done in the eye and foaming at the mouth', provided we remember that there are two contrasted memories ('George telling the story of Brenda' and 'George done in the eye and foaming at the mouth'), both sharply visualized. Fowler, I think, would have said that this should read: *'George's telling* the story of Brenda obliterated *George's being* (or *having been*) *done* in the eye and [on that account] foaming at the mouth', which, on first thoughts, may seem not merely feasible but preferable to the original. But is it equally convincing when we restore the sentence to its fuller form, 'The picture of George's telling the story of Brenda obliterated the picture of George's being (or having been) done in the eye and foaming at the mouth'? Does not the possessive + gerund construction destroy the vividness of the two pictures? Does it not even change two memory-*pictures* into two mental *ideas*? Both aesthetics and logic require the retention of 'George telling the story of Brenda', and 'George done in the eye and foaming at the mouth'. If *telling* and *done* and *foaming* are ordinary participles, no alteration of the sense will result from putting the sentence into the participial mode, thus: '[The picture of] George, telling the truth, obliterated the picture of George, done in the eye and foaming at the mouth'. It may be advanced that this is shorter than, but grammatically equivalent to, 'The first picture of George (a George telling [= that tells, or is telling] the story of Brenda) obliterated the second [or more remote] picture of George (a George done [= that has been done] in the eye and foaming [= is foaming] at the mouth)'. If that is so, the fused participle is not involved.

In Fowler's second example, 'Women's having the vote reduces men's political power', the subject is the gerund (or verbal noun, as some people prefer to designate it), *having* (*the vote*), and *women's* is the possessive case, i.e., an adjective-equivalent, attached to that verbal noun. About this type of sentence, there is no argument: all the authorities (Onions, Fowler, Jespersen, and the others) are agreed both on its correctness and on its convenience.

In his third example, 'Women having the vote reduces men's political power', the subject of the sentence is obviously, not *women* (for if *women* were the subject, the verb would be *reduce*), 'nor *having* (for if so, *women* would be left in the air without grammatical construction), but a compound notion formed by fusion of the noun *women* with the participle *having*. Participles so constructed, then, are called fused participles, as opposed to the true participle of No. 1 and the gerund of No. 2' (Fowler).

Probably one feels that 'Women's having the vote reduces men's political power' is preferable to 'Women having the vote reduces men's political power', but how far is that feeling the result of intellectual conviction and how far is it caused by the fact that here we have '*women* having the vote' and not '*woman* having the vote'? Most fair-minded citizens will readily admit that 'Woman having the vote reduces men's political power' rings much less oddly than 'Women having the vote reduces men's political power', especially if we balance the sense by changing 'men's' to 'man's'. Fowler would have done better to omit any reference to the grammatical number, for it is irrelevant to the discussion; to introduce it at all is to obscure the issue. Let us, then, take the revised sentence, 'Woman having the vote reduces man's political power', and see whether it will stand the various tests. 'Woman, having the vote, reduces man's political power'—the participial mode—makes poor sense; 'Woman's having the vote reduces man's political power'—the gerundial mode—is correct. But the correctness of the gerundial mode does not necessarily involve the incorrectness of the fused-participle mode. Grammar has many alternatives: the rightness of one construction does not preclude the rightness of the alternative.

If one compares '*Woman having* the vote reduces man's political power' with Dr Onions's example, 'His premature death prevented *anything's coming* of the scheme', one may, if one is an aesthete, be tempted to exclaim, 'Oh, but "anything's coming of the scheme" is so ugly that one simply couldn't use it! Only "anything coming of the scheme" is possible. "Woman's having the vote" is not so disgusting, so let it pass'. But is euphony the only—is it even the most important—reason why 'His premature death prevented anything coming of the scheme' is preferable to '. . . anything's coming . . .'? Dr Onions implies (for he does not actually state) that '. . . anything coming . . .' is idiomatic, for he goes almost so far as to say that '. . . anything's coming . . .' is unidiomatic—is, in short, un-English.

Now, in the idiomatic there is usually a basis of good sense—of logic—of ethnic necessity. As we have mentioned in the paragraphs taken from Dr Onions's *Advanced English Syntax*, the fused participle has historical precedent strongly behind it. Has it also reason, sense, necessity to support it? Dr Onions says that it is at least not illogical, nor inconsistent with other participial usages.

Let us return to 'Woman having the vote reduces man's political power'. This is equivalent to 'The female vote (or woman's vote) reduces man's political power' or 'Voting by women reduces man's political power' or even 'Woman's voting reduces . . .' But as 'woman's voting' = 'female voting', might not 'woman-voting' be so used? It is true that we speak of 'child-murder', not of 'child-murdering', but we do speak of 'pig-sticking'. Here 'child' and 'pig' are, as it were, accusatives after 'murdering' and 'sticking'. We could, however, use nominatives in the same way; primitive and savage peoples do; compare 'We hear of *it being* cold'. Moreover, *woman* (or, for that matter, *women*) *having the vote* may be regarded as a unit, with the two simple ideas *woman* and *having the vote*, which appears less odd if we write it *woman-having-the-vote* (= *female suffrage* or German *Frauenstimmrecht*). It seems likely that this unit-formation is, psychologically, at the back of Dr Onions's non-gerundial examples and that we need not rack our brains to find compounds.

This seems even more likely when we are confronted with such an example as 'For the first time the possibility of something serious having happened entered Jeffrey's mind' (F. W. Crofts, *The Loss of the Jane Vosper*, 1936). According to Fowler, this should be '. . . the possibility of something serious's having happened . . .',—which can hardly be called English. Consider, too, the following examples from Professor Jespersen's 'On ING' in his masterly paper, *Some Disputed Points in English Grammar* (S.P.E. Tract No. xxv, 1936), evoked in stern opposition to Fowler's article in *Modern English Usage* and based mainly on usage ('I have . . . examples of this construction from nearly every prose writer of repute from the beginning of the eighteenth century till our own days') and partly on convenience:—

'I cannot understand no *rain falling*', i.e., (the fact) that no rain falls or has fallen.

'Journeys end in *lovers meeting*' (Shakespeare).

'She had calculated on her *daughters remaining* at N.' (Jane Austen).

Note: 'He had every day a chance of *this happening*' (Fielding), 'He wouldn't hear of *that being* possible' (Dickens), 'We are mortified at the news of *the French taking* the town from the Portuguese' (Swift), 'I am not surprised at *young or old falling* in love with her' (Thackeray), 'No fear had they of *bad becoming* worse' (Wordsworth), 'Besides the fact of *those three being* there, the drawbridge is kept up' (A. Hope); here we have instances of words that cannot form a genitive; 'but are they therefore to be excluded from being used as the subject of an ing-combination?' as Jespersen pertinently asks. And he drives home his point by citing other examples of post-posed adjectives: that exquisitely finicky stylist, Walter Pater, could write, 'At the thought of *a man, a while since so strong, turning* his face to the wall'.

In many groups of words, it is difficult to form a genitive, and so the fused participle is preferred: 'The danger of *the chair and its occupant being* dashed against the rugged face of the precipice' (Scott)—not *the chair's and its occupant's* nor *the chair and its occupant's*; 'Laughing at *Sir John Walter and me falling* out' (Swift)—not *Sir John Walter's and my*, nor *Sir John Walter and my*; 'What is the good of *mother and me economising?*' (Hardy); 'We were talking about getting away. *Me and you getting* away' (Kipling) and 'There is the less fear of *you and me finding* one' (Conan Doyle),—'*I and your* or *All and your* or *my and your* getting away' being as unnatural as '*you and my* or *your and my* finding out'; *mine and yours* (for '*me and you* getting away') being even more absurd.

If the point is still not made, let us take a few more of Jespersen's pile-driving examples:—

'How could public justice be pacified by *a female cousin of the deceased man engaging* to love, honour and obey the clerk?' (De Quincey); 'It consists in *the heart and soul of the man* never *having* been open to Truth' (Carlyle); 'Without *either of us knowing* that the other had taken up the subject' (Wordsworth); 'Nor the slightest chance of *any of them going* in rags' (Ruskin); 'On *the door being* opened, she perceived a couch' (Hardy).

Jespersen calls the construction of '*woman having the vote* (reduces man's political power)' a nexus: this nexus arises from the feeling, or the subconscious understanding, that *woman having the vote* is a unit. Not merely is it a psychological unit. It is also a speech-unit; it is indivisible.

Such speech-units are in keeping with English idiom: witness the group genitive and the relative pronouns *that, which, who*, which can refer to a phrase or even a sentence as naturally as to a single word.

The final position is this:

When the participial construction (rightly used in 'Women, having the vote, share political power with men') fails to convey the sense intended *and* when the possessive + gerund (neat enough in 'Women's having the vote reduces men's political power') would be either clumsy or ambiguous, then the fused participle is, to guard against clumsiness, preferable, and to guard against ambiguity, inevitable; and it can be used without departing from English usage and without offending English good sense.

But this is not equivalent to saying that the *ing*-construction is not extremely clumsy at times. 'When it is clumsy, turn the sentence differently' is the safe and obvious practice to observe. It is, however, to be remarked that, even here, the fused participle is frequently less clumsy than is the possessive + gerund, as some of Jespersen's examples have shown.

And, whatever you do, avoid a mixture (unless there is an imperative reason for using the two different constructions). Sometimes a writer falls between two stools—between fusing and refusing, as in J. William Matthews's important book, *Cockney Past and Present*, 1938, where we find 'For my own part, I have no great objection to *Cockney being described* as vulgar or even to *its being denied* officially the status of a dialect' ('being officially denied' would have been preferable).

Postscript. There is a school of thought which holds that 'After verbs of reaction or feeling (*feel, blame, disapprove, approve, admire, dislike, resent, hate, like, love, adore*, etc., etc.), the genitive + gerund is obligatory; and after other verbs, the genitive + gerund is often preferable', the reference being to the object (the accusative); those who belong to this school of thought generally assert that even if the fused participle is sometimes defensible in the accusative, it is never defensible in the nominative (i.e. as subject)—a view that is untenable

for nouns, but has something to be said for it as to pronouns: 'He going away like that was a surprise' is less *idiomatic* than 'His going away like that was a surprise'.

With the second part of the above-quoted dictum, I have, by implication at least, dealt already. As for the first part, I concur so far as to say that after verbs of feeling and reaction, the genitive (or possessive) + gerund is sometimes felt to be more *idiomatic* than the fused participle: 'I resent his being away' sounds, perhaps, more natural than 'I resent him being away'; yet I still say that the latter is defensible and not un-English (for reasons into which I have already gone).

Note the difference between:

> I saw him cross the road.
> . . . crossing . . .
> . . . his crossing . . . .

and between:

> I felt it move
> . . . moving.
> . . . its moving.

In both sets, is there not something to be said for each form? And is it not that the criterion is not a mere grammatical one, but a criterion of *sense*? Does not the first form convey a sense different from that of the second? The third from that of the second, as well as from that of the first? If that is so, then the fused participle conveys one nuance, the genitive + gerund conveys another. But this is a point not fittingly to be developed here; it would require far too much space. [[There is an excellent discussion in Curme, *Syntax*, Ch. xxiv—Subject of the Gerund, pp. 485–490.]]

future refers to something that has not yet happened; do not, therefore, use it for *subsequent* or *after*, as in 'We do not know her future manoeuvres when she made the decision'.

G

gamble is to play games of chance for money, esp. for high stakes. It should not be applied to playing for trifling sums, for it is a pejorative term, whereas to *game* is neutral, literary, and slightly archaic: the same applies to the verbal nouns, *gambling* and *gaming*. (*The O.E.D.*) [[*Game* (v.), seldom occurs in American English as a synonym of *gamble.* The expression less deprecatory is to *play* one game or another *for stakes.*]]

game. 'Game in England—Hare, pheasant, partridge, grouse and moor fowl. Game in Ireland—Same as [for] England, with the addition of deer, landrail, quail, black game, and bustard. Game in Scotland—Same as [for] England, with the addition of ptarmigan.' (*Diary*, 1939, issued by Hay & Son, Ltd. of Norfold Street, Sheffield.) [[*Webster's:* 'The various animals (chiefly birds and mammals) which are considered worthy of pursuit by sportsmen. Among birds the order Galliformes, and the duck, plover, snipe, and rail families, contain the majority of those ordinarily considered game.']]

Gand for *Ghent.* See BRUXELLES . . .

gang of workmen or of criminals is correct. But to apply *gang* to a set, a clique, a fortuitous assemblage of idle and/or harmless persons is to fall into slang.

gantlet is in England an obsolete form of *gauntlet,* whether independently or in the phrase, *run the gauntlet.* In U.S.A., the phrase is written *run the gantlet,* in order to distinguish *gantlet* from *gauntlet* (glove), for *ga(u)ntlet* of the phrase is a corruption of *gantlope,* a totally different word. See esp. *The O.E.D.*

gaol, gaoler; jail, jailer. The former set is the earlier, but the latter is now the accepted one: *gaol, gaoler* are now literary and archaic. 'In literary and journalistic use both the G and J forms are now admitted as correct, but all recent dictionaries give the preference to the latter', says *The O.E.D.* in 1900: this tendency is, by now, even more marked. [[In the U.S.A., *gaol, gaoler* are 'obsolete, except for occasional legal use' (*Webster's*).]]

gargantuan, misused. 'The water was alive with traffic, Lilliputian tugs were performing gargantuan towing feats', Robert Eton, *Not in Our Stars,* 1937. The author (Laurence Meynell) means either *gigantic* or, better, *Brobdingnagian.*

gasolene and **gasoline** (likewise pronounced *-ene*) are equally correct. *Gas* is a colloquial abbreviation, originally American, and is in Britain used mostly in *step on the gas,* 'to make haste'. [The original noun *gas* was the invention of Van Helmont and is one of the most successful of invented words.]

gem for *something greatly prized* (a treasure') is colloquial and therefore to be avoided in formal or dignified contexts; and it can easily be overdone in any kind of context. Mr Frank Whitaker condemns it as a 'rubber-stamp' word.

gender refers to words; as a synonym for *sex* it is jocular and archaic.

general. See UNIVERSAL(LY).

generally for *usually* (as a general rule; in most instances) is not incorrect, but it may lead to ambiguity, as in 'It is generally wet and cold in S.W. New Zealand.'

generally always. The two adverbs used together are contradictory.

GENERIC AND PARTICULAR should not be confused—should not be interchanged. The theory is too obvious to be stressed; so obvious that one would think it impossible, in practice, to fall into this error. Yet the error occurs frequently in the use of the relative pronouns, *that, which, who(m)*; in sentences containing *man* or *mankind*; and in such a sentence as this, 'It would not be possible to call an angler [generic] a "worm" if one had seen the masterly manner in which he [particular] lands a large fish' (an essay script in the L.C.C. Major Establishment examination, 1938).

genetic, defined as 'pertaining to, or having reference to, origin' (*The O.E.D.*), must not be confused with *generative,* 'productive, able to produce'.

GENITIVE, GROUP. See GROUP GENITIVE.

GENITIVE*, VAGARIES OF THE. See also GROUP GENITIVE.

'"And did they compare for size?"— "About right. But then, so were that other clerk's, Mason, and Dr Parsons', and half a dozen other people's"',

Josephine Bell, *Death on the Borough Council,* 1937.

The basis from which we arrive at vagaries of the genitive (or possessive) case is the general rule that a singular *boy* takes apostrophe *s*: *boy's*; the plural *boys* takes apostrophe: *boys'*. The main exceptions are that those words whose interior changes take apostrophe *s* in both the singular and the plural: *man's*, plural *men's*; *woman's*, plural *women's*; *child's, children's; cow's, kine's; pig's, swine's*: and that nouns that remain unchanged also take apostrophe *s* in

---

* For an extremely good account of the genitive in general, see Geo. O. Curme, *Syntax,* 1931, pp. 70–88. The ensuing article is, in several parts, a précis of Curme's admirable chapter.

both numbers: *one sheep's (wool), two sheep's (wool)*.

Other exceptions are these: nouns ending in *-nce* take, in the singular, an apostrophe, as in *for patience' sake, for conscience' sake*, but in the plural they take *s'*, as in *for their consciences' sake*, in accordance with the general rule for the plural; *for goodness' sake* is a formula, —contrast *for mercy's sake*; nouns ending in *s*, followed immediately by a noun beginning with *s*, and nouns ending in *ses*, or *sess* or *sses* or *ssess*, or in *sis* or *siss* or *ssis* or *ssiss*, or in *-xes* (as in *Xerxes' army*), take in the singular an apostrophe, as in *Pears' Soap* (the three consecutive *s*'es in 'Pears's soap' being felt to be excessive) and in 'the *oasis'* verge', '*molasses*' attraction for children'.

In the past it was a very general, as it is now a not infrequent, practice to form the genitive singular of all nouns ending in *s* and especially those ending in *ss* (*hostess*) by adding an apostrophe to both the nominative singular (*a hostess' duties, your Highness' pleasure*) and of course in the plural ('The *three hostesses' houses* were in Park Lane'); but now it is usual to form the singular genitive by adding *'s* (*a hostess's duties, your Highness's pleasure*),—which seems to be a sensible idea, for if you can say *three hostesses' houses*, you can easily say *a hostess's duties*. There is, however, a strong tendency to retain *Jesus'* and *Demosthenes', Socrates'*, and other such genitives of Greek proper names.

In those three paragraphs, there are no vagaries properly so called, at least in the rules enunciated, although it is true that certain idiosyncratic, law-unto-themselves writers fall into vagaries when, in defiance of rule and clarity, they depart from those rules. [[American readers may wish to consult *Webster's* entry for '*possessive*', Perrin's discussion of *Jones*, and *A Manual of Style* [University of Chicago Press, 10th rev. ed., 1937], pp. 72, 95.]] Nor perhaps do the following paragraphs contain vagaries, unless we classify several idioms as vagaries.

In the group genitive (*the King of England's power*), a group of words is made to conform to the rule that governs single words: an economical idiom and a very great convenience. See GROUP GENITIVE.

The same principle determines the genitive ending of two or even three nouns in apposition. Thus, *John Williamson, the aforementioned tenant* becomes in the genitive *John Williamson, the aforementioned tenant's house*, or, for legal clarity, *John Williamson's (the aforementioned tenant's) house*; *Albert, the Prince Consort* becomes *Albert, the Prince Consort's home*; *Arthur Wellesley, Duke of Wellington, the Field-Marshal* becomes *Arthur Wellesley, Duke of Wellington, the Field Marshal's victory at Waterloo*. That these, or at least the shorter, genitival groups are equivalent to group genitives can be seen by the omission of the comma, as in *John Williamson the aforementioned tenant's house*—*Albert the Prince Consort's home*—but not in the third, for there *Arthur Wellesley Duke of Wellington* is possible, but *Duke of Wellington the Field Marshal* is impossible.

'If two names are connected by *and* and represent persons that are joined together in authorship, business, or a common activity, the second name alone assumes the genitive ending: "*Stevens and Malone's* Shakespeare", "in *William and Mary's* reign", but of course "*Steele's and Addison's* [work or] works" when we are speaking of the separate sets of two different authors' (Curme), and 'Elizabeth's and Victoria's reign [or, better, reigns]' when we are dealing with two separate reigns. In the same way, 'if two or more names connected by *and* represent persons that are joined together in possession, the second or [the] last name alone assumes the genitive ending: "*John and William's* uncle", "*John, William and Mary's* uncle". "We paid a visit to *Messrs Pike and White's* works." "My *father and mother's* Bible."—But we must give each genitive its genitive *-s* if there is no joint possession: "*My father's and my mother's* birthdays both fall in June, two days apart"' (Curme).

Two pronouns (*You and I*) or three pronouns (*he, you and I*) need careful handling: '*Your and my contract* (or *contracts*) has (or have) been signed'; '*His, your and my contract* (or *contracts*) has (or have) been signed'. An alternative to *your and my contracts*, where the contracts are separate, is *your contract(s) and mine*.

Noun and pronoun (*John and you*) or pronoun and noun (*you and John*) follow the same rule: *John's and your contract(s), your and John's contract(s)*.

There are to be noted several rules of

a different order. 'First [the] use [of the genitive case] is now in ordinary prose almost restricted to personal beings [and animals], and even such phrases as "society's hard-drilled soldiery" (Meredith), where *society* is personified, are felt as poetical; still more so, . . . "thou knowst not gold's effect" (Shakespeare) or "setting out upon life's journey" (Stevenson). But in some set phrases the genitive is [well] established, e.g. "out of *harm's* way"; "he is at his *wits*' (or *wit's*) end"; so also in the stock quotation from *Hamlet*, "in my *mind's* eye", etc. Then to indicate measure, etc.: "at a *boat's* length from the ship", and especially time: "an *hour's* walk", "a good *night's* rest", "*yesterday's* post"; and this is even extended to such prepositional combinations as "*to-day's* adventures", "*to-morrow's* papers."

'Secondly, . . . the subjective genitive . . . is in great vigour, for instance in "the King's arrival", "the Duke's invitation", "the Duke's inviting him [gave him much pleasure]", "Mrs Poyser's repulse of the squire" (G. Eliot). Still there is, in quite recent times a tendency towards expressing the subject by means of the preposition *by*, just as in the passive voice, for instance in "the accidental discovery by Miss Knag of some correspondence" (Dickens); "the appropriation by a settled community of lands on the other side of the ocean" (Seeley), "the massacre of Christians by Chinese". "Forster's Life of Dickens" is the same thing as "Dicken's Life, by Forster".—The objective genitive,—where the genitival noun or pronoun is affected by the following noun instead of affecting that following noun (*his defeat* = *the defeat of him*, not *the defeat by him*),—'was formerly much more common than now, the ambiguity of [this] genitive being probably the reason of its decline. Still, we find, for instance, "his expulsion from power by the Tories" (Thackeray)', where, however, 'by the Tories' dispels all ambiguity, '"What was thy pity's recompence?" (Byron). "England's wrongs" generally mean the wrongs done to England. . . . In "my sceptre's awe" [Shakespeare, *Richard the Second*, I, i, 118] we have an objective, but in "thy free awe pays homage to us" (*Hamlet*, IV, iii, 63) a subjective genitive. But on the whole, such obscurity will occur less frequently in English than in other languages, where the genitive is more fully used' (Jespersen, *Growth and Structure of the English Language*). The same ambiguity attaches to *of* + noun, as in *the love of God*, which only the context can—but sometimes does not—make clear, for by itself it may = 'the love felt by God' or 'the love felt for God'. But practised writers and speakers, and, indeed, all clear thinkers avoid these pitfalls almost by instinct.

Stylistically, the *'s* and the *of* forms of the possessive are often varied or mingled. Thus Elizabeth Barrett Browning's 'all the hoofs of King Saul's father's asses' would probably, in good prose, become 'all the hoofs of the asses of King Saul's father' or, better, 'all the hoofs of the asses owned by King Saul's father'; and Pinero's 'He is my wife's first husband's only child's godfather' might be rendered a little less monotonous by a change to 'He is the godfather of the only child of my wife's first husband'.

There is an excellent guiding principle set forth by George O. Curme, who acutely remarks, 'The inflected genitive that stands before the governing noun usually has a weaker stress than its governing noun, while the genitive after the governing noun has a heavier stress: *Mr Smith's new house'*, but *the new house of Mr Smith'*; stress, obviously, is laid on the important word, and if there are two stresses, the heavier stress falls on the more significant of the two important words, thus: *Mr Smith's' new house'* and *the new house' of Mr Smith'*.

Note too the place of the genitive in 'The desire *of my heart* for peace', *of my heart* being less important than *for peace*; to stress the genitive, put it last, as in 'the desire for peace *of every man, woman and child in that great nation'*. (Curme.)

Then there is the double genitive case, exemplified in such phrases as 'a friend of my *father's'*, 'three friends of *mine'*, 'that hat of *his'*, 'and dress of *Jane's'*. For the pronominal type of this strange genitive, see OF HER—OF HERS.

These pronominal examples are much less likely to lead to trouble than are the others: *that hat of his, that football of theirs, this pain of mine* are unambiguous; but what are we to say of *this beauty of my sister's* and *this famed beauty of my famous sisters'*? To the reader, they are clear; the listener, however, does not, in either example, know whether one or two or several sisters are concerned. Such double genitives as the two recorded in the last sentence but one are avoided by scrupulous writers, for the scrupulous remember the very sound rule that a piece of writing should be as clear to a listener as to a reader; especially do they avoid it with nouns in the plural, as in *in some retreat of his or his friends'* (John Burroughs, *Far and Near*), where the apostrophe after *friends* clarifies the thought of the author: listeners, unfortunately, do not hear an apostrophe. But nouns in the singular are often equally susceptible to misapprehension by a listener, as in ('It was no fault *of the doctor's*'). 'The *of*-genitive ['of the doctor'] is here, as often elsewhere [e.g., to distinguish between objective and subjective genitive], a clearer form, and is often preferred', remarks George O. Curme, who thereby implies a useful hint. The same authority has smilingly noticed that 'although the double genitive with nouns is in general subject to ambiguity, many [writers and speakers], desirous of its lively effect, take their chances with it, trusting to the [context or the] situation to help them out'. Make sure that the circumstances *do* make the reference clear.

'In the case of personal pronouns', Curme remarks, 'there has long been a tendency to differentiate . . . form and meaning, namely, to employ *his, her*, etc., in the possessive relation and *of him, of her*, etc., in the partitive relation, stressing the idea of an integral part . . . : "*His hair, his eyes*", etc., but "She was the daughter of a lumberjack and woodcraft was bred into the very fiber *of her*" (*Saturday Evening Post*, July 29, 1916). "The man had something in the *look of him*" (Browning, *An Epistle*). "I don't do it for the honour *of it*". As this differentiation has not become thoroughly established, we still more commonly employ here the old undifferentiated forms *his, her*, etc., for either the possessive or the partitive relation: "*his* eyes" and "The man had something in *his* look". But we now always use the form *of* when the pronoun is modified by a relative clause: "Then first I heard the voice of *her* to whom . . . the Gods Rise up for reverence" (Tennyson, *Œnone*, 1.105)', it being loose English to write such a sentence as 'I put the money into *his* hand *who* needed it'.

In general, the 'very fiber *of her*', 'something in the look *of him*' form is poetic or, at the least, literary; Carlyle says, 'The chief quality of Burns is *the sincerity of him*'; Jack London, in *White Fang*, has 'They were moulding *the clay of him*'. These examples are cited by Curme, who then adds:—'In a number of expressions the partitive genitive of personal pronouns is also common in plain prose, usually, however, without the poetic [connotation] of the preceding examples, [but] merely stressing the idea of an integral part: "That will be the end *of it*, the last *of it*". In a vague way we feel life and death as parts of us, vital parts of our human experience: "I couldn't do it for *the life of me*". "That will be *the death of you*".'

Worth noting, though it presents few difficulties, is the genitive absolute: that genitive in which the governing noun is omitted and which applies especially to residences and to places of business, as in 'Buy a loaf at the baker's in the next street', 'I spent a pleasant hour at Smith's [house, flat, apartment, 'diggings', etc.], after an unpleasant half hour at Robinson & Smith's [office or shop or factory]'; 'John has asked whether he might go for part of his holiday to his *uncle and aunt's*'; but if the uncle and the aunt occupy separate residences, the sentence must end: 'go . . . to his *uncle's and* (his) *aunt's*'. Now, 'the governing noun is regularly omitted when the possessive genitive points forward or backward to a preceding or following governing noun, for the genitive here is now felt as a possessive pronoun, like *mine, hers*, etc. . . . "John's auto is larger than *William's and* mine"' (Curme).

Finally we come to what Curme designates, by implication, as the Unclear Genitive and the Blended Genitive.

Unclear Genitives: 'The loss of distinctive genitive form . . . in a number of pronouns and limiting adjectives has weakened English expression.' Fielding wrote: '*Both their several talents* were excessive', whereas a Middle English author would have written *bother their* (or *their bother*) *talents*, where *bother*, in either *bother their* or *their bother*, is a distinctive genitive form—*bother* as distinctive from the nominative *both*. Fielding's *both their several talents* would, in correct Modern English, be *the several talents of both of them*, which is weak and wordy in comparison with the Middle English *bother their* (or *their bother*) *several talents*. 'This older usage', as Curme points out, 'is best preserved in the subjective genitive category in connection with the gerund: "Your mother will feel *your both* going away" (Mrs. Gaskell, *Wives and Daughters*, Ch. xiv). "Isn't it dreadful to think of *their all* being wrong!" (Sir Harry Johnston, *The Man Who Did the Right Thing*, Ch. ii).—It is also well preserved in the possessive category in such expressions as *both our lives* [are at stake], *both our minds* [are made up], but we now feel the old genitives as plural limiting adjectives. . . . This old usage survives in popular speech: "She is *both their mothers*, i.e., "the mother of both of them". "It is *both their faults*" [i.e., the faults of both of them]. In the literary language it lingers on in *for both their sakes, for both our sakes* [for the sake(s) of both of them—of us]. Similarly, when *of* is inserted after *all, both, none*, etc., to give expression to the partitive idea: "I'm taking the trouble of writing this true history *for all your benefits*" (Hughes, *Tom Brown's School-Days*, I, vi), instead of the correct *for the benefit of all of you*. "A painful circumstance which is attributable to *none of our faults*" (Thackeray, *Pendennis*, II, Ch. xxxv), instead of the correct *the fault of none of us*.' This difficulty affects also *each* and *either* (and *neither*): 'for each of our sakes' should be 'for the sake of each [or, all] of us'; 'It was neither of our faults' should be 'It was the fault of neither of us'. Note, however, that *neither of their faults*, like *both of their faults, all of their faults*, etc., is correct in such sentences as 'Smith's fault was gluttony; Robinson's avarice. But *both of their faults* paled into respectability in comparison with Jones's, for that was a tendency to murder those who contradicted him' and. ' . . . But *neither of their faults* seems of much account when set beside Jones's. . . .' This is a distinction that Curme failed to make,—perhaps he thought it too obvious to be worthy of his nicely discriminating mind.

Blended Genitives: These are more subtle: they constitute a nice test of the correctitude of even the best writers. 'In the partitive category', writes Curme, 'there is a tendency, once much more common than now, to blend the genitive with some other construction, resulting in illogical expression: "His versification is by far the most perfect *of any English poet*" (Saintsbury, *Nineteenth Century Literature*, 268), a blending of "His versification is far the most perfect *of all English poets*" and "His versification is more perfect than that *of any other English poet*"',—but should not the former sentence read '. . . *of all English poets*'? Such 'omission of the word *other* after *any* . . . is a form of blending still common. In comparisons where there is present the idea of a group or class, the superlative represents the group as complete, while the comparative represents the separation of one or more from all the others in the group. Hence we should say "[His versification] is [by far] the most perfect *of all English poets*"'— more logically, *of all English poets*'—'or "is more perfect [by far] than that *of any other English poet*"' (Curme). Curme, however, should add that Saintsbury could also have written: 'He, of all English poets, has by far the most perfect versification' or 'Of all English poets', his is by far the most perfect versification', or even 'Of all English versifications [= systems of versification, and performance therein], his is by far the most perfect', or several other modifications. (For the further infelicity, *the most perfect*, see COMPARATIVES, FALSE.) In 1938, an English journalist perpetrated this objectionable sentence, 'On President Benes's shoulders now devolves the greatest burden of any man in Europe'; for this, read 'On President Benes's shoulders now devolves a burden greater than that of any other man in Europe'.

genius, 'native intellectual power of an exalted type; instinctive and extraordinary capacity for imaginative creation, original thought, invention or discovery. Often contrasted with *talent*' (*The O.E.D.*), must not be debased to = *talent*, which should be confined to 'a special natural ability or aptitude; a natural capacity for success in some department of mental or physical activity' (*The O.E.D.*), but without inspiration or ultimate power. Do not confuse *genius* with *genus*, class, category, kind.

gent, 'a gentleman', is an illiteracy except when it applies to such a man as might be expected to use the word.

genteel; gentle; Gentile. The last = 'non-Jewish'; the second is now confined to the senses 'mild, not savage, not cruel, not rough', the senses 'well-born' being archaic; *genteel*, in Standard English, is now pejorative or, at best, playful,—the senses 'belonging to the gentry', 'appropriate to the gentry', 'having the habits characteristic of the gentry' being, except in sarcastic (or, occasionally, jocular) contexts, archaic.

gentleman. See LADY and MISTER.

GERUND. An admirably clear treatment of the subject is to be found in Dr C. T. Onions's *An Advanced English Syntax* (6th ed., 1932). Here are various examples of correct current usage:

'The *digging* of the foundations was hard work';

'The train will be long in *coming*';

'Now cease *complaining* and start work'.

With constructions dependent:

'He spoke of there *being a danger*';

'Your *being friends* will ease the situation';

'There are more ways of killing a cat . . .'.

With adverbial modifications:

'*Staring about aimlessly* will do no good';

'There is no *getting to the borders of space*'.

With adjectives:

'There's *no refuting* so cogent an argument';

'There was *some foolish staring, some more than foolish wondering*'.

Note that when the gerund governs— i.e., is followed by—an objective (an accusative), there are, in 20th Century English, two constructions:

'Much diffidence was felt about *demanding money*';

'The *demanding of money* was the cause of much diffidence'.

Demanding money is the more general usage when the gerund depends on a preposition. *The demanding money* is now obsolete: a good thing too, for it led to ambiguity: *the electing councillors* could either mean 'the election of councillors' (to the Town Council) or 'those Councillors who elect' (the Chairman of the council). Occasionally, even now, one sees *the mentioning this* for *(the) mention of this* or *the mentioning of this*.

The gerund governed (i.e., preceded) by *a* or *a-* (i.e., *on*), as in 'I went a-buying', is archaic,—when, at least, it is not dialectal. There is, however, a literary survival, with the preposition omitted: 'The church is *building*' (a-building,

or in the course of building—or being built);

'The reformation must still be *doing*, never done'.

A purely syntactic, one might call it an academic, difficulty occurs in such sentences as these:

'What a long time you are *dressing*!';

'He was too much occupied *watching* the passers-by to notice what was being discussed';

'They continued *eating* until they could eat no more'.

Thus:—'What a long time you are *a-dressing*', or 'What a long time you, dressing are';

'He was too much occupied, *a-watching* (or, in watching) . . .' or 'Watching, he was too much occupied . . .';

'They continued their eating . . .' or 'eating, they continued until they could eat no more'.

Finally, precisely as there are misrelated (or suspended) participles, so there are misrelated gerunds. 'The gerund', Dr Onions remarks, 'must be handled carefully with respect to its reference to the rest of the sentence. Do not write, e.g.:—"After *fighting* the flames for several hours the ship was abandoned." Here, *fighting* refers grammatically to "the ship", which makes nonsense; say: "After they (the crew . . .) had been fighting" or "After fighting the flames . . . the crew abandoned the ship". Correct the following: "By pouring hard peas upon the hatches they became so slippery that the boarders could not stand." [Who poured?]'

GERUND AND PARTICIPLE CONFUSED. (See also preceding article, last paragraph proper.) An example (Cameron McCabe, *The Face on the Cutting-Room Floor*, 1937) shows the error and affords material for the correction of the error. 'He describes . . . how Smith rang him up at my place. But he does not realise how very odd it is that Smith should ring him there . . . McCabe *goes on telling* us how he went back to the studio, how Smith took him up to Robertson's room, how Robertson . . ., and how Smith suggested that . . .' Written as printed here, *goes on telling* connotes that McCabe had already begun to tell how he went back to the studio, etc., etc., but the context shows that not the gerund but the present participle is required, thus: 'McCabe *goes on, telling* how he went back . . .' But a stylist

would have written 'He describes ...
ring him there. ... McCabe goes on to
tell how (or, unambiguously, that) he
went back ...'

gesture is now often inappropriately
used for speech or behaviour indicative
of new intention, good- or ill-will. *Daily
Mail*, 1922, 'The United States Cabinet
to-day sat ... to consider a world-
gesture which is intended, etc.' *Woman's
Journal*, 1929, 'The right gesture in
jewellery'. (*The O.E.D.*)

get. The verb *to get* implies always to
obtain, procure, acquire, attain (to), *receive*; its use, especially in the past tense,
got, to imply the mere fact of possession
is the commonest of colloquialisms, but
unnecessary and, strictly judged, incorrect. See example under HAVE GOT. See
also GOT.

get the best of; get the better of.
Properly, the former applies to swindling
and other trickery, whereas the latter
has no offensive connotation and simply
= to overcome, to defeat.

gibberish. See JABBER.

gifted (with *talented* and *moneyed* or
monied) was strongly condemned by
Dean Alford in 1870. He quotes Coleridge, 'I imagine other participles formed
by this analogy, and men being said to
be pennied, shillinged, or pounded'. But
the words are in idiomatic use and cannot be objected to.

gigantic, misused for *abundant, copious, heavy.* 'The waterfalls would have
been a great nuisance if we had not been
wet through, for the spray was so gigantic we couldn't have escaped a
soaking', Violet O. Cressy-Marcks, *Up
the Amazon and over the Andes*, 1932.

gigantic; titanic. In their transferred
senses, both of these words mean 'huge,
colossal', but whereas the former is
rarely, the latter is frequently employed
with the sub-sense of 'extraordinarily
powerful'. The stronger of the two words
is *titanic*, but both of them are to be
used in moderation.

gilded and **gilt** are both correct as
preterites and past participles, though
gilded is now much the commoner. But as
adjectives, *gilt* is now confined to the
literal sense, whereas *gilded* is not only
figurative ('A gilded pollution', Dean
Farrar), but also mediate as 'tinged with
a golden colour' ('The gilded summit of
that bright mountain') and literal; in
the literal sense, *gilded* is more dignified
than *gilt. Gilded*, moreover, appears in

certain set phrases—*the Gilded Chamber*
(the House of Lords), *gilded spurs* (of
knighthood), and *gilded youth* (the
French *jeunesse dorée*).

gipsy—gypsy; Gipsy—Gypsy. The
word being a corrupted form of *Egyptian*,
there is good ground for preserving the
latter spelling; the former is, however,
much more generally used,—perhaps,
as *The O.E.D.* suggests, because of the
awkward appearance of the two *y*'s; the
absence of this objection in the plural
may account for the more frequent
Gypsies. The capital *G* should be used
when the people or language is meant
(as *English, French*, etc.), but not when
gipsy, gypsy, is adjectival.

girl-wife for *a* (*very*) *young wife* is
shamefully overworked by those who
write for the sob-stuff and sensational
section of the Press.

give for *form* or *constitute*, as in 'Language gives a guide to national character', is not only misleading but also a
most damning indication of poverty of
spirit and vocabulary.

given name. See CHRISTIAN NAME.

glamorous for *romantic* or (of a scene,
a night, etc.) *lovely* or (of a woman)
beautiful and attractive or (of a way of
life) *exciting* or *adventurous* or (of a love-
affair or a flirtation) *sex-filled* or *amorous*
belongs to the advertising of films—and
should be treated as the dubious privilege
of boss-driven copywriters.

glassfuls and **glasses full.** Cf. the
comment at BASKETFULS.

glean, 'to gather in small quantities',
'to scrape together', is catachrestic when
it is used as a mere synonym of *acquire*
or *get* or *obtain* (as in 'He failed to glean
the sense').

globe. See EARTH.

glorious (as a vague but rapturous
expression of admiration or pleasure)
does not mean *delightful* but 'intensely
delightful'.

glycerine, glycerin. See '-ILE and
-INE'.

goanna is popularly used in Australia
for the monitor lizards (Varanidae); it is
a corruption of the word *iguana*, though
the true iguana is not found in that
country.

go by the name of. See BY THE NAME
OF.

going for *current* is unidiomatic, as in
'The going language of educators as
expressed in their learned papers ...',

Stuart Chase, *The Tyranny of Words,*
1938.

golf course and **golf links.** Properly,
the former is applied to an inland, the
latter to a seaside set of greens and
fairways. (With thanks to Mr Frank
Whitaker, lover of good English and
exponent of good golf.)

good few, a; a good many. What is
the difference? Cf. the entry at 'FEW and
A FEW'. *A good few* is 'a fair number'.
but it is a dialectism and a colloquialism.
A good many is also a colloquialism; its
sense is 'a very fair number'. Both
phrases are vague, but *a good many*
represents a slightly larger number than
a good few. '"Were there any others
there? There *were*! Quite a few?" "Oh,
Lord, yes! A good many, in fact".'
The American *quite a few* = 'a considerable number'.

good goods makes an ugly sound. Try
well-made, serviceable, excellent, superior,
etc.

good will; goodwill. In commerce, always *goodwill,* the privilege, granted by
seller to buyer, of trading as his successor, esp. the ready-formed connexion of
clients or customers, considered as part
of the saleability of a business and as
additional to the plant, the stock-
in-trade, the book-debts, etc. As 'the
state of wishing well (to a person, a corporation, a cause, etc.)', 'kindly or
favourable regard', and as 'cheerful consent or acquiescence', 'readiness or zeal',
it is written either *good will* (preferably)
or *goodwill. (The O.E.D.)*

goose, plural *geese,* except for *goose,*
'a tailor's smoothing-iron', which has
plural *gooses.*

got and **have got.** The too frequent
slovenly substitution of *got* for other
verbs expressive of *possession, acquiring,
attainment, arrival, achievement,* etc., was
noted as early as 1789 by the author of
*Aristarchus; or, The Principles of Com-
position. Containing a Methodical Arrangement of the Improprieties frequent in
Writing and Conversation, with Select
Rules for attaining to Purity and Elegance
of Expression.* (This anonymous work is
ascribed by the British Museum Library
to the Rev. Philip Withers, but John
Badcock ['Jon Bee'] says, in 1823, that
it is Dr Thomas Birch.)
At pp. 141–144 of the second edition,
1789, the author writes:—
'I GOT on Horseback within ten
Minutes after I received your Letter.

When I GOT to Canterbury, I GOT a
Chaise for Town. But I GOT wet through
before I GOT to Canterbury, and I
HAVE GOT such a Cold as I shall not
be able to GET rid of in a Hurry. I GOT
to the Treasury about Noon, but first
of all I GOT shaved and drest. I soon
GOT into the Secret of GETTING a
Memorial before the Board, but I could
not GET an Answer then, however I
GOT Intelligence from the Messenger
that I should most likely GET one the
next Morning. As soon as I GOT back
to my Inn, I GOT my supper, and GOT
to Bed, it was not long before I GOT to
Sleep. When I GOT up in the Morning,
I GOT my Breakfast, and then GOT
myself drest, that I might GET out in
Time, to GET an Answer to my Memorial. As soon as I GOT it I GOT into
the Chaise, and GOT to Canterbury by
three: and about Tea Time, I GOT
home. I have GOT Nothing particular
for you, and so Adieu.'
'Every phrase in this Extract,' says
the author, 'is in popular and perpetual
Use; and it is far from my Wish to deprive the Vulgar, and the wealthy illiterate of so convenient an Abridgement of
Terms. On the Contrary, I recommend
it to the pious care of Dr. —— to compose a History of the World, on this
elegant Plan of Abbreviation. All the
Events, from the Birth of Time to his
Majesty's Journey to Cheltenham may
be detailed without the Aid of a single
Verb in the English Language, the
omnipotent GET excepted.
This Verb is of Saxon Origin; *Arrival*
at the Place of Destination, the primitive
Idea; hence *Acquisition*; and hence *possession*. With the latter Idea, the Illiterate use it in Construction with *Have*—
I have GOT; in other Words, *I have*
HAVE. E.g.
I have got a Father ninety Years old.
For obvious reasons, *I have got a
Father* must be restricted to *I possess*;
consequently, it is absurd to prefix
HAVE—*I have* POSSESS!!
It may, therefore, be advanced as a
general Rule,—when *Possession* is implied, it is vulgar to use HAVE in Construction with GOT.
Permit me to add, our Ancestors have
furnished us with innumerable Terms to
express all the Ideas which the Vulgar
affix to their FACTOTUM—GOT.
Are you in Quest of any Thing? Do
not exclaim with the Illiterate—I HAVE

GOT it. But say—I have FOUND it or I HAVE it, HERE IT IS, etc.

Again. "I *mounted* my Horse, or I *was on Horseback* within ten Minutes after I *received* your Letter: as soon as I *arrived* at Canterbury, I *engaged* (or *hired* or *stept into*) a Post Chaise for Town. I *was* wet through before I *reached* Canterbury, and I *have* (or *I have taken*) such a Cold as I shall not easily *remove* (or *cure*). I *arrived* at the Treasury about Noon, having previously shaved and drest. I soon *discovered* the Secret of *introducing* a Memorial to the Board; I could not, however, *obtain* an immediate Answer, but the Messenger told me, that I should probably *receive* one, next Morning. I *returned* to my Inn, *Supt*, *Went* to Bed, and *Slept* well. I *rose* early, and *drest* immediately after *Breakfast*, that I might be in Time for the Answer to my Memorial. As soon as I *received* it, I *took* Post Chaise, *reached* Canterbury by three, and my home about Tea Time. I *have* nothing particular to add."

'It was not my Design to paraphrase the Extract in Terms of Elegance, I only wished to prove, that Men of common Education might express the usual Occurrences of Life, without the Aid of GET and GOT and I HAVE GOT, etc.'

gotten is obsolete in Great Britain, except in the cliché, *ill-gotten gains*; but in the U.S.A., *gotten* (past participle) is preferred to *got*.

gracile, properly meaning *slim* or *slender*, has been mistakenly used by some modern writers (e.g., D. G. Rossetti) for *graceful*.

graduate is 'to admit (a candidate) to a university degree' or (of the candidate) 'to take a university degree'; *to be graduated* expresses a different nuance—that of 'to be admitted to a university degree'.

grammar is perhaps obsolescent for *language*. 'Without a knowledge of the grammar of size and order, we cannot hope to plan an age of plenty', which is to be related to the statement, 'Hogben calls ordinary speech a language of "sorts", and mathematics a language of "size"': Stuart Chase, *The Tyranny of Words*, 1938.

GRAMMAR. (For the relation of grammar to logic, see the next article.)

This is no place for a general discussion of grammar, for in this book a knowledge of the essentials of accidence and the simplicities of syntax has been assumed.

For those who desire to examine 'the heart and soul' of grammar, there is one book that stands high above the rest: *The Philosophy of Grammar*, by Otto Jespersen, 1924. A simplified paraphrase (with comment) of the—to the general reader—most interesting part of Professor Jespersen's book will be found in my *The World of Words* (chapter entitled 'What Grammar Is—and *Why*').

Jespersen is the author of *A Modern English Grammar on Historical Principles*, 4 vols., 1909–1932: a masterly work, though less consecutively written than the warmly to be recommended *A Grammar of the English Language* (vols. 2 and 3, Parts of Speech, Accidence, and Syntax, 1931–1932), by George O. Curme. Prof. Hans Kurath has promised to complete his volume one, *History of the English Language* (etc.).

Syntax has been treated with admirable clarity and orderliness by Dr C. T. Onions in *An Advanced English Syntax*.

Of short grammars, Jespersen's *Essentials of English Grammar*, 1933, is perhaps the best; of medium-sized ones, J. C. Nesfield's *Manual of English Grammar and Composition* (in its latest edition) is still useful, but, owing to the modernization in terminology, E. A. Sonnenschein's *A New English Grammar*, 1916, is preferable. A suggestive and entertaining little book is C. C. Boyd's *Grammar for Grown-Ups*, 1927.

A bird's-eye view of comparative grammar is afforded by E. A. Sonnenschein's *The Soul of Grammar*, 1927: 'to the advanced student grammar is a fascinating subject, just because he knows that he is dealing with an organic writing'. But however far advanced he is, the student must beware of falling into the error of supposing that there is such a thing as a universal grammar, applicable to every language. Grammar is based on language —the particular language concerned— grammar has no existence apart from language; grammar is a set of rules codifying usage, not a code superimposed on language and predetermining usage; in short, grammar must modify itself if language changes, grammar being made for man, not man for grammar.

Nevertheless, where grammatical rules make for a clarity that would disappear with the disappearance of the rules, it is better to preserve and maintain the rules, —until, at least, a simpler or more satisfactory rule is devised or (more probably) evolved. For instance, to ignore the useful distinctions between *shall* and *will*, *that* and *who* (or *which*), is, in my opinion, to set up ambiguity without any fully compensating gain. Also see COMPOSITION.

GRAMMAR (and language in general) **AND LOGIC***.

'To write or speak, we must think; logic is the mechanism of formal reason, and grammar the mechanism of all writing and speaking; in so far as we think, we may—or may not—employ logic, for logical thinking is not the only kind of thinking, nor is it necessarily the most accurate. Logic may have been at the back of certain grammatical rules, but thought of some kind or other is at the back of all such rules.' *A Modern Scholiast*, 1938.

In *Logic and Grammar*, a paper read before the British Association in September, 1923, and published as S.P.E. Tract No. xvi in 1924, Professor Otto Jespersen is, to use a modern slang term, 'devastatingly' on the side of good sense as opposed to both the determinists and the nihilists among grammarians. From this paper, which every lover and student of language should con, study and remember, I take a few passages that not only illuminate the thorny path of theory but also establish a *modus vivendi* and a *modus operandi*—a practical ethic and a safe guide to the practice of speech and writing.

'In examining the relation between logic and grammar we are at once faced with two diametrically opposed views: one that grammar is nothing but applied logic, or, as John Stuart Mill has it, *"Grammar is the most elementary part of logic. The structure"*—? rather *the constructing*—*"of every sentence is a lesson in logic"*; the other that language has nothing to do with logic, but is essentially "alogical" [i.e., outside of logic, unconnected with logic]. The first view is found more frequently among philosophers or logicians than among philologists or linguists; it seems also to belong to a former period rather than to the present time ... The second and opposite view must often be considered a kind of reaction against the pedantry of many grammarians of the old school, who wanted to coerce or entrammel language so as to bring it into accordance with a set of rigid rules, condemning everything that did not agree with the strictest

* See also NEGATION, Section *A*.

classical'—rather, Classical—'standard of correctness. To this the school of historical grammar opposed the right of life and urged the inevitableness of change in the linguistic domain, pointing out the infinite diversity of human languages and thereby coming naturally to deny the possibility of one single strictly logical standard by which to measure correctness in every sentence and every language. These writers do not indeed maintain that language is *illogical*, because this expression implies that it is contrary to the laws of correct thinking, but they say that language has nothing to do with logic ...: linguistic laws, they say, are not logical, but merely psychological laws.'

'Which of these two opposed views', he asks, 'is the true one?' They cannot both be right, but they may both be wrong. Both of these views are one-sided, hence exaggerated, hence false. 'Many of the rules [of grammar] are so arbitrary that it is quite impossible to deduce them from the laws of universal logic; but, on the other hand, language as the vehicle of communication of thoughts cannot be exempt from obeying the most necessary laws of correct thinking. Grammar ... contains a practical, everyday logic; it embodies the common sense of untold generations as applied to those complex phenomena of human life which call for expression and communication: ... language has developed through an infinite number of momentary' and expedient 'solutions of such problems of communication as arise every instant of our daily life. Language has not come into existence as a well-thought-out system that would once for all preclude any possibility of misunderstanding; but the necessity for mutual comprehension has gradually eliminated all fruitful sources of permanent or continual misunderstanding. ... Language is never illogical where strict logic is required for the sake of comprehension, but neither is it pedantically logical where no ambiguity is to be feared in ordinary conversation: it steers adroitly between these two dangers.' In the conduct of his daily life, man proceeds by trial and error; he is quick to learn; he is shrewdly empirical. No less empirical in his language, he is quick to discard the useless and the grossly imperfect, the gravely obstructive.

Jespersen then becomes 'positively

shattering'. Concerning that stock syllogism, *All men are mortal; John is a man; therefore, John is mortal*, he asks, 'Do we ever reason that way?' and drives home his point of taking another simple syllogism, *Both my brothers are teachers; John is my brother; therefore, John is a teacher*. Here, as in the other syllogism, it is 'evident to the simplest mind' that the major premises connote or contain the conclusion; in other words, we could not know that *all* men are mortal unless we knew that *John* was mortal, and in my knowledge that both my brothers are teachers is implicit the (actually, prior) knowledge that John is a teacher. In Höffding's *Logic* there occurs this syllogism, *Neptune is a planet; every planet moves in an ellipse; therefore, Neptune moves in an ellipse*. There isn't a deduction here, for unless we knew that *Neptune* moves in an ellipse, we could not have known that *all* planets so move. 'The syllogism about John's mortality', continues Jespersen, 'is merely an illegitimate trick to disguise the real character of the conclusion, which is this: we have seen in innumerable instances that men have died, therefore we conclude that there is an overpowering probability that this man John, who has so many traits in common with those that have already died, will also some day die. This of course is no syllogism, but then the part played by syllogisms in everyday life, and consequently in everyday language, is really negligible.'

*But even in logicality, language is sometimes superior to logic itself. 'Sometimes the instinctive logic that underlies linguistic expression is subtler or suppler than the logic of the schools. Thus in

* Cf. NEGATION, third paragraph of Section *A*.

some cases with negatives. "He spends £200 a year" and "He lives on £200 a year" are practically synonymous, but if we negative them everything is changed, for "He doesn't spend £200 a year" means that he spends less than £200, and "He doesn't live on £200 a year" means that he spends more.' In the former instance the numeral is negatived; in the latter, 'live on £200 a year' is negatived. In language, the former negative yields 'less'; in the latter, 'more'. If we consider 'the way in which actual language uses two negatives together', we find that 'the result sometimes is a positive, sometimes a negative assertion'. See NEGATION.

In this relation of grammar and logic, there is a further aspect: Could our traditional system of grammar be more logically arranged? This is not the place for a detailed answer, which can be obtained in Jespersen's *The Philosophy of Grammar*; that great grammarian provides a short yet illuminating account on pp. 11–17 of his tract, *Logic and Grammar*. In brief, he urges us to consider all words (and word-groups) in their three aspects, form, syntactic function, and 'natural or logical meaning'; this third aspect he calls 'notional', the aspect itself being *notion*. Syntax, he remarks, stands between form and notion, and Janus-like, it faces both ways. 'If we take such an example as the English preterite, we find, first, that it is expressed by different forms in different verbs, and, second, that it corresponds to different time-divisions and other rational categories.' He establishes the following scheme, in which the criterion of form is not spelling but pronunciation:—

FORM	FUNCTION	NOTION
-ed, as in *handed* *-t*, as in *fixed* *-d*, as in *showed* *-t* with inner change (*left*) unchanged, as in *put* inner change, as in *drank* different kernel or radical (*was*)	Preterite	Past time: 'He *knew* it long ago'. Unreality in present time: 'If we *knew*' and 'I wish we *knew*' (or 'If only we *knew*', of which the past is 'If only we *had known*'). Future time: 'It is time you *went* to bed'. Shifted present time: 'How did you know I was a Dane?' All times (universality): 'Men *were* deceivers ever'.

This example serves to show, or at least to indicate, that 'the distinction between syntactic function and the notional meaning [or, briefly, notion] is extremely important, and may serve to settle disputed points in grammar'.

grammatic is archaic for *grammatical.*

grammatical error is rejected by purists on the ground that, *qua* grammar, an error that is ungrammatical cannot be grammatical: but this is folly: *grammatical* means 'in grammar or of grammar or pertaining to or like or characteristic of grammar' and therefore *grammatical error*, as any sensible person assumes, signifies 'an error in (or of) grammar'.

gramophone. See PHONOGRAPH.

grand as a passe-partout of admiration is to be avoided, not merely because it is a colloquialism (the adverb *grand*, 'He's doing grand', is, by the way, an illiteracy) but also and especially because it is not a precise term but a lazy man's substitute for thought. See also GRANDIOSE.

grandiloquent, magniloquent and **eloquent.** *Eloquent* is a favourable term; the other two are pejorative. For *magniloquent*, see the separate entry. *Grandiloquent* is applied to a person, his speech, his style, and it = 'characterized by swelling or pompous expression'. (*The O.E.D.*)

grandiose is more particular, more specific than *grand. Grandiose* = 'producing an effect or impression of grandeur or greatness; characterized by largeness of plan or nobility of design', as in 'The simple and grandiose taste of the Hellenic architects' (Leitch) and 'He recalls the past like "an Arab Ossian", monotonous and grandiose' (Dowden); also it = 'characterized by formal stateliness', a sense that is disparaging, as in 'Mr Urquiza entered first, with a strut more than usually grandiose', where the nuance is that of 'pompous' or 'aiming at grandeur'. (*The O.E.D.*)

grateful and **gratified.** *Grateful* = 'feeling gratitude' and (only of things) 'pleasing to the mind or the senses' (a literarism); but *gratified* = 'pleased— esp. pleased by compliance', 'satisfied, humoured, indulged', as in 'a gratified tone of voice', 'gratified acknowledgements', 'His vanity was gratified by the homage . . . paid him' (Prescott). (*The O.E.D.*)

gray—grey. Both are correct, and they are without real distinction of meaning, though certain writers have fancied a suggestion of lighter tint in *grey*, of darker in *gray*. [Webster prefers *gray*.]

great is an infelicity for *much* in such a context as the following:—'During the last few years great publicity has been given to the Physical Fitness Campaign', examination essay script, June, 1939.

Great Britain = England, Scotland, Wales; *the United Kingdom* adds Northern Ireland to these, but the official name is *The United Kingdom of Great Britain and Northern Ireland; the British Empire* adds to these, not only *Eiré* (the Irish Free State) but the dominions, dependencies, protectorates, etc.

greater part. See MAJOR PORTION.

greatly for *largely* or *mainly* is catachrestic. 'There is little doubt that hatred borne by one nation towards another is greatly due to a lack of understanding of their respective racial characteristics' (examination script, March, 1938).

Grecian and **Greek.** *Grecian* is gradually being superseded by *Greek* in almost every sense of both the adjective and the noun. As adj., it survives only in *Grecian bend* and *Grecian knot, Grecian bather* and *Grecian netting*, all in specialized, not general, senses; in short, the adjective is now rare 'except with reference to style of architecture and facial outline', and even *Grecian architecture* has become rarer than *Greek architecture*, except as an architectural technicality. As a noun, *Grecian* is extant in only three senses: (*a*) a person learned in the Greek language, a Greek scholar; (*b*) such a Jew of the Dispersion as spoke Greek, a Greek Jew; and (*c*) a boy in the highest form at Christ's Hospital, 'the Blue-Coat School'. Based on *The O.E.D.*

The Greeks is now obligatory. And the adj. Greek is preferred to *Grecian* in almost every context: e.g., *Greek art; Greek literature; Greek life; Greek history;* the *Greek character; Greek Earth*, as the title of Sydney Hopper's distinguished and delightful travel book *cum* aesthetic, literary, philosophical, and sociological commentary, published in 1939; *Greek cities; the Greek nation* and *people; the Greek army* and *navy*; etc., etc.

GREEK AND LATIN. To refrain from using Greek and Latin words when they are the best available, when indeed no others will perform the work that the Classical words will do, is childish. In science, philosophy, medicine, technology, they are inevitable.

But that Classicism may be overdone appears not only in JOHNSONESE (*q.v.*) but, as I see it, in such a sentence as this, 'Nor have I tried to plumb the subjects' minds for their fundamental credenda [? *beliefs*], philosophies and ideation' (G. J. Nathan, *The Intimate Notebooks of George Jean Nathan*, 1932).

On the immense number of current Latin words and phrases that an educated person must be familiar with, A. P. Herbert has eleven very useful pages (166–176), with notes on pronunciation, in *What a Word!*, 1935.

green house is a house painted green; **greenhouse** (or, now obsolescent: **green-house**) is a glass-house for the rearing and preservation of plants, esp. of tender and delicate plants.

grey. See GRAY.

grisly; grizzly; grizzled. *Grisly* = 'causing horror or terror', hence 'causing uncanny or extremely unpleasant feelings', 'grim', 'ghastly'; *grizzly* and *grizzled* = 'grey', esp. 'grey-haired'.

ground, misused for *floor*. Agatha Christie, *Murder in the Mews*, 1937, concerning a flat, 'Mrs Allen was lying in a heap on the ground shot through the head'.

GROUP GENITIVE. The rule governing the use of the genitive (*boy's, boys'*; *woman's, women's*) is extended to any phrase that can be regarded as a unit and that is not of an inordinate length. 'The position of the genitive now', says Professor Jespersen in *Growth and Structure of the English Language*, 'is always immediately before the governing word, and this in [conjunction] with the regularity of the formation of the [genitive] case has been instrumental in bringing about the modern group-genitive, where the *s* is tacked on to the end of a word-group with no regard to the logic of the older grammar: *the King of England's power* (formerly 'the kinges power of England'), *the bride and bridegroom's return, somebody else's hat,* etc.' Dr Onions adduces *A quarter of an hour's ride* and continues with the necessary caution:—'[The group genitive] must not be extended beyond reasonable limits; such ludicrous phrasings as the following will be avoided: "*the father of the child's* remonstrances" (instead of "the remonstrances of the child's father"), "that's *the man I saw*

yesterday's son", "that's *the passenger that missed the train's luggage*"': with which it is interesting and instructive to compare Shakespeare's 'I do dine to-day at the father's of a certain pupil of mine' (cited by Onions).

GROUP TERMS ('*flock* of sheep', '*herd* of cattle'). See SPORTS TECHNICALITIES.

grow smaller is condemned by many purists on the ground that it is impossible to *grow* smaller. A silly condemnation, for in idiomatic English *grow* has the derivative sense, 'to become'.

grudge. See BEGRUDGE.

guarantee is noun and verb; **guaranty** is noun only. The former noun is general, legal and commercial; the latter, legal and commercial, is the more usual for 'the act of guaranteeing or giving a security' and 'something given or already existing as security'. Avoid—though it is correct—*guarantee* and—because it is obsolete—*guaranty* in the sense 'a guaranteeing party', i.e., a *guarantor*, the person to whom the guarantee (or guaranty) is given being the *guarantee*. Cf. WARRANT and WARRANTY.

guarantee for is catachrestic for *guarantee*, or for *vouch for*. 'Who could guarantee for Mr McCabe' (a detective novel, 1937).

gubernatorial (mostly American) is permissible only when neither *governor's* nor *of the government* (or *the Government's*) will serve the purpose.

guer(r)illa (warfare) is correct, but the warrior is not *guer(r)illa* but *guer(r)-illero*. These are Spanish words. [[In American usage, *guerrilla* is a member of a group engaged in irregular warfare; in current slang, a hired murderer employed by underworld gangs; a tough. There is sometimes confusion of *guer(r)illa* with *gorilla*, the much more usual underworld form.]]

guess is colloquial in the senses 'believe, think, suppose, expect'. In current Standard English its predominant senses are 'to estimate' (to guess a weight, a direction, a value, etc.) and 'to form an opinion or hypothesis respecting (some unknown state of facts), either at random or from indications admittedly uncertain; to conjecture', as in 'we may guess when its growth began' (Bayard Taylor), 'I . . . little guessed the end' (Mrs Browning), and *as I guess, so I guess, one may guess*, etc.

gyne(i)ocracy is incorrect for *gynaeoc-*

racy, 'government by women' or, pejoratively, 'petticoat government'.

gypsy. See GIPSY.

H

habit, without a plural and without *a* or *the*, means *custom* or *usage*; but one does not, in good English, speak of *a* or *the habit* as = *a* or *the custom* (or *usage*), as in 'Politicians have a habit of promising the moon'.

habitable, inhabit, inhabitable, uninhabitable. Respectively 'liveable-in', 'to live in', 'liveable-in', 'not liveable-in'. *Habitable* is nowadays applied mostly to houses or flats, *inhabitable* to countries. (In French, *habitable* is English 'inhabitable', but Fr. *inhabitable* is English 'uninhabitable'.)

hacienda. See RANCH.

had. See WOULD HAVE.

had is improperly used by Eric Partridge (*French Romantics' Knowledge of English Literature*, 1924) in the following: 'At the former date, A. de Pontmartin's father had a prefect of police say to him, etc'. The idiom is common in America, where a man introducing a friend may say: 'I'd like to have you shake hands with Mr So-and-So'; here *have* means *cause to*. *The O.E.D.* confirms this definition: 'To cause, procure, or oblige (a person to do something)', and extends it thus: 'To wish, will, require that something be done', and gives examples: 'I would have you make an essay to accomplish it'; 'I would not have it spoken about'. Now 'A. de Pontmartin's father' did not *will* or *cause* 'the prefect of police' to say something to him, but happened to be spoken to by that official. (W.B.) ⟦*Webster's* does not discriminate against this usage and cites (under HAVE, 18) 'He had his leg broken'.⟧

had best; had better. See WOULD BEST and WOULD BETTER.

had have ('If you had have come'). Redundant *have*; an error by no means confined to the illiterate. This construction, in which the *have* is intrusive and which has the still more illiterate variant *had of*, is not an error I should have signalized here, had it not been for the following sentence met with in a very good novelist, 'But then, thought Rome [an educated woman], should I have been any more understanding if I hadn't have happened to have been there that after-

noon when Mark's name was mentioned.'

had rather. See WOULD RATHER.

had used to be for *had been* or *used to be*, or for preterite + *formerly* (before or after the verb), seems an odd mistake; but it is not so infrequent as the paragons would have us think. 'To Basil Woolrich, sitting in the room at the top of Rynox House which had used to be that of F.X., came the clerk Harris', Philip MacDonald, *The Rynox Mystery*, 1930.

hail and **hale** (v.) The former is 'to salute with "hail!"'; to greet; to welcome'; hence, 'to call to (a ship, a person) from a distance in order to attract attention', but *hale* is 'to draw or pull', hence 'to drag or bring violently', as in 'He was haled to prison'. (*The O.E.D.*)

half. See DEMI.

half a dozen and **half-dozen** in British usage are the better ways of writing these phrases. *The O.E.D.* gives them as equally good English. Whereas one says *a half-dozen*, one does not say *a half a dozen*, and *the half-dozen* is more idiomatic than *the half a dozen*. ⟦*Webster's* hyphenates the adj. *half-dozen*, but not the noun phrase.⟧

half after (8 o'clock), a, is less usual than *half-past* (eight), as Weseen points out. The same applies to *a quarter after* (for *a quarter past*).

hallelujah. See ALLELUIA.

handfuls and **hands full.** Cf. the remark at BASKETFULS.

handicap is not to be used loosely as a perfect synonym for *hindrance*, but Weseen's strictures are too severe. *The O.E.D.* accepts as Standard English the figurative sense, 'any encumbrance or disability that weighs upon effort and makes success more difficult'.

hangar; hanger. The former is used in only one sense, 'a shed for the shelter of aircraft'.

hanged is used of capital punishment only ('He was hanged'—not *hung*—'yesterday'; 'The executioner hanged the criminal'). *Hung*, preterite and past participle, is applied to things, as in 'The picture was hung too low', and 'I hung the picture as high as I could'.

happiness should not be debased to the sense, 'pleasure'.

harbour is sometimes confused with *arbour* (*q.v.*).

hardly and **scarcely** are virtual negatives. 'Hardly a man was there' and 'Scarcely a run was scored in the first half hour' are correct, but 'I didn't hardly (or, scarcely) know him' is incorrect. 'Touring arrangements have been made. Why? Nobody hardly tours in that country now' is another example of an error that is an illiteracy—a solecism—a damning social lapse!

hardly none is solecistic for *hardly any*.

hardly . . . than like *scarcely . . . than*, is a frequent misconstruction. 'Hardly was Edward dead than a struggle began for the possession of the reins of power', Ransome, *History of England* (Nesfield); Substitute *when* for *than*—Cf. BARELY . . . THAN.

hardly . . . until is catachrestic for *hardly when*, as in 'I had hardly begun my work until I was called away'.

hardwood is the correct form of those specific hard-wood trees which, from generic, have become particular.

hari-kari is a common misspelling and mispronunciation of the Japanese *hara-kiri*, a method of suicide sometimes practised in Japan. The error is made by E. C. R. Lorac, *A Pall for a Painter*, 1936, 'He'd have committed hari-kari himself before he tipped her off her pedestal'.

harmless. See COMPARATIVES, FALSE. —Cf. the synonymous INNOCUOUS.

haste; hasten. Keep the former as a noun, the latter as a verb (whether transitive or intransitive); as a verb, *haste* is obsolete, except as a literarism or as a poetic archaism.

hate is much stronger than *dislike*: do not, therefore, use these two terms synonymously.

have. See POSSESS.

have a right to is catachrestic when = *ought to*. Harold Herd happily cites the ludicrous 'He has a right to be hanged'. *Have a right to do* connotes privilege, not penalty.

have dinner. See DINE.

have got for *have*. 'I can truthfully say that I have not got an enemy in the world', Ethel L. White, *The Wheel Spins*, 1936. See GET.

haul is grossly overworked by journalists and by writers of crime novels. 'Meaning anything from herrings [properly, a *catch*] and diamonds [properly, a *theft* or a *booty*] to goals scored in a football match [properly, a *large number*]', Frank Whitaker, in *The J.I.J.*, January, 1939.

he. See at 'THEY . . . HE'.

healthful is archaic for *healthy* and should be reserved for 'promoting or conducive to bodily health'—hence, fig., '. . . to spiritual health'. (*The O.E.D.*)

Heaven (capital *H*) is 'the habitation of God and his angels'; *the heavens* (small *h*) are 'that expanse in which the sun, moon, and stars are seen' (*The O.E.D.*). Other senses are obsolete, archaic, poetic (or otherwise literary).

heavenward is the adjective and preferable adverb, *heavenwards* a later variant of the adverb.

Hebraic. See SEMITIC.

Hebrew. See at YIDDISH; also see SEMITIC.

hectic (adj.) 'applied to that kind of fever which accompanies consumption' (*The O.E.D.*), is, because of the flush which it causes, misapplied to any state of excitement, esp. enjoyment, as in 'We had a hectic time'.

heighth, a misspelling of *highth*, a variant of (preferred) *height*.

help (it), with **can** or **could**. *Not*, though necessary to the sense, is often erroneously omitted, as in Newman, *Apologia* (quoted by Whateley), 'Your name shall occur again as little as I can help, in these pages', the sense being'— shall occur only when I cannot help (or prevent) it'. See also NEGATION, the final sentence.

help but, cannot. See BUT.

helpmate and **helpmeet.** Both of these words are applied especially to a wife or a husband; the latter is archaic.

hemi-. See DEMI-, fourth paragraph.

hence is sufficient; *from hence* is tautological. *Hence* is redundant in such a sentence as 'It won't be a long time hence, before we sail'.

henceforth and **thenceforth.** The former = 'from this time or point'; both have the connotation of *onwards*. Except in legal and formal contexts, they are obsolescent.

her, of and **of hers.** See 'OF HER—OF HERS'.

her's for *hers*, a frequent illiteracy. Cf. *it's* for *its*, *their's* for *theirs*, *your's* for *yours*, *our's* for *ours*.

hereabout; hereabouts. Both = 'in this neighbourhood'; usage appears to be adopting the latter to the exclusion of the former.

heretofore and **theretofore.** See ARCHAISMS.—Cf. HENCEFORTH . . .

heroic; heroical. The latter is either obsolete or archaic for the former, in every sense of the two words.

herself. See MYSELF.

hesitate with for *be doubtful about* (the propriety of) is infelicitous—not to say ambiguous. 'I went on to argue that this inquiry must be philosophic, or—if you hesitate with that word, I do myself—that it must take charge of the criticism of its own assumptions', I. A. Richards, *The Philosophy of Rhetoric*. 1936.

hew—preterite, *hewed*—past participle, *hewn*: these are the correct forms of the verb.

hexarch, incorrect for *exarch*.

hide—hid—hidden (or, now obsolescent, **hid**). See also at CACHE.

hiding seek is solecistic for *hide-and-(go-) seek*.

high is, in my opinion, misused in the sentence, 'Mexico City is 7,350 feet high', Violet O. Cressy-Marcks, *Up the Amazon and over the Andes*, 1932, For *high* I should read *up*; in formal writing, 'M. C. is at an altitude of 7,350 feet'. [[*High* would seem colloquial but acceptable to an American, and preferable to *up*.]]

him, of. See GENITIVE, VAGARIES OF THE.

himself. See MYSELF.

Hindi and **Hindustani.** *Hindi*, the chief vernacular of northern India (it is, in fact, spoken by rather more than 60,000,000 people), is an Indo-Aryan language; it is divided into two groups, the Eastern Hindi dialects and the Western Hindi dialects. The most important Western Hindi dialect is Hindustani, which, containing—especially in its subdialect, Urdu—many words adopted from Arabic and Persian, is 'current as a lingua franca over nearly all India' (*Webster's*).

hindsight (or *hind-sight*) should be confined to the contrast of *hindsight* with *foresight*.

hire and **lease** and **let** and **rent**. Of these four verbs, only *let* (or *let out*) is univocal ('to grant the temporary possession and use of [property] to another in consideration of payments of money', i.e., of rent). The other three have opposite senses:

(1) to *let*; (2) 'to pay rent for, to take or occupy by payment of rent'. In England *rent*, however, is now used mostly in the second sense: it is the usual opposite of *let*. *Hire* is now little used of land or houses, and it is applied mostly in sense 2. *Lease* is a formal term; the one who lets is the *lessor*, he who pays rent is the *lessee*. Based on *The O.E.D.*

historic; historical. The latter = 'of the nature of history' (*historical novel*); the former = 'famous or important in history'.

hocus (v.) forms *hocussed, hocussing*, but *focus* (v.) forms *focused, focusing*: this is the ruling implied by The *O.E.D.*

hold up and **uphold.** Reserve the former for literal, the latter for figurative contexts.

holily is obviously much more economical than *in a holy manner*: and, after all, it is not so difficult to pronounce.

holocaust is 'destruction by fire': do not synonymize it with *disaster*. Moreover, it is properly an ecclesiastical technicality.

home is the residence of a family, a household; it should not be used as a synonym for *house*, as in 'Homes for Sale'.

home, be. To say that a person 'is home' for 'is at home' is, I think, both slovenly and ambiguous.

homicide. See MURDER.

honester is equally acceptable with *more honest*, but most of us avoid *honestest* as being difficult to pronounce with ease and dignity.

honeycombed has some odd uses: Mr A. P. Herbert learns from one newspaper that 'Kalat City is another wilderness honeycombed with corpses' and from another that 'Stresa is honeycombed with detectives'.

honorarium (plural, *-iums*; pedantically, *-ia*) is not synonymous with *salary*. Originally (as still) it was an honorary reward; thence it came to be, and predominantly it is, a fee for services rendered, esp. services rendered by a professional person (barrister, architect, doctor). Sometimes it is a complimentary fee paid to one who is not entitled to either salary or fee, as, e.g., to a nonprofessional club secretary. (*The O.E.D.*)

honorary; hono(u)rable. The latter is applied to that which is worthy of honour; the former, apart from legal phrases, has, as its predominant current sense, these two allied senses: 'holding a title or position conferred as an honour either without emolument and/or without the usual duties or obligations on the one hand, the usual privileges on the other', as in *honorary colonel, honorary magistrate*, and 'rendered or conferred merely for the sake of honour', as in *honorary colonelcy*; the oldest sense, not yet archaic, is that of 'denoting—or bringing—honour; conferred (or rendered) in honour', as in 'The simple crown of olive, an honorary reward' (Grote, *The History of Greece*, vol. ii, 1847). (*The O.E.D.*)

hooves as plural of *hoof*. See SPOOF.

horrible, like *awful*, *dreadful*, *terrible*, is overdone. Don't. Above all, do not so shear it of its virtue that it becomes a mere equivalent of *disagreeable*.

host. *The O.E.D.* does not record the word as a feminine; nor have I ever heard it so applied.

host for *large quantity*. 'Frank had arranged for a host of provisions to be laid up in the larder here', Cecil Freeman Gregg, *Tragedy at Wembley*, 1936. *Host* is properly a large number of individuals.

hot cup of cocoa, coffee, tea (etc.), is condemned by purists, who uphold *cup of hot cocoa* (etc.). The latter is more logical; but only at first sight.

house-clean or **houseclean** 'to clean (the) house', seems to me to be a permissible—and very convenient—word. But *housekeep* for *keep house* has not proved much of a success. (*The O.E.D.*)

how for *that* should be avoided except in indirect questions. Thus, 'He does not realise how very odd it is that Smith should ring him there' is correct and clear; but '[He] goes on telling me how he went back to the studio' is ambiguous for the intended meaning, which is 'that he went back to the studio', not 'in what manner' or 'in what conveyance he went back to the studio'.—'I do not know how you contrive to make ends meet' is correct; but 'I told him how I had spent four years in France' is ambiguous, for it may mean either plain fact or coloured manner.

how for *what* is illiterate or, at the best, slovenly. '"It will take my mind off the master, if you see how I mean"', John Bude, *The Cheltenham Square Murder*, 1937.

how, as, is vulgarly used for *that* or *whether*, e.g., 'He said as how he would be late tonight', 'I don't know as how I like that man'.

how long is insufficient in 'How long did Satan consume in rising through Chaos, etc.?' (quoted by Nesfield from *The School World*, February, 1901). It would be correct, being the established usage, to say 'How long did he take?', but 'consume' requires the noun *time* as

its object (*How much time?*, *How long a time?*).

however comes, not at the end of a sentence or clause ('He refused further refreshment, however', Inez Irwin, *The Poison Cross Mystery*, 1936), but after the first significant unit, as in, 'He, however, did not think so' (emphasis on 'He'), 'He flinched, however, when the gun went off' (although he had shown himself calm up to that point), 'In the morning, however, nothing was done' (in contrast to the preceding afternoon), and 'Germane to my subject, however, is the misplacing of *but*, *however*, *though*'.

HOWLERS are such schoolboys' (and schoolgirls') errors of fact as arise from misapprehension or confusion of sense. They are catachrestic or, more often, the result of confusing a word with a word similar to it in form or pronunciation. 'The bystanders expressed deep sorrow at the passing of the beer', 'Histology is the dry bones of history', 'A conjunction is where railway lines cross'. Sometimes an epigram is unintentionally achieved, as in 'Elizabeth was known as the Virgin Queen. She was a great success as a queen'. [Cecil Hunt collects these things—and publishes them. Good Hunting!]

human, 'belonging to or characteristic of mankind'; **humane**, 'kind' or (of knowledge) 'Classical'. As a noun, *human* is either a jocularity, or an affectation; it may, however, make its way as a convenience.

humble-bee and **bumble-bee** have caused a 'big-end, little-end' and a century-old discussion among the inexpert. The two forms are equally correct; the former is recorded by *The O.E.D.* in 1450, the latter (by the same authority) not until some eighty years later; *humble-bee* probably derives from 'to *hum*' (cf. *humming-bird*), the latter from 'to *bumble*'. [[*Humble-bee* is rare in American usage.]]

humbleness and **humility**. The former is now little used; all its nuances (meekness, lowliness; unpretentiousness, modest character) are included in *humility*. In opposition to *pride* or *haughtiness*, only *humility* is now admissible. Based on *The O.E.D.*

humorous; humoristic. The latter should never be used in any sense or nuance of the former: *humoristic* = 'of or like a humorist', as in 'He had a remarkable humoristic talent', 'humoristic cynicism'. Note the difference in spelling; *humorist*, by the way, is preferable to *humourist*.

hurricane. See CYCLONE.

hymenal, hymeneal, hymenial. The first is a physiological, the third is a botanical, technicality; only the second is in general use, and even that is a literary rather than an every-day term ('pertaining to marriage': *the hymeneal altar*). As a noun, *hymeneal* is a wedding-hymn, *hymeneals* being an obsolescent term for a wedding. (*The O.E.D.*)

hyper- and **hypo-** (both from Greek). *Hyper = over, above,* and *hypo = under.* Thus all words beginning with *hyper-* convey the idea of excess (*hypercritical =* too critical; *hyperbole =* exaggerated statement); words with *hypo-* convey the opposite idea though often indirectly (*hypocrite =* a person who simulates goodness, i.e., hides his real nature under a pretence).

HYPERBOLE, says Bain, 'is an effect gained by magnifying things beyond their natural bounds'; *The O.E.D.* defines it as 'A figure of speech consisting in exaggerated or extravagant statement, used to express strong feeling or to produce a strong impression, and not intended to be understood literally'.

Here are two examples of literary, justifiable hyperbole:—

Not in the regions
Of horrid hell can come a devil more damn'd
In evils, to top Macbeth;

I was all ear
And took in strains that might create a soul
Under the ribs of death.

But hyperbole may be incongruous or ludicrous or painful; in this form, it has a second name—Exaggeration or Over-Emphasis.

That the following examples are from one book by an American writer is accidental: one could easily find egregious examples from such English writers as Ossian and Hall Caine; and in any case the American was not an author.

'Crime, shielded beneath the garb of outward apparent virtue, stalks abroad unblushingly at noon-day, in the midst of society, or riots under cover of darkness, in its secretly guarded haunts of infamy. No community is free from its contamination': the opening words of the

Preface to Geo. P. Burnham's *Memoirs of the United States Secret Service,* 1872. 'It is probably true that New York City is annually the scene of more crimes than are committed in any other five cities in the United States. Yet, in other places, colossal offences occur, and great criminals flourish, in spite of all effort to prevent or suppress the evil-doings of the wickedly inclined. The cloak of piety and the outward garments of "eminent respectability" hide a multitude of iniquities and very few instances of well dissembled charity and righteousness which parallel in depth the following veritable occurrence—are found even in the annals of the romance of crime' (*ibid.,* p. 144).

hypercritical (excessively, unduly, or finically critical) is occasionally confused with *hypocritical.*

HYPHENATION. In the life of compound words there are three stages: (1) two separate words (*cat bird*); (2) a hyphenated compound (*cat-bird*); (3) a single word (*catbird*).

Apart from that general process of language, there are, however, (*a*) many instances in which the hyphen is necessary; and (*b*) others in which there is an important distinction between a hyphenated compound and two separate words; and others (*c*) in which the hyphen, by being misplaced, sets up an error or an ambiguity.

(*a*) *The hyphen that is necessary—or, at least, advisable.*

'They were using it to mark straight lines for relaying some flagstones' (F. J. Whaley, *Trouble in College,* 1936). *Re-laying* is intended: cf. the difference between 'That umbrella needs to be *re-covered*' and 'He has recovered the umbrella that he lost two days ago'.

That the hyphen is especially useful in objective combinations,—i.e., combinations in which the first noun is the virtual object of the action denoted or connoted by the second noun,—may be indicated by 'General Curley . . . known as "the Indian-fighter"' (Paul Horgan, *A Lamp on the Plains,* English edition, 1937), i.e., one who fights the Indians; General Curley is obviously not 'the Indian fighter', i.e., an Indian that is a fighter (subjective use).

In *Grammar for Grown-Ups,* 1927, C. C. Boyd quotes from a newspaper, in reference to a dog-show, the sentence, 'Every dog loving man should buy a ticket for this show', and remarks that 'without a hyphen between *dog* and *loving* it looks as if the editor had expected the dogs to buy the tickets'.

In *The Tyranny of Words*, 1938, Stuart Chase writes *antisurvival* for *anti-survival* (noun), *noneconomic* for *non-economic*, *nonresistance* for *non-resistance*, and *predepression* for *pre-depression*. Very little can be said in defence of his 'modernism', for *anti*, *non* and *pre* are strong prefixes. [[American readers will find that Mr Chase here follows good American usage; see *Webster's anti-, non-, pre-*.]]

'As for the little explored territory of [rhyming] slang, the fringe has been reached in . . .' (E. P., at *beef* in his edition, 1931, of Francis Grose, *A Classical Dictionary of the Vulgar Tongue*). For 'the little explored territory', read 'the little-explored territory'.

(b) *Hyphenated compound and two separate words.*

Compare 'The author's tense-sequence' (sequence of tenses) 'is defective in this passage' with 'A tense sequence of events'—a sequence of tense events—'succeeded a dull sequence'.

Compare also *bull's-eye* (a sweetmeat) with *bull's eye* (the animal's eye), as in 'He hit the bull's eye with a bull's-eye'.

(c) *Hyphen misplaced.*

'I am an old cloathes-man' (Israel Israel in *The Sessions Papers of the Old Bailey*, 3rd session, 1773). The reporter should have written, '. . . an old-cloathes man', the reference being not to his age but to his profession.

'The Queen's Head . . . where gin and water'—i.e., gin in water—'is sold in three half-penny bowls, called Goes' (Francis Grose, at *Go Shop*, in *A Classical Dictionary of the Vulgar Tongue*). For 'three half-penny bowls' read 'three-halfpenny bowls'.

In *The Times Literary Supplement* of April 8, 1938, appeared this very pertinent letter from Dr R. W. Chapman:—
HYPHENS.

'Sir,—All students of typographical practice must have noticed the awkwardness which results when a hyphen is used to connect compounds not themselves hyphenated. Thus "The Chipping Norton-Stony Stratford road" might be thought by a stranger to mean the road that leads from Chipping to Stratford by way of Norton Stony. The example which follows is extreme in my experi-

ence because the expression is tripartite. A writer in the American *Publishers' Weekly* (Feb. 11, 1939) explains that Mr Stanley Morison believes that early printing types were influenced not only by manuscript but also by engraved or carved letters. "He would like to replace our present concept of a dual relationship calligrapher-typecutter with a new calligrapher-letter engraver-typecutter triangle." It needs an effort to realize that the three sides of this triangle are (1) calligrapher, (2) letter engraver, (3) typecutter.'

Here, admittedly, I have merely skimmed the surface of Hyphenation. In the Fowlers' *The King's English* (3rd edition, 1930), there is, at pp. 284–289, an excellent short account; in *Modern English Usage* there is an admirable long account. See also pp. 79–84 of G. V. Carey's *Mind the Stop*, 1939. [[American readers may wish to consult *Webster's* dictionary at the entry *compound*, n.; also *The New Standard Dictionary*, 'Method of Compounding Words', pp. xxx–xxxi; and *The Style Manual of the Department of State* (Washington, D. C., 1937); and the *Manual of the Government Printing Office* (Washington, D. C.).]]

hyphenization is inferior to *hyphenation*.

hyphenize is inferior both to *hyphenate* and to *hyphen*; one would do well to adopt *hyphen*.

hypnotic, erroneously used for *narcotic* or *soporific*, e.g., 'The [sleeping-] draughts were merely a quite ordinary mild hypnotic', F. W. Crofts, *Sudden Death*, 1935. Though *hypnosis* is (originally) 'a state of artificially produced sleep', *hypnotism* has come to mean 'the artificial production of a state resembling deep sleep, in which the subject acts only on external suggestion' (*The Con. O.D.*); therefore *hypnotic* in the above is misleading.

I

I easily becomes egotistical, but it is preferable to 'your humble servant', 'the undersigned', 'your uncle', and all other such puerilities.

I is misused for *me* in such a sentence as: 'He could only get tickets for you and I'.—Boyd quotes 'a girl like I' from *Gentlemen Prefer Blondes*.

I (says). See SAYS.

ib. or **ibid.**, short for *ibidem* ('in the

same place'), is used chiefly in the sense, 'in the same chapter, passage; . . . to avoid the repetition of a reference', thus: 'R. Whiston, *Cathedral Trusts*, pp. 2–4 . . . *Ibid.*, pp. 10–12'. All forms of the word should be italicized; the same applies to the following three terms included in this entry:

id. is short for *idem*, 'the same word, name, title, author, etc., as mentioned before: used to avoid repetition'.

l.c. is the abbreviation of *locus citatus*, 'the passage quoted'; among printers, however, it = 'lower case' (small as opposed to capital letters).

op. cit. is short for *opus citatum*, the work (book, pamphlet, article) already mentioned as in 'Coleridge, *op. cit.*'

-ible and **-able.** The former represents Latin *-ibilis*, as in *audible, flexible, legible, permissible, possible, terrible, visible*. It is often displaced by *-able* in such Latin words as have come through French, also in such words as are regarded as having been formed immediately on an English verb: *convertable* for the usual *convertible*, *dividable, readmittable, referable, tenable*.

In phrases, only *-able* is permissible: *come-at-able, get-at-able.*

See *The O.E.D.* (at *-able* and *-ible*) and Jespersen's *Modern English Grammar*, Part I.

-ic and **-ical.** In general, the *-ical* form is obsolescent: except in certain formulas, *-ic* is fast dispossessing *-ical*, as in *comic(al), terrific(al), fantastic(al)*. There is, however, often a nuance at stake, as in *ethic, ethical; economic, economical; historic, historical*. See esp. *The O.E.D.*

ice coffee, ice tea. Incorrect for *iced coffee, iced tea*. Cf. the following entry.

ice-water; iced water. The former is correct only in the sense 'water formed by melting a piece or block of ice'; *iced water* corresponds to the terms forming the heads of the preceding entry.

id. See EGO.—See IB.

idea, misused for *principle* or *assumption*. 'Four kinds of explanations which people give to justify their beliefs: 1. *The impulsive:* Much used by primitive man in the idea that any explanation was better than none', Stuart Chase, *The Tyranny of Words*, 1938.

idea of (or **notion of**) for *idea* (etc.) *that* is occasionally ambiguous, as in 'This ties in' [= links up] with Korzybski's central idea of knowledge as structural' [= that knowledge is structural],

Stuart Chase, *The Tyranny of Words*, 1938.

ideagraph, idealogue, etc. Incorrect for *ideograph, ideologue*, etc.

ideal (adj.) does not admit of comparison. 'I think it is one of the most ideal spots in the whole of Scotland' (examination script, March, 1938). Moreover, *ideal* is catachrestic when it is used as a synonym of 'favourite', as in 'My ideal type of house is a [? the] bungalow' (*ibid.*). Cf. the list of uncomparable adjectives at COMPARATIVES, FALSE.

identic is confined to diplomacy.

identification. See IDENTITY.

identify is sometimes misused for *compare*. A candidate in the Scottish Leaving Certificate examination, March, 1938, in dealing with Burke's metaphor of the French Revolution described as a chemical reaction, wrote, 'In this metaphor the speaker is identifying the unruly state of France with liquor on the surface of which a froth had formed'.

Cf. *identify* for *connect*: a gross catachresis: as in, 'He has been identified with church work for many years'.

identity, 'a person's personality and individuality', must not be confused with *identification*, 'the establishment of a person's name and individuality'.

IDIOM AND IDIOMS.

'If there is one thing more than another that I have learnt in Fleet Street it is never to underrate the importance of usage. It is blind and often illogical, but when it makes its mind up nothing can withstand it; and whatever else may be said of it, it has done much to make our language the richest in the world.'
Frank Whitaker, in the *J.I.J.*,
January, 1939.

'Neither grammar nor rule governs the idiom of a people: and there will be a multitude of cases where *Sic volo, sic jubeo* is the only measure of the tyranny of usage.'
Dean Alford, *The Queen's English*, 1863.

The best account of idioms is that in Dr Pearsall Smith's *English Idioms*, S.P.E. Tract No. xii, 1923. The following remarks and quotations are based on and drawn from that delightful paper.

Generically, *idiom* is 'used . . . to describe the form of speech peculiar to a people or nation'. Particularly, *idioms* are 'those forms of expression, of grammatical construction, or of phrasing, which are peculiar to a language, and approved by its usage, although the meanings they convey are often different from their grammatical or logical significance'.

'The idiosyncrasy of English, like that of other languages, is perhaps most strikingly exemplified in the use of prepositions. Prepositional usage in all languages contains ... much that is peculiar and arbitrary; the relations to be expressed by prepositions are often so vague and indefinite, that many times one might seem logically just as right as another, and it is only "that tyrannical, capricious, utterly incalculable thing, idiomatic usage", which has decreed that this preposition must be used in this case, and that in another' (Jespersen, *Progress in Language*, 1909). For instance, 'we tamper *with*, but we tinker *at*; we find a fault *in* a person, but find fault *with* him; we act *on* the spur of the moment, but *at* a moment's notice; we are insensible *to*, but are unconscious *of*; we say *for* long, but *at* length. . . . Americans speak of getting *on* or *off* a train, in England of getting *in* or *out of* it; "*up to* time" is the English idiom, "*on* time" the American. The difference is one of usage; either is correct from the point of view of grammar.' Compare such terse prepositional phrases as *by fits, for ever, for good, in fact, in general*.

A large class of English idioms consists of phrases 'in which two words are habitually used together for the sake of emphasis', e.g., *hue and cry, fits and starts, free and easy, hard and fast; by and by, over and over, round and round; bag and baggage, safe and sound, spick and span; art and part, high and dry, fair and square; thither, from top to toe, as bold as brass, as large as life, as thick as thieves*.

Perhaps the most interesting class of idioms is that in which metaphor renders the idiom more telling, more effective. Originally confined to that trade or profession, sport or game, which originated them, these idioms 'are found to be capable of a wider use; ... and little by little the most vivid and useful of these phrases make their way into the common vocabulary and come to be understood by all'. From sailors we get *take in a reef, turn adrift, cut the painter, on the rocks, when one's ship comes home*, and a host of others; soldiers have passed on to us such phrases as *take alarm, pass muster, at close quarters, on the qui vive, to hang fire*, and *lock, stock and barrel*; from hunt-

ing (including dog-lore) come *to hunt down, to give tongue, to lead a dog's life, to have a hair of the dog that bit you*, and horses have given us *to saddle with, a run for one's money, out of hand, with a heavy hand*, etc., etc.; domesticity yields *to get on like a house on fire, next door to, on the shelf, a drop in the bucket, as stiff as a poker, to boil over, to butter up*, and so forth.

Though slightly less true now than in 1923, the following verdict is to be taken to heart:—'Idiom is held in little esteem by men of science, by schoolmasters, and old-fashioned grammarians, but good writers love it, for it is, in Landor's phrase, "the life and spirit of language". It may be regarded as the sister of poetry, for like poetry it retranslates our concepts into living experiences, and breathes that atmosphere of animal sensation which sustains the poet in his flights' (Logan Pearsall Smith).

if, omission of. 'And yet, come to the rights of it, he'd no business there at all' (Baumann); this colloquial abbreviation of *if you come* is slovenly.

if for *whether* is always wrong and often ambiguous, but the mixture of the two is wrong, ambiguous—and amusing. 'She was wondering if Rupert [her husband] would like an heir, and whether it was time that they moved from the doll's house in Bourdon Street into a house of more sensible proportions, and if Makepeace would keep a supply of records from *Private Lives* and the best honey and produce them placidly on a tray whenever they were needed', Barbara Worsley-Gough, *A Feather in Her Cap*, 1936. A particularly illuminating example is afforded by the second *if* in the following sentence from Margery Allingham's *The Fashion in Shrouds*, 1938, 'Rex was still speaking in an absent fashion, as if he were working round to a point and wondering if to make it'. [Many American grammarians grant the use of *if* for *whether* in informal style if the tag *or not* is omitted.]]

if is often misused by competent but hasty writers, where the right word is *and* or *but*, (as though I should have written 'by competent *if* hasty writers'); thus Arthur Bryant (*The Illustrated London News*, April 22, 1938), 'Which picture ... is likely to be nearest the truth?—that neat, simplified one which our descendants will master from their text-book histories, or that more complicated affair with which we are so painfully, if confusedly, familiar'. *If*, in such a sentence, implies a contrast between qualities unexpectedly found together, whereas no such contrast is seen in 'painfully' and 'confusedly'.

if and when is usually tautological for *when* (or *if*), as in 'I'll pay when I see you', 'I'll shout if it's necessary'.

if as how is an ugly solecism for *if*. E.g., 'If as how anyone had come up'. See also how, as.

if need be is correct with Present ('He always does that, if need be') or Future ('He will always do that, if need be'); but with Past, the correct form is *if need were* ('He always did that, if need were'). Those who feel that whereas *if need be* is literary, *if need were* is both literary and archaic (actually, it is not archaic), may, if they wish, use *if necessary*, which does away with the verb in the conditional, in all tenses.

Two variants are *if need require* (Present and Future; *if need required*, Past), now obsolescent; and *if need arise* (Past: *arose*).

When *if* = 'when', the indicative (*if need is, if need was;* etc.), not the subjunctive, is required.

if not, ambiguity of. An excellent example is quoted by A. P. Herbert (*What a Word!*): 'England's Captain . . . played one of the greatest, if not the most attractive innings of his career . . .' (*The Observer*). A.P.H. invites us to think this over: 'Was the innings "the most attractive" (as well as "one of the greatest") or not? Honestly, I do not know.'

The same ambiguity is to be noticed in the following: 'The war had found me still at school; I had left at once, of course, and done my share—with decent competence if not with distinction . . .', where '*though* not with distinction' would make the writer's lack of that quality definite; by '*if* not . . .' he appears to mean that he is merely too modest to claim the 'distinction' to which he would like to think himself entitled.

-ify is incorrect for *-efy*, *-ifaction* incorrect for *-efaction*, in the following verbs and their corresponding abstract nouns: *liquefy, putrefy, rarefy, stupefy, torrefy,* and in certain other scientific or technical terms.

ignoramus. See Plurals, un-english.

ignorant. See artless and illiterate.

-ile and **-ine,** words ending in. Alfred Ackermann, *Popular Fallacies*, 3rd edition, 1923, points to the almost universal error in pronouncing such words with the "i" long. 'Common examples are fragile, agile, turbine, profile, and projectile, in all of which the "i" should have its short sound.' *Glycerine* (or *glycerin*) must be added to this list, and the same rule applies in *apposite* and *opposite*. [[In American usage *profile* and *quinine* commonly have long *i* (*Webster's* first pronunciation), and *turbine* may have it (*Webster's* second pronunciation), especially among engineers and mechanics. The other words have short *i* in the speech tradition, but occasional spelling pronunciations with long *i* will be heard.]]

ilk, of that. *Of that ilk* means 'of the same (estate)'; thus *Guthrie of that ilk* means 'Guthrie of Guthrie' (Ackermann). Often erroneously used in journalism for 'of that family, clan, class or kind'.

ill and **sick,** as applied to persons. Both are used predicatively; the former, rarely otherwise: 'He is ill, or sick'. But 'He is a sick man'—not, in current usage, 'He is an ill man'. As applied to other than living things, *sick* has special reference to nausea, as 'a sick headache'. Cf. 'sick and sickly'.

ill of. See Prepositions wrongly used.

illegible. See unreadable.

illicit and **elicit.** See elicit.

ILLITERACIES, FALSE. See False illiteracies.

ILLITERACY. See Solecism.

illiterate and **ignorant.** The former = 'not knowing how to read or write', the latter = 'markedly deficient in knowledge'. An illiterate person is not necessarily ignorant.

illude, illusion, confused with *allude, allusion,* and *elude, elusiveness.* The indiscriminate fall into these errors. To *allude* is to 'refer casually' (to); to *elude* is 'to evade', and *illude* is 'to trick; to deceive with false hopes'. See also delude.

illume, illuminate; illumine. *Illume,* confined to poetry (and archaic even there), is a shortening of *illumine; illuminate* is, of these three words, the only one now used much in prose, *illumine* being now regarded as out of place in any but lofty prose or in poetry. (*The O.E.D.*)

illusion. See ILLUDE.

illustration and **example.** *Illustration*, in one of its derivative senses, does = *example* or *instance*; but it is more dignified than *example* and has a sub-tone connotation of 'image or picture', as in 'An illustration of the principle which runs throughout nature' (Tyndall), 'Charles James Fox afforded an excellent illustration of bohemianism-cum-integrity'. Based on *The O.E.D.*

Ilyssus is an error for *Ilissus*, the stream in Athens.

imaginary; imaginative. Respectively 'imagined', esp. in the sense 'unreal, non-existent'; and 'endowed with (a powerful or fruitful) imagination', 'pertaining to the imagination as a mental faculty', 'bearing evidence of high creative force' (e.g., *an imaginative poem*). (*The O.E.D.*)

imagine for *to suppose* is not bad, but rather familiar English.

imbue, misused for *instil.* One is *imbued* or *inspired with*: one *instils* something *into* a person. Incorrect is 'The courage he imbued into his men'; equally incorrect is 'The address instilled every citizen with fresh confidence'.

immanent, imminent, eminent. These and their corresponding nouns and adverbs are often interconfused; for their different meanings, see any good dictionary. But don't be too hasty in imputing error! Take 'Newt was aching with the immanence of what he had to tell Danny' (Paul Horgan, *A Lamp on the Plains*, English ed., 1937). One may at first think, 'Oh! he means *imminence*'; but reflection shows that *immanence* is, after all, intended.

immarcessible is incorrect for *immarcescible*, 'unfading', esp. in *immarcescible crown* (*of glory*).

immediately used in the sense of *as soon as* is bad English. '*Immediately* the police arrived the crowd began to disperse'; it is wrong here because 'immediately' applies not to the arrival of the police but to the dispersal of the crowd, and the sentence can be correctly arranged, 'When the police arrived the crowd dispersed immediately', or, of course, 'Immediately after the police arrived, the crowd began to disperse'.

immerge and **emerge.** For the sense of the latter (noun: *emergence*), see 'EMERGE and ISSUE'. *Immerge* is now comparatively rare for *immerse* ('to dip or plunge into liquid')—noun *immersion*.

immigrant and **emigrant.** See EMIGRANT . . .

imminent. See IMMANENT.

immoral. See AMORAL.

immortal. See DEATHLESS.—Also see COMPARATIVES, FALSE.

immunity and **impunity.** Apart from its technical senses in Law, Ecclesiasticism, Medicine, *immunity* = 'exemption from any usual liability; freedom from anything evil or harmful', as in 'immunity from pain', 'immunity from snakes', 'immunity from sin'. *Impunity* is less extensive in its meaning: it = 'exemption from penalty (e.g., a fine) or a punishment (e.g., imprisonment)', and, in a weakened sense, 'exemption from loss or injury, security': 'In England, one can't commit murder with impunity', 'Snake-venom may be swallowed with impunity'. (*The O.E.D.*)

impassable (**-ability**) and **impassible** (**-ibility**) are easily confused; the former = *that cannot be traversed*; the latter, *unfeeling, incapable of being hurt, impassive.*

impecunious is 'penniless, in want of money'; not 'unthrifty', as it is occasionally understood to be.

imperative and **imperious.** In 1794, Gouverneur Morris, American statesman and diplomat, wrote the useful words, 'Subject to the imperative, and too often the imperious, mandates of a committee'; 'An imperious ruler would naturally give imperative orders' (Weseen). The basic sense (apart from the grammatical one) of *imperative* is 'of or like or expressing a command', hence 'peremptory' ('He spoke in an imperative tone'); hence 'urgent' or 'obligatory', as in 'The condition of the sick and wounded made it imperative to ship them to Egypt', 'The work is imperative'. The predominant current sense of *imperious* is 'overbearing, domineering, dictatorial', as in 'A proud, imperious aristocrat, contemptuous . . . of popular rights' (Froude). (*The O.E.D.*)

implement, 'to complete, to fulfil' a contract, a promise, a condition, has been so much used by the cultured since ca. 1925, that it has acquired the stamp of a literarism. Avoid it.

implicit and **explicit.** *Implicit* is 'implied though not expressly stated; naturally or necessarily involved in, or inferable from, something else', as in 'Proofs are either implicit and indirect, or explicit and direct'; hence 'virtually or potentially contained *in*', as in 'The blessing implicit in all heaven's chastenings' (C. Kingsley). *Explicit* is '(of utterances) distinctly expressing *all* that is meant' (*explicit promises*); hence, '(of persons) saying all that one means; outspoken'. (*The O.E.D.*)

imply for **infer**. See INFER.

important must not be used as though it were a mere synonym of *chief*, *main*, *principal*. 'The important differences between Association football and Rugby football are in the number of players who compose a te m, the shape of the ball, the size of the pitch, the method of scoring, the carrying of the ball in Rugby football, the heading of the ball in Association football', from an examination script (Higher Grade, L.C.C.) written in June, 1938.

impossible. See COMPARATIVES, FALSE; and cf. POSSIBLE.

A thing is either possible or impossible; therefore 'more possible' is catachrestic for 'more feasible' or 'more practicable'.

impracticable and **impractical.** The former = 'that cannot be effected or dealt with; unmanageable, unserviceable', as in 'an impracticable road', 'an impracticable plan'; the latter = 'unpractical', 'having perhaps the theory but certainly not the practice', as in 'He was a great poet but an impractical man' (but see also at UNPRACTICABLE).

impressible and **impressive** are occasionally confused; so are the adverbs *impressibly* and *impressively*. *Impressible* = 'easily impressed'; *impressive* = 'likely or sure to impress others'. Misused in '"Don't forget," said my uncle impressibly, "that you are unable to articulate"' (Francis Beeding, *The Big Fish*, 1938).

impression. See EDITION.

imprimature, an obsolete word meaning *a print* or *impression*, may be met with in erroneous use for *imprimatur*, an official licence or permission to print.

impromptu; extempore. Both are adverbs = 'without preparation or premeditation'; only *impromptu* is a noun; both are adjectives, *impromptu* being 'improvised', as in 'an impromptu speech', hence 'makeshift', as in 'an impromptu raft'. An *extempore* speech may have been prepared, but not to the extent of being written down or memorized: it is not read, nor has the speaker any notes. *Extempore* is more usual than *extemporary*.

impudent, catachrestic for *impotent*, is recorded as early as 1612. Dekker, *O per se O*, represents the palliard (a beggar with artificial sores for the excitation of compassion) as employing this patter: 'Ah the urship'—i.e., worship—'if God looke out with your mercifull eyne, one pittifull looke upon sore, lame, grieved and impudent (for impotent) people, sore troubled with the grievous disease . . .'.

impunity. See IMMUNITY.

in and **at.** Concerning prepositional idioms, Dr Pearsall Smith in *English Idioms*, S.P.E. Tract No. xii, 1923, has posed the distinction better than I've seen it put anywhere else:—'More interesting are the cases where the difference of usage is not really arbitrary, but may express a shade of meaning which we are ourselves perhaps unconscious of. A curious instance of this is the way we use the prepositions *in* and *at* with the names of places. We say some one is *in* London, *in* Rome, *in* Paris, but usually *at* Oxford, *at* Rouen. The general rule is that we use *in* for large cities and capitals, *at* for smaller places'; (in a footnote) 'Shakespeare used *at* London, . . . when London was a smaller place than it is now'. He continues with the caution that, 'we commonly use *in* rather than *at* even for a small place if we ourselves are there, probably because then it bulks more largely in our imagination'.

in- and **en-** in verbs. See 'EN- and IN-'.

in- and **un-** in adjectives; **in** and **un** as prefixes. In general, *in* is the prefix that goes with words of Latin origin or with such words of French origin as spring from Latin; *un* is the prefix that goes with the words of Teutonic origin (i.e., from Old English, Scandinavian, German). Thus, *infelicitous*, but *unhappy*. But the influence of *un* is so strong that it is attached to many words of Latin origin: *unfortunate*, where French has *infortuné*.

in for *into*. 'Plane dives in reservoir', caption in *The Daily Mirror*, Aug. 24, 1937.—'I went in the Perla [a café], and sat down at a table', Ernest Hemingway, *To Have and Have Not*, 1937. 'Towards ten o'clock I slipped down in the street' (Interview reported in *The Daily Sketch*, Mar. 24, 1938) conveys only that the speaker *slipped and fell*, until we read that his object in 'slipping down' was 'to buy a paper'. Cf. the opposite error (*into* for *in*).

in for *within* causes ambiguity; e.g., 'I can get up in five minutes'.

in as much as, in so much as, in so far as may be written *inasmuch as, insofar as, insomuch as,* but not *in asmuch as, in somuch as, in sofar as.* The usual modern forms are *inasmuch as* and *insomuch as;* but *in so far as. In so far as* = 'in such measure or degree as', 'to such extent that'; *insomuch as* (slightly obsolescent) is virtually co-extensive with *inasmuch as,* which = *in so far as* (as here defined), but also = 'in proportion as' or 'according as', hence, 'in that', 'considering that', 'since', 'because'.—Nor can *in so far* (etc.) be made equivalent to *in so far as* (etc.): 'Winning this election meant nothing to me except in so far it was a fight' (Frank Tilsley, *I'd Hate to Be Dead,* 1938).

in behalf of. See BEHALF OF.

in comparison of. See PREPOSITIONS WRONGLY USED.

in consequence of. See CONSEQUENCE OF.

in despite of. See at DESPITE.

in excess of is not to be used indiscriminately for *more than,* as in 'The fee was in excess of £5', 'He rode in excess of twenty miles'.

in my opinion. See OPINION.

in respect to. See PREPOSITIONS WRONGLY USED.

in spite of. See at DESPITE.

in the circumstances. See CIRCUMSTANCES.

in the nature of for *about* or *approximately.* From a bank manager's letter of November, 1937: 'We are communicating with the Company to ascertain what rate of interest they charge and the amount they would be prepared to advance which we imagine would be in the nature of £450 if required.'

in view of the fact that is not quite the same as *in that:* to confuse them is to destroy a useful distinction. How oddly sounds this sentence from a Higher Grade L.C.C. essay (June, 1938): 'Both games' —Rugby and Association—'are good for character in view of the fact that they both call for team work.'

inapt, 'inappropriate', hence 'unskilful, awkward', is preferable to *unapt* (defended by Weseen); *inept* is the word to use for inappropriate words, speech, tone, allusions, and for 'absurd, foolish' actions, consequences, as in *inept interference;* in Law, *inept* = 'of no effect;

void'. The corresponding nouns are *inaptitude, ineptitude.* (*The O.E.D.*)

inasmuch as. See IN AS MUCH AS.

inaugurate, 'to begin formally or ceremonially', is grandiose and excessive as a synonym for *begin.*

incapable connotes innate or permanent lack of ability: *unable* connotes inability 'in a specific situation or at a specific time': 'He is incapable of doing such a thing' and 'He is unable to do it'.

incessant, 'unceasing, ceaseless' (actions; persons), is not to be used as a synonym for *everlasting.*

incident (adj.) and **incidental.** *Incident* is 'liable or tending to befall or affect; hence, naturally appertaining or attached *to*', either with *to* ('The physical weaknesses incident to human nature', 'powers incident to government') or absolutely ('The Puerto Rico expedition, and the incident aggressive steps taken in the campaign'). Do not use it in the senses of *incidental,* which = 'casual, fortuitous', as in 'Even corruptness may produce some incidental good', and (of a charge or expense) 'incurred apart from the primary disbursement', as in 'The house rent, and the incidental charges of a family' (W. Tennant) and the new set phrase, *incidental expenses.* And do not use *incidental* in the sense attaching to *incident.* (*The O.E.D.*)

incidently for *incidentally* is commoner than one might think; I have seen it in the writing of a good American journalist.

inclined for *likely* (or *apt*), when it is applied to things, is an odd usage: a usage to be avoided. In an Oxford and Cambridge School Certificate script (July, 1938) I felt myself pulled up with a jerk when I ran into this, 'They wrote the truth, which, though interesting, is inclined to shock us'.

inclosure. See ENCLOSE, ENCLOSURE.

including. See CONJUNCTIONS, DISGUISED.

incom'parable and **uncompa'rable.** See UNCOMPARABLE; also COMPARATIVES, FALSE.

INCOMPLETE INFINITIVE. See 'TO for *to* + infinitive'.

incomprehensive(ly) for *incomprehensible* (*-bly*). See COMPREHENSIVE(LY).

inconsequent; inconsequential. The two senses of *inconsequential,* 'characterized by inconsequence of reasoning, thought, or speech', hence 'of no consequence or importance', are covered by *inconsequent*, which is to be preferred in the former sense but is rare in the second —but then, so is *inconsequential*.

incontrollable is being superseded by *uncontrollable*.

incorrect and *uncorrected*, are the correct forms.

increase over. See DECREASE OVER.

incredible, incredulous, uncreditable. See CREDIBLE . . .

incubus. See SUCCUBUS.

incumbent. See RECUMBENT.

indestructible. See COMPARATIVES, FALSE.

indexes. See INDICES.

indicate, misused for *discover* or *guess at.* 'Before the first microscope was invented, no human being had knowledge of minute phenomena, and before atoms were *indicated*, there was no verifiable concept of the submicroscopic world', Stuart Chase, *The Tyranny of Words*, 1938.

indicated, be, is not good English for *advisable* or *that has been advised*, as in 'Prompt action is indicated'.

indices; indexes. The former is obligatory in Mathematics and Science; *indexes* is correct for 'an index of names, subjects, etc.'; in all other senses, *indices* is now the more usual plural.

indict and **indite** are pronounced alike, but the former = 'to accuse', whereas the latter = 'to write'.

indifferent to, misused for *unconnected with* or *dissociated from*, as in 'Public amusements, which are not indifferent to the manners of a nation, became disgraced by absurdities', A. Chalmers, Preface to Vol. I of *The British Essayists*, 1803.

indigestible and **indigestion,** but **undigested:** these are the correct forms.

indignant was confused with *indigent* by the blind beggar whose card was inscribed, 'Pity the indignant blind'.

INDIRECT SPEECH. See REPORTED SPEECH.

indiscreet and **indiscrete.** For the distinction, see DISCREET . . .

indiscriminate. See 'UNDISCRIMINATING and INDISCRIMINATE'.

indite. See INDICT . . .

individual is not synonymous with *person*; it connotes a person as an entity —as distinct from a class.

individually is often used unnecessarily and tautologically.

indoor is the adjective, **indoors** the adverb.

indorse and **approve.** The former is not to be used for the latter; nor the latter for the former.

indorse and **endorse.** The form *endorse* is preferred in English commerce, *indorse* in English legal and statutory use; in the U.S.A., *indorse* is used—and recommended—to the exclusion of *endorse*. (*The O.E.D.*)

indulge, misused for *satisfy*. 'Amateur theatricals indulge my real bent.'

indulge in; engage in. The former is catachrestic when used for the latter.

industrial; industrious. Respectively 'connected with or characteristic of industry' and 'diligent'.

inebriety is 'now chiefly applied to habitual drunkenness'. *Dipsomania* (violent and/or persistent drunkenness) is a stronger word, with a medical connotation.

inept. See INAPT.

inevitable has come to have what philologists term a pejorative connotation and what others call an unfavourable sense. It is, therefore, out of place in the following sentence: 'The most dramatic event was [Lord] Hawke's intrepidity in dropping Peel . . . when it would certainly rob Yorkshire of almost inevitable championship': substitute *certain* for *inevitable*. (And delete *certainly*, for *almost certain* is certainly not *certain*.)

inexplainable; inexplicable. Both mean 'that cannot be explained'; but the latter has what the former has not, an additional nuance, 'unaccountable'. Then there is the noun, *inexplicables*, 'that which cannot be explained'. (*The O.E.D.*)

infant, child; baby (poetic and archaic: **babe**). In general use, an *infant* is a child in arms (*babe in arms* is the set phrase); in law, a minor (a person under 21). A *child*, in general use, is under fourteen or, more logically, below the age of puberty; in law, (one of) the offspring; a *baby* is a child still at the breast or on the bottle.

infectious and **contagious.** (*Infective*, by the way, is a medical term only.) A *contagious* disease is one that is spread by actual contact, either with the person or with some object that has been in contact with him; an *infectious* disease is spread by germs, in the air or in water.

infer for *imply*. *Infer* is 'to deduce, to derive, as a fact or [a] consequence' (*Nuttall's Standard Dictionary*); *imply* is 'to include in reality, to express indirectly: to mean: to signify' (*Chambers's*), also 'to hint'. '"I had a detailed report from Penfold Travers. . . . Very terse indeed. . . . He inferred we were all blockheads in Bombay"', Graham Seton, *The K. Code Plan*, 1938, exemplifies the misuse.

inferior (or **superior**) **than** is a gross, yet alarmingly frequent error for *inferior* (or *superior*) *to*. Nesfield quotes *The Fortnightly Review*, September, 1898: 'A man of far inferior abilities than Bismarck', which contains a further error; it would be better to write either 'a man far less able than Bismarck' or 'a man of abilities far inferior to Bismarck's'.

inferiority complex. See COMPLEX.

infinite is a dignified word; an uncomparable adjective: do not debase it to equality with '(very) great' or 'vast', as it is debased in 'His infinite worries caused him to become a victim of insomnia'.

Infinitely small is loose, infelicitous English. *Infinitesimal* is the word required.

INFINITIVE, SPLIT. See SPLIT INFINITIVE.

inflammable and **inflammatory.** The former is applied to that which (fig., that person who) is combustible (or can easily be set fire to); the latter, to that which causes the fire; especially if it is particularly likely to cause it; hence, to 'stimulating' (liquors).

inflection and **inflexion.** See '-ECTION and -EXION'.

informant; informer. Respectively, anyone who gives information on a stated (or implied) occasion, and one who lays information against another, especially if he makes a habit of so doing.

-ing for **-ed.** Of this misuse ('I want my hair cutting', 'Do you want your car washing?'), 'Jackdaw' in *John o' London's Weekly*, Jan. 6, 1939, remarks that the examples (and the practice) 'seem to halt somewhere between idiom and idiocy; I leave them there'. There is confusion with 'My hair needs cutting' and 'Does your car need washing?', where *cutting* and *washing* are gerunds, and perhaps also with 'The cathedral was building', i.e., a-building. [[Unknown in America.]]

ingenuous, 'innocent, artless', is sometimes confused with *ingenious*, 'clever at contrivance'.

inhabitable. See HABITABLE.

inherent and **innate.** The latter (properly 'inborn', hence 'native' to a person, 'natural') is no longer used for the former. *Inherent* = 'existing in something as a permanent attribute; belonging to the intrinsic nature of that which is spoken of'; hence, 'intrinsic, indwelling'; hence 'essential', hence 'vested (*in*)', as in 'The supreme authority is inherent in the legislative assembly'. (*The O.E.D.*)

inhibit and **prohibit.** In Ecclesiastical Law, *inhibit* is to forbid or interdict; in general use, it is to restrain, check, prevent, stop, as in 'The reflex actions of the spinal cord may, by appropriate means, be inhibited'; in modern psychology, an *inhibition* is 'a (or the) restraining or checking of a thought or an action by the (unconscious) will'. *Prohibit*, in general use, is to forbid, as in 'The law prohibits larceny': cf. 'Fear can inhibit a man from action'. (*The O.E.D.*)

initial, for *primary* is not wrong; it is merely feeble. For *primeval* or *primitive* it is grossly erroneous.

INITIAL-WORDS. 'We must keep a sharp eye on these diehards of the style sheet'—an editor's list of stylistic *dont's* drawn up for observation by his staff— 'who are continually trying to drive useful [words and] phrases out of circulation and make language self-conscious.

'. . . [The particular fad of one of these diehards] is the use of the indefinite article before capital-letter abbreviations, such as L.C.C. and L.M.S. He would use "a" before the L's because they stand for "London". But may I remind him . . . that there comes a point in the life of initials as familiar as these when they take on an identity of their own. They become to all intents and purposes words in themselves. For one man who says "London County Council" a thousand say "Ellceecee", and euphony demands that this curious initial-word, and L.M.S. and F.J.I. should all be preceded by "an"', Frank Whitaker, in an address delivered on Dec. 13, 1938, to the Institute of Journalists and reproduced in the Institute's *Journal*, January, 1939. Mr Whitaker is undoubtedly right, and his rule should be extended to all initial-words beginning with any of the following letters: *E, F, I, L, M, N, O, R, S, X*. E.g., 'Where is that em-ess that came in yesterday?', 'Smith has received an O.B.E.', 'An X is rare in words of modern formation'.

initiate, 'to begin, to introduce, to originate', is a dignified word. Do **not**

use it as an easy synonym for *begin*. Its predominant sense is, 'to admit (a person) with due rites to a society, etc.', hence, 'to instruct in the elements of a subject, a practice', as in 'to initiate into freemasonry', 'to initiate in(to) physical science'. As v.i., it is rare.

initiate oneself for *insinuate oneself*. 'I initiated myself into the Esteem of a Master Builder under the Pretence of courting one of his Daughters', *The Life of Benj. Stratford by Himself*, 1766.

injured. See DAMAGED.

inmit and **emit.** See EMIT.

inmost; innermost. The former = 'most—or furthest—within', as in 'The third and innermost barrier' (Scott) and 'innermost thoughts'; but both spatially and figuratively ('most intimate or secret'), *inmost* is preferable and more usual. (*The O.E.D.*)

innate. See 'INHERENT and INNATE'.

innervation and **enervation.** These are the nouns for *innervate* and *enervate*; see ENERVATE.

innocuous. See COMPARATIVES, FALSE. —Cf. HARMLESS.

innumerable and **inumerable.** The former = uncountable, countless; the latter is incorrect for *enumerable* (countable)—itself a rare word.

inquire, inquiry. See ENQUIRE; also QUERY.

inquisitor is now rare except in its historical connexion with the Spanish Inquisition.

insensible, like *insensitive*, is now constructed with *to*; the latter word is gradually displacing the former.

insert in; insert into. The former emphasizes the general idea of the verb, the latter the inthrusting. *Insert in* = 'place in', whereas *insert into* rather = 'introduce into'. The former, in short, is static rather than dynamic; the latter is indubitably dynamic.

inside of. See OUTSIDE OF.

insignia is a plural; the rare singular is *insigne* (four syllables).

insignificant does not mean 'small', but 'unimportant'. (The sense 'small in size' does exist, but it is obsolescent.)

insinuate, now a pejorative, should not be flattened to equivalence with *to suggest*.

insipid. See VAPID . . .

insofar as; insomuch as. See IN AS MUCH AS.

insolate and **insulate.** The former is 'to expose to the rays of the sun'; the latter is used chiefly in reference to electricity.

insoluble and **insolvable.** The former is much the more general; the only sense of *insolvable* which is not possessed by *insoluble* is the obsolescent one, '(of a banknote or bill) that cannot be cashed'. (*The O.E.D.*)

inspect is 'to look closely into or at; to examine', not merely 'to see', as in 'Many citizens wish to inspect the new pool'.

instal is less usual than (to) INSTALL.

instance (n.). See EXAMPLE.—As a verb, it is not rare in the sense, 'to cite as an instance or example', as in 'I may instance olive oil, which is mischievous to all plants' (Jowett).

instance where ('This is an instance where a doctor is powerless') is incorrect for *instance in which*. Cf. EXAMPLE WHERE.

instant (n.). See 'MINUTE and MOMENT'.

instanter (instantly) is properly a legal term; its use in other contexts is—except perhaps as a humorous term—to be discouraged. Some good people employ it as an elegancy.

instead of for *than for* or *than with* is a strange error—not at all rare. 'The poor chap would probably be fifty times better off with a thousand pounds now instead of a lot more an unknown number of years hence', Rupert Penny, *Policemen in Armour*, 1937.

instil. See IMBUE.

instructional and **instructive.** Both = 'educational' and 'conveying instruction or information', but the former stresses the teaching, the latter the information imparted. 'An instructional course'—i.e., a course of instruction—'for young officers may be instructive' or informative, interestingly educative.

insuccess. See UNSUCCESS.

insurance. See ASSURANCE.

insure. See ENSURE.

intellectual. See following entry.

intelligent (of persons), 'having the faculty of understanding', especially in a high degree, or (of things) 'displaying that faculty'; *intelligible*, (of either persons or things) 'easily understood; comprehensible'; *intellectual*, 'relating to the intellect'. *Intellectual* should not be used as a synonym of 'learned'. The old gag that 'An intellectual is not necessarily intelligent' is made possible only by this catachresis.

intensely for *very* must be used with care. One may say 'intensely hot (or cold)', even 'intensely unpleasant', but not 'intensely wealthy' (Agatha Christie, *Death on the Nile*, 1937).

intension is a learned term, to be used with great care. It is not synonymous with *intention*, 'a purpose'.

intentionally. See ADVISEDLY.

intently is sometimes misused for *intensely*, as in '"Don't push your face so close to mine", Nigel begged. "I dislike your moustache intently"', Robert Eton, *The Journey*, 1938.

inter = 'between' or 'among', as in *intercede, intersection*; *intra* = 'within', as in *intramural, intravenous*.

intercalate. See at 'INTERJECT and INTERPOLATE'.

INTERCHANGEABILITY. See SYNONYMS.

interest. See INTRIGUE.

interesting. This passe-partout adjective is to be used very sparingly and, even when used, it must be only after soul-searching and intelligence-racking thought. If you mean 'puzzling', say so; if 'dramatic', say *dramatic*; if 'unusual', then *unusual*; if 'important', then *important*; if 'full of character or incident or implication(s)', then, for the sake of the right word, use the right words!

interject and **interpolate.** The former, intransitive, is to interrupt a conversation; the latter, transitive, is to insert something in a script or a publication—or indeed in a conversation, but without the abruptness or rudeness connoted by *interject*. To *intercalate* is to insert (a day) in a calendar or—a transferred use—to insert, in a series, something extraneous; generally in the passive.

interpellate (not to be confused with *interpolate, q.v.* at INTERJECT . . .) is extant in only one sense:—'To address an interpellation to (a Minister in Chamber, Parliament, Congress)' i.e., to interrupt him and ask him for an explanation of some matter belonging to his department; also absolutely, as in 'The Socialist from Newcastle interpellated'. (*The O.E.D.*)

interpretive. Usage has not adopted this variant of *interpretative*.

into for *in*. 'A far larger number [of compositions], cast (so to speak) into the same mould, have wearied the public', E. Partridge, *French Romantics, Knowledge of English Literature*, 1924; E. P. was wrong in speaking so. The error arises from the two meanings of 'cast' and from some ambiguity in his use of 'mould'. Another good example is 'He had understood at the beginning but failed to understand now as the threads ran away, on their own, into various directions' (a detective novel, 1937). And another is Fowler's example, 'Lord Rosebery took her into dinner'—which would have been very distressing for the lady.

intolerable, 'unbearable' (hence, 'excessive'); **intolerant,** 'unwilling—or unable—to endure (something specified)', hence, 'disposed to persecute those who differ'. (*The O.E.D.*)

intoxicated. See 'DRUNK (adj.); DRUNKEN'.

intra. See INTER.

intrigue and **intriguing,** 'to interest', 'to arrest the attention' and 'interesting' or 'arresting', are to be avoided: not only are they unnecessary, but they are wrongly derived from the French, for in that language *intriguer* means 'to puzzle', 'to exercise the wits (of a person)', as Mr A. R. L. Hudson pointed out in *The Observer* of Sept. 18, 1938.

intrude, misused for *obtrude* (to which the adjective is *obtrusive*). 'She was . . . a perfect companion, docile and admiring, never intruding her own personality', Louis Bromfield, *The Strange Case of Miss Annie Spragg*, 1928.

intrust; entrust. *The O.E.D.* treats the former as a mere variant of the latter and, in 1893, remarked that 'the form *intrust*, though preferred in many recent dictionaries, is now rare in actual use'. [[*Intrust* is regarded as a variant of *entrust* by *Webster's* (1934).]]

invalid; invalidated; invalided. *Inval'id* = 'not valid'; and *in'valid* = '(a person) that is ill', whence the pun 'An invalid invalid'; *invalidated*, 'rendered not valid; null and void' (e.g. *invalidated evidence*); *invalided* = 'rendered—or accounted—an invalid; disabled by illness or injury', and as in 'Invalided out of the Army'.

invaluable, like *priceless*, now means 'valuable to a high degree'; the senses 'without value', 'having no (high) price' are obsolete. The opposite of *invaluable* is *valueless*; that of *priceless*, is *worthless*.

invective. See SATIRE.

invent. See DISCOVER.

inverse. See CONVERSE.

Inverted Commas to Indicate Slang. See SLANG, Section III, last paragraph.

invite for (an) *invitation* is incorrect and ill-bred and far too common.

involved by. See PREPOSITIONS WRONGLY USED.

invulnerable, like *absolute* and *perfect* (see COMPARATIVES, FALSE), is a superlative, in that it implies a peak: one can say 'almost (or virtually) invulnerable' 'well nigh absolute', 'almost perfect', but, as one cannot say 'more absolute' or 'rather (or, more) perfect', so one cannot say 'rather invulnerable'. 'As long as he had Boss Warren's backing, he was fairly invulnerable', Milton Propper, *Murder at the Polls*, 1936.

inward, inwards. The latter is adverb only ('with scales turned inwards', 'duties paid inwards'); the former, both adverb (less usual than *inwardly* and *inwards*) and adjective ('inward vitality', 'inward experience').

IRISH BULLS. See BULLS.

ironical (laughter). We must quote from the last page of *Grammar for Grown-Ups*, by C. C. Boyd, 1927. 'The expression "ironical laughter", which often occurs in reports of Parliamentary debates, is wonderfully illogical. To be ironical, the laughter must mean the reverse of what it seems to mean. The laughter, so described, is never the pleasant kind, which expresses pure amusement and delight, but is meant to convey disagreement and contempt (not necessarily personal). If truly ironical, it would convey approval, while apparently expressing disapproval. It would be very difficult indeed to laugh like that; and it is certainly not what the reporter meant to describe.' *Ironical applause* is, however, legitimate.

IRONY. 'Irony consists in stating the contrary of what is meant, there being something in the tone or the manner to show the speaker's real drift', Alexander Bain, *English Composition and Rhetoric*, enlarged edition, 1887.

Bain gives many examples; several will suffice.

Job's address to his friends, 'No doubt but ye are the people, and wisdom shall die with you'; the Mark Antony oration ('honourable men') in *Julius Caesar*; Swift's *The Tale of a Tub*, *The Battle of the Books*, and *Gulliver's Travels*, all three for sustained irony; *The Spectator*, No. 239 (the various kinds of argument); Bentham's constant references to English law as a 'matchless institution'; in such commonplaces as 'so great a master',

a superior person', 'how very kind!', *too* charming!', 'It never entered his wise head'.

'The Socratic Irony', Bain remarks, 'consisted in an affectation of ignorance and a desire to be informed; but it was generally meant to be taken seriously by the hearer, at least at the beginning of a discussion.' It is a method of refutation.

Dramatic irony is that which consists in a situation—not in words; or rather, not in words alone, but in words plus situation; when the audience in a theatre or the reader of a book perceives a crux, a significance, a point, that the characters concerned do not perceive.

Irony must not be confused with sarcasm, which is direct: sarcasm means precisely what it says, but in a sharp, bitter, cutting, caustic or acerb manner: it is the instrument of indignation, a weapon of offence, whereas irony is one of the vehicles of wit. In Locke's 'If ideas were innate, it would save much trouble to many worthy persons', *worthy* is ironical; the principal clause as a whole is sarcastic—as also is the complete sentence. Both are instruments of satire and vituperation.

irreal is a gallicism for *unreal*.

irreligious. See UNRELIGIOUS.

irrespective of; irrespectively of. Usage tends to prefer the former, where, probably, *irrespective* has—or had originally—adverbial force. But where there is no *of*, *irrespectively* is obligatory.

irresponsive is being dispossessed by the longer established *unresponsive*.

irretentive is the learned and the technical, *unretentive* the lay and general word for 'lacking the power of retaining'; *irretentive memory*, *unretentive memory*.

irruption and **eruption** are often confused. A safe rule in such words is that the initial *i* signifies *in*; the *e*, *out*.—Cf. IMMIGRANT, EMIGRANT (see EMIGRANT).

is, stating identity, must be used with critical care.

is (or **are**) **to**—like *was* (or *were*) *to*—followed by an infinitive, is an ambiguous construction. Take 'He is to set a high standard, I believe': the context may or may not remove the ambiguity, but the sentence as it stands means either 'He is destined to set a high standard—such is my belief', or 'He has been instructed to set a high standard—or so I've been told', or 'It is planned (or, ardently desired) by others—he perhaps unknowing—that he shall set a high standard', or even 'He intends, I understand, to set a high standard'. Consider also 'He was to have departed yesterday', which may mean 'He intended to depart yesterday' or 'According to instructions, he should have departed yesterday' or 'It was planned (or ardently desired) by others—he perhaps unknowing—that he should depart yesterday'. A good writer will take care to convey the exact sense he intends.

is (or **are, was** or **were, shall** or **will be**) **to** + infinitive + preposition is so much less general than *is* (etc.) *to be* + past participle + preposition, that it rings oddly, as in 'So Christine wasn't to argue with in her choosing, so all I could aim at was [to] help as I might be able' (Michael Innes, *Lament for a Maker*, 1938), where *to be argued with* would be idiomatic. Compare 'She is not to contradict', which is idiomatic, with 'She is not to be contradicted', which is not only unidiomatic but ambiguous.

This stricture applies to the agent, not to the instrument: 'This gun is to shoot rats with' is idiomatic.

is when is a stupid beginning for a definition, as in 'Quadratics is when the highest power of the unknown is a square'.

-ise and **-ize** (verb endings). See -IZE . . .

ism, 'a theory', is disparaging; so is *ology*, 'an art, a science'. *Ism* comes direct from:—See following entry.

-ism. Its basic use, a suffix forming a noun of action (*baptism; heroism*), does not concern us. Derivatively, it indicates the name of a system, whether of theory or of practice—e.g., religious, philosophical, social, etc. etc.; it may derive from the subject (or the object) or from the name of its founder: *Buddhism, Catholicism, Protestantism*. Allied are class-names, or descriptive terms, for doctrines or principles: *atheism, bimetallism, scepticism*: whence such nonce-words and rarities as *rule-Britanniaism*. These two main groups lead naturally to that in which *-ism* denotes, not a system or a principle but a peculiarity, e.g., of language or style. *Americanism, Anglicism, Scotticism; archaism, colloquialism, witticism; Browningism, Carlylism, Micawberism*.

The corresponding adjectives are formed in *-istic. Ismatic* (rarely *ismat-*

ical) = (pertaining to *isms*, to an *ism*, or to the suffix *-ism'; ismatize* = 'to name (something) an *ism*, or to furnish a radical (or root or stem) with the suffix *-ism*). (*The O.E.D.*)

issue (n.) is misused in a dozen contradictory and confusing senses, especially by politicians and leader-writers. See A. P. Herbert for examples and comments.

issue (v.). See EMERGE.

issue with, 'to supply with', is condemned by Weseen but passed as permissible by *The O.E.D.*: and why not?

-istic. See second paragraph of the entry at -ISM.

it, misapplied. 'He put his feet up on the stove as it was very cold', meaning the weather, not the stove.—'Londonderry Corporation decided to reconsider the decision to ban jazz on the Guildhall organ as it was injurious to the instrument' (provincial paper quoted by *The New Statesman and Nation*); grammatically, the 'decision' was 'injurious to the instrument'.

it is me for *it is I* 'is a form of speech frequent in current English and is used even by educated speakers, who would not, however, say "it's *him*", "it's *her*", "it's *us*", or "it's *them*", these being generally regarded as vulgar or dialectal. The sound-analogy of [*it is*] *he*, [*it is*] *she*, and [*it is*] *we* has no doubt furthered the use of *me* as a regular and natural form of expression in such cases', which is not to say that Dr Onions (*An Advanced English Syntax*, 6th ed., 1932) recommends its use. It is to be noticed that those educated speakers who say 'it's me' or 'it is me' would not say 'It is me who wrote that essay'. *It is me* (or *It's me*) is defensible, however, when the statement is exclamatory: likewise *it's her* (or *him* or *us* or *them*) is justifiable when its use is exclamatory. [[In America, *it's me* is acceptable colloquial English; that is, it is used in good speech. There is no occasion to write it. *Us, him, her, them* are less common after *to be*, and their acceptableness is disputed. However, when a pronominal subject is not followed by its verb, the pronoun often appears in the objective case. That is, the habits of word-order are stronger than the habits of inflection. We expect subject + verb + object.]]

ITALICS. Italics should, in good writing, be used with caution and in moderation; their most legitimate purpose is to indicate emphasis in dialogue, and, everywhere else (but there too), to indicate foreign words and phrases and titles.

The whole title should be italicized; not, e.g., 'Carlyle's great work, the *French Revolution*'.

(For a fuller treatment, see G. V. Carey, *Mind the Stop*, 1939, and the Fowlers' *The King's English*, 3rd edition, 1930.)

item for *affair* or *matter* or *subject*, or *fact* or *incident* is not merely slovenly but misleading; it is almost as bad as falling weakly back on *you know what I mean* when one is too lazy to try to remember the precise term or is gravelled by one's astounding ignorance.

item for (specific) *object* is of the same order as the preceding error, but is perhaps more objectionable, for some particular object should be named. It is certainly less justifiable than *gadget* or *thingummy*, the tools-for-all-occasions of the incurably slothful and the unashamedly woolly.

item is often misused in non-commercial writing; e.g., 'The bed . . ., a table and a chair, were its only items of furniture' (Laurence Meynell, *The Door in the Wall*, 1937), where *pieces* would be better.

its is the genitive of *it*; **it's** = *it is*. The number of persons that one might suppose to know better, who fall into the error of *it's* for *its* (= *of it*) is a source of constant surprise to any keen observer. Cf. HER's for HERS.

it's me. See IT IS ME.

itself. See MYSELF.

-ization, -isation. These noun endings, like the participle-adjective endings *-ized, -ised*, correspond to:—See following entry.

-ize and **-ise,** verb-endings. Fowler, in *Modern English Usage*, has an admirable article on the subject. The following summary rule is based on *The O.E.D.*'s article (at *-ize*):—You will be safe if you make every verb, every derivative noun or participial adjective, conform to the *-z* type, for this suffix comes, whether direct or via Latin or French, from the Greek *-izein*: to employ *-ise* is to flout etymology and logic. Moreover, whether the spelling be *-ise*, or *-ize*, the pronunciation is *-ize*: another reason for using it.

And 'though I', who have for years foolishly resisted this scholarly and common-sensible rule, 'says it as shouldn't', yet the rule is single and exceptionless:

Where there are, in dictionaries, the alternatives *-ise* (etc.) and *-ize* (etc.), USE -IZE.

J

j' is a slovenly, illiterate pronunciation of *do you*, as in 'J'ever see the like of that, mate?'

jabber is an excellent term for 'incoherent, inarticulate, or unintelligible speech', a sense for which *gibberish* is also used; in the present century, however, *gibberish* is applied mostly to Ziph (*shagall wege gogo* = shall we go), to the Loucherbem of the Paris butchers (*loucherbem* for *boucher* is itself Loucherbem) and to other artificial addition, subtraction, reversion, or intercalation distortions of language. But as a synonym of 'chatter', 'prattle', 'voluble talk', *jabber* is somewhat discourteous.

Jack or **Jack Tar,** like *Middy* (*q.v.*), is now used only by the ignorant landsman. A similar ban affects *Tommy* (or *Tommy Atkins*).

jackeroo is an incorrect spelling and pronunciation of *jackaroo*. The word is a blend of *Jack* (from *Johnny Raw*, a 'new chum' or recent immigrant) and *kangaroo*. See especially Edward Morris, *Austral English*, 1898.

jail; jailer. See GAOL, GAOLER.

jalouse is catachrestic in the senses 'regard with jealousy' and 'begrudge jealously'. (*The O.E.D.*)

janders for *jaundice* is a solecism—when it's not dialect. Possibly influenced by *glanders*.

jannock (**jonnick, -ock**) is by some Lancashire people so frequently used that it seems to them to be the best of English, but I fear that it is still a rather provincial colloquialism.

Jap (n. and adj.) is a colloquialism—not to be employed in the society of a Japanese, any more than *Chinee* is respectful to a Chinese.

jarfuls; jars full. See the rule implicit in the entry at BASKETFULS.

JARGON. 'The pure research chemist will say, "Chlorophyll makes food by photosynthesis". The practical engineer does not know what he—the scientist—is talking about. But if that statement is rephrased, "Green leaves build up food with the help of light", anyone can understand it. So, says [C. F.] Kettering, if we are going to surmount the boundaries between different kinds of technical men: "The first thing to do is to get them to speak the same language".'—Stuart Chase, *The Tyranny of Words*, 1938.

In his masterly preface to *The Oxford English Dictionary*, Sir James Murray sets the stage thus:—'The English Vocabulary contains a nucleus or central mass of many thousand words whose "Anglicity" is unquestioned; some of them only literary, some of them colloquial [i.e., "used in speech": not in my sense], the great majority at once literary and colloquial—they are the *Common Words* of the language. But they are linked on every side with words that are less and less entitled to this appellation, and which pertain ever more and more distinctly to the domain of local dialect, of the slang and [peculiar expressions] of "sets" and classes, of the popular technicalities of trades and processes, of the scientific terminology common to all civilized nations, of the actual languages of other lands and peoples. And there is absolutely no defining line in any direction: the circle of the English language has a well-defined centre but no discernible circumference. The centre is occupied by the "common" words, in which literary and colloquial [i.e., spoken] usage meet. "Scientific" and "foreign" words enter the common language mainly through literature; "slang" words ascend through colloquial usage; the "technical" terms of crafts and processes, and the "dialect" words, blend with the common language both in speech and in literature. Slang also touches on one side the technical terminology of trades and occupations, as in "nautical slang", "Public School slang", "the slang of the Stock Exchange", and on another passes into true dialect. Dialects similarly pass into foreign languages. Scientific language passes on one side into purely foreign words, on another it blends with the technical vocabulary of art and manufactures.'

Jargon, originally (as in Chaucer) the warbling of birds, has been loosely employed for cant, slang, pidgin English, gibberish: it should be reserved for the technicalities of science, the professions, the Services, trades, crafts, sports and games, art, and Art. A synonym is *shop* or *shop talk*.

'Every social fact—and the language of a group is a social fact—is the result of two classes of cause: personal (or biological) causes, represented by the physiological and psychological characteristics of the individual; and external (or mesological) causes, represented by the great accumulation of the social pressures, economic and geographical and other factors, which so powerfully influence mankind', says Alfredo Niceforo (*Le Génie de l'Argot*, 1912). He makes the further distinction that sometimes it is feeling or sentiment, sometimes one's profession or trade which determines the nature of one's speech, whether it be Standard, dialectal, or unconventional. The specialization that characterizes every vocation leads naturally to a specialized vocabulary, to the invention of either new words or new senses (i.e., the re-charging of old words). Such special words and phrases become slang only when they are used outside the vocational group and, even there, only if they change their meaning or are applied in other ways. Motoring, aviation and the wireless have already supplied us with a large number of slang terms and colloquial or even Standard English metaphors.

It is important for us to be clear as to the difference between jargon and slang, and to be able to place them accurately in the hierarchy of language. In *La science du mot*, Professor Albert Carnoy remarks that '*Les langues spéciales* sont de deux types différents: 1. A la langue *soignée* (langue *noble*, langue *littéraire*) s'opposent le langage *familier* et la langue *triviale* (avec ses diverses nuances), qu'on emploie pour les usages ordinaires de la vie, les besoins journaliers, les sentiments élémentaires, etc.

2. A la langue *commune* (celle de tout le monde) s'opposent:

(*a*) le langage *intellectuel* (exprimant les notions philosophiques, morales, les conceptions que confère la culture) et les idiomes *techniques* ou *scientifiques* (en usage entre les gens du métier ou entre les initiés à une discipline).

(*b*) les langues développées plus ou moins *artificiellement* par des groupes sociaux particulars: *argots* [slang and cant] *et jargons* [non-slangy technicalities].' Carnoy rightly adds that the distinctions between these diverse types of speech are a little confused by the borrowings made by familiar and colloquial language from the jargons and slangs and by the borrowings made by the various jargons (or technical 'languages') from slang.

Niceforo has the following significant passage on an aspect common to jargons and cant; an aspect common, moreover, to the various jargons and all vocational and social slangs:—

'Les langages spéciaux, issus de la différente façon de sentir et de juger, et des différentes sortes de travail auxquelles chaque groupe est adonné, ne constituent pas l'argot [cant], qui est essentiellement un langage spécial né ou maintenu intentionnellement secret. Cependant, ils peuvent, spontanément, —nous dirions presque innocemment,— remplir de façon plus ou moins complete l'une des fonctions de l'argot [cant]: la fonction de protection du groupe.

'Tout langage spécial ne peut-il constituer, en effet, une protection du groupe qui le parle? Lorsqu'un groupe qui sent d'une façon spéciale et qui accomplit les gestes spéciaux se forge spontanément un langage traduisant ces deux spécialités, il ne fait pas acte prémédité d'hostilité ou de cachotterie envers le monde qui l'environne; mais, vus du dehors, ces hommes parlent une langue qui n'est pas de suite compréhensible dans toutes ses parties. Ils parlent, pour les non-initiés, une sorte de langue sacrée devenant par cela même un tissu de protection, formé spontanément autour du groupe social.

'Il est certain qu'un groupe parlant un langage spécial, s'apercevant que son dictionnaire tout naturellement éclos dans l'atmosphère spécial où le groupe vît, pense et agit, devient une sorte de protection,—tâche de tirer profit de ce fait; et on verra alors ces hommes complaire à leur langage. Mais il est également certain que ce dictionnaire n'en restera pas moins un dictionnaire de langage spécial' (i.e., a jargon).

A less specialist point of view is that expressed by Greenough & Kittredge:— 'The arts, science, philosophy, and religion are not alone in the necessity which they feel for a special vocabulary [*these vocabularies being jargons*]. Any limited circle [not necessarily so very limited, either!] having common interests is sure to develop a kind of "class dialect", such as that of schoolboys, of university men, of travelling salesmen, of . . . civil serv-

ants [these being either jargons or, as the case may be, slangs].' And these two authors display the same calm balance, the same exemplary 'stance', and that same sure 'seat in the saddle' which distinguishes the natural horseman, when they proceed to warn us of the cleavage between jargon and slang:—'A word or phrase which is slangy in general conversation stands in quite a different position when it is used in a limited circle, or under special circumstances. "Horsey" words are not slang when one is "talking horses", nor hunting terms in the hunting field, nor the [peculiar] phrases of politics on the hustings or on the stumps. They belong . . . to the category of jargons or technical dialects, and are comparable to the special vocabularies of commerce, or medicine, or the law.'

There is a jargon that calls for special attention: the jargon of Society, as distinguished from its slang and catchphrases. 'From the almost exclusive association of [the members of Society with one another] there arises a kind of special vocabulary . . . The society jargon is disseminated like the technical language of the philosopher or the man of science, by the same means and with even greater rapidity' (Greenough & Kittredge, 1901). We must, however, distinguish Society jargon from Society slang. And as the differences are, in the main, those between all jargon and all slang, we may dwell upon them for a moment. It is the procedure, the forms, the not so angelic 'hierarchy' of Society which make up almost the whole of its jargon, whereas the entire universe is the sport and plaything of the slang, properly so called, of Society. But, then, all jargon whatsoever consists of words and phrases concerning, or affected to the observance of, the letter of a profession, a trade, a social class, an art, a sport, whereas slang is concerned with the spirit of the universe, the world, life, and in that general, usually subconscious preoccupation, it also hovers, joyously or jauntily, or jaundicedly over the objects and the practices of the slangster's own vocation, but with this difference: jargon treats with solemnity and respect the avocation it serves; slang, even where—as seldom—it retains respect towards it, treats that avocation with the detached amusement that, viewed from afar, every human activity seems to invite. In Society, as in all close corporations, all groups, and all sections of society, jargon tends to develop in proportion to the degree of its own exclusiveness, to its own place in the world's esteem, and to the difficulty experienced in learning it or perhaps rather to its learnedness (not that erudition affects Society! It does, however, affect science, the law, the church, medicine, and so forth): but slang thrives only where this exclusiveness is tonic, not constrictive, and where, as among Cockneys and the Army, the users are very numerous. The more, for example in Society, jargon thrives,—the more, that is, the latter prevails,—the less does slang prosper. (Since the War of 1914–18, however, Society has become less walled-in, less snobbish, less clannish, with the result that its speech is being increasingly fertilized with technical terms from the trades and professions, from manufactures and processes, and, more importantly, with colloquial and slangy terms from the world of commerce and manual work, from journalism, art, the theatre, and, in short, from life as it is lived, not life as it is permitted by a comfortable income, and not life in which attention need be paid only to one's social equals.)

Let us turn to art. Of artistic jargon, John Camden Hotten makes fun; yet, having selected such terms as *aesthetic, transcendental, the harmonies, keeping harmony, middle distance, aërial perspective, delicate handling, nervous chiaroscuro,* 'and the like', he confesses that 'it is easy to find fault with this system of doing work',—or writing about art,—'whilst it is not easy to discover another so easily understood by educated readers, and so satisfactory to artists themselves. . . . Properly used, these technicalities are allowable'.

In the familiar speech employed by those who participate in, by those who watch, and by those who write about a sport (e.g., hunting) or a game (e.g., football, whether Rugby or Association, whether Australian or American, and, in Rugby, whether Union or League), one has to remember that what, to a complete outsider, seems mysterious and slangy may actually be mysterious but in no way slangy. Sport in general and every particular form of sport have their corpus of technical terms (their jargon). It is not always easy to say whether a term is jargon or slang; but a slang term is always a synonym of an accepted

term, and that accepted term, if a technicality, is jargon.

Sailors and soldiers have their jargon.

Les mathurins ont une langue
Où le verbe n'est point prison;
L'image y foisonne à foison,
Or vierge dans sa rude gangue.
            Jean Richepin, *La Mer,* 1886

The slang and the jargon of the sailor have exercised considerable influence upon familiar speech, whence they have sometimes passed into Standard English. 'Transporté dans un autre milieu, le professionnel', writes Albert Carnoy in *La science du mot,* 'conserve ses habitudes de pensée. Les objets et les activités qu'il rencontre lui rappellent des aspects et des expériences de sa vie de travail. Il les assimile donc en fonction de celle-ci et comme à travers celle-ci qu'il "projette" sur l'autre.—Rien de plus caractéristique à ce propos que le cas des hommes de mer qui trouvent de toutes parts des réminiscences de leur vie si spéciale.' Thus it is, he adds, that our everyday language has been affected by nautical terms: the *all aboard!* of bus, tram and train conductors; *to land,* e.g., on one's feet; *to be on the stocks,* to be in preparation; *to catch (the turn of) the tide,* to seize an opportunity; *to drift around,* to idle about.

Much the same applies to soldiers' language, especially their jargon (by which the civilian often affects to be annoyed). 'L'armée, comme tout corps étroitement constitué, ayant sa vie propre . . . et arrachant l'homme à sa vie normale, a toujours eu un parler propre très développé; qui, naturellement, comme celui des marins, a servi à désigner bien des idées extra-militaires' (Carnoy).

Those are special aspects* of jargon; but the subject of jargon is so important, and so often misunderstood, that it would be well to pose, more firmly than we have yet done, the basis and establish the generality of jargon: to treat it in the large. In *Words and Their Ways in English Speech,* 1901, Greenough & Kittredge include an excellent chapter on jargon; it is entitled 'Technical or Class Dialects', which exemplifies *dialect* employed in a way that I strongly object to—but let it pass!

'Every profession or trade, every art,

---

* Taken, in a modified form, from my *Slang To-Day and Yesterday,* revised edition, 1935.

and every science', they write, 'has its technical vocabulary, the function of which is partly to designate things or processes which have no names in ordinary English, and partly to secure greater exactness in nomenclature. Such special dialects, or jargons, are necessary in technical discussion of any kind. Being universally understood by the devotees of the particular science or art, they have the precision of a mathematical formula. Besides, they save time, for it is much more economical to name a process than to describe it. Thousands of these technical terms are very properly included in every large dictionary, yet, as a whole, they are rather on the outskirts of the English language than actually within its borders.

'Different occupations, however, differ widely in the character of their special vocabularies. In trades and handicrafts, and [in] other vocations, like farming and fishery, they have occupied great numbers of men from remote times, the technical vocabulary is very old. It consists largely of native words, or of borrowed words that have worked themselves into the very fibre of our language. Hence, though highly technical in many particulars, these vocabularies are more familiar in sound, and more generally understood, than most other technicalities. The special [jargons] of law, medicine, divinity, and philosophy have also, in their older strata, become pretty familiar to cultivated persons, and have contributed much to the popular vocabulary. Yet every vocation still possesses a large body of technical terms that remain essentially foreign, even to educated speech. And the proportion has been much increased [since about 1850], particularly in the various departments of natural and political science and in the mechanic arts. Here new terms are coined with the greatest freedom, and abandoned with indifference when they have served their turn.* Most of the new coinages are confined to special discussions, and seldom get into general literature or conversation. Yet no profession is nowadays, as all professions once were, a closed guild. The lawyer, the physician, the man of science, the divine,

* Note the corresponding process by which an entire set of words once so familiar to the educated as to be no longer jargon have fallen into so general a disuse that they are now, except by a few experts, regarded as 'deep' jargon: the nomenclature of Rhetoric.

associates freely with his fellow-creatures, and does not meet them in a merely professional way. Furthermore, what is called "popular science" makes everybody acquainted with modern views and recent discoveries. Any important discovery, [even if] made in a remote or provincial laboratory, is at once reported in the newspapers, and everybody is soon talking about it.'

They pass to a paramount point when they remark on the fact that 'the classifying habit of the natural sciences reacts on many scientific terms in a curious way. It is convenient for the naturalist to have the vernacular or "trivial" names of plants and animals coincide in their scope, so far as possible, with the orders and families and genera of his system. Hence we are bidden to limit the name *fly* to dipterous [two-winged] insects, *bug* to the hemiptera, *worm* to the order *vermes*, and are rebuked if we speak of a whale as a "big *fish*". This is all very well for the purposes of science, but we must not allow ourselves to be browbeaten. The whale was a "fish" when the "order *cetacea*" had never been heard of . . . The loose popular designations are quite as well established, and therefore as "correct", as the more limited terminology of science. Less "accurate" they may be, but language is not always bound to scientific accuracy. It has its inalienable right to vague terms when there is no question of system at stake.'—Which is all very refreshing and true.

Their summing-up is so sensible and practical and, from the viewpoint of usage, so sound, that it were a pity to refrain from quoting again from a book that had a very large sale in the first decade of this century and that deserves to go on selling. 'The position of technical dialects or jargons with respect to our language is this: so long as the terms in question are used in technical discussions only, they scarcely belong to the English vocabulary at all. If they wander out of their narrow circle and are occasionally heard in current speech, they become a part of our vocabulary, though they are still a very special or technical part of it. But the process may go much further: the objects or conceptions for which the [technical] terms stand may become very common, or the words may lose their strictly scientific sense and be applied vaguely or metaphorically. When this happens, the word has become fully naturalized, and its technical origin is pretty sure to be forgotten in the long run.

'The propriety of using technical terms in speaking or writing depends on a commonsense principle. A remark should be intelligible, not merely to the speaker, who is presumed to know what he wishes to say, but also to the person addressed. Otherwise, it can hardly be called language in any proper sense. To be very technical in conversation not only savors of pedantry but makes the speaker unintelligible; and the same is true of a book addressed "to a great variety of readers". Among specialists however, one can hardly go too far in the employment of technicalities, provided the terms belong to the accepted vocabulary of the science or art in question. That form of pedantry which consists in changing well-established designations for others that seem to the writer more appropriate is extremely common, and, indeed, may be called one of the weaknesses of the scientific temperament.'

(Anyone desirous of going further into the question of jargon should read the chapter entitled 'Technical Words' in Professor G. H. McKnight's *English Words and Their Background.* Certain aspects of the subject are briefly treated in Stuart Chase's *The Tyranny of Words.*)

jargoon, a variety of the mineral zircon, is better spelt thus than as *jargon,* which, to prevent confusion, should be reserved for the term in language-lore.

Jehosophat is incorrect for *Jehoshaphat.*

Jehu, 'a coachman', is outworn. Don't shred the tatters.

Jerry (a German, especially a German soldier) is inferior to *Gerry.* [[*Jerry,* not *gerry,* is given by *Webster's.*]]

jerrymander is incorrect for *gerrymander.* See esp. R. H. Thornton, *An American Glossary,* 1912.

jess, as a term in falconry, is wrongly defined in many good dictionaries. Properly, it is 'a short strap of leather, silk, or other material, fastened round each of the legs of a hawk used in falconry; usually bearing on its free end a small ring or *varvel* to which the swivel of the leash is attached' (*The O.E.D.*).

Jew; Jewish. See SEMITIC.

jim-jams; jitters. The former is now

a colloquialism, the latter is still a slang term: neither, therefore, has yet qualified to appear in serious writing or in impassioned oratory.

JINGLES; UNINTENTIONAL RHYMES. In prose, avoid these unsought, infelicitous solicitors of sense; avoid them anywhere. 'In most *prose,* and more than we ordinarily *suppose,* the opening words have to wait for *those* that follow' (I. A. Richards, *The Philosophy of Rhetoric,* 1936) is an excellent example of how *not* to write prose that is intended to be either effective or melodious.

This is the fault noticed by Alexander Bain when, in Part II (1888) of *English Composition and Rhetoric,* he says, 'Unpleasing are iterations within words or at the end of words: *indulgent parent, uniform formality, instead of a steady . . ., he is tempted to attempt.*

'Even a short interval is not enough to allow the repetition of very marked sounds: as "I confess with humility, the sterility of my fancy, and the debility of my judgment". "What is of more importance, the principles, being propounded with reverence, had an influence on the subsequent jurisprudence." "The art of politics consists, or would consist if it existed . . ."; "taking such directions as to awaken pleasing recollections".'

job for one's profession, trade, vocation is a colloquialism; *job of work* is Standard English, dating from the 16th Century. *Job* is an interesting word: look it up in *The O.E.D.* (and its *Supplement*) the next time you get the chance.

JOHNSONESE. *Johnsonian* is defined by *The O.E.D.* as 'a style in English abounding in words derived or made up from Latin, such as that of Dr Johnson'; but, in current usage, it is applied especially and indeed almost solely to 'stilted or pompous style, affecting polysyllabic classical words' (*Webster's*).

In *Squire's Companion to the British Pharmacopœia* I came upon the following definition of opium, 'the milky exudation of *papaver somniferum* obtained by incision from the unripe capsules, and inspissated by spontaneous evaporation', whereon I commented thus in *Literary Sessions,* 1932: 'If only the compiler had put *lacteal* for *milky,* and *immature* for *unripe,* Dr Johnson could not have bettered it. He would probably have been ungracious enough to translate the

Latin as "soporific poppy"; *inspissated* (i.e., thickened) was a favourite word of his.'

Dr Jespersen in *Growth and Structure of the English Language,* says, 'I can find no better example to illustrate the effect of extreme "Johnsonese" than the following:—

'"The proverbial oracles of our parsimonious ancestors have informed us, that the fatal waste of our fortune is by small expenses, by the profusion of sums too little singly to alarm our caution, and which we never suffer ourselves to consider together. Of the same kind is the prodigality of life; he that hopes to look back hereafter with satisfaction upon past years, must learn to know the present value of single minutes, and endeavour to let no particle of time fall useless to the ground". William Minto, in *A Manual of English Prose Literature,* translates that passage as follows:— "Take care of the pennies", says the thrifty old proverb, "and the pounds will take care of themselves." In like manner we might say, "Take care of the minutes, and the years will take care of themselves".'

Jespersen continues, thus:—'In his Essay on Madame D'Arblay, Macaulay gives some delightful samples of this style as developed by that ardent admirer of Dr Johnson. Sheridan refused to permit his lovely wife to sing in public, and was warmly praised on this account by Johnson. "The last of men," says Madame D'Arblay, "was Doctor Johnson to have abetted squandering the delicacy of integrity by nullifying the labours of talent." To be starved to death is "to sink from inanition into nonentity". Sir Isaac Newton is "the developer of the skies in their embodied movements", and Mrs Thrale, when a party of clever people sat silent, is said to have been "provoked by the dulness of a taciturnity that, in the midst of such renowned interlocutors, produced as narcotic a torpor as, etc." . . . In the nineteenth century a most happy reaction set in in favour of "Saxon" words and natural expressions . . . But still the malady lingers on, especially with the half-educated. I quote from a newspaper the following story. The young lady home from school was explaining. "Take an egg," she said, "and make a perforation in the base and a corresponding one in the apex. Then apply the lips to the aperture, and by forcibly inhaling the breath the shell is entirely discharged of its contents." An old lady who was listening exclaimed: by: "It beats all how folks do things nowadays. When I was a gal they made a hole in each end and sucked."'

In short, do not use a heavily Latinized style unless you wish to obtain an effect that can be obtained thus and only thus; an effect, maybe, of extreme formality or one of majestic impressiveness or again, one of sonorous euphony. *He died poor* is always preferable to *he expired in indigent circumstances,* but *a disastrous conflagration* might, in certain circumstances, be preferable to *a great fire*—especially if the results and not the extent are being referred to.

For further comments, see Jespersen, *op. cit.*

jonnick, -ock, -uck, -uk. See JANNOCK.

JOURNALESE. See OFFICIALESE.

journey. See TRIP.

judged as to whether it is (or **was** or **will be**) + adjective is a clumsy variation of *adjudged* + that adjective. Thus 'No word can be judged as to whether it is good or bad, correct or incorrect, beautiful or ugly, or anything else that matters to a writer, in isolation' (I. A. Richards, *The Philosophy of Rhetoric,* 1936) would be less wordy, more effective, if the author had written, 'No word can be adjudged good or bad . . .'. (Moreover, 'in isolation' is out of position.)

judgement and **judgment.** Although the latter has come to be the commonly accepted spelling there does not appear to be any reason for the omission of the *e*; many of the best writers retain the *e,* and many scholars have, since ca. 1920, recommended *judgement* as the more sensible and also as the more practical form.

judicial and **judicious** are frequently confused. The former = 'connected with, pertaining to, or proper to a court of law or a legal tribunal; belonging to or characteristic of a judge'; the sense 'showing sound judgement' fell into disuse so long ago as the 17th Century. *Judicious* = 'having sound judgement; wise in thought or behaviour; prudent; showing sound judgement'; the sense 'belonging or proper to a court of law or to a judge' dropped out of use in the 17th Century.

juncture, at this. Physically, 'at this joint or junction'; hence, 'at this crisis'. Even the sense 'at this particular point of time' is not incorrect, but its usage has been so debased that *at this juncture* is now avoided by self-respecting writers, public speakers, and private men of good sense and education.

junior. See 'SECUNDUS and JUNIOR'.

just is sometimes misused for *quite*. 'That forgetfulness had been well done, but not just well enough', Freeman Wills Crofts, *Found Floating*, 1937. (Possibly an uncorrected printer's error for 'just not well enough'.)

just means either *precisely* or *only*: obviously, therefore, it is to be used with care. Moreover, it has, in time-contexts, the sense of 'at, but certainly not later than'; sometimes, in this sense, it is preceded by *only*, as in '"Was it so late as 11 o'clock?" "Yes, but just"—*or* only just—"11"'. Hence, avoid *just* = 'precisely' except in time-contexts; and even there, *precisely* (or *exactly*) is preferable.

just as is catachrestic for *according as*. 'Liberty to individuals may be a good or a bad thing, just as they act, but liberty means power when men are in a body' (Examination script, March, 1938).

just exactly. This combination of almost synonymous terms is justly—and exactly—described by Fowler as 'bad tautology'.

just going to (do something), as Weseen remarks, 'has been much criticized. *Just about to* is preferable, as "I am just about to leave home".'

just the same does not equal *just as well*, as it is sometimes made to do. 'There is no need for grandeur in life to give happiness. The simple things provide it just the same' (Examination script, March, 1938).

justify, 'to excuse, to exonerate', is occasionally confused with *rectify*, 'to correct', 'to redress': one can *justify an error*, but it is something different from *rectifying an error*.

juvenile and **puerile.** Cf. the difference between *childlike* and *childish*. *Juvenile* is 'young', as in 'juvenile messengers', 'juvenile attendants'; hence 'belonging to, suited to, intended for youth', as in 'juvenile books'. *Puerile* is now confined to the sense 'childish'. Cf. 'YOUNG and YOUTHFUL'.

juwaub, 'a refusal, a dismissal', is better spelt *jawaub*.

K

kerb. See CURB.

ketchup, catchup, catsup. The earliest is *catchup* (late 17th Century); the prevalent 20th Century form is *ketchup*, the least used is *catsup*. (*The O.E.D.*) [[According to *Webster's*, *catchup* is the common form in American English.]]

kind . . . are for *kind . . . is*. 'Kittens and good scientists tend to let new experience pour in until some kind of workable relationships with past experience are established.'

kind of (e.g., rare) for *rather* (rare) is a solecism.

kind of, all. Not a serious solecism; according to *The O.E.D.*, 'still common colloquially, though considered grammatically incorrect'. (But *all manner of* is an established usage.) Similarly, *these* or *those kind of things*, pedantically judged incorrect, is a justifiable English idiom; Dean Alford (*The Queen's English*, 1870) is worth quoting on this point: '. . . it is evident that this tendency, to draw the less important word into similarity to the more important one, is suffered to prevail over strict grammatical exactness. We are speaking of "things" in the plural. Our pronoun "this" really has reference to "kind", not to "things"; but the fact of "things" being plural, gives a plural complexion to the whole, and we are tempted to put "this" into the plural. That this is the account to be given, appears still more plainly from the fact that not unfrequently we find a rival attraction prevails, and the clause takes a *singular* complexion from the other substantive, "kind". We often hear people say "this kind of thing", "that sort of thing". It must be confessed that the phrases, "this kind of things", "that sort of things", have a very awkward sound; and we find that our best writers have the popular expression, *These kind, those sort*. Thus we have in Shakespeare, *"King Lear"*, "These kind of knaves I know"; *Twelfth Night*, "that crow so at these set kind of fools"; in Pope: "The next objection is, that these sort of authors are poor".'
—In a gardening article in a daily paper, March, 1938, we find 'The newer kind (of aubrietia) spread rapidly', which is certainly incorrect and should be 'The newer kinds', or 'Those of the newer kind'.

kind of a for *kind of* is excessive, for

'What kind of a house do you live in?' means no more than 'What kind of house . . .?'

kindred to is wrongly used for *akin to* in the following: 'We need to know that other planets are inhabited by beings fulfilled and moved by a fire and spirit kindred to our own—otherwise what a dreadful loneliness oppresses us!', Don Marquis, *The Almost Perfect State*, 1927.

kinema, kinematic(al), kinematics, kinematograph, kinematographic, kineograph: these are etymologically correct, but usage is discarding them in favour of the *cine-* forms.

kingly, royal, regal. 'Who is able', asks Jespersen, 'to tell exactly how these adjectives differ in signification? And might not English like other languages (*royal* in French, *kongelig* in Danish, *königlich* in German) have been content with one word instead of three?' But only *kingly* can be used as the masculine counterpart to *queenly. Regal* is the least used of the three, and now is generally confined to the figurative or transferred senses, 'stately', 'splendid', as in 'She is a most regal woman', 'He wore his robes with a regal air'. *Royal* is the most general: 'of or pertaining to the sovereign; belonging to the royal prerogative', as in 'the Royal Family', 'royal power'; hence 'belonging to, or devoted to the service of the sovereign', as in 'the royal forest'; hence, 'befitting a sovereign; princely; munificent', as in 'royal splendour', 'royal hospitality', 'royal companions'—being in this nuance of 'splendid, magnificent', a synonym of *regal.* (*Webster's.*)

kneeled and **knelt** are equally correct as the preterite and past participle of *kneel.*

knit and **knitted.** Both of these forms are correct as the preterite and past participle of *knit.*

kodak is a trade-mark given at first to a special type of small photographic camera and later to other cameras and photographic supplies made by the same company. Properly it cannot be used for any small camera. ⟦This loose use seemed likely to become standard in America until the popularity of the so-called candid cameras brought a new type and other trade names into public favor.⟧

kotow is preferable to *kowtow* (n. and v.), especially in the literal Chinese sense. ⟦*Webster's* lists only *kowtow.*⟧

l.c. See IB.

L

L.L.A. (St. Andrews) is commonly taken to be a degree conferred by that University; it is, however, only a certificate of approximately the same standard as the Cambridge Higher Local. (Ackermann, *Popular Fallacies.*)

lactory is an erroneous form of *lactary* ('of or pertaining to milk').

laded; laden; ladened; loaded; loaden. *Laded* is the preterite and the past participle of *lade*, 'to put the cargo on board (a ship)'; but *laden* is the more usual past participle. *Ladened* is the preterite and past participle of *laden*, a mainly Scottish variant of *lade. Loaded* is the preterite and past participle of *load; loaden* is a dialectal past participle. (*The O.E.D.*)

lading. See CARGO.

lady, which has a social—almost a Society—connotation, should not be used as a synonym for *woman*, any more than *gentleman* should be used as a synonym for *man*. Only those men who are not gentlemen speak of their women friends as *lady friends*, and only those women who are not ladies speak of themselves as *charladies* and their men friends as *gentlemen friends.* Cf. the note at MISTER.

laid; lain. See 'LAY and LIE'.

lama, a Thibetan or Mongolian Buddhist priest, is sometimes confused with *llama*, a S. American animal between sheep and camel.

landscaper is a colloquial synonym of *landscape gardener; landscapist* is a Standard English synonym of *landscape-painter.*

LANGUAGE AND LOGIC. See GRAMMAR AND LOGIC.

lapse. See ELAPSE.

large is not—whereas *great* is—the adjective that should go with *breadth* (or *width*), *depth, distance, height, length.*

large-scale is correctly used of maps, in opposition to *small-scale*; but as a synonym for *large* it is both long-winded and unnecessary. It smacks, too, of 'big business', where the phrase 'large-scale operations' is not unknown. In an examination script (an L.C.C. Higher Grade essay) read by me in June, 1938, I met with this:—'He is able to see a large-scale result of his labours.'

large-size ('a large-size apple') is incorrect for *large-sized*, which many (myself included) would say is excessive for *large.*—Cf. the preceding entry.

last for *end*. Incorrect, as in 'Towards the last of the chapter'.

last for *latest* is incorrect for the sense 'most recent'. 'The last arrival' for 'the latest arrival', is not only incorrect but extremely ambiguous. Cf. 'LATTER for *last*'.

last, misused for *preceding*. 'The pioneers of semantics whose work we have attempted to summarize in the last four chapters have not . . .'.

last, at last . . . . 'At last the last forkful was pitched out', Adrian Bell, *By Road*, 1937. Not only does the repetition jar, but it sets up a contradiction that, though obviously apparent, is yet odd.

last, two; three last; four last, etc. English idiom demands *last two, three, four*, etc. For 'the three last chapters of the book' read 'the last three chapters . . .'; French idiom has 'les trois derniers chapitres du livre'.

last but one in such a phrase as 'in the last but one sentence' is top-heavy. Better 'in the last sentence but one'; or perhaps, 'in the penultimate sentence'; *last but one*, unchanged, should be used only in a predicate, as in 'In the sentence that comes last but one', 'It is the sentence last but one'.

last-mentioned. See 'LATTER and LAST-MENTIONED'.

late and **ex-.** 'The late President' is dead; 'the ex-President' is alive, *ex-* meaning 'former' but excluding death.

lately. See 'LATTERLY and LATELY'.

later and **latter.** *Later* is the comparative of *late* (in time), superlative *latest*; *latter*, the second of two things mentioned, has also the special sense 'near the end' of a period of time, as in 'the latter part of the year'.

later on for *later* (adv.) is an uneconomical colloquialism.

LATIN ADJECTIVES, USELESS. See USELESS LATIN ADJECTIVES.

LATIN TAGS. See CLICHÉ.

LATINISMS. See GREEK AND LATIN and JOHNSONESE.

latter, misused for *last*. John G. Brandon, *The Dragnet*, ca. 1936, 'Over all, was an aura of life, and youth, and happiness. But . . . there were others in that room whose countenances and general demeanour suggested anything but the latter emotion.' 'Latter' should be 'last' (of three). But *life* and *youth* are not *emotions*, and it is very doubtful whether *happiness* (except when *joy*) is one. See also SUPERLATIVE DEGREE.

latter and **last-mentioned** (or **named**) should be applied, respectively, to the second of two things, and to the last of three or more things: in 'Tennis and squash are good exercise but the last-mentioned is too strenuous', *last-mentioned* should be *latter*.

latterly and **lately.** Both refer to time; the former is rather literary in the sense 'of late' (*lately*), but is preferable to *lately* in the sense 'at the latter end' (of life or of some period); e.g., 'He died Sept. 23, 1766, at Hammersmith, though latterly he resided chiefly at Bath' (Horace Walpole). (*The O.E.D.*)

launder (preterite *laundered*) is the verb corresponding to *laundry*; in good English the latter is not used as a verb.

Lawd for *Lord*. Though the tendency in S. England and especially in Cockney is to eliminate *r* in pronunciation, the former spelling is incorrect and implies illiteracy where none exists.

lawyer; attorney; notary; solicitor, barrister. A *barrister* pleads in the courts; a *solicitor* does not,—he advises barristers in their cases and clients before, during and after cases, originally in equity only. An *attorney* performs the same work as a solicitor, but only in Common Law, and he is properly a *public attorney* (as opposite to a *private attorney* or *attorney in fact*, one who has *power of attorney* to act for another in business and legal affairs) or *attorney-at-law*; in current English, *solicitors* include *attorneys*. A *notary* (in full: *notary public* or *public notary*) is 'a person publicly authorized to draw up or attest contracts or similar documents, to protest bills of exchange, etc., and discharge other duties of a formal character' (*The O.E.D.*). *Lawyer* is generic: 'a member of the legal profession; one whose business it is to conduct suits in the courts, or to advise clients, in the widest sense embracing every branch of the profession, though in colloquial use often limited to attorneys and solicitors' (*ibid.*). [[The American terms are *lawyer* and, occasionally in certain phrases, *attorney* (*-at-law*), nowadays without difference in meaning. *Barrister* and *solicitor* are not current. *Notary* (*public*) is as defined above.]]

lay and **lie,** verbs active and passive, in the infinitive and present and past tenses, are continually misused and confused with each other, sometimes even in good literature; e.g., Byron, *Childe Harold*, iv. 7–9.

And send'st him . . . to his Gods, where
  haply lies
His petty hope in some near port or bay,
And dashest him again to earth:—there
  let him lay.

in which 'lies' is correct, but 'lay' incorrect. Dean Alford (*The Queen's English*, 3rd ed., 1870) remarks, 'I have observed that Eton men, for some reason or other, are especially liable to confuse these two verbs'. Ernest Hemingway falls into this trap in *To Have and Have Not*, 1937, thus, 'Eddy went forward and laid down'. *Lie—lay—lain; lay—laid—laid:* these are the correct forms. (*Lie*, to tell a falsehood, takes *lied* both in the preterite and in the past participle.)

'ld. See ''D and 'LD'.

leading question does not mean an unfair question but simply 'one that suggests the proper or expected answer', especially (in Law) 'a question which suggests to a witness the answer which he is to make' (Wharton). (*The O.E.D.*)

lean has preterite and past participle *leaned* (pron. *lēn'd*) or *leant* (pron. *lĕnt*); the latter usage is tending to become obsolete.

leap has preterite and past participle *leaped* (pron. *lēp'd*) or *leapt* (pron. *lĕpt*). Usage is gradually discarding *leapt*. Some good writers differentiate thus: *lean—leaned—leant; leap—leaped—leapt.*

learn has preterite and past participle *learned* and *learnt*. *Learnt* is disappearing from general use, but some discriminating writers and speakers retain it as past participle. Cf. LEAN and LEAP.—*Learn* for *teach* is a solecism.—The participial adjective *learned* is pronounced with two syllables.

lease (v.). See HIRE.

least for *lesser* (the smaller of two) is unfortunate; it destroys a valuable distinction.

leather and prunella, though once a well-worn cliché, is, I have found, frequently misunderstood. Trollope has 'The man to whom these delights of American humour are leather and prunella'—a matter of complete indifference. *The O.E.D.*, in a note, says that 'this is, strictly speaking, a misinterpretation [and misquotation] of Pope's words

[Worth makes the man, and want of it,
  the fellow:
The rest is all but leather or prunella,

Essay on Man, 1834]; the context refers to the difference of rank between the "cobbler" and the "parson", *prunella* being mentioned as the material for the clerical gown'. *The O.E.D.* defines *prunella* as 'a strong stuff, originally silk, afterwards worsted, formerly used for graduates', clergymen's, and barristers' gowns'.

leave, in *leave* a person *alone, leave me be, leave go of,* is a solecism for *let*. To *leave a person alone* is to allow him to remain in solitude; to *let him alone* is to cease from bothering him. [[Those Americans who know that to *leave a person alone* often means to allow him to remain in peace, undisturbed, will find authority in *Webster's*, LEAVE, 3. *Leave me be* is rustic or dialect; *leave go of* is vulgar.]]

legionary; légionnaire (properly: written in italics). The latter is, in English, noun only: 'a member of the French Foreign Legion', for which *legionary* is better, for *legionary* is 'a soldier of a legion, whether ancient (especially Roman) or modern (especially French)'. As an adjective, *legionary* = of or belonging to or characteristic of a legion'. Note, however, that *Legionary* or *Légionnaire* (or *Legionnaire*) also—since 1918—'a member of the British or the American Legion'. (*The O.E.D.*) [[Legionnaire is much more common than *legionary* for a member of the American Legion.]]

lengthways and **lengthwise**. Both are adverbs, with sense 'in the direction of the length' ('A hollow tube split lengthways', Coleridge; 'downward lengthwise', Goldsmith); the latter seems to be gaining the ascendant. Only *lengthwise* is an adjective. (*The O.E.D.*)

less for *fewer, not so many* is incorrect in the example given by C. C. Boyd, *Grammar for Great and Small*, 'There were less people at the match than I expected'. —In the correct 'the number of people was less', *less* qualifies *number*, not *people*. [[But *less* frequently occurs in place of *fewer* with collectives, as 'to wear less clothes' (*Webster's*); 'less people' is defensible, but not 'less persons'.]]

less and lesser. *Less*, adjective, is the comparative of *little*, with superlative *least*; it is also an adverb, the comparative of (the adverbial) *a little. Lesser* is adjective only—a double comparative (from *less*, with the comparative suffix *-er*). *Less* (adj.) is both attributive (as in 'in a less degree') and predicative ('And then the signs he would suppress

... grew less and less', Byron; 'It is less'); *lesser* is attributive only ('The lights of lesser craft dipped by', Howells). With reference to material dimension, *less* has given way to *smaller*, but it has been retained with reference to number or degree ('19 is less than 20'). (*The O.E.D.*)

lessee; lessor. See HIRE.

lest, misused. 'Walking to the *wagon restaurant* she looked enviously into each sleeping-car lest one would prove empty, and spare her the embarrassment of the couchette', Pamela Frankau, *I Find Four People*, 1935. For *lest one would* read *in case one should*: she hoped, not feared, to find one.

let takes the accusative, not the nominative; 'Let you and I go' is incorrect for 'Let you and me go'.—For *hire, let, rent,* see at HIRE.

LETTER-WRITING does not fall within the scope of this book. A useful guide is M. H. Weseen, *Everyday Uses of English*, 1922.

lexicon is often restricted to a dictionary of Greek, Hebrew, Syriac, or Arabic.

lexigraphy is 'a system of writing in which each character represents a word'; **lexicography** is 'the art or practice of writing dictionaries' (Johnson). (*The O.E.D.*)

liable (to do) for *likely* (to do), as in 'he is liable to make that mistake', is incorrect; but it is correct to say 'he is liable (i.e., subject) to error'.

liaison, apart from its technical senses in cookery, phonetics, and military organization, has only one sense, 'an illicit intimacy (generally of some considerable duration) between a man and a woman'. To apply it to other associations, to combinations, to alliances, to coalitions, is to commit an error.

libation is properly a pouring out of liquid—especially wine—in honour of a god, hence the drink-offering itself. Its use for a liquid poured out to be drunk by mere mortals is either jocular or pretentious. (*The O.E.D.*)

libel is printed (or written), whereas *slander* is spoken; to prove *slander*, an independent witness is required.

libellant and **libellous.** A *libellant* is 'one who institutes a suit in an ecclesiastical or admiralty court': note, any suit. Do not use it as a variant of *libeller*. The adjective *libellant* has the technical sense of the noun. *Libellous*

= 'of a libel; constituting a libel'. (*The O.E.D.*)

licence is the n., **license** the v. In *Six Years in the Prisons of England*, by 'A Merchant', 1869, the author gives a specimen of that form of licence which is familiarly called a ticket of leave and makes this comment:—'In the foregoing "ticket-of-leave" the word Licence is spelt with an *s*. In the Police Documents it is spelt with a *c*. So much for the education of Government Officials.' [[According to *Webster's*, the preferred spelling of both noun and verb is *license*.]]

lie. See 'LAY and LIE'.

lie-detector is merely a popular and journalistic name. 'Properly, this instrument is known as the Keeler Polygraph and consists of several instruments that measure ... pulse beat, blood pressure, rhythm of the chest in breathing, and electrical disturbances created by the activity of the sweat glands in the hands. A compensating device allows for what might be called normal irregularities of these and other functions, and the machine draws a graph on which are recorded states of normal and abnormal stress. A great deal depends upon the skill of the operator ...', Nigel Morland, *The Conquest of Crime*, 1937.

lifelong and **livelong.** The former is literal, 'lasting or continuing for a lifetime', as in 'The lifelong disability of deaf-mutism'; *livelong* is an intensive of *long*, as in 'Throughout the livelong day he had a presentiment of misfortune' and has come to have the connotation of 'long drawn out' or 'tedious'.

ligature. See DIPHTHONGS.

light, 'to dismount, to descend', is being displaced by *alight*.—The v. *light*, 'to give light; to set fire to', has preterite and past participle *lighted* or *lit*. As an attributive adjective, *lighted* is the more usual: *a lighted cigarette*.

lightening and **lightning** The former = '(a) making lighter or less heavy'; *lightning* is the visible discharge of electricity in the sky.

like for *as* is incorrect in: e.g., *to do like I do* (correctly *to do as I do*). It would appear to be going too far to call it an illiteracy; but it is at least 'a loose colloquialism ... avoided by careful speakers and writers' (Onions, *An Advanced English Syntax*). [[For comment on American use, see Perrin, *An Index to English*, pp. 366–367.]]

like for *as if* is incorrect. 'Carted her

out limp—looked like a chloroform-pad had been at work', John G. Brandon, *The Dragnet*, 1936.

like for *as though*. 'She was lying on the floor like dead with . . . wounds dark on her wrist and the blood squirting out' (a detective novel, 1937), where *like* should be *as though* (or *as though she were*) dead.

like for *likely* is incorrect, as in 'Is it like to happen soon?'

like as if, e.g., 'it looks like as if it would rain' is illiterate, but Nesfield, who had the nose of a sleuth hound for these errors, found it in *The Daily Telegraph* in May, 1900: 'The troop have set out with four days' supplies, so it looks like as if we were going no further than Ladybrand.'

like that, 'in that way', is not absolutely wrong, but it is vague; and often it is slightly ambiguous. 'Does he care for you like that' does not impress one as either vigorous or precise—or, for that matter, as elegant.

like which is incorrect for *the like of which*, Edwin Pugh, *A Street in Suburbia*, 1895, 'It give me a' insight inter 'is character like which I wouldn't otherwise ha' got'.

limited 'is not', Weseen pertinently remarks, 'in good use as a substitute for *small* or one of its synonyms. "A man of limited (meagre) education and limited (inadequate) capital is likely to be limited to a limited (scant) income."' Properly it = 'restricted, narrow, closely circumscribed'.

linage, less happily spelt *lineage*, is the number of lines of printed (or written) matter, or payment according to the number of lines; *lineage* is ancestry or pedigree. The former has long *i* and only two syllables; the latter, short *i* and three syllables. (*The O.E.D.*)

line, 'a profession or trade, an occupation, an activity', has been so overdone that one would be wise to avoid it—in good writing, at least. [[In the U.S.A., *line of goods*, trade jargon = the items dealt in.]]

lineament, 'a facial feature', is occasionally confused with *liniment*, 'an embrocation'.

linguistics, is rather 'the science of languages' and *philology* 'the science of a specific language or of language-as-communication'; the latter, however, is often used synonymously with the former. Meillet & Cohen's *Les Langues du*

Monde is linguistics, but the history of the English vowels is philology.

lit; lighted. See LIGHT.

literal. See LITERATE.—Do not confuse with *littoral*, 'adjacent to the shore'.

literally, when used, as it often is, as a mere intensive, is a slovenly colloquialism, its only correct use being to characterize *exactness to the letter*. 'William Hickie' once overheard the following in a woman's club:—'He literally turned the house upside down.'

LITERARISMS are either the journalese of the literary (these literarisms might almost be stigmatized as highbrow) or such unusual words as are used only by the literary or the learned.

And both kinds are to be distinguished from Elegancies (*q.v.*); for elegancies are the 'literary or cultured English' of those who, as a rule, are neither literary nor cultured.

If in doubt consult ELEGANCIES and also ARCHAISMS.

acerb
acolyte (non-ecclesiastically)
adumbrate
alchemy (figuratively)
alembicated
amplitude (non-scientifically)
arcana
aura
autochthonous
avid
avocation

balm
beatific
bedizened
bucolic

catharsis
certitude
cerulean
chieftain
chivalric
cognoscenti
confrère
continuum (used figuratively or non-technically)
converse (conversation)
couched (expressed)
crepuscular
crux

daedalian
darkling
deft and *deftly*
delectable and *delectation*

derogate from
descant
discrete
dolorous

effete
emanate (correctly used)
empyrean
encomium
envoy (of a poem)
esurient
eternize
ethereal
etiolated
exacerbate; exacerbation
excerpt (v.)
exemplar

feral
firmament
flee
fleece (to cheat)
fount
froward (also an archaism)
fulvid and *fulvous*

gelid
gilded youth
glabrous
grateful (of things: pleasing, acceptable)
gubernatorial

haste (v.)
heaven (sky)
helot
homo sapiens
hymeneal

immarcescible
implement (to fulfil)
in very truth
ineluctable
inexpugnable
imbrue (v.)
infinitude
intrinsic
inwardness
irrefragable
iteration and *iterate*

jocose

lassitude
laud (n. and v.)
Lethe
liege-lord (non-feudally; non-facetiously)
literati
longanimity
lustrum

mantle (figuratively)
meretricious

metempsychosis
mulct (*of:* to deprive of)

neophyte
nepenthe (or *N.*)
nimbus
no other, be able to do

obloquy
olden
opuscule
ordonnance
ordure
otherwhere

paramount
paramour
parergon
paucity
penumbra
perdurable
peripatetic
perspicacious; perspicacity
perspicuity
pestilence
plentitude
plenteous
plethora
polity
polymath
pother
prescience; prescient
proem
pusillanimous

quietude

regimen
Renascence, the
respire
retirement (see at RETIRACY)
r(h)odomontade

scabrous
sempiternal(ly)
significant (important)
similitude
smite
something (somewhat or rather)
straightway
supererogatory
supernal
superimpose
surcease (n.)
suspire
susurrus
suzerainty
swart

Tartarean (or *-ian*)
tantamount

thrasonical
toper
transpire (used correctly)
turpitude

umbrageous
unobtrusive(ly)
untoward

vacant (of persons: idle*)*
vault (to leap)
verdant
verisimilitude
verities, the
virtuoso (pl. *virtuosi*)
visitant

warranty (but not as a legal term)
what time (while; when)
whence
whither
wilderness
wondrous (adj.) and *wondrously*
writ (written)
wroth

LITERARY ALLUSION. Is literary
allusion a form of snobbery or is it not
rather—in the scholarly and the unpretentiously cultured, the genuinely well-
read—a legitimate source of pleasure and
a kind of subtlety? William Empson, in
Seven Types of Ambiguity, 1930, has
pertinently asserted that 'It is tactful,
when making an obscure reference, to
arrange that the verse'—he is speaking
of poetry—'shall be intelligible when the
reference is not understood'; the same
applies to prose. Those very sound
scholars and eminent philologists, J. B.
Greenough and G. L. Kittredge (*Words
and Their Ways in English Speech*, 1901),
have, apropos of fashions in language,
written thus:—'Another fashion is the
knack of literary allusion. It is akin to
the habit of quotation,—itself a fashion
. . . that comes and goes; but it shows
itself in a less formal and tangible way'—
less formal because less tangible.

LITERARY STANDARD. See STAND-
ARD ENGLISH, Section ii.

literate means 'able to read and
write'; the opposite of *illiterate*. For a
confusion with *literal*, see the passage
quoted at MALAPROPISMS.

literature for printed matter of any
kind, e.g., for advertising matter, is a
colloquialism—an extremely silly and
unfortunate one, for it tends to degrade
a good word and a fine thing.

littoral. See LITERAL.
livelong. See LIFELONG.
llama for *lama*. See LAMA.
lliana for *liana*. The former is a mere
misspelling of the latter, and is possibly
caused by confusion with *llano*, a S.
American level, treeless plain.

load. See CARGO.
loaded; loaden. See *laded*.
loan as a verb for *lend* is good American, but it is not yet good English.

loath; loathe; loth. *Loth* is an alternative form of *loath*, 'disinclined', 'reluctant', as in 'I am loath (or loth) to
believe it' or in the set phrase, *nothing
loath* ('not at all unwillingly'). *Loathe* is
a verb, 'to feel dislike or aversion for',
e.g. for food: 'To dictate their terms to
statesmen who loathe the necessity of
submission' (Bryce); 'Your stomach soon
must loathe all drink and meat' (J.
Thompson). (*The O.E.D.*)

locality and **location.** A *locality* is the
situation or position of an object, or the
place in which it is to be found; it is
applied especially to geographical position or place; also a district, a place,
regarded either as the site occupied by
certain persons or things or as the scene
of certain activities. 'A blind man . . .
feeling all round him with his cane, so
as to find out his locality' (Hawthorne);
'The tremendous rainfall of the Khasi
Hills, amounting in some localities . . . to
559 inches of annual rainfall' (Haugh-
ton). *Location* is local or definite
position, as in 'location in space'; the
two senses, 'a tract of land marked out
or surveyed', e.g., a mining claim, and
'place of settlement or residence', are
American, as also is the cinematic *location* ('on location'), 'an exterior place
where a scene is filmed'. (*The O.E.D.*)

locate, meaning *to place*, is misused
for *to find*; as the maid said about some
articles lost by the laundry, 'I expect
they'll be able to locate them'.

located. *To be located*, 'to reside'; 'to
live (in a place)', is an Americanism, as
in 'Are you located near here?'

locution and **circumlocution.** The
predominant 20th Century sense of *locution* is 'a form of expression; a phrase; an
expression', as in 'The introduction of
new words and locutions' and 'The brisk
and picturesque locutions of Cockneys'.
A *circumlocution* is a roundabout, esp. if
wordy, phrase or expression—e.g., *in
respect of* and *with regard to* for *about* or
concerning. (*The O.E.D.*)

LOGIC AND GRAMMAR. See GRAM-
MAR AND LOGIC.

lonely; alone. *Lonely* is solitary; *alone*,
by oneself. One may be alone in a wood,
yet by no means lonely; or one may be
walking in a crowded street, yet be
intolerably lonely.

look over. See OVERLOOK.

look well and **look good.** To *look good*
is to appear good; to *look well* is to be well
('She looks well'), hence to be attractive
('He looks well in that suit').

looker-ons is incorrect for *lookers-on*.

loose and **loosen.** The former is usual
in the sense, 'to undo, to unbind, set
free from material bonds', as in 'He
loosed the dog'; hence 'to loose an
arrow'. The latter is more general in the
sense 'to relax or slacken', as in 'to
loosen ligatures', 'loosen one's joints',
'loosen discipline'; hence 'to unfix or
detach; to render less firm or cohesive',
as in 'to loosen the stones in a wall',
'to loosen the soil'; cf. 'to loosen one's
tongue'. (*The O.E.D.*)

loose for *lose* is a misspelling not
infrequently met with; inexcusable, for
the two words are pronounced differently.

Lord's Day, the. See SABBATH.

lot. *A lot* for a large number or
quantity; *the lot* for the whole number
or quantity; are too common in our
speech to be condemned as incorrect,
but their use where any refinement or
elevation of language is required is impossible, for they are not Standard
English. *All the lot* is almost a vulgarism.

loud, 'showy', 'flashy' (*loud clothes,
loud colours*), is classified by *Webster's*
and considered by Weseen as a 'colloquialism, but it is Standard English;
familiar, if you like, but impeccable.
[But see *Webster's* definition of 'colloquialism'.]

loud speaker; loud-speaker. The
latter can refer only to the wireless-
telephony or radio broadcast instrument;
one who speaks loudly must be a *loud
speaker*. It is, therefore, advisable to use
the unhyphenated form only in reference
to the human speaker.

louring. See LOWERING.

love, in good English (whether spoken
or written), is not to be debased to
equivalence with *to like*, however amusing
it may be in conversation ('He just loves
cricket'). Extremely colloquial is 'What
a love of a child!'

lovelily is good English and it means
'beautifully; in such a way as to stimu-

late love', as in 'How lovelily do the
Graces cling to one another' and 'lovelily
shines the moon'. Where it is cacophonous, use *in a lovely manner*.

low. See LOWLY.

LOW LANGUAGE. See VULGARISMS
AND LOW LANGUAGE.

lowering (n. and adj.) = 'depression'
or 'depressing' ('Fever is very lowering')
and 'frowning; gloom or gloomy' (*lowering looks, lowering sky*); *louring* is used
only in the second sense. *The O.E.D.*
prefers the *lour* form for the 'frowning,
gloomy' sense.

lowly should be avoided as the adverb
of *lowly*, 'humble', for it is often ambiguous, as in 'The preacher spoke
lowly': for 'in a low voice', use *low*; for
'in a lowly manner', use either *in a lowly
manner* or *lowlily*. There is an adverb
lowly, and it occurs in both of these
senses: but avoid it!

luncheon is a formal (e.g., a civic)
lunch.

lure (v.). See ALLURE (v.).

lustful; lusty. The former = 'pertaining to or full of sexual desire;
libidinous', with adverb *lustfully*; the
latter (with adverb *lustily*) = 'vigorous',
as in 'He's a fine, lusty fellow', 'He
dealt the bully a lusty blow'.

luxuriant for *luxurious.* The former,
'producing abundantly, growing pro-
fusely', is an adj. of active properties;
the latter, 'given to luxury or self-
indulgence, of or pertaining to, or characterized by luxury' (*The O.E.D.*), is
passive. Often confused in application,
as are the adverbs *luxuriantly* and
luxuriously. For misuse of *luxuriantly*,
see the passage quoted at MALAPROP-
ISMS; of *luxuriously*, note: 'All the plants
in my garden are growing luxuriously'
(in a private letter received by the
author in July, 1938).

Lyon for *Lyons.* See BRUXELLES.

lyricist; lyrist. The latter is either 'a
player on the lyre', or 'a lyric poet';
the former, a rare word, is 'a lyric poet'.

M

macintosh, not *mackintosh,* is the
strictly correct name of the rain coat,
for it was called after one Charles
Macintosh; but the *ck* form has been
so widely used that one feels pedantic
in even mentioning the *c* form.

Maconachie is incorrect for *Macono-
chie* (*ration*).

mad for *angry* is a colloquialism.

Madam is the correct English form of the French *Madame*; the plural, however, is as in French: *Mesdames*.

maelstorm is incorrect for *maelstrom*; *maëlstrom* also is incorrect, for the word is dissyllabic.

magisterial and **magistral.** In current, non-technical usage, *magistral* = 'masterly' as in 'a magistral arrangement of complex facts' and 'Magistral as Milton at his greatest, but subtle beyond his scope' (J. M. Robertson, 1889). An adoption from France.

The predominant sense of *magisterial* is 'of, belonging to, proper to a magistrate; holding the office of a magistrate', as in 'my magisterial neighbour', 'a magisterial inquiry', 'magisterial duties'. Two obsolescent nuances are: 'authoritative', as in 'a magisterial utterance', *magisterial* being here synonymous with the preferable *magistral*; and 'invested with authority', as in 'a magisterial superintendent'. But a useful sense is that of 'assuming authority, schoolteacher-like', hence 'dictatorial', as in 'He delivered his instructions in a magisterial voice'. Based on *The O.E.D.*

Magna Charta, commonly so written and spoken, should be *Magna Carta* (Latin) or *The Great Charter* (English). *Charta* is neither Latin nor English.

magniloquent for *pompous* is an error due to misunderstanding, for by its Latin derivation *magniloquent* means 'talking big', a sense it retains in usage, although usage generally gives to it the meaning, 'lofty or ambitious in expression' (*The O.E.D.*); and pomposity is not a form of speech though it may accompany magniloquence. See also at GRANDILO-QUENT.

mail. See POST.

main. See COMPARATIVES, FALSE.

maintain, misused for the intransitive *obtain* ('to exist; be practised, be habitual; be thus'), as in 'Does that puerile practice still maintain?', Thorne Smith, *Topper Takes a Trip*, 1935. Perhaps cf. the French *se maintenir*.

major. See COMPARATIVES, FALSE. A thing or fact is either *major* or *minor*—and that is all there is to it.

major portion and **greater part.** The latter would be preferable in such a sentence as 'He devotes the major portion of his time to gardening.'

majority, misused for *larger part* of a thing; e.g., 'The majority of the book is instructive'. *Majority* applies only to numbers; it = 'the greater number'.

make an opinion should be *form an opinion*. Although the error is obvious and exemplifies a flagrant and wilful flouting of idiom, yet it is surprisingly common. 'One should not make strong opinions concerning liberty until one has looked deeply into the question' (examination script, March, 1938). [[Exceptional if found at all in American English.]]

Malapropisms. A malapropism—the adjective, by the way, is *malapropian*—is a 'ludicrous misuse of [a] word, especially in [a] mistake for one resembling it (e.g., *a nice derangement of epitaphs* for *arrangement of epitaphs*)', to quote *The Con. O.D.* The term derives from Mrs Malaprop in Sheridan's *The Rivals*, produced in 1775; she was 'noted for her aptitude for misapplying long words, e.g., "as headstrong as an allegory on the banks of the Nile"' (Sir Paul Hervey, *The Oxford Companion to English Literature*, 1932). This kind of mistake, which is a sub-division of the *genus* catachresis (*q.v.*), has been felicitously used by many writers. In the General English Paper set in the Oxford and Cambridge School Certificate examination of July, 1938, there occurred this question:

'Point out and correct any mistakes in word usage and idiom in the following passage:

'Mary entered the luxuriantly [*luxuriously*] furnished room and was welcomed by the baroness. She was indeed surprised by the warmth and pleasantry [*pleasantness*] of her reception considering all she had heard of her hostesses masterly [*hostess's masterful*] ways. It would not be difficult now, she thought, to explain her purport [*purpose*] in coming to the castle. Suddenly her eye was attracted by a small picture which hung [better, *was hanging*] between the tall French-windows, and the baroness interrupted her glance. "My dear, you are perspicuous [*perceptive*, or, preferably, *observant*]; I see you have already noticed my Orozzi. It is indeed quite unique [see UNIQUE] and priceless, though some people find the colours crude and the drawing primary [*primitive*: better *elementary*] and are worried [better, *perplexed*] because they find no allusion [*illusion*] of perspective in the background." "Ah yes," said Mary, "but these kind [*this* (or *that*) *kind*] of people always looks for a literate [*literal*] meaning in a work of art, and nothing else." "I see you are by no means *ingenious* (*ingenuous*: better, *ignorant*] in these matters," observed the baroness, and Mary smiled, well pleased with the complement [*compliment*].'

malapropos is the correct English way of writing the adopted French phrase, *mal à propos*. *Malapropos*, originally an adverb, has become also an adjective and even a noun.

Malay, used as the name of the country *Malaya*, *Malacca*, is a frequent error of ignorance. A *Malay* is a native of that country, *the Malay* (adj.) *Peninsula*.

male. See at MANLIKE.

maleficence; malevolence. See BENEFICENCE.

Mall, the. See PALL MALL.

Mall and **Pall Mall.** Uncertainty as to the pronunciation of these names is often shown and conclusive authority is wanting. In *the Mall* it may be *Mawl* or *Măl*, but *Měl* is considered incorrect, whereas in *Pall Mall* the pronunciation *Pĕl Mĕl*, usual in the 17th Century when the game from which it is derived was fashionable, has been retained and is correct, as is also *Păl Măl*, but not *Pawl Mawl*.

mammoth, as an adj. for *huge*, is questionable. We say 'elephantine', 'leonine', etc. Yet it is defended by a reviewer in *The Times Lit. Sup.*, March 20, 1937; he asks, 'If "demon" is an adjective, why not "mammoth"?'. In 'demon bowler', 'demon lover', only the hyphen is needed to show that each is a pair of nouns conveying that the subject is a demon as well as a bowler, or lover, whereas in 'mammoth show' only the adjectival quality of size is implied. A show cannot be a mammoth, though a mammoth would be a show.

man-like. See MANLIKE; MANLY; . . .

man of letters; writer; author. Whatever the nuances may have been in 1800 or 1850 or 1900, the differentiation now prevalent is this:—The term *author* is applied to a writer of *fiction*; *writer* to a writer of *fiction, history, biography, belles-lettres*; *man of letters* to such a writer of any or all of these, plus poetry, plus works of scholarship,—but if his fiction is preponderant, he is usually relegated to the rank of *writers*, precisely as a *writer* that produces very little except fiction becomes an *author*.

Note that a person that writes only—or mostly—poetry is generally called a *poet*, seldom a *writer*, never an *author*. A person that writes plays—or mostly plays—is generally called a *dramatist* (serious plays) or *playwright* (any kind, all kinds), not an *author* (despite the call 'Author! Author!'). One who writes reviews is a *reviewer*; if he writes a novel or two, he is usually spoken of as 'reviewer turned author', and all those novelists whom he has slated (and not a few others) rend him limb from limb—though not in the open; if he writes very well, he may become a *writer*, and if he not only writes very well but is a scholar, he may, by his friends, be described as a *man of letters*.

Man of letters, however, is, even among those who merit that designation, avoided by the modest, for it has a slight taint of highbrowism and, if used by themselves, more than a tinge of pretentiousness; they prefer to be called *writers*. *Author* has also a generic sense, as in 'The Society of Authors', 'The Authors' Club', and in legal and official documents (e.g., income-tax returns) and in semi-official publications (e.g., *Who's Who*); in its restricted sense (a writer of fiction), *author* is a useful welder of *novelists* and *short-story writers*—a combination that calls for some such neologism as *fictioner* or *fictionist*. *Writer* is probably the most useful of these three terms; it is certainly the least invidious; underwriters and copy-writers may generally be trusted not to usurp the more general—and more complimentary term.

mandatary; mandatory. The former is noun only ('a person to whom a mandate is given'); the latter, both adj. and noun, the latter both in the sense of *mandatary* and in that created by the League of Nations—'a Power selected by the League to administer (and develop) a territory; hence the territory or state thus assigned to a Power'. (*The O.E.D.*)

manifold; multifarious; multiform; multiple. For *manifold*, see the remarks at -FOLD; but it does also = 'consisting of many of one kind combined; operating many of one kind of object', as in 'a *manifold* bell-pull'; further, it = 'numerous and varied', as in 'O Lord how *manifold* are thy works!'

Multifarious emphasizes 'the diversity, sometimes even the incongruity, of the elements involved', as in 'The *multi-*

farious complexities of human character' (Hare).

Multiform = 'having many forms, shapes, or appearances', as in 'A plastic and multiform unit' (Hare).

Multiple (see also -PLE) = 'containing (something) more than once, or containing more than one (of a thing); consisting of more than one', as in *multiple stores, a multiple vote, multiple solutions* (of a problem).

mankind should be followed by *it*, not by *he*, for it = the human race. 'By [the middle of the 15th Century], through the application of science and invention, new possibilities were available to mankind which were likely to have an even larger effect on his future than those of agriculture and the techniques of early civilization', J. D. Bernal, 'The Social Function of Science', in *The Modern Quarterly*, January, 1938. Probably the confusion is caused by taking *mankind* to be a synonym of *man*, as of course it is—but of *man* generically, not of *man*, the male human being.

manlike (or **man-like**); **manly; mannish; male; masculine.** *Manly* (falling into disuse in the sense 'mannish') is favourable, connoting the good qualities of a man; *mannish* is unfavourable if it is applied to a woman, and it means 'resembling a man' (in dress, manners, speech), but as a synonym of *manly* and *manlike*, it is obsolescent; of *manlike* the predominant sense is, 'characteristic of a man as opposite to a woman or a child', but when applied to an animal (esp. an ape), it = 'resembling a human being',—its other senses ('mannish' and 'manly') being obsolescent; *male* is 'of the masculine sex, *qua* sex, as opposite to the feminine sex'; and *masculine*, the grammatical opposite of *feminine* (*gender*), is in general use in the senses 'peculiar to or assigned to males; consisting of males', as in *masculine attire, masculine primogeniture*, and 'virile; vigorous; appropriate to (excellences of) the male sex', as in *masculine licence, masculine force, masculine style*, the sense 'mannish' being obsolescent. (*The O.E.D.*)

MANNER AND MATTER. See SUIT-ABILITY.

manslaughter. See MURDER.

manuscript means 'written by hand' and *manuscripts* should be reserved for handwritten copies of, e.g., a book; that which is typed is a *typescript*. But *manu-*

script is often used for *typescript* (whether noun or adjective): which seems a pity!

map. See at CHART.

marionette. See PUPPET.

Marseille for *Marseilles*. See at BRUXELLES.

marshal for *martial* is an occasional error among the semi-literate. The former is n. and v.; the latter, adj. only ('warlike').

mart is slightly archaic, rather literary for *market*.

martyr (to) for *victim* (*of*) or *one suffering* (*from*) is hyperbolical and to be used with care: *a martyr to epilepsy* is admissible, *a martyr to colds* is absurd.

marvel and **miracle** are overworked—and too often used hyperbolically.

masculine. See MANLIKE . . .

masochism. See SADISM.

mass is sometimes used for *majority*, as in 'The mass of the people gained their enjoyment as spectators', examination essay script, June, 1939.

massacre (n. and v.) refers to wholesale killing, mass-slaughter, not to the murder of one person. 'He swore the most dreadful oaths that he would "massacre her"', Thomas Reid, *Two Voyages*, 1822.

masseur, masculine; **masseuse**, feminine. They may now be regarded as English words; do not, therefore print them in italic.

masterful; masterly. With a long interval between them, I wrote two accounts of this pair. Here is the later:

In current usage, they are distinguished thus:—*Masterful* is 'imperious' or (of actions) 'high-handed, despotic', as in 'She was proud and masterful' (Trollope), 'This masterful disregard of logical thought'; 'qualified to command; powerful and/or vigorous in command or in rule', as in 'Henry VIII was a masterful King'; as a synonym of *masterly*, it is obsolescent. *Masterly* is applied either to persons or their actions or abilities, and it = 'resembling or characteristic of a master or skilled workman; skilfully performed, done, exercised', as in 'a masterly sportsman', 'The thought is masculine and the expression masterly' (Leslie Stephen); 'a masterly stroke' (of painter, tactician, batsman). (*The O.E.D.*)

And here the earlier:

Masterful and *masterly* are often confused. In the Oxford and Cambridge School Certificate examination held in

July, 1938, the English General Paper contained this sentence for correction: 'She was indeed surprised by the warmth ... of her reception, considering all she had heard of her (hostess's) masterly ways'. And in the same month I found in the Introduction to Dr Selwyn Gurney Champion's remarkable book, *Racial Proverbs* (1938), this reference to Bonser & Stephen's *Proverb Literature* (1928), 'This unique and masterful compilation of the world's proverb literature is indispensable to the paroemiographer'. *Masterful* means 'self-willed', 'imperious', 'domineering'; *masterly* signifies 'worthy of a master (at, e.g., one's art)', hence 'very skilful or expert'.—The same remarks apply to *masterfulness* and *masterliness*.

materialize, 'to become visible or perceptible; to become real, actual, actual fact; against general opinion or serious obstacles to succeed, make its way', is overdone, as in 'There were doubts of his ability to come at all, but he materialized', 'After much discussion, a plan materialized', 'The house he longed to achieve did not materialize'.

materially is not incorrect in the sense 'to an important extent; substantially; considerably, greatly', as in 'Short cuts, by ... which the road was materially shortened' (Ralph Boldrewood), but there is, especially among journalists, a tendency to overdo it.

matter, misused for *material* or *article*. 'His breeches were of plain black cloth, and his black stockings were of cotton—matters entirely out of harmony with his magnificent coat'. Rafael Sabatini, *Scaramouche*, 1921.

maximum and **minimum,** meaning the absolute *most* and *least*, are often loosely used.

may and **can.** See 'CAN and MAY'.

may and **might.** See SUBJUNCTIVE.

may and **must.** See NEGATION, Section *A*, last five paragraphs.

maybe is to be preferred to the original *may be* as a colloquial synonym of 'perhaps'. '"You'll say it's likely enough that there was money and may be jewellery sent over to him from France"', Ronald Knox, *Double Cross Purposes*, 1937. It is permissible, though no longer usual, to write ' ... money and (it may be) jewellery'.

me for *I*. See IT IS ME.

me with ... See AND ME WITH ...

mean time and **meantime.** *Meantime*,

adverb, is short for *in the meantime* (originally *in the mean time*), 'during a specified interval'. In current usage, *mean time* is, by discriminating writers, confined to the sense *mean solar time*, i.e., the time of day as shown by the *mean sun*, i.e., the time shown by an ordinary clock, correctly regulated.

means, 'an instrument, agency, method, or course of action, by the employment of which some object is or may be attained, or which is concerned in bringing about some result' (*The O.E.D.*), is plural in form but singular in sense and construction, as in 'I was the means of this being done'. 'To speculate whether words are efficient means of communicating thought' is wrong; 'To speculate whether words are an efficient means ...' would be right. The error is taken from the blurb to the English edition of Stuart Chase's *The Tyranny of Words*, 1938. [[*Webster's* authorizes '... the plural form *means*, with either sing. or pl. sense and construction'.]]

meantime. See MEAN TIME ...

Mecca, being the birthplace of the Prophet, is a place of religious pilgrimage for Mohammedans, but to say (as the Southern Railway's *Holiday Hints*, 1938, says) that 'Ryde Pier is a Mecca for anglers' is to debase metaphor from the sublime to the ridiculous.

media. See MEDIUMS.

medium-size (adj.) is incorrect for *medium-sized*, and often *medium-sized* is unnecessary for *medium* or *average*.

mediums are spiritualistic, or (or persons) 'intermediaries' or 'mediators', or absolute as in 'The large hats are ugly, the mediums are tolerable, the small ones are pretty'; in all other senses, the plural is *media*, although *mediums* is gaining ground at the expense of *media* and will probably—except perhaps in scientific jargon—become the accepted plural in all senses.

mellifulous, an occasional mispronunciation of *mellifluous* by people who have a difficulty with the consonants.

memoranda is the plural of *memorandum*; and because the plural is more often used than the singular it is occasionally taken for and construed as a singular (cf. STRATA). The English plural, *memorandums*, is gaining ground: and there is no reason why you should not use it if you wish. The unforgivable sin is to form the plural in -*as*; *memorandas* is as absurd as *stratas*.

menace, 'a threat', should not be overdone. That Kenneth Farnes is a better bowler than writer appears from: 'McCabe is a good second-string to the Bradman menace', *Lyons' Sports Sheet*, May 8, 1938.

mendacity and **mendicity.** The former is habitual lying or deceiving; the latter, the habit of begging, or the existence of the begging class (*mendicants*). See *Webster's* and *The O.E.D.*

mental to describe a mentally disordered person is a modern term—and no better than slang.

mephites for *mephitis* is an error.

mere is often unnecessary. Properly, it is a strong word and therefore should not be used weakly, as in 'Sometimes this "frankness" [about sexual matters] is mere vulgarity', where the simple *vulgarity* would be stronger.—*Merely* also is misused. See PURE and ONLY.

mesdames. See MADAM.

Messrs should be confined to commerce; elsewhere *Messieurs*. The best abbreviation, in English as in the French original, is, in my opinion, *MM*.

metal has been displaced by *mettle* for '"the stuff" of which a man is made, with reference to character' (*The O.E.D.*).

METAPHOR.

I, General Considerations; II, Confused or Mixed Metaphors.

I. *General Considerations.*

Metaphor, as defined by *The O.E.D.*, is that 'figure of speech in which a name or descriptive term is transferred to some object different from, but analogous to, that to which it is properly applicable'; derivatively, an instance of this, i.e., a metaphorical expression—a transference or transferred usage. The word comes from the Greek μεταφορά, 'a transference (of the sense of one word to another), and its Latin synonym is *translatio*, lit. 'a carrying across'.

But, as the following précis of certain passages from 'Metaphor' and 'The Command of Metaphor' in Dr I. A. Richards's *The Philosophy of Rhetoric*, 1936,—the two best chapters in a provocative and illuminating book—will (I hope) make clear, that is an insufficient definition.

Aristotle, in *The Poetics*, went so far as to declare that 'the greatest thing by far is to have a command of metaphor' and added that, 'to employ metaphors

happily and effectively', it was necessary to have 'an eye for resemblances'. On this matter, Dr Richards says:—'We all live, and speak, only through our eye for resemblances. Without it we should perish early. Though some may have better eyes than others, the differences between them are in degree only and may be remedied, certainly in some measure, as other differences are, by the right kinds of teaching and study. . . . As individuals we gain our command of metaphor just as we learn whatever else makes us distinctively human.'

Richards passes to that further assumption made by the 18th and 19th Century writers on Rhetoric—'that metaphor is something special and exceptional in the use of language, a deviation from its normal mode of working, instead of the omnipresent principle of all its free action.

'Throughout the history of Rhetoric', continues this able pleader for a revival and a re-assessment of Rhetoric, 'metaphor has been treated as a sort of happy extra trick with words, an opportunity to exploit the accidents of their versatility, something in place occasionally but requiring unusual skill and caution. In brief, a grace or ornament or *added* power of language, not its constitutive form'. He notes that Shelley developed his view that 'language is vitally metaphorical': and remarks, 'But that is an exceptional utterance and its implications have not yet been taken account of by rhetoricians'.

Richards proceeds to deal with a matter of primary importance:—'That metaphor is the omnipresent principle of language can be shown by mere observation. We cannot get through [even so much as] three sentences of ordinary fluid discourse without it. . . . Even in the rigid language of the settled sciences we do not eliminate or prevent it without great difficulty. In the semi-technicalised subjects, in aesthetics, politics, sociology, ethics, psychology, theory of language and so on, our constant chief difficulty is to discover how we are using it [i.e., metaphor] and how our supposedly fixed words are shifting their senses. In philosophy, above all, we can take no step safely without an unrelaxing awareness of the metaphors we, and our audience, may be employing. . . . And this is the more true, the more severe and abstract the philosophy is. As it grows more abstract we think increasingly by means of metaphors that we profess *not* to be relying on. The metaphors we are avoiding steer our thought as much as those we accept.

'In the simplest formulation, when we use a metaphor we have two thoughts of different things active together and supported by a single word, or phrase, whose meaning is a resultant of their interaction. . . . There is an immense variety in [the] modes of interaction between co-present thoughts . . . or, in terms of the context theorem, between different missing parts or aspects of the different contexts of a word's meaning. In practice, we distinguish with marvellous skill between these modes of interaction, though our skill varies. The Elizabethans, for example, were far more widely skilled in the use of metaphor—both in utterance and in interpretation—than we are. A fact which made Shakespeare possible. The 18th Century narrowed its skill down, defensively, to certain modes only. The early 19th Century revolted against this and specialized in other modes. The later 19th Century and [the 20th] have been recovering from these two specializations.'

Dr Richards then 'gets down to brass tacks'. 'The traditional theory noticed only a few of the modes of metaphor; and limited its application of the term *metaphor* to a few of them only. And thereby it made metaphor seem to be a verbal matter, a shifting and displacement of words, whereas fundamentally it is a borrowing and [an] intercourse of *thoughts*, a transaction between contexts. *Thought* is metaphoric, and proceeds by comparison, and the metaphors of language derive therefrom.'

Having established a background and a principle, Richards asks us to consider certain simple analytic steps that render more facile the translation of our skill with metaphor into an explicit art. 'A first step is to introduce two technical terms to assist us in distinguishing from [each other] what Dr Johnson called the two ideas that any metaphor, at its simplest, gives us. Let me call them the tenor and the vehicle. . . . At present we have only some clumsy descriptive phrases with which to separate [the two halves—or members—of a metaphor]. "The original idea" and "the borrowed one"; "what is really being said or thought of" and "what it is compared to"; "the underlying idea" and "the imagined nature"; "the principal subject" and "what it resembles"; or, still more confusing, simply "the meaning" and "the metaphor", or "the idea" and "its image".

'How confusing these must be', he continues, 'is easily seen. . . . We need the word "metaphor" for the whole double unit.' The 18th Century rhetoricians assumed 'that figures [especially metaphors] are a mere embellishment or added beauty and that the plain meaning, the tenor'—the surface meaning, the general tenor of the discourse at any given point or stage of the discourse—'is what alone really matters and is something that, "regardless of the figures", might be gathered by the patient reader'.

To this, 'a modern theory would object, first, that in many of the most important uses of metaphor, the co-presence of the vehicle and tenor results in a meaning (to be clearly distinguished from the tenor [; a meaning richer, subtler, fuller than that conveyed by the tenor alone]) which is not attainable without their interaction'. Modern opinion would object, secondly 'that the vehicle is not normally a mere embellishment of a tenor which is otherwise unchanged by it, but that vehicle and tenor in co-operation give a meaning of more varied powers than can be ascribed to either [the tenor alone or the vehicle alone]. And a modern theory would go on to point out that with different metaphors the relative importance of the contributions of vehicle and tenor to this resultant meaning varies immensely. At one extreme the vehicle may become almost a mere decoration or coloring of the tenor, at the other extreme the tenor may become almost a mere excuse for the introduction of the vehicle, and so no longer be "the principal subject".

'How about [Lord Kames's] suggested rule that we should carefully avoid mounting metaphor upon metaphor? What would be the effect of taking it seriously? It would, if accepted and observed, make havoc of most writing and speech. It is disregarding the most sustaining metaphors of all speech. It would make, I think, Shakespeare the faultiest writer who ever held a pen; and it turns an obstinately blind eye upon one of the most obvious features of current practice in every minute of our speech.'

Arrived at 'the command of metaphor', Dr Richards remarks upon the contrast between our use of metaphors and our awareness of them. 'Our skill with metaphor, with thought, is one thing—prodigious and inexplicable; our reflective awareness of that skill is quite another thing—very incomplete, distorted, fallacious, over-simplifying. [The business of reflective awareness is] to protect our natural skill from the interferences of unnecessarily crude views about it; and, above all, to assist the imparting of that skill—that command of metaphor—from mind to mind!

'A very broad division can ... be made between metaphors which work through some direct resemblance between the two things, the tenor and vehicle, and those which work through some common attitude which we may ... take up towards them both. *That we like them both* is ... a common property that two things share, though we may, at the same time, be willing to admit that they are utterly different. . . . This division, though it does not go very deep, may ... help us sometimes to avoid one of the worst snares—the assumption that if we cannot see how a metaphor works, it does not work.'

Let us take the simple word *leg*. 'We notice that even there the boundary between literal and metaphoric uses is not quite fixed or constant. To what do we apply it literally? A horse has legs literally, so has a spider, but how about a chimpanzee? Has it two legs or four? And how about a star-fish? Has it arms or legs or neither? And, when a man has a wooden leg, is it a metaphoric or a literal leg? The answer to this last is that it is both. It is literal in one set of respects, metaphoric in another. A word may be *simultaneously* both literal and metaphoric, just as it may simultaneously support many different metaphors, may serve to focus into one meaning many different meanings. This point is of some importance, since so much interpretation comes from supposing that if a word works one way it cannot simultaneously work in another way and have simultaneously another meaning.'

From that important point, Richards passes to another—'the varying relations between tenor and vehicle. It is convenient to begin with the remark ... that a metaphor involves a comparison. What is a comparison? It may be several different things: it may be just a putting together of two things to let them work together; it may be a study of them both to see how they are like and how unlike [each other]; or it may be a process of calling attention to their likenesses or a method of drawing attention to certain aspects of the one through the co-presence of the other. [Thus] we get different conceptions of metaphor. If we mean calling attention to likenesses, we get a main 18th Century doctrine of metaphor. Dr Johnson ... praises Denham's lines on the Thames because "the particulars of resemblance are so perspicaciously collected" ...

O could I flow like thee, and make thy
     stream
My great exemplar as it is my theme!
Though deep, yet clear; though gentle,
     yet not dull;
Strong without rage; without o'erflow-
     ing, full.

'Here the flow of the poet's mind, we may say, is the tenor [or the subject of discourse, the primary matter under consideration], and the river the vehicle; and it is worth noting ... that in the last two lines there is a repeated alternation of the relative positions of tenor and vehicle and of the direction of the shift between them. "Though deep, yet clear": the words are literally descriptive of the vehicle, the river; derivatively or metaphorically descriptive of the mind. "Though gentle, yet not dull": "gentle" certainly is literally descriptive of the mind, the tenor, derivatively of the river, the other way about; but "dull", I suppose, goes from the river to the mind again'; *dull*, as applied to a river, means 'sluggish',—cf. Spenser's 'Thenceforth her waters waxed dull and slow'. '"Strong without rage" goes, for me, unquestionably from mind to river, and "without overflowing, full" goes back again from river—does it not?—to mind. . . . The more carefully and attentively we go over the senses and implications of *deep, clear, gentle, strong* and *full* as they apply to a stream and to a mind, the less shall we find the resemblances between vehicle and tenor counting [= significant] and the more the vehicle, the river, comes to seem an excuse for saying about the mind something which could not be said about the river. . . . But the river is not a mere excuse, or a decoration only, a gilding of the moral pill. The vehicle is still controlling the mode in which the tenor forms.

'Comparison, as a stressing of likenesses, is not the whole mode of this metaphor though it commonly is in the 18th Century writing—where, too, the tenor is usually the [more] important partner in the metaphor. The opposed conception of comparison—as a mere putting together' (or juxtaposition) 'of two things to see what will happen—is a contemporary fashionable aberration, which takes an extreme case as the norm. . . . This is André Breton, the leader of the French Super-Realists, stating the doctrine very plainly: "To compare two objects, as remote from [each other] in character as possible, or by any other method [to] put them together in [an abrupt] and striking fashion, this remains the highest task to which poetry can aspire" . . . That as "the highest task to which poetry can aspire"! . . . Like Mr Max Eastman, with his insistence (in *The Literary Mind*) that metaphor works by attempting "impracticable identifications", M. Breton sees no need to consider what should be put with what—provided they are sufficiently remote from [each other]—nor does he distinguish between the very different effects of such collocations . . . Mr Eastman shares this indifference as to the precise effect of the encounter of disparates.* For him the poet "communicates a kind of experience not elsewhere accessible", and, to do so, . . . he "must arouse a reaction and yet impede it, creating a tension in our nervous system sufficient and rightly calculated to make us completely aware that we are living something" . . . This . . . heroism comes, I think, from a crude conception of the mode of action of metaphors, a conception which is an excessive reaction from' the equative of metaphor to a mere comparison of likenesses.

'I conclude that these contemporary exploiters of the crude "clash them together—no matter what" view of the metaphor are beguiling themselves with by-products of the process of interpretation and neglecting the more important cares of critical theory. But . . . one point of importance emerges clearly from examining these exaggerations. We must

not, with the 18th Century, suppose that the interactions of tenor and vehicle are to be confined to their resemblances. There is disparity action too. When Hamlet uses the word '*crawling*'—'What should such fellows as I do crawling between earth and heaven?'—'its force comes not only from whatever resemblances to vermin it brings in but at least equally from the differences that resist and control the influences of their resemblances. The implication there is that man should not so crawl. Thus, talk about the identification or fusion that a metaphor effects is nearly always misleading and pernicious. In general, there are very few metaphors in which disparities between tenor and vehicle are not as much operative as the similarities. Some similarity will commonly be the ostensive ground of the shift, but the peculiar modification of the tenor which the vehicle brings about is even more the work of their unlikenesses than of their likenesses.'

Richards then leads us gently to the crux. 'Words cannot, and should not attempt to "hand over sensations bodily"; they have very much more important work to do. So far from verbal language being a "compromise for a language of intuition" . . ., language, well used, is a *completion* and does what the intuitions of sensation by themselves cannot do. Words are the meeting points at which regions of experience which can never combine in sensation or intuition, come together. They are the occasion and the means of that growth which is the mind's endless endeavour to order itself. That is why we have language. It is no mere signalling system. It is the instrument of all our distinctively human development, of everything in which we go beyond the other animals.

'Thus, to present language as working only through the sensations it reinstates, is to turn the whole process upside down. It overlooks what is important in Mallarmé's *dictum* that the poet does not write with thoughts (or with ideas or sensations or beliefs or desires or feelings, we may add) but with words. "Are not words", Coleridge asked, "parts and germinations of the plant? And what is the law of their growth? In something of this sort", he wrote, "I would endeavour to destroy the old antithesis of Words and Things: elevating, as it were, Words into Things and living things

---

* *Disparates* are 'things so unlike that they cannot be compared with each other' (*The O.E.D.*).

too." We must do so if we are to study metaphor properly . . . It is the word which brings in the meaning which the image and its original perception lack.'

Richards then attacks 'the mistaking of what I have been calling the tenor-vehicle antithesis for that between the metaphor (the double unit including tenor and vehicle) and its meaning'. He attacks, too, 'those anxious, over-careful [and erroneous] attempts to *copy* perceptions and feelings *in words*, to "hand over sensations bodily", of which modern prose at its most distinguished too often consists. Words are not a medium in which to copy life. Their true work is to restore life itself to order.

'We are accustomed to distinguish between taking an utterance literally and taking it metaphorically, but, at the simplest, there are at least four possible modes of interpretation to be considered, not two. And the kinds of believing that will be appropriate will as a rule be different. We can abstract the tenor and believe that as a statement; or abstract the vehicle; or, taking tenor and vehicle together, contemplate for acceptance or rejection some statement about their relations; or we can accept or refuse the direction which together they would give to our living. We need not go to the Alexandrian schools of early Christian interpretation, or to the similar exegetical developments of other religions, to find instances to show how immense the consequences for belief of these choices may be. The varying possibilities of understanding of any metaphoric utterance will show them.'

That is but a poor and meagre presentation of Dr Richards's two perceptive and highly acute lectures on metaphor: if I succeed in sending readers to the source, I shall have achieved my purpose.

II. *Confused or Mixed Metaphors.*

In Alexander Bain's *English Composition and Rhetoric*, enlarged edition, Part I, 1887, at pp. 165–168, there is a sound though perhaps unimaginative and rather too formal, section on mixed metaphor.

Bain introduces the section with the sibyllic words, 'The brevity of the Metaphor renders it liable to the vice called Mixing Metaphors': is it the brevity or is it not rather the confused thinking of the perpetrator?

'This arises', Bain says, 'when meta-phors from different sources are combined in the same subject: as "to *kindle* a *seed*". We may *sow* a *seed* or *kindle* a *flame*; but kindling a seed is incongruous and confusing to the mind.

'The following example from Addison is familiar—

I *bridle* in my struggling muse with pain
That longs to *launch* into a bolder *strain*.

Three different figures'—horse, ship, music—'are conjoined in one action.

'"The very *hinge* and *centre* of an immense system": "hinge" is out of place': but is it? Here we have not a mixing but an adding or a collocation of metaphors, for 'centre' is as much a metaphor as a 'hinge'.

'"All my pretty *chickens* and their *dam*" is the mixing of two metaphors. . . .

'"Physiology and psychology thus become united, and the study of man passes from the uncertain *light* of mere opinion to the *region* of science."

'"The very recognition of these by the jurisprudence of a nation is a *mortal wound* to the very *keystone* upon which the whole vast arch of morality reposes."'

After citing other examples, of which several would, to the modern mind, seem not merely permissible but admirable, Bain goes on to say, 'There is no objection to different metaphors being successively applied to the same subject, provided they are kept distinct. Thus: "They admire the profundity of what is mystical and obscure, mistaking the *muddiness of water* for *depth* (1), and *magnifying* in their imaginations what is *viewed through a fog* (2)." (Whately)'

Nor do we now subscribe to the dictum that 'the mixture of the metaphorical and the plain or literal is also objectionable. Dryden, speaking of the aids he had in his translations, says, "I was sailing in a vast ocean without other help than the *pole-star* of the ancients, and the *rules of the French* stage among the moderns"': *rules* itself is naught but a metaphor—originally.

Let me now adduce a few instances of a more glaring kind. Sir Boyle Roche (1743–1807), Irish politician, is reported to have said, in the version given in *Stevenson's Book of Quotations:*—

'Mr Speaker, I smell a rat; I see him forming in the air and darkening the sky; but I'll nip him in the bud.'

But some 19th Century wit elaborated the original, and the form in which most of us know this delightful mixture is:—

'Mr Speaker, I smell a rat. I see it floating in the air; and if it is not nipped in the bud, it will burst forth into a terrible conflagration that will deluge the world.'

'A house mortgaged up to the hilt.' Two from Mr A. P. Herbert's *What a Word!*, 1935:—

'. . . Ideas of individuality, freedom, tolerance, and eternal youth with which the aftermath of war was impregnated.'

'The Irish Free State had held out the olive branch but nothing concrete had come out of it' (Mr James Maxton, M.P.).

Two examples of a different kind, from my own reading:—

'They alone were concerned about the sharing of the bear's skin after the bear had been killed—perhaps because they are possessed by the illusion that they can win the election off their own bat' (leading article in *The Daily Telegraph*, June 6, 1938): not a mixing but a confusingly rapid change of metaphors.

'When Einstein broke . . . open [the old concept of length], knowledge jumped forward' (Stuart Chase, *The Tyranny of Words*, 1938): 'jumped *out*' would have been preferable.

METAPHORS, OUTWORN. See CLICHÉS.

meticulous is erroneously used to mean 'careful of detail in a praiseworthy manner'; properly, it imples excess of care and an overscrupulousness caused by timidity. It is also misused in the sense of *neat* and *tidy*, e.g., 'He was ushered into a small, meticulous inner office of white enamel', Milton Propper, *Murder at the Polls*, 1936. Here the writer means *carefully tended*. To be meticulous is a quality possible only to a conscientious person.— Occasionally it is misused for 'timid' (in the 16th and 17th Centuries, good English).

METRES, POETICAL. Fascinating; but none of my business. For a first-class exposition, see Fowler's *Modern English Usage*, at 'Technical Terms'.

mid, preposition, is—except in traditional and scientific phrases—rather literary (and poetic). Write *mid*, not *'mid*.

middle. See CENTRE.

Middle West; Middle Western. See MIDWEST.

middy. 'Traffrail' writes: 'We read in newspaper articles and boys' books of adventure of "middies". We sometimes even hear the term used in conversation round tea-tables ashore, but to call a present-day midshipman a "middy" to his face would make him squirm.'

'midst is inferior to *midst* (whether noun, adverb or preposition); now rather literary than spoken English, it has, for the most part, been superseded by *among* or *in the midst of*.

Midwest, Midwestern; Middle West, Middle Western. As applied to the central United States. 'Usage', remarks Weseen, 'seems to favour *Midwest* and *Midwestern* as adjectives and . . . *Middle West* as the noun. But *Midwest* [not *Midwestern*] is sometimes used as a noun and *Middle West* and [less often] *Middle Western* are often used as adjectives.'

might for *would*. See SUBJUNCTIVE (near end).—*Might* for *may*. See PAST SUBJUNCTIVE . . .—For the correct use of *may* and *might*, see the same article.

Milady, as a term of address, is not English but Continental—as Continental as *Milord* in the vocative. As generics, they are written in italic and have the senses 'an English noblewoman', 'an English nobleman'.

millenary and **millinery.** The latter is noun only ('articles made and/or sold by milliners; the business of a milliner'); the former, both noun (a thousand years) and adjective ('consisting of, belonging to, characteristic of a thousand'—especially a thousand years, a millennium).

milliad is incorrect for *milliard*, a thousand millions (i.e., an American or Continental *billion*).

Milord. See MILADY.

mind, 'to remind', is obsolescent; *mind*, 'to remember' (v.t.) is archaic, except in dialect.

miniature should, as an adjective, be used with care. It is not a synonym of *small* or *little* or *dainty*. For a misuse, see the quotation at SOUND (v.).

minify, 'to diminish, to lessen', is a word that we can well do without.

minimize: 'to reduce to the smallest possible size, amount, or degree', as in 'Clerical vestments are minimized', and 'to estimate at the smallest possible amount (or value of importance)', as in 'Jesus did not minimize sin': is not to be degraded to equivalence with to *decrease*, *diminish*, *lessen*, as in 'Why seek to minimize the danger?' (*The O.E.D.*)

minor. 'Of very minor importance' is ludicrous. Cf. MAJOR, *q.v.*

minute (n.) and **moment.** A *minute* is (or should be) an objective, precise period or measure of time; a *moment* is a subjective, imprecise period (not a measure) of time. Do not, therefore, exclaim impatiently, 'Oh, tell him I'll see him in a minute' if all you mean is 'in a moment'. A *moment* is vaguer—and usually longer than an *instant*.

miracle. See MARVEL.

mischievious is a too frequent mispronunciation of *mischievous*.

MISPRONUNCIATIONS. I do not include these. For an excellent list, see pp. 263–298 of Whitten & Whitaker's *Good and Bad English* (London, 1939).

MISQUOTATIONS. '"Similarity of style. . . . Two or three times the fellow tried to disguise it . . .". "Oh, but there was more than that!" cried the other. . . . ". . . Now, look at this. The Minister of Imperial Finance, in his efforts for advancement of self, would do well to remember that hackneyed line of Pope: "A little learning is a dangerous thing". "Did you see that?"—Anthony opened his eyes. "I did. And thought how refreshing it was to see the quotation given right. They nearly all get it wrong, though you'd think anyone could see that Pope couldn't have been such a fool as to say a little knowledge was dangerous. Knowledge is always useful; learning isn't, until you've got plenty. But go on . . ."—Masterson was searching feverishly. ". . . here we are! Listen . . . 'when Greek joins Greek then comes the tug of war!' . . . How many times d'you see that given right?"—"Never" said Anthony. "They all say 'meets'."—"There you are then. . . . Style—similarity of style, I mean—isn't proof; but this orgy of correctitude *plus* that similarity is. . . . There are plenty more instances . . . There's one I remember well . . . It said . . .: *'facilis descensus Averno'*. What about that?"—Anthony sat up. "*Averno*' is very rare", he said slowly. "But it's a better reading . . .".' From Ch. xiii, sec. ii, of Philip MacDonald's first-class 'deteccer', *The Rasp*, 1924.

As this brief entry is not intended to cope with even the commonest of the many misquotations, I shall note only a few others; but these others are, at least, extremely common.

'That he who runs may read' should be '[Write the vision, and make it plain upon tables] that he may run that readeth it' (*Habakkuk*, ii, 2.); the meaning was that 'he who reads the information may run away and act upon it (Alfred Ackermann, *Popular Fallacies*, 3rd ed., 1914).

'Fresh fields and pastures new' should be 'Fresh woods and pastures new' (Milton).

'A parting shot' was originally 'a Parthian shot', and originally 'All that glitters is not gold' was 'All that glisters . . .'.

'Water, water everywhere, and not a drop to drink' should be 'Water, water everywhere, nor any drop to drink (Coleridge).

'Of the making of books there is no end' is properly (and originally) 'Of making many books there is no end', which occurs in the Bible. In

To die—to sleep
No more; and by a sleep we say we end
The heart-ache, and the thousand natural shocks
That flesh is heir to,—'tis a consummation
Devoutly to be wished (Shakespeare),

shocks is frequently misquoted as *ills*.

Prunes and prisms is incorrect for *prunes and prism*; and *leather and prunella*—see the separate entry—is incorrect for *leather or prunella* (Pope).

'Cribbed, cabined and confined' is incorrect for Shakespeare's '[Now am I] cabin'd, crib'd, confin'd, bound in' (*Macbeth*, III, iv. 24).

'Flat, stale and unprofitable' (or 'improfitable') is a misquotation of Shakespeare's 'How weary, stale, flat, and unprofitable, Seem to me all the uses of this world'.

MISRELATED GERUND. See GERUND, last paragraph.

MISRELATED PARTICIPLE. See CONFUSED PARTICIPLES.

misremember is correct in the sense 'to remember incorrectly or incompletely'; dialectal in the sense 'to forget'.

miss for *escape* (*the notice of*). 'The mere sight of Osaki du Channe is enough to give any C.I.D. man the idea that I'm somewhere about. But, if you're travelling entirely alone, the fact may miss them' (John G. Brandon, *The Mail-Van Mystery*, ca. 1937).

Miss and **Misses.** The formally correct plural of *Miss Hume* is *the Misses Hume*; but *the Miss Humes* is permissible.

MISSPELLINGS. One cannot satis-

factorily generalize about these evidences
of human fallibility. A few particularly
confusing examples are included in this
book: but those persons who are genuinely concerned to know precisely how
vulnerable they are to error, should be
duly chastened by a study of W. S.
Sonnenschein's *Five Thousand Words
frequently misspelt*, 1906.

missis (or **missus**), **the,** is at best a
colloquialism for '(one's) wife' and (also
without *the*) 'the mistress' of the house.

mistaken; misunderstood. 'I was
mistaken' = 'I was wrong, in error'; 'I
was misunderstood' = 'Somebody (or
some persons) failed to understand me'.

Mister, as a vocative (or term of address) without the surname, is avoided
by the polite.

MIXED METAPHORS. See META-
PHORS, Part II.

MM. See MESSRS.

mob is a dangerous or at least a potentially disorderly crowd; do not use it
of any crowd, nor of companies of animals. (Australians, however, ignore both
of these rules.)
  The mob is the populace, the masses.

model is a pattern or a representation
in scale or proportion; do not use it
where *copy, reproduction,* or, esp., *replica*
is the precise word. See, above all, *The
O.E.D.*

modest is often misused for *moderate.*
The former is defined by *The O.E.D.* as
'unobtrusive, retiring, bashful; decorous
in manner and conduct; scrupulously
chaste in feeling, language and conduct';
the latter as 'avoiding extremes; of
medium or middling size, quality, price,
etc.'—As applied to persons, the two
terms have a kindred, though not the
same meaning; a 'modest' man is naturally of 'moderate' language and behaviour, but one has no right to speak
of, e.g., 'a modest rate of interest'.

MODIFIED STANDARD. See STAND-
ARD ENGLISH, Section ii.

Mohammed, Mohammedan are the
correct and accepted forms, though
Mahomet, -an, and other spellings are
frequently found.

moiré for *moire.* The fabric is *moire;*
and *moiré* is an adjective or as a noun it
is the watered or cloudy appearance
characteristic of moire. The verb is
moiré or *moire,* to create such an appearance.

moment. See MINUTE.

momentary is (of things) 'transitory';

(of persons or animal life) 'short-lived'—
an obsolescent sense. But *momentous* is
'important' of events, and 'weighty' of
statements or decisions.

monies is incorrect for *moneys;* after
all, the singular is *money,* not *mony.*

monologue. See DIALOGUE.

Mons., whether written or spoken, is
regarded by Frenchmen as a gratuitous
insult. Say or write *Monsieur;* write *M.*
(Weekley.)

monstrous, even when it means
enormous, has a connotation either of
abnormality or of ugliness. Subjectively,
it means 'horrible, atrocious' or 'out-
rageously wrong; contemptibly absurd'.
As an adverb ('exceedingly'), it is
archaic. See esp. *The O.E.D.*

MOOD IN SYNTAX; right use of
mood. See esp. SUBJUNCTIVE and TENSE-
SEQUENCE: but also CONCESSIVE CLAUSES
and CONDITIONAL SENTENCES and FINAL
CLAUSES.

moonlight, adjective, except in the
unconventional *moonlight flit(ting), moonlight dancing,* and derivatives, is now less
used than *moonlit.*

moral and **morale.** In regard to the
power of usage, Mr Frank Whitaker, in
The J.I.J., January, 1939, selects an
excellent example. 'Take', says he, 'the
word "moral", meaning "of good morals". We had used it for centuries in that
sense when somebody discovered that
the French used it [as a noun] to mean
"the spirit of the troops". "Ah", said
this person, "a useful word. We must
bag that." So we took it, added an "e" to
distinguish it both in spelling and [in]
pronunciation from "moral", and made
it our own. It didn't matter a pin to Mr
Usage that the French have the two
words, and use them in precisely the
reverse sense. But although this happened years ago, it still matters to *The
Times* . . . It still spells it without an
"e" to remind us that we mustn't play
tricks with other people's words. It
might as well talk to the moon. The distinction is useful, and because it is useful
it has established itself.'

Fowler upholds *morale* (pronounced
morahl) and—for what that is worth—
so do I.

more for *other* is to be avoided, for
often it leads to ambiguity, as in 'Most
people have heard of Shaftesbury, South-
wood Smith and Chadwick, but there
were many more ardent reformers who
are now forgotten' (an essay script in the

L.C.C. Major Establishment examination, 1938).

more -er (e.g., *more brighter*). Now a solecism, though in Middle and Early Modern English it was common and permissible.

more often. See OFTENER.

more or less certain, though illogical (see COMPARATIVES, FALSE), is idiomatic English. 'It expresses a valuable shade of meaning, and has earned its keep over and over again', Frank Whitaker, in *The J.I.J.*, January, 1939.

more perfect, like *more inferior, more superior, more unique, more universal,* is an absurdity. See COMPARATIVES, FALSE; and also TAUTOLOGY.

Mormons is the popular name of the members of the *Church of Jesus Christ of Latter-day Saints*; cf. QUAKERS, the popular name of the members of the Society of Friends. In official and formal contexts, the longer names should, in mere respect and decency, be used.

moron is properly 'one of the highest class of feeble-minded; an adult having an intelligence comparable to that of a normal average child between eight and twelve years of age'; hence, as a colloquialism, 'a stupid person; a fool'. (*The O.E.D.*)

Morpheus, in the arms of, is commonly used to mean 'asleep', whereas Morpheus was god of dreams (maker of changing shapes); the god of sleep was Hypnos. Not only, therefore, is the phrase an intolerably overworked cliché: it is also an inaccurate one.

mortal, whether 'human' ('mere mortal man') or 'death-causing', is an uncomparable adjective. See the list at COMPARATIVES, FALSE.—As meaning 'wearisome', it is a colloquialism.

mortar. See CEMENT.

Moslemin is plural of *Moslem,* though sometimes ignorantly used as the singular. It is safer to treat the word as English and to say *Moslems*.

most is pleonastic before superlative of adjj. and advv. Shakespeare's 'This was the most unkindest cut of all', effective in its emphasis, affords no excuse.

most should not be used of comparison between two; 'Of those two men, Jack is the most intelligent' should be '. . . more . . .'

most and **mostly.** See MOSTLY.

most and **the most** are occasionally confused, with resultant ambiguity. 'What I should most like to do would be to die without knowing I was even in danger of dying'; but 'Which do you like the most—cricket, lawn tennis, or golf?' In other words, *most* is absolute, whereas *the most* is relative.

most and **very.** 'All those stories were most interesting' is ambiguous.

most all, properly *'most all,* for *almost all,* is an illiteracy. [[In American usage, *most* for *almost* is dialectal or colloquial.]]

most part is incorrect for *greater* (or *greatest*) *part* or *main part* except in the phrase *for the most part* (whence springs the error). 'It was rough going, and more than once Philip blessed the broad pair of bucolic shoulders which were doing the most part of the work', Laurence Meynell, *The Door in the Wall,* 1937. There are several alternatives, all to be preferred: 'doing most of the work', '— the biggest share of the work', '— the larger part of the work'.

mostly is 'in the main; for the most part', as in 'A man whose mind had been mostly fallow ground will not easily take to the mental plough and hoe' (H. Black). Do not misuse it for *most,* as it is misused in 'The people mostly in need of assistance do not ask for it'. (*The O.E.D.*)

mother-in-laws is incorrect for *mothers-in-law.*

motif is not a synonym of *motive.* It has four specific uses:—

i. In painting, sculpture, architecture, decoration, etc., it is a constituent feature of a composition or a distinct part of a design, hence a particular type of subject, hence the principal feature or the predominant idea of a work; as in 'The *motif* is simple', 'That painter's favourite *motif* is cherubs'.

ii. Hence, in a novel, a biography, etc., a type of incident, a dominant idea, the predominant idea or theme.

iii. In dress-making, an ornament (e.g., of lace or braid) sewn on to a dress.

iv. In Psychology. But here it is obsolescent.

v. In Music, be careful! (*Leitmotiv* or *subject* or *figure* is safer.)

Originally an adoption from French, it should now be written in roman characters. *Motiv,* a German term, has not been anglicized, except in *leitmotiv* (a technical word). Based on *The O.E.D.*

motion pictures; moving pictures; the pictures; the movies. The fourth is slang, the third is a colloquialism. *Moving pictures* is more usual than *motion pictures*, although the latter is the more sensible term. The building in which a cinematographic programme is shown is in England a *cinema* [[in the U.S.A. a (*moving* or *motion picture*) theater]]. *Talkies* is slang for *talking pictures* as opposed to *silent pictures*.

moustache. See WHISKERS.

mouthfuls and mouths full. Cf. the remark at BASKETFULS.

mowed and mown as past participles. Usage prefers 'He has mowed the grass', 'The grass was mowed yesterday', but 'Mown grass smells sweet', 'A mown field looks bare'. As a true participle, *mown* is archaic.

Mr. See MISTER.—Write *Mr*, not *Mr.*; if you desire pedantic accuracy, write *M'r*,—but nobody does so write it.

Mrs, not *Mrs.*, is the form preferred in England; the pedantically correct form would be *M'r's*. [[In American usage, *Mr.*, *Mrs.*, and similar spellings are considered abbreviations, not contractions; they are therefore followed by a period.]]

MS. (permissibly *Ms.*, *Ms*, or *m.s.*) has plural *MSS.* (etc.)

much and many. Do not use the former where the latter is idiomatic, as in 'As much as twenty members have resigned'; *many* is the word for separables, for units, for entities. Weseen cites the absurd *much clothes* for *many clothes* —or *much clothing*.

much and muchly. Avoid the archaic *muchly* unless you are sure that as a jocularity it is inoffensive.

much and very. With ordinary (i.e., non-participial) adjectives and with adverbs, use *very*: not 'much unkind' but 'very unkind'; not 'much soon' but 'very soon'. With participial adjectives, *much* is permissible, as in 'He was much pleased', though 'very pleased' is more usual; *much obliged* is a set phrase. Note, however, that one says 'much too soon', 'much sooner', 'much worse', 'much better', 'much the more praiseworthy', 'much the largest'.

much less (or still less) is sometimes illogically used through lack of clear thinking, by writers usually competent; e.g., 'The task of keeping the fire under, much less of putting it out, was beyond the resources of the fire-engines', G. B. Besant, *London Bridge*, 1926. Obviously, if 'the task of keeping the fire under' was difficult, that of extinguishing it was *much more* so.

much the same is a common but clumsy way of saying 'about the same'. Very weak in literary use, as e.g., in Alfred Austin's poem on the illness of Edward VII,—

Across the wire the electric message came.
He is no better, he is much the same.

MUDDLING THROUGH, otherwise known as Hoping for the Best, is seen, in its results, in the article entitled WOOLLINESS.

mulct does not mean 'to *cheat* (a person)'. Correctly it = 'to punish (a person) by a fine', either as in 'The master was mulcted all his pay' or as in 'The new sect were . . . mulcted in heavy fines'; hence, 'to deprive or divest *of*', as in 'Every third year each tree is mulcted of her spreading boughs'—a permissible sense, which, however, I do not recommend, for it seems to me to be a literarism. (*The O.E.D.*) [[*Webster's* gives as a derivative meaning 'to deprive of, as by deceit or trickery'.]]

multifarious; multiform; multiple. See MANIFOLD.

murder; manslaughter; homicide. These three terms are often confused. In the British Empire, *murder* is planned, intentional killing; *manslaughter* is unplanned, though possibly intentional killing; *homicide* is the generic term for all killing of one person by another. More precisely:—
Murder is 'the unlawful killing of a human being with malice aforethought; often more implicitly *wilful murder*'. In the U.S.A. there are two kinds of murder: *murder in the second degree*, where there are mitigating circumstances; *murder in the first degree*, where there are no such circumstances.

Manslaughter (in Scotland: *culpable homicide*) is 'committed when one person causes the death of another either intentionally in the heat of passion under certain kinds of provocation, or unintentionally by culpable negligence or as a consequence of some unlawful act' (*The O.E.D.*).

Homicide, which includes both *murder* and *manslaughter*, occurs chiefly in

culpable homicide, which is *manslaughter*;
excusable homicide, which is killing in self-
    defence or by accident or mis-
    adventure;
justifiable homicide, which is a killing in
    the performance of certain legal
    duties (e.g., the hangman's), by
    unavoidable necessity, or to pre-
    vent the commission of an atrocious
    crime. (*Webster's*.)

[[In the U.S.A. *the Homicide Squad* is
that section of the detective force which
deals with homicide.]]

mush-melon is dialectal for *musk-
melon*; **mush-rat** for *musk-rat*.

musical is adjective; **musicale** is
noun. *Musicale* has taken on in America;
not in England, where *musical evening*,
musical party, *musical reunion*, etc., are
preferred.

must and **may**. See NEGATION, Section *A*, last five paragraphs.

mutual = 'reciprocal', as in 'mutual
fear', 'mutual friendship',—this being
the safest sense in which to use it;
'respective' as in 'the difference in their
mutual years',—correct but obsolescent,
so avoid it!; and 'pertaining to both
parties; common; in common', since ca.
1900 regarded as incorrect when applied
to things, actions, sentiments, as in 'our
mutual front door', (of a collaboration)
'their mutual work', 'your mutual opinion',—certainly a usage to be avoided;
and in the same general sense, but
applied to 'a personal designation expressive of a relation'—an application
now regarded as incorrect except in
mutual friend(s) and *mutual acquaintance*(s), where the strictly correct *common* is ambiguous (still, one can always
say *friends*—or *acquaintances—in common*), such collocations as *mutual father*,
mutual brother now sounding very odd.
(*The O.E.D.*)

**myself, yourself, herself, himself,
itself, ourselves, yourselves, themselves.** There is a tendency to employ
these pronouns where the simple *I* (or
me), *you*, *she* (or *her*), *he* (or *him*), *it*, *we*
(or *us*), *you*, *they* (or *them*) are sufficient
The *self* forms are either reflexives, as in
'I hurt *myself*', or emphatic additions, as
in 'He *himself* did not know' (avoid the
ambiguity of 'He did not know *himself*').
Here are three misuses:—

'You and myself will arrange this between
    us'

'Herself and himself will soon be getting
    married'
'He sent the enquiry to yourself'.

mystery is not used as an adjective
by self-respecting writers. When Anthony
Berkeley, in *Not to Be Taken*, 1938, writes
that 'The local police were half disgruntled at being cheated of their mystery murder and half thrilled at being
caught up into issues so far outside their
own experience', he is poking fun at
popular journalists. There is some—
though inadequate—excuse for *mystery
man* (short for *man of mystery* or
mysteries).

mystic, as an adjective, is more
rhetorical and more formal than *mystical*,
where the two forms are synonymous:
cf. 'the mystical relation of man and
God' and 'the mystic union of the soul
with Christ'.

N

naif, naïf; naive, naïve. *Naif* is inexcusable; in English, *naïf* is unnecessary,
being the masculine of Fr. *naïf, naïve*,
'artless'. *The O.E.D.* implies its recommendation of *naïve*, written in roman
and pronounced as a dissyllabic.

name (v.). See DENOMINATE.

name of, of (or **by**) **the**. See BY THE
NAME OF.

name . . . who (or **that**). It is permissible to say, 'The editor telephoned to a
big name from whom he wanted an
article', although the present writer does
not recommend such looseness. But the
following use of *name* passes the bounds
of decency: 'Picking up his telephone,
he called for a certain number . . . Getting it, he asked for a certain name, who,
in less than a minute, was upon the
'phone to him' (John G. Brandon, *The
Mail-Van Mystery*, ca. 1937).

nary, 'not a; not one; no; neither', is
a dialectalism.

nasty. Weseen is wrong in condemning
this word as a colloquialism in the senses
'unpleasant, disagreeable' (as in 'a nasty
day'), 'mean' ('a nasty trick'), and 'ill-
natured, ill-tempered' ('to turn nasty'):
they are faultless Standard English:
admittedly not literary, they are familiar
Standard. [[*Webster's* and Krapp agree
with Weseen. This use of *nasty* is much
more common in England than in the
U.S.A.]]

native(s). There is something not only

inexact but offensive in the general use of this word for the dark-skinned inhabitants of Africa, India, etc., as though it applied exclusively to them and implied an inferiority of race. The inhabitants born in England or any other country are the 'natives' of that country.

natty. See TASTEFUL.

naught. See 'NOUGHT and NAUGHT'.

nauseation for *nausea* is, to put it mildly, unfortunate. 'Slowly he read the story from beginning to end, and finished up with a feeling of nauseation' (John G. Brandon, *The Mail-Van Mystery*).

naval (adj.); **navel** (n.).

near and **near to.** *Near* and *near to* can be used of literal position, as in 'We lived quite near them', or, less usually, '. . . near to them'; *near to* is more general than *near* in transferred or derivative senses—sometimes, indeed, *near* would be wrong in such instances. As Dr C. T. Onions remarks in *An Advanced English Syntax*, 6th ed., 1932, 'Notice that the different senses of *near* take different constructions, e.g., "The Prince of Wales stood *near* (or *near to*) [i.e., close *to*] *the throne*" and "The German Emperor [was] *near to the throne* of Great Britain" (i.e., in respect of succession). In the second sentence "near the throne" would be undesirable, as being ambiguous and suggesting the wrong meaning'; a neat exemplification of the difference.

near-by, as an adverb, is English dialectal and American; as a preposition, English dialectal; as an adjective, American.

nearly is an adverb, not a preposition. It is wrongly used in 'She came nearly falling' (for '. . . near to falling . . .' or colloquially '. . . near falling').

'neath (or **neath**) is on the one hand dialectal, on the other poetic, for *beneath*.

necessaries and **necessities.** The former = 'essentials; requisites', as in 'A father provides his children with necessaries' and 'Food, sleep and shelter are necessaries of life'. In this sense, *necessities* is obsolete—or, at the least, obsolescent. The predominant current sense of *necessities* is 'pressing needs or wants; a situation of difficulty or of hardship', as in 'The necessities of every newly colonised country' and 'We must aim at a habit of gratitude, which has no relation to present necessities' (J. B. Mozley).

The adjective *necessitous* = 'living or placed in poverty' or 'characterized by poverty'. (*The O.E.D.*)

necessity is a misuse when made to synonymize (an) *essential*. 'Without the necessities of a good internal government, liberty is not likely to last long' (examination script, March, 1938), meaning 'the needful elements' or 'essentials'.

NEGATION.

'And we none of us never said nowt'
A Yorkshire song, broadcast on December 9, 1937.

The subject of negation may be divided into three sections: *A, THE MEANING OF NEGATION; B, NEGATION IN SYNTAX; NEGATIVE CONJUNCTIONS (OR CONNECTIVES);* and *C,* esp. the *DOUBLE NEGATIVE.*

A. THE MEANING OF NEGATION.

'A linguisitic negative', writes Professor Otto Jespersen in *Negation**, Copenhagen, 1917, 'generally changes a term into what logicians call the contradictory term (A and not-A) comprising everything in existence and is thus very different from a negative in the mathematical sense, where −4 means a point as much below 0 as 4 (or +4) is above 0.' There are, however, 'instances in which a negative changes a term into the "contrary term", as when *he begins not to sing* (for *he begins not-to-sing*) comes to mean "he ceases singing".

'If we say, according to the general rule, that "not four" means "different from four", this should be taken with a general qualification, for in practice it generally means, not whatever is above or below 4 . . ., but only what is below 4, thus less than 4, something between 4 and 0, just as "not everything" means something between everything and nothing (and as "not good" means "inferior", but does not comprise "excellent").' So, too, in 'He does not write three books in a decade', 'The mountain is not 10,000 feet high', 'He does not go to Paris once in three years', 'His income is not £300 a year'. When '*not* + a numeral is exceptionally to be taken as "more than", the numeral has to be strongly stressed [in conversation], and [in writing] generally to be followed by

---

* Perhaps the most acute and subtle, yet gloriously practical and serviceable, of all Jespersen's works; it is only his *The Philosophy of Grammar* which makes one write 'perhaps'.

a more exact indication', as in 'The mountain is not 10,000 feet high, but 11,000', 'His income is not £300 a year, but £400', 'Not once, but two or three times' (Defoe), and 'Not one invention, but fifty—from a corkscrew to a machine-gun' (W. J. Locke), 'He would bend to kiss her, not once, not once only' (E. F. Benson). 'But *not once or twice* always means "several times", as in Tennyson, 'Not once or twice in our rough island-story The path of duty was the way to glory.'

*The import of 'a negative quantitative indication' often depends 'on what is expected, or [on] what is the direction of thought'—the trend of the conversation, the general sense of the subject-matter. Whereas 'the two sentences "he spends £200 a year" and "he lives on £200 a year" are practically synonymous, everything is changed if we add *not*: "he doesn't spend £200 a year" means [that he spends less than that sum]; "he doesn't live on £200 a year" means [that he spends more than £200 a year]; because in the former case we expect an indication of a maximum, and in the latter of a minimum.—Or, perhaps the explanation is rather this, that in the former sentence it does not matter whether we negative the nexus** or the numeral (he does-not-spend £200 he spends not-£200), but in the latter it changes the whole meaning, for "he does-not-live on £200" states'—? rather 'connotes'—'the impossibility of living on so little, and "he lives on not-£200 a year" (which is rendered more idio-matic if we add an adverb: "on not quite £200 a year") states the possibility of living on less than £200.

'. . . Compare also: *He is not content with £200 a year* and *he is content with not £200 a year.*

'Where a numeral is not used as a point in an ascending scale, its negative is really contradictory; "the train doesn't start at seven" says nothing about the actual time of starting, which may be either before or after seven. But "he won't be here at seven" implies "we can't expect him till after seven", because an arrival before 7 o'clock would naturally imply his being here also at that hour.'

Compare the point raised by Jespersen in the following:—'*Not above 30* means either 30 or less than 30. But *less than 30* may in English be negatived in two ways: *not less than 30* means either 30 or more than 30, and *no less than 30* means exactly 30, implying surprise or wonder at the high number.

"He has not less than ten children"— I am not certain of the number, but it is at least ten. "He has no less than ten children"—he has ten, and isn't that a large family?' Cf. 'He has not more than ten books' and 'He has no more than ten books'.

And here is an interesting case: *a little* is positive, *little* a virtual negative (cf. *absent* as contrasted with *present*). Jespersen equates these two terms with *a few* and *few* and arranges them thus:—

1. *much:* much money	*many:* many people	*very:* very careless
2. *a little:* a little money	*a few:* a few people	*a little:* (He's) a little careless
3. *little:* little money	*few:* few people	*little:* little [idiomatically: slightly] careless.

If we negative these, we find that (1) becomes (3): *not · much (money)* becomes (*little*) *money*; *not many (people)* becomes *few (people)*; *not very (careless)*

* Cf. GRAMMAR AND LOGIC, par. 5 of the article proper.
** *Nexus:*—'The negative notion may belong logically either to one definite idea'—Special Negation—'or to the combination of two ideas' —Nexal Negation, the notional combination being the Nexus. In 'never', 'unhappy', 'impossible', 'disorder', '*non*-belligerent'—as also in '*not* happy' and '*no* longer', we have special negation; in 'He does *not* come' the combination of two positive ideas, *he* and *coming*, and in 'He doesn't come to-day', the combination of *he* and *coming to-day*, are negatived, both sentences affording examples of negatived nexus.

becomes *little* (idiomatically, *slightly*) *careless*. But by negativing (2) we arrive at something that is either almost synonymous with (1) or standing between (1) and (2): *not a little (money)* becomes, or almost becomes, *much money*; *not a few (people)* roughly = *many (people)*; *not a little (careless)* is approximately equivalent to *very (careless)*.

Now, 'if we lengthen the series given above (*much—a little—little*) in both directions, we get on the one hand *all* (*everything*), on the other hand *nothing*. These are contrary terms, even in a higher degree than *good* and *bad* are, as both are absolute. Whatever comes in between them (thus all the three quantities mentioned above) is comprised in the term *something*, and we may now arrange these terms in this way, denoting by *A* and *C* the two absolutes, and by *B* the intermediate:—

A	*B*	*C*
all [noun] *everything*	*something*	*nothing*
and correspondingly:		
all [plural] ⎫	*some*	⎧ *none*
everybody (everyone) ⎭	*somebody (someone)*	⎨ *nobody (no one)*
all girls	*some girls (a girl)*	*no girls (no girl)*
all the money	*some money*	*no money*
So too with the adverbs:		
always	*sometimes*	*never*
everywhere	*somewhere*	*nowhere*

If we negative the *A* terms we get *B* terms; or, if you prefer it, *A* negatived = *B*; thus:

not all, not everything = something
not all, not everybody = some
not all girls   = *some girls*
not all the money   = *some (of the) money*
not always   = *sometimes*
not everywhere   = *somewhere*

In other words, when we negative an *A* term, word-group or phrase, we negative the *absolute* element in that *A* term or phrase. 'Thus always when the negative precedes the absolute word [etc.] of the *A*-class', as in 'We are not cotton-spinners all, But some love England and her honour yet' (Tennyson); 'I do not regard every politician as a self-seeker'; 'Not all Hugh's letters were concerned with these technicalities' (H. G. Wells).

That is a sensible as well as a logical positioning of the adverb *not*, but in *all*-sentences, *all* is frequently placed first for emphasis, and the negative is attracted to the verb in accordance with the prevailing tendency seen in 'He does not come to-day but to-morrow', which is so much more general than the more logical 'He comes not to-day but to-morrow'. 'All that glisters is not gold' is more usual than 'Not all that glisters is of gold', despite the fact that the latter is clear, the former ambiguous— but idiomatic. (Not that the latter is *unidiomatic*.) In 'Thank Heaven, all scholars are not like this' (Richardson) the context removes all ambiguity, precisely as, in conversation, emphasis would make the statement clear. In 'For each man kills the thing he loves, Yet each man does not die' (Wilde), the first *each* = *every*, but *each man does not die* does not mean that every man dies (for a given reason). 'All men aren't fools' should, logically, mean 'All men are sensible'; idiomatically it means 'Some men aren't fools' or 'Not all men are fools'.

'On the other hand', continues Jespersen, 'when a word of the *A*-class (*all*, etc.) is placed in a sentence with a special negative (or [a virtual or] an implied negative), the result is the same as if we had the corresponding *C*-word and a positive word; . . . the assertion is absolute':

All this is unnecessary = none of this is necessary*
Everybody was unkind = nobody was kind
He was always unkind = he was never kind
Everybody fails   = *nobody succeeds*
He forgets everything = he remembers nothing.

If we examine what happens when a word of the *C*-class is negatived, we get the *not for nothing* = 'not in vain' or even 'to good purpose', as in Shakespeare's 'It was not for nothing that my nose fell a bleeding on Black Monday last' and in Professor Sir Walter Raleigh's 'He was not the eldest son of his father for nothing'. The result falls into class *B*: 'He was his son for something'. The same applies to 'It's not good for a man to have no gods'.

'Inversely if we begin with the word belonging to class *C* and place the negative adverb after it', we get an *A* result, as in Latin *nihil no videt* = *omnia videt*. Such sentences do not exist in English—not in workaday English, anyway; but precisely 'the same result is

---

* Jespersen's *nothing is necessary* is misleading, so I have taken the liberty of changing it.

obtained when one of these words is followed by a word with a negative prefix or [as in *fail*] with implied negative meaning':

Nothing is unnecessary = *everything is necessary*
Nobody was unkind = *everybody was kind*
He was never unkind = *He was always kind*
Nobody fails = *everybody succeeds*
He forgets nothing = *he remembers everything.*

(It may be remarked that the second and third equations imply a gracious opinion of humanity.)

'When the negative is a separate word, the result is the same; but . . . such sentences are generally avoided because they are not always clear or readily understood': thus Thackeray's 'Not a clerk in that house did not tremble before her' is an obscure and verbose way of saying 'Every clerk (or, all the clerks) in that house trembled before her'. 'There is, however, no difficulty if the two negatives are placed in separate clauses, as in "There was no one present that did not weep" (= everybody wept).'

Moreover, if we negative a *B* term (*something, somebody*), we get a *C* term: 'I met somebody' becomes 'I met nobody'; more generally, however, we use the *not* form: 'I did not meet anybody'. 'Obviously, obviously!' murmurs some intelligent person. Quite! Yet we find the intelligent Mr Cameron McCabe writing 'Maria looked back with a dead expression on her face—pale, indifferent, non-committal. She was not trying to hide something [properly, 'She was not trying to hide anything']: nothing she might have tried to hide was left in her' (*The Face on the Cutting-Room Floor*, 1937).

In the preceding paragraphs we have been dealing with the tripartite (threefold) arrangement of *A*: *all*—*B*: *some*—*C*: *none*. There is another tripartition that concerns both logicians and students of grammar in particular and of language in general:

A: necessity
B: possibility
C: impossibility.

'If closely inspected, these categories',

as is remarked by Professor Jespersen, who is nobody's dupe, 'are found to be nothing else but special instances of our three categories above, for necessity really means'—and fundamentally connotes—'that *all* possibilities are comprised.' *Not necessary* = *possible*, or perhaps rather *not necessary* involves *possible*; *not impossible* = *possible*; *it is impossible not to admit* (that Shakespeare was a good writer) certainly implies that it is *necessary* to admit it.

The verbal correspondences, equivalences, counterparts, expressions of these three categories (*A*: necessity—*B*: possibility—*C*: impossibility) are:

A: *must* (or, *need*)
B: *can* (or, *may*)
C: *cannot* (or, *be unable to*).

Their interrelationship is evident in such instances as these:

He *must* run = he *cannot* but run (or, cannot help running)
No one *can* deny = everyone *must* admit
Nobody *need* be present = everybody *may* be absent
He *cannot* succeed = he *must* fail
He *cannot* forget = he *must* remember.

If to these three categories (necessity, possibility, impossibility) we add an element of desire (or will) as it affects another person, we get the instructive tripartition:

A: command
B: permission
C: prohibition.

'But these three categories are not neatly separated in actual language, at any rate not in the forms of the verb, for the imperative is usually the only form available for *A* [command] and *B* [permission]. Thus *take that!* may have [either] of two distinct meanings, (*A*) a command: "You must take that", (*B*) a permission: "You may take that", with some intermediate shades of meaning (request, entreaty, prayer). Now a prohibition (*C*) means at the same time (1) a positive command to not (take that), and (2) the negative of a permission: "You are not allowed to (take that)"; hence the possibility of using a negative as a prohibitive:

Don't take that!
Don't you stir!'

This possibility helps us to understand certain peculiarities in the use of *must* and *may*. In *you must* (positive command) *not take* (negative) *that*, 'we have the usual tendency to attract the negation to the auxiliary . . ., and thus we get: *you mustn't take that*, which . . . has become the ordinary prohibitive auxiliary'. But in *you may not* (negative) *take* (positive) *that*, properly the negative of a permission, 'we have the competition with the usual combination of (positive) *may* + negative infinitive, as in "He may not be rich, but he is a gentleman"; this makes people shrink from *may-not* in a prohibition, the more so as *may* is felt to be weaker and more polite than . . . *must*. The result is that to the positive "we may walk on the grass" corresponds a negative "we mustn't walk on the grass". . . . The old *may not* in prohibitions . . . is now comparatively rare, except in questions implying a positive answer (*mayn't I* = "I suppose I may") and in close connexion with a positive *may*, thus especially in answers', as in '"Perhaps I may kiss your hand?"—"No, you may not".'—'"May I tell you?" "No, you may not".'

'Positive *may* and negative *must not* are frequently found together:

'Ruskin . . ., Your labour only may be sold; your soul must not.

'Stevenson . . ., Prose may be rhythmical . . ., but it must not be metrical.

'Shaw . . ., You may call me Dolly if you like; but you mustn't call me child. . . .

'*May* is thus used even in tag questions after *must not*: [Jane] Austen . . ., "I must not tell, may I, Elinor?"

'Dickens . . ., "You mustn't marry more than one person at a time, may you?" "Certainly not." "But if you marry a person, and the person dies, why then you may marry another person, mayn't you?" "You *may*, if you choose."

'On the other hand, *must* begins to be used in tag questions, though it is not possible to ask *Must I?* instead of *May I?* Thus: George Eliot . . ., "I must not go any further, must I?"'

But this tendency is to be strongly resisted: any further break-down in the differentiation of *may* and *must* can result only in the blunting of the instrument and the slurring of the effect.

Two further points concerning *may*

here present themselves: and Jespersen, as always, is lucid and helpful. *May* + a negative infinitive denotes possibility (*you may not know* = 'it is possible that you do not know"); usually, the *not* is attracted to the verb, in accordance with the general tendency of *not* to slip from its logical to what seems to be its idiomatic position. Shaw, 'Newcomers whom they may not think quite good enough for them'; A. Hope, 'I may not be an earl, but I have a perfect right to be useful'; W. J. Locke, 'What may be permissible to a scrubby little artist in Paris mayn't be permitted to one who ought to know better'. Then there is the semantic change caused by a negative. To the positive *may*, (past) *might*, there 'corresponds a negative *cannot*, *could not* (or *may not*, *might not*)': Kingsley, 'His dialectic, though it *might* silence her, *could not* convince her'; Geo. A. Birmingham, 'He *might* be a Turk.—No, he couldn't'; 'This cannot do harm and *may* do good'.

Section *B* falls into two parts:— i. *NEGATION IN SYNTAX*; ii, *NEGATIVE CONJUNCTIONS (OR CONNECTIVES)*.

B. i.: *NEGATION IN SYNTAX*.

Obviously, much of the practice, as opposed to the theory, of negation has been dealt with or touched on in the preceding section; and much of it is being deferred to *B*, ii (Negative Connectives). Nevertheless, a few general remarks may usefully be made at this point. The following short account is taken from George O. Curme's *Syntax*, 1931.

In general, the negative is a sentence adverb and, like the other sentence adverbs, it is, as a rule, stressed weakly and placed between subject and predicate, as in 'I never do such things'. If there is an auxiliary in the sentence, the negative *not* (or *n't*), as is the way of sentence adverbs, 'stands before the stressed verbal form: "He has*n't* come yet." "He does*n't* do such things." "He can*'t* do such things." The perfect infinitive without *to* is usually considered as a unit, so that the negative stands before the unaccented tense auxiliary of the infinitive: "He can *scarcely have arrived* by this time" [*scarcely* being a virtual negative] . . . "He had spoken late, but he need *not have spoken* at all."

'In abridged infinitival or participial

clauses the subject is usually understood, so that the negative stands before
the verbal form: "He promises *not to
do it again*", or now sometimes with
split infinitive . . ., since there is a
tendency here to place the sentence
adverb immediately before the stressed
verb, as in the full clause: . . . "There
can be nothing between you and me,
dear mother, that we can *not talk
about*". . . . In the compound form of
the infinitive the negative usually stands
before *to*, or now sometimes in accordance with the new drift, after the
auxiliary, as in the full clause: "He
claims *not* (or *never*) *to have seen her
before*", or sometimes *to have not* (or
never) *seen her before*, as in "He claims
that he has not (or *never*) *seen her
before*".'

In 'abridged participial clauses', as
Curme designates them, *not* stands before the participle, whether simple
('*Not knowing the subject*, I failed in the
examination'), or compound ('*Not having
met him*, I failed to recognize him from
his photographs in the newspapers').
Never is more amenable: '*Having never
met him*, I . . .' or, more emphatically
but less usually, '*Never having met him*,
I . . .', as in the fuller sentences: '*As I
had never met him*, I . . .', or, less generally, '*As I never had met him*, I . . .'

When a statement as a whole is
stressed, the negative (like other sentence adverbs) is stressed: 'I *never* did
it'; 'I have *not* done it'. When the *not*
merges with the auxiliary, the auxiliary
receives the stress, as in 'I *didn't* do it',
'I just *can't* do it!'

'Usually the negative constitutes a
sentence adverb and stands before the
verbal form, but sometimes the negative
is felt as 'a distinguishing adverb, i.e.,
as belonging to some particular word,
phrase, or clause which is prominent in
the sentence as a whole, and is then
placed immediately before this word,
phrase, or clause: "*He* did it, not I."
"He hit *me*, not *him*."'

In 'I hope *not*' as an answer to 'You
will shortly be dismissed' or as a comment on 'He thinks that soon he will
die', and 'I thought *not*' as a comment
on 'He didn't get what he expected',
not 'represents all that is left of a subordinate clause, such as "that is *not* so".
It does not strictly qualify "hope",
"thought"' (Onions). Logically the construction is 'I hope that . . . *not*', 'I

thought that . . . *not*', 'I feared that . . .
not', not 'I do not hope that', 'I did not
think that', 'I did not fear that'. Here,
as in so many English constructions,
Latin influence (*non spero* . . ., *non
arbitrabor*, etc., etc.) has perhaps been
at work.

B. ii: *NEGATIVE CONJUNCTIONS
(OR CONNECTIVES).*

In his book *Negation*, Jespersen sets
forth seven types of negative connection
of sentences.

(1) '*Nor* seeks *nor* finds he mortal
blisses', where *nor* . . . *nor* represents
a shortening of 13th to 15th Century
nother . . . *nother* (neither . . . nor):
archaic and/or poetical.

(2) 'I could *neither* run with speed, *nor*
climb trees' (Swift); '*Neither* he nor his
sister has come'; 'He neither loves nor
hates her'; 'Neither are we ready, nor
are you willing': the usual formula; the
norm.

Where there are more than two
alternatives, it is not uncommon to omit
the connective with the middle terms
(or one of them): thus Shakespeare,
Measure for Measure, 'Thou hast neither
heat, affection, limb, nor beauty'. *Julius
Caesar*, 'I have neither writ nor words,
nor worth, Action nor utterance, nor the
power of speech'.

'The conjunction may even be omitted
poetically before all except the first
alternative: Shakespeare, *Lear*, Nor rain,
wind, thunder, fire are my daughters.'

(3) The *neither* . . . *or* type, which is
wrong in 'Having *neither* weapons *or*
clothes' or 'He neither knew that fellow
or wished to know him', is, in short,
usually wrong; but it is correct in
'*Neither* she nor your brother *or* sister
suspected a word of the matter' (Jane
Austen), for the principal dissociation
(*neither* . . . *nor*) is that between 'she'
on the one hand, 'either your brother
or your sister' on the other hand, and
'brother or sister' is felt as one idea, as
indeed it is, being the second of the
two parties concerned in the statement.
Another good example of the correct use
of *neither* . . . *nor* . . . *or* is afforded by
the sentence, 'He wants neither [*a*] to
solve any questions nor [*b*] to set them
or [*b¹*] to evoke them in his readers'
minds' (Cameron McCabe, *The Face on
the Cutting-Room Floor*, 1937).

Compare the following sentences,
where the negative word, be it adverb

(*never*, *not*) or pronoun (*nobody*), covers everything: 'Faustus vows *never* to look to heaven, *Never* to name God, *or* to pray to him' (Marlowe); Jane Austen, 'She knew not what to think, *or* how to account for it' (Dickens), where 'knew not' = 'was ignorant'; 'He lived alone, and *never* saw her, or inquired after her' (Dickens); 'Nobody was singing or shouting' (H. G. Wells).

(4) 'They threatened that the cage *nor* irons should serve their turn' (Bunyan); 'She *nor* her daughters were . . .' (J. Austen); 'My father, *nor* his father before him, ever saw it otherwise',—these are correct examples of a now archaic type, wrongly used in 'She struggled against this for an instant or two (maid *nor* anybody assisting)', perpetrated by Carlyle. The *nor* casts backward as well as forward.

(5) 'Never attaching herself much to us, *neither* us to her' (Ruskin); 'The royal Dane does not haunt his own mother,—*neither* does Arthur, King John; *neither* Norfolk, King Richard II; *nor* Tybalt, Romeo' (Ruskin); 'Nothing makes us think . . . *Nor*, I believe, are the facts ever so presented . . . *Nor*, lastly, do we receive the impression . . .' (Bradley); 'She said nothing, neither did I' (W. J. Locke). But *neither* constitutes a slight variation: 'He did not for a moment underestimate the danger; *but neither* did he exaggerate its importance' (J. MacCarthy).

(6) 'I know nothing, *nor* you *neither*' is the double-negative form, now incorrect, of 'I know nothing; *nor* you *either*' (or, more neatly, 'I know nothing; nor do you').

(7) Analogous is 'Blush not . . . *and* do *not* laugh *neither*' (Scott); 'I had no companions to quarrel with, neither' (Ruskin). This type is now frowned on: rightly, for it is misleading, clumsy, tautological.

An instructive example of the necessity for clear thinking in the use of negative connectives is afforded by this quotation from *A Ship of the Line*, by that excellent novelist, C. S. Forester:— 'Close overside he saw a woman . . . blubbering unashamed. . . . It was *no more* than an even chance that she would *never* see her man again', where *never* should be *ever*, the author having been misled by *no*.

Summing up, we may say that *neither* calls for *nor*, as *either* calls for *or*; if *neither* appears in the second half, it is preceded not by *neither* but by *no* + noun and *not* (or *never*) + verb; *nor* unpreceded by *neither* properly = *and not*, but now improperly = *and no* (for examples, see *no . . . nor*).

C. THE DOUBLE NEGATIVE.

The most comprehensive, subtle and informative treatment of the double negative—abstractly, a repeated (or even reiterated) negation—is that given by Professor Jespersen in *Negation*, 1917: but as it is designed rather for the professional grammarian and as it presupposes a considerable knowledge of comparative linguistics, I shall do no more than recommend it to the curious. The following account falls into two parts: (a) the double negative in its relation to logic and to good sense; (b) the double and the pleonastic negative in practice.

(a) *Logic and the Double Negative.*

In his *Logic and Grammar*, S. P. E. Tract No. xvi, 1924, Jespersen puts the case thus:—

Both philosophers, especially logicians, and old-fashioned grammarians (back-to-the-wallers; last-ditchers, die-hards) insist, with an absoluteness proper enough to cloudland metaphysics but improper to an empiric world, 'that two negatives make an affirmative, and that therefore those languages are illogical which use a double negative as a strengthened negative'. These intransigents generally refer to the mathematical law that $- - 1 = + 1$ (i.e., 1); but a linguistic* negative is not equivalent to a mathematical negative. In actual as distinct from vacuum'd language, a combination of two negatives leads sometimes to a positive, sometimes to a negative.

'The first rule', says Jespersen, '. . . is that when two negatives are special negatives'—a negative applying to one idea only is a special negative, whereas a nexal negative applies to two ideas [section *A*, third par., footnote]—'the meaning is always positive; . . . [as in] "not uncommon", "not infrequent", "not without fear", &c. But it is important to observe that the double negative always modifies the idea, for "not uncommon" does not mean exactly the same thing as "common"; it is weaker; "this is not unknown to me"

* Cf. GRAMMAR AND LOGIC, par. 5.

means "I am to some extent aware of it", &c. The psychological reason for this is that the *détour* through the two mutually destructive negatives weakens the mental energy of the listener and implies on the part of the speaker a certain hesitation which is absent from the blunt, outspoken *common* or *known.* "Not uncommon", therefore, cannot be classed exactly with the mathematical— (− 1); the result is similar, though not identical.'

Now for the second rule: two nexal negatives may produce a negative result, as, e.g., in the French *on ne le voit nulle part,* literally 'one not him sees no place' (one does not see him nowhere), but idiomatically 'one sees him nowhere' (or, in familiar English, 'you don't see him about at all').

'But wherever this cumulative negation is found, the negative elements are attached not to the same word, but to different words, even though these belong to the same sentence, and under these circumstances . . . we may say that though logically one negative suffices, two or three in the same sentence cannot be termed illogical; they are simply a redundancy, which may be superfluous from a stylistic point of view, just as any repetition [is] in a positive sentence (*every and any, always and on all occasions*), but is otherwise unobjectionable. There is no logical objection to combinations like these: "I shall never consent, not under any circumstances, not on any conditions, neither at home nor abroad"; it is true that here pauses, which in writing are marked by commas, separate the negatives, as if they belonged to so many different sentences [whereas] in "he never said nothing" and in similar phrases . . ., the negatives belong to one and the same sentence. But it is [difficult*] to draw the [line] between what constitutes one and what constitutes two sentences. We see this in such resumptions as "he never sleeps, neither by night nor by day" and "he cannot sleep, not even after taking an opiate" [—two sentences in which the substitution of dashes for the commas would perhaps make the point clearer]; in such cases, with "neither—nor"**

* Jespersen wrote 'impossible': to me, 'impossible' seems rather too strong.
** A good example is this:—'He hated Jensen with the sound hatred of a jealous lover. He never hid either sentiment, neither his hate nor his jealousy' (C. McCabe, *The Face on the Cutting-*

and "not even", all languages freely admit double negatives, though even here precisians object to them'.

The psychological reason for the use of a double negative in the majority of such sentences has been neatly posited by Jespersen, thus:—'Double negation in one and the same sentence generally arises under the influence of a strong feeling: the speaker wants to make absolutely sure that the negative sense will be fully apprehended; therefore he attaches it not only to the verb, but also to any other part of the sentence that can be easily made negative. . . . [Further,] it may be said that it requires greater mental energy to content oneself with one negative, which has to be remembered during the whole length of the utterance both by the speaker and [by] the hearer, than to repeat the negative idea whenever an occasion offers itself.

'. . . We have also what may be called paratactic negation, a negative being placed in a clause dependent on a verb of negative import like "deny", "forbid", "hinder", "doubt", as if either the corresponding positive verb had been used, or the clause had been an independent sentence; cf. "What hinders . . . that you do not return to those habits?" (Lamb) . . . Here, too, we have redundancy and over-emphasis rather than irrationality or want of logic.

'Redundancy in the negatives should be judged in the same way as redundancies found in other departments of grammar. . . . Languages differ greatly in their demands on explicitness . . .; that, however, is a question of the economy of speech, but hardly one of logic.'

(b): *The Double and the Pleonastic Negative in Practice.*

Practice, obviously, has been indicated and even stressed in the preceding sub-section (from the fourth paragraph to the end); all that is necessary, now, is to state that 'I don't know nothing' is psychologically defensible but contrary to the present idiom of the educated, whereas, 'He can't sleep, not even after taking an opiate' is both psychologically justifiable and idiomatically justified; and to remark that 'What hinders . . . that you do not return to those habits?'

Room Floor, 1937), for the insertion of 'he hid' before 'neither his hate nor his jealousy' renders the sentence both logical and idiomatic.

is perhaps based on the Latin *quominus* and *quin* and on that French *ne* which does not demand a succeeding *pas*.

But Dr George O. Curme's verdict on 'Double Negation' and 'Pleonastic Expression with Negatives' is so concise and pithy that to reproduce it here will probably be a meritorious action. 'In older literary English, as in current popular speech, two or three negatives were felt as stronger than a single negative, on the same principle that we drive in two or three nails instead of one, feeling that they hold better than one: "I *can't* see *no* wit in her" (Lamb in a letter to Coleridge in 1797). "I *don't* know *nothing* about it" (current popular speech). Under Latin influence'—e.g., *non nihil vidi*, I did see something—'we have come to feel that two negatives make an affirmative statement, although we still in an answer say *no, no*, to strengthen our negative reply. Even in the literary language, however, there is a survival of older usage after verbs like *doubt, wonder*, which are affirmative in form but negative in meaning. We sometimes still use the negative *but* after these words when preceded by a negative, not feeling that the two negatives make the statement affirmative without the help of *but*, so that *but* is really pleonastic: "I do not doubt *but that* (now usually simple *that*) you are surprised". "I wouldn't doubt *but* Hannah's upstairs all the while, splitting her sides (St John Ervine, *John Ferguson*, Act II). . . . Not feeling that *but* (= *only*) is a negative, we sometimes put a *not* before it, so that here *not* is pleonastic: "It will *not* take but a few minutes to dispose of it" (Mr Blanton, of Texas, in the House, Aug. 12, 1919)'. 'On the other hand, not feeling that *help* is negative with the force of *avoid*, we often say, "I won't do any more *than I can* (instead of the correct *can't*) help", after the analogy of *than I have to* or *than I must*.'

neglect is *negligence* exemplified. When they are approximate equivalents ('Guilty of negligence', 'guilty of neglect'), *neglect* is the stronger word.

negligence should be used for *indifference* only in the senses 'careless indifference concerning one's appearance' and 'unaffected style'; not for *callousness*, as in 'Feigned negligence and real anxiety as it were cancelling each other out in his voice and rendering it quite

toneless', Nicholas Blake, *There's Trouble Brewing*, 1937.

negligent; negligible. Respectively 'careless' and 'not worth care (or attention)'.—Cf. the entry at INTELLIGENT.

negro (capitalized). [[In America Negro is not so acceptable as *colored* (*person*) to descendants of African races, except in formal statements. Of recent use is *race* (n. and adj.), e.g., 'race (phonograph) *recordings*' for recordings made by Negroes.]]

neighbourhood of, in the. 'The story . . . on the making of which Hollywood is said to have lavished in the neighbourhood of £300,000' (*The Sphere*, 15th Jan., 1938). Here the expression is a bad and wholly unnecessary substitute for 'about' or 'nearly'.

neither followed by a plural verb: See EITHER. But an excellent example of *neither . . . are* for *neither . . . is* is furnished by the following:—

DESPATCH FROM THE BRITISH MINISTER AT PEKING TO THE CHINESE FOREIGN OFFICE

As printed in White Paper *China*, No. 2 (1898).
Sir C. MacDonald to the Tsung-li Yamen
Peking, February 9, 1898.

MM. Les Ministres.

Your Highnesses and your Excellencies have more than once intimated to me that the Chinese Government were aware of the great importance that has always been attached by Great Britain to the retention in Chinese possession of the Yang-tsze region, now entirely hers, as providing security for the free course and development of trade.

Strictly speaking, this is not grammar. 'China' has not been mentioned, only 'Chinese possession' and the 'Chinese Government' neither of which are in the feminine gender. 'Hers' can only refer, according to the ordinary rules of grammar, to Great Britain.

However, I suppose we must not be pedantic, but must leave Sir C. MacDonald and the Yamen to use bad grammar if they prefer.

I shall be glad to be in a position to communicate to Her Majesty's Government a definite assurance that China will never alienate any territory in the provinces adjoining the Yang-tsze to any other Power, whether under lease, mortgage, or any other designation. Such an assurance is in full harmony with the observations made to me by your Highnesses and your Excellencies.

I avail, etc.
(Signed) CLAUD M. MACDONALD.

ELUCIDATORY NOTE.

Paragraphs 2 and 3 are marginal notes by Curzon, then Under-Secretary for Foreign Affairs, and form no part of the actual despatch which is composed of paragraphs 1 and 4. By some mishap in the printing the marginal note (which should have been suppressed) got incorporated in the text with the above result.

It is amusing to note that the careful grammarian has himself made a slip in "neither of which *are*".

(With thanks to Valentine Williams, *The World of Action*, 1938, and to Professor A. W. Stewart.)

neither should be restricted to two, things, persons, actions, sets, groups companies, etc. For three or more, *not any* or *none* is required. In 'Jack, Jill and Jim were present; neither had much to say', substitute *none* (*of them*) for *neither*.

neither . . . nor. See NEGATION, Section *B*, ii.

neither . . . nor, misplaced. 'Bertrand Russell has characterized pure mathematics as "that science in which we neither know what we are talking about, nor whether what we say is true" (Stuart Chase; *The Tyranny of Words*, 1938). Read '. . . we know neither what we are talking about nor whether what we say is true'.

neither . . . nor . . . nor. See NO . . . NOR.

neither of their (sakes). See GENITIVE, VAGARIES OF THE: penultimate paragraph.

neither . . . or should (except in *neither . . . nor . . . or:* see NEGATION) invariably be *neither . . . nor*. A writer of detective 'thrillers' perpetrated this in 1932, 'Looking neither to the right or the left'.

NEOLOGISMS. 'A novel word or phrase which has not yet secured unquestioned admission into the standard [language] is called a *neologism*, which is simply a "new form of speech". There

is no test but time. If a neologism seems to most speakers to supply a lack in the language, or to be peculiarly fit for the expression of some special idea, it is sure to maintain itself against the protests of the literary and scholastic guild.—On the other hand, nothing can force a new term into any language against the inclination of a large majority of those who speak it. The field of language is strewn with the dry bones of adventurous words which once started out with the paternal blessing to make their fortune, but which have met with an untimely end, and serve only, when collected, to fill the shelves of a lexicographical museum.' (The Fowler brothers.)

Concerning the origin of neologisms, the Fowlers, in *The King's English* (3rd. ed., 1930), have written thus judiciously: —'The motive may be laziness, avoidance of the obvious, love of precision, or desire for a brevity or poignancy that the language as at present constituted does not seem to him to admit of. The first two are bad motives, the third a good, and the last a mixed one. But in all cases it may be said that a writer should not indulge in nonce-words unless he is quite sure he is a good writer.' (A *nonce-word* is 'a word apparently used only for the nonce', in the definition of *The O.E.D.*)

Neologisms, moreover, should be formed with some regard to etymological decency; the marriage of so very English word as *swim* with a so very Greek vocable as *stad* strikes one as an unseemly misalliance. And what reason for *swimstad* when we have *swimming-bath*? *Swimstad* has not even the excuse of necessity.

To neologisms adopted direct from foreign languages there is less objection, provided always that the new words fill a gap.

neophyte: 'a beginner, a novice, a tyro': is not to be overdone!

nett for *net*, as in *nett profit, nett result*, is without justification.

neurasthenic and **neurotic.** There is a scientific distinction between *neurasthenia*, 'a nervous weakness', and *neurosis*, 'a nervous disease' (*The O. E.D.*), from which the adjectives are derived. Such terms should be left to the doctors who understand them; it is offensive to a person to be called 'neurotic' if he is only 'neurasthenic'.

never, as a mere equivalent of *not*

is a colloquialism and should, in serious writing, be used only after careful consideration. 'He never knew it was so chilly' for 'He did not know it was so chilly' is natural in dialogue, but incongruous in formal writing; cf. 'He spoke never a word' for 'He spoke *not* a word' (emphatic) or 'He did not speak a word' (neutral). In familiar speech 'He spoke never a word' is stronger than 'He did not speak a word'; in writing it is no stronger than 'He spoke not a word'. Students will find this matter treated suggestively in Jespersen's monograph, *Negation*, Copenhagen, 1917, pp. 17–18.

never expected is incorrect—or, at best, loose—for *expected never*, as in 'I never expected to see her there'.

never so is no longer good English for *ever so*, as in 'Beer is beer, be it never so weak'.

nevertheless. The combination, *but nevertheless*, is tautological for *nevertheless*.

new and **novel.** The former refers to time ('It is new to me') or to state or condition ('His suit was new'); the latter to kind ('It's a novel way or method'). *New* is opposed to *old*, *novel* to *common* or *well-known*.

New Year Day is incorrect for *New Year's Day.*

New York City. The official name is *The City of New York*, rare except in official papers or formal statements. *New York City* (abbr. *N.Y.C.*) is common in both speech and writing, as is simple *New York* except where it leads to confusion between the city and the state. *New York, N.Y.* is a variant in writing and is sometimes preferred to *New York City*. Mail is addressed to *New York, N.Y.* or *New York City*. Pretentious and formal communications such as wedding invitations may bear *New York, New York.*

news. Anxiety to be correct causes people sometimes to put the verb in the plural, but the singular has been accepted as Good English, as in 'No news is good news'.

nice is a verbal counter, a passe-partout, a word-of-all-pleasant-work; permissible—though an indication of laziness—in conversation, it is to be avoided in serious writing.

nicely for *satisfactorily* or *well*, or *very well* is not, as Weseen states, a colloquialism; it is, however, far too common and should, as a general rule, be avoided. [[According to *Webster's, nicely* (adj.) meaning *well, in good health*, is colloquial; *nicely* (adv.) is standard for *precisely, scrupulously, satisfactorily*.]]

NICKNAMES are permissible among friends, and, for the great or the famous or the notorious, among all men (and women): but in writing, unless they are so apposite and effective that other considerations become negligible or inoperative, they are to be avoided. Gossip writers affect them, for nicknames in a gossip column give the impression that the writer knows intimately the person nicknamed or is at least in the enviable position of knowing the name if not the person; and readers, in the glow induced by intimacy at second hand, forgive the writer the gross tactlessness or the childish impertinence of this excessive familiarity. Especially offensive is the nicknaming of royalty: it is comparable with journalists' references to film and lawn-tennis stars by their pet names, as in 'Betty plays magnificently in Wimbledon doubles' and 'Where is Greta?' [[There is an increasing tendency in American businesses—e.g., in radio—to call nearly everyone by his first name or by a nickname. It may produce a friendly atmosphere but it does not keep John from firing Charlie.]]

nigger belongs only, and then only in contempt or fun, to the dark-skinned African races and their descendants in America and the West Indies. Its application to the native peoples of India is ignorant and offensive. See NEGRO.

nigh (adv.) for *near* is archaic in prose; current usage reserves it for poetry. Do not employ it as an adjective. *Well nigh* for *almost* or *very nearly* is a cliché.

no. See at NONE.

no, as in 'I didn't want no tellin'' (Baumann). An example of the double negative, common in illiterate speech.

no + superlative + noun ('no slightest sign') = '*no* + that noun, *not even the slightest*'. Idiomatically, 'There was no slightest sign' = 'There was no sign at all, not even the slightest', and not, as one might think, 'There was no very slight sign, but there was a big sign'.

no admission is occasionally used ambiguously for *no admission-charge*, to which *admission (is) free* is preferable.

no more . . . than. A curious slip is made by that brilliant American writer, George Jean Nathan (*The Intimate Note-*

books of George Jean Nathan, 1932) in this sentence: 'Napoleon returned and had no more taken up his knife and fork than he was again called out of his tent . . .', where the meaning is '. . . had no more than taken up his knife and fork when he was called out . . .', or 'had no sooner taken up [etc.] . . . than he was called out'.

no . . . nor for *no . . . and no* and *no . . . or.* This *no . . . nor* is permitted by *The O.E.D.* in its use as an equivalent of *no . . . and no,* as in 'We had no revolutions to fear, nor fatigues to endure' (Goldsmith, 1766). This equivalence, however, is obsolescent. The man in the street tends now to say, 'We had no revolutions to fear and no fatigues to endure', and the modern stylist would write, 'We had no revolutions to fear; [or,:] no fatigues to endure'. 'She took no interest nor part in outdoor sports' seems nowadays old-fashioned. Sometimes *or* would be preferred to *and no* as the modern equivalent of this *nor,* as in 'He had in him . . . no tincture of Scottish, Irish, Welsh, French, German, Italian, American nor Jewish [blood]' (Arnold Bennett, *Imperial Palace,* 1930), where a modern stylist would write 'He had . . . no tincture of Scottish, Irish, Welsh . . . American, or Jewish [blood]', with a comma after *American* to ensure dissociation. In the following sentence from Hugh Walpole's *John Cornelius,* 1937,— 'They say that no novel in the first person can ever be true because no one can recall conversations as they actually occurred nor remember the physical details of past scenes',—I should have preferred '. . . no one can [either] recall conversations . . . or remember the physical details', which is neater than 'no one can recall conversations . . . and no one can remember the physical details'. Here, as in all nuanced writing, discrimination is required; not the bull-at-a-gate courage of desperation!

no object. See OBJECT, NO.

no one; noone. The latter is incorrect.

no one (or **nobody**) . . . **they.** See ANYONE . . . THEY.

no one's (or **nobody's**) **else** (or **else's**). See ELSE'S.

no place is illiterate for *nowhere,* as in 'The jewel was no place to be found'.

no such. Freeman Wills Crofts, *The Cask,* 1920, 'You can't have seen a letter from me, because no such exists', should be *no such letter* (or *thing*), for *such* ought

not to be used as a pronoun except in the time-honoured formulas, 'such is life', 'such was the decision'.

no thing. See 'NOTHING and NO THING'.

no use is incorrect—or, at best, colloquial—for *of no use* or, more economically, *useless,* as in 'This pen is no use'.

noble for *charming, very kind, unselfish* is slang. Originally it was schoolgirls' slang.

nobody's else. See ELSE'S.

nom de plume is to be avoided: there is no such term in the best French (*nom de guerre* being usual). The correct English is *pen-name* or (literary) *pseudonym,* of which the former is a translation of the pseudo-French *nom de plume;* but in post-War French, *nom de plume* is very often employed: the popularity of *pen-name* + that of *nom de plume,* as used in England, have engendered a genuinely French *nom de plume* which is a writer's *nom de guerre.*

nominal is incorrectly used by Nigel Morland (*The Conquest of Crime,* 1937) in 'The figures are nominal'; he means *approximate,* 'nominal' is 'existing in name only, in distinction to real or actual' (*The O.E.D.*). *Nominal,* in *at a nominal charge* or *cost, for a nominal fee,* is not 'low' but 'so low' as not fairly to be considered a charge, a cost, a fee. In short, *nominal* is not synonymous with *low.*

nominate. See DENOMINATE.

NOMINATIVE ABSOLUTE. There's nothing mysterious about this! But example is better than precept: 'She failing to keep the appointment, he went off and got drunk'.

none. (i) When *none = not one,* use the singular, as in 'None of the newspapers has appeared this week'.

(ii) When *none = no one, no person, nobody,* the singular is correct; but, as indeed for (i) also, the plural is not regarded as a solecism: in both (i) and (ii), the plural is merely an infelicity, a defect that will not hinder the good-enoughists.

(iii) When *none = no persons,* the verb is plural, as in 'None have been so greedy of employments . . . as they who have least deserved their stations' (Dryden). The corresponding singular pronoun is *no one.* Based on *The O.E.D.*

none, misused with genitive. See GENITIVE, VAGARIES . . ., penultimate paragraph.

none such is very awkwardly, if not

absolutely incorrectly used in 'When he asked for the name, he was told that none such was in the register', Nigel Morland, *The Conquest of Crime*, 1937. —Cf. NO SUCH.

noone. See NO ONE.

nor (in **neither . . . nor**). See NEITHER . . . OR.

nor for *or* and for *and no*. See 'NO . . . NOR for NO . . . AND NO'.

nor for *than*, as in Thackeray, 1840. 'You're no better nor a common tramper' (*The O.E.D.*), is still frequent in low colloquial speech, but is a mark of illiteracy.

nor . . . neither. In general, see NEGATION, *B* (Negation in Syntax).

Occasionally, *nor . . . neither* is misused for *nor . . . either*, as in 'You've had a Boy Scout's training and they never have. Nor I neither', Inez Irwin, *The Poison Cross Mystery*, 1936. One negatives not both members of *or . . . either* (that would produce a double negative) but the first only in this formula, which is quite different from '*neither* (you) *nor* I'; *nor I either* is merely an elaboration of *nor I*.

nor none is occasionally misused for *nor any*. '"They have no Libel Law in France." "Nor none in Brazil", says Miles', Beatrice Kean Seymour, *The Happier Eden*, 1937; this Miles was a novelist.

normal, the. See the following entry.

normalcy, normalism, normality and **normalness.** The fourth is incorrect; the second, which is rare, has no special, no technical senses; the first is more American than English, but it is catching on in Great Britain; *normality* is the usual English form, although *the normal* is fast displacing it in the sense 'a normal variety of anything; an individual or specimen possessing normal characteristics or faculties' (*The O.E.D.*).

north is inferior to *northward(s)* as an adverb.

northernly is inferior to *northerly* (adjective).

northward and **northwards.** The former is adjective and adverb; the latter, adverb only. Usage apparently prefers adverbial *northward* to the longer-established *northwards*.

not a one and **not one.** The former is incorrect: for 'Not a one of them did that' read 'Not one of them did that'.

not . . . any more is both wordy and colloquial for *no longer*, as in 'He was

not hungry any more' (= 'He was no longer hungry').

not anything like. See NOTHING LIKE . . .

not hardly is incorrect for *hardly*. So too NOT SCARCELY.

not . . . nor, in the following sentence (J. B. Priestley, *English Humour*, 1929), is not only incorrect in itself, but leads Mr Priestley into a contradiction of his own meaning: 'He asks what it is that governs the Englishman. After replying that it is certainly not intelligence, nor seldom passion, and hardly self-interest, he goes on, etc.' The meaning is 'seldom passion' or 'not often passion'. It is unsafe for the ordinary person to use *nor*—except after *neither* (*q.v.*).

not . . . nor . . . nor is permissible when it is used instead of *neither . . . nor . . . nor*. Gladstone, 1870, writes 'Not a vessel, nor a gun, nor a man, were on the ground to prevent their landing', which, woolly though it is, is preferable to 'Neither a vessel, nor a gun, nor a man . . .'

not only . . . but (also), misplaced. 'This necessitated, not only the resignations of Essex and Manchester, against whom it was chiefly aimed, but also such valuable men as Lord Warwick, who as Lord High Admiral had successfully held the seas for Parliament during those anxious years': should read: 'This necessitated the resignations not only of Essex and Manchester, against whom it was chiefly aimed, but also of such valuable men as Lord Warwick, who . . .' Quoted by G. V. Carey, *Mind the Stop*, 1939; he adds: 'If you prefer to put "not only" after the first "of", you will not need a second "of" before "such".' [[*Not only . . . but (also)* is overworked by writers of too little rhetoric. In short sentences a simple *and* is more emphatic.]]

not . . . or for *not . . . nor*. 'Making certain that there was not, or was there likely to be, any alteration in the time of the boat's usual midday sailing . . . he disappeared' (John G. Brandon, *The Mail-Van Mystery*, ca. 1937).

not scarcely. See NOT HARDLY.

notable and **noted.** The former stresses worth or worthiness; the latter, celebrity. The former is potential; the latter, actual. A notable man may not be noted; a noted man may not be notable—his fame may be notoriety, his title to fame may be factitious, adventitious, or meretricious. Cf. the entry at NOTICEABLE.

notary; notary public. See LAWYER.— The plural of *notary public* is *notaries public*.

note and **notice** (vv.). *Note*, as merely 'to take notice of', is fortunately passing out of use. Usage now prefers *note* to = 'to *notice closely*'.

nothing and **no thing.** In the latter, the stress is on *thing*, as in 'No thing perturbs him; many persons do'. 'Nothing perturbs him' connotes absence of, or freedom from perturbation. Whereas *nothing* is inclusive and general, *no thing* is exclusive and particular.

nothing but. In *nothing but* + a noun, it is *nothing* which determines the number of the verb; in other words, the verb after *nothing but* . . . should be in the singular. 'Nothing but dreary dykes occur to break the monotony of the landscape' should be 'Nothing but dreary dykes occurs . . .' (Onions, *An Advanced English Syntax*, 6th ed., 1932).

nothing like, adverbial ('Nothing like so fast'), is a colloquialism for *not nearly*.

notice. See 'NOTE and NOTICE'.

noticeable and **notable.** The former merely = 'worthy of notice', not—as *notable* does—'worthy of fame'; *noticeable* has the derivative sense, 'capable of being noticed; perceptible'.—See also 'NOTABLE and NOTED'.

notorious and **famous.** Both mean 'very well known (to the general public)'; but the former is unfavourable, the latter favourable; thus, 'a famous writer' but 'a notorious criminal'. *Notorious*, in short, is 'famous in a bad way—for crime or excessive vice'. The cliché *it is notorious that* properly means no more than 'it is common knowledge that . . .', but current usage invests it with pejorative connotation. Note, however, that a person may in his lifetime be so notorious that after his death he becomes famous: e.g., Charley Peace the murderer.

n't for *not* is colloquial and familiar: it should, in serious writing, be used with caution—or not at all.

nought and **naught.** For the cypher or zero, use *nought*; for 'nothing' use *naught*,—that is, if you use it at all, for it is archaic except in poetry. [For the cypher or zero, *Webster's* prefers *naught*.]

NOUN ADJECTIVES. In *The J.I.J.*, January, 1939, Mr Frank Whitaker, having attacked the anti-possessive (or -genitive) craze (*q.v.* at AMBIGUITY),

continues thus, under the caption, 'Dangerous Noun-Adjectives':—

'The noun-adjective mania is even more dangerous, in the sense that it is driving a wedge between written and spoken English. I read in a recent issue of the "Daily Sketch", picked up haphazard, these headlines: "Minister's Milk Bill Climb-down" (we must be grateful for the possessive there: "Minister Milk Bill" would have been a little difficult); "Navy bid to save stranded Britons" (no possessive there, you will notice), and "Brothers' big boxing bid". Now I know what is meant by the first two of those headlines—the third puzzles me—but heaven forbid that one man should ever go up to another in the street and say "Have you heard the latest about the Minister's Milk Bill Climb-down, or of the Navy bid to save stranded Britons?"

'I read in another paper, "Crime chief to retire", and I think I know what that means. But I am wrong. The man who is about to retire is not a gangster but a Scotland Yard superintendent. And what are we to make of the headline noted by William Empson in his book, "Seven types of Ambiguity", which reads, "Italian assassin bomb plot disaster"? We must be grateful again that the sub-editor did not follow the current fashion and write, "Italy assassin bomb plot disaster". But what did he mean? Was the assassin Italian? He was not. It was the disaster that was Italian. And what is an "assassin bomb plot"? I give it up.'

novel. See NEW.

noway; noways; nowise. All are correct; the third is the best; the second is the least used nowadays.

noxious. See OBNOXIOUS.

number (v.), for *possess*. 'My *locum tenens* consented to perform the office of best man for me, since I numbered no personal friend to meet the occasion', Eden Phillpotts, *Physician Heal Thyself*, ca. 1937. Rather too pregnant for *number among one's acquaintances*.

number: whether it takes a singular or a plural verb. 'If a group of words, especially a partitive group, conveys the idea of plurality, a number of individuals, the verb is in the plural, even though the governing noun is singular, [but] the verb is singular if the group conveys the idea of oneness: "The greatest *part* of these years *was* spent in philosophic retirement", but "The greatest *part* of the

Moguls and Tartars *were* as illiterate as their sovereigns". In *"a large number* of the garrison *were* prostrate with sickness" and *"*There *are a large number* of things that I desire to say" *number* is now felt not as a collective noun but as a component of a compound numeral, [and] the indefinite . . . *a large number* [as having] plural force, so that the verb is in the plural. . . . *Number* as a singular noun is still found occasionally where a writer follows the outward form rather than the inner meaning: "Chicago has as many more [models] and besides these there *is* probably *an equal number* of occasional sitters, transients" (Beecher Edwards, "Faces That Haunt You", in *Liberty*, May 22, 1926).' Such is the pronouncement of that great American grammarian, George O. Curme, in *Syntax*, 1931.

O

O and Oh. Is there a shade of human feeling which cannot be conveyed in speech by this simple vowel-sound? Yet we have no signs but these to represent to the eye their infinite variety of meanings, which prayer and imprecation, surprise, disgust, horror and delight, dubiety, incredulity, and a dozen phases of interrogation can hardly summarize. '"Here I am", said he; "Oh", said she': and how shall we indicate whether she was glad to see him? In the dialogue of a play, a stage direction might be required for the guidance of a (perhaps) stupid actress.—To come to modern practice: *O* and *Oh* were at one time used indifferently, but now the use of *O* is almost confined to poetry. *O* without punctuation is an invocation (vocative case) to some person or object named in the words that follow it, as in Milton:

O thou that with surpassing glory crowned,
Look'st from thy sole dominion, etc.,

or in the humbler verse, O lovely night! O! [or Oh!] lovely night!', which is two exclamations, the second explaining the cause of the first. But *Oh,* (a) *lovely night, isn't it?* is not exclamatory; *Oh* in such cases implies a momentary pause for thought before speaking. Often it seems to call attention to a change of subject, a new idea: *Oh, have you heard, etc.?* Real hesitancy would be conveyed

by *Oh—.* The mark of exclamation (*Oh!*) will always indicate some degree of feeling, surprise, pleasure or the reverse. In James Thomson's tragedy, *Sophonisba* (1730), there is a line much quoted as an instance of unconscious bathos, i.e., strong feeling made ridiculous by affected and inadequate expression:

Oh! Sophonisba! Sophonisba! Oh!

It is spoken by a young lover in a frenzy of delight and is perfectly natural in the circumstances. Each word is a separate exclamation capable of any change of intonation; spoken by a good actor as the author intended, it would be free from bathos and not open to ridicule.

John Evelyn, *Diary*, May 26th, 1671, wrote thus: 'This was the very first suit at law that ever I had with any creature, and that it might be the last!' I do not find any other instance of this device, which he seems to have invented for the occasion.

Dean Alford (*The Queen's English*, 1870), complaining of the compositors' habit of inserting unnecessary and often misleading stops, says: 'If one has written the words *O sir* as they ought to be written, and are written in Genesis xliii, 20, viz., with the plain capital "O" and no stop, and then a comma after "sir", our friend the compositor is sure to write "Oh" with a shriek (!) and to put another shriek after "sir".' (W.B.)

object, no. E.g., 'distance no object', and especially, 'price no object': catachrestic when 'no obstacle' or 'not an objection' is meant. The correct sense, 'not a thing aimed at or considered important' has been vitiated by confusion with *no objection*. Its flagrant absurdity is seen in the undertaker's advertisement: 'Distance no object'.

objectionable, 'open to objection; disagreeable; unacceptable'; *objectional,* 'of or involving or like an objection'. Though the latter has been used in the sense of the former, it is better to differentiate sharply between the two words.

obligate (adj.), defined by *The O.E.D.* as 'that is of necessity such', is applied with scientific meaning by biologists, but is better avoided by all others.—As verb it is sometimes used for *oblige*, but means rather *to bind* (a person) *under an obligation*. An ugly and unnecessary word.

obliged. Correct uses:—

(1) 'I am obliged by circumstances to do it.'

(2) 'I am much obliged to you for your kindness.'

(3) 'I shall be obliged if you stop making that noise.'

(4) 'I am'—or 'He or she is'—'your obliged servant', an old-fashioned letter-ending.

Of Nos. 2 and 3, *The O.E.D.* remarks, 'Now said only in reference to small services'. Except in dialogue, avoid the colloquialism exemplified in 'He obliged with a song'.

oblivion for *ignorance*. 'The necessity of keeping the common people in oblivion of the shortcomings of their material welfare.' (In reference to Germany and Italy.)

oblivious for *unconscious (of)*. *The O.E.D.* quotes Buckle, *History of Civilization*, 1862, 'He was so little given to observation as to be frequently oblivious of what was passing around him'. Noun and adjective refer only to what has been known and is forgotten. Indeed, *oblivious* for *unconscious*, or for *impervious*, is a rather serious misuse. 'Fraim Falloway crouched morosely . . ., his face a puzzled mask' ['puzzled mask' is contradictory]; 'and when I offered him a cigarette he seemed utterly oblivious to my gesture', S. S. Van Dine, *The Kidnap Murder Case* (English edition), 1936; moreover, one says *oblivious of*. Cf. 'She continued brightly, oblivious to Martha's expression', Jennings Rice, *The Somers Inheritance* (English edition), 1938.— An error more common in the U.S.A. than in Great Britain. [[*Oblivious* for *unobservant* is a colloquialism in American English.]]

oblivious to. See PREPOSITIONS WRONGLY USED.

obnoxious, 'aggressively disagreeable', must not be confused with *noxious*, which means 'injurious', e.g., of poison gas.

OBSCURITY.* 'It may be better to be clear than clever, it is still better to be clear and correct', as we are told by a correspondent in *The J.I.J.*, 1938.

'Without distinction of speech there is never much distinction of idea', remarks Frank Binder in Dialectic, 1932. And without distinction of idea there cannot be distinction of speech—or style.

* The beginner will find some useful and pithy matter in Harold Herd, *Watch Your English* 1925, at pp. 42–43.

'Real and offensive obscurity comes merely of inadequate thought embodied in inadequate language', declared Swinburne in 1870. On the other hand, as a certain grammarian has said, 'In contemplating the way in which our sentences will be understood, we are allowed to remember, that we do not write for idiots'.

To begin with, three examples of that obscurity which arises from the desire to be brief ('I labour to be brief and become obscure', as Horace once remarked).

'The foreign elements . . . played a large part in the formation of the Romantic drama and constituted a large proportion of its maturity in the 'Forties' (Eric Partridge, *The French Romantics' Knowledge of English Literature*, 1924).

'I began to get excited over my new photographic outfit. It was natural, since it was new' (Violet O. Cressy-Marcks, *Up the Amazon and over the Andes*, 1932).

'The bright naves of the wheels caught and played with the sun in their slow turning; and . . . at every fourth revolution, one of them creaked with a sort of musical complaint at a world which was perfect but for a drop of oil' (Robert Eton, *The Journey*, 1938). One is abruptly pulled up: *but for the lack of a drop of oil* would be better: *but for* (= except for) makes the phrase almost too pithy.

And then a number of miscellaneous examples; for all their miscellaneity, they do, I think, serve to show the dangers of obscurity.

'There are, of course, many uses of *colorful* which have no such [damning-with-faint-praise] implications—where, for example, that a thing should be full of colour is all we can ask where no ironical reserves and no disparagement can be intended' (I. A. Richards, *The Philosophy of Rhetoric*, 1936).

'It is the rest of the poem that makes the connection easy and obvious, which witnesses to a general truth' (*ibid.*). *That* should be *which*. But to what does *which* (*which witnesses*) refer? To *rest* or to *poem* or to the sentence, 'It is the rest of the poem that makes the connection easy and obvious'? Presumably to the sentence.

'There is no warrant for the placing on these inevitably rather light heads and hearts, on any company of you, assaulted, in our vast vague order, by many pressing wonderments, the *whole* of the burden of a care for tone' (Henry James, *The Question of Our Speech*, 1905). Cited by I. A. Richards (*op. cit.*) without comment. I pass it on—without comment.

'This common professional attitude [courage and self-abnegation] to sea-going both sides of the pay-desk has one odd result' (Richard Hughes, *In Hazard*, 1939). The author might perhaps have written, 'This . . . attitude—common to sea-going, on both sides of the pay-desk —has one odd result'.

'No, there was nothing left for him [David] in business . . . he was surfeited with success . . . David, too, though, had ideas. Vague, true, but ideas' (Frank Tilsley, *Devil Take the Hindmost*, 1937). *Though* (= however) causes part of the trouble; *true* is so short for 'it is true' that ambiguity has arisen. What the author intended was, 'No . . . David, however, had ideas. *Vague ideas*, it is true; yet ideas'.

'He watched David talk, not too closely to make him self-conscious' (*ibid.*). The sentence would have been clear had it been written, '. . . not too closely, lest he should make him self-conscious' or 'not so closely as to make . . .'

'I suppose that a few days before the place must have given some impression of a dwelling. Now . . . there hung about it the atmosphere of an ancient monument. The tenancy of Ronald Guthrie had been a thread holding it to the present; that thread broken, *it* had slipped into the past as inevitably as a ripe apricot falls to the ground' (Michael Innes, *Lament for a Maker*, 1938). To what does the italicized *it* (italicized by me) refer? To 'the place' in the first sentence—rather too far away.

'Dales went first next day to the Registrar of Births and Marriages' (Vernon Loder, *The Button in the Plate*, 1938). Dales was not the first to go there; probably not the first on even that day. The author meant, 'Next day, Dales went, first to the Registrar (and then elsewhere)'. Not content with that piece of obscurity, the author continues, 'He found him a young man'.

'It was not Carol Berman alone to whom the jury's verdict came as a bewildering shock. Inspector Cambridge felt almost as dazed as she' (Sidney Fowler, *Four Callers in Razor Street*, 1938). Obviously the passage should begin thus: 'It was not to Carol Berman alone that the jury's verdict came as a bewildering shock.'

'Power Age communities . . . rely increasingly on printed matter, radio, communication at a distance. *This* has operated to enlarge the field for words, absolutely and relatively, and has created a paradise for fakirs. A community of semantic illiterates, of persons unable to perceive the meaning of what they read and hear, is one of *perilous equilibrium*' (Stuart Chase, *The Tyranny of Words*, 1938). The italics are mine.

observance and **observation.** The latter is no longer used for the former. *Observance* = 'the action or practice of keeping or paying attention to (a law, custom, ceremony, etc.)'; also 'an act performed in accordance with prescribed usage; a practice customarily observed'. Thus 'the sternest observance of discipline'; 'religious ceremonies and observances'. (*The O.E.D.*)

observe is incorrect when used for 'to preserve' or 'keep' or 'retain'.—In the sense 'to make a remark', to 'remark' (v.t.), it is not incorrect but merely feeble.

obtain is incorrect when used for *to effect*. It seems to have arisen from a confusion of two senses, 'to gain or acquire'; and 'to reach'. George Parker, *A View of Society*, 1781, 'A very small boy is carried by a gang . . . in the dead of night to a house. . . . When this gang is pretty certain that the family is in bed, they despatch . . . the boy, or Little Snakes-man, to obtain their admittance.' See also 'PROCURE and SECURE'.

obverse. See CONVERSE.

OBVIOUS, THE. *Punch* (Aug. 16, 1938) quotes from *The Rugeley Mercury*: 'One effect of the better lighting' (of a church) 'is the improved visibility'.

occupy for *run to*, or *have*, or *comprise*, is loose. 'Such preparation may occupy six or seven stages', Nigel Morland, *The Conquest of Crime*, 1937.

octopi, a mistaken plural of *octopus* by those who suppose it to be from Latin. The English termination should be used, *octopuses*; the pedantic prefer *octopoaes*. [[*Webster's* lists as plurals of *octopus* (New Latin): *octopuses, octopodes, octopi.*]]

odd, 'strange', and **odd,** 'and a few more' (300 *odd*), must not be allowed to set up ambiguity, as in 'These 300 odd pages'. Write 'These 300-odd pages' or 'These 300 and odd pages'.

odd number (or **odd-number**) is incorrect for *odd-numbered* in 'the odd-number tickets'.

odious and **odorous.** The former = 'hateful or detestable'; the latter = 'having a smell', i.e., *odoriferous*, which is generally used in the favourable sense, 'sweet-smelling, fragrant', the opposite being *malodorous* ('evil-smelling'). *Odorous* is never a pejorative.

of, carelessly omitted. This happens especially in *of which* clauses; e.g., 'The Colonel . . . departed to make arrangements, the exact nature of which Topper decided he would be more comfortable to remain in ignorance' (Thorne Smith, *Topper Takes a Trip*, English edition, 1935), where *the exact nature of which* should be *of the exact nature of which*.

of for *have* is a gross solecism, as in 'If I had of done it'. And *have* is illiterate.

of, for *in*, is careless. 'The task of finding concepts which shall adequately describe nature and at the same time be easily handled by us, is the most important and difficult of physics', cited (from whom?) by Stuart Chase in *The Tyranny of Words*, 1938.

of in *doing of* ('What are you a doin' of?') is common only in vulgar speech, especially Cockney.

of in *off of* is also a Cockneyism and incorrect. *Off from* may in certain cases be allowed, but *away from, down from*, would always be better. [[In American English *off of* is colloquial and vulgar; *inside of, outside of* are colloquial and informal.]]

of, preposition. Incorrect uses of both *of* and *for* are exemplified in the following sentence (from *Swift or the Egotist* by M. M. Rossi and J. M. Hone, 1934), 'Even the very recent explanation of Mr Aldous Huxley for Swift's misanthropy is influenced by the theory of psycho-analysis'. Here 'of' should be 'by' and 'for' should be 'of'.

of all others. See OTHER, OF ALL.

of her—of hers; of his (+ noun)—**of his; of my—of mine; of your—of yours.** 'Note that "These are three friends *of mine*" and "These are three of *my friends*" have different implications; the second implies that I have more than three friends; the first does not' (Onions), though it does not exclude that possibility. There is, however, a further difference: 'A friend of the King' connotes dignity, whereas 'a friend of Bill Brown's' connotes familiarity in speech.

Certain writers have sought to confuse the issue by asking, 'What about *that long nose of his*?'; they point out that *his* cannot refer to more noses than one. Jespersen, in his admirable S.P.E. tract *On Some Disputed Points in English Grammar*, 1926, deals fully with the entire *of my—of mine* question, and he shows that *that long nose of his* = *that long nose which is his*; he calls 'of his' (in *that long nose of his*) an appositional genitive.

Dr George O. Curme, in *Syntax*, 1931, shrewdly remarks that 'There has become associated with the double genitive a marked liveliness of feeling, so that it now often implies praise or censure, pleasure or displeasure: "that dear little girl *of yours*", "that kind wife *of yours*", "this broad land *of ours*", "that ugly nose *of his*". "Thus Professor Blackie, in that vituperative book *of his*, 'The Natural History of Atheism' . . . says" (John Burroughs, *The Light of Day*, Ch. vi).' For the difficulties of this double genitive when a noun, not a pronoun is involved, see GENITIVE, VAGARIES OF THE, at the paragraph on the double genitive.

of old, as in 'A boy of twelve years old', is incorrect for *of age*. Or re-write thus, 'A boy twelve years old'.

of the name of. See BY THE NAME OF.

of whether. See WHETHER, OF.

of which. See WHOSE.

off of. See OF in *off of*.

off-handed (adj.) is unnecessary for *off-hand; off-handedly* (adv.) is unnecessary for *off-hand*. These terms may be written as one word.

official = 'of, pertaining to, characteristic of office; authoritative; governmental'; whereas *officious* = 'meddlesome, interfering, obtrusive, pettily fussy'.

OFFICIALESE, JOURNALESE, COMMERCIALESE.
Perhaps the most sensible order is Journalese, Officialese, Commercialese.
I, JOURNALESE. 'The style of language supposed to be characteristic of public journals; "newspaper" or "penny-a-liner's" English' (*The O.E.D.*). *Webster's*, 2nd edition, defines it more fully and exactly thus:—'English of a style featured by use of colloquialisms, superficiality of thought or reasoning, clever or sensational presentation of material, and evidences of haste in composition, con-

sidered characteristic of newspaper writing.'

Journalese hardly needs exemplifying; but here is one example: 'Notwithstanding the genuine literary productions that have sprung out of the haunts of cotton-mills and weaving sheds, they have only here and there penetrated far beyond the immediate neighbourhood that called them into existence' (a Manchester journalist, 1850: cited by E.P. in *A Critical Medley*, 1926).

II, *OFFICIALESE* is that type of wordy English which has been—often justifiably—associated with Government offices.

In *The Star* of Feb. 11, 1938, we find this piece of news:—'The Central News reports that unrest prevailed among certain "military and political elements". The elements, it was added, were being "energetically suppressed"': which sounds very totalitarian.

The Evening News, Feb. 25, 1938, gives the following instance:—

'WORK THIS ONE OUT!

'What is the position now? Reduced to simple terms, it is this:

'If A has a small business, he may open his shop for the sale of the goods specified in the schedules to the Act—and none other—during the permitted hours.

'If, however, he cares to place his goods (without restriction as to quality or variety) on a barrow or in a cart and perambulate the streets on Sunday, he is outside the scope of the Act, for in the words of Lord Hewart he is using "a movable and peripatetic apparatus by means of which sales are enabled to be made at every sort of point in streets and roads over a large area—no fixed locality, no identifiable place".

'Apart from avoiding the heavy penalties provided for an infringement of the Act, such a person will be freed from many burdens—not the least of which is to understand provisions in the statute such as this:

"... the following provisions of this Act shall extend only to shops that is to say those provisions of section six and section eight which relate to the approval by occupiers of shops of orders made under those sections the provisions of paragraph (c) of sub-section (1) of section seven and the provisions of paragraph (a) of section twelve."'

In *The Times* of August 8, 1939, occurs this letter (which contains examples of both officialese and elegancies):—

'PLAIN ENGLISH

'To the Editor of *The Times*.

'Sir,—May I contribute an example to Mr. Herbert's instances of deviations from "plain verbiage"? I had occasion some time since to ask a Government Department to supply me with a book for official use. I was informed in reply that, although the Department was not in a position to meet my request, I was "authorized to acquire the work in question by purchase through the ordinary trade channels". Or, as we should say, "buy it".

'It would be easy to add to Mr. Herbert's list of words which mark the tendency he deplores. "Assist" for "help", "endeavour" for "try", "proceed" for "go", "purchase" for "buy", "approximately" for "about", "sufficient" for "enough", "attired" for "dressed", "inquire" for "ask", are general in speech as well as print. I have noticed that whereas the waste in old lavatory-basins is marked "Shut", the up-to-date ones prefer the more refined "Closed". And, no doubt, some of these words and expressions are what Mr. Fowler, in his Modern English Usage, aptly termed "genteelisms". But others seem not to have even this justification.

'Mr. Herbert says with truth that even the Fighting Services have been corrupted. I have known one of them to be responsible for the use of "nomenclature" as a preferable equivalent for "name".

'August 3.   Your obedient servant,
CLAUD RUSSELL.'

III, *COMMERCIALESE OR BUSINESS ENGLISH* (or, as A. P. Herbert calls it, *Officese*).

A few examples of words and phrases used in commercial offices—and avoided by all self-respecting persons:—*advise* (inform), *as per, be in receipt of* ('We are in receipt of your letter'), *beg* ('We beg to bring to the notice of . . .'), *duly noted, esteemed favour* and *esteemed order,* (of) *even date, favour* (letter), *friends* (competitors: 'Our friends in the trade have been guilty of price-cutting'), *kindly* (for *please!*), *per, proximo, re,* (of) *recent date, same* (for *it*: 'We have received same'), *service* (verb), *shop-lady state* (for *say*), *a substantial percentage* (much; or merely some), *thanking you in advance, transportation* (a ticket), *ultimo, under one's signature, valuable asset, valued favour, your good self* (or *selves*).

A. P. Herbert, in *What a Word!*, 1935, has, at pp. 69–87, a delightful section on commercialese. To those lively pages we send all those who wish a wittily scathing attack on the sort of English affected by business men (at least, in their offices). Mr Herbert gives one example that simply cannot be omitted:—

'Madam,

We are in receipt of your favour of the 9th inst. with regard to the estimate required for the removal of your furniture and effects from the above address to Burbleton, and will arrange for a Representative to call to make an inspection on Tuesday next, the 14th inst., before 12 noon, which we trust will be convenient, after which our quotation will at once issue.'

Taking that letter as it stands, Mr Herbert reduces it thus:—

'Madam,

We have your letter of May 9th requesting an estimate for the removal of your furniture and effects to Burbleton, and a man will call to see them next Tuesday afternoon if convenient, after which we will send the estimate without delay': not counting 'Madam', we notice that the revised letter contains 42 words instead of 66. But Mr Herbert goes further, by recasting, thus:

'Madam,

Thank you for your letter of May 9th. A man will call next Tuesday, forenoon, to see your furniture and effects, after which, without delay, we will send our estimate for their removal to Burbleton' (or 35 words against the original 66; or 157 letters against 294 letters).

Business English, in short, is extremely un-businesslike.

officious. See OFFICIAL.

offspring is properly used as a plural ('What offspring have you?'); as a singular it may have a curious ring, as in 'Here is my offspring, what do you think of him?'

oft is to be avoided as an archaism; *many times and oft*, as a cliché.

often. According to *The Con. O.D.*, to pronounce the *t* is 'vulgar'. It is certainly unnecessary and is usually due to an affectation of refinement. [[On the pronunciation in American English, see *Webster's*.]]

To use *often* for *in many instances* sets up an ambiguity, as in 'A Danish house is often thatched with straw' (cited by Weseen).

oftener, oftenest are, by current usage, regarded as no less correct than *more often* and *most often*.

oftentimes and **ofttimes.** Both are obsolescent, though the latter still occurs in conventionally phrased poetry. Neither word means more than what is conveyed by *often*. [[*Oftentimes* still occurs in American speech.]]

old age, at an. Incorrect—or rather, unidiomatic—for *at an advanced age*.

older. See 'ELDER and OLDER'. Only *elder* is now used as a noun.

ology. See ISM.

omission. See OVERSIGHT.

omnibus. See BUS.

omnipotent; omniscient. See COMPARATIVES, FALSE.—The former = 'all-powerful'; the latter, 'all-knowing'.

on, misused for *at*. 'Anyone who was in the vicinity of New Cavendish Street *on* or about one a.m. on the morning of March 31st', Anthony Weymouth, *Tempt Me Not*, 1937.

on, used for *for*, is an error. 'To lay down the concept of free speech as practised in America *on* Asiatic peoples . . . is consistent if you like, but meaningless', Stuart Chase, *The Tyranny of Words*, 1938.

on, misused for *on to*, e.g., 'I never notice what happens on the road, hanging on the back takes me all my time', a pillion passenger in a motoring case at Willesden (*The Evening News*, Dec. 13, 1937). The first 'on' is correctly used, the second incorrectly; to *hang on* anything is literally to be suspended, but to *hang on to* something is to cling or hold on with difficulty. This misuse, in such a phrase as 'The cat jumped on the table', was obstinately defended by Dean Alford in *The Queen's English*, 3rd ed., 1870, after much argument; despite the popular use of *on*, I believe his defence is indefensible.

on and **upon.** See 'UPON and ON'.

on account of is unnecessary after *cause* or *reason*. For 'The reason is on account of (something or other)', read 'The reason is that . . .' or 'On account of something or other, something else happened'.

on behalf of. See BEHALF OF.

on time; in time. The former is colloquial, and American rather than English. *In time* = 'soon enough'; *on time* = 'punctually'.

on to. See ONTO.

one is often used unnecessarily or, at best, verbosely, as in 'If the opinion expressed is not one worthy of repetition, circulation should be restricted accordingly', examination essay script, June, 1939.

one, use of plural in v. after. The rule is that the formula, *one of* + plural noun or pronoun, requires the ensuing verb to be in the plural. Thus 'He's one of those chaps who plays a lone hand' (E. R. Lorac, *Death of an Author*, 1935) should be '. . . play a lone hand'. The rule becomes clear from an equation:

The cows
The red cows
The cows that *are* red in colour
One of the cows that *are* red in colour
It is one of the cows that are red in colour.

Therefore the *one* requires a singular verb:

One of the cows that *are* red in colour *is* for sale.

one and **he.** Nesfield condemns the use of *his* in: 'There are few demonstrations of affection; one is made to feel that he must trust himself', *The British Weekly*, Jan. 16, 1902. It is strictly correct, but reads awkwardly; it would be better to say 'a man', 'each man' (is made to feel that he must trust himself). Correct, too, is the *one . . . one* mode; I confess that I prefer *one . . . one*, for it is less ambiguous than *one . . . he*.

Compare 'One readily admits that one may be wrong' (unambiguous) with 'One readily admits that he may be wrong'; in the latter it is not clear whether *he* refers to *one* or to a third person. Perhaps the simplest procedure is to determine whether the *one . . . one* or the *person . . . he* or the *you . . . you* mode is to prevail in the expression of your thought, and then to adhere to the mode chosen.

ONE and YOU modes (with a note on the *we* mode).

The *we* mode is—or should be—left to royalty, the Vatican, and editors of newspapers and other periodicals; the popularity of 'We are not amused' has waned.

In friendly or familiar speech and in familiar writing, the *you* mode is permissible and often preferable: but care must be exercised against confusing the personal *you* ('When are you going to Town?') with the generic or impersonal *you* ('When you're dead, you're a long, long time dead').

In formal speeches and addresses, as in formal and literary writing, the *one* mode is preferable ('One does one's best to live the good life; but that best may fall so far short of merit as to seem, in the result, evil; nevertheless, it is one's effort which counts as virtue'). To employ the *one* mode in conversation, unless one does it with consummate skill, may produce a comic effect ('If one does one's best, one does all that one can be expected to do, doesn't one?').

one for *a* or *any*. 'Never has there been one complaint of any person having been robbed there' (John G. Brandon, *The Mail-Van Mystery*, ca. 1937).

one another and **each other.** See 'EACH OTHER and ONE ANOTHER'.

one in (two . . . five, etc.) . . . takes a singular verb, and *two* (or *three* or *five*, etc.) *in* . . . takes a plural verb. The subjects respectively are simply *one* (amplified) and *two*, etc. (amplified), precisely as in *one horse in a million, one horse* is singular, and in *two horses in a thousand, two horses* is plural. In *John o' London's Weekly*, Jan. 6, 1939, 'Jackdaw' defends the advertisement-slogan 'Only one in five *clean* their [properly *his*] teeth . . .' on the unconvincingly ingenious ground that '"one-in-five" contemplates not *one*, but as many *ones* as there are *fives*'. Am I, then, to presume that 'One horse in a million has a purple coat' should be '. . . have . . .' on the ground that there are as many *ones* as *millions*! Compare 'In every five [i.e., in every set of five persons], only one cleans his teeth' and 'Of every five, only one cleans his teeth'.

one or other is incorrect for *the one or the other* or *one or other of them*. 'Bennett . . . fought back [against Thoms], and only the interference of the Cut and Come Again staff prevented serious damage to one or other', E. R. Punshon, *The Dusky Hour*, 1937.

ones for *those* is not wholly wrong, but it is loose and unidiomatic, as in 'Eminence is an accident in [the United States of] America, and it might befall anyone. —It does befall the most unlikely ones. *Ones* who are not prepared for it. . . .

Ones who hoard fame and batten on it', (Paul Horgan, *A Lamp on the Plains*, English edition, 1937).

one's for *his* or other pronoun. In 'Who would not wish to retrace the path of one's hero in the hope of becoming a hero on one's own?', A. R. Orage, *The Art of Reading*, *one's* is not incorrect; it is inelegant. In comparison with Orage's sentence, the revision 'Who would not wish to retrace the path of his hero in the hope of becoming a hero on one's own [account]' is preferable.

oneself and **one's self.** The difference between these two forms is precisely that between *myself* and *my self*, *yourself* and *your self*, *herself* and *her self*, *himself* and *his self*, *ourselves* and *our selves*, *yourselves* and *your selves*, *themselves* and *their selves*. The *oneself*, *yourself*, *themselves* form is that of the reflexive pronoun ('He hurt himself'), the appositive pronoun ('I myself did not understand what was happening'), and—in poetry—the emphatic pronoun ('Myself would work eye dim and finger lame', Tennyson—cited by Onions). In the *my self*, *their selves* form, *self* is synonymous with 'personality or personal entity'.

only, conjunction (approximately = *but*), should have a comma after it, for, otherwise, ambiguities are needlessly created, as in 'I do not know, only he does'. A semi-colon or a colon should precede *only*, as in 'I'd like to do it; only, I don't know how', for a comma looks odd and produces ambiguity, as in 'He came, only, he stopped for but a day'.

only, misplaced. Jespersen, *The Philosophy of Grammar*, 1924, 'The plural *feet* from *foot* was formerly only mentioned as one of a few exceptions to the rule that plurals . . . were formed in *-s*'. Not 'only mentioned' but 'mentioned only as one, etc.'—'We only heard it yesterday' should be 'We heard it only yesterday'. Shakespeare makes this mistake in

The summer's flower is to the summer sweet
Though to itself it only live and die.

There is also ambiguity in the use of *only* where *alone* would be clearer, as in Nesfield's example from Johnson (*Letter to Rev. Mr White*), 'No book has been published since your departure of which much notice is taken. Faction only fills the town with pamphlets, and greater subjects are forgotten.' Nesfield takes

'only' to be an adjective qualifying 'faction', but might it not be an adverb qualifying 'fills'? Coleridge, a careful writer, at least once committed a misplacement: 'The wise only possess ideas; the greater part of mankind are possessed by them' ('Notes on Robinson Crusoe', 1830): properly, 'only the wise'. Even G. K. Chesterton fell into the error of a misplaced *only*, as in 'His black coat looked as if it were only black by being too dense a purple. His black beard looked as if it were only black by being too deep a blue' (*The Man Who Was Thursday*, 1908). Nor are philosophers exempt: 'We can only substitute a clear symbolism for an unprecise one by inspecting the phenomena which we want to describe' (read '. . . one only by inspecting'), Ludwig Wittgenstein, 'Logical Form', in *The Aristotelian Society*: *Supplementary Volume* ix, 1929.—*Merely* is subject to the same vagaries. [[Many American grammarians would suggest that in citing these examples of misplaced *only*, Mr Partridge defeats his own case. They are obviously good English. An account of *only* in accord with the facts of usage will be found in Perrin, *An Index to Usage*, pp. 423–24; see also Curme, *Syntax*, pp. 135–36.]]

only, tautological. See BUT.

only and **only not** for *excepting* or *but*. 'But for all 'is bein' nothink only a stoker, the contractors would at whiles put 'im on for boss', Nevinson, 1895; and again from the same author, 'Mrs Simon would 'ave 'eaved at 'er 'ead whatever else she's 'ad in 'er 'and, only not the baby'. These examples are both illiterate and colloquial, especially Cockney.—Cf. 'He never drinks, only when it's somebody's birthday', where *only* should be *except*.

only alternative. See ALTERNATIVE.

only too is defensible when it is used literally, as in 'One who has committed murder once is, as a rule, only too ready to commit it again'. But it should be avoided as a loose synonym of *very*: for instance, 'Only too pleased to help in a good cause' is absurd. But the finest example comes in 'The Necklace of Pearls', one of the stories in Dorothy Sayers's *Hangman's Holiday*, for the sentence is luxuriantly tautological. '[He also made out a list of the persons to whom the pearls might be useful or desirable. . . .] The search for motives was *only too fatally easy*' (the italics being mine).

onomatopœia. See ECHOISM.

onset should not be used for (first) *sign* as it is in E. R. Lorac, *Death of an Author*, 1935, 'I'm getting stylised, and that's the onset of fossilisation via coagulation'.

onto is misused for *on to* in such a phrase as 'to walk onto the next station'. (Cf. 'INTO for IN TO'.) Wherever the *on* is simply an adverb, *on to* is the correct form. But 'in the sense in which it corresponds to *into*, *onto* is a real compound', pronounced differently from *on to* (*on' to'*), for *onto* is a trochee (*on' to*), as *The O.E.D.* points out.

onus and **gravamen.** The former is 'a burden or charge, a duty or responsibility'; the latter is 'that particular part of an accusation which bears most heavily on the person accused' (*The O.E.D.*). *The onus of proof* (L. *onus probandi*) is the accuser's obligation to prove the accusation he has made. The 'grievance' sense of *gravamen* is obsolescent.

op.cit. See IB.

operative and **operator**, nouns. *Operative* is now confined to workmen in mills or factories; it is common in American usage, whereas English usage prefers *mill-hand* and *workman* respectively. Not that *operative* is not used in Great Britain (and the Empire), but it is a technical word of industry, sociology and politics.

An *operator* may be a surgeon or a dentist, a telephone or telegraph operator, or, especially, one engaged in the buying and selling of stocks, shares, commodities, or in some speculative business; of a workman or mill-hand, it is to be avoided. Based on *The O.E.D.*

ophthalmologist is a person versed in the structure and functions of the eye; an *optician* is a maker of or—the usual current sense—a dealer in optical instruments, an *optometrist* is one who measures and tests vision (without the use of drugs) and adapts lenses to the vision he examines. (*The O.E.D.*)

opinion, in my; I (myself) think, etc. Frequently, these phrases are unnecessary: usually, the context and the circumstances of one's statement make it clear that it is only an opinion; and if one wishes to stress *I*, it is enough to write (or say) '*I* think'.

opponent. See ANTAGONIST.

opposite (adj.) takes *to*, as in 'His house is opposite to mine'; the noun takes *of*, as in 'His is the opposite of that'. Incorrect are 'This is the opposite to that' and 'His house is opposite of mine'. ('His house is the opposite of mine' means something different and requires a particularization.)

opposite (n. and adj.). Constantly mispronounced with long *i*; the correct pronunciation is *oppozit*. See '-ILE and -INE'. [[The pronunciation with long *i* is not heard in American English.]]

opposite and **contrary.** See 'CONTRARY and OPPOSITE'.

optimistic, 'inclined to optimism, i.e., to take a favourable view of circumstances and therefore to hope for the best', should not—as Weseen very properly remarks—be debased to equivalence with *hopeful* on the one hand nor with *cheerful* (or *sanguine*) on the other.

option, have no. This should be avoided, especially in 'I have (or, had) no option but to go'; 'I had to go' is infinitely better.

or and **nor.** Both *or* and *nor* are dissociative, not associative; these conjunctions 'do not link words so as to form a Compound Subject. The Verb is therefore not necessarily Plural.

Either he or she *is* in fault. . . .

Constructions like the following should be avoided: "Neither death nor fortune *were* sufficient to subdue the mind of Cargill" (Fox, *History of James II*).'

If either of the two subjects joined by *or* or by *nor* is plural, the ensuing verb must be plural; stylistically, it is advisable to set the plural subject the nearer to the verb, as in 'Neither Britain nor the Dominions desire war'.

In sentences where the subjects are of different persons (*he* and *I*, *I* and *the dog*, *you* and *your brother*, *you* and *I*), the verb should agree with the subject nearer to it, as in

'Either my brother or I *am* going';
'Neither you nor he *is* in fault';
'Neither he nor we *have* any doubt of it'.

These examples have been taken from *An Advanced English Syntax*, by Dr C. T. Onions, who adds:—'In the majority of cases, however, this form of expression is awkward, and is especially so when the sentence is a question, *e.g.*, "Is he or we wrong?" Avoid the difficulty by saying:

Either my brother is going, or I am.
You are not in fault, nor is he.
He has no doubt of it, nor have we.
Is he wrong, or are we?'

As a general caution:—Where *nor* is preceded by *neither* (whether explicit, or, as in 'Friend nor foe can help me now', implicit), *nor* presents no difficulties; in all other instances, *nor* is—or should be —synonymous with *and not*; but if it isn't, then be careful!

or for *and*. 'As matters stood, no power the police had, or'—properly 'and'—'no action they could take, could prove Granadi to be lying' (John G. Brandon, *The Mail-Van Mystery*, ca. 1937).

oral. See AURAL.

oral and **verbal.** In its general sense, *oral* is applied to that which is 'communicated in or by speech', i.e., 'spoken', as in 'Oral teaching is the best' and 'oral evidence'; it has two technical senses: (a) in Physiology and Medicine, 'of the mouth', 'pertaining to the mouth', the *oral cavity* being the cavity of the mouth; (b) in Theology, 'by or with the mouth', as in *oral communion* (the partaking of bread and wine at the Eucharist).

Verbal is applied to all words, not merely to spoken words, and it emphasizes the letter as opposed to the spirit, as in 'a verbal translation', 'verbal criticisms' (criticism rather of the words than of the ideas and sentiments), 'a difference that was verbal rather than real'; a *verbal agreement*, however, is simply an agreement in speech only. In the sense 'verbatim', it is obsolescent. In Grammar, it is the adjective corresponding to the noun (and notion), *verb.*

orate for 'deliver a speech', 'to speak (in public)', is now either facetious or sarcastic—or both.

ORDER OF SENTENCES AND CLAUSES. There is no point in theorizing on this subject. And no use. Sentences and clauses follow—or should follow— the natural flow of effective presentation: the minor is subordinated to the major: clarity is preserved, ambiguity avoided.

ORDER OF WORDS. Wrong order leads to ambiguity. 'All persons, events and places on the journey as far as Trieste, are entirely fictitious', author's note to Ethel Lina White's *The Wheel Spins*, 1936. Better: 'All persons, events and, as far as Trieste, places, are entirely fictitious'.

'An inquest was held only where the corpse existed, not merely where one was suspected' should read 'not where one was merely suspected', Milton Propper, *The Great Insurance Murders*, 1937.

'. . . She said, as she made room for him on a settee beside her' (Humfrey Jordan, *Roundabout*, 1935) should be '. . . made room for him beside her on a settee'.

'I saw a man in the room, who looked very ill' should be 'I saw, in the room, a man, who [or, a man that] looked very ill' or 'In the room I saw a man, who [or, a man that] looked very ill'.

A. After those examples, which may serve as a warning to the incautious, we shall proceed to a few general remarks, based on ch. xvii, 'Word-Order', in vol. iii of Curme's *A Grammar of the English Language*, 1931.

'In English', says Dr George O. Curme, 'there are three word-orders: the verb in the second, the third, or the first place.'

I. *Verb in Second or Third Place.*

'The most common order is: subject in the first place, verb in the second: "*The boy loves* his dog". This is called *normal order.*' Even when a sentence is inverted, it is usual to keep the verb in the second place; inversion, by the way, is now common only when it conveys interrogation or ensures emphasis. 'Bitterly did we repent our decision', 'Never had I dreamed of such a thing', 'Only two had merciful death released from their sufferings', 'When did you meet him?', 'Where did you say she put it?', 'Only when the artist understands these psychological principles can he work in harmony with them' (Spencer).

'When the principal proposition'—i.e., the principal clause—'is inserted in a direct quotation or follows it, the principal verb may sometimes still, in accordance with the old inverted order, . . . stand before the subject, but it is now more common [? usual] . . . to regulate the word-order by the modern group stress, so that the heavier word, be it subject or verb, stands last in the group.' Contrast: '"Harry", *continued the old man*, "before you choose a wife, you must know my position"' with: '"George", *she exclaimed*, "this is the happiest moment of my life"'. Contrast also: '"You have acted selfishly", *was her cold retort*' with: '"You have acted selfishly", *she replied*'.

Compare too: 'The wind whistled and moaned as if, *thought Michael*, all the devils in hell were trying to break into the holy building' (Compton Mackenzie) and 'The wind whistled and moaned as if, *it sounded to him*, all the devils in hell...' To the latter arrangement, which Mr Compton Mackenzie would never have tolerated, it must, however, be objected that it is ambiguous.

Another type of inversion is that in which the subject comes at the end for emphasis. 'Now comes *my best trick*', 'To the list may be added *the following names*', and, from Galsworthy's *The Man of Property*, 'Fast into this perilous gulf of night walked *Bosinney* and fast after him walked *George*', where there is a lesser stress on 'fast' (in both instances).

Inversions are the usual reason for a verb to go into the third place, as in 'Very grateful they *were* for my offer', 'Lucky it *is* that we know her name', 'This threat he *was* unable to carry out'. The verb goes into the third place also in exclamations. Thus, 'What cheek he *has!*', 'What good friends horses *have been* to us for thousands of years!' The old inverted order, however, is retained in 'How pleasant *is* this hill where the road widens!'

Dr Curme sums up in this way:—'The normal word-order [i.e., the subject before the verb, with the complement, adverb, or object after the verb] has become the form of expression suited to the mind in its normal condition of steady activity and easy movement, from which it only departs'—better, 'departs only' —'under the stress of emotion, or for logical reasons, or in conformity to fixed rules'.

II. *Verb in the First Place.*

In modern English the first place in the sentence—an emphatic position—is occupied by the verb 'in expressions of will containing an imperative and often in those containing a volitive subjunctive, also in questions that require *yes* or *no* for an answer', as in:

'*Hand* me that book!'
'*Were* he only here!'
'*Come* what will.'
'*Did* he go?'

B. From these generalities, let us pass to the position of the adverb in the sentence or clause and to the order of adverbs or

adverbial phrases when there are two or more.

For the splitting of the infinitive (*to earnestly pray*), see SPLIT INFINITIVE.

*The fear of an imaginary split infinitive has caused this monstrosity (cited by Fowler): 'The awkward necessity for getting to work and working as hard as possible and with hearty goodwill *altogether* seems to be forgotten', for . . . '. . . seems to be altogether forgotten'.

'Spare the infinitive, split the verb', as Wilson Follett says. In a compound verb (*have seen*) with an adverb, that adverb comes between the auxiliary and the participle ('I have *never* seen her'); or, if there are two or more auxiliaries, immediately after the first auxiliary ('I have *always* been intending to go to Paris'); that order is changed only to obtain emphasis, as in 'I never have seen her' (with stress on 'have') or 'Never, never have I seen her'. Failure to ensure the necessary emphasis accounts for such an infelicity as '*No one has probably seen you*—so you can go home in peace' (a detective novel, 1937), instead of '*Probably no one has seen you* . . .' There is, however, a tendency to move an adverb from its rightful and natural position for inadequate reasons, as in 'Oxford must *heartily* be congratulated on their victory', where 'heartily' modifying 'must' instead of 'be congratulated' is as absurd as—if 'certainly' was substituted for 'heartily'—'certainly' would be if placed after 'be': logically, 'must *heartily* be congratulated' (instead of 'must be *heartily* congratulated') is no less absurd than 'must be *certainly* congratulated' (instead of 'must *certainly* be congratulated'). Or as in 'The importance which *quite rightly* has been given to their meetings', instead of 'The importance which has quite rightly been given . . .'

On the same footing are the errors in 'It would be a different thing if the scheme had been *found fundamentally to be faulty*, but that is not the case' (where '. . . *found to be fundamentally faulty* . . .' would be correct) and 'In these times it is rare that the First Lord of the Treasury *also is Prime Minister*' (where *is also* would be correct).

To separate a transitive verb from its object leads to awkwardness and generally discomfits the reader. 'I had to *second by all the means in my power*

*See especially *The Position of Adverbs*, S.P.E. Tract, No. xv.

diplomatic action' should be 'I had, by
all the means in my power, to second
diplomatic action' or, less forcibly and
less happily, 'I had to second diplomatic
action by all the means in my power'.
There the adverbial phrase is long and
the error glaring. (Cf. 'How right were
those peoples who *filled with lamentations
the house* when a female child was born',
Richard Aldington, *Women Must Work*,
1934,—a passage exemplifying Gallic
influence, English idiom demanding 'filled
the house with lamentations', which is
also euphonious.) But the rule holds
good, however short the adverb. 'Have
you *interpreted rightly the situation*?'
should be 'Have you rightly interpreted
the situation?' 'I should *advise, then, the
boy* to take plenty of exercise' should
be 'I should, then [better: therefore],
advise the boy to take plenty of exercise'.
'It is probable that the Allies will *regard
favourably Belgium's request'* should be
'It is probable that the Allies will favourably regard Belgium's request'.

'There are', Fowler cautions us, 'conditions that justify the separation, the
most obvious being when a lengthy
object would keep an adverb that is not
suitable for the early position too remote
from the verb ... But anyone who applies
this principle must be careful not to
reckon as part of the object words that
either do not belong to it at all or are
unessential to it.' In 'These men are
*risking every day with intelligence and
with shrewdness fortunes on what they
believe*', *fortunes* is the object; not *fortunes on what they believe*. Put *fortunes*
immediately after *risking*. But the sentence needs re-ordering: 'Every day,
though with intelligence and shrewdness,
these men are risking fortunes on what
they believe'. In 'I can set most of the
shocks that flesh is heir to at defiance'
(Joan Jukes, 'On the Floor', in *New
Stories*, 1934), *at defiance* should follow
set, not only because it is too far separated from its verb but also because *set at
defiance* is a verbal unit—*defy*. In
'Failure of the Powers to enforce their
will as to the Albanian frontier would
expose to the ridicule of all the restless
elements in East Europe their authority,
which, as it is, is not very imposing',
*their authority, which, as it is, is not very
imposing* should immediately follow *expose*. But had *to the ridicule* . . . *East
Europe* been *to ridicule* (two words instead of eleven), then the sentence would

properly have read 'Failure of the Powers
to enforce their will as to the Albanian
frontier would expose to ridicule their
authority, which, as it is, is not very
imposing', for to put the very long object
in front of the short adverbial phrase
would be to remove the adverb too far
from the verb.

The fear of splitting the infinitive has
been so insidious that it has become a
fear of 'splitting' even a gerund, as in
'To reduce the infantry for the sake
unduly of increasing the artillery', where
the sensible (and correct) order is '. . .
sake of unduly increasing'.

Many of the preceding examples seem
to have sprung from wrong ideas of
correctness. Probably, however, the most
frequent cause of error is that which one
would expect: carelessness. (For the misplacing of *only*, see 'ONLY, misplaced'.)
'The Freudian theories in the last few
years have influenced the novelists
greatly' should be 'In the last few years
the Freudian theories have greatly influenced the novelists', for the original
position of *in the last few years* makes it
appear that the Freudian theories began
to exercise an influence not until the
middle-1930's; *greatly* was also out of
position. 'It has been implied that Germany is a collectivist State, or, if not,
that it has at least far advanced in Socialism' should be '. . . has at least advanced far in Socialism'.

See, too, the four examples set at the
head of this article: all four result from
carelessness, although the fourth might
have been given in the FALSE AGREE-
MENT article.

These misplacings of the adverb (or
the adverbial phrase) exemplify the need
of caution. But all errors exemplify that
need: and errors of word and errors of
syntax are instructively frequent in the
work of those popular authors who turn
out three or four or five books a year—
often under two (or even three or more)
names.

But adverbs may depart from the positions recommended in the foregoing
paragraphs—if there is a good reason.
The best reason of all is clarity: but then,
we hardly need give examples of this. The
reason next in importance is that of
emphasis. 'I met your father *yesterday*'
is the normal order; 'I met *yesterday* your
father', as we have already seen, is abnormal and unidiomatic in English
(though correct in French); '*Yesterday*

I met your father' stresses the day—the time—*yesterday*; 'I *yesterday* met your father' is now affected, although it was common enough in the 18th Century ('The jury now will examine the [article]', *The Sessions Papers of the Old Bailey*, 1751).

The *yesterday* example comes from Geo. O. Curme's *Syntax*, where it is also pointed out that sometimes the adverb (or adverbial phrase) modifies, not the verb alone but the sentence as a whole. 'In this case the adverbial element usually precedes the verb, verbal phrase, or predicate noun or adjective' (i.e., the object or the complement), as in 'He *evidently* thought so' or, more strongly, '*Evidently* he thought so'; 'He not only believes in such books, but he *even* reads them to his children'; 'He *absolutely* lives from hand to mouth', where 'lives *absolutely*' would, at best, change the sense or, at worst, create confusion; 'She *always* lets him have his own way' or, more emphatically, '*Always* she lets him have his own way'.

For adverbs such as *not*, *never*, *nowhere*, see NEGATION.

ordinance; ordnance; ordonnance. An *ordinance* is a regulation, by-law, rule, that is less permanent, less constitutional, less general than a law or a statute; especially a municipal or other local enactment; also it is a religious observance, and a decree, and a dispensation of Providence or merely of destiny.

As a military term, *ordnance* = 'cannon' (mounted guns); but the chief sense of the term is, 'the public establishment concerned with the military stores and materials, the management of the artillery, etc.'

Ordonnance is a systematic arrangement, e.g., of parts or features in a piece of architectural or artistic work, or of literary material; Sir Joshua Reynolds spoke of 'disproportionate ordonnance of parts' (*The O.E.D.*).

orient (v.). See ORIENTATE.

Oriental and **Eastern.** *Eastern* refers to the East portion (or part or region or land) of any part of the world; *Oriental* only to the countries, regions, etc., lying to the east of the Mediterranean, and especially to Asia or rather to Asia-without-Siberia. *Eastern Europe, the Orient, Oriental lands, Oriental drugs,* and similar expressions require a capital letter, but one may with propriety drop the capital both in 'the eastern part of the island', 'the eastern extremity of Great Britain', and in *oriental* as an adjective in astrology or astronomy, or in *oriental stitch* (a technicality in needlework).

orientate and **orient** (v.). (Noun: *orientation.*) As an intransitive, 'to face in some specific direction, originally and especially to the east' (an ecclesiastical term), *orientate* is correct; in all other senses, *to orient* is preferable. One can *orient* one's behaviour, one's conscience, one's ambition, or another person, or one can, reflexively, *orient oneself*, i.e., guide or direct it, him, oneself, or to get one's bearings, put another on the right path or track. [[*Orientation course*, American pedagoguese for an introductory, general or historical study, usually of the social sciences, designed for college freshmen or sophomores.]]

ostensible and **ostensive.** The former = 'declared, avowed; pretended or merely professed', as in 'Her ostensible demand was for English aid in her restoration to the throne' (J. R. Green), 'His ostensible reason was that . . .' *Ostensive* is to be avoided in this sense, both because it is obsolescent and because it may set up an ambiguity. In Philosophy, *ostensive* = 'declarative', as in 'Reason is heuristic, not ostensive: it asks questions but does not supply the answers'; applied to a proof, it means 'specious'; in Logic it = 'directly demonstrative', 'setting forth a general principle manifestly including the proposition to be proved'. (*The O.E.D.*)

other, omitted after *any*. See GENITIVE, VAGARIES OF THE, last paragraph.

other, used intrusively. *Other* is incorrectly and ambiguously introduced in the following (quoted by Nesfield from *The Daily Telegraph* in August, 1900): 'The Jingo element is strong in London, stronger than it is in the *other* provincial towns.'

other, the. Avoid clumsy use. How awkward is the following! 'While one man was baling out the water from his canoe, another tipped up the boat so that it shipped bucketsful. It was the fun-maker who suffered, for *the other* man got out and landed while *the other* sank with the canoe', Violet O. Cressy-Marcks, *Up the Amazon and Over the Andes*, 1932.

other . . . except. An article in *The News Chronicle*, March 4, 1938, speaks of 'every other country except ours'.

Our country, to be excepted from, must first be one of those 'others', which is absurd. The sense is expressed either by 'every country except (or, but) ours', or by 'every other country than ours', which is correct but clumsy.

other than is the correct form (as also the similar combinations, *different from*, *opposite to*, *contrasted with*). In *other than*, etc., writers occasionally forget that *other*, *different*, etc., are adjectives, not adverbs. Thus *other than* should be *apart from* in this sentence by C. G. Macartney in *The Observer*, July 31, 1938: 'Other than that'—a missed catch—'the batsmen were quite comfortable'.

other than that, misused for *apart* (American: *aside*) *from that*. 'A particularly smart job—with the exception of the murder of this poor fellow. . . . Other than that, I'm bound to say that I quite appreciate a neat bit of work' (John G. Brandon, *The Regent Street Raid*, ca. 1938).

other to. *Other to* is occasionally misused for *opposite to* or *across from*, as in 'On the other side to mine', 'In the other room to mine'.

others, of all, is a form of false comparison. The 'he' referred to in 'he was the best (cricketer) of all others' is not *one of the others*, but *best of all* (the cricketers), or *better than any of the others*. This illogicality was frequently committed by Southey, Thackeray and many other esteemed writers, but it is unjustifiable. Nesfield (*Errors in English Composition*, 1903) puts it thus: 'The thing to which the Superlative refers must be *included* amongst things of its own class; otherwise no such comparison can be made'. E.g., 'The place which of all others in the wide world she had wished most to see' (Southey, *The Doctor*).

othertimes (at other times) is incorrect; *otherwhere* is literary; *otherwhile(s)*, when not dialectal, is archaic.

otherwise for *other* is misused. 'What he expected from life, otherwise than a day-by-day relish of experience and some eventual recognition of his disinterestedness, could not be seen'. Frank Swinnerton, *Harvest Comedy*, 1937.

ought (n.). See AUGHT.

ought is stronger than *should*. 'You ought to do it' is stronger than 'You should do it'. See also the entry, PAST SUBJUNCTIVE . . .

ought, didn't — hadn't — shouldn't. '"He shouldn't ought to behave like that. It's hardly decent"', Ernest Raymond, *We, the Accused*, 1935 (in dialogue), for 'he ought not to behave like that'. *Ought* never requires the auxiliary, the use of which can lead to the most ridiculous grammatical confusion, as in: 'He didn't ought to have done it, had he?' or 'He hadn't ought . . ., did he?'

-ourous for **-orous**, as in Galsworthy, *The Silver Spoon*, 1926, 'The rumourous town still hummed', is incorrect.

ourselves. See MYSELF.

out loud, colloquial, is stylistically inferior to *aloud*, as in 'She sobbed out loud'; also it tends to be ambiguous.

outcast (one who has suffered expulsion from society) and **outcaste** (one who has lost caste or has no caste) have often been confused.

outdoor is the adjective, **outdoors** the adverb, as in 'She put on her outdoor clothes to go outdoors into the rain and wind'. Oddly enough, the corresponding noun is *outdoors*, as in 'The outdoors is stimulating' although *out-of-doors* is perhaps more usual ('He prefers the out-of-doors to the most comfortable house').

outline is a skeleton preliminary plan; **summary** an abridged restatement.

outside of is incorrect in 'Outside of the house, he could see quite well; inside of the house, he could hardly see'. Read 'Outside the house . . ., inside the house . . .', for the prepositions are *outside* and *inside*. [[In American usage, *outside of* and *inside of* may occur in informal writing as well as in conversation.]]

outskirt (adj.); **outskirts** (n.) (the singular being obsolete).

outward and **outwards.** The former is both adjective and adverb; the latter is only adverb. Of the two adverbs, *outward* is used of position or situation, to mean 'on the outside; without', as in 'Sheepskins, with the wool outward' (Defoe), although *outside* is now more usual; and 'from the soul or mind into external actions or conditions', as in 'His life radiated from within outward', but the adverb for the literal 'in an outward direction; towards that which is outside or without', is *outwards*, as in 'To cut a semicircular flap from within outwards'. (*The O.E.D.*)

over for *about* or *concerning* is catachrestic or, at best, very colloquial, as in 'He was anxious over your misfortune', 'He was happy over your good fortune'.

over should, to avoid ambiguity, be *for over* in the following: 'It was audacious, perhaps foolhardy. But not too daring for a determined man who at last had an opportunity to satisfy a grudge he had nursed over a decade' (actually, thirteen years at least), Milton Propper, *Murder at the Polls*, 1936.—*Over* in the time-sense is normally 'for the duration of', or 'spread over', not, as in the example, 'more than'.

over and **above**. See 'ABOVE and OVER'.

OVER-EMPHASIS, OVER-STRESS-ING, etc. See TAUTOLOGY. But we give one example here, just to show what we mean:—'The general appearance of the road—as regards traffic and pedestrians—presented quite a usual aspect', John Ross, *The Moccasin Man*, 1936.—But the more usual kind of over-stressing is that which is present in HYPERBOLE, *q.v.*

overlay and **overlie**. The latter = 'to lie over or upon', lit. (as in Geology) or fig.; hence, 'to smother by lying upon', more generally *overlay* ('She overlaid her child'). *Overlay* is much wider in its application: e.g., 'to cover *with*', 'to deck all over', 'to conceal or obscure as if by covering up', 'to overburden'. Do not use *overlay* in the first sense of *overlie*. *Overlay—overlaid—overlaid; overlie—overlay—overlain.*

overlook and **look over**. The latter = 'to look at, to inspect, to read through'; the former = 'to look over the top of', 'to look down upon', (of a place) 'to command a view of'; also, 'to disregard, to ignore; to fail to see'.

overly (for *excessively*, as in 'overly enthusiastic') is an Americanism; *over* ('over ready to . . .') or *excessively* is preferred in the British Empire.

oversight; omission; supervision. *Oversight* = 'supervision, superintendence; care or management', but is slightly obsolescent in this sense. Its dominant current sense is 'failure or omission to see', hence 'inadvertence', hence 'a mistake of inadvertence', as in 'It may have been an oversight'. (*The O.E.D.*)

overwhelming is misapplied when it is used as a mere synonym of *vast*, as in 'Though it can be said that, in the overwhelming majority of cases, secret messages can be deciphered and read by the trained expert, the fact remains that the time factor may make the decipherment valueless', Nigel Morland, *The Conquest*

of *Crime*, 1937. So, too, *an* (or, *the*) *overwhelming proportion of* is infelicitous for *by far the larger part of* or *the vast majority of.*

overflowed; overflown. The preterite of *overflow* is *overflowed*; so too is the past participle, in current usage. Reserve *overflown* for *overfly*, 'to fly over', hence 'to surpass in flight' (i.e., to fly faster or further or higher).

owing to. See CONJUNCTIONS, DISGUISED.

ozone should be used neither as a synonym of *air* (especially, good or healthy air), as so many advertisers use it; nor of *oxygen*, for properly it = 'an altered condition of oxygen, existing in a state of condensation, with a particularly pungent and refreshing odour'. Mortimer Collins employed it correctly in 'Exhilarated by the fresh ozone of the mountains', though he need not have used *fresh* at all. (*The O.E.D.*) [[The misuse of *ozone*, once so common in advertisements, is now rare in American English.]]

P

pacifist and **passivist**. A *pacifist* opposes war, proposes peace (though not necessarily at any price). A *passivist*—not in *The O.E.D.*, but duly recorded in the new edition of *Webster's*—is 'a passive resister' (of anything including war). There is, in cultured usage, a tendency to make *pacifist* an active, *passivist* an inactive, indeed a negatively passive, opponent of war.

pact is 'an agreement made between persons or parties, a compact' (*The O.E.D.*): a dignified word, it should not be debased to trivial uses. Properly, it is applied to *formal* agreements; to solemn or weighty or important or significant agreements.

pailfuls and **pails full**. See the remark at BASKETFULS.

palate; palette; pallet; pallette. *Palate* is 'the roof of the mouth', hence one's sense of taste; *palette*, that tablet of wood (or occasionally porcelain) on which an artist lays and mixes his colours; *pallet* is a straw bed, hence a mean or humble bed or couch; and *pallette* (but more usually *pallet*) is a piece of armour for the head, hence in Scottish, the head or pate. (*The O.E.D.*)

Pall Mall is pronounced *pell-mell* (as

in the game); **(the) Mall** (like *mall*, 'mallet') is pronounced *maul*. See MALL.

palmistry. See CHIROGNOMY.

panacea should not be used for a cure for a particular ill, for *panacea* means 'a catholicon', i.e., 'a universal remedy'. Therefore to speak of 'a panacea for gout' is absurd.

panegyric is not merely *praise*, but either a public speech, or a public writing, in praise of a person, thing, achievement; a laudatory discourse; 'a formal or at least an elaborate eulogy', or, derivatively, 'laudation' or any 'elaborate praise'. (*The O.E.D.*)

panic (v.i. and v.t.), has present participle *panicking* and past participle (and tense) *panicked*.

panta- for *panto-*. Wrong spellings of pantomime are *pantamime* and *pantamine* and *pantomine*.

paragon and **parergon.** A *paragon* is 'a model or pattern of excellence', whether person ('a paragon of virtue') or thing ('the paragon of easy chairs'); for things, it is now slightly obsolescent. It has two technical senses: 'a perfect diamond that weighs more than 100 carats'; in printing, 'two-line Long Primer'. A *parergon* is 'a literary by-work' (done at an idle period or off one's usual track) or 'employment supplementary or secondary to one's principal or recognized work'; as a term in 17th and 18th Century painting, it meant 'a grace, embellishment, ornament'. The plurals are *paragons*, *parerga*; but *parergons* will be correct if ever *parergon* comes into general use.

The adjectives are *paragon* and *parergic.*

PARAGRAPHING. In the words of that eminent philosopher and rhetorician, Alexander Bain (1818–1903), 'The division of discourse next above the Sentence is the Paragraph. It is a collection, or series, of sentences, with unity of purpose'—an orderly collection, a natural sequence.

'Between one paragraph and another, there is a greater break in the subject than between one sentence and another. The internal arrangement comes under laws that are essentially the same as in the sentence, but on a greater scale.

'The Paragraph laws are important, not only for their own sake, but also for their bearing on an entire composition. They are the general principles that must regulate the structure of sections, chapters, and books. The special laws applying to different kinds of prose composition—Description, Narrative, Exposition, and Persuasion—cannot supersede those general principles; they only deal with the matter in hand from a higher point of view. Apart from the application of these higher laws, we may adapt an old homely maxim, and say, "Look to the Paragraphs, and the Discourse will take care of itself"': each paragraph (or, on a larger scale, each section of a chapter) corresponds to a point to be made, described, narrated; to a head of discourse, a topic, an aspect. If you establish the ordonnance of your theme, you will find that there is one order superior to all others; in establishing the order in which you desire to make the points of your exposition or your argument, to set forth the incidents in your narrative, the aspects in your description, you simultaneously and inevitably establish the division into paragraphs and the order of those paragraphs. That is the nearest sensible thing to a general rule.

But here are several minor precautions.

I. If a paragraph shows signs of becoming tediously long, break it up into two or three or even four parts, linked one to another and casting back to the first head by such a conjunction or such a conjunctival phrase (e.g., 'in such circumstances as these, it was natural that . . .') as indicate the dependence of the second, third, fourth of the theme-involved paragraphs on the first and the relation of the second to the first, the third to the second, the fourth to the third.

II. Do not shred the story or the discourse, the essay or the whatnot into a sequence of very short paragraphs, for this is an irritating trick beloved of slick journalists.

III. But to interpose a one-sentence paragraph at intervals—at longish intervals—is prudent. Such a device helps the eye and enables the reader (especially if 'the going is heavy') to regain his breath between one impressive or weighty or abstruse paragraph and the next.

IV. If the development of the theme is logical, natural, easy, one paragraph follows on its predecessor so inevitably that a conjunction may often be unnecessary. A long procession of *but*, *however*, *nevertheless*, *therefore*, *moreover* can become a weariness—and generally does.

V. Examine the paragraphing in the longer articles of this book. I do not pretend that it is perfect, but I believe that it is both simple and adequate.

⟦An interesting treatise is E. H. Lewis, *The History of the English Paragraph* (Chicago 1894), referred to by Perrin.⟧

paramount ⟨either 'superior' or, in modern usage, 'supreme' in rank or authority; hence, 'preëminent'), as in 'of paramount importance', is sometimes misused for *tantamount* (to), 'equivalent (to)'.

paraphrase, misused. 'The young man was fully clothed—to complete the paraphrase—presumably in his right mind', Cecil Freeman Gregg, *Tragedy at Wembley*, 1936. Presumably *parallel* is intended.

parasol is a (carried) sunshade; an *umbrella* is a (carried or not carried) protection against rain or sun. The distinction between *parasol* and *sunshade* is that the former is small and umbrella-shaped; the latter may be anything designed to protect against the sun's rays, be it visor, large umbrella, lattice or awning.

parentheses. See BRACKET.

PARENTHESIS, USE AND DANGERS OF. The danger of losing the thread of grammatical sequences is illustrated by the following sentence from Sir Arthur Evans's Lecture, 'The Minoan World', Oct. 16, 1936:—

'But the present Exhibition, arranged by him in connexion with the Jubilee of the British School of Athens (though the results of the discoveries at Knossos itself naturally still form the main theme on an amplified scale), the object has been to supply as far as possible the materials for a general survey of the Minoan culture in its widest range, etc.' Charles C. Boyd, in *Grammar for Great and Small*, 1928, hit the nail on the head when he remarked that 'The test of a parenthesis is whether the other words make sense without it'. See also PUNCTUATION.

pardon me! See EXCUSE ME!

parergon. See at PARAGON . . .

parson, technically, is 'a holder of a parochial benefice in full possession of its rights and dues; a rector'. Hence, colloquially, any beneficed clergyman —any clergyman, whether Anglican or Nonconformist: but in this extended, this colloquial sense, it is—except in rural use—slightly, occasionally very, depreciatory ('dyslogistic', as the philologists and grammarians have it). In favourable or neutral contexts, therefore, *parson* is to be avoided, as of course it is also in formal speech or writing except in its technical sense. Based on *The O.E.D.* ⟦In American usage, *parson* may have a familiar, affectionate connotation. *Parsonage* is in more regular use.⟧

part: whether singular or plural. See NUMBER.

part, misused for *some*, as in 'Part of the students fail their examinations'. See also PORTION.

partake of is not simply 'to *take*': it means 'to take one's share of', 'to share in'. 'Being alone, I consoled myself by partaking of a glass of stout' is silly; 'Your papa invited Mr R. to partake of our lowly fare' (Dickens) is sensible.

partiality. See PREJUDICE.

partially, wrongly used for *partly*. Mr Harold Herd in *Watch Your English* gives an excellent example of the ambiguity caused by this misuse: 'The appeal was partially heard before the Lord Chief Justice . . . yesterday', where the proper meaning of 'partially' is *unfairly*, with a bias towards one side. However, the adj. *partial*, 'incomplete', as in *a partial success*, can hardly be avoided. Don Marquis, that admirable and witty American writer, in *The Almost Perfect State*, 1927, falls into this error: 'They will work all the harder on account of all this, and they will get more work done in four hours than is done in eight hours now—partially because they will be more vigorous nervously and mentally and physically, partially because they will each be working for himself, partially because they will use better machines than exist today, etc.'

PARTICIPIAL PHRASES, DISCONNECTED. 'Upon landing at the quay the little town presented a strong contrast in styles', Hulbert Footner, *The Obeah Murders*, 1937.—'Listening, there was much to stimulate both mind and imagination' (Arthur Bryant, *The Illustrated London News*, Jan. 8, 1938).— 'After walking about two miles from Llangollen, a narrow valley opens on the right', W. W. Davies, *A Wayfarer in Wales*, 1930.

For a fuller treatment, see CONFUSED PARTICIPLES.

PARTICIPLES, FUSED. See FUSED PARTICIPLES.

party should not, in formal English, be used for *person*: 'The old party looked ill' should be 'The old man'—or 'woman' —'looked ill'. A *party* is a group or body of persons; in legal phraseology, *party* does not denote 'one person': it denotes each side (one or more persons) in a contract or an action. [With acknowledgements to Mr Harold Herd.]

pass, misused for *meet*. A train *passes* another going in the same direction; *meets* one that is coming in the opposite direction.

passable and **passible**. The former = 'traversable or viable', hence 'tolerable', '(almost) satisfactory'; the latter is a theological technicality, meaning 'capable of suffering', 'exposed to suffering'.

passed and **past**. *Past* was formerly the common spelling of the past participle of *pass*, but this use is now obsolete and is confusing: *passed* is the past participle, and *past* is adj. or noun. We write 'the past month' 'in the past', but 'the month has passed quickly'.

passion and **Passion**. The former is now current in two main senses: '(violent) anger' and 'amorous feeling' (hence 'a vehement liking or enthusiasm' for, e.g., philately); the latter is 'the sufferings of Jesus Christ on the Cross (also often including the Agony in Gethsemane)'. (*The O.E.D.*)

passivist. See PACIFIST.

PAST SUBJUNCTIVE FOR PRESENT (OR FUTURE) INDICATIVE or for **PRESENT SUBJUNCTIVE** 'softens the form of the expression', as in 'You *should*' for 'It is your duty to' (do something); '*Would* you help him?' for '*Will* you help him?'; '*Might* I say what I think?' for '*May* . . .?'; '*Could* you come a little earlier than we arranged?' for '*Can* you . . .?' The same applies to 'You *should* not speak so disrespectfully of your parents' for 'You *ought* not to speak. . . .'
Based on *The O.E.D.*'s remarks at *ought*, v., iii, 5b.

pastor should not be used as an exact synonym of *minister* or *clergyman*; it should be restricted to a 'minister in charge of a church or congregation, with particular reference to the spiritual care of his "flock"' (*The O.E.D.*). [[When one American church member meets another, he may ask, 'Who is your . . .?' (minister, pastor, priest, rector). Methodists and Baptists seem to prefer *pastor* or, old style, *preacher*; Presbyterians, *minister* or *pastor*; Congregationalists, *minister*; Episcopalians, *minister* or *rector* (High Churchmen, sometimes, *priest*); Roman Catholics, *priest*. *Preacher* and *parson* (Protestant) are now old-fashioned. *Clergyman* is usually Episcopalian, though *clergy* is a common term. The Methodist pastor lives in a *parsonage*; the Presbyterian and the Congregationalist minister in a *manse*; the Episcopalian rector and the Catholic rector (priest in charge, sometimes *pastor*) in a *rectory*.]]

pastoral; pastorale; pastourelle; pastural. The second and third are nouns only, *pastorale* being a musical term for an instrumental composition in rustic style or of pastoral scene, or an opera or cantata with a rustic subject, and not to be taken as a variant of *pastourelle*, a quadrille dance-figure resembling the dance of shepherds and shepherdesses. *Pastural* means 'of pasture, belonging to pasture, characteristic of pasture'; *pastoral* = 'used for pasture' ('Epirus is essentially a pastoral country', Grote), and also 'of or pertaining to shepherds; relating to, occupied in, consisting of, (the care of) flocks and/or herds', as in 'pastoral farms', 'Agricultural and Pastoral Show', hence 'of a Church pastor' or 'relating to the guidance of a "flock" of Christians', and as a term in music, art, literature, 'setting forth the shepherd's life', with the corresponding noun *pastoral*, (Literature) 'a play, a dialogue, a poem, dealing with the life of shepherds, or, more widely, the rural life', and (Art) 'a picture of the same or a similar kind'. (*The O.E.D.*)

pathos. See BATHOS.

patina and **patine**. The latter is the French form of the former in its current sense, 'a film or incrustation produced by oxidation on the surface of old bronze —hence, a similar alteration of the surface of other substances, especially marble or flint. It is of a green colour and esteemed as an ornament' (*The O.E.D.*). But Louis Bromfield went, perhaps, a little too far when, in *The Strange Case of Miss Annie Spragg*, 1928, he wrote of 'a copper bell-handle . . . covered with a patine of verdigris'.
As = *paten*, the Eucharistic dish, *patine* is obsolete. *Patine* may, however, win its way as the verb corresponding to *patina*.

'**patron** of the arts', but not of a greengrocer or a bookmaker. Tradesmen have *customers*, professional men have *clients* —though doctors have *patients*.

See also 'CLIENT and CUSTOMER', and cf. the following entry.

patronize for *trade with* (a grocer) or *at* (his shop) is commercial pretentiousness.

pavement is the usual English, *sidewalk* the usual American term for 'the paved footway at the side of a street, as distinct from the roadway' (*The O.E.D.*). If at the side of a country road, it is a *footpath* in England, a *path* in America.

pay away; pay down; pay off; pay out; pay over; pay up. To *pay down* is to pay part of a due or a debt, also to pay on the spot or immediately; *pay off* is to pay a person in full and discharge him, whereas *pay up* is to pay in full for something or to discharge a debt in full; to *pay over* is to hand money (*to* a person) either in part or, less generally, in full; *pay away* is pay unexpectedly or reluctantly or with difficulty or (e.g., of a bill) to a third party; and *pay out* is to pay a sum from one's account or a fund, or to get rid of a person (e.g., an undesirable partner) by paying (e.g., his share of the capital). Based on *The O.E.D.*

peaceable and **peaceful.** The former is now restricted to persons, their character, their actions, their feelings, etc., as in 'She shall give security for her peaceable intentions' (Goldsmith) and 'The inhabitants are shepherds, . . . simple, peaceable, and inoffensive' (Elphinstone). *Peaceful*, 'full of or characterized by peace; undisturbed, untroubled, quiet', is applied to periods, occasions, countries, scenes, parties, states of mind, appearances, faces, as in 'The Thames Valley affords many peaceful scenes and vistas', 'In death, peaceful is the face that in life was either anxious or stormy', 'Peaceful Italy involv'd in arms' (Dryden). (*The O.E.D.*)

peculiar(ly) is better avoided in the sense of *particular(ly)* or *especial(ly)*; e.g., Helen Harris, 1891, 'The Arabs regard the spot as peculiarly sacred' (*The O.E.D.*).

-ped, as in the adjectives (hence nouns) *biped, triped, quadruped*, means 'footed' (*biped* = two footed); 'five-footed' is *quinqueped* (noun) or *quinquepedal* (adjective), 'eight-footed' is *octoped*, 'ten-footed' is *decapod*. The series extends to *multiped* (many-footed), which may be more or less than *centiped*

(hundred-footed, the insect being a *centipede*) and is generally less than *milliped* (thousand-footed, the insect being a *millepede*). But *centipede* and *millipede* are also adjectives. In *-ped*, the *e* is short; in *-pede* it is long.

PEDANTRY. 'O, in what a mightie vaine am I now against Horn-bookes! Here before all this companie, I professe myself an open enemy to Inke and paper. Ile make it good upon the Accidence body, that in speech is the devils Pater noster: Nownes and Pronounes, I pronounce you as traitors to boyes buttockes, Syntaxis and Prosodia, you are tormentors of wit, and good for nothing but to get a schoolmaster two pence a weeke. Hang copies, flye out phrase books, let pennes be turned to picktooths: bowles, cards and dice, you are the true liberal sciences, Ile ne're be Goosequil, gentlemen, while I live.'

Thomas Nashe, *Summers last Will and Testament* (written in 1593).

Pedantry, says *The O.E.D.*, is 'the character, habit of mind, or mode of proceeding, characteristic of a pedant' (one who overrates book-learning or technical knowledge); mere learning without judgement or discrimination; conceit or unseasonable display of learning or technical knowledge'; hence 'undue insistence on forms or details; slavish adherence to rule, theory, or precedent, in connexion with a particular profession or practice'. An alternative definition is the Viscount Stranford's (ca. 1869), 'Undue stress laid on insignificant detail, and over-valuation of petty accuracy'.

The pedant, then, maintains tradition against usage in speech and in writing; he is the trouble-feast at every linguistic banquet, the spoil-sport in all word-fun, the wet blanket on all stylistic ardour, the kill-joy of every verbal or syntactical exuberance, the 'sour-graping' *écrivain manqué* that crabs the work of the successful or the copious creative writer; the scholar that believes scholarship to be a close corporation of university professors, readers, lecturers, lectors, demonstrators and what have you, and denounces every outsider as 'unscientific' or 'brilliant but not sound', his work as 'spectacular but not scholarly', 'interesting but untrustworthy', and drags in irrelevance to prove his charge; the research student that believes research superior to creation, the history of the vowel *e* from Noah's stepping into the

Ark to Norma's stepping into the Austin to be more important than *Tom Jones*; the sort of fellow who calls Shakespeare a bad writer because he breaks so many rules; who prefers Whittier to Whitman; who thinks *aggravation* (annoyance) a crime and *psychological moment* a sin, *different to* a solecism, and *under the circumstances* an impossibility. But why allow oneself to grow angry? for pedants, like the poor, are always with us. See also PLURALS, UN-ENGLISH.

peer, misused for (a person) *superior.* 'He is the equal if not the peer of anyone in the club' (vouched for by Weseen). [[The belief that *peer* means superior or at least connotes *superiority* is exceedingly common among Americans—so common and so strong that it actually has this meaning more often than not. And unfortunately, correction at school only drives the word from the vocabulary of expression (as opposed to the vocabulary understood).]]

pence is the collective, PENNIES the distributive (or separative) plural of *penny.* Thus, 'The fare was fivepence', 'Two insular and pence-paying realms' (*The O.E.D.*); 'I gave him three pennies', three coins, whereas 'I gave him threepence' refers to the sum, paid either in a threepenny piece or in three separate pennies; 'The miser counted his great heap of pennies'; 'Pennies are brown, pence are money'. [[In American English, *penny* colloquially = *cent*; pl. *pennies* (pence does not occur).]]

pendant, -ent. See DEPENDANT.

penetrant, for *penetrating* (of mind: 'subtle', 'acute') is not wrong; but it is disappearing from general use. It should be reserved for 'physically penetrating or trenchant', 'deeply cutting' or 'entering deep'.

penetrate is incorrectly used for PERVADE: an interesting error, because of the etymological approximation. '[Marxism] effectively separates the metaphysical elements which throughout the whole course of its history'—the history of science—'have penetrated scientific thought', J. D. Bernal, 'The Social Function of Science', in *The Modern Quarterly*, January, 1938.—And *penetrate into* is redundant.

penultimate is the last but one; **antepenultimate,** the last but two. Noun and adjective.

people, 'a nation, race, tribe, community', is singular, with plural *peoples*; *people,* 'persons', is plural. *The people,* 'the electorate', is singular, as is *the people,* 'the laity'; but *the people,* 'the common people', i.e., those who do not belong to the nobility or the ruling (or official) classes, is plural.

per is commercialese—and permissible in a Latin phrase, *per annum.* But it should not be allowed in good writing. 'Mr Chamberlain went to Munich per aeroplane.'

per cent. is occasionally misused for *percentage;* properly, *per cent.* is used after a numeral. [[American usage prefers *per cent* or *percent* (without period).]]

per day; per month; per week; per year. Inferior to *per diem, per mensem, per hebdomadem, per annum;* much inferior to 'a day' ('twelve shillings a day'), 'a year' ('£300 a year'), etc., or 'by the day or month or week or year'. Be either learned in Latin or easy in English; don't be mongrel in both. [[For American usage this is a command not to use *per.* Probably *per mensem,* certainly *per hebdomadem* would not be intelligible.]]

percentage for *proportion.* 'In motor racing, the machine—not the man—does the larger percentage of the work'. Idiomatically, one would go a step further and write, 'In motor racing, the machine does most of the work'.

perceptible; perceptive; perceptual. In current usage, *perceptible* is 'able to be perceived by the senses or the mind; observable'; 'a perceptible difference' is a difference that can be seen, felt, or understood, but it is not synonymous with *considerable,* as certain careless writers have supposed.—*Perceptive* is 'capable of perceiving, belonging to or instrumental in perception', as in 'perceptive faculties'; hence, 'quick in perception, quick to notice; intelligent', as in 'Dickens was a most perceptive man'.—*Perceptual* is a learned term, meaning 'of or belonging to perception; consisting in, or of the nature of, perception or the things perceived', as in 'perceptual images'. (*The O.E.D.*)

perception and **apperception.** To sum up the lengthy definitions of *The O.E.D.*: the former is awareness of things external, the latter an inner consciousness.

perennially = 'permanently', 'constantly', 'perpetually', not 'year after year' as in 'Perennially subject to attacks of gout'. The same applies to the adjective, which does not = 'recurring year after year'.

perfect, more, most; less, least; all these are inadmissible. See COMPARATIVES, FALSE.—Used for *complete*, it is incorrect, as in 'The ship is a perfect loss'.

PERFECT INFINITIVE, w r o n g l y used. The perfect infinitive seems to unpractised writers to accompany 'I (or you or he) should, or would, have liked', or 'He had intended', as in 'They would have liked to *have been* there, I'm sure', 'I should have liked to *have gone* to the cricket match', 'If he had intended to *have done* that, he might at least have told me': whereas the correct forms are 'They would have liked to *be* there', 'I should have liked to *go*', 'If he had intended to *do* that'. Compare 'If he had intended *doing* that'. The idea of the past is already in the finite verb ('would have liked', 'should have liked', 'had intended'): why repeat it? To good sense as to logic, the repetition is always irritating and occasionally confusing. Based on Onions, *An Advanced English Syntax* § 179.

perfectly for *entirely* or *wholly*, as in 'A perfectly good motor-car', is a colloquialism that rings rather oddly in formal prose.

perform one's ablutions. See ABLUTIONS.

permit; allow. The former is active, the latter neutral; the latter is the more formal; the former connotes forbearance, sufferance, mere toleration, whereas the latter connotes approval and denotes sanction. One *allows* a thing by default or out of weariness; one *permits* it by express action—one states or even legalizes (certainly one formalizes) it. 'I allow him to come here; I permit him to stay past the agreed time.' 'That may be tacitly allowed which is not expressly permitted' (*Webster's*).

permit of. See ADMIT, ADMIT OF.

perpetually and **continually.** In current usage, *perpetually* means 'incessantly; persistently; constantly recurrent; continually';—not necessarily 'eternally' or 'for the rest of one's life'.

perquisite, misused for *privilege.* (Concerning a fancy-dress ball) '"I never dress up", said Maxim. "It's the one perquisite allowed to the host"', Daphne Du Maurier, *Rebecca*, 1938.

persecute and **prosecute** are occasionally confused. The former is to 'pursue with malignancy or with enmity and injurious action'; to *prosecute* is 'to institute legal proceedings against' (a person). *Persecute* used to mean 'prosecute at law'; a sense now obsolete except in dialect and in humorous writings or speech.

persistently. See CONSISTENTLY.

personage, misused for *person.* 'She looked exactly the same cool, cynical personage as when she had spoken to him at the bank that morning', John G. Brandon, *The Dragnet*, ca., 1937. 'That entirely mythical personage, "the man in the street"' (from an essay script in the L. C. C. Major Establishment examination, 1938). A *personage* is somewhat important.

personal and **personally.** 'My personal opinion', 'I personally think', 'to pay a personal visit' are excessive—not to say absurd—for 'my opinion', 'I (*or* I*) think', 'to pay a visit'. If you must have emphasis and wish to avoid italics, you can say 'my own opinion', 'I myself think'; and for 'to pay a personal visit' (as though one could visit otherwise than in person!) it is best to substitute some more sensible phrase. Instead of saying, 'Tom Mix paid a personal visit to London', say 'Tom Mix paid a visit to London' or, if you consider that event to be remarkable, 'Tom Mix actually paid a visit to London',—although 'actually visited' is more economical and telling than 'paid a visit to'.

personal is an adjective; **personnel** (stress on last syllable) is a noun, meaning 'the body of persons working in an establishment, especially of a public institution', and often opposed to *matériel.*

PERSONAL REMARKS, or **PERSONALITIES** as they are sometimes called.

Personality is 'the quality of being directed to or aimed at an individual, especially in the way of disparagement or unfriendly reference'; e.g., 'Personality in his satires . . . accorded with the temper and the talent of Pope', as Disraeli the Elder suggested. That sense leads to and merges with this:—(Generally in plural) 'A statement or remark aimed at or referring to an individual person, usually of a disparaging or offensive kind'; e.g., 'The Court cannot and will not stand journalistic personalities about its members' (C. Lowe). [With thanks to *The O.E.D.*]

Avoid personalities except when they are *not*, in the usual sense, personalities:

be personal only in a friendly, pleasant or respectful way. It is easy to give offence unwittingly: the loss of a friend is too high a price to pay for a witticism at his expense; the enmity of a stranger outweighs the pleasure of relieving oneself of a brilliant *mot*.

And in any event, remember that in these polite days, it is dangerous to put personalities into print. Cases of libel are distressingly frequent, and even though that person who is the object of a personality may not take offence (at least to the extent of instituting a lawsuit), his friends may say, 'Look here, A., this is going too far: you *can't* lie down under that, you know'. Or one of the sharking firms of shady solicitors that specialize in libel—and keep someone constantly on the watch for potential libel—will offer to take up the matter in the courts or obtain a fat sum out of court.

personality. In addition to retaining the basic sense, 'the fact (or the quality) of being a person, not, e.g., a thing', and the sense 'personal existence or personal identity', *personality* is now used chiefly in the sense 'distinctive personal or individual character, especially when *of a marked or notable kind*' (*The O.E.D.*; italics mine); but that kind need not necessarily be *a pleasing* (attractive) *personality*; therefore a modifying word is advisable.—e.g., *attractive, lovable, remarkable*—See also the following entry.

personality and **personalty** are occasionally confused. *Personalty* is a legal term for 'personal estate'; or, as Henry Stephen defines it in his famous *New Commentaries on the Laws of England*, 1841–45, 'Things personal (otherwise called personalty) consist of goods, money, and all other moveables, and of such rights and profits as relate to moveables'. *Personality* = 'personal existence, a distinctive personal character' (Harold Herd); do not loosely use it as a synonym of 'famous person'. For the literary or grammatical sense of *personality*, see PERSONAL REMARKS.

PERSONIFICATION. In personification, a quality is represented as a person: 'Confusion spoke', 'Vice is a monster', 'Poetry is a mellifluous rhetorician'. Or, more fully: 'The attribution of personal form, nature, or characteristics; the representation of a thing or abstraction

as a person, especially as a rhetorical figure' (*The O.E.D.*).

Once so common, especially in poetry and perhaps above all in odes, personification is now suspect. When a writer personifies, he is looked at askance: 'He's ranting', say the critics; 'Getting a bit above himself', say his friends; and maybe he feels not too comfortable about it himself.

But in impassioned verse and poetic prose, personification is permissible. It is, however, to be used sparingly and with the nicest discretion.

(For a goodish, though rather old-fashioned account of this subject, see Alexander Bain, *English Composition and Rhetoric*, II, 1888, at pp. 21–29.)

personnel is singular. Wrong in: 'There are few more gloomy places in the early morning than a restaurant. Both the personnel—such as are about—as well as the furniture are in *déshabille*', Anthony Weymouth, *Tempt Me Not*, 1937.—Also see 'PERSONAL . . . PERSONNEL'.

persons is now less usual than *people* except after a numeral, as in 'eighty persons were present': 'Eighty *people* . . .' would be extremely colloquial. In short, *people* is the indefinite, *persons* the precise or definite plural.

perspective and **prospective.** Except in heraldry, *prospective* is obsolete or rare as a noun; as an adjective, it means, on the one hand, 'regarding or concerned with or operative in the future', and on the other, 'future; expected or hoped for'. *Perspective* = 'of or belonging to perspective', i.e., to a particular 'art of delineating solid objects on a plane surface', hence 'the relation—especially the proportion—in which the parts of a subject are viewed by the mind; the aspect of an object of thought', and several technical senses.

perspicuity, 'clearness of statement' (*The O.E.D.*), and *perspicacity*, 'clearness of understanding' (*ibid.*), are easily and often confused. Perspicacity is required to grasp the distinction, and perspicuity to explain it. The same applies to the adjectives, *perspicuous* and *perspicacious*.

PERSPICUITY. In general, this subject is treated at OBSCURITY. Very little, therefore, need be said at this point.

Within the scope of the sentence, perspicuity is clear statement; viewed more broadly, it is clear ordonnance in composition: in either case, lucidity is attained not only negatively by freedom from the ambiguous and the obscure but, positively, by an unassailable univocality.

perspiration and **perspire.** See SWEAT.

persuasion. Correctly used for 'religious (and less often political) beliefs or opinion', it is classified by *The O.E.D.* as 'slang or burlesque' when used for nationality, sex, kind, sort, description, as in 'She said she thought it was a gentleman in the haircutting persuasion', F. Anstey, *The Tinted Venus*, 1885.

peruse is not synonymous with '**to** *read*', for it means to read thoroughly, read carefully from beginning to end. One *peruses* a contract, one *reads* an (ordinary) advertisement,—that is, if one does not merely glance at it.

pessimistic is 'pertaining to or like or suitable to pessimism'; hence, 'disposed to take the gloomiest view of circumstances': but do not debase it to meaning nothing more than 'gloomy'.

petit; petite. The English adjective *petit* is obsolete; *petite* (no longer written as a foreign word) is now applied to a woman, a girl, or rarely a female child, of small size or stature, and it has a connotation of daintiness of figure.

phantasy. See FANTASY.

phenomena is plural (see PHENOMENON), not singular as it is made to be in 'The phenomena will not have been considered in all its bearings unless I add . . .' (M. D. Eden, translation of Freud, *On Dreams*, 1914).

phenomenal should not be debased to equivalence with *unusual*; it can, however, be used as a synonym of *prodigious*, as in 'The success of Miss Kate Greenaway's "Birthday Book" was phenomenal' (*The Athenaeum*, Jan. 7, 1882).

phenomenon; scientific plural, *phenomena*; ordinary plural, *phenomenons*; incorrect plural, *phenomenas* (cf. STRATAS and DATAS). In the sense 'a prodigy', it is a colloquialism. Not to be used of anything unremarkable, nor to be confused with *feature* or *quality*.—And see PHENOMENA.

phonograph and **gramophone.** A *gramophone* is 'a kind of phonograph', says *Webster's*, and a *phonograph* is 'an instrument for mechanically recording and reproducing human speech and other sounds'. The earlier term *record*

is now competing with *recording*, a useful word as it prevents confusion, especially when a (written) record is kept of (sound) recordings. An *electrical transcription* is in American English a recording used for 'radio broadcasting'.—See also VICTROLA.

phosphorous (adj.) is a not infrequent misspelling of *phosphorus* (n.).

photo is a colloquial abbreviation of *photograph*. It may be used, with lamentable ignorance or levity, for any *portrait* (drawn or painted). [[In the U.S.A. this usage is not known.]] A young lady who is supposed to be well educated and is herself an instructor of youth, speaks of a friend of the family who 'had his photo in the Academy last year'.

phrenetic, 'delirious, crazy', and *phrenic*, a scientific term for 'pertaining to the diaphragm' (*The O.E.D.*), are sometimes mistaken, the one for the other.

picture is colloquial (and trivial) for 'a (very) beautiful or picturesque object', as in 'The room, when decorated, was a picture', 'The child was a picture'. For *portrait* or *photograph* it is obsolescent in Standard English.

picturedrome is affected (and silly) for *picture-house* or, better, *cinema*.

piece is now dialectal only, in the sense 'a portion of space' i.e., a short distance, a part of the way, or 'a portion of time', i.e., a while, especially a short while. As applied to a woman or a girl, it is depreciatory or, at best, trivial.

pierce for to *peer*. 'Beady eyes piercing around at all objects', John G. Brandon, *The Pawnshop Murder*, 1936. Glances (but not *eyes*) may be said to *pierce*; and they pierce not *at*, but *into* or *through*.

pinchers is dialectal for *pincers*. But whereas *pincers* has no singular, *pinchers* has a technical singular: '*Pincher* . . . a nipping tool fitting the inside and outside of a bottle, in order to shape the mouth' (Knight's *Dictionary of Mechanics*, Supplement, 1884). (*The O.E.D.*) [[In American English *pinchers* is probably more common than *pincers*. However, small pinchers are nowadays called *pliers* and *nippers*. These are the terms used in the catalogues of Sears, Roebuck and Co. and Montgomery Ward and Co.]]

pipefuls and **pipes full.** Cf. the remark at BASKETFULS.

pistol is the weapon, **pistole** (accent on second syllable), an obsolete Spanish or French gold coin.

piteous; pitiable; pitiful. (And the corresponding adverbs in *-ly*.) In current usage, *piteous* is 'appealing for pity or exciting it; deserving it', hence 'lamentable' or 'mournful', as in 'a piteous groan'; but it is now less common than *pitiable*. *Pitiable* is used mostly in the sense 'deserving or needing pity, or exciting it; lamentable', as in 'The beggar was in a pitiable condition'. *Pitiful* can be used in this sense, but one would do well to confine it to the sense 'full of pity, feeling pity, characterized by pity', hence 'compassionate' or 'merciful'; as a pejorative, it = 'miserably insignificant' ('A pitiful attempt to ape Royalty'), 'contemptible'.

placable for *quiet*, *peaceable* is misused; its true sense, *easily appeased*, *forgiving*, is distinct.

placable, placeable; placatory, placating. *Placeable* = 'capable of being placed'; *placable* = 'gentle, mild, forgiving; especially, easily pacifiable or appeasable', as in 'Though irritable, he was placable'. *Placatory* (rarely of persons) = 'conciliatory or propitiatory', as in 'a reply both dignified and placatory', 'a placatory offer or offering'. As an adjective, *placating* is a synonym of, and less formal, less literary than, *placatory*; like *placatory*, it is not used of persons themselves.

The respective adverbs are *placably*, (*placeably* doesn't exist), *placatorily*, *placatingly*.

The respective opposites are *implacable*, *unplaceable*, *unplacatory*, *unplacating*, but the third and fourth are not much used. (*The O.E.D.*)

place is incorrect for *where* in *anywhere*, *everywhere*, *nowhere*, *somewhere*. More than that, it is illiterate.

placent, an unnecessary word meaning *pleasing*, *agreeable*, is occasionally misused for *propitious*.

plain, like *homely*, is to be avoided in descriptions of women, for, there, it is a euphemism for *ugly* or, at best, *unbeautiful*. *Homely*, however, is inoffensive (or it should be!) in England, where it has the connotation of 'home-loving', 'unpretentiously housewifely'. [[In American usage *homely* usually means plain and even unattractive when applied to persons and things. *Homelike* and *homey* (colloquial) preserve the connotation of affectionate welcome and comfortable ease.]]

PLATITUDES are, to thinking, what clichés are to writing. 'The platitude is the prince of spiritual peace; his yoke is easy, his burden is light' (Frank Binder, *Dialectic*, 1932).

-ple, as in the series *triple*, *quadruple*, *quintuple*, *sextuple*, *septuple*, *octuple*, *decuple*, and ending with *multiple*, has a meaning easily deducible from the entry at 'TREBLE and TRIPLE', *q.v.* The *-ple* represents Latin suffix *-plex*, which (e.g., in L. *duplex*, *triplex*) corresponds exactly to the English suffix *-fold* (*q.v.*).

Duple is obsolete as a general term in the series, but it is retained in mathematics and music.

For *multiple*, see the entry at MANIFOLD.

plead—preterite, *pleaded* (colloquial American, Scottish dialect: often *pled*)—past participle, *pleaded*.

PLEONASM. See VERBOSITY.

PLEONASTIC NEGATION. See NEGATION, Section *C. b.*

plethora is not mere *abundance*, but *superabundance*.

PLURALS, UN-ENGLISH. Jespersen, in *Growth and Structure of the English Language* (sec. 141), speaks of those 'abnormal plurals which break the beautiful regularity of nearly all English substantives—*phenomena, nuclei, larvae, chrysalides, indices,* etc. The occasional occurrence of such blundering plurals as *animalculae* [the correct plural is *animalcula*, singular *animalculum*; the English is *animalcule*, plural *animalcules*] and *ignorami* [as if from a Latin noun, *ignoramus*, 'an ignorant person', whereas *ignoramus* = 'we are ignorant': English usage has given us *ignoramus*, singular, with plural *ignoramuses* (against which pedants inveigh)] is an unconscious protest against the prevalent pedantry of schoolmasters in this respect.'

The general rule is: Add *s* (or, to nouns ending in *s* or *x* in the singular, *es*). Therefore *nucleuses* and *chrysalises*. *Indices* differs from *indexes*—see the separate entry. For *phenomena*, see *phenomenon*. This rule applies not only to Greek and Latin words (*octopus—octopuses; rhinoceros—rhinoceroses*), but to words from modern languages: thus, the plural of *stiletto* is *stilettos*; not, as in Italian, *stiletti*. For those who wish to go further into the matter, there is no better authority than the excellent Tracts of the Society for Pure English.

plurocentral for *pluricentral* ('having more than one centre or nucleus', *The*

O.E.D.), is typical of an error common among writers on science. The combining form of L. *plus*, 'more', is *pluri*.

p.m. See A.M.

POETIC PROSE. Poetic or imaginative prose is prose that so far partakes of the nature of poetry as to possess the vocabulary—the words and the phrasing—of poetry and some of its rhythms. But it is not—or should not be—metrical, except for sequences of not more than (say) eight syllables: the metrical character should be broken up.

Poetic prose is out of fashion. Yet it may be found in such twentieth-century writers as G. K. Chesterton, Hilaire Belloc, Santayana, Frank Binder. The golden age of poetic prose was the approximate period, 1810–1850; perhaps the greatest master was De Quincey. Both Walter Savage Landor and Robert Eyres Landor occasionally wrote pages of splendour in a genuinely poetic prose; William Sharp, a lesser man, employed poetic prose in most of his imaginative work.

To those who would essay this difficult and demoded genre, I recommend a study of all the writers I have named; to these names I add those of Shelley (*The Defence of Poetry*), Edgar Allan Poe, and the two-centuries-earlier Thomas Browne (*Urn Burial, The Garden of Cyrus, Religio Medici*), who sometimes achieves effects unsurpassed by even De Quincey.

POETS' LICENCE. A learned professor objected to A. E. Housman's 'The bells, they sound on Bredon' that the 'they' is superfluous and the line ungrammatical, and went so far as to say that 'a man who cannot write better English than that has no business to write at all.' Such a rash judgement would condemn most of our greatest writers, for they have all made such 'mistakes'. Indeed, as Flaubert remarked in a letter to Turgenev, it is not to the greatest, but to lesser masters that we look for models of style. The pedant critic overlooked the fact that this ungrammatical construction is an idiom so characteristic of English ballad poetry that modern poets writing in that style have adopted it as a matter of course.

He rendered Tunstall all his right,
Knowing his valiant blood unstained,

The king he caused this trusty knight
Undefiled Tunstall to be named.
    An Elizabethan ballad of
        the Battle of Flodden.

The silly buckets on the deck,
    That had so long remained,
I dreamed that they were filled with dew,
    And when I woke it rained.
        S. T. Coleridge, *Ancient Mariner*.

Lars Porsenna of Clusium,
    By the nine gods he swore,
That the great house of Tarquin
    Should suffer wrong no more.
        T. B. Macaulay, *Lay of Horatius*.

'Last night the moon had a golden ring
    And tonight no moon we see.'
The skipper he blew a whiff from his pipe
    And a scornful laugh laughed he.
        Longfellow, *The Wreck
            of the 'Hesperus'*.

The fays that to my christening came,—
    For come they did, my nurses taught
    me,—
They did not bring me wealth or fame,
    'Tis very little that they brought me.
        Andrew Lang.

Mrs Jones gave a musical party,
    Her friends she invited them all;
There was old Mr Jenkins so hearty
    And young Mr Jenkins so tall.
        Mid-Victorian comic song.

This idiom is particularly common in rustic speech, to which ballad poetry always tends, and sometimes, as in the line of Housman quoted above, serves to suggest the homely character of the person speaking. It also falls naturally from the lips of a Shakespearean character of the utmost beauty and dignity, Viola (*Twelfth Night*), when, on learning that the coast on which she has been shipwrecked is that of Illyria, she says meditatively, 'My brother, he is in Elysium'. It is a matter of emphasis and of the subtle process of thought. Nevertheless, this construction is strictly incorrect and should not be used in mere imitative carelessness, but only when it is necessary to the expression of a shade of meaning.

Within an hour or two of writing the above I had occasion to buy some flowers in Holborn from a man who complained,

'The growers and the dealers, they fix the price between 'em'.

An error of a different and more serious kind is that of Shakespeare in the song:

Hark, the lark at heaven's gate sings,
  And Phoebus 'gins arise
His steeds to water at those springs
  On chaliced flowers that lies.

But Shakespeare wanted his rhyme, and the words were to be sung to the accompaniment of music; the error would pass unnoticed. Scholars suggest that *lies* is here a plural form borrowed from the Northern dialects.

There are grave blemishes in Keats's famous odes. Take the first stanza of *To a Nightingale*, which stanza it is necessary to quote in full:

My head aches, and a drowsy numbness pains
My sense, as though of hemlock I had drunk
Or emptied some dull opiate to the drains
One minute past and Lethewards had sunk.
'Tis not through envy of thy happy lot,
  But being too happy in thy happiness
    That thou, light-wingèd dryad of the trees,
      In some melodious plot
  Of beechen green and shadows numberless
    Singest of summer in full-throated ease.

It may be mentioned first that the idea of *emptying . . . to the drains* is too suggestive of the kitchen-sink; and again, that one does not *empty* a liquid, but the vessel containing it. The latter part of the stanza, however, is mainly in question; for the grammatical skeleton of the long unbroken sentence is ' '*Tis not through envy of thy happy lot . . . that thou . . . singest of summer*', which is mere nonsense. It is to his own 'envy', to himself as 'too happy', that the poet means to refer, but grammatically the words can apply only to the bird itself.

The *Ode on Melancholy* is addressed to a hypothetical listener: *Go not to Lethe . . .*; *Make not thy rosary of yew-berries . . .* and Keats ends the second stanza with:

Or if thy mistress some rich anger shows,
  Emprison her soft hand and let her rave,

And feed deep, deep, upon her peer-less eyes.

Then immediately he begins the third: *She dwells with beauty . . .* Who can 'she' be but the lady with the peerless eyes? It is only in the sixth line, with,

Ay, in the very temple of delight
  Veil'd Melancholy has her sovran shrine . . .

that we first hear of the personified subject of the title.

These are the errors of a concentrated passion, knowing its own meaning too well to see that the chosen words and images are not clear to another.

Common in 18th Century poetry is the use of *thou* and *you* (singular) indifferently in the same poem; a typical example is this from a political poem against Defoe, about 1703:

When you and I met slyly at the *Vine*,
To spin our Legion-letters o'er our wine,
These were the useful flams and shams,
  thou know'st,
Which made thy passage easy to thy post.

Probably both usages were at that time colloquially current, and the employment of both seemed to a writer to bring variety to his verse. Today there is a certain remote dignity in the use of 'thou', which if chosen must be maintained.

Byron, with all his rhetorical splendours, was not impeccable. Notorious is his *. . . there let him lay*, in the address to Ocean (*Childe Harold*, IV), which is thrown into greater prominence by his correct—*where haply lies* two lines earlier. Elsewhere he writes, *Awaking with a start, The waters heave around me*; an instance of false agreement; as also is:

The thunder-clouds close o'er it, which when rent
The earth is covered thick with other clay,
Which her own clay shall cover . . .
          Childe Harold, III.

Swinburne, a great scholar, who wrote well in Greek, Latin, Italian and French, is seldom at fault, but perpetrates a grammatical offence in writing, 'Woe are we that once we loved and love not'. *Woe is me* meaning *woe is to me* or *woe is mine*, the plural form must be *Woe is us*. But Swinburne, perhaps unconsciously, preferred euphony to sense.

Not a misuse of words but a confusion of his metaphor is Tennyson's 'Then I shall see my pilot face to face when I have crossed the bar'. The poet's image is of a divine guide who takes him in charge when, having passed the dangers of mortality, he reaches the open sea; whereas the marine pilot steers the vessel past those dangers and, when the open sea is reached, turns his back on it and leaves it.

It is risky to base one's poetical imagery on objects or actions requiring technical knowledge.

That singular genius, Gerard Manley Hopkins, whose poems, though written in the eighties of last century, were first published in 1918 and have strongly influenced contemporary writers, allowed his search for novel and individual forms of expression to draw him into strange and inexcusable distortions of syntax:

What life half lifts the latch of,
What hell stalks towards the snatch of,
Your offering, with dispatch, of!
Morning Midday and Evening Service.

Recorded only, I have put my lips on pleas
Would brandle adamantine heaven with ride and jar, did Prayer go disregarded:
Forward-like, but however, and like favourable heaven heard these.
The Bugler's First Communion.

When will you ever, Peace, wild wood one, shy wings shut,
Your round me roaming end, and under be my boughs?
Peace.

Thou knowest the walls, altar and hour and night:
The swoon of a heart that the sweep and the hurl of thee trod
Hard down with a horror of height:
And the midriff astrain with leaning of, laced with fire of stress.
The Wreck of the Deutschland.

Patient analysis may reveal the meaning of the poet, but his experimental eccentricities are no safe guide to lesser men.
Wilson Benington.

poetize is gradually displacing *poeticize.*

point of view. See STANDPOINT.

policy and **polity.** The latter means 'civil organization; civil order', also 'civil

government' or 'a particular form of government', 'a state'; it is no longer used synonymously with *policy*, 'a *course* of action intended, or adopted and pursued by a ruler or a government'. Weseen gives a good example in 'The United Kingdom is democratic in polity, but each party has its own policy, and so has each cabinet' (adapted). (*The O.E.D.*)

Political Economy. H. D. Dickinson, in his review of *Political Economy and Capitalism*, by Maurice Dobb, in *The Modern Quarterly* of January, 1938, writes:

'Sixty years ago "economics" began to supplant "political economy" as the name of the science that studies the material conditions of social well-being. This change in linguistic habits reflected a profound change in the method of the science itself. Instead of studying the *productive* relations of a human *society*, as Adam Smith and the classical economists had done, the vulgar economists (to give them Marx's designation) studied the *market* relations of isolated *individuals*. Dobbs's use of the almost obsolete term "political economy" in the title of the present work is a banner of revolt against contemporary individualist tendencies and marks a return to the methods and outlook of the classical economists.'

politician and **statesman.** In the U.S.A., *politician* has a connotation of intrigue and jobbery; in Great Britain, where it is not so sinister a word, it means 'one skilled—or engaged—in politics', all M.P.s being politicians. A *statesman* is a Cabinet Minister—a good one —or, at the least, an M.P. that has much influence and uses it sagaciously.

polyarchy is not, as it is occasionally misunderstood to be, 'a group of kingdoms', but 'the government of a state by many (associated rulers)'.

populace is a noun, *populous* an adjective. *Populace* is now, for the most part, derogatory: instead of meaning 'the common people', as it used to do, it = 'the mob' or even 'the rabble'.

portend, misused for *signify.* 'The window had been open at the time . . ., though what it might portend Higgins was not prepared to say', Cecil Freeman Gregg, *Tragedy at Wembley,* 1936.

portent is equally unfortunate when used for *significance,* as in: 'For signature there was the interlocking-squares symbol that had come to have such a sinister portent for us all', S. S. Van Dine, *The Kidnap Murder Case* (English edition), 1936.

portentious for *portentous* is seldom written but often uttered: cf. PRESUMPTIOUS for *presumptuous*. Probably on the analogy of *pretentious*.

portion and **part.** *Portion* = 'share' (one's portion of food; of an estate); it is short for *marriage portion*; it is one's lot or fate ('Brief life is here our portion', Neale); a (limited) quantity; not now used often for 'a part of *any* whole'. Roughly, a *portion* is an entity cut or taken from a mass or conglomerate, whereas a *part* is a fraction or a constituent ('part of a house, a pen, a body, a country, etc.'), as in 'Five portions cut from that cake will leave only a small part'. (*The O.E.D.*)

PORTMANTEAU WORDS. The coining of these should be done with care— and with especial attention to the avoidance of ambiguity. When, in Robert Carson's very fine novel, *The Revels Are Ended* (English edition), 1937, I read that a man breathed 'stentoriously' I thought, 'Oh, he means *stertorously*'. But Carson writes so well that I then reflected that he intended a portmanteau, or a blend (as Americans prefer), of *stentorianly* and *stertorously*, for he wishes to convey the senses of an extremely noisy stertorousness.

See especially 'Word-Making' in my *For These Few Minutes*, 1938.

POSITION OF WORDS. See ORDER.

positive for 'merely *sure*' or 'merely *certain*' is hyperbolical and misused; the correct nuance is 'very sure' or 'dogmatically (or assertively) sure'. There is something odd about this sentence from Stuart Chase's *The Tyranny of Words*, 1938: 'The scientist finds his referents and makes positive that others can find them in the dark': despite the fact that *positive* is used as = 'very sure'. Idiom demands 'makes certain that . . .'

For 'thoroughgoing', 'complete', as in 'He's a positive fool', *positive* is a colloquialism.

possess is stronger than *have*. Where the two words are synonymous, euphony or dignity will decide which is the better. *Possess* is, for instance, never derogatory: one *has* faults, one does not possess them. Generally, however, these two words are not synonymous.

POSSESSIVE, DUPLICATED. 'Seyss-Inquart's sentimental contact with Austria has been very different from that of Hitler's' should be either '. . . different from that of Hitler' or '. . . different from Hitler's'. (G. V. Carey, *Mind the Stop*, 1939.)

POSSESSIVE ADJECTIVE, omission of. Alexander Smith, in *The History of the Highwaymen*, 1714, begins the chapter on 'Tom Sharp, Murderer and House-Breaker', thus: 'He was not only *Sharp* by name, but also sharp by Nature, as appears by dressing himself in an old suit of black clothes . . .', where 'by his dressing himself' would be correct.

POSSESSIVE ADJECTIVE, unnecessary. 'Mr Garston's, the pawnbroker's, voluntary contribution', Cecil Freeman Gregg, *Tragedy at Wembley*, 1936. Contrast the preceding entry.

POSSESSIVE CASE. See GENITIVE.

POSSESSIVE PRONOUN. See PRONOUN, POSSESSIVE.

possibility is sometimes misused for *chance*. 'I had no possibility to eschew the confusion' (a detective novel, 1937). The author might, however, have written, 'There was no possibility of my eschewing the confusion'—but the sense would have been slightly changed.

possible. See COMPARATIVES, FALSE. Cf. IMPOSSIBLE.

possible for *necessary* or *unavoidable* would seem to be an improbable error. Nevertheless, it occurs—surprisingly often. In *Mr. Pendlebury Makes a Catch*, 1939, Anthony Webb permits an educated character to say, 'They [the police] have their duty to do, but I am sure they will do their best not to make things more difficult for you than possible' (for 'than necessary' or 'than is unavoidable').

possibly for *perhaps*. In conversation it is both permissible and, in general, clear, but in writing it is sometimes ambiguous. Consider 'He cannot possibly do it' and 'He cannot, possibly, do it': the first is clear, the latter becomes ambiguous if a careless writer omits the commas.

possum is now colloquial for *opossum*.

post. In North America, one *mails* a letter; in England and most of the British Empire, one *posts* it.

postcard; postal card. In the British Empire, a postcard may be already postage-stamped or it may require a postage stamp; in the U.S.A., it requires one, an already postage-stamped card being in the States a *postal card*.

postscript and **p.s.** (or *P.S.*). Strictly

the latter is an abbreviation of the former; to say *p—s* is to speak colloquially, but it is not reprehensible. The plural of the word *p.s.* is *p.ss.*; but in a letter one's second *p.s.* is generally written *pp.s.*, one's third *pp.ss.* [[American usage: *p.p.s.*]]

post-meridian is incorrect for *post meridiem*, Latin for 'afternoon', as in

'Twas post meridian, half past four,
By signal I from Nancy parted,

C. Dibdin, 1795 (adduced by *The O.E.D.*).

potent and **potential**. *Potent* is 'powerful', whether of person or liquor; *potential* is 'possible as opposed to actual; latent'. A potential statesman is one who has the ability: all he needs is the opportunity.

pother is a literarism; it is now pronounced to rhyme with *bother*.

pot-herb, mistakenly supposed to be a plant growing in a pot, is one growing in the kitchen-garden, *for the pot*.

pot-walloping, misused for *big and clumsy* (or slang, *pot cleaner*), is from *pot-walloper*, explained by *The O.E.D.* as an independent householder, who, boiling his pot on his own hearth, was entitled to a vote.

practical, misused for *practicable*. 'She tried to open the window on the right, but it didn't seem practical', G. M. Marlowe, *Pictures on the Pavement*, 1938.

practical, when misused for *virtual*, leads to strange ambiguities; this misuse springs from that *practically* which means, not 'in a practical manner', but 'almost', 'virtually'.—'It provides proof positive that forgery by typewriter is a practical impossibility' (Nigel Morland, *The Conquest of Crime*, 1937), a very odd statement indeed. (Here, exaggeration or overstatement may have originated the error, '. . . is an impossibility' being all that was required.)

practically. In *What a Word!*, 1935, Mr A. P. Herbert—that intellectual swashbuckler in, and sturdy champion of, the cause of good English—writes thus:—'As a rule, "practically" means *"Not* practically" or "Nearly". For example, we [foolishly] say of a reluctant engine that it *"practically* started" when it did not start but made a bronchial sound and is now silent.—Do not misunderstand me . . . Life would be impossible if we never said "practically". You may say that a family is "practically extinct" when the only survivor is a

dying old man', although a stylist would much prefer *'virtually* extinct'. 'But', Mr Herbert resumes, 'it would be silly to say that the horse placed second "practically" won the Derby. A boxer may be "practically" knocked out, though still on his feet: but you cannot "practically" hit the bull's-eye, unless you do hit it. It is not the word but the habit that is bad.' I should go further and say: Avoid the word when it synonymizes *almost* or *virtually*—*as good as*—*to all intents*—*in effect*—*though not formally* (or *explicitly*), and select whichever of those seven synonyms is the most suitable to the context. (Eschew *to all intents and purposes*, which, now, means no more than *to all intents*.)

practice (n.), **practise** (v.), are often confused in spelling. [[*Webster's*: *practice* (n.); *practice* or *practise* (v.)]]

precedence, precedent. *Precedence* means superiority, especially socially, as in 'An earl takes precedence of a baronet'; cf. 'The moral always takes precedence of the miraculous' (A. Davidson, quoted by *The O.E.D.*). A *precedent* is a previous example or case that establishes a moral, social, or legal ruling; a lawyer has virtually won his case when he has found a precedent. *Precedence* is wrongly used in this sentence, 'There is, he thinks, no precedence for the admission of such evidence' (Anthony Weymouth, *Tempt Me Not*, 1937). (*Precedence* is stressed on the second syllable, *precedent* (n.), on the first.)

precession and **procession**. The former implies a *going before*, the latter a *going forward*, but is usually applied to a body of persons marching in ceremonial order. The man in the street knows *precession* only in *the precession of the equinoxes*; that is, if he knows it at all!

PRECIOUSNESS (or Preciosity). See also AFFECTATION

The O.E.D.'s definition is 'affectation of refinement or distinction, especially in the use of language; fastidious refinement in literary style' and one of that dictionary's quotations is, 'this . . . may be described as the *reductio ad absurdum* of the preciosity of Pater and Stevenson'. It is at times difficult to distinguish between art, artifice, and affectation: preciosity ensues when subtlety or delicacy or both subtlety and delicacy are employed in contexts that do not call for them.

Here are several brief examples. Preciousness can be satisfactorily judged only in long passages; but long passages cannot be quoted here; therefore I recommend that those who wish to go further into the subject should read extensively in Pater, Symonds, Hewlett (the romantic novels).

From Pater's essay, 'Aesthetic Poetry' (1868) in *Appreciations*, 1889, comes this:—'The choice life of the human spirit is always under mixed lights, and in mixed situations, when it is not too sure of itself, is still expectant, girt up to leap forward to the promise. Such a situation there was in that earliest return from the overwrought spiritualities of the Middle Age to the earlier, more ancient life of the senses; and for us the most attractive form of the classical story is the monk's conception of it, when he escapes from the sombre atmosphere of his cloister to natural light. Then the fruits of this mood, which, divining more than it understands, infuses into the scenery and figures of Christian history some subtle reminiscence of older gods, or into the story of Cupid and Psyche that passionate stress of spirit which the world owes to Christianity, constitute a peculiar vein of interest in the art of the fifteenth century.'

John Addington Symonds, usually ornate, is, at times, precious, as in the following reference* to a passage ('L'altra mattina in un mio piccolo orto . . .') in Lorenzo de' Medici's *Corinto*:—'Here we have the *Collige virgo rosas*, "Gather ye roses while ye may", translated from the autumn of antique to the April of modern poetry, and that note is echoed through all the love-literature of the Renaissance. Lorenzo, be it observed, has followed his model, not only in the close, but also in the opening of the passage. Side by side with this Florentine transcript from Ausonius I will now place Poliziano's looser, but more poetical handling of the same theme, subjoining my version of his ballata.'

And now two or three examples from Maurice Hewlett, *The Forest Lovers*, 1898:

'The time of his going-out [*departure*] was September of the harvest: a fresh wet air was abroad.'

'There was a tall lady. . . . She was dainty to view, her hands and arms

* Page 210, vol. ii, *Essays Speculative and Suggestive*, 1890; Essay on 'The Pathos of the Rose in Poetry'.

shone like white marble; but apart from all this, it was clear to Prosper that she lacked the mere strength for the office she had proposed herself!

'Next day he rode fast and long without meeting a living soul, and so came at last into Morgraunt Forest, where the trees shut out the light of day, and very few birds sing. He entered the east purlieus in the evening of his fifth day from Starning, and slept in a rocky valley. Tall black trees stood all round him, the vanguards of the forest host.'

In Robert Louis Stevenson also are there examples of preciosity; for instance, in *Markheim*.

precipitate and **precipitous**. See following entry.

precipitously is erroneously used for *precipitately* in 'She looked around her wildly, and precipitously left the room', Peter Traill, *Half Mast*, 1936; *precipitous* meaning 'very steep', and *precipitate* 'violently hurried'. One might leave a room 'precipitously' by jumping out of the window or falling downstairs.

precisian (not *precision*); **precisionist** (not *precisianist*). A *precisian* is a person rigidly precise; but one who makes a profession or practice of precision is a *precisionist*. Hence, *precisianism*, the abstract noun corresponding to *precisian*; *precisionism*, to *precisionist*.

PRÉCIS WRITING. 'If we try to analyze any given propositions we shall find in general that they are logical sums . . . But our analysis, if carried far enough, must come to the point where it reaches propositional forms which are not themselves composed of simpler propositional forms. We must eventually reach the ultimate connexion of the terms, the immediate connexion which cannot be broken without destroying the propositional form as such. The propositions which represent this ultimate connexion of terms I call, after B[ertrand] Russell, atomic propositions. They, then, are the kernels of every proposition, *they* contain the material, and all the rest is only a development of this material. It is to them that we have to look for the subject matter of propositions.'

L. Wittgenstein, 'Some Remarks on Logical Form' in *Knowledge, Experience and Realism* (Aristotelian Society, Supplementary Volume ix), 1929.

The O.E.D. gives the word 'précis' as not yet naturalized: spells it not only with an accent (a procedure both justifiable and indeed necessary) but in italics, which, I propose should be discarded. The plural is 'précis's'. [[For American usage, *Webster's* gives the plural *précis*.]] The verb 'précis', to make a précis of, has present participle 'précising' and past tense (and participle) 'précised'; I must say that I prefer 'précis'ing' and précis'd'.

By the same authority, the term 'précis' is defined as 'a concise or abridged statement; a summary; an abstract'. My impression is that *summary* is an exact synonym of *précis* and that *abstract* might be usefully restricted to a summary or epitome of scientific or technical information—above all, of figures (e.g., statistics). Admittedly, an *abridgement* is also either a compendium or an epitome: but the terms are not interchangeable at will, and it is better to maintain distinctions than to destroy them.—From *The O.E.D.*'s definition it would be dangerous to deduce that *abridgement* and *précis* are synonymous: one makes a précis of a paragraph, a passage, even a chapter, or of a letter, a report, a document; not of a book of any considerable size, the summary of a book being either (large scale) an abridgement or a compendium, or (small scale) a synopsis. An *abridgement* (which form I prefer to *abridgment*), as *The O.E.D.* says, is either 'a compendium of a larger work, with the details abridged, and less important things omitted, but retaining the sense and substance' or 'an epitome or compendium of any subject that might be treated much more fully'; it is also, *The O.E.D.* allows, a synopsis,—but that is a sense we should do well to ignore, at least to the extent of avoiding it. [[In American usage the term *digest*, as synonymous with *abridgment* and *abridge*, has been popularized by the magazines *The Literary Digest* (now defunct) and *The Reader's Digest*. The term was borrowed from the law, where it means a compilation, systematically arranged, of legal rules, decisions, and statutes.]]

There are four main ways in which a précis can be made:—

I. To summarize in one's own language and to cast the summary into Reported Speech (*oratio obliqua*)—or to retain reported speech if the original itself is oblique.

II. To summarize in one's own language and, unless the original is itself in Reported Speech, ignore the convention of reported speech—i.e., leave the summary in Direct Speech.

III. To retain so far as possible the language of the original and, unless the original is already oblique, to cast the summary into Indirect or Reported Speech.

IV. To retain, so far as possible, the language of the original, but to ignore the convention of Reported Speech, —unless the original is in Reported, in which case there is no sense in turning the Indirect into the Direct mode.

A certain Examining Board (one of whose revisers I have the honour—and I mean 'honour'—of being) says, in its instructions concerning précis, that 'generally the recognized technique of "reported speech" should be expected, together with a formal title, and the date if relevant'; but it does not insist on Reported Speech. The custom of putting a précis into Reported Speech is an old one. That something is to be said for it—e.g., that the précis gains in impersonality (if that *is* a gain)—I admit. But much more can be said against it: one takes longer to cast a précis into Indirect Speech than into direct, unless the original is in Indirect Speech; a précis in Indirect is more difficult to make; therefore, the proportion of errors will be larger in an Indirect than a Direct précis; and the potentiality of ambiguity is much higher in Indirect than in Direct Speech. As a school exercise, Reported Speech has its intellectual value; but in the practical world, to turn Direct into Indirect Speech is a waste of time. Moreover, it is a relic of a rigid Classicism: why should we be forced to imitate Livy?

Examining Boards, in general, recommend Method I: a summary couched in one's own words and cast into Reported Speech. Failing that, they tolerate Methods II and III: III, a summary that, cast into Reported, retains much or even most of the wording of the original; II, a summary not in Reported, yet written in one's own words. But they frown on IV, which, abandoning the convention of Reported, yet sticks as close as possible to the wording of the original.

Now I plead for the abolition of Reported Speech (unless the original is

Indirect) from précis-writing. Which, then, of Methods II and IV do I prefer?

As a literary exercise, as a training in composition, Method II (one's own language, in Direct Speech) is superior to Method IV; but as précis *qua* précis, IV (Direct Speech in words keeping as close as is idiomatically possible to those of the original) is superior, for this is the method that precludes error more than any other method does.

In short, there is précis by recast and there is précis by reduction; the *literary* ideal is a recast of the reduction. If the reduction is carefully made, it will require only a slight recasting.

For easy reading, it is advisable to break a long, unparagraphed passage into paragraphs—not arbitrarily but according to the divisions of the subject. (Do not tinker with an already satisfactory paragraphing.) And do not alter the order of the narrative or the discourse unless the order is faulty: remember that you're not supposed to be presenting yourself; you are required to represent the author in brief. Don't show off by changing the ordonnance of a good writer: he knows better than you do how *he* wishes to set forth his subject.*

Here follow three passages set in a certain School Certificate examination, the first of 1937, the second of 1938, the third of 1939. Before each of the to-be-précis'd passages come these instructions:—'Write a Précis giving clearly the substance of the following passage and presenting *in a consecutive and readable shape*, briefly and distinctly expressed, the main points of the argument, so that anyone who has not time to read the actual passage may learn the substance of it from the Précis.'

The Functions of a Cabinet.
(to be reduced to 280-300 words)

A German professor in a lecture on anatomy is reported to have said to his class, 'Gentlemen, we come now to the spleen. About the functions of the spleen, gentlemen, we know nothing. So much for the spleen.' It is with much feeling that one enters upon the task of writing a chapter upon the cabinet; although that body has become more and more, decade by decade, the motive power of all political action. The fact is that the cabinet from its very nature can hardly have

* See also my *Précis Writing* (Routledge, London).

fixed traditions. In the first place, it has no legal status as an organ of government, but is an informal body, unknown to the law, whose business is to bring about a cooperation among the different forces of the state without interfering with their legal independence. Its action must, therefore, be of an informal character. Then it meets in secret, and no records of its proceedings are kept, which would in itself make very difficult the establishment and preservation of a tradition. This could, indeed, happen only in case of a certain permanence among the members who could learn and transmit its practice. But a new cabinet contains under ordinary circumstances none of the members of its predecessor. A Conservative minister knows nothing of the procedure under Liberal administrations; and we find even a man of the experience of Sir Robert Peel asking Sir James Graham about the practice of a Liberal cabinet, of which that statesman—who at this time changed his party every decade—had formerly been a member. No doubt the mode of transacting business varies a good deal from one cabinet to another, depending to a great extent upon the personal qualities of the members. Still, the real nature of the work to be done, and hence the method of doing it, have changed during the last half century less in the case of the cabinet than of any of the other political organs of the state, and one can observe certain general characteristics that may be noted.

The conventions of the constitution have limited and regulated the exercise of all legal powers by the regular organs of the state in such a way as to vest the main authority of the central government—the driving and the steering force—in the hands of a body entirely unknown to the law. The members of the cabinet are now always the holders of public offices created by law; but their possession of those offices by no means determines their activity as members of the cabinet. They have, indeed, two functions. Individually, as officials, they do the executive work of the state and administer its departments; collectively they direct the general policy of the government, and this they do irrespective of their individual authority as officials. Their several administrative duties, and their collective functions are quite distinct; and may, in the case of a particular person, have little or no connection. The

Lord Privy Seal, for example, has no administrative duties whatever; and it is conceivable that the work of other members might not come before the cabinet during the whole life of the ministry.

The essential function of the cabinet is to coordinate and guide the political action of the different branches of the government and thus create a consistent policy. Bagehot called it a hyphen that joins, a buckle that fastens, the executive and legislative together; and in another place he speaks of it as a committee of Parliament chosen to rule the nation. More strictly it is a committee of the party that has a majority in the House of Commons. The minority are not represented upon it; and in this it differs from every other parliamentary committee. The distinction is so obvious to us to-day, we are so accustomed to government by party where-ever popular institutions prevail, that we are apt to forget the importance of the fact. Party government as a system has developed comparatively recently; but it has now become almost universal.

Lowell, *The Government of England.*

Here is a précis by reduction, with a few slight recastings that are demanded by the laws of composition, logic, good sense.

Functions of the Cabinet

The Cabinet has become, increasingly, the motor of all political action. The Cabinet* can hardly have fixed traditions. Firstly, it has no legal status as an organ of government, but it is an informal body, unknown to the law; its business is to co-operate the different forces of the state without interfering with their legal independence. Its action, therefore, is informal. It meets secretly; no records of its proceedings being kept, the establishment and preservation of a tradition is difficult. This could, indeed, happen only with permanent members. But a new Cabinet normally contains none of the members of its predecessor. A Conservative minister knows nothing of the procedure under liberal administrations; and vice versa. The transaction of business varies from one Cabinet to another, according to the members' personalities. Still, the nature of the work to be done, hence the method, have changed during the last half century less

* Not *it*: *it* would be ambiguous.

in the Cabinet than in any other political organ: one can observe certain general characteristics.

The conventions of the Constitution have so limited and regulated the exercise of all legal powers by the regular organs of the state as to vest the main authority of the central government in a body unknown to the law. The members of the Cabinet are the holders of public offices created by law; but their possession of those offices by no means determines their activity as members of the Cabinet. They have two functions. Individually, they do the executive work of the state and administer to departments; collectively, they direct the general policy of the government, irrespectively of their individual authority as officials.

The Cabinet's essential function is to co-ordinate and guide the political action of the different branches of the government. It is a committee of the party that has a *majority* in the House of Commons; in this it significantly differs from every other parliamentary committee. It affords a remarkable illustration of party government, which, though developed comparatively recently, is now general.

The Capture and Defence of Arcot
(to be précis'd in 280–320 words)

Clive was now twenty-five years old. After hesitating for some time between a military and a commercial life, he had at length been placed in a post which partook of both characters, that of commissary to the troops, with the rank of Captain. The present emergency called forth all his powers. He represented to his superiors that, unless some vigorous efforts were made, Trichinopoly would fall, and the French would become the real masters of the whole peninsula of India. It was absolutely necessary to strike some daring blow. If an attack were made on Arcot, the capital of the Carnatic, and the favourite residence of the Nabobs, it was not impossible that the seige of Trichinopoly would be raised. The heads of the English settlement, now thoroughly alarmed by the success of Dupleix, and apprehensive that, in the event of a new war between France and Great Britain, Madras would be instantly taken and destroyed, approved of Clive's plan, and intrusted the execution of it to himself. The young captain was put at the head of two hundred English soldiers, and three hundred Sepoys armed and disciplined after the European fashion. Of the eight officers who commanded this little force under him, only two had ever been in action, and four of the eight were factors of the company, whom Clive's example had induced to offer their services. The weather was stormy; but Clive pushed on, through thunder, lightning, and rain, to the gates of Arcot. The garrison, in a panic, evacuated the fort, and the English entered it without a blow.

The intelligence of these events was soon carried to Chunda Sahib, who, with his French allies, was besieging Trichinopoly. He immediately detached an army of ten thousand men, under his son, Rajah Sahib, to invest the fort of Arcot, which seemed quite incapable of sustaining a siege. The walls were ruinous, the ditches dry, the ramparts too narrow to admit the guns, the battlements too low to protect the soldiers. The little garrison had been greatly reduced by casualties. It now consisted of a hundred and twenty Europeans and two hundred Sepoys. Only four officers were left; the stock of provisions was scanty.

During fifty days the siege went on. During fifty days the young captain maintained the defence, with a firmness, vigilance, and ability, which would have done honour to the oldest marshal in Europe. The breach, however, increased day by day. The garrison began to feel the pressure of hunger. Under such circumstances, any troops so scantily provided with officers might have been expected to show signs of insubordination. But the Sepoys came to Clive, not to complain of their scanty fare, but to propose that all the grain should be given to the Europeans, who required more nourishment than the natives of India. The thin gruel, they said, which was strained away from the rice, would suffice for themselves.

An attempt made by the government of Madras to relieve the place had failed, but Rajah Sahib learned that the Mahrattas were in motion; their chief, Morari Row, roused by the fame of the defense of Arcot declared that he had never before believed that Englishmen could fight, but that he would willingly help them since he saw that they had spirit to help themselves. It was neces-

sary to be expeditious. Rajah Sahib offered large bribes to Clive; they were rejected with scorn, and he determined to storm the fort.

The enemy advanced, driving before them elephants whose foreheads were armed with iron plates. It was expected that the gates would yield to the shock of these living battering-rams. But the huge beasts no sooner felt the English musket-balls than they turned round and trampled on the multitude which had urged them forward. The rear ranks of the English kept the front ranks supplied with a constant succession of loaded muskets, and every shot told on the living mass below. After three desperate onsets, the besiegers retired.

The struggle lasted about an hour. Four hundred of the assailants fell. The garrison lost only five or six men. The besieged passed an anxious night, looking for a renewal of the attack. But when day broke, the enemy were no more to be seen. They had retired, leaving the English several guns and a large quantity of ammunition.

Lord Macaulay.

My version (by reduction and slight recasting) is this:—

The Capture and Defence of Arcot

Clive, promoted commissary captain at 25, represented that, unless vigorous efforts were made, Trichinopoly would fall: the French become masters of India. If an attack were made on Arcot, capital of the Carnatic and residence of the Nabobs, the siege might be raised. The heads of the English settlement approved of Clive's plan. He was put in command of 200 English soldiers and 300 Sepoys, with eight officers. Clive pushed on, through storms, to Arcot. The garrison, panicking, evacuated the fort; the English entered.

Intelligence was soon carried to Chunda Sahib, who, with French allies, was besieging Trichinopoly. He immediately detached 10,000 men, under his son, Rajah Sahib, to invest Arcot fort, which seemed incapable of sustaining a siege. The garrison now consisted of 120 Europeans and 200 Sepoys with four officers and scanty provisions.

During fifty days Clive maintained the defence like a veteran. The breach, however, increased. The garrison began to feel hunger. But the Sepoys proposed that the grain should be given to the Europeans, who required more nourishment: the thin gruel strained from the rice would suffice for themselves.

An attempt by the Madras government to relieve Arcot had failed, but Rajah Sahib learned that the Mahrattas were moving; expedition was necessary. Rajah offered bribes to Clive; they were rejected; he determined to storm the fort.

The enemy drove before them elephants forehead-armed with iron plates: battering-rams. But the huge beasts, feeling the English bullets, trampled on the multitude behind; every shot told on the living mass below. After three desperate onsets, the besiegers retired.

There fell 400 assailants, only six defenders. The besieged passed an anxious night, but when day broke, the enemy had retired, leaving several guns and much ammunition.

Here is a passage to be précis'd in 260–300 words.

The Pitt-Newcastle Coalition.

The two most powerful men in the country were the Duke of Newcastle and Pitt. Alternate victories and defeats had made them sensible that neither of them could stand alone. The interest of the State, and the interest of their own ambition, impelled them to coalesce. By their coalition was formed the ministry which was in power when George the Third ascended the throne.

The more carefully the structure of this celebrated ministry is examined, the more shall we see reason to marvel at the skill or the luck which had combined in one harmonious whole such various and, as it seemed, incompatible elements of force. The influence which is derived from stainless integrity, the influence which is derived from the vilest arts of corruption, the strength of aristocratical connection, the strength of democratical enthusiasm, all these things were for the first time found together.

Newcastle brought to the coalition a vast mass of power, which had descended to him from Walpole and 'Pelham. The public offices, the church, the courts of law, the army, the navy, the diplomatic service, swarmed with his creatures. The great Whig families, which, during several generations, had been trained in the discipline of party warfare, and were accustomed to stand together in a firm phalanx, acknowledged him as their captain. 'Pitt, on the other hand, had what Newcastle wanted, an eloquence which stirred the passions and charmed the imagination, a high reputation for purity, and the confidence and ardent love of millions.

The partition which the two ministers made of the powers of government was singularly happy. Each occupied a province for which he was well qualified; and neither had any inclination to intrude himself into the province of the other. Newcastle took the treasury, the civil and ecclesiastical patronage, and the disposal of that part of the 'secret-service money which was then employed in bribing members of Parliament. Pitt was Secretary of State, with the direction of the war and of foreign affairs. Thus the filth of all the noisome and pestilential sewers of government was poured into one channel. Through the other passed only what was bright and stainless. Mean and selfish politicians, pining for commissionerships, gold sticks, and ribands, flocked to the great house at the corner of Lincoln's Inn Fields. There, at every levee, appeared eighteen or twenty pair of lawn sleeves; for there was not, it was said, a single Prelate who had not owed either his first elevation or some subsequent translation to Newcastle. There appeared those members of the House of Commons in whose silent votes the main strength of the Government lay. One wanted a place in the excise for his butler. Another came about a prebend for his son. A third whispered that he had always stood by his Grace and the Protestant succession; that his last election had been very expensive; that he had been forced to take up money on mortgage; and that he hardly knew where to turn for five hundred pounds. The Duke pressed all their hands, passed his arm round all their shoulders, patted all their backs, and sent away some with wages, and some with promises. From this traffic Pitt stood haughtily aloof. Not only was he himself incorruptible, but he shrank from the loathsome drudgery of corrupting others. He had not, however, been twenty years in Parliament, and ten year in office, without discovering how the Government was carried on. He was perfectly aware that bribery was practised on a large scale by his colleagues.

Hating the practice, yet despairing of putting it down, and doubting whether, in those times, any ministry could stand without it, he determined to be blind to it. He would see nothing, know nothing, believe nothing.

It may be doubted whether he did not owe as much of his popularity to his ostentatious purity as to his eloquence, or to his talents for the administration of war. It was everywhere said with delight and admiration that the Great Commoner, without any advantages of birth or fortune, had, in spite of the dislike of the Court and of the aristocracy, made himself the first man in England, and made England the first country in the world; that his name was mentioned with awe in every palace from Lisbon to Moscow; that his trophies were in all the four quarters of the globe; yet that he was still plain William Pitt, without title or riband, without pension or sinecure place. Whenever he should retire, after saving the State, he must sell his coach horses and his silver candlesticks. Widely as the taint of corruption had spread, his hands were clean. They had never received, they had never given, the price of infamy. Thus the coalition gathered to itself support from all the high and all the low parts of human nature, and was strong with the whole united strength of virtue and of Mammon.

Lord Macaulay.*

The following is my suggestion:—

The Pitt-Newcastle Coalition.

The most powerful men were the Duke of Newcastle and Pitt. Alternate victories and defeats had made them sensible that neither could stand alone. The interest of the State, and their own ambition, impelled them to coalesce, in the ministry that was in power when George the Third became king.

The more carefully the structure of this celebrated ministry is examined, the more we marvel at the skill or the luck that had harmoniously combined such various and seemingly incompatible forces. The influences deriving from stainless integrity and from the vilest arts of corruption, the strength of aristocratical connection, and democratical enthusiasm, all merged for the first time.

* This passage is reprinted, as are the preceding passages, with the very kind permission of the Oxford & Cambridge Schools Examination Board.

Newcastle brought a vast mass of power; the public offices, the church, the courts of law, the army, the navy, the diplomatic service, swarmed with his creatures. The great Whig families, trained in party warfare, acknowledged him as their captain. Pitt had what Newcastle lacked, an imaginative and passionate eloquence, a high reputation for purity, and the confidence and ardent love of millions.

The partition of government was singularly happy. Each man occupied a province for which he was well qualified; and neither wished to intrude into the other's. Newcastle took the treasury, the civil and ecclesiastical patronage, and the bribing of members of Parliament. Pitt was Secretary of State, with the direction of the war and of foreign affairs. Thus all the filth was poured into one channel. Through the other passed only what was bright and stainless. Mean, selfish, self-seeking politicians flocked to Newcastle's great London house. There appeared ambitious Prelates and those M.P.s in whose silent votes the strength of the Government lay,—one wanting this; another, that. The Duke pressed all their hands, and sent away some with wages, some with promises. From this traffic Pitt stood haughtily aloof. Incorruptible, he shrank from the drudgery of corrupting others. He inevitably knew, however, how the Government was carried on; that bribery was practised on a large scale: but doubting whether any ministry could stand without it, he determined to be blind to it. He would know nothing.

Perhaps he owed as much of his popularity to his ostentatious purity as to his eloquence, or to his talents for the administration of war. It was everywhere said with delighted admiration that the Great Commoner had, in spite of the Court and the aristocracy, made himself the first man in England, England the first country in the world; that his name was mentioned with awe in every Palace of Europe; yet that he was still plain William Pitt, without title, pension, or sinecure. Whenever he should retire, after saving the State, he would be poor. Widely as corruption had spread, *his* hands were clean. Thus the coalition was strong with the united strength of virtue and of Mammon.

precognition and **preconization.** The former is knowledge beforehand, the latter the public confirmation of an appointment by the Pope.

predicate is occasionally misused for *predict*; and vice versa. The former = to declare, assert, affirm; the latter = to foretell.

prefer ... than. See THAN.

preferable, more. See COMPARATIVES, FALSE.

pregnant of. See PREPOSITIONS WRONGLY USED.

prejudice (n.) **against**, but *partiality for*. The former word (except in legal terminology) is now unusually pejorative, the latter usually favourable.

premise, misused for *presumption, assumption*. 'Since then, nothing has been seen or heard of him, and as that is the case, the premise is that he's still there', John G. Brandon, *The Dragnet*, ca., 1937. The author here misunderstands the meaning of *premise*, a legal term for 'the previous statement from which another is inferred' (*The Con. O.D.*); the assertion that 'nothing has been seen or heard of him' is the premise from which it is inferred that 'he's still there'. The error occurs also in John Ross, *The Black Spot*, 1936. And elsewhere.

prepared to admit, confess, state, etc., **be**. 'I am prepared to confess that I am the culprit' is absurd; the verbosity is undignified; one confesses, or one doesn't. (Mr. A. P. Herbert attacks *prepared to admit*.)

PREPOSITION AT END. Instances of the extreme awkwardness, and even ambiguity, of this construction, are the following: 'The paper so praised Boswell himself was the author of', (J. Timbs, *The Romance of London*, 1865); the author should rather have said 'Boswell ... was the author of the paper ...'. 'When she prattles about herself and her admirers, she makes the reader blush for the shamefacedness she evidently does not even guess at the lack of' (quoted by Nesfield from *The Spectator*, Jan. 31, 1903); here one cannot be sure whether 'the reader' blushes for (but why *for*?) his own shamefacedness or the prattler's lack of it.

Yet too great a fear of putting the preposition at the end sometimes leads to even worse errors, e.g., Joan Grant in *Winged Pharaoh* (1937), 'They who come here see it as though it were a place of earth records, in the form that in their own countries such things are

kept', meaning 'are kept in', or better, 'the form in which such things are kept'; here the writer shirks the necessary repetition of *in*, and writes ungrammatically. The same error, and for the same reason, occurs in the inscription on the monument to John, Duke of Argyle, in Westminster Abbey: 'A General and Orator exceeded by none in the Age he lived' [in].

Dr Pearsall Smith, in *English Idioms* (S.P.E. Tract No. xii, 1923), called the preposition at the end of a clause or a sentence an anglicism; he added that it should not be discouraged. In Tract No. xiv, 1923, the late H. W. Fowler wrote thus:

'It is a cherished superstition that prepositions must, in spite of the ineradicable English instinct for putting them late ("They are the fittest timber to make great politics of" said Bacon; and "What are you hitting me for?" says the modern schoolboy), be kept true to their name and placed before the word they govern. ... The fact is that the remarkable freedom enjoyed by English in putting its prepositions late and omitting its relatives is an important element in the flexibility of the language. The power of saying *A state of dejection such as they are absolute strangers to* (Cowper) instead of *A state of dejection of an intensity to which they are absolute strangers*, or *People worth talking to* instead of *People with whom it is worth while to talk*, is not one to be lightly surrendered. ... *That depends on what they are cut with* is not improved by conversion into *That depends on with what they are cut*; and too often the lust of sophistication ... becomes uncontrollable, and ends with *That depends on the answer to the question as to what with they are cut*. Those who lay down the universal principle that final prepositions are "inelegant" are unconsciously trying to deprive the English language of a valuable idiomatic resource, which has been freely used by all our greatest writers, except those whose instinct for English idiom has been overpowered by notions of correctness derived from Latin standards. The legitimacy of the prepositional ending in literary English must be uncompromisingly maintained; in respect of elegance or inelegance, every example must be judged not by any arbitrary rule, but on its own merits, according to the impression it makes on the feeling of educated English readers.'

PREPOSITION REPEATED UNNEC-ESSARILY. 'An order, this, at which the taximan would have jibbed at violently . . .', John G. Brandon, *The Dragnet*, 1936; 'The weak estate in which Queen Mary left the realm in' (Milton: cited by Onions).

PREPOSITIONS, DISGUISED. See DISGUISED PREPOSITIONS.

PREPOSITIONS WRONGLY USED. The idea is owed to Charles Boyd's very useful little book, *Grammar for Grown-Ups*, 1927; Mr Boyd gives a tabulated list of words, with the wrong and the right prepositions to accompany them. I have drawn a few examples from his valuable list, and added a few of my own. For a fuller list than mine, see Nesfield's *English Composition*, ch. on 'Errors in Prepositions', and his *Errors in English Composition*, pp. 178–187.— Here, the error precedes the correct use.

(of things) *accompanied by* for *accompanied with*; a person, however, is accompanied *by* another
accounted for in consequence of for *accounted-for by*
acquiescence to for *acquiescence in*
adherence of for *adherence to*; *an adherent to* for *an adherent of*; *adherent* (adj.) *of* for *adherent to*
aim for for *to aim at*
assist (him) *to do* for *assist* (him) *in doing*
(of things) *attended by* for *attended with*
(one's) *belief of* (e.g., *revelation*) for *belief in*
careful with for *careful of* (e.g., one's money or reputation)
(one's) *character of honesty* for *character for honesty*
comment (n. and v.) *to* (a thing) for *comment on*
conducive of for *conducive to*
[*different to* is not a solecism, but the scholarly prefer *different from*; *different than*, however, is incorrect, though increasingly common]
disgust at (or *of*) for *disgust with*
embarrassed at for *embarrassed by*
end by for *end with*, as in 'The service ended by a prayer'; or for *end in* (as in 'It all ended by his going off in a huff')
equal as (or *with*), for *equal to*
familiar to (the idea) for *familiar with*
favourable reception with (the public) for *favourable reception by*

ill of is now rare for *ill with*
in comparison of for *in comparison with*
in respect to for *in respect of*
in search for for *in search of*
inculcate (a person) *with* (something) for *inculcate* (something) *on* (a person)
inferior than for *inferior to*
instil with for *instil into*
involved by for *involved in*
judged on (certain standards) for *judged by*
knowledge on for *knowledge of*
listen at for *listen to*
oblivious to for *oblivious of*
pregnant of for *pregnant with*
protest at for *protest against*
receptive to for *receptive of*
(one's) *relations towards* (another person) for *relations with*
sensible to for *sensible of*; contrast *sensitive of*, which is incorrect for *sensitive to*
solicitous to for *solicitous of*
sparing with for *sparing of*
suffer with for *suffer from*
superior than for *superior to*
tendency for for *tendency to*
tolerant to for *tolerant of*
with a view of for *with a view to*
write (*up*) *on impulse*, ambiguous for *write from impulse*.

prescience, misused for *presentiment*. (With reference to 1936) 'The prescience [his own] of another European War harassed him', Gilbert Frankau, *Royal Regiment*, 1938; the error occurs at least three times in the book.

prescribe and **proscribe** are sometimes confused. The former, 'to appoint, advise, order', is not to be confused with the latter, which has an opposed meaning: to *prohibit* or *condemn*.

present-day for *present* or *contemporary* is an unnecessary synonym; and why use two words for one? 'The present-day system in politics' drew my attention to this particular piece of ineptitude. [['Present-day English' is the awkward name of an American group devoted to the study of contemporary English.]]

presentative and **presentive.** The former is the more usual; *presentive* is the opposite of *symbolic*, i.e., it = 'presenting an object or an idea direct to the mind' and is a philological term. In addition to its ecclesiastical sense, *presentative* is used in Psychology and Metaphysics in a sense wider than that of *representative*. Both are learned words, to be used with great care.

present writer, the, is inferior to *the author* in the sense 'I (or me), the writer'; and usually *I* is preferable to either.

preservitor is occasionally misused for *preservator*. So, too, is *preservitive* for *preservative*.

president for *presidency* or *Presidency*. The American *run for president* (properly *President*) and *candidates for President* are colloquialisms for *run for the Presidency, candidates for the Presidency*.

presume. See ASSUME.

presumptious for *presumptuous* is a misspelling and a mispronunciation: in brief, an illiteracy. Cf. VOLUPTIOUS.

presumptive for *presumptuous*. 'If I am unhappy it is my own fault for being a presumptive fool' (from novel read in typescript on Jan. 22, 1938); in this sense never correct and now obsolete. *Presumptive* is defined as 'based on presumption or inference', and *presumption* as 'a belief deduced from facts or experience' (*The O.E.D.*) or even from imagination. *Presumptuous* is 'unduly confident or bold'. The presumptuous man is too ready to act on a merely presumptive opinion.

pretend dominantly = 'to feign, represent falsely', and, although the sense 'to profess' is admissible, it is better to use the word *profess*.

preventitive, preventative, preventive, are easily confused. The first is incorrect for either of the other two; *preventive* is the best form, whether for the noun or for the adjective.

previous is frequently used of a person acting too hastily, especially as in 'You have been much too previous'; this is slang. The meaning of *previous* is 'preceding' or 'former': 'The previous question', that came last before the one under discussion.

previous to for *before* or *until* is commercialese.

previously to this is catachrestic for *previous to this*, which is itself verbose for *before this* or *previously*. 'Previously to this we could toy with various ideas', E. R. Lorac, *Death of an Author*, 1935. Perhaps the author hesitated between *previously* and *prior to this*. (I have seen the error made elsewhere.)

priceless. See INVALUABLE.

primeval (now considered preferable to *primaeval*) and **primitive.** Both words = belonging to or characteristic of the first age of the world or of anything ancient. But only *primitive* = rough, elementary; old-fashioned. *Primitive*, moreover, has learned senses (in, e.g., anthropology, medicine and philology) not possessed by *primeval*.

primordial; principal. See COMPARATIVES, FALSE.

principate and **principiate.** The former is the rule of the Princeps, the latter an obsolete adjective for 'original'.

principal, confused with *principle*. F. R. Burrow, *The Centre Court*, 1937, writes, 'On the principal of taking the biggest first, I will begin with Eastbourne'.

probe, misused for *prod*. 'He probed about the hedge'. To *probe* is to *penetrate*.

procession. See CAVALCADE.

procure and **secure.** To *procure* is 'to gain or win; to obtain by care or effort'; to secure is 'to obtain for certain; to obtain for safe possession'. *Procure* and *secure* should not be so weakened that they become synonymous with the neutral *obtain*.

pro et con is absurd pedantry for *pro and con*.

professor is illicitly used by pill-vendors, mountebanks, showmen of all sorts. To speak of a *professor of music* (or of *singing*) is permissible, if he be prominent or very capable in his profession. In general, it is best to reserve the term for university professors.

PROGRESSIVE INFINITIVE. See BE, BEING . . .

PROGRESSIVE (or CONTINUOUS) TENSES are often, by stylists, employed to avoid ambiguity: 'Fruit was eaten in large quantities' may refer either to habitual action or to a certain occasion; 'Fruit was being eaten in large quantities' is—or *should* be—applicable only to continuous action on a certain occasion. Based on Onions.

prohibit. See INHIBIT.

prohibit (a person) to (do something) is archaic. Either one *prohibits* a person *from* doing something, or one prohibits the thing in question: thus, 'The Prime Minister prohibits them from discussing the matter in public' or 'The Prime Minister prohibited public discussion of the matter'.

prolific is often misused for *profuse*. The former = 'fertile; abundant.'

PROLIXITY. See VERBOSITY.

promote should not be used with bad or evil things, for it means 'to further, to advance'. Do not say 'Drink promotes idleness' but 'Drink increases (or leads to) idleness'.

prone and **supine**. 'To lie *prone*' is to lie, face downwards, on one's belly, as in (normal) rifle-shooting; 'to lie *supine*' is to lie flat on one's back, face to the zenith. Both of these words may be applied to the person (or his body) or to the position.

PRONOUNS, CONFUSED. In *The Queen's English*, Dean Alford writes:— 'The following note has been sent me, received'—wrong agreement, Dean!— 'after a tithe dinner in Devonshire: "Mr T. presents his compliments to Mr H., and I have got a hat that is not his, and if he have got a hat that is not yours, no doubt they are the expectant ones".'

See also AMBIGUITY, towards end (particular examples: pronouns group).

PRONOUN, POSSESSIVE. Arthur Bryant, *The Illustrated London News*, Nov. 27, 1937, '. . . the sound of martial music would be borne to eager . . . ears as regiment after regiment made their way, etc.' The nominative 'regiment' is in the singular and the pronoun should be *its*.

Ezra Pound, in *Moeurs Contemporaines*, 'At a friend of my wife's there is a photograph . . .', omits a possessive; the sentence needs to be recast.

PRONOUNS JOINED by *and* or dissociated by *or* must not be in different cases, as they are in 'You and me will go now'; 'She didn't hit him or I'.

PROOF CORRECTING, HINTS ON. Not a subject to be treated in this book. But the curious—and the inexperienced —should consult G. V. Carey, *Mind the Stop* (1939), last chapter.

propaganda is a singular (not, like *data* and *strata*, a plural); its plural is propagandas.—See also PUBLICITY.

propellant and **propellent; propulsion; propulsive.** 'Wind is a propellant, that is to say, a propellent [= driving] force', Weseen; although *The O.E.D.* (which gives *propellent* for both noun and adjective) does not recognize *propellant*, *Webster's* has -ent form as n. and adj.

Propulsion is the action of driving or pushing forward or onward, or the being so driven, or the effort required therefor; *propulsive* is its adjective.

properly so called is needed in contradistinction to 'falsely (or improperly) so called', but generally it is a wordy synonym for *proper* (after, not before,

the noun it qualifies). Thus 'The dialects properly so called' are merely 'The dialects proper'.

prophecy and **prophesy**. The latter is the verb, the former the noun, *the thing prophesied*.

proponent (opp. *opponent*) is a proposer or propounder; the term, therefore, is not—as it is sometimes supposed to be—synonymous with *supporter*. 'The proponents of the President called at noon.'

proportion should not be used for *portion* (or *part*), or *number*, as in 'The greater proportion of journalists are men'.

proportions is commonly misused for *size* in such a sentence as 'the chair is not suited to a man of his proportions'; *proportions* being the relation of one part to another, whether large or small.

propose and **purpose**. To *purpose* is 'to set before *oneself* for accomplishment', as in 'My friend purposes to open an office' (Johnson), 'His mother purposed that he should be a preacher' (Lynch), 'I purpose . . . keeping a sort of journal' (Francis Kemble); also in the passive (though this is obsolescent), as in 'I am purposed instantly to return' (Scott) and 'The whole nation was . . . fully purposed that the next brood of Æthelings . . . should be . . . Englishmen' (Freeman). In short, *propose* is encroaching far too freely on the territory of *purpose*. (*The O.E.D.*)

proposition, fast becoming a passepartout word, is in constant misuse. A *proposal* of marriage is not a 'proposition', but the word is properly applied to a draft of the terms for a business agreement. *Proposition* is not synonymous with *affair*, *matter*, *task*, *undertaking*. For a slashing attack on the word see Fowler's *English Usage*; consult also Horwill's *American Usage*.

proprietrix for *proprietress* is absurd. Nor is *proprietress* necessary, unless one wishes to draw attention to the sex of the *proprietor*.

prosaic and **prosy**. Both = 'commonplace, matter-of-fact', but *prosy* has the connotation of tedious, so that its sense is 'commonplace *and* tedious; dull and wearisome'. Neither is now used for 'consisting of, or written in prose', *prose* being the current adjective. (*The O.E.D.*)

proscribe. See PRESCRIBE.

prosecute, confused with *persecute*. See 'PERSECUTE and PROSECUTE'.

proselyte, a noun, is misused as a verb by Don Marquis (*The Almost Perfect State*, 1927): 'It is far from our purpose to proselyte'. The verb is *proselytize*. [[*Webster's* enters the verb, to *proselyte*, t. & int.]]

prospective. See 'PERSPECTIVE and PROSPECTIVE'.

prosy. See 'PROSAIC and PROSY'.

prostrate (adj.) and **supine** are sometimes inexactly used. The former is lying face downwards, the latter face upwards, on the back. Two different states of mind or feeling may be expressed in these attitudes. [[*Webster's* equates *prostrate* (adj.) with *prone* or *supine*.]]

protagonist is occasionally confused with *antagonist*, which is almost its opposite. In literary terminology, *protagonist* (Greek *protos*, 'first', and *agonistes*, 'a contender for a prize') means 'the chief character in a drama; hence in a novel, a story, etc.'; derivatively, 'a person prominent in any contest or cause; a champion of a cause'. (*The O.E.D.*)

protagonist should not be used loosely for any *supporter* (or *partisan*) or *upholder*, for in its derivative sense it means 'a *prominent* supporter or champion of any cause' (*The O.E.D.*).

protest, incorrect for *protest against*. 'They bitterly protest attempts by the Government to aid stability', Stuart Chase, *The Tyranny of Words*, 1938. [[*Webster's* quotes with approval 'to protest a witness'. *Protest* may be used for *protest against* in American usage.]]

protest at. See PREPOSITIONS WRONGLY USED.

Protestant and **protestant**. The former is the opposite of a Roman Catholic, the latter is a protester—and the term is so obsolescent as to be virtually obsolete.

prototype, misused for *predecessor* or *similar*. 'The book . . . would have passed into the limbo of the remainder lists with thousands of its prototypes had not the quality of one of the wilder anecdotes . . . earned it a place in the news columns of a Sunday paper', Margery Allingham, *Dancers in Mourning*, 1937. There can be only one prototype.

protrude, obtrude, intrude. 'I hope I don't protrude', said the foreign gentleman, joining the company uninvited.

To *obtrude* (a thing) is to force it on a person's attention.

prove, in 'the exception proves the rule', is used in its primary sense, 'to test; to make trial of', as in the Biblical 'Prove all things and hold fast to that which is good'. (Weseen.)

provide, misused for *form* or *constitute*, as in 'Darts provides one of the most interesting games of skill and can be played almost anywhere', examination essay script, June, 1939.

provided and **providing** are less correct (and often less clear) than *provided that* and *providing that* in the sense 'it being stipulated that', as in 'Provided that all is safe, you may go' and 'I shall pay the money, providing that you prove to me the necessity'. It is, however, both permissible and indeed usual to omit *that* when the sense is 'on condition that; in case that, if only' as in 'Provided the temperature remain the same, the volume which a gas occupies is . . .' and 'Freytag proposes a concert, providing somebody will pay for it'. Based on *The O.E.D.*

A certain writer errs when he says that *providing* (either with or without *that*) is 'misused for the conjunction *provided*'; and, by the way, *provided* was originally no less of a participle than *providing* is.

P.S. See POSTSCRIPT.

psychological moment, at the, is, in post-War usage, a mere synonym—and how pompous!—for *in the nick of time*. In the sense 'at the psychologically, most favourable moment', it is permissible, though hackneyed. It came into English as the translation of a French mistranslation of the German *das Moment*, which = 'momentum', not 'moment of time'. See especially Fowler's *Modern English Usage*.

psychology. Be sure to use this vague term so precisely that its volatility is crystallized, for it can be distressingly ambiguous. E.g., 'Shakespeare's psychology' has at least four meanings, the two most obvious being: 'Shakespeare's opinion of or theories about the mind' and 'the way in which Shakespeare's mind worked'. In *The Philosophy of Rhetoric*, 1936, at p. 82, Dr I. A. Richards has a most illuminating paragraph on the subject.

publicity; propaganda. The latter is 'any association, systematic scheme, or concerted movement for the propagation of a particular doctrine or practice' (*The O.E.D.*), whereas *publicity*, in its 20th Century sense, is 'the business [or the practice] of advertising or making articles, schemes, or persons publicly known' (*ibid.*). *Propaganda* cannot be applied to the advertising of articles (goods).

punctilious and **punctual.** A punctilious person,—one who is scrupulously observant of fine points, or of details of action or behaviour,—is always *punctual*, i.e., scrupulously observant of an appointed time (or, of trains, 'not late').

PUNCTUATION. In a curious little treatise published in 1644, *The English Primrôse*, by one Richard Hodges, a schoolmaster in Southwark, occurs this sentence: 'Great care ought to be had in writing, for the due observing of points: for, the neglect thereof will pervert the sence. As for example, My Son, if sinners intise thee consent thou, not refraining thy foot from their way. Which ought to bee written thus, My son, if sinners intise thee consent thou not, refraining thy foot, etc.'

Here is a newspaper article that calls attention to the importance of punctuation:—

PUNCTUATION AND SPELLING

Dr Temple's Views

A Word To "Idle Examiners"

The Archbishop of York, Dr Temple, thinks that correct punctuation is more important—intellectually—than correct spelling. He said so yesterday when he presented the school prizes at the Royal Infant Orphanage at Wanstead.

"In writing essays," said Dr Temple, "there are two things one has difficulty with—spelling and stops. Nearly everybody says it is the spelling that matters.

"Now spelling is one of the decencies of life, like the proper use of knives and forks. It looks slovenly and nasty if you spell wrongly, like trying to eat your soup with a fork.

"But, intellectually, spelling—English spelling—does not matter. Shakespeare spelt his own name at least four different ways, and it may have puzzled his cashiers at the bank.

"Intellectually, stops matter a great deal. If you are getting your commas, semi-colons, and full stops wrong, it means that you are not getting your thoughts right, and your mind is muddled." *The Observer*, Oct. 23, 1938.

Granted health and time, I shall, a few years hence, write a treatise (full-dress, serious, no-nonsense) on punctuation; but, before making a few remarks on punctuation in general and then giving some significant examples of mispunctuation, I shall refer the reader to some authorities to be studied:—

Dean Alford (Henry Alford), *The Queen's English*, 1863 (7th ed., 1888), pp. 124–125, 130–131.
Alex. Bain, *English Composition and Rhetoric*, 2 vols., 1887–88, at I, 89–90.
Alex. Bain, *A Higher English Grammar*, 2nd ed., 1897, at pp. 335–339.
F. Howard Collins, *Authors' and Printers' Dictionary*, 1905; 8th ed., 1938.
F. G. & H. W. Fowler, *The King's English*, 1906; 3rd ed., 1930, at pp. 228–229 (excellent).
Maurice H. Weseen, *Everyday Uses of English*, 1922, pp. 313–333 (useful).
H. W. Fowler, *Modern English Usage*, 1926 (excellent).
W. Whitten & F. Whitaker, *Good and Bad English*, 1939 (short but valuable).
But best of all: G. V. Carey, *Mind the Stop*, 1939. (Cambridge University Press; English ed., 3*s*.6*d*.)

Before coming to intrinsic punctuation, let us for a moment consider extrinsic punctuation—punctuation in reference to quotation marks. There is a tendency among printers to put the period (full-stop) and comma inside the 'quotes', but the semi-colon and colon outside (though one often sees this sort of monstrosity: 'He was "hot-stuff;" he was "no fool:" he was formidable'), as in:—

'The word "breakfast," now always written as one word, was, before that, a hyphenated word, "break-fast." The natural course is for such words to begin as two vocables, "care free"; to become hyphenated words, "care-free": and to end up as single words, "carefree."'

But careful printers are beginning to follow the more logical rule of putting punctuation inside the 'quote' only when the punctuation mark is actually *part* of the quotation and also serves to round off the entire phrase or sentence that is concluded. A good writer will punctuate the above example thus:—

'The word "breakfast", now always

written as one word, was, before that, a hyphenated word, "break-fast". The natural course is for such words to begin as two vocables, "care free"; to become hyphenated words, "care-free": and to end up as single words, "carefree".'

If one is quoting a person's actual words, the same rule should be observed as is observed in that example: with the caution that 'he said', 'as he said', etc., are to be treated as parenthetical; indeed, if you are in doubt, use parentheses.

'It was', he remarked, 'easy enough to find her.' Or 'It was' (he remarked) 'easy enough to find her.' In such an example, the quotations marks come *inside* the comma and outside the period, for the statement is obviously more important than the 'he remarked'. If you are in doubt, omit the quotation marks, provided that you make it clear that these are the actual words. (In the English Bible (A.V.), there are no quotation marks.)

In support of Dr Temple (as cited early in this article), I quote from Mr Frank Whitaker's practical, sane, suggestive address in *The J.I.J.*, January, 1939: 'Of punctuation I have time only to say this: that we ought to deplore the growing tendency to use only full stops and commas. Punctuation is an invaluable aid to clear writing, and I suggest that far too little importance is attached to it by many journalists.'

In very short sentences, the period (which marks the end of a statement) and the comma (which signifies apposition, as in 'Edward VII, King of England', or divides principal from subordinate clauses, as in 'When the girl arrived, the boy sat down') can—though not always happily—be made to suffice; but once you begin using long sentences, you need either the semi-colon, for a pause—a break—more important than that which is marked by a comma, as with the semi-colon in this sentence, or the colon, for a counterbalancing, a poising of the importance-stresses or significance-divisions: or for an addition that is too immediate and so final a stop as the period,—such an addition as you will have noticed in this, my rather long sentence, which (as at '. . . for a pause—a break—more important . . .') exemplifies the ordinary dash and the strong or intensive comma-dash ('. . . the period,—

such an addition as you will have noticed . . .').—And, of course, there is the period-dash, which marks a rather abrupt resumption or a dissociative break in the discourse. Such a break (if in the nature of a parenthesis: herein exemplified) may conclude with '.—' as well as begin with one. The stop written ':—' is the colon-dash; it serves to introduce a list or anything else that has been formally announced; it might, in short, be defined as 'annunciatory'. Nowadays, however, the colon-dash often gives way to the simple period, especially when the list or more especially the illustrative sentences or passage (e.g., 'The word "breakfast", now always written as one word . . .' earlier in this article) begins on a new line.

But there are fine shades of distinction between the following:—

(a) 'The man rose to his feet, his opponent rushed at him, and both fell heavily to the ground.'

(b) 'The man rose to his feet; his opponent rushed at him; and both fell heavily to the ground.'

(c) 'The man rose to his feet: his opponent rushed at him: and both fell heavily to the ground.'

I think that, here, (c) is affected, for it is too literary for the context. In (a), the first comma is perhaps too weak to mark adequately the ensuing pause. Of these three, (b) is the best: but better still is the more varied:—

'The man rose to his feet; his opponent rushed at him, and both men fell heavily to the ground'. If, however, 'and' were omitted, the most effective and suitable punctuation would be

'The man rose to his feet; his opponent rushed at him; both fell heavily to the ground',

although some writers might prefer

'The man rose to his feet. His opponent rushed at him; both fell heavily to the ground', or
'The man rose to his feet; his opponent rushed at him. Both fell heavily to the ground'. The objection to

'The man rose to his feet. His opponent rushed at him. Both fell'—but certainly not 'And both fell'—'heavily to the ground' is that the sentences are too nearly equal in length for so sharp a dissection as that which is given by three periods.

At this point, I should like to draw attention to the recent revival, in literary prose, of the 18th Century use of the semi-colon: that use which produces the effect of a stressed pause or of a rhetorical break, as in the following example from Michael Harrison's novel (or rather, one of his novels), *When All the Trees Were Green*, published in 1936:—'And now we are coming to a clearing in the woods; a little glade, bright green with the soft moss-grass; in the centre of which glade a stream ran between deep banks . . .'.

There are, in fact, five ways of indicating a break or a pause.

(1) Parentheses, as in 'He was (God forgive him) a scoundrel'.
It is worth one's while to remember that the contents of a parenthesis (the words between parentheses) must be such that their omission would neither alter the syntactic flow nor materially affect the pause.

(2) Dashes, as in 'He was—God forgive him!—a scoundrel'. This is stronger than (1).

(3) Commas, as in 'He was, God forgive him!, a scoundrel': but here the exclamation mark virtually precludes the use of commas.

(4) Semi-colons, as in 'He was; God forgive him!; a scoundrel!', though here, too, an exclamation mark looks odd in conjunction with a semi-colon.

But (3) and (4) are viable in: 'He was, as all men knew, a scoundrel' and 'He was; as all men knew; a scoundrel', the latter being very literary.

(5) Colons, as in 'He was: God forgive him!: a scoundrel', where, again, the exclamation mark induces a feeling of discomfort; a discomfort absent both from 'He was: as all men knew: a scoundrel' and from the preferable 'He was: all men knew (*or* knew it): a scoundrel', which is perhaps even more literary than (4).

The importance of punctuation—an importance that could hardly be over-emphasized—may be illustrated by the following example: the letter of invitation to Jameson at the time of his raid into the Transvaal. In telegraphic form, the text runs thus:—'It is under these circumstances that we feel constrained to call upon you to come to our aid should a disturbance arise here the circumstances are so extreme that we cannot but be-

lieve that you and the men under you will not fail to come to the rescue of people who are so situated.'

If you put a full stop after 'aid', the message contains an unequivocal invitation ('Come at once!'). But if you put the full stop, not after 'aid' but after 'here', the message becomes merely a conditional invitation depending on a circumstance arising at some indefinite time in the future.

Now, it is believed that the authors meant it to be conditional. But when it was cabled to *The Times*, the period was inserted after 'aid': as a result, the message was made to appear to justify Jameson's precipitancy.

[With thanks to Professor **A. W.** Stewart, who is, to many, better known as J. J. Connington.]

Now for some examples, this article being but short and readers desirous of detail being recommended to refer either to *The King's English* or to *Mind the Stop*.

In a publisher's list of books there appears:

'**ANARCHY** or **HIERARCHY**

by S. de Madariaga

Author of *Englishmen, Frenchmen, Spaniards, Disarmament, The Genius of Spain,* etc.'

Very confusing, that list of the author's works! Read, 'Author of *Englishmen, Frenchmen, Spaniards; Disarmament; The Genius of Spain;* etc.'

'The only student I have ever met who ever believed his ears was blind': the lack of punctuation is defensible on the score of fluency; but 'The only student I have met who ever believed his ears, was blind' does away with that ambiguity which may strike others as it did me— with a jar. (The sentence needs to be rewritten, perhaps in the form, 'Of all the students I have met, only one believed his ears: and he was blind' or '. . .; and he was blind'.

From the same author (Frank Binder, *Dialectic*, 1932) comes 'It is not enough to lead a student by the still waters, one must lose him at last in the stormy ones', the comma is inferior to a semi-colon or, as this example occurs in literary English, a colon.

'Bush and Brown slept in cloak and blanket on the bare soil, probably, Hornblower anticipated, most uncomfortably' (C. S. Forester, *Flying Colours*, 1938). The comma after 'soil' is too weak; I suggest, 'B. and B. slept . . . on the bare soil; probably (Hornblower anticipated) most uncomfortably'.

In the British Museum copy of H. A. J. Munro's *Criticisms and Elucidations of Catullus*, 1878, someone has, against the sentence 'The latest editor of the text Baehrens believes it like me to be one poem', the criticism, 'not grammatical'. (Munro had very odd ideas about punctuation; usually, he eschewed it—except for the period.) Rewrite, 'The latest editor of the text, Baehrens, believes it, like me, to be one poem' or, better, 'The latest editor of the text, Baehrens, like me believes it to be one poem' or 'Like me, the latest editor of the text, Baehrens, believes it to be one poem'.

'There was no villa to be seen . . . As they drew near it became evident that the narrow road ended by the villa itself' (Louis Bromfield, *The Strange Case of Miss Annie Spragg*, 1928). This passage obviously requires a comma after 'near'.

'For all the Loyalist Party know the girl may turn up at any second' (Laurence Meynell, *The House in the Hills*, 1937). Punctuate, 'For all the Loyalist Party know, the girl . . .'

'The crowd was thinning, many of the girls, among them Joan and Valerie, finding it chilly standing about in their scanty costumes, had gone up to dress' (W. H. Lane Crauford, *Murder to Music*, 1936). Anyone would feel chilly if he (or she) were stranded in such a sentence as that! Re-punctuate in some such fashion as this:—'The crowd was thinning; many of the girls (among them Joan and Valerie), finding it chilly standing about in their scanty costumes, went up to dress.'

'The night it all began torrential rain fell' (Dale Collins, *Lost*, 1933): insert a comma after 'began'.

'"You don't really like it, you're only pretending to please me"' (Muriel Hine, *Clear as the Sun*, 1938): a comma is required after 'pretending'; but that insertion weakens the comma after 'it'. Punctuate, 'You don't really like it; you're only pretending, to please me'.

'If there was any previous connection between Bennett and the Oultons that, and not Mrs O'Brien's name and address on their back, might account for Bennett's interest in Miss Molly's sketches' (E. R. Punshon, *The Dusky Hour*, 1937): put a comma after 'Oultons'.

'Can he, he has admittedly made money in America, be the confidence trickster . . .?' (*ibid*): not commas but dashes are required; parentheses would destroy the inference.

'And once I had discovered that there was no longer any doubt as to whether a spark of life still lingered in him' (Stephen Maddock, *Doorway to Danger*, 1938). I had reached the end of the sentence before I realized that not the whole sentence but only 'once I had discovered that' is an adverbial clause; a comma is needed after 'that', which is pronoun, not conjunction.

'He trod over to the window . . . His torch explored the shadows cast by the flowering shrubs without, however, revealing anything but a nondescript cat' (Georgette Heyer, *A Blunt Instrument*, 1938). When I came upon this sentence, I read 'two flowering shrubs without' (i.e., outside the house) and was then pulled up with a jerk. After 'shrubs', either a comma or, better, a semicolon is required.

'Shall we borrow one of Torquemada's witticisms and call them four more "little grey sells!"' (publishers' foreword to Agatha Christie's four stories in one volume, *Murder in the Mews*, 1937). Instead of '. . . "little grey sells!"' we require '. . . "little grey sells"!'; and a question mark would have been preferable to the exclamation mark.

In 'The opposite arrangement—that is to say, an abundance of short and unaccented syllables, and the more abrupt consonants alternated with the vowels, by making the pronunciation rapid, light and easy, corresponds to quickness of motion in the subject' (Alexander Bain, *English Composition and Rhetoric*, 1887–88, at II, 292) the punctuation is vague, probably incomplete, and certainly ambiguous. Instead of the comma after 'easy', a dash is required, to correspond to the first dash. I myself would use a comma-dash (,—), both after 'arrangement' and after 'easy'; or a colon. The colons would produce a more elegant effect.

In 'When the dreadful plague was mowing down the terrified people of London in great swathes, this brave man, instead of flying quietly, remained at his house' (Walter Thornbury), it is obviously the printer, not the author, who has erred by putting a comma after 'quietly' instead of before it.

'He had opposed the policy of alliance with Egypt against Assyria, . . . but when war came, in spite of his efforts, he heartened the spirit of King Hezekiah to fight to the death' (Introduction to Isaiah, in *The Bible as Literature*, 1937). Remove the comma from after 'came'. Better rewrite thus, '. . . but when, in spite of his efforts, war came, he heartened . . .'.

And, finally, two examples from Stuart Chase's *The Tyranny of Words*, 1938:—
'What is the ultimate nature of matter? The question we know by now is meaningless.' Punctuate thus:— '. . . The question, we know by now, is meaningless.'

'A bank studied on the basis of what is going on inside without recourse to abstractions like "credit", "liquidity", "soundness", is a pretty whimsical thing.' A comma after 'inside' would remove an ambiguity.

⟦To American readers Mr. Partridge's recommendations of the colon may seem strange, though perhaps in his examples the colon has 'a more elegant effect'. Certainly it should remind readers of the punctuation in their Bibles. For American usage an important authority is the University of Chicago Press *A Manual of Style*.—Double marks of punctuation, such as :— and ,—, have almost disappeared from American printing.— Many American printers prefer a general practice of setting all periods and commas within the quotation marks, all semicolons and colons outside of the quotation marks. The small points dangling after the broad double quotes of American use are curious-looking. However, in typescripts, where every symbol takes an em space, double quotes after period or comma may jut out ridiculously, especially when only the last word is quoted.—Mr. Partridge's account of punctuation shows by its wealth of possible effects that punctuation can be made a part of the art of writing— instead of the simple, almost mechanical routine that American schools recommend.⟧

PUNS. The pun is the lowest form of wit.

'. . . The universal Elizabethan habit of punning, which pervaded conversation and literature alike. Every kind of play on words was common, from the merest jingle in sound to the most elaborate calembour. Puns are now out of favour, probably because we think that the punster wishes us to laugh at them. We should be careful, however, not to take the punning habit of the Elizabethans too seriously. Clearly the Elizabethans did not laugh at puns, unless they were peculiarly amusing. They got merely a certain intellectual titillation out of the grotesque association of ideas which punning induced.'
Greenough & Kittredge, *Words and Their Ways in English Speech*, 1901.

Briefly, a pun is 'a play upon words'; more fully and more precisely, 'the use of a word so as to suggest two or more meanings or different associations, or the use of two or more words of the same or nearly the same sound with different meanings, so as to produce a humorous effect' (*The O.E.D.*).

Despite the epigraph, many puns are far from being 'the lowest form of wit': superficially these superior puns are still mere puns (why *mere*?); but they may comport a wealth of connotation that raises them to the upper regions of wit and they may have undertones and (to the ordinary reader) buried meanings that spring—can spring only—from profundity. From William Empson's acute and provocative *Seven Types of Ambiguity*, 1930, I select a few examples.

In *Macbeth* we have the verses,

Augurs, and understood relations, have
By maggot-pies, and choughs, and rooks,
    brought forth
The secret'st man of blood (III, iv.
    125–7).

Set beside this passage the significant

        Light thickens, and the crow
Makes wing to th' rooky wood (in III, ii).

'Macbeth looked out of the window because Banquo was to be killed soon after dusk, so he wanted to know how the time was going. . . . The peaceful solitary *crow*, moving towards bed and the other crows, is made unnaturally like Macbeth and a murderer who is coming against them; this is suggested . . . mainly, I think, by the use of the two words *rook* and *crow*.—*Rooks* live in a crowd and are mainly vegetarian; *crow* may be either another name for a *rook*, especially when seen alone, or it may mean the solitary

Carrion crow. This subdued pun is made to imply' this, that, and the other.

Having mentioned euphuistic conceit and the paradoxes cultivated in the 'nineties, 'which give a noun two contradictory adjectives and leave it to the reader to see how the adjectives are used', Mr Empson subtly continues thus:—'In an extended sense . . . this in itself is an ambiguity, just as a pun may repeat its key word once in each sense and be not less a pun. These tricks demand some thought and much awareness of the nature and pitfalls of language; it is not altogether a good sign when they are despised.'

Remembering that, in Shakespeare's day, *quibble* meant 'a pun', and that, in 1711, the swift-minded Shaftesbury could write, 'All humour had something of the quibble. The very language of the Court was punning', we may, after Empson, quote from Johnson:—'A quibble is to Shakespeare what luminous vapours'—probably mirages; possibly mists sun-thinned—'are to the traveller; he follows it at all adventures; it is sure to lead him out of his way and sure to engulf him in the mire. It has some malignant power over his mind. . . . A quibble was for him the fatal Cleopatra for whom he lost the world, and was content to lose it.' Empson's comment is, 'Nor can I hold out against the Doctor, beyond saying that life ran very high in those days, and that he does not seem to have lost the world so completely after all'. But he deplores the fact that Shakespeare was 'so fearfully susceptible to puns'. I merely add the well-known facts that punning was in the literary air, a literary exercise, a Court exercise, of Shakespeare's time, and that he wrote not merely for himself but also for his audiences; even the groundlings expected puns and enjoyed them.

Even Milton punned,—punned even in the bare and virile *Samson Agonistes*, where, at least once, there occurs a weighty and effective pun-by-etymology; Delilah is, in Samson's words,

'That specious monster, my accomplished snare'.

As Empson points out, the pun or rather puns are worked out thus:—'*Specious*, "beautiful and deceitful"; *monster*, "something unnatural and something striking shown as a sign of disaster"; *accomplished*, "skilled in the arts of

blandishment and successful in undoing her husband". The point here is the sharpness of distinction between the two meanings [of each of the three words, *specious*, *monster*, *accomplished*], of which the reader is forced to be aware; they are two pieces of information, two parts of the narrative; if ingenuity had not used an [etymological] accident, they would have required two words [each].' This quotation from Milton prompts Mr Empson to laugh quietly—or so I gather—at those who are 'mainly conscious of the pun'—any pun—'not of its consequences'.

He then adduces, from *Paradise Lost* (vi, 565–7), the words,

> Ye, who appointed stand,
> Do as you have in charge, and briefly touch
> What we propound, and loud that all may hear,

and comments thus:—'It is a bitter and controlled mood of irony in which Satan gives this address to his gunners; so much above mere ingenuity that the puns seem almost like a generalisation. But here, as for ironical puns in general, to be put into the state of mind intended you must concentrate your intention on the ingenuity; on the way the words are being interpreted both by the gunners themselves and by the angels who have not yet heard of artillery; on the fact that they are puns.'

He goes on to note that the pun has become more obvious; has become overt; has become 'less intimately an expression of sensibility'. (Here I interpolate a wish that the Miltonic puns and the subtler of the Shakespearian puns, in their essence, their principles, their dignity, their verbal richness, their sophistication and depth and variety of meaning, should be revived.) 'Thus', Mr Empson continues, 'its most definite examples are likely to be found, in increasing order of self-consciousness, among the seventeenth-century mystics who stress the conscious will, the eighteenth-century stylists who stress rationality, clarity, and satire, and the harmless nineteenth-century punsters who stress decent above-board fun.' He then, sarcastically, analyzes the kinds of pun that are considered, by the ordinary person, to be justifiable—puns for which the reader or the auditor has been prepared; puns so obvious that no preparation was necessary; puns that 'demand an attention . . . not absorbed into the attention demanded by the rest of the poem, and are a separate ornament on their own'; puns that are explicit only, not puns that are both explicit and implicit; puns that pose no strain on the intellect, no premium on imagination, no price on aesthetic awareness. In his implicit defence of the stronger, subtler, richer pun, he is, perhaps unconsciously, pleading for a departure from the standard of nit-witticism, for a proper contempt of the non-compulsive prohibitions set up by morons. (Not that Empson is wholly contemptuous of the 'curiously worldly' use of the pun in the 18th Century; he admits its virtues, as he admits the virtues of the 19th Century pun.)

Yet even the simple, obvious puns of the 19th Century are not always either obvious or simple—except to the cultured and intelligent reader or auditor. As exercises of wit, many are salutary; nor, all of them, the worse for the fact that, abstracted from their context, they can 'stand on their own feet'—no inconsiderable feat for a pun.

Charles Lamb, who once said 'May my last breath be drawn through a pipe, and exhaled in a pun', punned inveterately. Here are several of his witticisms, culled from Walter Jerrold's *Bon-Mots of Charles Lamb and Douglas Jerrold*, 1913. 'Charles Lamb and Ayrton were playing at whist, when Ayrton took a trick by trumping.

"Ah!" said he, "when Greek meets Greek"—Jerrold failing to indicate that here is a goodish pun on *Greek*, 'a card-sharper'—"then comes the tug of war."

"But when *you* meet Greek," retorted Lamb, "you can't read it."'

'An old lady, who was fond of her dissenting minister, once wearied Lamb by the length of her praises.

"I speak because I *know* him well", said she.

"Well, I don't," replied Lamb; "I don't, but damn him! at a venture."'

'You have no mock modesty about you—no, nor real either.'

From the same small volume, I take a few puns made by Douglas Jerrold (1803–57).

'Someone praised the *mise en scène* at one of Kean's revivals at the Princess's Theatre, to which Jerrold retorted, "Oh yes, it is all scenery and Keanery".'

'A friend was one day reading to Jerrold an account of a case in which a person named Ure was reproached with having suddenly jilted a young lady to whom he was engaged.

"Ure seems to have turned out to be a base 'un", said Jerrold.'

'Jerrold said to an ardent young gentleman, who burned with a desire to see himself in print:—Be advised by me, young man—don't take down the shutters before there is something in the window.'

'Discussing Mrs Grundy and her "set", a member of the same club said, "They'll soon say marriage is improper".

"No, no," said Jerrold, "they'll always consider marriage good breeding."'

'A lawyer's smile Douglas Jerrold described as "dirt cheap at six and eight-pence".'

'He kissed her and promised. Such beautiful lips! Man's usual fate—he was lost upon the coral reefs.'

'To a very thin man, who had been boring him, Jerrold said: "Sir, you are like a pin, but without either its head or its point".' [sharp as a needle, in fact.]

'A certain pretty actress being mentioned, Douglas Jerrold praised her early beauty. "She was a lovely little thing," he said, "when she was *a bud* and—(a pause)—"before she was *a blowen*."'

'On the carrying of Free Trade, Douglas Jerrold, an earnest free trader, immediately proposed the following epitaph for Protection—

Here Lies
PROTECTION
It lied throughout its life
and now
Lies Still.'

Which reminds one of the epigram,

And in her wondrous eyes
Love lies—and lies and lies

(or words to that effect).

Let us pass from the two wisely-simple, not-so-simple, witty Charles Lamb and Douglas Jerrold to the sophisticated James Abbott McNeill Whistler (1834–1903) and Oscar Wilde (1856–1900). Here I draw upon Walter Jerrold's *A Book of Famous Wits*, 1912. Whistler, however, was not a frequent punster; he was a frequent wit. But we may record that, Whistler 'having made some happy remark, Wilde showed his appreciation by saying, "I wish I had said that, Whistler". "You will, Oscar; you will", said Whistler dryly. . . . 'One of Wilde's retaliations may perhaps be recognized in his remark that "Whistler, with all his faults, was never guilty of writing a line of poetry".'

Sir Lewis Morris (author of *The Epic of Hades*), feeling disgruntled by the neglect with which he met while successors to the Laureateship were being discussed after Tennyson's death; 'It is a complete conspiracy of silence against me! What ought I to do, Oscar?' 'Join it', said Wilde.

'"It appears that I am dying beyond my means", was his whimsical comment on the straits to which he was reduced in his last illness.'

Of recent punster-wits, I shall cite only Mr Humbert Wolfe (poet and wit and able Civil Servant). Of a certain intellectualist critic of poetry, he remarked that he spoke on the subject as a professor *ex cathedra ignorantiae*. Asked how a woman politician, not long inducted into office, was progressing, he said, 'Oh, she's still *virago intacta*'.

pupil and **student**. A *pupil* at a school, a *student* at a university. [[In American usage we cater to the young people and speak of *high school students* as well as *college* and *university students*; and *grammar school pupils*. But a professor may talk of 'a former pupil of mine'. Musicians and painters have *pupils*, not *students*, though these are 'students of painting or of music' and some of them may study at 'the Art Students League'.]]

puppet and **marionette**. A *puppet* is any figure representing a human being; usually it is small; generally it is a doll. Also it is 'a human figure, with jointed limbs, moved by means of a string or wires; especially one of the figures in a puppet-show; a marionette' (*The O.E.D.*); but in this sense, *marionette* is now more usual.

pure does = *mere*, but avoid it if, as in 'pure Nudism', it sets up an ambiguity.

PURE ENGLISH. See STANDARD ENGLISH, II.—For the limits of pure English, see Section iii of STANDARD ENGLISH.

Puritan and **puritan**. A *Puritan* is a member of that party of English Protestants who, in late 16th-mid 17th Century, desired a further purification of the Church and, especially, a simpler form of worship. A *puritan* is 'one who is, affects

to be, or is accounted extremely strict, precise, or scrupulous in religion or morals' (*The O.E.D.*); it is now a pejorative term.

purport in the sense of 'purpose' is now so rare—so nearly obsolete—as to make its employment inadvisable; see the passage quoted at MALAPROPISMS. The general sense of the noun is 'meaning' or 'tenor'; and, properly used, the word is restricted to documents and speeches. As a verb, it is confined to documents and speeches and it signifies 'to have as its meaning' or 'to be intended to seem', 'to be made to appear', as in 'He received a letter purporting to be written by me and to contain my decision on an important matter'. Adapted from *The Con. O.D.*

PURPOSE. See FINAL CLAUSES.

purpose (v.). See 'PROPOSE and PURPOSE'.

purposely. See ADVISEDLY.

putter and **potter** (v.). The latter is Standard English and American, the former is English dialectal and American Standard

Q

quadra-; quadri-; quadru-. The first is always wrong; the second is the usual form, except in *quadrumanous* and in such other nouns as have a second element that begins with *p* (as in *quadruped*). The sense is 'having *or* consisting of *or* connected with four (things specified)'. (*The O.E.D.*)

quaint is 'unusual, uncommon, or even odd', but at the same time either 'attractive' or 'agreeable' especially if it is either 'pretty or dainty in an old-fashioned way'. Do not use it to mean either 'merely odd' or 'amusing (or droll)': those are a slangy or, at best, a colloquial usage.

Quakers. See at MORMONS, where it occurs, not by association of ideas (no association is possible), but for the sake of convenience.

qualitive is incorrect for *qualitative* (referring to quality), which is often contrasted with *quantitative* (referring to quantity).

quality of is correct in 'a certain quality of paper' but wrong in 'To finish up in some club of the same quality of his own' (John G. Brandon, *The Mail-Van Mystery*, ca. 1937), where the first 'of' seems to have led the author astray.

quantative is incorrect for *quantitative*; cf. QUALITATIVE.

quantity and **number.** It is better not to speak of *a large* (or *a small*) *quantity* of things or persons when one means *a large* (or *small*) *number*; but in familiar (though not in literary) Standard English, *a quantity* may be used of an indefinite, i.e., of a fair or considerable number of persons or things, as in 'Four chairs and a quantity of pillows' (Mrs Carlyle, 1852). But avoid it if it leads to ambiguity; it is better to differentiate, as in 'It takes a large number of nuts to make such a quantity as there is in this bag' and 'He gave away a large quantity of canned goods but still has a number of cans'. (*The O.E.D.*)

quarter after, a. See HALF AFTER, A.

query and **inquiry; quest.** A *query* is a specific question, a question of limited or particular or *singular* reference, whereas an *inquiry*, though it may simply mean 'a question', more usually means a set or a series of questions, an investigation, as in 'an official inquiry into the fate of *The Thetis*'. A *quest*, in current usage and apart from technicalities, is a search or pursuit, especially of something remote, or figuratively; e.g., 'the quest of the Holy Grail'. (*The O.E.D.*)

question (v.) is used in a misleading manner in the following from Eric Partridge, *The French Romantics' Knowledge of English Literature*, 1924, 'Despite this popularity, Scott was questioned as to whether he was a suitable source for dramatists'. The meaning is not that someone asked Scott this question, but that *the question was raised* or *the suitability was called in question*.

questionary is an adjective; 'having the form of, or consisting of, questions; conducted by means of questions', as in 'a questionary interview'; *questionnaire* is a list of questions; especially an ordered list—or a skilful set—of questions, designed to cover a certain field, or to fulfil an educational or official purpose. *Questionnaire* has—more's the pity!—displaced *questionary* in this sense ('Answers to the society's questionary of sociology and ethnography', *The Athenaeum*, 1887: cited by *The O.E.D.*).

quiescent; quiet. *Quiescent* means 'inactive, at rest, motionless', as in 'a quiescent star', 'He lay quiescent', and, in Philology, (of a letter that is) 'silent, not sounded'. (*The O.E.D.*)

quit—quitted. The form *quit*, whether in the preterite or in the past participle, is English dialectal. [[In American it is a standard variant of *quitted*.]]

quite cannot properly qualify a noun. 'Quite the sensation of the day' and 'Not quite the thing' are colloquial phrases, better avoided in writing.

quite does not—in good English—mean 'rather', its two Standard senses being (i), 'completely, wholly, entirely, to the fullest extent', as in 'Haws . . . which often quite cover the hawthorn bushes' (Jefferies), 'Here have I sat . . . Quite by myself', 'quite certain', 'a quite separate question' or 'quite another question (or, thing)'; and

(ii) 'actually; truly; positively', as in 'He died quite suddenly', 'She was so perturbed that she felt quite ill'. The exclamatory *quite* (or *quite so*!) ('I agree with you' or 'I heartily approve') is colloquial.

quite a for *a quite*. E.g., the colloquial 'He stayed there quite a long time' should be '. . . a quite long time'. But 'quite a while' is correct, because *a while* is indivisible (it is often spelt *awhile*).

quota, 'a predetermined share or proportion', is used unhappily in 'The Queen's Road was busy with its usual quota of life', Laurence Meynell, *The Dandy*, 1938.

QUOTATION. See MISQUOTATIONS.

QUOTATION CLICHÉS. See CLICHÉ.

QUOTATION MARKS, unnecessary use of; e.g., in 'It would seem that over all was hanging some menace which was real but intangible, something against which the sling-shots, the knives, the "silenced" automatics of gangdom, could not prevail'. The quotation marks would be appropriate only if the word *silenced* were a technical or slang term of which the reader was presumably ignorant.

QUOTATION MARKS TO INDICATE SLANG. See SLANG, Section III, last paragraph.

quote. See CITE.

R

'Rabbit, Welsh, generally supposed to be a corruption of -*Rarebit*, is actually a slang nickname for a local dish, similar to "Norfolk Capons" for red herrings, "Irish apricots" for potatoes, etc.', Ackermann. The form *rarebit* is incorrect.

racquet, a frequent spelling of (tennis-) *racket*, is quite incorrect; 'in some mysterious way', says Sir Gordon Lowe (*Lowe's Lawn Tennis Annual*, 1935), 'it has got mixed up with the French spelling "raquette"'.

radical, Radical; radicle. A *Radical* is 'one who advocates sweeping changes, esp. in government and the social order'; *radical* means 'basic, fundamental'; but a *radicle*, is, in Botany, an embryonic primary root, or, more generally, a rootlet; in Philology, however, a root or stem is a *radical*, not a *radicle*.

radio (radiotelegraphy) for *wireless* (broadcasting), has been opposed by many Englishmen on the ground that it is an Americanism: regarded closely, it is seen to be at least as unobjectionable as *wireless* (whether noun, adjective, or verb). *Radio*, as verb, means either 'to send a message by radio' or 'to broadcast'; but in England, it has been, for the most part, restricted to the former sense; *radio*, moreover, is also short for *radiogram*. Both 'to *radio*' and 'to *broadcast*' are infinitely preferable to either *radiocast* or *radiobroadcast*.

radius ignorantly confused with *diameter, circumference*, as in John G. Brandon, *The Pawnshop Murder*, 1936, 'objects which came within the radius lit by her torch'.

rail for *railroad, railway*, is a 'rubberstamp word' that should be eschewed by self-respecting writers. [[In American usage the phrase *by rail* is probably standard.]]

railroad is the usual term in the U.S.A., **railway** the usual term for the British Empire. But *railway* is much more widely used (witness Weseen) in the States than is generally believed in England, and in England *railroad* was, until ca. 1900, at least as common as *railway*. [[*Webster's* states a distinction often made in American English: *railroad* for heavy steam transportation; *railway* for the lighter street-car (or tram) lines, for shop railways, crane railways, or any way for wheels. *Webster's* admits *railway* for *railroad* as defined above; but by some opinions it is old-fashioned and probably obsolescent.]]

raise is transitive, *rise* is intransitive. The noun is *rise*, but *raise* is permissible (though less usual) in the sense 'an increase in amount (especially of money)' and correct in the sense 'a rising road or passage' ('Sometimes at the top of a long raise they stopped to breathe the horse', Hall Caine), though for 'a piece of rising

ground; a hill', *rise* again is more usual. (*The O.E.D.*)

raise and **rear.** One *rears* children; animals are either *reared* or *raised*. As applied to human beings, *raise* is depreciative, facetious. [[Not so in American English. In the U.S.A. 'born and raised' is much more common than 'born and reared'. Teachers fought for the latter but they did not convince the generations now mature.]]

raison d'être is a wholly unnecessary Gallicism for *reason*, or, occasionally (and incorrectly), *explanation*.

ranch and **rancho; range; hacienda.** A *range* is 'the region in which cattle or sheep may pasture' (but chiefly the former), or, without *a* or *the*, 'grazing ground'. A *rancho* is 'a large grazing farm; a ranch;—distinguished from *hacienda*', a *hacienda* being a Spanish American term (*rancho* is Spanish American too, but also Southwestern U.S.) for 'a cultivated farm, with a good house, in distinction from a farming establishment with rude huts for herdsmen, etc.', i.e., a *rancho*. In Western U.S.A. and Canada a *ranch* is 'an establishment, with its estate, for the grazing and rearing of horses, cattle, or sheep' (not cattle only, as *The O.E.D.* has it); especially 'the buildings occupied by owner and employees, with the adjacent barns, corrals, etc.; also, the persons on the estate collectively'. Loosely [and commonly] any farm in the West, esp. if large.

rang. See RING.

range (n.). See RANCH.

rapt. See at WRAPT.

rare and **scarce.** Weseen has neatly established the difference, thus:—'The adjective *rare* is often misused for *scarce*, as "Potatoes are rare this winter". *Rare* applies properly to things that are infrequent at all times and usually to things that have superior qualities, as "Great leaders are rare". *Scarce* applies to ordinary things that are temporarily not plentiful, as "Jobs are scarce this winter".'

rarely or ever. See 'SELDOM OR EVER.'

rather, had; rather, would. 'I had rather oppose prejudices than confute arguments'; but *would rather* when an hypothesis is expressed; e.g., 'were a patriot reduced to the alternative of death or political slavery, I am confident he would rather die than live' (or 'he would, I am confident, rather die than live'). [This is taken from a source to which the reference has been mislaid. *Auctori ignoto gratias habeo.*]

rather a . . ., misused for *a rather . . .* 'He was rather a dandy' is correct, for 'a dandy' is, here, indivisible in the sense that one cannot say 'a rather dandy'; but 'He was rather a conceited dandy' is incorrect for '. . . a rather conceited'; cf. 'a very conceited dandy'.

A parallel is afforded by 'quite a dandy' and 'a quite recent dandy' (*not* 'quite a recent dandy').

rather than for *than*. 'All this was new to him, his experience having made him more knowing about bookies rather than books' (John Ferguson, *Death of Mr Dodsley*, 1937). To correct this sentence, omit 'rather', or write '. . . having made him knowing about bookies rather than about books'.

rational ('endowed with reason'); hence, 'sane, sensible, reasonable' is now rare as a noun; *rationale*, 'a reasoned exposition of principles; hence, an explanation', also 'the logical or the rational basis (*of* anything)', is only noun. (*The O.E.D.*)

re from *in re* (Latin), 'in the matter of', which is supposed in commercial offices to be an abbreviation of 'referring to', can be properly used only in the dryest of business communications.

re- and **re** (v.). If *re* = 'again', then hyphenate, as in *re-sound*; if it = 'back-(wards)', then write the verb as one word, as *resound*. Note especially *re-cover*, 'to cover again', and *recover*, 'to have good health again'.

reaction is occasionally misused for *attitude* or *opinion*.—Cf. the next entry.

reaction is correctly used in *one's reaction to*, 'one's response (whether conscious or sub-conscious) to' or 'one's behaviour in relation to an influence (actual or presumed)', as in 'His reaction to the doctor's treatment was, all in all, satisfactory' or 'I fear that my reactions to his proposal were not quite what he expected'. But *reaction on* is incorrect, as in 'The reaction of the doctor's treatment on the patient was alarming' or 'The reactions of Belgravia on Suburbia are snob-making'. One's reaction is one's action in reference *to* something, not one's influence *on* something.

reactionary. Says A. P. Herbert:— 'The word is not needed. Speak, if you like, of the forces of Obstruction, the foes of Change, the apostles of Privilege, the enemies of Reform and Progress (though

Progress is another "Question-Beggar"); but kill this mean and imbecile sneer-word, whose history is a long procession of errors.' (*What a Word!*, p. 28.)

real is often unnecessary. Particularly unnecessary in the phrase in which it so often occurs: *in real life*, as, e.g., in 'Very often in fiction, as in real life, one is appalled . . .', where *in life* (or *in reality*) would be much superior to *in real life*. That example occurs in a review written by a novelist that prides himself on his economical style.

Always ask yourself whether *real* or *mere* or *actual* is necessary [not '*really*']: if it is not, then omit the excrescential word. And cf. REALLY.

realize for 'to *obtain* or *gain*' is loose.

really, actually and **definitely** are generally unnecessary. The frequent use of 'really', 'definitely', 'actually', 'as a matter of fact', 'to tell you the truth', etc., shows the speaker's lack of confidence in his own credibility; he seems to need additional assurance that what he asserts is not a fabrication or a mere conjecture. He whose Yea is Yea and his Nay Nay has no need of these adverbial supports. Father Ronald Knox, in *Double Cross Purposes*, 1937, says that 'They found Victor Lethaby a tornado of well-bred apologies, all punctuated with an irritating repetition of the word "actually"—a habit of modern youth, particularly when he is lying'. It is a well known fact that *as a matter of fact* often prefaces either a lie or a deliberate half-statement.

realm. See SPHERE.

realty is the legal term for 'real property', 'real estate': it can never be used as a synonym of *reality*.

reason. See CAUSE.

reason . . . because, or **why . . . because,** is often used redundantly for *reason . . . that*, as in 'The reason he does this (or, why he did this) is because he knows no better'.

receipt is now archaic for *recipe* (in cookery); a *receipt* is a written acknowledgement of money or goods received, or the receiving itself (as in 'On the receipt of the recipe, the cook immediately went to the kitchen and made the new dish'). [[In American usage *receipt* is still current in cookery though less common than *recipe*.]]

RECEIVED STANDARD. See STANDARD ENGLISH, II.

receptacle, of a thing; **recipient,** of a

person. 'The recipient of the ornate receptacle was less pleased than its donors had hoped he would be.'

recipe. See RECEIPT.

recollect and **re-collect.** Respectively 'to recall to mind' and 'to collect again', as in 'I do not recollect re-collecting my MSS, but as they're here, I suppose I must have done so'.

recollect and **remember.** The former may be synonymous with the latter; but discriminating writers and speakers—discriminate. '*Recollect*, when distinguished from *remember*, implies a conscious or express effort of memory to recall something [that] does not spontaneously rise in the mind' (*The O.E.D.*), as in 'At last I recollected what, during my illness (lasting, you may recall, some nine weeks), I had failed to remember, important though it was'.

recompense is the v.; either *recompence* or, etymologically, *recompense* is then.

recondition, (**-ing**), in constant use in official documents, is a bastard and illegitimate word, with which Mr A. P. Herbert deals very trenchantly (*What a Word!* pp. 22–24), pointing out that *improve* or *reconstruct* conveys the meaning. [[In American usage *recondition*, (*-ing*) is standard in the sense *renovate*, *renovation*, for automobiles and other machines and equipment such as electrical refrigerators, gas stoves, typewriters.]]

recountal occurs in *The O.E.D.* with the implication that its use is mainly journalistic. There can be little doubt that it arose through a confusion of *account*, *recounting*, *recital*, and it jars one to find it in a reputable novelist such as Miss Georgette Heyer: 'She chose the luncheon hour as a suitable time for the recountal to Jim of the whole affair of the letter' (*They Found Him Dead*, 1937).

recopy is the verb, **re-copy** the noun. But as we may copy a copy, no less than we may copy an original, *re-copy* and *recopy* are pointless except on rare occasions.

recourse for *resource*. 'Most of us read detective stories and know all the tricks of the trade of the fiction-detective—but how many of us know how the *real* criminal investigators work, and what recourses they have at their command to help them in their fight against crime?': blurb of Nigel Morland's *The*

Conquest of Crime, 1937. See also RESOURCE.

recover and **re-cover.** Respectively, 'to get (a thing) back' and 'to cover again', as in 'I succeeded in recovering that excellent chair which, sent to be re-covered, had gone astray'.

recreation and **re-creation** are to be kept distinct: the latter = 'creation anew', the former = 'refreshment, physical or mental or spiritual'. In 'This was a temperament singularly fitted for the recreation of life's little comedies and tragedies' (John Galsworthy, Preface to Stacy Aumonier's *Ups and Downs*, 1929), *re-creation* is the word required. The corresponding adjectives are *recreational* and *re-creative* (generally written *recreative*).

recrudescence has been so strongly and wittily condemned by Fowler that I, who have sinned but do now repent, need only point out that, etymologically, it = 'a breaking out again of a wound', 'a becoming raw of the flesh'; hence, it is used of a disease, a sore, an epidemic. Hence, figuratively, a renewal or a return of a quality, or a state of things, especially and *properly* if they are regarded as evil or objectionable, as in 'a recrudescence of calumny', 'the recrudescence of a metaphysical Paganism' (*The O.E.D.*). Any extension of that 'figuratively' leads inevitably to absurdity.

rectify. See JUSTIFY.

recto. See VERSO.

rector and **vicar** puzzle all except the cleric and the knowledgeable. A *rector* is 'a parson [*q.v.*] or incumbent of a parish whose tithes are not impropriate' (i.e., held by the parson); a *vicar's* tithes, however, are impropriate (held by him). (*The O.E.D.*)

rectoral is applied only to God (as spiritual Ruler); *rectorial* to a rector. (The adjective corresponding to *vicar* is *vicarial*, which is not to be confused with *vicarious*.)

recumbent and **incumbent; super-incumbent; decumbent.** *Recumbent* is 'lying down'; 'reclining' ('His recumbent form was scarcely visible'); so too is the now rare *decumbent* ('The advantages of a decumbent'—now preferably *recumbent*—'position'), which has in Botany the technical sense, (of plants) 'lying or trailing upon the ground, but with up-pointing extremity'. In *incumbent*, the stress is on the weight of the 'lier'; cf. the figurative *incumbent on* ('obligatory upon'), as in 'It is incumbent on him to look after his aged mother'. In Geology, *incumbent* has, like *superincumbent*, the sense, 'overlying'; *superincumbent*, however, is not properly a geological term, though it is applied, in a general way, to overhanging rocks. (*The O.E.D.*)

recurring for *frequent* is wholly unnecessary; and it is also catachrestic, for, as an adjective, it should be applied to that which recurs either at irregular intervals or, as in *recurring decimals*, to infinity, and for irregular recurrence the correct adjective is *recurrent*; 'It might well be that here the scientific criminologist will find one more means of dealing with a problem that is one of the most recurring in his work', Nigel Morland, *The Conquest of Crime*, 1937.

REDUNDANCY. See VERBOSITY, last paragraph.

re-enforce is still current in the U.S.A. (though less common than *reinforce*); it is rare in England, where *reinforce* is preferred.

refer to. See ALLUDE.

reflection and **reflexion.** 'The etymological spelling with *x* is the [earlier], and is still common in scientific use, perhaps through its connexion with *reflex*; in the general [i.e., the non-scientific] senses the influence of the verb has made the form with *ct* the prevailing one' (*The O.E.D.*).

reform and **re-form.** To *reform* is 'to improve, to correct'; *re-form* is 'to form anew'. Thus, one re-forms clay models, but one reforms criminals (or tries to).

refute and **deny.** To *deny* an accusation is merely to assert that it is false; to *refute* an accusation is to prove that it is false. One can also *refute* (or *confute*) the accuser; and one may *confute* an accusation. Perhaps it would be wise to reserve *confute* for proving accusers and arguers to be wrong, and *refute* for proving accusations, arguments, theories to be wrong; certainly *refute* is much the more common in the latter application. A further distinction between *confute* and *refute* is that the former is the stronger word.

regal. See KINGLY.

regalia, 'emblems (or insignia) of royalty', is a plural.

regard. One says *in regard to* and *without regard to*, but *as regards*.

regarding. See CONJUNCTIONS, DISGUISED.

regarding, preposition = 'in respect

of', can be ambiguous, as in 'He [an idiot] would have a child's mentality too, regarding likes and dislikes', Daphne Du Maurier, *Rebecca*, 1938.

regime is an English word. If it is italicized and so treated as a French word, it must bear an accent, thus: *régime*; cf. ROLE.

REGIONAL DIALECTS. See DIALECT and STANDARD ENGLISH, II.

regret (v.) is frequently ambiguous; as in 'For an instant Mr Pendlebury regretted the freshness of Berkshire. Then his natural buoyancy reasserted itself. After all, though it was hot here . . ., Central London must be an inferno', Anthony Webb, *Mr Pendlebury's Second Case*, 1938. The meaning is that Mr Pendlebury, who was not in Berkshire at the time, longed for—*not* 'was repentant (or apologetic) about'— the pleasant county of Berkshire.

regulate and **relegate** are often confused by those who know the former but have merely heard the latter. *Relegate* is 'to consign to an inferior position, or to hand over to another to deal with'.

reinforce. See RE-ENFORCE.

reiterate and **repeat.** The latter is general; the former, particular, being applied only to words, statements, requests, expressions of feeling. *Iterate* (*q.v.*) is a literarism.

rejoinder is either 'the defendant's answer to the plaintiff's replication' (plaintiff's reply to defendant's plea) or, in general usage, 'an answer to a reply': it is a pity to weaken it to synonymity with '*any* reply'. (*The O.E.D.*)

relation and **relative.** The writer is one of those who prefer *relative* to *relation* in the sense 'kinsman'.

relations towards. See PREPOSITIONS WRONGLY USED.

RELATIVE CLAUSES. For the use of *that, which, who* (the why and the when), see 'WHICH and THAT'.

'A moderate number of relative clauses may give charm and ease to the style, many consecutive ones are often felt as heavy and cumbersome', writes Professor Otto Jespersen in *Notes of Relative Clauses* (S.P.E. Tract No. xxiv, 1926). He gives an excellent example from Medwin's *Life of Shelley*, 1847):—

'Lewis told that [i.e., the story] of Minna, *which* first appeared in *The Conversations of Lord Byron*; and one also sketched there, *which* is more stirring, of a haunted house, at Mannheim, *which* he had inhabited, *that* had belonged to a widow, *who* to prevent the marriage of her only son with a poor but honest maiden, had sent him to sea, *where* he perished in a wreck.'

The sentence might be rewritten thus:—

'Having told that story of Minna which first appeared in *The Conversations of Lord Byron*, Lewis went on to relate another and more stirring story, which had been briefly outlined there. It concerned a haunted house, which, inhabited later by Lewis, had belonged to a widow. This widow, to prevent her son's marriage with a poor but honest maiden, had sent him to sea—and to his death in a wreck [*or*, to sea, where he perished in a wreck].'

RELATIVE CLAUSES, WRONG POSITION OF. See AGREEMENT, FALSE.

RELATIVE PRONOUN, attached to wrong noun. See AGREEMENT, FALSE.

RELATIVE PRONOUN, omitted. In many instances, the omission of the relative pronoun leads to 'a form of expression which can hardly be matched for conciseness in English or any other language' (Onions), although this omission is generally avoided in dignified or literary writings. Thus 'The man I was talking about is a well known author', *that* being omitted and this shorter form being preferred to 'The man about whom I was talking'; 'The etymology (*that*) you met with' rather than 'The etymology with which you met'. As Jespersen has remarked, this omission of the relative pronoun, so far from being a fault, 'is a genuine English idiom of long standing' (*Growth and Structure of the English Language*, p. 118).

relegate. See REGULATE.

relevant. See at REVELANT.

relic is incorrect for *relict*, 'a widow'. In all other senses, *relict* is either obsolete or obsolescent.

remain uncovered is often very ambiguous, for it means not only 'to stay uncovered after having one's (or its) cover (hat, etc.) removed' by oneself or another, or by an action or process, but also 'to stay without a cover that has never been put on'.

remediable; remedial. The former is passive, 'able to be remedied or redressed; curable', as in 'Where injustice, like disease, is remediable, there the remedy must be applied in word or deed' (Jowett); the latter is active, 'affording

or constituting a remedy, tending to remedy, relieve, or redress; potentially curative, potentially effective in providing a remedy', as in 'The remedial part of a law' (Blackstone).

'Every good political institution must have a preventive operation as well as a remedial' (Burke), and 'Tribulation is a remedial (though bitter) pill'.—The adverbs are *remediably* and *remedially*; the opposites of the adjectives are *irremediable* (adverb in -*bly*) and—what? Perhaps *inefficacious* and *ineffectual*. There seems to be no such adjective as *irremedial*, though it is hard to see why there shouldn't be one! Based on *The O.E.D.*)

remembrance and **reminder.** *Reminder* is rare for 'memento'; *remembrance* is rare and obsolescent for *reminder*, 'something that reminds, or is intended to remind, a person; a mention designed to remind a person of something'; *remembrance* cannot be interchanged with *reminder* in the latter's sense of 'a person that reminds'. In short, *remembrance* and *reminder* are, in current usage, never interchangeable.

remember. See RECOLLECT.

reminisce, though 'still somewhat colloquial or jocular' (*The O.E.D.*), is almost certain to be adopted as Standard English, for it is so very convenient for 'to indulge in reminiscences; (of a person) to be reminiscent'; in the sense 'to recollect or remember', it serves no useful purpose and is already obsolescent. (*The O.E.D.*)

reminiscent of for *indicative of* or *redolent of* is feeble: and incorrect.

remit and **send.** Remit = 'to *send*' only in the specific sense, 'to send or transmit (money or valuables) *to* a person or a place'. In any other sense of *send*, *remit* is either incorrect or unthinkable.

remunerate. See 'RENUMERATE and REMUNERATE.'

Renaissance and **Renascence; renaissance** and **renascence.** As a synonym of 're-birth', only *renascence*; for a revival, e.g., in art or literature, either *renaissance* or *renascence*, though preferably the latter. For that great European revival of art and letters which began in the 14th Century and reached its English peak in the 16th Century, or the period itself or its architecture, *Renaissance* is the more usual, the other being literary and perhaps a trifle affected: the adjectives are *Renaissance* or *Renascence*, preferably the former. The adjective corresponding to the 're-birth' sense of *renascence* is *renascent*; there is no such adjective as *renaissant*, and *Renaissant* is virtually obsolete. (*The O.E.D.*)

rend, 'to tear, to tear apart'; preterite *rent*; past participle, *rent*.

render a decision and **render decisions** are inferior to *make a decision* and *make decisions*.

rendition, 'surrender (of a garrison or a person)', is obsolescent; as 'a performing or a performance', it is frowned upon in England, even in a musical connexion (*rendering* or *playing* is preferable); and as 'the amount produced or rendered; the yield (especially of silk)', it is an Americanism.

rent (v.). See HIRE . . . And cf. the entry at REND.

rent is misused when it is made synonymous with *let* or *lease*. The lessee, not the lessor, 'rents' a house, a room; the lessor 'leases' or 'lets' it. [[In American English *rent* and *lease* are used of both the tenant and the landlord.]]

renumerate, 'to enumerate again', is obsolete; *remunerate* = 'to repay or requite; to reward'. But people that have never heard of *renumerate* (and, if they did, wouldn't know what it meant), often allow their undisciplined tongues to say *renumerate* when they intended *remunerate*.

reoccurrence is incorrect for *recurrence*; *reoccur* is rare for *recur*.

repairable can be used for *reparable* only of material things (buildings, roads, boots); in the sense 'falling due to be repaired, due (if occasion arises) to be repaired', either form is correct, but for material objects, *repairable* is to be preferred.

repast. See ELEGANCIES.

repeat. See 'REITERATE and REPEAT'.

repellent and **repulsive.** *Repellent* is confined to persons, their faces or expressions, their statements or demands; *repulsive* is synonymous with *repellent* in the sense 'repelling by coldness or excessive austerity or by some disagreeable feature; affecting one with distaste or aversion', though here, *repulsive* is the stronger word; but *repulsive* also = 'repellent *to the mind*, i.e., disgusting', as in 'repulsive tropical plants, repulsive manners', 'Balzac . . . is often repulsive, and not unfrequently dull' (Leslie Stephen). (*The O.E.D.*)

repent for *regret* or *resent* is a misuse.

'She had treated them well and he no longer repented her coming to Grakenhill', H. W. Freeman, *Joseph and His Brethren*, 1928.

repertoire and **repertory.** The latter is a storehouse (lit. or fig.) where something may be found, as in 'The established repertory of our statutes and usages' (Milman); it may be, but is better not, used as a synonym of *repertoire*, 'a stock of plays or musical pieces with which either a company or a player is accustomed—or prepared—to perform', hence one's stock of, e.g., stories; the adjective of *repertoire*, however, is *repertory*, as in *repertory company* and *repertory theatre*. (*The O.E.D.*)

REPETITION, needless, has been described as 'a mark of illiteracy—or of a minor intelligence'. 'It looked bad, that it did! With all the . . . Very bad, it looked. Hersey wouldn't half be interested, he wouldn't!' (Freeman Wills Crofts, *Sudden Death*, 1935). Nor is repetition particularly effective or even useful in 'Denis had met the girl at Stern Bridge, and had gone there without going through Isle by going some roundabout way' (John Chance Newton, *Wheels in the Forest*, 1935): which is, moreover, an ambiguous sentence.

Words or phrases should be repeated only if the repetition is effective or if it is essential to clarity: two occasions that occur often enough. Macaulay is an excellent writer to study in this respect.

replace is frequently misused for *displace* (or *supplant*) or *put something* (or *someone*) *in the place of*. 'From the Post-Bag', *The Observer*, Sept. 20, 1936, contained this:—'May I call attention to a regrettable misuse of English perpetrated—of all places!—at the Journalists' Congress? The point under discussion was the pressure alleged to be brought to bear on editors, with the result that "in more than one instance the correspondents have been replaced". To replace means, and can only mean, to put back in its place. Obviously the meaning was intended to be the opposite to displace.—Stephen Tone, *Coventry*.'—Jespersen, *The Philosophy of Grammar*, 1924, 'Irregular forms are those which [speakers] will often tend to replace by new forms created on the principle of analogy'. Dean Alford drew attention to this error in *The Queen's English* as long ago as 1865, 'Lord Derby went out of office and was replaced by Lord Palmerston', pointing out that this literally means 'Lord D. went out and Lord P. *put him back again*'. The error seems, however, to be incurable; we find it again in *The Evening News*, March 7, 1938, 'But surely the time has come to replace complaints by action . . . to replace those deplorable examinations by a better and more practicable system'. It is diverting to record the following misuse taken from Ludwig Wittgenstein's paper, 'Logical Form', which was read in 1929: 'Where ordinary language disguises logical structure, where it allows the formation of pseudo-propositions, where we must replace it by a symbolism which gives a clear picture of the logical structure, excludes pseudo-propositions, and uses its terms unambiguously' (*The Aristotelian Society: Supplementary Volume ix*, 1929). [[In American usage (as seemingly in British usage) *replace* means to *place again*, to *take the place of*, to *fill the place of*.]]

replete is debased to mean *complete* or *furnished with*, in the announcement by a catering firm of a branch café 'replete with every modern convenience'; *replete* means 'quite full', 'full to overflowing'. — See also COMPARATIVES, FALSE.

replica should not be used as a synonym of *repetition*, as it is in 'His speech was an almost exact replica of one delivered by Disraeli'. Be careful with *replica*, which might well be restricted to its use as an art term; and as an art term, it is properly 'a copy, duplicate or reproduction . . . made'—not by another but—'by the original artist' (*The O.E.D.*)

reported. See 'REPUTED and REPORTED'.

REPORTED SPEECH. One excuse for reported speech is a desire to break up the monotony of verbatim dialogue by making it impersonal: but reported or indirect speech (*oratio obliqua*) is, because of its artificiality, more apt than direct speech (*oratio recta*) to become monotonous. What, in 'They declare that they refuse to fight' or 'They declared that they refused to fight', is there that is preferable to '"We refuse to fight"', they declare' or 'They declare: "We refuse to fight"'?

The Classics started this cumbrous metamorphosis of the speaker's actual words, and despite the fact that the Romans often made a sad mess of it,

we stick to an outmoded vehicle of thought. Newspaper reporters of Parliamentary (and other) speeches continue to use it; examiners of the young still set questions on it. The best justification is that it exercises the wits: but why exercise the wits in steering one's verbal craft between the Scylla of pedantry and the Charybdis of unwieldiness?

Nevertheless, for the sake of those who contrive to believe in the virtues of reported speech, perhaps I ought to say that an excellent exposition is made by Dr Onions in *An Advanced English Syntax*. Of the different kinds of reported speech, he gives an illuminating example.

He points out that the passage:—
'Croesus, king of the Lydians, said to Solon, the Athenian: "My Athenian guest, *your* great fame has reached even to *us*, as well of *your* wisdom as of *your* travels, how that as a philosopher *you have* travelled through various countries for the purpose of observation. *I am* therefore desirous of asking *you* a question. *Tell me*, who *is* the most happy man *you have* seen?"'—can be reported in three different ways, i.e., from the viewpoint of Croesus, from that of Solon, and from that of an outsider.

I. Croesus would say:—

'I said to Solon that *his* great fame *had* reached even to *us*, as well of *his* wisdom as of *his* travels, how that as a philosopher *he had* travelled through various countries for the purpose of observation. *I was* therefore desirous of asking *him* a question. *I asked him to tell me*'—or *would he tell me*—'who *was* the most happy man *he had* seen', the *would he tell me* representing a possible 'Will you tell me?'

II. Solon would say:—

'Croesus told me that *my* great fame *had* reached even *to them*, as well of *my* wisdom as of *my* travels, how that as a philosopher I *had* travelled through various countries for the purpose of observation. *He was* therefore desirous of asking *me* a question. *He asked me to tell him*'—or *would I tell him*—'who *was* the most happy man *I had* seen.'

III. An outsider's account (being in the 3rd Person throughout, this is the most usual form of reported speech) would run:—

'Croesus, king of the Lydians, said to

Solon, the Athenian, that *his* (Solon's) great fame *had* reached even to *them* (the Lydians), as well of *his* wisdom as of *his* travels, how that as a philosopher he *had* travelled through various countries for the purpose of observation. That *he* (Croesus) *was* therefore desirous of asking *him* (Solon) a question. *Would he tell him*, who *was* the most happy man he *had* seen?'

[For an excellent grammatical survey of reported speech, see Jespersen's *A Modern English Grammar on Historical Principles*, Part iv, ch. xi, 'Indirect Speech'.]

I am prepared to admit that there may be occasions when reported speech is a convenience; but is that convenience sufficiently great to outweigh the consequent lack of clarity and brevity? In brief, reported speech may serve to introduce variety: but variety—especially, as here, a very limited variety—cannot compensate for ambiguity, ponderousness, and verbosity. Moreover, it is slowly becoming recognized that it is important, often indeed essential, to have the speaker's exact words: and quite apart from the fact that reported-speeches sometimes misrepresent, carelessly or unthinkingly, the actual speech, it does seem unnecessary that we should be forced to view words (elusive enough, ambiguous enough, at the best of times) through a blur-glass darkly.

How darkly may be perceived from the following passage:—'The Belgae gave evidence that they themselves heard the enemy say that they stated that they possessed firm allies in the Suevi, who had promised to join them; but it appeared as if the latter had seceded from them and come over to their own party.' Broken up into Direct Speech, that Chinese puzzle would have been sun-clear: as it stands, it needs a running gloss. For the sake of the curious, here is the sentence divided and (to some extent) clarified; and on the right the translation made for me in 1913 by Mr G. P. Barbour, that sound scholar, fine headmaster (T.G.S., Queensland), first-class cricketer and lawn tennis player who,—when as a young teacher I was private-studying for a, to me, important examination,—corrected the Greek and Latin prose I sent to him each week. He had, I think, a shrewd idea that I had concocted the English for my own delectation and his puzzlement.

The Belgae gave evidence	Belgae indicaverunt
that they themselves heard the enemy say that they [the enemy] stated	se quidem ab hostibus accepisse eos dixisse
that they [the enemy] possessed firm allies in the Suevi, who had promised to join them;	Suevos esse socios fidelissimos, qui promisissent se in societatem cum ipsis ituros;
but that [the Belgae stated] it appeared as if the Suevi had seceded from them [the enemy] and come over to their own party.	Suevos autem, ut appareret, ab hostibus sejunctos in fidem secum ipsis rediisse.

reprehend, 'to reprove, rebuke, find fault with', is occasionally confused with *apprehend*, and even *represent*.

reprehend is 'to blame'; **apprehend** is 'to seize or grasp' (physically or mentally); **comprehend** is 'to understand'.

reprint. See EDITION.

repulsive. See 'REPELLENT and REPULSIVE'.

reputed and **reported.** The former is occasionally misused for the latter (or for *said*), as in 'It is reputed that he tried to escape'.

requirement and **requisite.** A *requirement* is 'a want, a need; that which is needed', as in 'the requirements of a hospital', '£10,000 would meet the requirements of capitalization'; also 'a condition that must be fulfilled', as in 'The other professors are under more stringent requirements to teach' (Mark Pattison). A *requisite* is 'something indispensable, especially an indispensable quality or property', as in 'The form of febrifuge which combines . . . the two requisites of efficacy and economy' (C. R. Markham, concerning Peruvian bark). A *prerequisite* is 'something required beforehand' (there being no such term as *prerequirement*) or 'a condition previously necessary' (as in 'The . . . prerequisites of success are ability, courage, and luck'): there is, in the latter sense, very little difference between *requisite* and *prerequisite*; the latter does, however, stress the fact that before anything can be done at all, certain conditions must already have been complied with. (*The O.E.D.*)

reserve and **preserve**. A *reserve* (in addition to non-competing senses) is 'something set apart for a specific purpose', including a district or a place; if for a native tribe, it is a *reservation*. A *preserve* is 'a piece of ground, especially a wood, set apart for the rearing (and protection) of game', also 'a pond for fish; a vivarium'; often figurative, as in *to poach on a person's preserves*.

reside and **live; residence** and **house.** To *reside* is to live permanently or at least for some considerable time *in* or *at* a particular place; to live officially (i.e., to *be in residence*) at a place. One's *residence* is one's settled abode, especially the house or mansion of a person of rank or distinction: you and I have a *house*, the President or the Prime Minister has a *residence*. (*The O.E.D.*)

residuum is a legal and scientific variant of *residue*, which is for general purposes much the more serviceable and unaffected.

resin and **rosin**. *Rosin* is *resin* 'in a solid state obtained as a residue after the distillation of oil of turpentine from crude turpentine' (*The O.E.D.*).

resolve (n); **resoluteness; resolution.** As 'steadfastness of purpose', *resolve* is archaic, as in the set phrase, *of high resolve*; *resoluteness* is now the usual word in this sense. The dominant sense of *resolve* is 'a (specified) resolution or determination', as in 'She made up her mind never to marry again, and she kept her resolve' (Jessopp); as 'a formal resolution of a deliberative body', it may occur in American English, though *resolution* is the common term. As an abstract, *resolve* = 'determination': cf. *resoluteness* above. But as a scientific, medical, or musical term, *resolution* has no rivals. (*The O.E.D.*)

resource is occasionally confused with and misused for *recourse*. You examine your *resources* (stock that can be drawn on to supply some need), and decide which of them *to have recourse to*, i.e., to adopt as means of help.—See also RECOURSE.

respectable, 'worthy of respect'; **respectful,** 'showing respect'; **respective,** as in 'The practical sovereignty of all

three brothers was admitted in their respective territories' (Bryce: in *The O.E.D.*). These adjectives and their adverbs are occasionally confused by the slovenly.

respecting. See CONJUNCTIONS, DISGUISED.

respectively, misused for *both*. In 'He is a member of the hockey eleven and the "Rugger" fifteen respectively', omit *respectively*; or rewrite thus, 'He is a member both of the hockey eleven and the Rugger fifteen'.

responsible should be restricted to human beings. [[American usage permits such sentences as 'Great heat is responsible for many deaths', but here *responsible* is inferior to *the cause of*.]] *Responsible* is wrongly used also in 'The same year was responsible for a thoroughly Classic attack on Shakespeare'. E. Partridge, *French Romantics' Knowledge of English Literature*, 1924. Surely the responsibility rested on those who made the attack in that year!

restive and **restless.** Of horses, *restive* = 'refractory' or 'intractable'; the same applies to human beings. *Restless* = 'averse to being still, settled or quiet', or 'deprived of rest; hence, uneasy'. (*The O.E.D.*)

restrain. See CONSTRAIN.

result for *fact* is feeble, as in 'The autopsy shows the curious result that Jensen was dead before the shot that was supposed to have killed him had been fired', Cameron McCabe, *The Face on the Cutting-Room Floor*, 1937.

N.B.: an action, process, etc., *has a result* or *shows* (or *discloses* or *proves*) *a fact*.

results. See ACCIDENT.

resurrect is occasionally misused for 'to *find*', as in 'Where did you resurrect that hat?', when the hat is new; but if the speaker says 'When did you resurrect that hat?' and means 'When did you rescue it from the rubbish-heap?', he is simply using *resurrect* figuratively in the sense, 'restore to life, or to view, again' ('Slavery is already dead, and cannot be resurrected'). (*The O.E.D.*)

retiracy; retiral; retirement. *Retiracy*, an Americanism (nowadays rare), means either 'seclusion or privacy' (one of the two main senses of *retirement*) or 'a sufficient fortune to retire upon' (Bartlett); *retiral* is now rare in the sense 'an act of withdrawal or retreat' (the opposite of *advance*), and less common than *retirement* in the sense, 'the act—or the fact—of withdrawing from, or surrendering, an office, a position, a vocation' or from, say, street to house, drawing room to w.c., or from noise to quiet, publicity to peace. In military terminology, *retirement* is now less common than *retreat* (though one's own forces tend to *retire*, the enemy to *retreat*). A further sense of *retirement* is 'a place or abode characterized by seclusion or privacy', as in 'Exmouth; where, as they say, he has a sweet country retirement' (John Wilkes, 1772), but this, now, is slightly obsolescent and more than slightly literary. (*The O.E.D.*)

retort and **riposte** should not be used as colourless synonyms of *reply*; *retort* is to reply wittily; *riposte* (a term from fencing) is to reply sharply and wittily. '"I love you", he said ardently.—"I love you too", she retorted [or riposted]' shows up the absurdity.

revelant, revelatory; relevant; also **revelative** and **revealing.** The first is a common solecism for the third (*relevant*, 'pertinent; in question or under consideration or bearing upon the matter in hand'); *revelatory* is the adjective corresponding to 'to *reveal*' and it = either 'serving or tending to reveal' or '(actually) yielding a revelation', as in 'a revelatory gesture', 'a most revelatory autobiography', 'a physic manifestation startlingly revelatory of the unseen'; *revelative* has the nuance, 'conveying a revelation', as in 'The Bible, to one who comes upon it for the first time, is a tremendously revelative book'. Ordinary people—perhaps rightly—prefer *revealing*, as in 'A most revealing oath fell from his lips', 'a revealing book', 'a revealing ray of light'. Based on *The O.E.D.*

revelation for *disclosure*—a strong word for a weak one—is not to be overworked. (Journalists are a shade too fond of it.)

Revelations is incorrect for *Revelation* as the short title of *The Revelation of St. John the Divine. Revelation* is lit. 'a drawing back of the Veil', whereas *Apocalypse* (as in Vulgate) is 'an uncovering'.

revenge and **avenge** (vv.); **revenge** and **vengeance** (nn.). See AVENGE.

reverent must not be confused with *reverend*; the former applies to the worshipper, the latter to the object of worship (or reverence).

reversal; reversion. The former is the noun corresponding to *reverse* ('to reverse the order'). *Reversion* is a legal term, but it also = 'the right of succession to a thing or an office'; and it is the abstraction of *reversal*.

reverse (n.). See CONVERSE.

revolutionist (n.) is an unnecessary variant of *revolutionary*, which serves very well as both noun and adjective. This variant is surprisingly common.

revue is confined to the theatrical entertainment. Do not italicize it: there's no other name for this form of serial diversion.

RHETORICAL, THE. Rhetoric, as Lord Baldwin of Bewdley once remarked, is the harlot of the arts.

There are two Rhetorics: the old and the new. Of the old, a typical expositor is Alexander Bain, who died early in the present century; of the new, the best expositor is Dr I. A. Richards, whose *The Philosophy of Rhetoric*, 1936, has done so much to rehabilitate both the art and the study thereof.

In *English Composition and Rhetoric*, enlarged edition, Part II, 1888, Bain says in the Preface:—'I do not here enter on a defence of the utility of Rhetoric in general, though many persons are still disposed to question it. Since the art first took form in Greece, it has seldom been neglected by writers aiming at superior excellence of style. In order to vanquish the difficulties of the highest composition, it is necessary to attack them on every side. . . .

'The direct bearing of the Rhetorical art is, of course, not Invention, but Correctness; in other words, polish, elegance, or refinement. It deals with curable defects and faults, and with such merits as can be secured by method. It aids, without superseding, the intuitive perception of what is excellent in a literary performance.

'There is not wanting, however, a possibility of rendering assistance to invention proper; somewhat similar to the contribution of Logic to the Art of Discovery. All right criticism, in helping to reject the bad, urges to renewed search for the good. Nor is this all. By taking a broad and systematic view of the possibilities of style, Rhetoric prevents the available means of effect from being overlooked, and draws attention to still unoccupied corners of the literary field.'

There you see—or can at least perceive—the defects of the old rhetoric: it is, in the best sense of the word, superficial: on the one hand, it is a superior art of composition; on the other, it is a means of exciting certain emotions in an audience.

'I need spend no time, I think, in describing the present state of Rhetoric. To-day it is the dreariest and least profitable part of the waste that the unfortunate travel through in Freshman English, [especially in the United States]! So low has Rhetoric sunk that we would do better to dismiss it to Limbo than to trouble ourselves with it—unless we can find reason for believing that it can become a study that will minister successfully to important needs.

'As to the needs, there is little room for doubt about them. Rhetoric . . . should be a study of misunderstanding and its remedies. . . . "How much and in how many ways may good communication differ from bad?"'

In reference to the traditional expositors of Rhetoric, Dr Richards says that, 'instead of tackling, in earnest, the problem of how language works at all, they assume that nothing relevant is to be learnt about it; and that the problem is merely one of disposing the given and unquestioned powers of words to the best advantage. Instead of ventilating by inquiry the sources of the whole action of words, they merely play with generalizations about their effects.

'To account for understanding and misunderstanding, to study the efficiency of language and its conditions, we have to renounce, for a while, the view that words just have their meanings and that what a discourse does is to be explained as a composition of these meanings—as a wall can be represented as a composition of its bricks. We have to shift the focus of our analysis and attempt a deeper and more minute grasp and try to take account of the structures of the smallest discussable units of meaning and the ways in which these vary as they are put with other units. . . . Most words, as they pass from context to context, change their meanings; and in many different ways. It is their duty and their service to us to do so.'

Dr Richards then touches on one of his main theses: 'the Proper Meaning Superstition . . . the common belief . . . that a word has a meaning of its own (ideally, only one) independent and controlling its use and the purpose for which it should be uttered'.

'A revived Rhetoric', he says, returning to the attack, 'or study of verbal understanding and misunderstanding, must itself undertake its own inquiry into the modes of meaning—not only, as with the old Rhetoric, on a macroscopic scale, discussing the effects of different disposals of large parts of a discourse—but also on a microscopic scale by using theorems about the structure of the fundamental conjectural units of meaning and the conditions through which they, and their inter-connections, arise.'

One of these theorems is 'the context theorem of meaning', which, he says, 'prevents our making hundreds of baseless and disabling assumptions . . . about meanings, over-simplifications that create false problems. . . . Preëminently what the theorem would discourage, is our habit of behaving as though, if a passage means one thing it cannot at the same time mean another and an incompatible thing. . . . This theorem goes further, and regards all discourse—outside the technicalities of science—as over-determined, as having multiplicity of meaning.

'The next problem concerns what happens when we put words together in sentences. . . . The theorem recommends us rather to turn the problem round and ask what happens when, out of the integral utterance which is the sentence, we try to isolate the discrete meanings of the words of which it is composed. . . . It is there that the most deep-rooted, systematic and persistent misunderstandings arise': to Richards the sentence, not the word, is the unit of speech.

'The context theorem of meaning will make us expect ambiguity to the widest extent and of the subtlest kinds nearly everywhere, and of course we find it. But [whereas] the old Rhetoric treated ambiguity as a fault in language, the new Rhetoric sees it as an inevitable consequence of the powers of language and as the indispensable means of most of our important utterances—especially in Poetry and Religion.

'The extra meaning that comes in when a sentence, in addition to making a statement, is meant to be insulting, or flattering, or is interpreted so—we may call it emotive meaning—is not so different from plain statement as we are apt to suppose. As the word means the missing part of its contexts and is a substitute for them, so the insulting intention may be the substitute for a kick. The same general theorem covers all the modes of thought.

There is a progression of some sort in every explicit sentence [—e.g., in "The cat is on the mat", to take the simplest sentence-type]. But in the strictest prose the meanings of the separate words theoretically stay put and thought passes from one to another of them. At the other end of the scale the whole meaning of the sentence shifts, and with it any meanings we may try to ascribe to the individual words. In the extreme case it will go on moving as long as we bring fresh wits to study it. When Octavius Caesar is gazing down at Cleopatra dead, he says,

> She looks like sleep,
> As she would catch another Antony
> In her strong toil of grace.

"Her strong toil of grace." Where, in terms of what entries in what possible dictionary, do the meanings here of *toil* and *grace* come to rest? . . . In most prose . . . the opening words have to wait for those that follow to settle what they shall mean—if indeed that ever gets settled.

'All this holds good not only as to the *sense* of the waiting words but as regards all [those] other functions of language which we can distinguish and set over against the mere sense. It holds for the *feeling* [of my audience] towards what I am talking about, for *the relation towards my audience* I want to establish or maintain with the remark, and for the *confidence* I have in the soundness of the remark—to mention three main sorts of these other language functions. In speech . . . I have the aid of intonation for these purposes.

'. . . In writing we have to [substitute for] intonation as far as we can. Most of the more recondite virtues of prose style come from the skill with which the rival claims of these various language functions are reconciled and combined.'

We pass to the essence of Dr Richards's attack upon 'the Usage Doctrine':—'Its evil is that it takes the sense of an author's words to be things we know before we read him, fixed factors with which he has to build up the meaning of his sentences as a mosaic is put together of discrete independent tesserae. Instead, they are resultants which we arrive at only through the interplay of the interpretative possibilities of the whole utterance. In brief, we have to guess them and we guess much better when we realize we are guessing, and watch out for indications, than we think we know.'

No less acute, illuminating and, in its dignified sense, entertaining is his arraignment of what he calls 'the Club Spirit'; but for this, I must refer the reader to pp. 77–80 of *The Philosophy of Rhetoric*.

And with the conclusion of Dr Richards's own eloquent peroration, this faulty gist of some of his views on Rhetoric may fittingly end:—'It is an old dream that in time psychology might be able to tell us so much about our minds that we would at last become able to discover with some certainty what we mean by our words and how we mean it. An opposite or complementary dream is that, with enough improvement in Rhetoric we may in time learn so much about words that they will tell us how our minds work. It seems modest and reasonable to combine these dreams and hope that a patient persistence with the problems of Rhetoric may, while exposing the causes and modes of the misinterpretation of words, also throw light upon and suggest a remedial discipline for deeper and more grievous disorders; that, as the small and local errors in our everyday misunderstandings with language are models in miniature of the greater errors which disturb the development of our personalities, their story may also show us more about how these large-scale disasters may be avoided.'

[I take the greater pleasure in recommending all serious students of semantics and of the art of writing to read and ponder *The Philosophy of Rhetoric* for the very reason that Dr Richards and I do not always agree on literary and linguistic questions. I do not agree with everything in the foregoing abstract, but his provocativeness is so tonic and bracing that I do not wish to obscure the issue with demurrers, modifications, precautions.]

rhyme and **rime**. Although the former is the usual spelling, the latter is not incorrect and has historical justification; it has of late years been to some extent revived to make clear its distinction from *rhythm*.

rid—preterite, *rid*—past participle, *rid*; *ridded* is permissible but now less common in both preterite and past participle.

ride—preterite, *rode*—past participle, *ridden* (rarely *rid*).

riddle should not be used as a co-extensive synonym of *puzzle*. A *riddle* is an enigma or dark saying ('When is a door not a door?'), *puzzle* being no longer used in this sense; a mystery (*The Riddle of the Sands*), hence a mysterious person. On the other hand, *puzzle* may be applied to a person or a thing that puzzles us (He's a bit of a puzzle'), though not with quite the sense of 'mystery'; and whereas a *puzzle* is used of any toy, device or (non-verbal) problem designed to exercise the brain, *riddle* is applied only to a verbal problem. In his important address to the Institute of Journalists on Dec. 18, 1938, Mr Frank Whitaker classed it among the 'rubber-stamp words'.

right of ways is incorrect for *rights of way*.

right to, have a. See HAVE A RIGHT TO.

rigorous. See at VIGOUR.

rime. See RHYME.

ring (of bells)—preterite, *rang* (or *rung*: but avoid it)—past participle, *rung*. But 'to ring' a tree has both preterite and past participle *ringed*.

riposte. See RETORT.

rise. See RAISE.

Rockefeller is, except among Americans, often misspelt *Rockfeller*; and, except among Englishmen, *Rosebery* is often misspelt *Roseberry*.

role, without accent or italic, is correct; so is *rôle*, with accent and italic, but it is, in English, obsolescent; *role*, without accent but in italic, is incorrect; cf. REGIME.

Roman Catholic; Catholic; catholic. The first two are both noun and adjective; the third, adjective only. In the sense 'universal', *catholic* is obsolescent. The prevailing nuances of *catholic* are 'of universal human interest or use'; 'touching the needs, interests, or sympathies of all men', as in 'What was of catholic rather than national interest' (Froude); (of persons) 'having sympathies with all' ('He is catholic in his tastes', (of things) 'embracing all' ('The sun poured its clear and catholic looks', Stevenson). *Catholic Church* or *Church Catholic* formerly meant 'the Church universal, the entire body of Christians'; but since the Reformation it has also and more generally meant 'the Church of Rome', now usually and more clearly designated *the Roman Catholic Church*; *Catholic* may suffice in opposition to *Protestant*, but it is safer to distinguish *Roman Catholic* from *Anglo-Catholic*.

rooves as plural of *roof*. See SPOOF.

Rosebery. See ROCKEFELLER.

rosin. See 'RESIN and ROSIN'.

rotal; rotary; rotatable; rotating; rotational; rotative; rotatory.
Rotal: of a wheel; like or characteristic of a wheel ('vocal or rotal tumult'); also, 'of or pertaining to rotation or circular movement', a sense in which *rotatory* is the usual adjective.

Rotary (adjective): (of motion) circular, i.e., taking place round a centre or axis; also, operating by means of rotation, especially in reference to that large class of machines in which the main action is dependent on the rotation of an importantly operative part; also as in 'Storms that are cyclonic; i.e., rotary and progressive'; (of persons) acting in rotation—for which the dominant adjective is *rotational*. In the U.S.A., *Rotary* = 'belonging to one of the Rotary Clubs, of which the first was formed in 1905 by P. P. Harris of Chicago'.

Rotatable: capable—or admitting—of a rotatory movement, as in 'a sounder [a surgical instrument], rotatable on a long shaft'.

Rotating (adjective): (*a*) turning round a centre (or an axis),—for which *rotary* is commoner; (*b*) causing rotation,—for which *rotatory* is more usual and less ambiguous.

Rotational: acting in rotation, as in 'rotational members'; also of or belonging to rotation, as in 'motion, whether orbital or rotational', *rotatory* being the dominant adjective.

Rotative: turning round like a wheel, acting by or operating in circular motion: a sense in which *rotary* and *rotatory* are more strongly established. Producing—or produced by—rotation, as in the astronomical 'rotative forces'; hence, connected with rotation: in these three nuances, *rotatory* is at least equally common; in the 'of the nature of rotation' sense of *rotative, rotatory* is more usual. But a useful sense is 'recurrent', as in 'Cotton was cultivated in India as a rotative and not as a special crop' (Sir R. A. Arnold, *The Cotton Famine*, 1864), a further synonym being 'seasonal'.

Rotatory: in rotation, *rotational* being preferable.—Causing rotation (cf. *rotative*), especially in *rotatory apparatus*.—Working by means of rotation; and of things that *rotate* (v.i.): as in 'rotatory storms' and 'cruel rotatory spurs' (Stevenson).—Of the nature of,—or connected with, rotation, as (of a wheel) 'having a rotatory motion', 'a rotatory velocity'.

Rotation, basically, is either the action of moving or turning around a centre or axis (or on an axis), or the action of producing such a movement. (*The O.E.D.*)

round for *on* or *about* is a characteristic of Cockney speech: e.g., 'Meet me round seven o'clock', and from Edwin Pugh's *Harry the Cockney*, 1912, '"If you don't gimme a bit . . . I shall punch you round the jaw"'. Also see AROUND. [[*Round* (*around*) for *about* is colloquial in American English.]]

round house; roundhouse. The former is any house that is circular, whereas a *roundhouse* is, in the U.S.A., 'a circular shed for locomotives, with a turn-table in the centre', and, in Britain, either a cabin—or a set of cabins—on the afterpart of a ship's quarter-deck, or, though now only historical, a lock-up, or a place of detention for arrested persons,—but all three senses have the alternative forms *round-house* and *round house*. (*The O.E.D.*)'

route is occasionally misused for *method* or *manner* or *procedure* or *process*, as in 'attaining fame by the political route'. [[*Route* is generally pronounced *root*, but in the U.S.A. the pronunciation with the diphthong of *out* survives in military use, railroad use, and often in business ('milk route', 'bread route', 'paper route'). (*Webster's.*)]]

royal tennis. See TENNIS.

RUBBER-STAMP WORDS. See AMAZING.

rung. See RING.

rush (n. and v.) is being overworked by journalists: on Dec. 8, 1938, Mr

Frank Whitaker included it in his list of 'rubber-stamp words' (see AMAZING). It is not an exact synonym of *haste*.

S

Sabbath, the, and **Sunday;** not forgetting **the Lord's Day** and **the Day of Rest.** But the best of these is *Sunday, the Sabbath* being slightly affected where it is not Scottish; in good, normal English, *sabbath* is short for *witches' sabbath* (a midnight meeting of demons, wizards, witches, Devil-presided). The only serious objection to *the Lord's Day* is that it is so much longer than *Sunday*, than which it is also more formal; *the Day of Rest* is a rather trivial synonym—a lazy man's variation.

sabotage, used as verb, for *to wreck,* is unhappy and introduces a mechanical note that is out of keeping. In *What a Word!*, Mr A. P. Herbert attacks it and quotes, as an example of its misuse, 'Sabotaged the Peace issue'.

sacred. See SACROSANCT.

sacrilegious is a frequent misspelling of *sacrilegious*.

sacrosanct and **sacred.** The former is, stylistically, an intensive of the latter; prudent writers, however, use it only in the specific sense (of persons; laws, customs, obligations; authority) 'secured by a religious sanction from violation, infringement, or encroachment', as in 'Truth, which alone of words is essentially divine and sacrosanct' (John Morley, 1871). Based on *The O.E.D.*

sadism and **masochism.** In generalized and (at first) loose usage, the former is desire to hurt others and the ability to enjoy their pain; the latter is the desire to be hurt and especially the enjoyment derived from being hurt. But in medical and strictly correct usage, *sadism* is 'a form of sexual perversion marked by a love of cruelty' (*The O.E.D.*), the name deriving from the Comte (*not* Marquis) de Sade †(1814); and *masochism*, from the Austrian novelist, Sacher-Masoch, is 'sexual perversion, in which a member of one sex takes delight in being dominated, even to the extent of violence or cruelty, by one of the other sex' (Dunglison). Both are morbid faults: the former is dangerous, the latter pathetic.

saeter. See 'SATIRE; SATYR; SAETER'.

said, the ('the said act'), is permissible for *this* in legal phraseology—and nowhere else. See also THE SAID.

sailer is either *a sailing ship*, or a ship (or vessel) with reference to her sailing powers ('A very strong tight ship, and a pretty good sailer', Defoe); a **sailor** is a seaman, a mariner.

sake and **sakes.** 'When the preceding genitive is plural, the plural *sakes* is often used', as in 'For both our sakes, I would that word were true' (Shakespeare), 'Put yourself to no further trouble for our sakes' (Addison). (*The O.E.D.*) True; but there are two points to be made:—(i) '"For our sake" implies a common concern or purpose. "For our sakes" implies a difference of concern or purpose' (Weseen): a valid and valuable distinction. But (ii) except where metre needs *both our* (or *your* or *their*) *sakes*, a good writer would today write 'for the sake of both of us' (jointly) and 'for the sakes of both of us' (separately).

salary. See HONORARIUM (and also WAGE).

salam; salams. Incorrect for *salaam* (v.) and *salaams*, implying as they do a wrong pronunciation; the former occurs in Smyth's *Sailor's Word Book*, 1867.

salon and **saloon.** *Saloon* is American (pre-Prohibition era) for a barroom, and general for a public room on a passenger-boat; American for a drawing-room (especially a large one); and general for a large apartment or hall in a hotel or restaurant. *Salon* is a reception-room of a Parisian lady of fashion, hence a gathering (more or less recurrent) of notabilities at her house; hence, either the room or the gathering in other capitals. Also, a drawing-room on the Continent, especially in France. (*The O.E.D.*)

same (adj.)—used tautologically. 'The comedian has repeated the same joke at least a thousand times.'

same (n.). 'We are in receipt of your favour of the 2nd inst., and thank you for same': *the same* would be correct, but it is stilted and too commercially conventional; '*it*' would be better.

same and **similar.** The former denotes identity; the latter implies mere likeness. 'He was positive it was the same man.' —'It is a house of similar design to ours' (or 'It is a house of a design similar to that of ours'), Harold Herd, *Watch Your English*, 1925.

same, the, is incorrectly followed by *which* in such a sentence as 'Is the agency referred to the same agency which the honourable gentleman repudiated the other day?' The correct form would be 'the same agency as that which' or 'as the one which'; but 'the same' is itself unnecessary, and the hon. member would have better expressed his meaning, 'Is the hon. gentleman referring to the agency which he repudiated the other day?' Cf. 'The post which the judge subsequently received is not the same that he was originally offered' (C. Daly King, *Arrogant Alibi*, 1938): where 'not the same that' should be 'not the same as that which' or 'not the one that' or, better, 'not that which'.

same . . . of, incorrect for *same . . . as that of.* 'It was the same colour of'— properly *same colour as that of*—'the moundy platform where they stood', Paul Horgan, *A Lamp on the Plains*, English ed., 1937.

sample. See EXAMPLE.

sanatarium; sanatorium; sanitarium. The first is an occasional misspelling of the second; a misspelling probably caused by confusion with *sanitarium* (a variant—except for a school hospital or sick room—of *sanatorium*). The plurals are *sanatoria, sanitaria*, but soon the plurals in *-iums* will (as they should) oust the others.

sanatory and **sanitary** must be carefully distinguished, the former meaning 'conducive to healing', the latter 'intended or tending to promote health' or healthy conditions. (*The O.E.D.*) [[*Webster's*: '*Sanatory* signifies *conducive to health*; *sanitary* has the more general meaning of *pertaining to health*; as, the camp is not *sanatory*, its *sanitary* conditions are bad'.]]

sang. See SING.

SARCASM. See IRONY, last paragraph.

sateen and **satin.** *Sateen* is a cotton (or woollen) fabric that has a glossy surface like that of satin; but sateen is to satin what *near silk* is to (*sheer*) *silk*. *Satin* is a silk fabric that has on one side a glossy surface produced by such a method of weaving as ensures that the warp threads are 'caught and looped by the weft only at certain intervals' (*The O.E.D.*).

SATIRE. 'Satire, in its literary aspect, may be defined as the expression in adequate terms of the sense of amusement or disgust excited by the ridiculous or unseemly, provided that humour is a distinctly recognizable element, and that the utterance is invested with literary form. Without humour, satire is invective; without literary form, it is mere clownish jeering' (Richard Garnett, in *The Encyclopaedia Britannica*, 1911).

satire; satyr; saeter. *Satire* is that which has been briefly treated in the preceding entry; a *satyr* is a woodland god (in form: part man, part beast) that tends to Bacchic revelry and sexual pursuits. *Saeter:*—In the Orkneys and the Shetlands, it is 'a pasturage attached to a dwelling'; in Scandinavia, 'a mountain pasture for cattle in the summer', hence a farm (especially a dairy farm) on a saeter. (*The O.E.D.*)

save is obsolete for *unless*; 'elegant' for the preposition *except*. The conjunctival *save that* ('Then all was still, save that a vast gush of fire rose up for a moment', R. I. Wilberforce, 1842) is archaic in prose, literary in verse. (*The O.E.D.*)

saw—preterite, *sawed*—past participle, *sawed* or *sawn*. The past participle used predicatively is either *sawed* or *sawn*, but preferably *sawed* ('The wood to be sawed is in the yard, over there'); attributively, in England always *sawn* ('Sawn wood is easier to handle'); [[in the U.S.A. *sawed* or *sawn*]].

says for *say* is illiterate, as in 'I says, says I' and 'Says you' (generally spelt *sez*), which, by the way, is fly-blown—as blown upon and stale as *oh, boy!*

scan, as Alfred Ackermann (*Popular Fallacies*) points out, is erroneously used for, and taken to mean, 'to glance through hurriedly and casually', but as will be found in the best dictionaries, it means *to examine closely or minutely, to scrutinize*. When one scans verse, one metrically analyses it.

scarcely. See HARDLY.

scarcely . . . than. See HARDLY . . . THAN.

scared of is incorrect for *afraid of* (or *frightened by*). [[*Scared* has homely and forceful qualities in American English, and one may well hesitate to proscribe any of its idiomatic uses. *Scared to do it* is dialect or colloquial speech; *scared by dogs* is standard English; *scared of dogs* is probably standard on a familiar level.]]

scatheless and **unscathed.** *Scatheless* = 'without scathe', i.e., without harm or injury, as in 'It is a game from which you will come out scatheless, but I have been scalded' (Trollope). *Unscathed* =

'unharmed, uninjured', as in 'Whatever his experiences of this kind may have been, he passed unscathed through them' (A. W. Ward). (*The O.E.D.*) The distinction, therefore, is very fine; but clear.

Sceptic is not synonymous with *infidel*, and its use for 'one who maintains a doubting attitude with reference to some particular question or statement' is a popular looseness that is so very loose as to deserve the stigmatic label, 'catachresis'. In Philosophy, a *Sceptic* is one who doubts—or even denies—the possibility of real knowledge of any kind; also (but not of Pyrrho or his disciples) one who denies the competence of reason, and the possibility of certitude, in all matters that lie outside the bounds of experience,—and he is in lower case (*s.* not *S.*).

In theological and other religious writings, a *sceptic* is one who doubts—but will not absolutely deny—the truth of Christianity or, at the least, of one or more of the important among the Christian dogmas. (Cf. AGNOSTIC, *q.v.* at 'AGNOSTIC and ATHEIST'.)

Among etymology-worshippers, a *sceptic* (late Latin *scepticus*, 'inquiring', from Greek *skeptikos* akin to *skeptesthai*, 'to look out; to consider') is a seeker after truth.

But in general (and, of course, correct) use, a *sceptic* is one who, in reference to a department of inquiry (e.g., natural science, spiritualism, psychology), doubts the validity of what is there set forth, or claimed, as knowledge. Hence, a person that, by habit, tends rather to doubt than to believe any apparent fact, any assertion, that comes under his notice or to his attention. [With due acknowledgements to *The O.E.D.*]

sceptic, sceptical; skeptic, skeptical. The *sk-* forms are the usual ones in the U.S.A.; *sceptical* is preferred to *sceptic* for the adjective. (The *sc* is pronounced as *sk*; there is an ancient pun about *sceptics* that are *septic*.)

Scot, Scotch, Scots, Scottish, adjectives; **Scotchmen** (or **-women**), **Scotsmen**, **Scots** and **the Scotch,** nouns.

Of the nouns, the usual English name is *Scotchmen*; the usual Scottish one, *Scotsmen*. Of the noun *Scot*, *The O.E.D.* says that 'since the 17th Century till recently chiefly Historical except in jocular and rhetorical use. In Scotland there has latterly been a tendency (especially in newspaper writing) *to the more extended use of the word*'; *the Scotch* is unobjectionable but slightly obsolescent.

Of the adjectives, *Scot* is a solecism, now rare; the other three are admirably treated in *The O.E.D.* at *Scotch* (adjective); their use is 'somewhat unsettled'. Since about 1870, there has, in Scotland, been an increasing tendency to discard *Scotch* and to use *Scottish* or, less frequently, *Scots*; in England, *Scotch* is the usual adjective in speech, but good writers prefer *Scottish* in reference to the nation (*the Scottish people*), the country at large (*Scottish scenery, the Scottish border*), its institutions, and characteristics (*a Scottish lawyer, the Scottish character, Scottish poets*); nevertheless, it would be an affectation to speak of *a Scottish gardener* or *girl*, usage prescribing *a Scotch gardener, a Scotch girl*, and there simply isn't an alternative for *Scotch whiskey* and *Scotch tweeds*. Usage —that is, current usage—favours *Scots* in *Scots law*; and *Scots* is obligatory in *a pound Scots, a shilling Scots, a penny Scots*, and in such variations from English weights and measures as *Scots acre, Scots mile, Scots pint, Scots stone*; moreover, in language contexts, we say *a Scots dialect* or *phrase*, although *a Scottish dialect* or *phrase* would not be incorrect; as a noun, *Scots* = the language spoken by the inhabitants of the Lowlands. *Scots* is invariable in such regimental names as *Scots Guards* and *Scots Greys*, and for those bodies of mercenaries serving abroad, *the Scots Brigade* and *the Scots Dutch*. For fuller details, see *The O.E.D.*

scrip and **script.** 'In loose or popular language', *scrip* is 'applied to share certificates in general'; properly, it is 'a provisional document entitling the holder to a share or shares in a joint-stock undertaking, and exchangeable for a more formal certificate when the necessary payments have been completed'; it is 'short for the obsolete *subscription receipt*'. But *script* is handwriting ('His is a beautiful script'), hence a kind or system of writing ('a cuneiform script', 'the Babylonian script', 'the complicated Japanese scripts'); in Law, it is the original document in opposition to a counterpart (or *rescript*). (*The O.E.D.*) [[In American usage *scrip* may also = a certificate of indebtedness used in place of government currency. *Script* in thea-

ter, movie, and radio jargons = manuscript or typescript—for theater and radio, the play; for motion pictures, the synopsis, scenario, dialogue, etc.]]

Scylla and **Charybdis** constitutes a cliché when the two names are used in combination to signify the danger of running into an equal or greater evil or peril in the (hasty) avoidance of its opposite. But many who use the cliché forget the origin:—Scylla is a rock (personified as a horrible and dangerous sea-monster) on the Italian side of the Straits of Messina; opposite is Charybdis, a once-dangerous whirlpool on the coast of Sicily.

seamstress. See SEMPSTRESS.

seasonable is 'suitable to or to be expected in the season referred to': 'It's seasonable weather' is that infuriating remark for which we must be prepared when, in winter, one experiences weather that might be more aptly described as a blight. *Seasonal*, however, means 'in season', 'characteristic of the seasons or, especially, of a particular season' ('seasonal variations of weather'); hence (of trades) 'dependent on the season' or (of employees) 'engaged only in or for a particular season' ('Seaside-hotel waiters are mostly seasonal'); applied to diseases, it = 'recurrent' or 'periodical', as in 'Hay-fever, fortunately, is a seasonal complaint'. *Seasoned* is 'matured' (worked on by the season) or (of wood) 'dried—hence, hardened—by keeping'; of persons or animals it = 'acclimatized', 'fortified by habit, especially familiarized with a certain occupation' ('4000 seasoned troops'). (*The O.E.D.*)

secretarial is the adjective corresponding to *secretary*; **secretariat** is the official, especially governmental, establishment of a secretary, hence the staff and the place where a secretarial department works or records are preserved. The position of a non-official secretary is a *secretaryship*.

secretion for **concealment** is an error not often met with, but Dean Alford quotes *The Times* as referring to 'the secretion of tobacco and written communications in the food sent in (to prisoners)', and points out that 'secretion' means 'that agency in the animal economy that consists in separating the various fluids of the body'.

sector is a technical term; **section** is (for the most part) a general one ('part, portion, division, subdivision, and slice').

The only sense in which they are confused the one for the other is the military one, 'a portion or section of a front, corresponding generally to a sector of a circle the centre of which is a headquarters', the correct term being, not *section* but *sector*. A sector was that portion of the front which was, in practice during the War of 1914–18, occupied by a division. *The O.E.D.; Larousse du xx² siècle.*

secundus and **junior.** *Junior* is 'the younger' and it is appended to a full name (*James Smith, Junior*) 'to denote the younger of the two bearing the same name in a family, especially a son of the same name as his father'; also after a simple surname (*Smith, Junior*), to denote the younger of two boys of the same surname at school. *Secundus* is 'the second'. Appended to a personal name, it means 'the second of the name' (*Dr Monro, secundus; James Thomson, secundus; Robert Chambers, secundus*), but it is not usually applied to a son in relation to his father. ⟦In American English *second* is used instead of *secundus.*⟧

secure (v.). See 'PROCURE and SECURE'.
—It is misused for *ensure* (or *effect*) in 'The police have got frightfully swollen heads; the conditions of the modern world all tend to secure that', Laurence Meynell, *The Dandy*, 1938.

see, do you. The frequent introduction, in conversational narrative and description, of *d'you see?, you see?,* or *see?,* is a bad habit with very many people, and is always a sign of uncertainty and a lack of clear thinking. It is no new fault, for it was censured in 1789 by "Aristarchus", who says 'would it not be somewhat extraordinary if I asked him at every third word—*Are you blind?*' ⟦*Listen!* as well as *See?* is a frequent interjection in low colloquial American.⟧

see where is incorrect for *see that* (and an astonishingly common error it is!), as in 'I see where they've had another storm at home', for 'I see'—i.e., have read in the newspaper—'that they've had another storm'.

seeing. See CONJUNCTIONS, DISGUISED.

seldom is not now to be used as an adjective, though it was formerly so employed by good writers; e.g., Thackeray (in *Esmond*), 'My Lord Duke's entertainments were both seldom and shabby'.

seldom ever is pleonastic for *seldom* in such a sentence as 'I seldom ever go to town nowadays'. Cf. the following entry.

seldom or ever, like *rarely or ever,* is a not uncommon error for *seldom or never* (or for *seldom if ever* in the same sense.) Thus, George Parker, *A View of Society,* 1781, 'Red Sail-Yard Dockers [a cant term] are people who live by buying and selling the king's [naval] stores, and who are seldom or ever detected, from the king's mark not being commonly known'; (with reference to a trencher) 'That is, —a square piece of deal board, seldom or ever scraped, (never wash'd) off which the younger part of the University dine', Anon., *A Day in Vacation at College,* 1751. Nesfield finds this error committed by Sydney Smith:—'Those who walk in their sleep have seldom or ever the most distant recollection that they have been dreaming at all.'

selection and **composition.** *Selection* = an or the act of selecting or choosing, or a thing selected. Therefore, it should not be employed where there is no idea of selecting or choosing, as in 'What selection of Bach's do you like best?' Weseen pertinently remarks that 'When the reference is to a programme [or, e.g., an anthology] some other word such as *number, piece, composition,* or a more specific word such as *waltz, poem, essay* is always preferable to *selection*'.

self is incorrect for *I* in, e.g., 'Self and family desire to extend to you our sympathy'. The plural is *selves* ('their dead selves'), not *selfs* as so often in A. S. M. Hutchinson's novel, *As Once You Were,* 1938.

semi. See DEMI.

semi-monthly; semi-weekly. See BI-MONTHLY.

semi-yearly is a hybrid for either *semi-annual* or the more English *half-yearly.* (Adverbs: *semi-annually, half-yearly.*)

seminar and **seminary.** The former is a university technicality for 'a select group of advanced students associated for special study and original research under the guidance of a professor' (or other head of department); hence, 'a class that meets for systematic study under the direction of a teacher'.

A *seminary* is any place of Secondary education; and specifically 'an institution for the training of those destined for some particular profession'—in the Roman Catholic Church, a college for training youths and young men to become priests.

The learner in either a seminar or a seminary is a *seminarist* or a *seminarian*. (*The O.E.D.*)

Semitic; Hebraic, Hebrew; Jewish. *Semitic* = 'belonging to or concerned with the Semitic group of languages' (Hebrew, Aramaean, Arabic, Ethiopic, Ancient Assyrian), as in 'a Semitic verb', 'a Semitic scholar', 'Semitic studies'; as a noun, *Semitic* is the Semitic family of languages; *Semitics* is the study thereof, or of the Semitic peoples.

Hebraic = 'of, concerning, or characteristic of the Hebrews or their language; having a Hebrew style or character', as in 'His features were Hebraic', 'His perception of nature . . . is mystical and Hebraic' (Emerson). A *Hebraist* is one versed in the Hebrew language, a Hebrew scholar.

Hebrew (n.) is an Israelite; historically, it is 'applied to the early Israelites'; 'in modern use', says *The O.E.D.*, 1901, 'it avoids the religious and other associations often attaching to *Jew*', but *Jew* is rapidly acquiring dignity and is now generally preferred to *Hebrew*; also the language spoken by the Hebrews. As an adjective, it = 'Israelitish, Jewish', and 'of, concerning, like or characteristic of the Hebrew language'.

Jewish is now the predominant adjective in reference to the modern Jews (the nation, religion, literature, art, character, customs), precisely as *Jew* is the predominant noun. (*The O.E.D.*)

sempstress and **seamstress.** The former is obsolescent; the latter, almost literary. *Sewing woman* or *sewer* is rather more common in general use for a professional, *needlewoman* for a nonprofessional 'woman that sews'. The male is *seamster* or *sempster*: but both are archaic.

send a remittance is inferior to *make a remittance*.

SENSE-CONSTRUCTIONS. Senseconstructions are those in which—according to their upholders—grammar (whether accidence or syntax) is set aside in the interest, and to the increase, of ready understanding. Rarely are they justifiable: for, in almost every instance, the breaking of the rule tends to set up or does actually set up an ambiguity, or else it so shocks the cultured reader (or listener) that the intended advantage is wholly lost.

For three excellent examples, see BETWEEN YOU AND I, EVERYONE . . . THEY, and FRIENDS WITH.

With the second, cf. ANYONE . . . THEY in the following extract from a letter that appeared in *The Observer* of March 12, 1939:—'"Anyone can call *their* house a hall" is a subtle recognition of the virtual plural in "anyone"' (H. B. Bullen): but has not almost every noun or pronoun a virtual plural? Can that virtuality (so far taken for granted that one never thinks of it) be held to be a sufficient reason for dispensing with a simple and sensible rule? I think not.

Here are two other examples of senseconstruction.

(Concerning a man that died with his hand outstretched to feed a beacon fire) 'Death had taken him in the act of feeding his last desperate signal' (Michael Innes, *Lament for a Maker*, 1938). 'His act' for 'the act' would have been logical, but unidiomatic; but even 'his act' leaves us with an ambiguity,—an ambiguity resolved by the fact that there is a unit: *him — in — the — act — of — feeding — his — last — desperate — signal*. Where sense-construction is idiom, it is folly and presumption to meddle with it.

'Of clearing or settlement or homestead, white man or blackfellow, there was no slightest sign' (*ibid.*). *No slightest sign* conforms to a formula; it = 'no sign, not even the slightest'. Literally, *no slightest sign* = 'no very slight sign' (but, on the contrary, an important sign); but actually (or idiomatically), it is a sense construction for *no sign at all*.

See also COLLECTIVE NOUNS; collectives afford an example of legitimate as opposed to illegitimate or, at best, disputed sense-constructions.

sensible and **sensitive.** The former is now obsolete for the latter in the nuances, 'having more or less acute power of sensation or feeling', 'apt to be quickly or acutely affected by some object of sensation', 'capable of delicate or tender feeling', and 'readily accessible to some specified emotional influence' (*The O.E.D.*). Those persons who have some French (but not enough) are misled by the French *sensible*, which = 'sensitive'. The English *sensible* is the French *sensé*; the English *sensitive* is the French *sensible*.

sensitiveness and **sensitivity.** The former is the general, the latter is the psychological term (as in 'sensitivity to stimuli', 'cutaneous sensitivity'). In short, *sensitivity* is merely the psychological version of *sensitiveness*, which is both 'the power or the capacity of sensation (feeling)' and especially 'a highly developed capacity or power of sensation; keen or delicate susceptibility to outward impressions'; hence, '(excessive) touchiness', also 'the quality of being easily affected by or quickly indicating changes of condition', as in photography. (*The O.E.D.*)

sensual, sensuous, sensory. *Sensory*, being the most technical of these three terms, is much less likely to be confused with either of the other two than *sensual* is with *sensuous* or vice-versa. *Sensory* = 'of or relating to the sensorium' (physiology) or 'relating to sensation or sense-impressions' (psychology).

Sensual is obsolete in the nuances 'sensory'; pertaining to physical sensation; perceptible by the senses'. As 'physical' (or 'sensuous') it is so moribund that it should be avoided—all the more that to use this sense is to confuse the issue. Its predominant senses are 'lewd' or 'unchaste', and 'voluptuous' (as in *sensual pleasure*) or 'excessively inclined to the gratification of the senses' (especially in sexual activities). In philosophy it = 'materialistic'.

Sensuous should be avoided in the now rare, almost dead sense 'excessively addicted to the pleasures of the senses, especially to sexual pleasure'. Its nuances are these:—'Of or pertaining to the senses', 'derived from or perceived by or affecting the senses', 'concerned with sensation (feeling) or sense-perception'; (of pleasure) 'received through the senses' and 'sensitive, or keenly alive, to the pleasures of sensation'. Thus, a *sensuous* artist is not necessarily a *sensual* man; the pleasure derived from music is *sensuous*, not *sensual*. [Definitions: *The O.E.D.*]

separate for *dissociate* is incorrect, as in 'It was intolerably easy to separate mentally the academic theories of war from the human side of it, even when one was engaged in it oneself', C. S. Forester, *A Ship of the Line*, 1938.

separate between. Freeman Wills Crofts, *Mystery in the Channel*, 1931, 'He had to separate between what was essential and what was accidental', where *distinguish between* or *separate . . . from* is meant.

SEQUENCE OF TENSES. See TENSE-SEQUENCE.

series, 'one set of . . .', is occasionally misused as a plural. Thus, 'A series of cellars provide the various parts of our dressing-station'.

sermo pedestris (pedestrian style) is incorrect for *sermo pedester*, which occurs in Horace's *Ars Poetica*. The confusion arose from *pedestris sermo* (in Flavius, a Silver not a Golden Latin historian), or perhaps from the genitive *sermonis pedestris*.

serried, 'closely ranked', and **serrated**, 'saw-toothed in shape', are sometimes confused.

service (n.) is, as Weseen has remarked, 'a much overworked word', especially in commercialese; *duty* is, in many contexts, preferable, and in others *expert advice* or *expert assistance* or *expert attendance*.

service (v.) should not be loosely used for *to serve*. [[*Service* in the sense of repair or keep in operating condition a car, a radio, or other machine is general American usage.]]

session and **cession.** The former = a sitting, a séance; the latter, a surrendering, a surrender (of territory or rights).

set for 'to *sit*, be seated' is now a solecism—when it's not dialectal. The same remark applies to figurative uses ('The matter sets heavily on her mind'; 'The food does not set well on her stomach').

sets-off, sets-out, sets-to. Incorrect for *set-offs, -outs, -tos*; but these awkward combinations should be avoided.

several for *some* or *fairly numerous*. ' "Found these, sir", he said, producing several pieces of broken glass, some of which were evidently fragments of a spectacle-lens or lenses, and some of which had formed part of a tube with engraved markings on it', W. Stanley Sykes, *The Missing Moneylender*, 1931.

sew, sewed, sewed or, archaically, **sewn.** *Sewn* survives in *hand-sewn* and *machine-sewn*.

sewage; sewerage. *Sewage* is refuse matter conveyed in sewers; *sewerage* is 'drainage or draining by means of sewers; a system, a method, of draining by sewers', hence 'sewers collectively; the system of sewers belonging to a particular locality'. Although *sewerage* can be used in the sense of *sewage* as here defined, careful writers do not so use it. (*The O.E.D.*)

sewn. See SEW.

sex. See GENDER.

sez. See SAYS.

shadow in the sense of *reflected image* and conveying the idea of *an exact likeness* was at one time common, but is incorrect and can be confusing; the latest example quoted by *The O.E.D.* is from Scott, 1813, 'The planets which shine above us as little influential of our destiny as their shadows, when reflected in the river, are capable of altering its course'—in which Scott was doubly wrong, for it is 'the planets' themselves that are 'reflected', not their 'shadows'.

To a modern reader for whom a shadow is the dark figure thrown by a body intercepting light, a figure whose likeness to that body is often grotesquely distorted, certain passages of literature are puzzling until he realizes that 'shadow' is used in the sense of 'reflection', as in Shakespeare's Sonnet LIII:

What is your substance, whereof are you made,
That millions of strange shadows on you tend?

shake—shook—shaken. *Shook* as past participle is solecistic when not dialectal.

shall and **will.** Letter signed 'R. C.', *The Daily Telegraph*, Nov. 18, 1937, 'Sir—Englishmen have long been accustomed to the misuse of "will" and "would" in the writings of Americans, Celts and others who do us the honour of using our language.

'But within the last few years "shall" and "should" have become increasingly neglected by the English themselves—at any rate, among the more uncultivated and slovenly. I suppose this is to be put down to the influence of the insidious cinema.

'The question I should like to raise is whether or no we must regard the traditional English usage as doomed? To read "I would like", "We will be glad to", etc., still sets the teeth of some Englishmen on edge. Will that be so in a generation's time?

'I cannot help thinking that English newspapers might help more than they do to preserve an idiom the abandonment of which will mean a loss to the language of a fine shade of expression—

    Yours, etc.'

'Shall the material universe be destroyed?' was the subject of debate in a young men's institute in Scotland, according to a correspondent of Dean Alford in 1870, who, seeing that the universe remains intact, concludes that the decision must have been 'No'.

'The faultless idiomatic use of *shall* and *will* is one of the points which are regarded as infallible tests of the correct English speaker; it offers peculiar difficulties to Scots, Irishmen and Americans', says Dr C. T. Onions in *An Advanced English Syntax.*

(The same rules affect all three kinds of future tense: the simple, 'I shall go'—the progressive, 'I shall be going'—and the perfect, 'I shall have gone'. Indeed they affect also the corresponding pasts, *would* of *will*, and *should* of *shall*; but for the purpose of reference, *should* and *would* are in the present work treated separately.

Mere futurity is expressed by *shall* in the first person ('I shall go', 'We shall go') and by *will* in the second and third persons ('You *or* he will go', 'They will go'): this may be regarded as the ordinary, the regular, the basic usage in modern Standard English, and it should be departed from only for a specific reason. In this usage *shall* and *will* are mere indications of time—formulas expressive of futurity—auxiliaries of tense.

The chief modification of that general rule is a survival of the original (the Old English) senses of *shall* and *will*. Dr Onions summarizes thus: '*Shall* denoting obligation, necessity, or permission; *will* denoting resolve or willingness'. And the following are his examples:—*

(1) 'I *will* (= am resolved to) live a bachelor.'
(2) '*Will* you (= do you intend or wish to) take it with you, or shall I (=am I to) send it?' [But does not post-War usage tend to: '*shall* you take it with you, or *will* I (or, am I to) send it?']
(3) 'We *will* send someone to fetch you.' [= 'We are resolved to send someone to fetch you'; mere futurity would require 'shall']
(4) 'He *will* (= is determined to) go, say what you may.' [But if *will* be employed, it must be stressed; otherwise 'is determined *or* resolved to go' is usual.]
(5) 'Thou *shalt* not steal'; 'You (he, they) *shall* go this instant'. [With the

*The parentheses *within* the example-sentences are Dr Onions's; the square parentheses following the example-sentences are mine.

latter might be compared this: 'Westwood said, *hale him away, dead or alive, for go he shall*' (*The Sessions Papers of the Old Bailey*, 1741).]

(6) 'Where the tree falls, there it *shall* lie.' [I.e., 'it must lie'.]

(7) 'He found the country in a state of unrest, for reasons which you *shall* hear.' [I.e., 'for reasons which you will be permitted to hear'. This usage is now a literary, not a spoken one.]

(8) 'You *shall* repay me at your convenience.' [This stresses the obligation or the permission, according as the speaker intends his statement to be understood. More gracious is, 'You will, please, allow me to add (or, I should like to add), repay me at your convenience'.]

(9) '*Wilt* thou have this woman to be thy wedded wife?' Answer: 'I *will*'. I.e., 'Do you wish to have . . .?' Answer: 'Yes, I do wish to . . .'

Dr Onions modifies his general modification, thus:—'*Shall* is sometimes stronger than *will*; e.g., "You will not go away?"—"I *shall*". *Will* is occasionally used to express command; e.g., "You *will* not go out to-day; you *will* stay in and work".' Closely connected with this use of *will* is that use whereby *will* serves to to soften a request, as in 'You *will* have breakfast ready by eight o'clock' (of which a still milder alternative is 'You *might* have my breakfast ready by eight o'clock'), and also in the interrogative '*Will* you tell me the time, please', which is rendered still more polite by substituting *would* for *will*.

Dr Onions notes that the future tense is 'not uncommonly employed to express an inferential fact of the present: 'This *will* no doubt be the book he referred to.' But such an inferential fact is equally well and idiomatically expressed by '*This*, doubtless, is the book he referred to'. Compare the tense but contrast the usage in Sheridan's 'Courage *will* come and go', where *will* connotes (rather than expresses) tendency or present habitual action; an even better example is 'These things *will* happen', for it shows that 'courage' and 'these things' are invested with will-power, intention, determination (cf. the thought behind 'The cussedness of the universe tends to a maximum'). The past of this *will* is *would* (see 'WOULD and SHOULD').

He further notes that in independent questions, the rule for the employment of *shall* and *will* is the same as in independent statements; 'but in the 2nd Person that auxiliary is used which is expected in the answer: '"*Shall* you go to London to-morrow?" (The expected answer is "I *shall*".) The substitution of *will* would convert the sentence into a kind of request.' But not if the progressive tense be used, for '*Will* you be going to London to-morrow?' asks what the addressed person intends to do on the morrow, and 'Are you going to London to-morrow' stresses not so much intention as futurity.

Literary uses of *shall* for all three persons are these:—

(*a*) In those clauses in which the action is mentioned or implied as being under consideration or in prospect:— 'Permission to use the reading-room will be withdrawn from any person who *shall* write on any part of a printed book.' (This might have been included under OFFICIALESE; logic and good sense and idiomatic usage would seem to prefer 'Permission . . . will be withdrawn from any person who [or, that] writes on any part of a printed book'.) 'There will I hide thee, till life *shall* end.' (I.e., 'There am I resolved to hide thee. . .'. The corresponding past is 'There did I'— or 'was I resolved to'—'hide thee, till life should end'.)

(*b*) In implied commands, e.g., 'My aunt intends that you *shall* accompany us'. Current idiom, however prefers 'My aunt intends you to accompany us'.

In colloquial and indeed all spoken English, however, *will* is fast displacing *shall* in all cases in which *shall* was formerly used and in which we are recommended to use it. That there should be this tendency is a pity, for once *shall* has disappeared, we shall have lost many subtle and useful distinctions.

Mr Wilson Benington, who does not profess to be a grammarian and who has no need to claim that he is a sensitive writer, responded thus to my invitation to give me his immediate reaction to the question of the distinction between *will*, *would*, and *shall*, *should*:—'The distinction may be indicated in this way: '*I will* (*do it*) has originally the sense, *I do it because I wish to*; *I shall* (*do it*) = *I do it because I ought to*. This applies particularly *to* the past tense and subjunctive mood: "Yes, you *would* do that!" has a meaning quite different from that of "You *should* do that".'

From that starting-point we may proceed along the lines so clearly laid down by Dr C. T. Onions.

⟦On the American usage there is a particularly interesting article by C. C. Fries, 'The Expression of the Future', *Language*, iii, 87–95.⟧

shape of, in the, is incorrect for *in the form of* in such sentences as these cited by Weseen:—'He gets his pay in the shape of commissions'; 'He gets his exercise in the shape of golf'. But even *in the form of commissions* (or *golf*) is verbose for *by commissions*, *at golf* or *by golfing.*

shape—shaped—shaped. The past participle *shapen* survives in the obsolescent *well shapen* and, though even there somewhat archaic, in poetry.

share and **part.** Cf. the entry at 'POR-TION and PART'. Do not misuse *share*, 'an allotted portion', for *part*, as in 'A large share of the meadow'.

sheared. See SHORE (v.).

shelffuls; shelves full. Cf. the remark at BASKETFULS.

shew; show. The latter is now the usual spelling. Don't show off by using *shew.* (But *shew-bread* has survived.)

shine (v.i.); preterite *shone*; past participle, *shone.* But the v.t. has preterite and past participle *shined.* 'The sun shone yesterday', 'The sun has not shone the last few days'; 'He shined *or* has shined my boots': these are correct. ⟦The old-fashioned *shined* for *shone* may occur in American usage.⟧

shipment. See CARGO.

shook. See SHAKE.

shop. See JARGON, par. 2.

shore of an ocean, a sea, a lake, or even of a great river; *bank* of all other rivers.

shore is archaic for *sheared* as the preterite of 'to *shear*'; the past participle is either *sheared* or *shorn*, the former only as a verb, the latter as both verb and adjective ('the shorn lamb').

short. See BRIEF.

shortly is to be avoided as a synonym of *briefly* in such a sentence as 'She spoke shortly', which conveys the idea of curtness or abruptness. Still more ambiguous is 'She will speak shortly', which conveys that 'she will speak before long'.

should and **would.** See 'WOULD and SHOULD'.

show. See SHEW.

show—showed—showed or, preferably, **shown.** In the passive, *shown* is obligatory ('He was shown to be a thief'); in the active, *showed* is less common than *shown.* (*The O.E.D.*)

shut. See CLOSE.

sick. See 'ILL and SICK'.

sick and **sickly.** The former refers to temporary, the latter to habitual illness; *sickly*, to be more precise, means 'habitually ailing'.

sick of, 'ill with', is now *sick with*; *sick of* is familiar (not slangy) for 'thoroughly weary of', with intensive *sick and tired of.*

sidewalk. See PAVEMENT.

sideward is adverb and adjective; **sidewards,** adverb only.

sideway; sideways; sidewise. *Sideway* is obsolescent as an adverb (= sideways) and as an adjective (= sidelong); as a noun (= byway or rarely sidewalk), it is American.

Sideways is current, in good use, only as an adverb, 'with the side foremost; facing the side' ('Two people could not pass in the passage without turning sideways'); 'in a lateral direction; obliquely' ('The lark came down sideways on its wing'; 'inclining to one side' ('with head bent sideways').

Sidewise is occasionally used as an adjective = 'sideward' ('Each man gave a sidewise bow'). As an adverb, it = 'sidewards', 'to one side', 'laterally', as in 'He glanced sidewise at me'; it is less common than *sideways* both in 'a house standing sidewise to the street' and in 'to hold the head sidewise'; in 'Viewed sidewise, the castle looked magnificent', it = 'from the side'. (*The O.E.D.*)

signature. See SUPERSCRIPTION.

sillily may be difficult to pronounce, but it is easy to write and so much more economical than *in a silly manner.*

silly (n.). See at STUPID PERSON.

similar, exactly, is a misuse for either *same* or *very closely resembling*; 'similar' is too vague to be made 'exact'. *The Daily Express* often uses it: and on Nov. 27, 1937, it defended the phrase, 'This thing is exactly similar to that'.

similar and **analogous.** *Similar* is 'having a marked resemblance or likeness; of a like nature or kind' ('We are on our guard against similar conclusions', Burke); constructed with *to* ('This is similar to that'). It has technical senses in mathematics and music. *Analogous* is 'having—or, characterized by—analogy*; similar in certain attributes, circumstances, relations or uses; having something parallel'; it is constructed with *to*; 'Disorders analogous to those of Syracuse' (Grote). It has a technical sense in Natural History. In the sense 'expressing an analogy', it is inferior to *analogical*.

similar and **same**. See 'SAME and SIMILAR'.

similar for *corresponding*; **similarly** for *correspondingly*. 'In accepting a definition wider than political for Left and Right, we must similarly accept a definition of Socialism wider than that of a particular political programme.' Misuse

similar as for *similar to* or *same as* is probably caused by a confusion between those two phrases. It is an odd mistake to find in so competent a writer as Nicholas Blake, yet in *There's Trouble Brewing*, 1937, we come on: 'The remains appear to be of similar height and physique as Bunnett': either for 'of height and physique similar to Bunnett's' or, more probably, for 'of the same height and physique as Bunnett [was]' or 'as Bunnett's'.

similar to, misused for *the same as*. J. H. Vaux, the convict, writing from Newcastle (New South Wales) and speaking of robbery with violence, says, in 1812, 'This audacious game is called by *prigs* [i.e., thieves] *the ramp*, and is nearly similar to *the rush*'. (Or is it possible that by 'nearly' Vaux meant 'closely'? In that now obsolete sense he would have been correct.) Cf. preceding entry.

similarly for *correspondingly*. See 'SIMILAR for CORRESPONDING'.

SIMILES, BATTERED. Here is a short list of similes that have been—and still are—working overtime. Think twice before you use any of the following.

as similes: see the key-words
aspen leaf, shake (or *tremble*) *like an*

bad shilling (or *penny*), turn up (or *come back*) *like a*
bear with a sore head, like a
behave: see *bull*
black as coal—or *pitch*—or *the Pit, as*

* *Analogy*. Apart from its technical senses in Logic, Philology, Natural History, and its loose sense, 'similarity', it = 'resemblance of things with regard to some circumstances or effects', 'resemblance of relations'. 'Knowledge is to the mind, what light is to the eye' is an excellent example of analogy.

blush like a schoolgirl, to
bold (or *brave*) *as a lion, as*
bold as brass, as
bright as a new pin, as [obsolescent]
brown as a berry, as
bull in a china shop, (behave) *like a*
cat on hot bricks, like a; e.g., *jump about . . .*
caught like a rat in a trap
cheap as dirt, as
Cheshire cat, grin like a
clean as a whistle, as
clear as crystal (or *the day* or *the sun*), *as;* jocularly, as *clear as mud*
clever as a cart- (or *waggon-*) *load of monkeys, as*
cold as charity, as
collapse like a pack of cards
cool as a cucumber, as
crawl like a snail
cross as a bear with a sore head (or *as two sticks*), *as*

dead as a door-nail, as
deaf as a post (or *as an adder*), *as*
different as chalk from cheese, as
drink like a fish, to
drop like a cart-load of bricks, to
drowned like a rat
drunk as a lord, as
dry as a bone (or *as dust*), *as*
dull as ditch-water, as
Dutch uncle, talk (to someone) *like a*
dying duck: see *look like . . .*
dying like flies

easy as kiss (or *as kissing*) *your hand, as;* also *as easy as falling off a log*

fight like Kilkenny cats
fighting cocks: see *live . .*
fit as a fiddle, as
flash, like a
flat as a pancake, as
free as a bird, as; as free as the air
fresh as a daisy (or *as paint*), *as*

good as a play, as; i.e., very amusing
good as gold, as; i.e., very well behaved
good in parts, like the curate's egg
green as grass, as
grin: see *Cheshire cat*

hang on like grim death
happy (or *jolly*) *as a sandboy* (or *as the day is long*), *as*
hard as a brick (or *as iron* or, fig., *as nails*), *as*
hate like poison, to
have nine lives like a cat, to
heavy as lead, as
honest as the day, as

hot as hell, as
hungry as a hunter, as

innocent as a babe unborn (or *as a newborn babe*), *as*

jolly: see *happy*

keen as mustard, as
Kilkenny cats: see *fight*

lamb to the slaughter, like a
large as life (jocularly: *large as life and twice as natural*) *as*
light as a feather (or *as air*), *as*
like similes: see the key-words
like as two peas, as
like water off a duck's back
live like fighting cocks
look like a dying duck in a thunder-storm
look like grim death
lost soul, like a

mad as a March hare (or *as a hatter*), *as*
meek as a lamb, as
memory like a sieve, a
merry as a grig, as [obsolescent]

nervous as a cat, as

obstinate as a mule, as
old as Methuselah (or *as the hills*), *as*

plain as a pikestaff (or *the nose on your face*), *as*
pleased as a dog with two tails (or *as Punch*), *as*
poor as a church mouse, as
pretty as a picture, as
pure as driven snow, as

quick as a flash (or *as lightning*), *as*
quiet as mice, as

read (a person) *like a book, to* (*be able to*)
red as a rose (or *as a turkey-cock*), *as*
rich as Croesus, as
right as a trivet (or *as rain*), *as*
roar like a bull
run like a hare

safe as houses (or *as the Bank of England*), *as*
shake: see *aspen leaf*: also *shake like a jelly*
sharp as a razor (or *as a needle*), *as*
sigh like a furnace, to
silent as the grave, as
sleep like a top, to
slippery as an eel, as
slow as a snail (or *as a wet week*)
sob as though one's heart would break, to
sober as a judge, as
soft as butter, as
sound as a bell, as
speak like a book, to

steady as a rock, as
stiff as a poker (or *as a ramrod*), *as*
straight as a die, as
strong as a horse, as
swear like a trooper
sweet as a nut (or *as sugar*), *as*

talk like a book; and see *Dutch uncle*
thick as leaves in Vallombrosa, as [Ex. Milton's 'Thick as autumnal leaves that strow the brooks In Vallombrosa']
thick as thieves, as
thin as a lath (or *as a rake*), *as*
ton of bricks, (e.g., *come down* or *fall*) *like a*
tough as leather, as
true as steel, as
turn up: see *bad shilling*
two-year-old, like a

ugly as sin, as

warm as toast, as
weak as water, as
white as a sheet (or *as snow*), *as*
wise as Solomon, as
work like a nigger (or *a horse* or *a Trojan*)

simpleness is being superseded by *simplicity*, except in the sense, 'foolishness; lack of intelligence; lack of shrewdness'.

SIMPLICITY. Simplicity of language or style is 'absence or lack of elegance or polish' or, in the modern acceptation, 'freedom from ornateness or overelaboration; plainness or directness of an attractive kind' (*The O.E.D.*); also 'freedom from or lack of obscurity or abstruseness'.

Simplicity is an admirable ideal; it can, however, be pushed to that extreme wherein the style becomes inadequate to the subject.

This is not a theme that can be satisfactorily treated within the limits of an article. But to those who feel that any guidance is better than none, I recommend 'Simplicity' in Alexander Bain's *English Composition and Rhetoric*, 1887–88, at I, 247–258; and to those who prefer example to precept, I suggest a perusal of my *English Prose*: 1700–1914, to which must be added a patient study of *The Bible* in the Authorized Version.

simply should, in many contexts, be avoided in the sense of *merely* (as in 'He is simply careless'), for it often sets up an ambiguity. Note, too, that 'He spoke simply' = 'in a simple, unaffected, sincere manner', whereas 'He simply spoke' = 'He only spoke; he spoke but did not act, sing, etc., etc.' As an intensive, *simply* is familiar English—not quite reprehensible, but to be avoided in good writing or dignified speech; 'simply too lovely for words' may be amusing, but it is also trivial.

simulate and **dissimulate.** The difference is important. To *dissimulate* is to hide or disguise one's real thought or feeling, to pretend not to have or feel; to *simulate* is to pretend to be, have or feel that which one is not, has not, or does not feel.

simultaneous. See COMPARATIVES, FALSE.

since (adv.) for *ago* is, says Weseen, 'incorrectly used . . . in such expressions as "It was a long time since" and "I was there two weeks since"'; but *The O.E.D.* makes no discouraging remark concerning this usage and gives these examples:—'A merchant . . . bespoke it not half an hour since'; 'Literati long since defunct' (De Quincey: *long ago* would be contrary to *usage*); 'He went out a little while since' (T. L. Peacock): nevertheless, in Weseen's second example, *ago* would be much superior to *since*, and in the first, rather better. Weseen makes an excellent point when he says that '*since* carries the mind forward from a starting point in the past to the present and applies to the intervening period', whereas '*ago* refers to a point in past time and carries the mind back from the present'.

since (conj.) leads to errors in the use of tense. It is obviously incorrect to write 'He is a notability since he has written that book'; less obviously incorrect is 'He has been a notability since he has . . .', the logical (and correct) form being 'He has been a notability since he wrote . . .'.

'You had a row with him and are not'—it should be *have not been*—'on speaking terms since', Vernon Loder, *The Button in the Plate*, 1938. Advertisement in a tube train: 'What a difference since I have used—soap!' should read 'since I used, or began to use'; here the verb must be in the preterite.—And see AS.

sing—preterite *sang*—past participle *sung*. *Sung* is the only form possible for the participle, but the preterite has the alternative *sung*, which, however, is gradually falling into disuse.

sink—**sank**—**sunk** are the usual forms in current speech and in prose.

The preterite *sunk* is becoming rare (cf. SUNG in preceding entry). The alternative past participle *sunken* is attributive, as in 'a sunken road', 'sunken cheeks', 'sunken rocks': yet *sunk* is preferred where (deliberate) human agency is implied, especially in certain technical senses, e.g., in architecture: 'a sunk ditch', 'sunk [= submerged] lands', 'sunk carving', 'sunk cistern', 'sunk panel', etc. (*The O.E.D.*)

sinus: plural **sinuses**.

situate; situated. In general, *situated* is to be preferred; in legal phraseology, *situate* is sanctified by custom, but elsewhere it is an absurd affectation, much affected by estate agents.

size; sized. *Every-size, fair-size, medium-size, middle-size, small-size, large-size,* etc., as adjectives are incorrect for *fair-sized, medium-sized, middle-sized, small-sized, large-sized; every-sized* seems illogical, and *of every size* (after the noun) is preferred. So too *larger-sized, smaller-sized* are correct—but unnecessary—for *larger* and *smaller*.

size of, the, as in 'That's the size of it' (= that is what it amounts to, that is what it signifies), is a colloquialism; it rings oddly in formal, impressive or beautiful contexts.

skilful; skilled. Possessing skill; showing skill. Usage, however, restricts *skilled* to labour—to craftsmen or technicians—and to their work. E.g., 'a skilled wool-sorter' but 'a skilful batsman'. (Harold Herd.)

sky-light (or, better, **sky light**) and **skylight.** *Sky light* is precisely what one would expect it to be: light from the sky. *Skylight* is that small opening in a roof (or a ceiling) which, filled in with glass, admits daylight.

slack is, in the sense 'to *slake* (one's thirst), said by Weseen to be incorrect: *The O.E.D.* admits it; so does *Webster's*. It is, however, unnecessary.

slander. See at LIBEL.

slang is incorrect for *slung* (preterite of *sling*); the past participle is *slung*.

SLANG.

I. DEFINITIONS; EXAMPLES.

The O.E.D.—that ever present help in time of doubt, and that *monumentum aere perennius*—defines the almost undefinable *slang* as 'language of a highly colloquial type, considered as below the level of standard educated speech, and consisting either of new words or of current words employed in some special sense'; H. W. Fowler, as 'playing with words and renaming things and actions; some invent new words, or mutilate or misapply the old, for the pleasure of novelty and others catch up such words for the pleasure of being in the fashion'; *Webster's* 'Language comprising certain widely current but usually ephemeral terms having a forced, fantastic, or grotesque meaning, or exhibiting eccentric or extravagant humor or fancy'.

It stands below colloquialisms, but above cant; it excludes dialect; and it is now improperly applied to solecisms, illiteracies, pidgin English, and all jargons. If a cant word gains wider currency, it is by its admission to the vocabulary of slang; if a slang word is promoted, it is to the ranks of colloquialism. [See the articles CANT, COLLOQUIAL, DIALECT, JARGON, SOLECISMS.] That, in the past, *slang* was applied, at different times, to all of these grades except dialect is no reason for so using it now. Moreover, don't call slang *cant*, nor *lingo*, nor *argot*.

In the matter of fine distinctions, example, as the worthy proverb assures us, is better than precept.

Here are a few examples exhibiting the difference between slang and colloquialism and Standard English (or Standard American). Standard *man* is colloquial *chap* and slang *bloke* or *cove* or *cully* or *guy* or *stiff* or *bozo*, of which slang terms the first three were originally cant; and *old man* is colloquial *old* (or *ancient*) *chap* (or *fellow*) and slang *old buffer* or *old geezer*; *money* is colloquial *wherewithal* or *shekels* and slang *spondulicks* (originally American) or *tin*; *doctor* becomes the colloquial *doc* and the slang *vet, croaker, pill-shooter; lawyers' clerk* becomes colloquial *limb of the law; lawyer*, colloquially *pettifogger*, becomes in slang, *landshark* (English), *mouthpiece* (English and American), *fixer* (American); a clergyman is colloquially *parson* and slangily *amen wallah, fire escape, holy Joe, sky pilot.*

Or consider this piece of English racecourse dialogue,* in which Gus is a bookmaker; 'Fairy' Smith is his clerk: 'Fat' Wilkins is his 'tictac man' or signaller; a 'shark', 'squib', and 'knowing one', or professional punter, and a 'steamer' or ordinary punter, are participants.

* The basis is slang, but some of the words are cant.

Gus (to the public at large). Pick where you like; I don't care. Shoot it in; shoot it in! It won't grow in your pockets, my lads. The jolly old favourite at two to one before he's a lot less.

Fat. Finith to fere! Finith to fere [Five to four.]

Gus. Evens on the field—what did I tell you? Bet levels, you devils. Shoot it in! Shoot it in!

Shark. Cow's calf [ten shillings] on *Fish.*

Gus (interpreting to 'Fairy'). Three halves on *Physic*. [*Psyche* is the horse's name.]

Steamer. Three tossaroons [half-crowns] each way on *Treacle Tart.*

Gus (to 'Fairy'). Treacle Tart: seven and six at fours to win; evens a place.

Fat (in a hoarse stage whisper). Scrub [cancel the previous odds on] *Treacle Tart*. A bice [two] and a half is the best. [I.e., 2½ is the best odds.]

Gus (incredulously). Come orf it!

Fat (waving as if demented). Scrub it! You'll do your dough. *Treacle Tart's* a springer [a dark horse]. It's deuces [odds of two to one]; it's exes to fere [six to four].

Gus (altering his board). Two late will be the cry. Shoot it in!*

II. ORIGIN; REASONS FOR USE.

†Slang, being the quintessence of colloquial speech, is determined by convenience and fancy rather than by scientific laws, philosophical ideals and absolutes, and grammatical rules. As it originates, so it flourishes best, in colloquial speech. 'Among the impulses which lead to the invention of slang,' Henry Bradley remarked, some years ago, 'the two most important seem to be the desire to secure increased vivacity and the desire to secure increased sense of intimacy in the use of language.' The most favourable conditions of growth are those of 'crowding and excitement, and artificial life. . . . Any sudden excitement or peculiar circumstance is quite sufficient to originate and set going a score of slang words', said John Camden Hotten in his dictionary of slang. Its origin and its use become more

* The rest of this delectable dialogue, which is six times as long as this excerpt, will be found in my *Slang To-Day and Yesterday*.
† The ensuing paragraphs represent a condensation and modification of chapters II–IV of my *Slang To-Day and Yesterday*, revised edition.

interesting as we bear in mind one of its primary laws: slang is not merely employed as a means of self-expression: it connotes personality: 'its coinage and circulation comes rather from the wish of the individual to distinguish himself by oddity or grotesque humour' (Greenough & Kittredge). Another aspect is presented in Earle Welby's dictum that 'some slang originates in an honourable discontent with the battered and bleached phrases in far too general use', this fresh slang being 'the plain man's poetry, the plain man's aspiration from penny plain to two-pence coloured'.

One of the most interesting pronouncements on the origins and uses of slang is that made by Mr H. L. Mencken in his invigorating *The American Language*. 'What slang actually consists of doesn't depend . . . upon intrinsic qualities, but upon the surrounding circumstances. It is the user that determines the matter, and particularly the user's habitual way of thinking. If he chooses words carefully, with a full understanding of their meaning and savor, then no [?] word that he uses seriously will belong to slang, but if his speech is made up chiefly of terms poll-parroted, and he has no sense of their shades and limitations, then slang will bulk largely in his vocabulary. In its origin it is nearly always respectable; it is devised not by the stupid populace [Cockneys are certainly not stupid], but by individuals of wit and ingenuity; as Whitney says, it is a product of an "exuberance of mental activity, and the natural delight of language-making". But when its inventions happen to strike the popular fancy and are adopted by the mob, they are soon worn threadbare and so lose all piquancy and significance, and, in Whitney's words, become "incapable of expressing anything that is real". This is the history of such slang phrases as . . . "How's your poor feet?" . . . "Have a heart!", "This is the life".'

But why is slang used at all?

Slang, I believe, is employed for one, or several, of the following sixteen reasons—and there are doubtless others.

(1) In sheer *joie de vivre*, by the young in spirit as well as by the young in years; 'just for the hell of it'; playfully, waggishly.

(2) As an exercise either in humour or in wit and ingenuity. The motive is usually self-display, snobbishness, emulation; or responsiveness; or a quasi-professional delight in virtuosity.

(3) To be different from others; to be novel.

(4) To be picturesque—either from a positive desire or, as in the wish to avoid insipidity, from a neutral or negative volition.

(5) To be arresting, striking, or even startling. (*Epater les bourgeois.*)

(6) To avoid clichés.

(7) To be brief, concise.

(8) To enrich the language. This purposiveness and deliberateness is rare except among the well-educated, Cockneys forming the most important exception; in general, therefore, it is literary and pondered rather than popular and spontaneous.

(9) To impose an air of solidity and concreteness on the abstract; of earthiness on the idealistic; of immediacy and appositeness on the remote. (In the cultured the effort is usually premeditated; in the uncultured it is almost always unconscious or perhaps rather subconscious.)

(10) To lessen the sting of, or on the other hand to give additional point to, a refusal, a rejection, a recantation; to reduce, perhaps also to disperse, the solemnity, pomposity, or excessive seriousness of a conversation—or on rare occasions, of a piece of writing; to soften the starkness, to lighten or to "prettify" the inevitability of death, the hammer-blow of madness, or to mark the ugliness or the pitiableness of profound turpitude (e.g., treachery, barbarous ingratitude); and thus to enable the speaker, or his auditor, or both, to endure, to 'carry on'.

(11) To talk, or to write, down to an inferior, or to amuse a superior, public; or merely to be on the same speech-level with one's audience or one's subject-matter.

(12) For ease of social intercourse: an affable attitude, this.

(13) To induce friendliness or intimacy of a deep or durable nature.

(14) To show that one belongs to a certain school (especially if it be Public or fashionable), trade or profession, artistic or intellectual set, a social

class; in brief, to establish contact or to be 'in the swim'.

(15) To show or prove that someone else is not 'in the swim'.

(16) To be secret—not understood by those around one. (Children, students, lovers, members of forbidden political societies are the chief exponents.)

III. ATTITUDES TO SLANG.

Slang now excites less disapprobation than was its lot before the present century; disapproval, indeed, had coloured the views of some notable 19th Century philologists and grammarians; nor is the condemnatory attitude yet dead. In 1825, J. P. Thomas, in *My Thought Book*, bluntly declared that 'the language of slang is the conversation of fools'; O. W. Holmes was scathing at its expense. Greenough & Kittredge condemn it on the ground that, being evanescent, vague and ill-defined, slang has a deleterious effect on those who use it often, for it tends to destroy all those delicate shades of meaning which are at the root of a good style; they hold that it is the speech of lazy persons; and assert that when a slang word becomes definite in meaning it has almost ceased to be slang,—which is manifestly false, for most slang words are unconventional synonyms of conventional words. A fairer view is that expressed by Professor H. C. K. Wyld: 'While slang is essentially part of familiar and colloquial speech, it is not necessarily either incorrect or vulgar in its proper place', which, the Fowler brothers assert in *The King's English*, 'is in real life'—that is, in conversation. The Fowlers continue by saying that, 'as style is the great antiseptic, so slang is the great corrupting matter; it is perishable, and infects what is round it'. The same thought is conveyed from a different angle by Professor G. H. McKnight, who remarks that, 'originating as slang expressions often do, in an insensibility to the meaning of legitimate words, the use of slang checks an acquisition of a command over recognized modes of expression . . . [and] must result in atrophy of the faculty of using language'. This applies mainly to authors and orators. But no stylist, no one capable of good speaking or good writing, is likely to be harmed by the occasional employment of slang; provided that he is conscious of the fact, he can even employ it freely without stultifying his mind, impoverishing his vocabulary, vitiating the taste or impairing the skill that he brings to the using of that vocabulary. Except in formal and dignified writing and in professional speaking, a vivid and extensive slang is perhaps preferable to a jejune and meagre vocabulary of Standard English; on the other hand, it will hardly be denied that, whether in writing or in speech, a sound though restricted vocabulary of Standard English is preferable to an equally small vocabulary of slang, however vivid that slang may be.

With regard to the use of slang, the Fowlers raise an important point when they say that 'foreign words and slang are, as spurious ornaments, on the same level. . . . The effect of using quotation marks with slang is merely to convert a mental into a moral weakness'. But there I must join issue with the authors of *The King's English*. They say that if a man uses slang at all (they advise him not to use it) in writing, let him do so in a courageous, not a cowardly manner: let him use it frankly, without quotation marks. So far as it goes, that is admirable; it does not go far enough. A good writer wishes to indicate that the word or phrase he puts into inverted commas is *not* Standard English, is not pure English, is not to be aped by the young nor unreflectingly copied by a foreigner; its status, he implies, is suspect, but he is using it because it is necessary to the atmosphere or to the characterization he wishes to make. True; he will use slang sparingly; he will use it only when it is necessary to the effect he is desirous of creating: but, precisely because he employs words scrupulously and precisely because he is anxious to avoid being taken as an exemplar of slang, a supporter of this particular word or phrase, he fences it off with quotation marks. 'This is not Standard English; I am using slang with the reservation that a Standard English term might, after all, have been preferable; however justifiable it is here, it is not always justifiable.'

IV. THE ROLE OF SLANG.

'An analysis of modern slang', wrote Brander Matthews in 1893, 'reveals the fact that it is possible to divide [it] . . . into four broad classes, of quite different origin and very varying value. Two

unworthy, two worthy. Of the two
unworthy classes, the first is that which
includes the survivals of "thieves'
Latin". . . . Much of the distaste for
slang felt by people of delicate taste is,
however, due to the second class, which
includes the ephemeral phrases fortui-
tously popular for a season [e.g., *Where
did you get that hat?*]. . . . The other two
classes of slang stand on a different
footing . . . They serve a purpose.
Indeed, their utility is indisputable, and
it was never greater [—the remark is still
valid—] than it is today. One of these
consists of old and forgotten phrases
and words, which, having long lain dor-
mant, are now struggling again to the
surface. The other consists of new words
and phrases, often vigorous and expressive, but . . . still on probation': these
two classes help to feed and refresh the
vocabulary. 'It is the duty of slang to
provide substitutes for the good words
. . . which are worn out by hard service.'
Of the fourth class—vigorous new slang
—he goes on to say that it is 'what idiom
was before language stiffened into literature': compare Lounsbury's description
of slang as 'the source from which the
decaying energies of speech are constantly refreshed'.

V. THE ESSENCE OF SLANG.

Two writers have been particularly
successful in attempting to set forth the
essentials of slang. Professor Albert
Carnoy, very briefly, in *La science du
mot*, 1927; Mr Frank Sechrist, at some
length, in 'The Psychology of Unconventional Language' (*The Pedagogical
Seminary*, December, 1913). 'L'argot',
writes Carnoy, 'est constitué par un
vocabulaire particulier dans lequel la
fantaisie intentionnelle joue un rôle dominant. Il tend à produire une sensation
de nouveauté, d'imprévu, d'ingéniosité
en donnant à certains mots un sens
inusité et "piquant". Les procédés em-
ployés à atteindre à ce but sont analogues
à ceux qui président en général à
l'évolution du sens, ceux notamment qui
produisent le langage "imagé", "ex-
pressif" et "affectif". Toutefois dans
l'argot, la part de la conscience [con-
sciousness] est plus grande, et toujours
se fait sentir un effort pour parler
autrement que la façon naturelle, pour
être drolatique, contourné ou ironique.
L'argot correspond à un état d'esprit
dédaigneux ou bon enfant qui ne prend

pas trop au sérieux les chose dont on
parle.'

To précis and paraphrase Sechrist is
difficult. Here, however, are a few of
his remarks:—

'[Slang] is purely unsentimental.'

'It is superior to accepted use through
its emotional force.'

'Slang phrases often possess a greater
wealth of association than others because they appeal to recent experiences
rather than to dim memories.'

'The emotional tension produced by
slang is greater than that of more customary and conventional language, and
the mind in time seeks a relief from it.'

'Slang is radical. It looks to the present, puts off restraint, and does not
concern itself with limits in speech.'

'[It] keeps close to the objective world
of things. . . . It is the language of
reality as common sense.'

'Slang will often be clear, even though
it must be distasteful; it will be familiar,
even though it must be coarse. It is
realistic, naturalistic, unromantic.'

Anthropomorphically considered, slang
'is the individual speaking from the racial
substratum, while conventional language
is the language of expediency, of social
deference, and reverence for the past'.

Sechrist's long article, which was reprinted in book form, should be read by
all those who are interested in the
psychology of language. To his illuminating remarks, I add a summary of my
own views:—

Slang tends to be 'Saxon' rather
than 'Latin-Greek'—native rather than
learned in its elements; except among
the very cultured and the innately supple
and subtle, it is simple and direct rather
than complex and concealed or insinua-
tory; it reduces the peculiar and the
particular (in which, nevertheless, it
rejoices and is, on occasion, 'at home')
to the level of general comprehension;
it abridges rather than develops or
elaborates; so far from padding, it omits
the incidental and the contingent; rather
than divest them of colour, it renders
them pictorial and metaphorical; except
in humour and wit, it eschews sentimental hyperbole and philosophical high-
falutin'; it takes nothing too seriously,
yet (very faintly) it implies a moral or
an intellectual standard, usually at the
level of good sense or, at the lowest, of
common sense; it universalizes words
and phrases rather than exclusively or

snobbishly confines them to one social class; it refers itself to human nature rather than to Nature; it dispels hypocrisy and humbug; in short, it is catholic, tolerant, human and, though often tartly, humane.

Inherent in human nature as a psychological tendency and potentiality, slang is indicative not only of man's earthiness but of his indomitable spirit: it sets him in his proper place: relates a man to his fellows, to his world and the world, and to the universe.

slank is archaic—now incorrect—for *slunk*, the preterite of *slink*; *slunk* is also correct for the past participle.

slant (n.). See STANDPOINT.

slattern. See SLOVEN.

slayed is incorrect for *slew*, the preterite of *slay*; the correct past participle is *slain*.

sled, sledge, sleigh, as vehicles. As 'a vehicle running on ice or snow', the three terms are synonymous, *sledge* being in the U.S.A. the least used, *sled* the most; in the British Empire, *sledge* is the most used, *sled* the least. *Sleigh* has a technical military sense, 'a carriage on which heavy guns are moved in store'. (*The O.E.D.*) ⟦In the memory of many Americans, a *sleigh* was a more comfortable and stylish vehicle than a *sled*. The two compared much as a car and a truck today. A *sledge*, sometimes called a *sled*, is a low vehicle on runners used for very heavy work in summer or winter. Cf. *stone-sledge* and *stone-boat*. Every child in the snow country has a small *sled* (or *handsled*) for his pleasure and, formerly, his chores.⟧

sleuth for *detective* should be employed only in a facetious way: used seriously, it is journalese.

slippy for *slippery* is described as 'vulgar' (*The Con. O.D.*), and *look slippy* for *be quick* as slang.

sloven and **slattern.** The former is common to the two sexes; the latter is used only of the female—'a woman or girl untidy and careless in clothes and cleanliness (and other habits) and/or in housework'. A *sloven* is any untidy or dirty person; hence also a careless, slipshod workman, craftsman, or writer. *Slut*, by the way, is stronger than *slattern*: a *slut* is a foul *slattern*; hence, a low or loose woman or girl, or a forward, impudent one (especially of a girl); and, unlike *slattern*, it may be used playfully ('Ah!

you're a wheedling slut', Swift). (*The O.E.D.*)

slow, slower or **more slow,** adverbially *more slowly—slowest* (rarely *most slow*), adverbially *slowest* (occasionally *most slowly*). 'He walks slowly' and 'go slowly' (literal) or 'go slow!' (figurative). The forms *more slow(ly), most slow(ly)* are literary or poetical. ⟦*Go slow* is literal as well as figurative in American usage. *Slow* adv. is occasionally interchangeable with *slowly* adv. Sometimes it is more forceful; sometimes it better suits the rhythm of the sentence.⟧

slut. See SLOVEN.

small fry is occasionally misused as a singular. 'Garston takes your overcoat on Monday and lets you have it back again on Saturday night—for a consideration. Or will buy it for that matter. Small fry', Cecil Freeman Gregg, *Tragedy at Wembley*, 1936. It is also misused in the following: 'It resulted in murder [the murder of a prominent lawyer politician] —and not just the usual shooting of some small fry', Milton Propper, *Murder at the Polls*, 1936. *Fry* is 'a collective term for young or insignificant beings' (especially newly-hatched fish), as *The O.E.D* tells us.

smell — smelled, smelt — smelled, smelt; but in both preterite and past participle, *smelt* is now the usual form. 'I smell something' but 'something smells unpleasantly' and 'something smells of (e.g.) oil'.

snicker is obsolescent for 'to *snigger*', to laugh in a half-suppressed manner. *Snigger* has a connotation of slyness in the laughter and/or of fault or absurdity in the object. To say, as Weseen does, that *snicker* and *snigger* are 'colloquial substitutes for *giggle*' is not only to classify them wrongly but also to misunderstand them.

snout is obsolescent for the trunk of an elephant, pejorative for the nose of a man. Properly it is the projecting part of an animal's head; it includes nose and mouth, and is applied also to insects and fishes. (*The O.E.D.*)

so (adv.), emphasizing the adj. following, as in *I was so pleased*, is a weak and slovenly form of expression. *Much* or *very* is preferable.

so, ambiguous. 'A prosperous, carefree foreigner, probably visiting Monte Carlo for the first time in his life, and so eager for adventure', Mrs Belloc Lowndes, *The House by the Sea*, 1937. Should not *so* be *therefore*? *So* for *therefore* or *accordingly* is much overworked.

so for *so that* or *in order that* is always colloquial and sometimes ambiguous, as in 'I don't know why I did that exactly' [—he means, 'I don't precisely know why' or 'I don't know precisely why . . .'] '—Perhaps a kind of dim hope that I'd find something . . . , but more to be alone and quiet—*so* I could think', Inez Irwin, *The Poison Cross Mystery*, 1936. (It is but fair to the author to add that she puts this statement into the mouth of a youngish detective that is better at detecting than at talking.)—'I do not ask you to believe these things, but I will give you proof, so you can judge them for yourself', in a novel published in 1937.

so, pronoun, is frequently misused: sometimes because it is asked to do too much. In *The World of Words* I found that I had written: 'A young child is not told, "The subject usually precedes the verb", yet that child has no difficulty in learning to do so', instead of the correct . . . 'yet that child has no difficulty in learning to set [or, place] the subject before the verb'. There is a considerable strain on *so* in 'King Carol to-day . . . proclaimed to his people: "Rumania must be saved, and I have decided to do so"' (*The Star*, Feb. 11, 1938); and here is a parallel misuse in *The Daily Herald* of the same date, 'Mr B. said later: "Much as we hate doing so, we are reconciled to the fact"'.

so, superfluous. As, e.g., in 'Both Karl and his mother discussed the crisis with Sir Oscar Bloom, but separately so, and from different viewpoints', Warwick Deeping, *Sackcloth and Silk*, 1935.

so as for *so that*, in the sense *in order that* is catachrestic, for *so as*—if used at all—should be confined to consequence. And in any event, it should be followed by *to* + the infinitive. Therefore 'He did this so as he might win the prize' is doubly unfortunate. 'He did this vigorously—so as to fall down exhausted' (result) is not incorrect; but it is clumsy for 'He did this so vigorously as to fall down exhausted'.

so . . . as, omitted. Do not omit this preparatory, this ordering, this clarifying formula: to omit *so* necessary and basic a piece of sentence-material is to incur the certainty of ambiguity and abruptness. 'It may turn out that nature can be so embraced,'—i.e., embraced in any one formula,—'but thinking must be organized not to demand it as a necessity' (Stuart Chase, *The Tyranny of Words*, 1938) should read '. . . but thinking must be so organized as not to demand it . . .'. I cannot bring myself to believe that Mr Chase deliberately omitted *so . . . as* on the grounds that a second *so* would render the sentence inelegant.

so far as. See AS FAR AS.

so that = *with the result that* (generally) and *in order that*. Keep it for the former. Also, its use is occasionally ambiguous, as, e.g., in the quotation at OTHER, THE.

sociable and **social.** *Sociable* is 'naturally inclined to be in company with others', hence 'inclined to seek their company and to enjoy it', 'affable'; hence of occasions, 'of or characterized by companionship, especially friendly or at least pleasant companionship' (*sociable habits* or *manners*, *sociable life*, *sociable talk*). *Social* is now rarely applied to persons: in the foregoing senses of *sociable* it is so very obsolescent as to be almost a catachresis. *Social* = 'consisting (or composed) of persons associated in—or for the purpose of—friendly intercourse or pleasant companionship' (*in every social circle*, *a social club*); 'living—or desiring to live—in communities' ('Man is a social being', Jowett); 'of or like, connected with or due to society as an ordinary condition of human life' (*social usefulness*, *social sympathy*, *the social order* or *state*, *social rank*); 'concerned with or interested in the constitution of society and its problems' (*a social reformer*, *social reform*). (*The O.E.D.*)

society and **Society.** The former = 'companionship, fellowship; the state or condition of living in association with others of the same species; and especially the aggregate of persons living together in a more or less ordered community'. The latter = 'the aggregate of leisured, cultured, or fashionable persons regarded as forming a distinct class or body in a community'. (*The O.E.D.*) The capital *S* serves to indicate the distinction in a way so convenient that it is not to be lightly disregarded.

SOCRATIC IRONY. See IRONY, third paragraph.

solar topi is incorrect for *sola topi* (or *topee*). The pith helmet used in India is so called from the sola, a swamp plant producing the pith, and is misspelt *solar* from the mistaken idea that the adjective refers to the *solar rays* (the rays of the sun, from which the helmet protects the wearer's head). (Ackermann, *Popular Fallacies*.)

sole is obsolescent in the following senses:—(Of places) 'lonely or secluded'; 'unique, unrivalled'; (of actions) 'exercised by one person only'; 'uniform or unvaried' (as in 'a sole colour'). In Law, it = 'unmarried'; a *corporation sole* is vested in one person (e.g., 'a parson is a corporation sole'). It is rare in the sense 'alone or solitary', and mostly predicative. The two commonest senses in non-technical English are 'one and one only', as in 'the sole support of his mother', 'the sole manager of these estates'; and (of properties, rights, privileges, duties, obligations) 'exclusive', as in 'A theory of which he claims the sole invention', 'This is a task in which he has the sole obligation'. (*The O.E.D.*)

SOLECISM AND SOLECISMS. *Solecism*, the Greek *soloikismos*, derives from the offensive and illiterate corruption of the Attic dialect as spoken by those Athenian colonists who settled at *Soloi* (Soli), in Cilicia, a province of Asia Minor. (The Greek word was probably slang, originally.)

The O.E.D. defines it, in the social sense, as 'a blunder or impropriety in manners'; in the linguistic sense, as 'an impropriety or irregularity in speech or diction'—a gross mispronunciation, a stress wrongly placed (especially in a well-known word); 'a violation of the rules of [accidence] or syntax; properly, a faulty concord', or, as Bentley has it, 'The last part of the sentence not agreeing nor answering to the first; which is the proper definition of a Solœcism': such a faulty concord as, e.g., 'He and I was in town'. In the 20th Century, however, its linguistic sense is generally taken to be a faulty pronunciation, an ignorant syntaxis, a gross fault in accidence ('two mans').

In short, it is approximately synonymous with *illiteracy*, which, however, includes also misspellings. ''E ain't a-comin' 'ere' contains three solecisms ('e, comin', 'ere) and five illiteracies ('e, ain't, a-, comin', 'ere).

solicitor. See LAWYER.

solidity should not be made synonymous with *solidarity* ('community or perfect coincidence *of* (or *between*) interests'), as Graham Seton makes it in

The *K. Code Plan*, 1938, nor with *stolidity*, which is 'dull impassiveness' or 'a natural incapacity for feeling', the former sense being favourable, the latter unfavourable. (*The O.E.D.*)

some, ambiguous. 'In particular propositions the adjective *some* is to be carefully interpreted as *some, and there may or may not be more or all*. An interpretation *some, not more nor all* often leads to trouble. 'If I say "some men are sincere", I must not be taken as implying that "some men are not sincere"; I must be understood to predicate sincerity of some men, leaving the character of the remainder wholly unaffected. It follows from this that, when I deny the truth of a particular, I must not be understood as implying the truth of the universal of the same quality. To deny the truth of "some men are mortal" might seem very natural, on the ground that not *some* but *all* men are mortal; but then the proposition denied would really be *some men are not mortal* . . . Hence, when I deny that "some men are immortal" I mean that "no men are immortal"; and that when I deny that "some men are not mortal" I mean that "all men are mortal"' (Jevons & Hill, *The Elements of Logic*, 1883).

some for *about, approximately, nearly, not many more than* is condemned by a rhetorician, who cites 'Some sixty men were present': but this is impeccable English.

some for *part* is misused, as in 'I shall spend some of the day in Town'.

some for *somewhat* (or *rather*) is a solecism ('He is some better to-day'); for *very* (or *much*), *very pleasant, large*, it is slang ('He speeded some'; 'We had some holiday'). See especially my *A Dictionary of Slang*.

some few. See 'FEW and A FEW'.

some place, some place else: solecisms for *somewhere, somewhere else*: as in 'The enemy was some place near', 'The jar is obviously some place else'.

some reason or another. See SOME WAY OR ANOTHER . . .

some thing and **something; some time** and **sometime.** Written as separate words, these two expressions are dissociative ('I'll see you at some time before midnight'; 'Some thing, not some person, was revealed'). When units are required, *something* and *sometime* are required. In current usage, *sometime* has two main senses, 'at some future time' ('Will you tell me?'—'Yes, sometime') and 'at some indefinite or indeterminate point of time; at some time or other' ('The prisoner escaped, sometime after nightfall'); in the sense 'now and then; occasionally', *sometimes* is the right word. (*The O.E.D.*)

some way or another; some reason or another. These are inferior to—indeed, wrong for—*some way or other*, *some reason or other*, e.g., 'In some way or other they escaped', 'For some reason or other, he left home'.

somebody (or someone) . . . they. See ANYONE . . . THEY.

somebody's (or someone's) else or else's. See ELSE'S.

someday is incorrect for *some day* ('I'll come some day soon').

somerset; somersault. The former is either dialectal or obsolescent (and slightly solecistic) for the latter.

something of that extent is misused for *something of that kind* or *sort*.

somewhat the same. Eric Partridge in *The French Romantics' Knowledge of English Literature*, 1924, speaks of 'a group of critics . . . possessing similar literary opinions as well as ability of somewhat the same high standard', but his subsequent study of English leads him to condemn this use of *somewhat* in the sense of *approximately* or *nearly* or *the like*.

somewhere near is infelicitous and slovenly for *somewhere about*, 'at (or in) approximately' (a specified period or date), as in 'I woke up somewhere about five o'clock', and also for *approximately*, as in 'He was ill somewhere about a month'. Note, too, that *somewhere about*, in these two nuances, is a trifle clumsy for *about* or *approximately*. (*The O.E.D.*)

somewheres is solecistic (when not dialectal) for *somewhere*.

son-in-laws is incorrect for *sons-in-law*.

sooner is familiar but good English for *rather* in 'He'd sooner play than work'; not a colloquialism. One would not, however, employ it in formal or lofty prose.

sophisticate (adj.) is obsolete for *sophisticated*. But *sophisticate* (n.) is both convenient and justifiable for *sophisticated person*: *Webster's*, 2nd edition, recognizes it as unexceptionable.

sort of for *rather*, *somewhat*, is generally regarded as vulgar or low colloquial. At the end of a sentence and usually following an adjective, it is a slovenly form of modification. 'He is queer, sort of'. 'He is rather queer' or 'He is, in a way, queer' is much to be preferred. Cf. KIND . . . OF.

sort of, these or those. In 'these sort of things are done by conjurers' (well-known novelist) there is a confusion between 'this sort of thing is done . . .' and 'these sorts of things are done . . .' (Baumann). Cf. KIND . . . OF, ALL.

SOULFULNESS. The only profitable thing to say about soulfulness is: avoid it in speech, if you wish to retain your self-respect and your friends; avoid it in writing if you wish to be ranked as a writer at all or if you have any regard for your correspondents. (I use the term in its modern sense, 'undue or affected emotionalism'.) Perhaps the best—or should I say the worst?—example of soulfulness is afforded by the more emotional novels of that almost forgotten best-seller, Marie Corelli: *God's Good Man*, *The Sorrows of Satan*, *Wormwood*, and the others.

sound (v.). One may say that 'A thing sounds all right' (which is rather colloquial, of course), but *sound* is misused in 'In a moment or two blows would be exchanged and after that anything might happen, but most likely a miniature razor battle, particularly as the voices of both parties sounded to be of foreign origin' (John G. Brandon, *The Mail-Van Mystery*, ca. 1937), where 'seemed to be' would be better, as also would 'the voices . . . sounded like those of foreigners'.

SOUND AND SENSE. In his *English Composition and Rhetoric*, 1887–88, Alexander Bain treats this subject under two headings: Melody and Harmony. But there are at least two other things to be taken into consideration: (1) alliteration; (2) adequacy of sound to sense.

'The Melody or Music of Language involves both the Voice and the Ear. What is hard to pronounce is not only disagreeable as a vocal effort'—though, to some authors, easy enough to write—'but also painful to listen to': and hardly less painful to those of us who read with the inner ear.

Bain examines certain sound-combinations that are melodious, others that are harsh, unmusical (see II, 280–90): but his findings are so obvious, his remarks

so unilluminating (because so trite),
that they are useless to the learner and
extremely tedious to the student: and
both useless and tedious to anyone who
is interested in the subject. But perhaps
we may quote his summary. 'The melodious flow of speech', he says, 'is dependent
upon the lengthening out of the pronunciation through the presence of long
vowels and continuing consonants. Rapidity and ease can be given by the
alternation of abrupt consonants and
short vowels; but it is hardly possible
to introduce musical tone without the
means of delaying and prolonging the
vocal strain.'

At 'Harmony of Sound and Sense',
Bain says, 'It is possible to make the
Sound of the language an echo to the
Sense', and first of all considers echo-
words and echoic collocations—which
formerly were called onomatopœia (*q.v.*).

Passing over such obviousness as
bang, crash, hiss, munch, thunder, whirr
and *whizz*, we see that imitation is most
effective when the echoism and sound-
effects extend over a succession of words.
Milton excels at such effects, as in

The hoarse Trinacrian shore;

Hell's gates open thus harshly:

On a sudden open fly
With impetuous recoil and jarring sound,
The infernal doors; and on their hinges
    grate
Harsh thunder;

whereas of Heaven's, he says that

Heaven opened wide
Her ever-during gates, harmonious sound,
On golden hinges turning;

a battle:

Arms on armour clashing, bray'd
Horrible discord: and the maddening
    wheels
Of brazen fury raged;

compare the meagre discordance of

Grate on their scrannel pipes of wretched
    straw.

The use of sibilants constitutes perhaps the most obvious echo-effect, especially as *s* is so seldom missing in a sound-
collocation of any length greater than
half a dozen syllables. Whittier ripples
thus the sea-shore:

And so beside the silent sea
    I wait the muffled roar;

and Poe achieves a rustling in

And the silken sad uncertain rustling of
    each purple curtain.

But language can by imitation represent
more impressive or more cumulative
movement: 'a series of long syllables, or
of words under accent [i.e., stressed
words], with the frequent occurrence of
the voice-prolonging consonants, being
necessarily slow to pronounce, is appropriate to the description of slow and
laboured movement. As in Pope's couplet
on *The Iliad*:—

When Ajax strives some rock's vast
    weight to throw,
The line too labours, and the words move
    slow.

. . . The opposite arrangement—that is
to say, an abundance of short and unaccented syllables, and the more abrupt
consonants alternated with the vowels—
by making the pronunciation rapid,
light and easy, corresponds to quickness
of motion in the subject', as in Gray's
Ode on the Spring:—

Yet hark! how through the peopled air
The busy murmur glows!
The insect youth are on the wing,
Eager to taste the honied Spring,
And float amid the liquid noon;
Some lightly o'er the current skim,
Some shew their gaily-gilded trim,
Quick-glancing to the sun.

Of the numerous special effects, we
shall note several. Keats is a master of
drowsy, headily sensuous effects, but he
can, when he wishes, be admirably precise,
even where precision is not the quality
that one would most expect—or expect at
all—as when, by using liquid consonants,
he brings before our eyes 'the gliding
motion of the clouds' (Bain), in

And let the clouds of even and of morn
Float in voluptuous fleeces o'er the sea.

Compare a similar use of liquids here:—

O what can ail thee, knight-at-arms,
    Alone and palely loitering?

. . . Tennyson's ingenuity is conspicuous.
The movement of a wave at the beach is
described—

Till last, a ninth one, gathering half the
    deep

And full of voices, slowly rose and
plunged
Roaring.

But then, Tennyson is perhaps as
skilful, subtle and delicate as anyone in
the entire range of English poets in the
suiting of sound to sense. So well-known,
so often quoted in his subtle skill, that
only two other examples need be given
here—

The moan of doves in immemorial elms;

and, to express the feeling of hopeless-
ness, a harsh rhythm with alliteration
magistrally employed to heighten the
effect—

And ghastly through the drizzling rain
On the back street breaks the blank day.

Obstructed movement, toilsome striving
are characterized in the following description of Sisyphus at his task (Pope's
The Iliad):

With many a weary step, and many a
groan,
Up the high hill he heaves a huge round
stone;
The huge round stone resulting with a
bound,
Thunders impetuous down, and smokes
along the ground.

Huge, unwieldy *bulk* implies slowness
of movement, and may be expressed by
similar language:

O'er all the dreary coasts
So stretch'd out, huge in length, the
arch-fiend lay.

But ended foul in many a scaly fold
Voluminous and vast.

But for alliteration, see the entry at
that term. And as for the psychological
adequacy of sound to sense,—well, that
is a big subject: See SUITABILITY.

sound out is tautological—and it
rings oddly—for *sound*, 'to test'. Perhaps
on the analogy of *try out*. 'President is
sounding out sentiment by undercover
[= secret] observers in European capitals', cited—from an American financial
weekly market letter—by Stuart Chase
in *The Tyranny of Words*, 1938.

source and **cause**. *Source* cannot be
used indiscriminately for *cause*, as in
'The source of his injury was a motor
collision', but, despite Weseen, it is permissible in 'The source of many failures
is neglect of duty'. *The O.E.D.* makes it

clear that a *source* is 'the chief or prime
cause *of* something of a non-material or
abstract character', as in 'The free election of our representatives . . . is the
source and security of every right and
privilege' (Junius) and 'This intellectual
perversion is the source of a systematic
immorality' (Manning); generally, however, there is a reference (actual or
implied) to the quarter whence something non-material or abstract arises, as
in 'Evil-smelling gases are a source of
annoyance to all those who live within
a mile of the factory' and 'One source of
danger is the carelessness of the garrison'.

sourkrout is incorrect for *sauerkraut*:
the German *sauer* means 'pickled', not
'sour'.

southernly is obsolete for *southerly*;
and *southerly* is obsolescent for 'situated
in—or towards—the south', for which
southern is the correct term. *Southerly*
is reserved for '(wind) blowing from the
south', as in 'In the greater part of
Europe the southerly and westerly winds
bring rain' (T. H. Huxley) and for 'facing
southwards or tending southwards', as
in *A southerly aspect, a southerly direction*. (*The O.E.D.*)

southward; southwards. The latter
is adverb only; the former is both adjective and adverb, and even as the latter,
now more usual than *southwards*.

sow—**sowed**—**sowed** (or, in poetry
and as adj. before a noun, **sown**). The
verbal noun is *sown*, as in 'The desert and
the sown'.

spake is archaic for *spoke*.

span is archaic for *spun* (preterite).

sparing with. See PREPOSITIONS
WRONGLY USED.

spat is said by Weseen to be archaic
as the preterite of *spit* (to expectorate);
but it is the usual form in Britain. See
also SPIT.

special. See ESPECIAL.

speciality and **specialty.** *Specialty* is
now preferred to *speciality* in the following senses:—A special line of work (including study and research); a manufacture or product characteristic of a
certain locality, firm, factory, etc.; 'an
article specially dealt in or stocked' by,
e.g., a shopkeeper: thus, 'His specialty
was inlaid-work' (Leland), 'The brass
work of Birmingham has long been one
of its specialties', 'He had selected as his
specialty currency and finance' (Mark
Pattison). In the abstract, 'the quality
of being special, limited, or restricted

in some respect', *speciality* is the right word ('Some . . . are general and vague directions, . . . others . . . the extreme of speciality', Grote); and as a plural, in the sense 'particulars, details', only *specialities* is possible ('A practical position chains the mind to specialities and details', Mill). (*The O.E.D.*)

specie and **species.** *Specie* is coined money; *in specie* = in actual coin; *specie* has no plural. *Species* is both singular and plural, and it = 'a class composed of individuals [animate or inanimate] having some common qualities or characteristics, frequently as a subdivision of a larger class or genus' (*The O.E.D.*).

species for *sex* is a curious error. 'It was not difficult to catalogue Miss Woods. But there was one consolation—J. L. was even more adept with her species', Robert George Dean, *The Sutton Place Murders*, 1936. Perhaps from 'The female of the species is the more dangerous'.

spectators. See AUDIENCE.

speed—sped—sped. But *speed*, 'to drive a motor-car very fast', and *speed up*, 'to hasten the acceleration or tempo of' (e.g., a business, a dance), more often than not have their preterite and past participle in the form *speeded*.

spell—spelled or **spelt—spelled** or **spelt.** Purists prefer *spelled* for the preterite, *spelt* for the past participle; usage accepts either form in the preterite but prefers the shorter form in the participle.

Spencer, philosopher (adj. *Spencerian*); **spencer,** a wig, a garment, a lifebelt; **Spenser,** poet (adj., *Spenserian*).

sphere (or **realm,** or **world**) **of** (e.g., **sport**) for *sport*. 'In the sphere (or realm or world) of sport, one should play for the side, not for oneself' would not be weakened by reducing it to 'In sport, one should . . .'.

spill—spilled or **spilt—spilled** or **spilt.** Those who like to differentiate, reserve *spilled* for the preterite, *spilt* for the participle; but usage scarcely supports them, except that it prefers *spilt* as a participial adjective, as in 'His words are like spilt water' (Carlyle) and *to cry over spilt milk.*

spit, 'to expectorate'—preterite, *spat* [in U.S.A., generally *spit*]—past participle, *spit*; but *spit*, 'to transfix'—*spitted* —*spitted.*

spite of. See DESPITE.

splendid, 'excellent' ('He was a splendid shot with a revolver'), is not a colloquialism, but it is familiar English—much overdone, and to be avoided in reputable writing or impressive speech. *Splendacious* and *splendiferous* are to be avoided as humorous slang or colloquialisms for 'magnificent'.

SPLIT INFINITIVE, THE. Dean Alford in *The Queen's English*, 3rd ed., 1870, scarcely troubles to discuss the matter, but seems to raise his very reverend eyebrows in sheer astonishment at the admission of such an error.

Dr C. T. Onions in *An Advanced English Syntax*, 1904 (6th ed., 1932), is much more tolerant. 'The construction known by this name consists of the separation of *to* from the Infinitive by means of an adverb, e.g. "He used *to continually refer* to the subject", instead of "He used *continually to refer*", or "He used *to refer continually*". The construction is becoming more and more frequent, especially in newspapers, but it is generally admitted that a constant and unguarded use of it is not to be encouraged; some indeed, would refuse altogether to recognize it, as being inelegant and Un-English. (Instances like "For a time, the Merovings continued to *nominally rule*" are particularly ugly.) On the other hand, it may be said that its occasional use is of advantage in cases where it is desired to avoid ambiguity by indicating in this manner the close connexion of the adverb with the infinitive, and thus prevent its being taken in conjunction with some other word': e.g., 'Our object is to further cement trade relations', is obviously preferable to 'Our object is to cement further trade relations' (which yields a sense different from the one intended), and is less obviously but no less surely preferable to 'Our object is further to cement trade relations', which leaves it 'doubtful whether an additional object or additional cement is the point' (Fowler). H. W. Fowler writes thus:— 'We maintain that a real split infinitive, though not desirable in itself,'—he implies that the sentence ought to be differently constructed,—'is preferable to either of two things, to real ambiguity, and to patent artificiality' (*The Split Infinitive*, S.P.E. Tract No. xv, 1923). As an example of patent artificiality he cites 'In not combining to forbid flatly hostilities', instead of the natural and sensible 'In not combining to flatly forbid hostilities'; 'In not combining flatly to forbid hostilities' would obviously have been ambiguous.

Fowler, we see, speaks of 'a real split infinitive'. Is there, then 'an unreal split infinitive'? I myself have used one in the preceding paragraph: 'The sentence ought *to be differently constructed*', which is as blameless as '*to be mortally wounded*' or '*to have just heard*'. There is a 'split' only when an adverb comes between *to* and an infinitive '*to clearly see*'.

Avoid the split infinitive wherever possible; but if it is the clearest and/or most natural construction, use it boldly. The angels are on our side.

spoil—spoiled, spoilt—spoiled, spoilt. *Spoiled* is the correct form in both preterite and participle, but *spoilt* is permissible in the senses 'so to damage as to render unfit or useless' ('Supper had been waiting until it was quite spoiled *or* spoilt'); 'to affect detrimentally or injuriously (an immaterial object)', as in 'His day will, I fear, be spoiled *or* spoilt by rain'; 'to injure (a person's character) by excessive leniency' (*spare the rod and spoil the child*), as in 'She spoiled *or* spoilt her only son'; and intransitively, 'to deteriorate; to decay', as in 'The fruit soon spoiled or spoilt in the very hot weather'. (*The O.E.D.*) As adjective, *spoilt* is usual; 'A spoilt child is an unhappy child'.

spoof and its plural. A correspondent wrote as follows to *The Radio Times* of Jan. 15, 1938: 'In a recent *Radio Times* the plural of the word hoof is spelled hooves in two instances. One would not spell the plural of roof rooves, and how supremely ridiculous the plural of spoof would appear if it were spelled spooves!' *Hooves* is allowed by *The O.E.D.*, though it is less commonly used than *hoofs*; but good authors have preferred it. *Rooves* also was common in our early literature, and is (like *loaf, loaves*) consistent with the genius of our language; a writer that prefers it could not be condemned for error and hardly for eccentricity. But *spoof* is quoted as analogous. Has *spoof* a plural? Originally a game, it was no more capable of taking a plural form than *cricket* or *golf*. *Spoof* is the abstract quality of jocular deception inspiring some trick or practical joke; it is in fact an adjective derived from the game. If it is to be used in such a sense that a plural is required for it, there will be nothing in *spooves* more 'ridiculous' than

in *spoof*, which has a comic intention from the first. (W.B.)

spoonfuls and **spoons full.** Cf. the remark at BASKETFULS.

SPORTING PLURALS. Sportsmen (big-game hunters, anglers, and others) tend to use the singular for the plural—*trout* for *trouts*, *lion* for *lions*, etc., etc. —and to look with scorn upon those who speak of *trouts* and *lions*. The ordinary person, unacquainted with the jargon of these very superior specialists, should not allow himself to be intimidated by the snobs of sport. If you wish to shoot three *lions* or to hunt *tigers*, do so.

SPORTS (field-sport) **TECHNICALITIES.** There are, in field sports, numerous terms that baffle or are unknown to the ordinary man and woman. The best book I know on the subject is Major C. E. Hare's *The Language of Sport*, 1939 (published by *Country Life*, London, at 7s. 6d. net).

From Major Hare's invaluable work, to which I refer the laudably curious reader, I select a few groups: animals' footmarks; retirement to rest; cries; tails; the marks on horses. And Company (or Group) Nouns.

A. i. Footmarks.

For the footing and treading of a hart, we say: *slot**;

buck, and all fallow deer: *view*;

all deer, when on grass and hardly visible: *foiling*;

a fox†: *print*;

similar vermin: *footing*;

an otter: *marks* or *seal*;

a boar: *track*.

ii. Retirement to rest.

A badger *earths*;

a boar *couches*;

a buck *lodges*;

a coney *sits* (or *burrows*);

a fox *kennels*;

a hare *seats* or *forms* or (less generally) *squats*;

a hart *harbours*;

a marten *trees*;

an otter *watches* or, if inland, *couches*

a roe *beds*;

a wolf *trains*.

* Also applied, derivatively, to a deer's foot.
† A fox's feet are *pads*, its face a *mask* or (rarely) *front*.

The corresponding nouns are:—

The bed of a badger is an *earth*;
    buck, a roebuck, or a hart is a *lair* (or, in English dialect, a *ligging*);
    coney is a *burrow*;
    fox is a *kennel* or, more usually, an *earth*;
    hare is a *form*.

iii. *Cries.*

A bittern *booms*;
a bull *bellows*;
a panther *saws*;
a sambur (Indian elk) *saws*;
a stag *roars* (at the end of September).

At rutting time, a badger *shrieks* or *yells*;
    a boar *freams*;
    a buck *groans* or *troats* (hoots);
    a ferret, like a polecat and a stoat, *chatters*;
    a fox *barks* (or *whines*);
    a goat *rattles*;
    a hare or a rabbit *beats* or *taps*;
    a hart *bells*;
    an otter *whines*;
    a roe *bellows*;
    a wolf *howls*.

iv. *Tails.*

The tail of a boar is a *wreath*;
    a buck, a hart, or other deer, is a *single*;
    a coney or a hare is a *scut*;
    a fox is a *brush* or *drag*, the tip at the end being a *chafe* or a *tag*;
    a foxhound, a greyhound, a wolf, is a *stern*;
    an otter is a *rudder* or a *pole*;
    a roe is a *target*.

v. *The Marks on Horses.*

A *blaze* is 'a white marking spread over the forehead, and sometimes down the whole width of the face. An exaggerated blaze is called "white face"' (Hare);
flesh marks are such patches of skin as have no colouring matter;
a *list** or *ray* is that dark line which

* Perhaps from *list*, a strip (e.g., of cloth).

runs along the back of some horses, many mules, and all donkeys;
lop ears are such ears as are 'set on in rather a loose and pendulous manner' (Hare);
a *race* or *stripe* is a white marking,—it is a thin line,—that runs down the nose;
a *snip* is a white or pink patch on nostril or lip;
sock: see *stocking*;
a *star* is a small white patch in the centre of the forehead;
a *stocking* is such an area of white on the leg as extends from the coronet (the lowest part of the pastern) to the knee or hock, but when the white ascends for a short distance only it is called a *sock*;
a *wall-eye* is an eye that has a bluish-white appearance (caused by lack of pigment);
white face: see *blaze*;
a *zebra mark* is any stripe (but generally applied when there are more than one stripe) on body or limb, but, common in donkeys and mules, it is rare in horses.

B. *GROUP TERMS:* Nouns of Assemblage or Company*

i. *Birds, Animals, Fishes* and *Insects.*

(a) *Birds.*

Birds in a company are called a *flock* or a *congregation*
Bitters or herons: a *siege*
Bustards: a *flock*
Chickens: a *brood*
Choughs: a *clattering*
Cranes and Curlews: a *herd*
Crows: a *murder*
Doves: a *flight*
Ducks (in flight): a *team*; (on the water) a *paddling*
Eagles: a *convocation*
Finches: a *charm*
Geese (on the water): a *gaggle*; (on the wing) a *skein*
Goshawks: a *flight*
Grouse (a single family): a *covey*; (larger band): a *pack*
Gulls: a *colony*
Hens: a *brood*
Jays: a *band*
Lapwings: a *deceit*
Larks: an *exaltation*
Mallard(s): a *flush*
Nightingales: a *watch*

* See Hare's book and, esp., R. J. Nicol, *A Collection of Terms, denoting Assemblages,* 1933 (privately printed).

Parrots: a *flock*
Partridges: a *covey*
Peacocks: a *muster* (mediaevally) an *ostentation* or a *pride*)
Pheasants (a family): a *brood*; (a large group) a *rye*
Pigeons: a *flight* or a *flock*
Plovers: a *congregation*
Poultry: a *run*
Quails: a *bevy*
Ravens: an *unkindness*
Rooks: a *clamour*
Snipe: a *walk*
Sparrows: a *host*
Starlings: a *chattering*
Storks: a *mustering*
Swallows: a *flight*
Swans: a *herd* or, less usually, a *weage*
Swifts: a *flock*
Widgeon(s), in the air: *flight*; on the water: *bunch, company* or *knob*
Wildfowl(s): *plump* or *trip*
Wrens: a *herd*

(b) *Animals.**

Antelopes in company are a *herd*
Asses: a *herd*; also a *drove* or a *pace*
Boars: a *sounder* (mediaevally, a *singular*)
Bucks: a *herd*
Buffaloes: a *herd*
Camels: a *flock*
Cats (tame): a *cluster*; (young) a *kindle*
Cattle: a *herd* or *drove*; *mob* is Australian
Chamois: a *herd*
Conies: a *bury*
Cubs or whelps: a *litter*
Deer (all sorts): a *herd*
Dogs: a *kennel*
Elephants: a *herd*
Elk(s): a *gang*
Ferrets: a *business*
Foxes: an *earth* or a *skulk*
Frogs: an *army*
Giraffes: a *herd*
Goats: a *herd, flock* or *trib* (mediaevally, a *trip*)
Hares: a *drove* (mediaevally, a *trip*)
Horses: a *herd*
Horses (stabled): a *stable*; (stud) a *harras* (obsolete)
Hounds: a *pack*
Kangaroos: a *troop*
Leopards: a *leap*
Lions: a *flock, pride,* or *troop*
Mice: a *nest*
Monkeys: a *tribe, troop* or *troupe*

* In this list *herd* occurs 13 times; *flock*, 4; *troop*, 3; *drove*, 4.

Mules: a *barren* or a *rake*
Oxen: a *herd* or a *drove*
Piglets or pups: a *litter*
Racehorses: a *field*; a *string*
Rhinoceroses: a *crash*
Sheep: a *flock*
Squirrels: a *dray*
Stoats: a *pack*
Swine: a *sounder*
Toads: a *knot*
Wolves (wild): a *pack*; also a *herd* or *rout*

(c) *Fishes and Insects.*

Eels in a company are a *swarm*
Dogfish: a *troop*
Fishes: a *school* or a *shoal* (see also Hare's book)
Herrings: *army, glean* or *shoal*
Mackerel and minnows, perch and pilchards: a *shoal*
Porpoises: a *school*
Roach: a *shoal*
Seals: a *herd*
Sticklebacks: a *shoal*
Trout: a *hover*
Turtles: a *bale*
Whales: a *school*
Whales, sperm: a *herd*
Whiting: a *pod.*

ii. *Persons—and Objects.*

Apart from generally accepted terms like *crowd* and *host*, suggestions have, at various times, been made for new ones, on the lines of certain fanciful mediaeval Company Terms (e.g., in *The Book of St. Albans*, 1486), such as a *bevy* of ladies, a *blast* of hunters, a *blush* (or *rascal*) of boys, a *boast* of soldiers, a *charge* of curates, a *dignity* of canons, a *gaggle* of gossips, a *hastiness* of cooks, a *laughter* of eggs (modern), a *skulk* of thieves, and so on. Here are some of the modern suggestions:—

(a) *Objects*

Aeroplanes: a *buzziness*
Bicycles: a *wobble*
Cocktails: a *shake* or *scatter*
Motor-cars: a *maze* or a *stink*
Sausages: a *sizzle*
Whiskey: a *want.*

(b) *Persons.**

Actors: a *condescension* (N)
Aldermen: a *guzzle* (P)

* H = Major C. E. Hare; N = Colonel R. J. Nicol; P = *Punch*; S.D. = *The Sunday Dispatch*; B.D. = Lt.-Col. C. Bartley-Denniss; E.P. = Eric Partridge.

Americans: a *Mayflower* (E.P.)
Anglers: an *elongation* (E.P.)
Announcers (radio): an *accent* (E.P.)
Aunts: an *anticipation* (E.P.)
Aviators: an *annihilation* or a *celerity* (E.P.)
Babies: a *dampness* (E.P.)
Bachelors: a *debauchery* (N)
Bandsmen: a *furore* (H)
Barbers: a *botheration* or a *loquacity* (E.P.)
Bathers (seaside): a *bareness* or *nudity* (E.P.)
Beggars: a *whine* (E.P.)
Bishops: a *psalter* (P); an *unction* (E.P.)
Bookmakers: a *surge* (H)
Bores (club): a *geyser* (P)
Boys: a *riot* (H)
Bridge fiends: an *argument* (P)
Butchers: a *bloodiness* (E.P.)
Children: a *scamper* (E.P.)
Chinese: a *jaundice* or a *piety* (E.P.)
Choir Boys: an *angelry* (E.P.)
Chorus Girls: a *click* (B.D.); a *giggle* (N)
Civil Servants: a *file* (E.P.)
Clergymen: an *offertory* or a *vestry* (E.P.)
Clerks: a *ledger* (E.P.)
Clowns: a *guffaw* (P)
Colonels: a *blimp* or an *explosion* (E.P.)
Colonials (British): a *dominion* or a *loyalty* (E.P.)
Commercial Travellers: a *brazenness* (E.P.)
Commissionaires: a *chestiness* (E.P.)
Communists: an *envy* (E.P.)
Company Promoters: a *boodle* (P)
Confidence men: a *plausibility* (E.P.)
Conservatives: a *stodge* (P)
Cooks: a *burning*, a *caprice* or a *hash* (E.P.)
Councillors: a *corpulence* (S.D.)
Cousins: a *countryside* (E.P.)
Cricketers: a *pavilion* or a *test* (E.P.)
Curates: a *coyness* (S.D.)
Damsels: a *spray* (H)
Dancers: a *clutter*, a *jazz*, a *rhythm*, or a *swing* (E.P.)
Daughters: a *dependence* (E.P.)
Débutantes: a *curtsy* or a *diffidence* (E.P.)
Dentists: a *removal* (E.P.)
Diplomats: a *suavity* (E.P.)
Doctors: an *emulsion* (B.D.)
Dramatists: a *dialogue* (E.P.)
Dutchmen: a *courage* or a *comfort* (E.P.)

Editors (newspaper): an *erudition* (S.D.); a *rejection* (E.P.)
Englishmen: an *insularity* (E.P.)
Fairies: a *charm* (H)
Families: a *garden suburb* (E.P.)
Farmers: a *grousing* (E.P.)
Fathers: a *fatuity* (S.D.); an *overdraft* (E.P.)
Film stars: a *screen* or a *transience* (E.P.)
Financiers: a *corner* (E.P.)
Fishermen: see Anglers
Flappers: a *frolic* (P)
Footballers (Association): a *dribble* (E.P.)
Footballers (Rugby): a *tackle* (E.P.)
Frenchmen: a *gesticulation* (E.P.)
Garage-Proprietors: an *Ali Baba* (E.P.)
Gardeners: a *growth* or *offshoot* (E.P.)
Generals: a *blather* (N); an *importance* (E.P.)
Germans: a *blitz* or *momentum* (E.P.)
Girls: an *evasion* (E.P.)
Gods: a *gatheration* (B.D.); an *omnipotence* (E.P.)
Gold-diggers: a *daddy* (E.P.)
Golfers: a *bogey* or a *mouth-disease* (E.P.)
Governesses: a *pathos* or an *effacement* (E.P.)
Grocers: an *imposition* (E.P.)
Highbrows: an *altitude* (P); a *high-falutin'* or a *depression* (E.P.)
Hikers: a *hustle* (E.P.)
Housewives: a *duster* (E.P.)
Husbands: a *futility* (N); an *unhappiness* (B.D.); a *duty* (E.P.)
Indians (Asiatic): a *pagoda* (E.P.)
Insurance men: a *prospect* (E.P.)
Irishmen: an *eloquence* (E.P.)
Italians: an *opera* (E.P.)
Japanese: an *adaptation* (E.P.)
Journalists: a *column* (E.P.)
Lawn-tennis players: a *love* or a *service* (E.P.)
Lawyers: a *surplus* (E.P.)
Liberals: a *brace* (P)
Loafers: a *saunter* (H)
Lovers: (women) a *delight*; (men) a *flattery* or a *pressure* or a *cornucopia* (E.P.)
Lowbrows: an *earthiness* (E.P.)
Majors: a *Poona* (E.P.)
Mannequins: a *slink* (P); an *undulation* (E.P.)
Members of Parliament: a *chatter* (B.D.); a *promise* (E.P.)
Milkmen: a *clatter*; a *watering* (E.P.)
Millionaires: a *Mammon* (E.P.)
Miners: a *muttering* (H)

Misers: a *proximity* (E.P.)
Mothers: a *patience* (E.P.)
Mothers-in-Law: an *interference* or *management* or *pestilence* (E.P.)
Motorists: a *licence* or a *mania* (E.P.)
Navvies: a *neckerchief* (E.P.)
Nazis: a *hail* (E.P.)
Old Maids: *see* Spinsters
Pacifists: a *propaganda* (E.P.)
Pedestrians: a *morgue* (E.P.)
Peeping Toms: a *Godiva* (E.P.)
Playwrights: a *caste* (E.P.)
Plumbers: a *procrastination* (E.P.)
Poets: a *gush* (P); a *cacophony* or a *prosiness* (E.P.)
Policemen: a *college* or a *politeness* (E.P.)
Politicians (tame): a *plethora* (B.D.); an *indifference* (E.P.)
Portrait painters: a *palliation* or an *improvement* (E.P.)
Postmen: a *delivery* (E.P.)
Prohibitionists: a *gargle* (P)
Publicans: a *pint* or a *pot* (E.P.)
Publishers: an *optimism* (E.P.)
Punters: a *fleece* (P)
Racketeers: a *protection* (E.P.)
Rascals: a *parcel* (B.D.)
Readers (British Museum): a *somnolence* (E.P.)
Relatives: a *poverty* or an *invasion* (E.P.)
Russians: a *gloom*, a *lustrum* or a *steppe* (E.P.)
Sailors: a *wave* (E.P.)
Saints: a *severity* (E.P.)
Schoolteachers: an *unselfishness* (E.P.)
Scholars: a *collation* (E.P.)
Scientists: a *quantum* (E.P.)
Scotches (whiskeys): a *skinful* (S.D.); a *headache* (E.P.)
Scotchmen: a *generosity* (E.P.)
Servants: a *dearth* (B.D.); a *departure* (E.P.)
Socialists: a *heckle* (P)
Soldiers: a *canteen* (E.P.)
Sons: an *independence* (E.P.)
Spaniards: a *discord* or a *revolution* (E.P.)
Spectators (at English field games): a *shiver* (E.P.)
Spinsters (of any age): a *flutter* (P)
Spinsters (old maids): an *anxiety* (E.P.)
'Stars' (cinema): a *constellation* or a *Hollywood* (E.P.)
Statesmen: a *pact* (E.P.)
Stockbrokers: a *margin* (E.P.)
Surgeons: a *see-saw* (E.P.)
Sweet young things: a *rapacity* (E.P.)
Tailors: a *long credit* (E.P.)

Taxi-drivers: a *tardiness* or an *expectation* (E.P.)
Telephone Operators: an *apology* (E.P.)
Thieves: an *honour* (E.P.)
Topers: a *continuity* (E.P.)
Tourists: a *drove* (B.D.)
Turks: a *delight* (E.P.)
Tyrants: an *egotism* or a *Hit-or-Muss* (E.P.)
Uncles: a *disappointment* (E.P.)
Urchins: a *mischief* (H)
Vicars: a *vicariousness* (S.D.)
Virgins: a *trace* (H); a *malaise* or a *misfortune* (E.P.)
Waiters: a *dawdling* (B.D.)
Welshmen: an *eisteddfod* (E.P.)
Wives: a *questionnaire* or a *quo vadis?* (E.P.)
Women: a *millinery* (E.P.)
Writers: a *sufficiency* or a *vanity* (E.P.)
Young people: a *superiority* (E.P.)
Zealots: a *preachment* or a *proselytism* (E.P.)

Too late for inclusion in the alphabetical list are these three small sets, handed to me by friends.

(1) Mr F. G. Rendall (of the British Museum): a *foozle* of golfers, a *fraud* of Freudians, a *frowst* of philosophers.

(2) Major C. H. Wilkinson (Worcester College, Oxford): a *cheat* of bursars, a *dread* of deans, a *lakh* (or *lac*) of principals (of colleges), a *prowl* of proctors,—of which the first and last are in actual use among the dons.

(3) Sir Harry Luke (K.C.M.G., D. Litt): a *cuddle* of nurses, a *galaxy* of milkmaids, a *swell* of admirals.

sprain and **strain** (v.). The former is 'so to twist or wrench (a part of the body) as to cause pain or difficulty in moving', now mostly confined to wrenching one's ankle. To *strain oneself* is so to exert oneself physically as to be in danger of injury.

spring—sprang, or, less generally **sprung—sprung.**

squirt. Blood *spirts*, not *squirts*, from a wound; here is an idiom that careless writers tend to ignore. Such writers appear to act, not on the epigram, 'The best is good enough for me', but on the assumption, 'Anything is good enough for the public'.

St, not **St.,** is, in my opinion, the best form; to be pedantically accurate, you would write it *S't*; thus *Ste*, not *Ste.*, nor *S'te.*

staff of persons, pl. *staffs*; *staff*, a stick,

rod, pole, pl. *staffs*, although the earlier plural, *staves*, is still preferred in the senses 'a stick carried in the hand as an aid in walking', 'a rod used as an instrument of divination or magic', 'a stick or pole used as a weapon', 'a spear- (or lance-) shaft'. In music, *staff* has plural *staffs*, but obviously the variant *stave* has plural *staves*. (*The O.E.D.*)

staid and **stayed.** Reserve the former for the adjective ('of grave or dignified or sedate deportment, demeanour, conduct'), the latter for the verb. 'The staid fellow stayed at home', 'The staid girl has stayed—a girl'.

stair; stairs. A *stair* is one of a succession of steps leading from one floor to another; *stairs* means either the steps of staircases or a series or 'flight' of such steps; *staircase* is usually one flight of steps, occasionally a series of flights. *Stairs*, as the plural of *stair*, hence as '(two or more) steps', is now avoided, *steps* being used instead to minimize the likelihood of ambiguity. (*The O.E.D.*)

stalactite and **stalagmite.** The former deposit of calcium carbonate is one that forms downward from the roof of cave or cavern; the latter, one that forms upward from the floor.

stanch and **staunch.** For the adjective, much the commoner form is *staunch*; for the verb, *stanch* is preferable. [For verb, noun, and adjective, *Webster's* gives *stanch, staunch*.]

stand for *withstand* is, to put it mildly, unhappy. Whereas *stand* for 'tolerate, endure, bear' is a colloquialism to be avoided in good writing, *stand* for 'withstand' or 'resist' is the product of a meagre vocabulary; and it may be a rank mistake, leading to ambiguity, as in 'The avaricious man could not stand the solicitations of easy money'.

standard is incorrect when it is used as a synonym for a person's physical stature, as in 'John was a stoutly-made man; his standard about five feet ten inches' (adduced by *The O.E.D.*).

STANDARD AMERICAN. See Section v of the following entry.

STANDARD ENGLISH and **STANDARD AMERICAN.** If we take the definition, 'Standard English and Standard American are the speech of the educated classes in the British Empire and the United States' (when, of course, they are not speaking slangily), as sufficient for the moment, we may yet desire to know where, and how, Standard English arose. That rise* provides material for an interesting story.

I. HISTORY.

Old English had a standard (witness Old English literature), but that standard disappeared with the Norman Conquest. In the victorious reigns of Edward I (1272–1307) and Edward III (1327–77), there was a strong growth of national feeling; national consciousness was certainly accompanied by, and probably it was in part the source of, an increasing hostility to the use of French in England and consequently an increasingly favourable attitude towards the use of English. 'In the second half of the Fourteenth Century', says McKnight, 'the English language came once more to its own, into use not only in Parliament and the law courts and in schools, but in the literary productions composed for English cultured society.'

In this revival of English as a literary language, after it had so long been a merely spoken language, the particular kind of English adopted was the East Midland dialect. The reasons for this adoption, says McKnight, are these:— 'The dialect of the East Midland district lay between Northern and Southern dialects and, as the Northern differed considerably from the Southern, the Midland served as a midway compromise understandable by all; it formed the speech of Oxford and Cambridge, the two great centres of higher education and of a culture more profound and mellow than that of London; it formed also the dialect of London itself, the centre of the political, official and commercial life of the country. And thus it was the speech of Chaucer, who, the greatest English writer until the 16th Century and, during the 11th–14th Centuries, the only great writer to employ English at all, passed most of his life in

* For the advanced student, Professor H. C. K. Wyld's books are inescapable and invaluable; so too is Professor G. H. McKnight's *The Making of Modern English*. But here I draw, for the most part, on McKnight's 'Standard English', the opening chapter of his *English Words and Their Background*. Another excellent book for the general reader and the less advanced student is Henry Bradley's *The Making of English*. This article follows very closely, in outline and often in detail, the 'Standard English' section of the chapter entitled 'English: Good; Bad; and Worse' in my *The World of Words*, 2nd edition (revised), 1939.

London; as the dialect spoken at Oxford, it was used by Wycliffe, who discarded his native Yorkshire for this smoother speech; as the dialect of London and hence of the Court, it was used by Gower, who might have been expected to employ the Kentish dialect.' Chaucer's and Gower's best work appeared in the last twenty years of the 14th Century; in the 15th, their disciples—and others—followed their lead and wrote in the East Midland dialect. Standard English, then, began in the second half of the 14th Century as the East Midland dialect; and in the 15th Century that dialect was established as the correct one to use for general literary purposes. It was the more readily adopted because it had not the harshness of the Northern dialects, very little of the rather drawling softness of the Southern. The supremacy of the East Midland dialect was unquestioned by the dramatists and the poets of the Elizabethan age.

The language of the 16th and early 17th Century, however, was far from being so fixed and regularized as that of the 19th and, though less, the 20th Century. Spelling was idiosyncratic, syntax experimental, and vocabulary a glorious uncertainty; these features and tendencies were counter-balanced by 'the freedom enjoyed by the writers of that period in the adoption of new words and the combination of existing words in word-compound and in phrase'. Regularity in spelling and vocabulary, along with order in accidence and syntax, came in the approximate period, 1660–1800. 'In the 18th Century, especially near the end, the influence of grammars and dictionaries made itself fully felt. Words admissible into literary use were registered with their meanings in dictionaries, which also more and more undertook to indicate the pronunciation. English grammar became a subject for school study, and conformity to the use authorized by dictionary and grammar became the test of [culture] in language.'

For more than 300 years the East Midland dialect, 'at first, no doubt, merely held to be the fashionable mode of speech, has gained in prestige, until, at the present day, it is spreading all over [Great Britain], and among all classes' (Wyld, *The Growth of English*). This dialect has become Standard English: the criteria of that standard are the choice of words and phrases, the syntax, the pronunciation. Of Standard English as we know it in the 20th Century, we may say that it 'is a kind of English which is tinged neither with the Northern, nor Midland, nor Southern peculiarities of speech [and] which gives no indication . . . of where the speaker comes from. . . . It is the ambition of all educated persons in [Great Britain and Northern Ireland] to acquire this manner of speaking, and this is the form of our language which foreigners wish to learn' (*ibid.*).

But it is important to bear in mind that 'no form of language is, *in itself*, [originally] better than any other form. A dialect gains whatever place of superiority it enjoys solely from the estimation in which it is commonly held. It is natural that the language of the Court should come to be regarded as the most elegant and refined type of English, and that those who do not speak that dialect naturally'—that is, as birthright or as environmental training—'should be at the pains of acquiring it. This is what has happened, and is still happening, to the dialect which is called Standard English',—although Standard English is to be no longer regarded as a dialect properly so called. 'Of course, since this form of English is used in the conversation of the refined, the brilliant and the learned, it has become a better instrument for the expression of ideas than any other [variety] of speech now spoken.'

'When', continues Professor Wyld, 'we speak of Good English, or Standard English, or Pure English, as distinct from . . . Provincial English [the dialects proper], we must remember that there is nothing in the original nature of these . . . dialects which is in itself inferior, or reprehensible, or contemptible. In a word, the other dialects are in reality and apart from fashion and custom, quite as good as Standard English [[—the same holds, of course, for Standard American in relation to American dialects—]], considered simply as forms of language; but they have not the same place in general estimation, they have not been so highly cultivated' (nor have they become so subtle and delicate), 'and they have not the same wide currency.'

II. STANDARD ENGLISH: DEGREES AND KINDS.

There are, however, different kinds of Standard English:—The best of these is Received Standard*, for it fulfils all the requirements of good speech; Modified Standard is Standard English that differs from Received mainly in pronunciation; and Literary Standard lies beyond any matter of pronunciation, and is confined to written English,—and should it be used in speech, it is too bookish to be Received.

Of Literary English—Literary Standard—it is necessary only to say that it is the more conventional, stylized, and dignified, more accurate and logical, sometimes the more beautiful form that Received Standard assumes, like evening dress, for important occasions; it is also more rhythmical and musical. The prose of Sir Thomas Browne, Gibbon, De Quincey, The Landors, Pater is in Literary English. With dialect, colloquialism, slang, cant, it has nothing to do unless they possess a long pedigree—and then only in rare instances.

What then of Received Standard and Modified Standard? 'It is proposed', says Wyld in his *Short History of English*, 'to use the term *Received Standard* for that form which all would probably agree in considering the best, that form which has the widest currency and is heard with practically no variation among speakers of the better class all over the country. This type might be called Public School English.' (The stress here, you see, is on pronunciation and enunciation.) 'It is proposed to call the vulgar English of the Towns, and the English of the Villager who has abandoned his native Regional Dialect'—dialect in the ordinary sense of the term—'*Modified Standard*. That is, it is Standard English, modified, altered, differentiated, by various influences, regional and social. Modified Standard differs from class to class, and from locality to locality; it has no uniformity, and no single form of it is heard outside a particular class or a particular area.' Very obvious, as Professor Wyld is the first to admit; very important, as he was the first to emphasize.

* 'Received Standard' and 'Modified Standard' are Professor Wyld's designations, whereas 'Literary Standard' is a designation proposed—after due thought—by myself.

III. THE LIMITS OF PURE (or, RECEIVED STANDARD) ENGLISH*

There is a perhaps startling difference between pure English and the English spoken by the uncultured.† In the American 'Them guys ain't got no pep' and the English 'Them blokes ain't got no go', not even a single word satisfies the standard exacted by pure English, whether American English or British English. In both versions, the first word (*them*) is ungrammatical (for 'these' or 'those'); the second is slang (for 'men'); the third (*ain't*) is illiterate; the fourth (*got*) is unnecessary—and colloquial; the fifth (*no*) is illogical, the sense demanding *any*; and the sixth (*pep*: *go*) is slang. Both versions are not merely uncultured but illiterate; yet the speech is straight from the shoulder, the meaning unmistakable.

There are, however, inestimable advantages to be obtained from uniformity of vocabulary and from regularity of syntax: that uniformity and that regularity do at least make understanding much easier: and communicability is the primary requisite of both speech and writing.

Since the 17th Century, English has gained tremendously in precision. Language has not been evolved to be the sport of the illiterate, any more than to be the plaything of the highbrow or the chopping-block of the journalist. Language is a means—the chief means—of communication, not merely between two Chicago gangsters or two Soho toughs, but among all the members of a nation; internationally too. 'It is important that the language medium should offer as little as possible resistance to the thought current, and this end is attained only when the symbols of language are ones that convey precisely the same meaning to all who use the language.'

But we may raise a question concerning the degree to which a language can be healthily standardized. Too often are spoken English and spoken American criticized as though it were impossible for them to have any laws of their own—a freedom not shackled at every turn by the rules explicit or implicit in Literary Standard.

A language cannot be at the same time

* In this section I draw heavily on G. H. McKnight's *English Words and Their Background*.
† Dialect is considered as of an essentially different order from illiterate speech—as indeed it is.

entirely standardized and truly vital: a rigorously regimented language would die from stiffness of the joints and atrophy of the spirit. 'Ideas inherited from the past . . . may find adequate expression in the idiom of the past. . . . The shifting, developing forms assumed by living thought, however, demand the plastic medium of a living language.' It is only natural that new systems of thought and new modes of living should, by the very strength of their processes and by their widespread currency, generate new words, new compounds, new phrases and even new modes of expression: in linguistics, as in politics, the will of the nation is all-powerful; it is of no use for the pedants to deplore and lament the misuses implicit in (say) *aggravating* or *the psychological moment*, for usage has consecrated the original errors and turned them into correct currency.

On this question of the limits of pure English (Received Standard), Logan Pearsall Smith, an American long resident in England, has, in 'Popular Speech and Standard English' (an admirable article to be read in full), in *Words and Idioms*, written as follows:—'Since our language seems to be growing year by year more foreign, abstract and colourless in character, it stands in greater need than ever of this vigorous and native reinforcement' which we could obtain from dialect in particular and popular speech in general. This reinforcement could be enlisted and fruitfully employed by all of us, 'were we not paralysed by that superstitious feeling of awe and respect for standard English [i.e., Received Standard] which is now [1925] spread by the diffusion of education'. We are enslaved by the tyrant Correctitude.

But why should Standard English have to resort to dialectal and popular speech for vitality and picturesqueness instead of drawing on its own resources? 'It is inevitable', Pearsall Smith continues, 'that when any form of speech becomes a standard and written language, it should as a consequence lose much of its linguistic freedom. All forms of speech have of course their rules and usages, but in a written language these rules and usages become much more settled and stereotyped': so that, finally, words and phrases are adjudged to be good or bad, not by their strength, clarity and aptness of expression, but by the external criterion of correctness. 'Such an attitude . . . tends . . . to fix grammar and pronunciation, to discourage assimilation [of picturesque or vigorous outsiders], and to cripple the free and spontaneous powers of word-creation'. Then, too, 'a standard language, in modern conditions, tends to be rather a written than a spoken language. The printed word becomes more and more the reality, the spoken word an echo or [a] faint copy of it. This inversion of the normal relation between speech and writing, this predominance'—almost, tyranny—'of the eye over the ear, of the written symbol over its audible'—i.e., spoken—'equivalent, tends to deprive the language of that vigour and reality which comes, and can only come, from its intimate association with the acts and passions of men, as they vividly describe and express them in their speech.'

The foregoing, however, is not to be taken as an attack on, nor as a depreciation of, the *virtues and the advantages* of Standard English, for this, the accepted form of English, with its national scope and its national use, with its rich and varied vocabulary, with its often subtle and, for the most part, flexible syntax, with all the historical associations inevitably and naturally garnered in the course of centuries, and these and other associations enriched by successive generations, is the inestimably precious inheritance of the English people, as any such language is of any ancient people. The position of good (or pure) English is, in essentials, impregnable: for as it arises from, so does it serve, a social need. The danger lies, not in its being set aside (with the result of linguistic chaos, and hence of a lack of national unity), but in its being so unreflectingly and blindly respected that we may forget the very existence of popular speech and widespread colloquialism, of slang and dialect, and thus forget both their intrinsic value and their value as readily available sources of freshness and invigoration.

No standard language exists on its own capital; no standard language can thus exist,—if it is to continue to be a language and not become a mausoleum. Standard English, sprung from a dialect, has never, for long, disregarded the other dialects, over which, by a geographical, political and social accident, it has been exalted: those others have always had too much to offer in potential enrichment of the triumphant dialect. Like dialect, popular speech abounds in uncouth phrases and low words and absurd (or, at the least, hasty) perversions and inaccuracies; but it also abounds in vivid phrases, in racy and vigorous words, in strong monosyllables and picturesque compounds, and also in ancient words that have, unfortunately for us, dropped out of cultured speech. How useful, how valuable, how fitting it would be if many of these words and phrases were to be admitted, or re-admitted, to standard speech and were, in their turn, to become Received Standard, whence there would duly be expelled those learned terms which had become synonyms of these racier or stronger or more musical terms adopted from dialect and from the popular speech of the towns. Their adoption would not merely enrich but also improve the material stock, hence the cultural and spiritual value and potentialities, of Standard English, which they would strengthen and render less standardized.

'Human speech', as Pearsall Smith has remarked in that work which we have already quoted, 'is after all a democratic product, the creation, not of scholars and grammarians, but of . . . unlettered people. Scholars and men of education may cultivate and enrich it, and make it flower into all the beauty of a literary language', but they should not, in their efforts to keep the language pure, forget that it should also be kept vigorous; they are too apt to forget that the 'rarest blooms are grafted on a wild stock, and [that] its roots are deep-buried in the common soil. From that soil it must still draw its sap and nourishment, if it is not to perish [from inanition], as the other standard languages of the past have perished, when . . . they have been . . . cut off from the popular vernacular.'

Nevertheless, as McKnight has excellently said in his excellent *Modern English in the Making*, 'the standardization of modern English is not as nearly complete as is sometimes supposed. The language ideal of philosophers like [Wilkins and] Locke has never been realized. Idealistic efforts . . . have been only partially successful. The English language has not been subjected to absolute rule. . . . In other words, English

is not yet a dead language. . . . "Law," says Roscoe Pound, "must be stable and yet cannot stand still." The statement applies with little modification to . . . language. Language, though regulated, . . . must change in company with changing conditions of life.'

Let us, therefore, have purity, so far as possible. But not to the detriment of raciness and vigour.

IV. STANDARD ENGLISH IN THE DOMINIONS AND COLONIES.

Except among Public School men and women resident there, the Dominions and Colonies have not a Received Standard pronunciation, although the vocabulary is, among the cultured and the well educated, that of Received Standard. They may be said to speak Modified Standard. One may hope that, in the Dominions (especially, perhaps, Canada and Australia), the clarity and subtlety of the best Standard English will always exercise a beneficent influence. Certainly it would be idle to fear that these Dominion writers might be unduly cramped thereby.

Colonial scorn of Public School English, like English scorn of Colonial accents, should be allowed to die. There is a reason for Colonial accents; much virtue in Public School English.

V. STANDARD AMERICAN SPEECH AND WRITING.

The United States presents a knottier problem, for, there, a much larger population is concerned than that of the English-speakers in the Dominions.

In writing, there is an American Literary Standard, which so closely resembles English Literary Standard as to establish no basic, no important difference. But is there, in American speech, a Received Standard? Or is there nothing but a number of Modified Standards? One might, on first thought, say that there are only Modified Standards, although one might add that some of these modifications are more pleasing to the British ear or more widely used than others. But the fact remains that, although there is, in the United States, no speech that can be classified as Received Standard with the same feeling of certainty as Public School speech can be said to be Received Standard in England, yet the speech of the cultured elements of American society is as close to being a Received Standard as can be expected in so vast and many-peopled a land as the United States. That the criterion is neither so severe nor so rigid as that of English Received Standard does not make it any the less a genuine criterion.* But in America even more than in Great Britain, the speakers of Modified Standard are more numerous than the speakers of Received Standard. It must, however, be remembered that the differentiation between Standard and popular speech, between Standard and slang, between slang and cant, is, on the whole, less marked in the United States than in the British Empire.

standpoint, point of view, viewpoint; angle and **slant.** The first is a blameless variant of the second, whether literal or figurative. *Viewpoint*, however, though admitted (without comment) by *The O.E.D.*, has been deprecated by purists; not being a purist, I occasionally use it, although I perceive that it is unnecessary.

Angle, modern and permissible, is not to be used to the exclusion of *standpoint*; Americans tend to overdo *slant* in the figurative sense ('mental point of view'), but in England it has not yet been acclimatized.

stanza. See at VERSE.

starlight (or **star-light**) and **starlit** (or **star-lit**). The former is a noun, and attributively an adjective ('a starlight night'); *starlit* is only an adjective ('a starlit night'). But *starlit* is the commoner ‚ adjective predicatively: 'The night was starlit' is—quite apart from euphony—preferable to 'The night was starlight'. *Starlit* = 'lit up, or lighted, by the stars' ('The whole of the star-lit sky', Proctor), and so does *starlight* ('A starlight evening, and a morning fair', Dryden): in this sense, *starlit* is to be preferred. But in the transferred sense, 'bright as the stars', only *starlight* is used, as in 'starlight eyes'. Based on *The O.E.D.*

start for *begin* is familiar—not literary—English, whether it is used transitively or intransitively; but for inanimate objects, *begin* is better, 'That story begins on page 79' being superior to '. . . starts on page 79', 'He began to work when he was only twelve' to 'He started . . .'. To

start in to do something is an American colloquialism for 'to start [preferably *begin*] to do something'.

state (n.). See EDITION.—In the sense 'alarm, fuss, anxiety, distraction', it is a colloquialism.

state and **say.** *State*, being much stronger than *say*, should be reserved for formal or impressive contexts. 'I wish to state that I like fish' is an absurd overstatement.

stately is now rare as an adverb; so is *statelily. In a stately manner* is the locution sanctified by usage.

States, the. See AMERICA.

statesman. See 'POLITICIAN and STATESMAN'.

stationary is the adjective ('static; not moving'); *stationery*, the n. ('writing materials').

statute and **statue** are occasionally confused by the ignorant. A *statute* is a (formally enacted) law.

staunch. See STANCH.

staves. See STAFF.

stay, in law = 'to delay', 'to arrest (an action) for the time being'—not 'to put an end to'.

stayed. See 'STAID and STAYED'.

steal, 'a theft', 'something stolen', 'a corrupt transaction or a fraudulent one', is an American and Canadian colloquialism.

sticker and **stickler.** A *sticker* is a person constant to a cause or persistent (or persevering) in a task, whereas a *stickler* (for something) is a pertinacious contender for, or supporter or advocate of, a cause or a principle, a person or a party, also one who insists on the letter as opposed to the spirit of, e.g., a form or ceremony, a custom or habit. (*The O.E.D.*)

still more yet is redundant for *still more* or *yet more*, as in 'Still more yet is to be said for a strong defensive force'. *Still* (or *yet*) *more* is an intensive of *more* and should not be used unless an intensive is required.

stimulant and **stimulus.** *Stimulant*, in medicine and physiology, is 'something that temporarily quickens some vital process, or the function of some organ', as in 'The abuse of stimulants, in the form of alcohol, tobacco, tea, and coffee'; hence, in general use, 'alcohol; an alcoholic drink', as in 'In one of his many serious illnesses he refused all stimulants' (A. C. Benson, concerning Archbishop Benson). *Stimulus* is a medical synonym

---

* ⟦The best account of American pronunciation is Professor Kenyon's admirable 'Guide to Pronunciation', *Webster's New International Dictionary*, Second Edition.⟧

of the medical sense of *stimulant*, and also, in medicine, it = 'the resulting stimulation'; in general use it is 'an agency or influence that stimulates [or excites] to action or that quickens an activity or process'; hence, 'a quickening impulse or influence' (as in 'Difficulty is a stimulus'). Plural, *stimuli*. (*The O.E.D.*)

sting—**stung** (archaic and dialectal: **stang**)—**stung**.

stingy and **economical**. An *economical* person is careful of his money, but when occasion calls for liberality he may be generous; a *stingy* person is one who, too careful of his money, is always niggardly.

stolidity. See at SOLIDITY.

stomach. See BELLY.

stop in the sense of *stay, remain, sojourn* (at a place or with a friend), though general, is strictly a misuse of the word; *The O.E.D.* allows it, only cautiously saying that *stay* 'is more correct'. To *stop off* or to *stop over* at a place, to *stop in*, e.g., a hotel, are American colloquialisms.

STOPS. See PUNCTUATION.

storey and **story.** In the British Empire it is possible and useful to reserve *story* for 'a narrative', *storey* for 'a set of rooms on (or, one large room constituting) one floor or level': this is merely a matter of convenience, for etymologically *storey* is a mere variant of *story*. The use of *storey* is to be recommended on the score of clarity: 'the story of a story' is readily distinguishable from 'the story of a storey'; consider, too 'the storey in this story is the fifth'.—See also 'FLOOR and STOREY'. [[In American English the spelling *storey* for *story* is exceedingly rare.]]

strait, 'narrow, constricted', is occasionally confused with *straight*, 'direct, unswerving'.

strata is a plural ('layers') and should not be used as a singular, the correct singular being *stratum*. 'Woman, from her childhood, except perhaps in that strata of society which has divorced itself from the common cause of mankind, is ever the mother' (Graham Seton, *The K. Code Plan*, 1938). *Data* (singular *datum*) is occasionally misused in the same way. [[*Webster's* notes that data is 'not infrequently used as a singular'; it b'ings no such comfort, however, to the users of *strata* as a singular, and for good reason. It is important to distinguish one stratum from another; but data is usually collective.]]

stricken. See following entry.

strike—**struck**—**struck** (archaic, **striken**). But *stricken* as a participial adjective is actively extant in *a stricken deer* (wounded in the chase); in the science of percussion, it = 'struck with a blow'; in music, *a stricken note* is one produced by striking a blow; *fever-stricken, poverty-stricken, sorrow-stricken*; in the sense of '(mind, heart) afflicted with frenzy or madness'; jocularly *love-stricken* (*maiden* or *swain*); *stricken measure* (a measure 'having its contents levelled with the brim'); and *stricken field*, 'a pitched battle' (*not* a ravaged field); a rare variant is *stricken battle*. The archaism *stricken hour* means a full hour (from one hour-striking to the next).

string—**strung** (dialectal or solecistic, **strang**)—**strung** (except as in next entry).

stringed, not *strung*, is the participial adjective to be used
(*a*) of musical instruments ('wind and stringed orchestras'); hence it = 'produced by strings or stringed instruments' (stringed music);
(*b*) in heraldry;
(*c*) and of a running-track divided into 'lanes'.

strive—**strove**—**striven** (solecistic: **strove**).

student. See PUPIL.

studio and **study.** A *study* is a room in which a student or a scholar studies or works, or a room in which a writer writes, whereas a *studio* is the work-room of a painter or a sculptor—or of a photographer; hence, in cinematography, a room in which cinema-plays are staged; in wireless, a room in which items to be broadcasted are produced; and a room in which gramophone records are made.

stupid person. See at MORON.—By the way, the noun *stupid* (for a *stupid person*) is a colloquialism, as *silly* is for a *silly person*.

STYLE.

Le style, c'est l'homme même.
Buffon.

An aesthetic discussion of style would be out of place in this book. Moreover, many of the practical questions of style are dealt with elsewhere: especially, on the positive side, at SUITABILITY and, on the negative side, at WOOLLINESS. Particular aspects are treated here; for instance, the use of the SUBJUNCTIVE

FALSE AGREEMENT, ARCHAISMS, AM-
BIGUITY, COLLOQUIALISMS and DIALECT
and SLANG, CLICHÉ, CONFUSED PAR-
TICIPLES and FUSED PARTICIPLES, ELE-
GANCIES, GRAMMAR AND LOGIC, JARGON,
LITERARISMS, METAPHOR, NEGATION,
OBSCURITY, ORDER, PRECIOUSNESS,
PUNCTUATION, RHETORIC, SIMPLICITY,
SOUND AND SENSE, STANDARD ENGLISH
AND AMERICAN, SIMILES (battered),
SYNONYMS, TAUTOLOGY, TENSE-
SEQUENCE.

But it may be well to recall to the
aspirant writer's as to the student's and
even the critic's mind, the too often
forgotten fact that style is not something
that one assumes on special occasions
(like dress clothes), but that which one
is when one writes; so far from being
compelled to seek it, one cannot avoid it.

In writing, hence in style, the primary consideration is comprehensibility
—therefore clarity; one's first duty is
to make oneself understood.

The second is to be adequate to one's
theme: the style should be thoroughly
suitable to the subject.

The third, which is partly implied in
the second, is to write well: forcibly when
force is required; beautifully when love-
liness is to be described or conveyed;
concisely when concision is necessary or,
at the least, advisable.

(When, in 1938, Mr G. M. Young
wrote in *The Observer*, 'Good writing is
the most efficient mode of communicating in words made visible', he gave 'too
bare a definition of literary style in
general' as Mr Frank Whitaker remarked
in *The J.I.J.*, January, 1939.)

'Without distinction of speech', says
Frank Binder*, 'there is never much
distinction of idea, and therefore it need
hardly be said that in no age have men
so striven [as in the 20th Century] to be
different and yet so frantically failed to
be anything but the same. That the
style is the man, we know, but this is
one of those unfortunate truths which
have the licence of all lips and the hospitality of few hearts, and whilst everyone
is sighing for personality in others, he
shuns the labour of attaining it for himself. He is pleased with such facility as
he has, the facility that comes not of
power but of habit, the averaging habit
of familiar fluency and of the practised

* In his remarkable (and remarkably unknown)
Dialectic, 1932, pp. 21–22.

drumming of ordinary ideas. And the
thinner the fluid the faster the flow.'

Here is a very brief list of *some* of the
more important books on style.

Walter Pater: *Appreciations* (with an
    essay on style), 1889.
John Addington Symonds: 'Notes on
    Style' in *Essays, Speculative and
    Suggestive*, 1890.
Herbert Spencer: *The Philosophy of
    Style*, edited by Fred Newton Scott,
    1895.
Remy de Gourmont: *Le Problème
    littéraire*, 1902.
Robert Louis Stevenson: *Essays on
    the Art of Writing*, 1905.
Sir A. Quiller-Couch: *On the Art of
    Writing*, 1916.
Fred Newton Scott: *Contributions to
    Rhetorical Theory*, 1918 and after.
J. Middleton Murry: *The Problem of
    Style*, 1922.
Vernon Lee: *The Handling of Words*,
    1923.
Joseph Warren Beach: *The Outlook for
    American Prose*, 1926.
Herbert Read: *English Prose Style*,
    1928.
John Brophy: *English Prose*, 1932.
F. Duchiez & P. C. Jagot: *L'Education
    du style*, 1934.
Bonamy Dobrée: *Modern Prose Style*,
    1934.
S. P. B. Mais: *The Fun of Writing**,
    1937.

Of this list, it can at least be said that
every one of these works will be found
to contain matter invaluable to the
student of style, to the writer, to the
critic, no matter how experienced or
inexperienced, how conceited or how
humble, he may be.

For those who wish to know something of the history of English Prose,
without having to wade through ponderous tomes, an excellent book is George
Philip Krapp's *The Rise of English
Literary Prose*, 1915.

(For the practical side, see COMPOSI-
TION.)

subconscious. See 'UNCONSCIOUS and
SUBCONSCIOUS'.

subject (n.). In 'Roberts shared in all
the contraband—many and various in
subject—that Smith managed to get
hold of' (George Ingram, *Stir*, 1933),
subject is misused for *kind, sort*.—See
also TOPIC.

* A book for young people.

subject (v.) is occasionally used catachrestically for *subordinate*, as in '[Newspaper] editors must subject their personal interests to the interests of the community', examination essay script, June, 1939.

subject to and **addicted to.** Subject to = liable to (a disease); liable to the recurrence (or merely the incidence) of an action, a process, a state or condition; exposed to, open to, liable to suffer from something damaging, harmful, disadvantageous, e.g., peril, violent treatment, bad weather, etc.: as in 'subject to social disadvantages', 'subject to insolence', 'subject to earthquakes', 'subject to epileptic fits', 'subject to exception', 'subject to personal examination'. The noun is *subject*, as in 'The poor fellow is an epileptic subject'. But *addicted to* is 'given to a harmful practice or an evil habit' (*addicted to drugs, addicted to alcohol*); the noun is *addict*, as in 'He is a drug addict'.

SUBJUNCTIVE. The whole vexed question of the subjunctive mood has been admirably posited and explained by Dr C. T. Onions in *An Advanced English Syntax*. That most lucid and, in the best sense, methodical grammarian gives the history of the subjunctive—a subject that would be extraneous here. But on his exposition of the nature and the uses of the subjunctive, rests the whole of the following article.

'The Subjunctive is a Mood of *Will*; in its simplest uses it expresses *desire*, and all its uses can be traced to this primary meaning.'

In modern English, especially from the middle of the 17th Century, the subjunctive is much less used than formerly—much less, too, than in many of the other European languages. In short, the English subjunctive is, and has long been, in a state of decay*: partly because the English people has become increasingly careless of distinctions of thought; partly because, in subordinate clauses, *may, might, shall, should* have been increasingly substituted for the true or simple subjunctive. For

* In *We Who Speak English* Prof. C. A. Lloyd discusses 'the living subjunctive' and the contemporary use of the present subjunctive in substantive clauses after *beg, command, arrange, ask, warn, insist, suggest*, etc. This usage is not noticed by Jespersen or Fowler, and it seems to be an American phenomenon, though, as Professor Lloyd reports, Fowler himself uses it in the article on *foam, froth* (*Modern English Usage*, p. 184): 'One demands of foam that it *be* white'.

example, *lest he die* has, for the most part, been supplanted by *lest he may die* or *lest he should die*. Actually, these auxiliary words (*may, should*, etc.) are Subjunctive in origin.

But, although it is freely admitted that the use of the subjunctive has been restricted and even, in its survivals, modified, it is foolish 'to say (as is sometimes said) that the Subjunctive, except in the case of *be* and *were*, is an extinct Mood. . . . A careful examination of both the [spoken] and the literary language shows that the Subjunctive is really a living Mood, and that it can never become extinct without an entire reconstruction of certain classes of sentences, e.g., the Conditional sentences [of Group ii]. In these sentences we have the Past Subjunctive referring not to Past time but to Present or to Future time, which a Past Indicative could not do', as in '*Were* my brave son at home, he *would* not suffer this' (Present) and in 'If he *were* to do this (or, If he *did* this), he *would* sin' (Future).

Except in certain forms (e.g., *be* and *were*), the subjunctive has been *disguised*: that which, by itself, appears to be an Indicative, may, from the context, emerge clearly as a subjunctive: to the test of form and inflexion must be added the test of *meaning*.

Here is a test of Mood:—In 'It is necessary that I remain here', *remain* is subjunctive because we can also say 'It is necessary that he *remain* here'. In 'I wish I had a violin', *had* is subjunctive because we could change the sentence to 'I wish it *were* possible for me to have a violin'.

The most important point, for practical purposes, is the uses of the subjunctive; the most difficult point is the correct tense to employ.

Let us examine the uses of the subjunctive, *A*, in simple sentences and the principal clauses of complex sentences, and *B*, in subordinate clauses.

A. In Simple Sentences and Principal Clauses the subjunctive is used to express 'a wish or request that something may be', as in 'God *bless* you' and 'So *be* it'; or a concession, as in '*Be* that as it may . . .' These subjunctival wishes and concessions are confined to the present tense.

Also 'in the principal clause of conditional sentences implying a negative', as in 'I *would* not say, even if I knew' and

'Had we done it, we *should* have let you know'. It is worth remembering that the only verbs so used are *could*, *would*, *should*, *might* and *must*, although in poetry and poetic prose two others are permitted—*were* (= would be) and *had* (= would have), as in 'If thou hadst been here, my brother *had* not died' (the Bible).

So, too, where the *if*-clause has been omitted, as in 'I *should* like to go' (i.e., if I could), 'How *would* you express it?' (i.e., if you were asked), and 'Anyone *might* see that he is not well' (i.e., if he looked).

B. In Subordinate Clauses the uses of the subjunctive are more numerous— as might be expected.

i. In conditional sentences of Group II; the tense is either the past or the pluperfect. See CONDITIONAL SENTENCES.

ii. In clauses introduced by *if* or *though* subordinated to *as* or *then* representing a comparative clause, as in 'I feel as if I *were* going to fall'. See COMPARATIVE CLAUSES.

iii. In conditional sentences of Group III, 'where the Subjunctive implies *reserve*, or is *restrictive*', as in 'If it *be* so. . . .' See CONDITIONAL CLAUSES.

iv. In noun clauses depending on a verb of *will* or *request*. This is usual in statutes and notices. 'It is requested that letters to the Editor *be* written on one side of the paper only'; 'The regulation is that no candidate *take* a book into the examination room.' Also 'It was requested . . . *should be* written . . .'; 'The regulation was that . . . should take . . .', though even here the present subjunctive is more common, this present-for-past-subjunctive being a hall-mark of officialese.

In noun clauses dependent on *it is right* (or *not right*), *it is wrong, it is necessary, it is not possible,* and *is it possible?* as in 'It is right (or, not right; or, is it right?) that you *be* dismissed', 'It is necessary that he *go*'. Note, however, that the simple subjunctive is less usual than a subjunctive-equivalent, as in 'It is right (etc.) that he *should be* dismissed' and 'Is it necessary that he *should go?*' After *is it possible?* and *it is impossible* the subjunctive-equivalent, as in 'Is it possible that he *should be* such a fool?', is almost obligatory, for 'Is it possible that he *be* such a fool?' is intolerably archaic and 'It is impossible that he *be* such a fool' is almost intolerable.

Where, however, 'is it possible?' is merely exclamatory, the indicative is obligatory, as in 'Is it possible that he *has* left England?'

In noun clauses dependent on *wish* and the archaic *would*, to indicate the object of the wish, as in 'I wish I *were* there' or 'had been there' or 'could have been there'; and in '*Would* that he *had* lived', where *would = I would.*

In noun clauses dependent on a verb of emotion, 'where the speaker contemplates the *thought* of something happening rather than its actually happening'; not the simple subjunctive but the *should*-equivalent is used here. 'I grieved that you *should* be so angry'; 'It cannot be wondered at that he *should* have been so anxious'; 'That he has acted thus is a misfortune, but that he *should* have acted thus is not surprising'.

v. In temporal clauses (clauses of time) of a certain type, i.e., when the action of the Temporal Clause is prospective; or, in other words, when the temporal clause refers to the future, whether from a present or from a past viewpoint. The simple subjunctive is now confined to poetry and poetic or, at the least, lofty prose, as in 'This night, before the cock *crow*, thou shalt deny me thrice' and 'The sun a backward course shall take ere aught thy manly courage *shake*'. But the *shall* and *should* equivalents,—in which, by the way, it is *shall* or *should* in all persons and both numbers,—are common in ordinary good prose as well as in lofty prose, as in 'When his eyesight *shall fail*, he will apply for a pension' and 'He decided to wait until the car *should pass* him'; here too, however, the indicative is fast becoming more usual, as in 'He decided to wait until the car passed him'. Perhaps I should have written 'apparent indicative', for is not *passed* a virtual subjunctive in this sentence, whereas it is indubitably indicative in 'He decided to wait—until the car passed him. The car's passing made him immediately change his mind, and he walked hurriedly on.' It is obvious that the discarding of the subjunctive in such temporal clauses as these would lead to ambiguity.

In vi-ix, which follow this interpolated paragraph, the subjunctive is archaic except in poetry and in poetic and other lofty prose. A good case for its retention could be argued in every instance; after all, there is no good reason why the

English language should be reduced to the level of the gangster and the professional thief, the half-wit and the nit-wit; they get quite enough of their own way as it is!

vi. In final clauses (clauses of purpose) introduced by *lest*:

Lord God of Hosts, be with us yet,
Lest we *forget*, lest we *forget* (Kipling);

the *forget* would still have been *forget*, i.e., a subjunctive, had that sinewy Imperialist been prophetically speaking of (say) the Fuehrer:

Lord God of Hosts, be with him yet,
Lest he *forget*, lest he *forget*.

vii. In concession clauses:

'Though he *do* his best, his best is bad';
'Try as he *might*, he failed'.

viii. In general relative clauses. especially in the past

(Calm, but not overcast, he stood
Resigned to the decree, whatever it *were*,
Byron),

where it would now be avoided even in poetry; Bacon's 'However it *be* between nations, certainly it is so between man and man' is archaic, though not ludicrously so, but if we change his sentence, to 'However it *may be* . . ., certainly . . .' we get an effect of good prose, not necessarily poetic nor even literary; the substitution of the subjunctive-equivalent for the simple subjunctive has made all the difference, as indeed it would in a general relative clause in the past tense: change Byron's two verses to prose and you get 'He stood calm, but not overcast: resigned to the verdict, whatever it *might be*', which is ordinary good prose— certainly not poetic nor (except in sentiment) lofty.

ix. In dependent questions:
'All men mused [= wondered] whether he *were* Christ' (The Bible); 'Even those who had often seen him were at first in doubt whether he *were* the brilliant and graceful Monmouth' (Macaulay).

(Note how feeble would have been the catachrestic *if* in these two examples; see 'IF for WHETHER'.)

TENSES OF THE SUBJUNCTIVE. In the subjunctive, as in the indicative, the tenses are those which conform to that general and invaluable principle which is known as the sequence of tenses. See TENSE-SEQUENCE.

'I have told you that you *may* know';
'The headmaster said that we *might* have a holiday';
'He took care that his form master *should* not see him';
'If you *did* it [either now or in the future], you *would* repent it' (either now or in the future);
'She looked as though she *were* fainting'.

There are, of the subjunctive, at least two forms that seem to be rather too 'refayned' for my simple taste: *I could wish* for *I wish*, as in 'I could wish that he had written a better book'; and *it were to be wished* for *it is to be wished*, as in 'It were to be wished that princes would lay aside their ambitious projects'. In this matter, it is to be remembered that the objection is being made to positive, unconditional statements, which require nothing more subtle than an indicative. Used correctly, *I could wish* refers to a wishing in past time, *could* being the past of *can*; correctly used, *it were to be wished* can occur only in subordinate clauses—e.g., 'He gently inquired whether it were to be wished that the wretched men should suffer so undignified a death', and even that is a trifle clumsy for 'whether it were desirable'.

Two errors of the same kind are made in the following sentence from John G. Brandon's *The Mail-Van Mystery*, ca. 1937:—'The thing that struck "The Wallflower" most, was the air of furtivity [—see FURTIVITY—] with which the newcomer glanced here, there and everywhere, as though he might be fearing [i.e., as though he feared] that some entirely unwelcome person might pounce [?would pounce] out upon him from any corner at any moment.'

sublimate is occasionally misused for '*to subordinate*', as, e.g., in J. D. Griffith Davies, *Revolt and Reaction*, 1939.

sublime, sublimated; subliminal. Of these three terms, the first is the only one now in general as distinguished from psychological use. *Sublime* = 'elevated, lofty, exalted', literally and figuratively; hence, 'supreme', 'perfect'; in literature and aesthetics, it = 'apt or designed to inspire awe, deep reverence, lofty emotion, by beauty or grandeur'. *Sublimated* in the sense 'lofty, sublime', is obsolescent: better discard it! In chemistry, it = 'produced by the process of sublimation'; in psychology, it = (of a primitive impulse) 'modified and adapted, especially to the needs of civilization', as in *sublimated sex, sublimated savagery. Subliminal* is also a psychological term; it = 'below the threshold of sensation or consciousness, pertaining to the subliminal self', as in *subliminal consciousness.*—The corresponding nouns are *sublimity* or *the sublime; sublimation; a* or *the subliminal.*

Note that in *sublime* and *sublimated,* the etymology is *sub,* 'up to', and *limen,* 'the *head*-piece or lintel'; but in *subliminal, sub* = 'below' and *limen* = 'footpiece or threshold'.

submit for *subject* is not wrong, but it is so obsolescent as to be virtually obsolete, as one realizes on encountering such a sentence as this:—'He submitted the carpet . . . to the same microscopic scrutiny', Inez Irwin, *The Poison Cross Mystery,* 1936.

submittance is obsolete for *submission.*

subnormal. See ABNORMAL.

subscription. See SUPERSCRIPTION.

subsequent. See CONSEQUENT.

subsist. See EXIST.

substantial and **substantive.** Apart from technical senses, these terms are synonymous except in the following senses of *substantial:*—real or true in the main ('On the whole, substantial justice had been done'); of real worth, repute, reliability ('The substantial intellect of the country'); (of persons) wealthy, weighty, influential ('A substantial Scottish grazier'); (of structures) made of solid material, of good workmanship ('a substantial house'); (of food) very nutritious, (of a meal) solid. And except in these senses of *substantive:*—(Of persons, nations, groups or associations of persons) independent ('substantive inventors'); not transitory ('Let us call the resting-places the "substantive parts", and the places of flight the "transitive parts", of the stream of thought', Wm. James). The chief senses in which *substantial* and *substantive* are synonymous are:—Material or essential; not imaginary, not illusory; i.e., real; having a firm basis, solidly established; of considerable amount or quantity, valuable or effective because of large numbers. (*The O.E.D.*)

substitute, misused. 'He must substitute sugar by saccharin' should be 'He must substitute saccharin for sugar'.

substract is a surprisingly common error for *subtract. Subtract* and *detract* are occasionally confused. Both mean to deduct, but *detract* is applied only to virtue, reputation, status (see DETRACT . . .); *subtract* is rare in a figurative sense, George Eliot's 'The transient pink flush . . . subtracted nothing from her majesty' now seeming slightly obsolescent; indeed, *subtract* is, in current usage, confined—or virtually confined—to mathematics.

subtile is archaic for *subtle* in every sense except the now (in the main) medical one: (of feeling or sense) 'acute, keen', as in Longfellow's 'A secret Subtile sense crept in of pain'; in Dorland's *Medical Dictionary* (7th ed., 1913) it is defined as 'keen and acute, as, a subtile pain'.

succeed and **follow** are not synonymous; the latter having usually 'a literal and physical sense' and being applicable 'to many persons or things at the same time' ('A thousand sheep followed the bellwether'); *succeed* 'usually means to come next after and take the place of. It implies only two individuals' or two groups or bodies viewed as units, as in 'Haig succeeded French', 'Winter succeeds autumn', 'A National government succeeds a Labour one', 'An eldest son succeeds his father'.

successively and **successfully** are sometimes confused. The latter = 'with success', the former = 'in succession', 'consecutively'.

succubus and **incubus.** A *succubus* is a female demon supposed to have sexual intercourse with men in their sleep; hence, a demon or evil spirit or, metaphorically, a whore; *succuba,* a variant, is rare. Etymologically, 'a person lying *under* another'.—An *incubus* is a male demon that seeks sexual intercourse with women in their sleep; hence, a nightmare; hence, a person or thing that oppresses one as does a nightmare. Etymologically, 'a person lying *on* another'.

such for *any* or *any such* or *this* or *that* (or *these* or *those*). 'For the sake of verisimilitude the scenes of this story have been laid in real places. All the characters introduced, however, are wholly imaginary, and if the name of any living person has been used, this has been done inadvertently and no reference to such person is intended', Author's note to *The Loss of the Jane Vosper,* 1936,

F. W. Crofts; 'Of the Roman's earthworks, if such were made, no traces remain', Francis Brett Young, *This Little World*, 1934.

such for *of them.* This odd misusage occurs in Carolyn Wells's *The Clue of the Eyelash*, 1933:— '"Will you suggest some names as possibilities?"—"No, there are too many such."'

such for *similar* should be used with caution.

such for *so* (pronoun). *The New Statesman and Nation* of Feb. 5, 1938, quotes from a Selfridge advertisement written by a Public School member of the staff; it ends thus: 'With this being such he will always be an ever-awake and useful member of society.'

such for *some one.* '"Can you suggest . . . anyone who wished his death?"— "Mercy, no!"—"Yet there must have been such. Somebody killed him"', Carolyn Wells, *The Clue of the Eyelash*, 1933.

such for *such a thing.* 'No unauthorised objects or materials could . . . have been included. He wished to take strong exception to the suggestion that such might have occurred', F. W. Crofts, *The Loss of the Jane Vosper*, 1936.

such for *such part* or *such portion.* 'His eyes ran quickly over such of the interior . . . as they could reach', John G. Brandon, *The Mail-Van Mystery*, ca. 1937.

such for *such things.* '. . . Cabalistic figures . . . French kept all such, though he doubted they would be helpful', Nigel Morland, *The Conquest of Crime*, 1937; also, 'They [500 petrol-electric sets] were to be larger than such are usually made', *ibid.*; Mr Arthur Bryant, *The Illustrated London News*, March 5, 1938, 'We had seen enough of the folly of complete strangers maiming and slaughtering each other under conditions of extreme discomfort and degradation for the sake of national honour and glory. Like Old Caspar, we had come to recognise from bitter experience, that no good ever came of such.' Mr Bryant so often uses 'such' in this manner that he would no doubt defend it; but brevity is its only merit. [['He was the father of *such* as dwell in tents' (Gen. iv. 20), cited by *Webster's.*]]

such (or **such a**) for *very* should not be overdone; 'Such charming people!', 'Such a bright boy'. Not a colloquialism, but familiar English.

such, none. See NONE SUCH.

such a (or **an**) + adjective + noun for *so* + adjective + *a(n)* + noun or for noun + *so* (or *thus*) + adjective, is to be avoided. In the sentence:

'The critics attacked McCabe, the author, for having invented such an unbelievable character [the detective, Smith], instead of attacking Smith, the [actual] man, for being what he was': write, 'for having invented so unbelievable a character' or, better here, 'a character so [or, thus] unbelievable', for any of these three changes (especially the third) would dispel the ambiguity; 'such an' leads some readers to suppose that the sentence will continue in some such way as this—'[The critics attacked McCabe . . . for having invented such an unbelievable character] as he, the author, makes him out to be'.

such a much. 'That is why . . . Rugby is such a much better game than Association' (Wodehouse, *A Prefect's Uncle*, 1903) is ugly and incorrect; for it should be 'Rugby is so much better a game . . .'; 'She was going to copy her stepfather, who was such a much smarter proposition than her own father' (Ernest Raymond, *The Marsh*, 1937), where 'So very much smarter a proposition' would be preferable.

such another, a transposition of the correct *another such,* Edwin Pugh, *A Street in Suburbia*, 1895. '"Ah, that was a funeral!" "I'm sure Marsh Street ain't likely to see sech another for many a, etc."'

such as for *as, for example* or *for instance.* 'When the resistance to the complex is weakened, such as in sleep, the complexes may reappear', Isador Coriat, *The Hysteria of Lady Macbeth*, 1912. 'The same language may predominate over a very large area, such as the English language predominates in England.'

such as for *what* or *so much as.* 'Then he mooched to another window and surveyed such as was to be seen of the rear of the place from that point', John G. Brandon, *The Pawnshop Murder*, 1936.

such . . . that for *such . . . as.* 'He was even allowed to dust such objects of the precious collection that were not kept under glass', Wilfranc Hubbard, *Orvieto Dust*, 1925.—Cf. the next entry.

such . . . which (or **who**) is incorrect for *such as.* 'Such trifling variations which make [Portuguese] be a mere dialect of

[Spanish]', for '*such . . . as*' (Letter in *The Observer*, Aug. 29, 1937); '[She had] a real compassion for such cases of hardship which were clamped [? clumped] down under her eyes', Ethel Lina White, *The Wheel Spins*, 1936; 'Such of my acquaintances who care to submit themselves . . .' (John Rhode, *The Hanging Woman*, 1931); 'The very fact that they lived in an enclosed intimacy not to be found in an ordinary road is sufficient to exaggerate such small annoyances and dissensions which from time to time arise', John Bude, *The Cheltenham Square Murder*, 1937. The mistake probably arises from a confusion with *those . . . which*.—Cf. SUCH . . . THAT.

suffer with for *suffer from* a disease or disability is bad English; the 'suffering' is caused by and derived *from* the disease.

sufferance; suffering. The former is archaic as a synonym of the latter noun. Except for a legal sense, *sufferance* is extant only as = 'acquiescence, consent, sanction, permission, toleration', and mostly in the phrase *on sufferance*; 'He is on sufferance', 'liberty on sufferance', 'a Cabinet on sufferance', 'to woo on sufferance'. (*The O.E.D.*)

sufficient and **enough.** The main difference between them as adjectives is that, before a noun, *enough* takes no article; *sufficient* does take one, or omits it, according to the context ('a sufficient income' but 'sufficient money'). The adverbs are *sufficiently* and *enough*. The nouns are *sufficient* and *enough*; despite Weseen, *sufficient*, which never takes an article, is faultless English in 'Sufficient has been done for pride; now let us think of comfort'; 'We saw sufficient to account for the noise'. *Sufficience* is archaic; *sufficiency*, which generally takes an article (except in the sense 'adequate provision of food; adequate bodily comfort'), has three main senses:—A competence ('to retire on a sufficiency'), though this is obsolescent; adequacy ('to report on the sufficiency of an examination candidate's work'); enough ('a sufficiency of wood for fuel'). (*The O.E.D.*)

suffragette; suffragist. The former is—or rather, was—a rabid female supporter of female suffrage (votes for women); the latter is merely any supporter (not necessarily violent nor militant) of female suffrage.

suggested plan; suggestive plan. The former has been suggested by someone; the latter is 'a stimulating plan'. *Suggestive*, in this sense, is applied also to remedies.

SUITABILITY AND ADEQUACY. *Ingenium par materiae* (ability equal to one's theme).

To write satisfactorily on the subject of suitability and adequacy would be to write a treatise on style: and obviously that cannot be done here.

Broadly, adequacy* is such treatment of a theme as is felt to be not only and merely in keeping (i.e., suitable) but also worthy of it—fully worthy of it, no matter how profound, moving, subtle or lovely the theme. To be adequate, therefore, is more than to be suitable; one may have—or adopt—a style suitable to a subject and yet one may prove to be unequal to that subject. One's conception may be excellent, but one's execution may be faulty: the road to style is paved with good intentions. Style must be clear, effective, aesthetically and emotionally adequate.

Here, more than anywhere else, practice is better than precept. And so I give a certain number of passages in which the manner suits the matter and the style is adequate to the theme. But first, one brief example on the negative side:— 'And the place thereof was unknown. . . . It is an astonishing commentary on the way man had been born and then cut down so much like grass that weeds had been his only memorial—till some explorer came along' (Violet O. Cressy-Marcks, *Up the Amazon and over the Andes*, 1932). The inadequacy of 'came along' is pathetic; such triviality of language is one of the commonest sorts of inadequacy.

(The ensuing examples of adequacy on the positive side have been taken from Sir Arthur Quiller-Couch's *The Oxford Book of English Prose*, 1925).

'Let us now praise famous men, and our fathers that begat us. The Lord hath wrought great glory by them, through his great power from the beginning. Such as did bear rule in their kingdoms, men renowned for their power, giving counsel by their understanding, and declaring prophecies: leaders of the people by their counsels, and by their knowledge of learning meet for the people, wise and

---

* I use the word, not as = bare adequacy (cf. the common phrase, 'barely adequate'), but as = complete adequacy.

eloquent in their instructions. Such as found out musical tunes, and recited verses in writing. Rich men furnished with ability, living peaceably in their habitations. All these were honoured in their generations, and were the glory of their times. There be of them, that have left a name behind them, that their praises might be reported. And some there be, which have no memorial, who are perished as though they had never been, and are become as though they had never been born, and their children after them. But these were merciful men, whose righteousness hath not been forgotten. With their seed shall remain a good inheritance, and their children are within the covenant. Their seed stands fast, and their children for their sakes. Their seed shall remain for ever, and their glory shall not be blotted out. Their bodies are buried in peace, but their name liveth for evermore.'

Ecclesiasticus (Authorized Version, 1611).

That is a rhetorical style, drawing much of its beauty and effectiveness from rhythm, sense-repetition, word-repetition. Contrast it with:—

'All the powder of the *Revenge* to the last barrel was now spent, all her pikes broken, forty of her best men slain, and the most part of the rest hurt. In the beginning of the fight she had but one hundred free from sickness, and four-score and ten sick, laid in hold upon the ballast. A small troop to man such a ship, and a weak garrison to resist so mighty an army. By those hundred all was sustained, the volleys, boardings, and enterings of fifteen ships of war, besides those which beat her at large. On the contrary, the Spanish were always supplied with soldiers brought from every squadron: all manner of arms and powder at will. Unto ours there remained no comfort at all, no hope, no supply either of ships, men or weapons; the masts all beaten overboard, all her tackle cut asunder, her upper work altogether razed, and in effect evened she was with the water, but the very foundation or bottom of a ship, nothing being left overhead either for flight or defence. Sir Richard, finding himself in this distress, and unable any longer to make resistance . . .; and that himself and the ship must needs be possessed by the enemy . . .: commanded the master gunner, whom he knew to be a most resolute man, to split and sink

the ship; that thereby nothing might remain of glory or victory to the Spaniards . . .'

Sir Walter Raleigh, The Last Fight of the Revenge, from a Report, published in 1591.

With this plain prose compare the following passage on death from Raleigh's *A History of the World*, 1614, concerning 'the kings and princes of the world':—

'They neglect the advice of God while they enjoy life, or hope it; but they follow the counsel of Death upon his first approach. It is he that puts into man all the wisdom of the world without speaking a word. . . . He tells the proud and insolent that they are but abjects, and humbles them at the instant; makes them cry, complain, and repent, yea, even to hate their forepassed happiness. He takes the account of the rich and proves him a beggar. . . . He holds a glass before the eyes of the most beautiful, and makes them see therein their deformity and rottenness; and they acknowledge it.—O eloquent, just and mighty Death! whom none could advise, thou hast persuaded; what none hath dared thou hast done; and whom all the world hath flattered, thou only hast cast out of the world and despised: thou hast drawn together all the far-stretched greatness, all the pride, cruelty, and ambition of man, and covered it all over with these two narrow words, *Hic jacet*.'

With Raleigh on death, compare Bacon:—

'Men fear Death as children fear to go in the dark; and as that natural fear in children is increased with tales, so is the other. Certainly, the contemplation of Death, as the wages of sin and passage to another world, is holy and religious; but the fear of it, as a tribute due unto Nature, is weak. . . . It is as natural to die as to be born; and to a little infant perhaps the one is as painful as the other. He that dies in an earnest pursuit is like one that is wounded in hot blood, who, for the time, scarce feels the hurt; and therefore a mind fixed and bent upon somewhat that is good doth avert the dolours of Death: but, above all, believe it, the sweetest canticle is *Nunc dimittis*, when a man hath obtained worthy ends and expectations. Death hath this also, that it openeth the gate to good fame, and extinguisheth envy.'

More effective is this 'Of Studies',

wherein Bacon speaks with weighty and indisputable authority:—

'Read not to contradict and confute, nor to believe and take for granted, nor to find talk and discourse, but to weigh and consider. Some books are to be tasted, others to be swallowed, and some few to be chewed and digested; that is, some books are to be read only in parts; others to be read but not curiously, and some few to be read wholly, and with diligence and attention. Some books also may be read by deputy, and extracts made of them by others; but that would be only in the less important arguments and the meaner sort of books; else distilled books are like common distilled waters, flashy things. Reading maketh a full man; conference a ready man; and writing an exact man; and therefore, if a man write little he had need have a great memory; if he confer little he had need have a present wit; and if he read little he had need have much cunning, to seem to know what he doth not. Histories make men wise; Poets, witty; the Mathematics, subtle; Natural Philosophy, deep; Moral, grave; Logic and Rhetoric, able to contend: *Abeunt studia in mores.*'

I have spoken elsewhere of poetic prose, but there I gave no example. Here is one, chosen from Thomas Traherne's *Centuries of Meditations* rather than from Sir Thomas Browne's more famous works.

'You never enjoy the world aright, till the Sea itself floweth in your veins, till you are clothed with the heavens, and crowned with the stars: and perceive yourself to be the sole heir of the whole world, and more than so, because men are in it who are every one sole heirs as well as you. Till you can sing and rejoice and delight in God, as misers do in gold, and Kings in sceptres you never enjoy the world.—Till your spirit filleth the whole world, and the stars are your jewels; till you are as familiar with the ways of God in all Ages as with your walk and table: till you are intimately acquainted with that shady nothing out of which the world was made: till you love men so as to desire their happiness, with a thirst equal to the zeal of your own: till you delight in God for being good to all: you never enjoy the world.'

In *Some Fruits of Solitude* (1693), William Penn, on 'The Comfort of Friends', wrote thus:—'They that love

beyond the world cannot be separated by it.

Death cannot kill what never dies.

Nor can spirits ever be divided, that love and live in the same divine principle, the root and record of their friendship.

If absence be not death, neither is theirs.

Death is but crossing the world, as friends do the seas; they live in one another still.

For they must needs be present, that love and live in that which is omnipresent.

In this divine glass they see face to face; and their converse is free, as well as pure.

This is the comfort of friends, that though they may be said to die, yet their friendship and society are, in the best sense, ever preserved, because immortal.'

Let us turn to Addison and take a short passage from his paper on the Royal Exchange (*The Spectator*, 1711–14):—

'Our ships are laden with the harvest of every climate: our tables are stored with spices, and oils, and wines: our rooms are filled with pyramids of China, and adorned with the workmanship of Japan: our morning's draught comes to us from the remotest corners of the earth: we repair our bodies by the drugs of America, and repose ourselves under Indian canopies. . . . For these reasons there are not more useful members in a commonwealth than merchants. They knit mankind together in a mutual intercourse of good offices, distribute the gifts of Nature, find work for the poor, add wealth to the rich, and magnificence to the great. Our English merchant converts the tin of his own country into gold, and exchanges his wool for rubies. The Mahometans are clothed in our British manufacture, and the inhabitants of the frozen zone warmed with the fleeces of our sheep.'

From Chesterfield:

'London, January the 8th, O.S. 1750.
Dear Boy,

I have seldom or never written to you upon the subject of Religion and Morality: your own reason, I am persuaded, has given you true notions of both; they speak best for themselves; but if they wanted assistance, you have Mr Harte at hand, both for precept and example: to your own reason, therefore, and to Mr Harte shall I refer you, for the reality of both; and confine myself, in this letter, to the decency, the utility, and the necessity, of scrupulously preserving the appearances of both. When I say the appearances of Religion, I do not mean that you should talk or act like a missionary, or an enthusiast, nor that you should take up a controversial cudgel, against whoever attacks the sect you are of; this would be both useless, and unbecoming your age: but I mean that you should by no means seem to approve, encourage, or applaud, those libertine notions, which strike at religions equally, and which are the poor threadbare topics of half-wits, and minute philosophers. Even those who are silly enough to laugh at their jokes, are still wise enough to distrust and detest their characters: for, putting moral virtues at the highest, and religion at the lowest, Religion must still be allowed to be a collateral security, at least, to Virtue; and every prudent man will sooner trust to two securities than to one.'

From Gibbon comes this:

'It is a very honourable circumstance for the morals of the primitive Christians, that even their faults, or rather errors, were derived from an excess of virtue. The bishops and doctors of the church, whose evidence attests, and whose authority might influence, the professions, the principles, and even the practice, of their contemporaries, had studied the scriptures with less skill than devotion, and they often received, in the most literal sense, those rigid precepts of Christ and the apostles to which the prudence of succeeding commentators has applied a looser and more figurative mode of interpretation. Ambitious to exalt the perfection of the gospel above the wisdom of philosophy, the zealous fathers have carried the duties of self-mortification, of purity, and of patience, to a height which it is scarcely possible to attain, and much less to preserve, in our present state of weakness and corruption. A doctrine so extraordinary and so sublime must inevitably command the veneration of the people; but it was ill calculated to obtain the suffrage of those worldly philosophers who, in the conduct of this transitory life, consult only the feelings of nature and the interest of society. ... It was not in *this* world that the primitive Christians were desirous of making themselves either agreeable or useful' (*The Decline and Fall of the Roman Empire*, 1776–1781).

With that, the grand style, contrast this simpler style of Robert Southey in *The Life of Nelson*, 1813:—'Early on the following morning he reached Portsmouth; and having dispatched his business on shore, endeavoured to elude the populace by taking a by-way to the beach; but a crowd collected in his train, pressing forward, to obtain a sight of his face: many were in tears, and many knelt down before him, and blessed him as he passed. England has had many heroes; but never one who so entirely possessed the love of his fellow-countrymen as Nelson. All men knew that his heart was as humane as it was fearless; that there was not in his nature the slightest alloy of selfishness or cupidity; but that, with perfect and entire devotion, he served his country with all his heart, and with all his soul, and with all his strength; and, therefore, they loved him as truly as and as fervently as he loved England. They pressed upon the parapet, to gaze after him when his barge pushed off, and he was returning their cheers by waving his hat. The sentinels, who endeavoured to prevent them from trespassing upon his ground, were wedged among the crowd; and an officer, who, not very prudently upon such an occasion, ordered them to drive the people down with their bayonets, was compelled speedily to retreat; for the people would not be debarred from gazing, till the last moment, upon the hero—the darling hero of England.'

And now, one of the great masters of prose—Walter Savage Landor ('Aesop and Rhodope', *Imaginary Conversations*, 1824–29):—

Rhodope. . . . Let me pause and consider a little, if you please. I begin to suspect that, as gods formerly did, you have been turning men into beasts, and beasts into men. But, Aesop, you should never say the thing that is untrue.

Aesop. We say and do and look no other all our lives.

Rhodope. Do we never know better?

Aesop. Yes; when we cease to please, and to wish it; when death is settling the features, and the cerements are ready to render them unchangeable.

Rhodope. Alas! Alas!

Aesop. Breathe, Rhodope! breathe again those painless sighs: they belong to thy vernal season. May thy summer of life be calm, thy autumn calmer, and thy winter never come!

Rhodope. I must die then earlier.

Aesop. Laodameia died; Helen died; Leda, the beloved of Jupiter, went before. It is better to repose in the earth betimes than to sit up late; better, than to cling pertinaciously to what we feel crumbling under us, and to protract an inevitable fall. We may enjoy the present, while we are insensible to infirmity and decay; but the present, like a note in music, is nothing but as it appertains to what is past and what is to come. There are no fields of amaranth on this side of the grave; there are no voices, O Rhodope, that are not soon mute, however tuneful; there is no name, with whatever emphasis of passionate love repeated, of which the echo is not faint at last.

Rhodope. O Aesop! Let me rest my head on yours: it throbs and pains me.

Aesop. What are these ideas to thee?

Rhodope. Sad, sorrowful.

Aesop. Harrows that break the soil, preparing it for wisdom. Many flowers must perish ere a grain of corn be ripened. And now remove thy head: the cheek is cool enough after its little shower of tears.

Again in contrast, an extract from that admirably lucid and effective writer, Macaulay (from his essay on Clive):—
'The river was passed; and, at the close of a toilsome day's march, the army, long after sunset, took up its quarters in a grove of mango-trees near Plassey, within a mile of the enemy. Clive was unable to sleep; he heard, through the whole night, the sound of drums and cymbals from the vast camp of the Nabob. It is not strange that even his stout heart should now and then have sunk, when he reflected against what odds, and for what a prize, he was in a few hours to contend. . . . The day broke, the day which was to decide the fate of India. At sunrise the army of the Nabob, pouring through many openings from the camp, began to move towards the grove where the English lay. Forty thousand infantry, armed with firelocks, pikes, swords, bows and arrows, covered the plain. They were accompanied by fifty pieces of ordnance. . . . The cavalry were fifteen thousand. . . . The force which [Clive] had to oppose to this great multitude consisted of only three thousand men. But of these nearly a thousand were English; and all were led by English officers, and trained in the English discipline. . . . The battle commenced with a cannonade in which the artillery of the Nabob did scarcely any execution, while the few field-pieces of the English produced great effect. Several of the most distinguished officers in Surajah Dowlah's service fell. Disorder began to spread through his ranks. His own terror increased every moment. . . . He ordered his army to fall back, and this order decided his fate. Clive snatched the moment, and ordered his troops to advance. The confused and dispirited multitude gave way before the onset of disciplined valour. No mob attacked by regular soldiers was ever more completely routed. The little band of Frenchmen, who alone ventured to confront the English, were swept down the stream of fugitives. In an hour the forces of Surajah Dowlah were dispersed, never to reassemble.'

Before passing to an example of contemporary prose, I should like to give John Henry Newman's definition of a gentleman (*The Idea of a University*, 1852):—'It is almost a definition of a gentleman to say he is one who never inflicts pain. . . . He is mainly occupied in merely removing the obstacles which hinder the free and unembarrassed action of those about him; and he concurs with their movements rather than takes the initiative himself. . . . The true gentleman . . ., carefully avoids what may cause a jar or a jolt in the minds of those with whom he is cast;—all clashing of opinion or collision of feeling, all restraint, or suspicion, or gloom, or resentment. . . . He has his eyes on all his company; he is tender towards the bashful, gentle towards the distant, and merciful towards the absurd; he can recollect to whom he is speaking; he guards against unseasonable allusions, or topics which may irritate; he is seldom prominent in conversation and never wearisome. He makes light of favours while he does them, and seems to be receiving when he is conferring. He never speaks of himself except when compelled, never defends himself by a mere retort. He has no ears for slander or gossip, is scrupulous in imputing motives to those who interfere with him, and interprets everything for the best. He is never mean or little in his disputes. . . . He has too much good

sense to be affronted at insults, he is too
well employed to remember injuries, and
too indolent to bear malice. He is patient,
forbearing, and resigned, on philosophical
principles; he submits to pain, because
it is inevitable, to bereavement, because
it is irreparable, and to death, because
it is his destiny. If he engages in controversy of any kind, his disciplined intellect
preserves him from the blundering discourtesy of better, though less educated
minds. . . . He may be right or wrong in
his opinion, but he is too clear-headed
to be unjust; he is as simple as he is
forcible, and as brief as he is decisive.'

In conclusion, I give two extracts from
Frank Binder, *Dialectic*, 1932.

'To know how a man is educated we
require to know how he is examined—
and no more. For it is by examinations,
which are the rudder of study, that all
effort to pass them is determined. Let
these be altered a little and education
alters in turn, adapting itself to demands
which are thought to prove not only the
students but the studies themselves.
Indeed if the dream of Swift were true,
and the highest of honours awaited him
who could stunt on the tight rope, climb
the greasy pole, and chase the slippy
pig with success, our schools would be
closed on the instant, and with every
scholar a trickster and with every university an open vanity fair we should
all go pantomiming on the boards of
education. For the weathercock goes as
the wind blows, and students who are
weathercocks in practice to much east
wind of theory turn here and there and
everywhere as their tails and not their
heads direct them. And rightly, as students enter a higher school not to prepare
for an examination but to pass it. . . .
All reforms of education therefore must
begin where education concludes—in the
examination room. It is here that attempts have been made, and whereas
once we used to test for attainments we
now test for potentiality. Years ago we
were content to ask what a student had
done, and nowadays what he is likely to
do at some future date. Nowadays we
seek to measure not his knowledge but
his ability, not his actual possessions but
his coming power to obtain, not the
capital he may chance to have but the
income he is certain to command. And
then above the evidence of intelligence
some proof of personality is required—
a quality best appraised in the absence

of it—and students who have impressed
us by the keenness of their wits are
asked to impress us still further with
their independence of character and
originality of thought. . . . To test for
intelligence is perhaps easy when the
examiner has some himself, but personality, which is too often beyond the
experience of both parties, is likely to
prove its obscurity. For even in broad
daylight it is a grand dabble in the dark
to seek what we have never seen or to
know what we cannot recognize, and as
yet we have no scales for character. We
may affect the things of the spirit but
we still traffic in things of earth, and
candidates in examinations like the sup-
plicants in the temple must always compact with herdsmen and changers of
money. But before we test for personality we must first learn what it is and
not expect teachers to impart what they
do not possess themselves. In this respect
we are worse than we were. With cram
as our aim and with a stick as our means
we at least gave what we had, but in
this palaver of personality and distillation of ideals we are fast coming to a
state when the deaf dun the ears of the
deafened and where the blunders of a
one-eyed guide are the only wisdom of
his blind disciples.'

And in a loftier mode:

'Life has its alternative, the ironic one
of being angled at the bank or netted at
the weir. We may escape the philosophy
of form with its interplay of fate and
personality, of the world without and the
will within, and flee to the philosophy
of measures with its processes of evidence, fact and proof. Here at least we
are safe, or think we are, from the flats
and shifting sands of superstition, and
may sail on our daylight ways, scientific,
assured, and open-eyed, along the charted
paths of the seas. The port is fixed, the
track defined, the times determined,
yet even these our modern ways, like
all the wisdom of the world, are writ
on water. For just as religion is fallibly
poised on the floating mote of faith, so
science is no less parlously embarked
on the dubious bubble of a measure, on
something that has no absolute standing,
a something that, in want of niches in
space and time, cannot be measured
itself nor be assessed in ultimate units.
Indeed, were the world in flux, pulsating
to all sizes yet keeping the ratio in every
part, or speeding and staying the flight

of time with proportional pace and delay in ourselves, we should not know it, and still should deem our measures, which swelled and lapsed in concert, as fixed and final for the universe itself. And to this myth of immutable measures comes the illusion of simultaneity, since for all experiments, comparisons, and proofs, whereby a synchronism is assumed, there is a passage through space and time, the measure being brought to the object measured, the proof following by an interval of thought. Yet we are asked to believe that in transpositions from spot to spot, and in references from a moment to a moment succeeding, there is a constancy in the object thought of, that it keeps a congruence in all its motions, and ceteris paribus always is what it was before. But how are we to prove this when no two points in space or time may be placed together for comparison? and since by the latest theory matter determines the space whereby it is contained, so with equal truth may space determine matter. With an equal truth we may assume that change is a change in the medium which surrounds us, that we fall like a fluid into the mould of the world, into the play of its principles and lineament of its seasons, and take on by adaptation the idiosyncrasies of time. And though we scout the thought as dialectic, how without a synchronism is this to be proved?'

A careful study of the preceding examples will show what is meant by *adequacy*, for these examples are in styles that are more than merely *suitable*.

summary; précis; abstract; abridgement. See PRÉCIS, par. 2; for *summary*, see also at OUTLINE.

Sunday. See SABBATH.

sung. See SING.

sunk. See SINK.

sunlight and **sunlit**, adjectives. Cf. the entry at 'STARLIGHT and STARLIT'.

sunlight; sunshine. The former is simply the light of the sun, whereas the latter is the shining of the sun, but also 'direct sunlight uninterrupted by cloud' (*The O.E.D.*). 'Sunshine peeping through some little window' (Dickens), 'There was a long fight between mist and sunshine' (Tyndall), 'He sat in the sunshine'; 'When we pass from open sunlight to a moderately illuminated room' (Tyndall), 'Sunlight is dispensed mainly from carbon'. (*The O.E.D.*)

sunshade. See PARASOL.

super, in the sense of 'very good', 'very modern', 'very efficient (or, effectual)', is becoming so general that even tolerably educated persons are beginning to forget that it is slang.

supercede is now incorrect for *supersede*.

superincumbent. See RECUMBENT.

SUPERIORITY. Do not be superior. No man (or woman) is entitled to take a lofty tone unless he first makes it clear that he in no way considers himself to be better than his fellows and that he offers moral advice or takes a high tone in the spirit of 'Do as I say, not as I do'. If we are better than our neighbour, the superiority may be accidental: we have been luckier, not felt the workings of some dark god.

superior than. See INFERIOR THAN.

superlative. See COMPARATIVES, FALSE.

SUPERLATIVE DEGREE. The general rule is that the superlative is to be used only when there are three or more persons or things, as in 'He is the better runner of the two', 'She was the prettiest of them all'. But the pair *the former . . . the latter* ('There were two battles, A. and B.: the former was at X., the latter at Y.') is beginning to break down—to yield to *the first . . . the second*: a tendency to be resisted. Where only one of the two is mentioned, *former* and *latter* retain their potency: we say 'There were two battles . . .; only the former was important' or '. . . only the latter can be described here'.

superscription; subscription; signature. The first does not, the second does (though now rarely), mean a .signature. *Subscription* is an act, or the action, of affixing a signature or of signing one's name; *superscription*, a heading, a piece of writing at the beginning of a document, is archaic in the sense 'address (on an envelope containing a letter)'. (*The O.E.D.*) The same remarks apply to the verbs *subscribe, superscribe*.

supersede (to take the place of, to serve instead of) is occasionally misused for *surpass*. Weseen quotes a newspaper headline, 'Women supersede men in scholarship'.

supine. See PRONE.

supple is sometimes ignorantly confused with *subtle*. (As, e.g., in Desmond Coke, *The School across the Road*, 1910.) If, greatly daring, one speaks of 'a supple mind', one means, not a subtle but an agile mind or a mind readily adapting itself.

supplement and **complement.** Whereas a *complement* is an integral second part or portion, a *supplement* is additional to something that was at first thought to be complete. To *supplement* is to augment or to add something to (to supplement something *with* something else; to supplement an income); to *complement* is to complete by adding an essential part, to supply what is (conspicuously) wanting. The adjectives are *complementary* and *supplementary*.

suppose. See SUSPECT.

supposedly, misused for *presumably*. 'X. is supposedly the guilty party' should be 'X. is presumably the guilty party'.

supposititious and **suppositious; suppositional.** For 'supposed; based on—or at the least, involving—supposition', *suppositional* is now more common than *suppositious*. *Supposititious* (child) is one 'set up to displace the real heir or successor'; do not use it for an illegitimate child; as applied to a writing, or a passage or even a word therein, it = spurious, counterfeit, false, forged. (*The O.E.D.*)

supra-normal. See ABNORMAL.

surmise. See SUSPECT.

surprise. See ASTONISH.

surprised; astonished, amazed, astounded. As adjectives expressive of the feeling of wonder, these four are in ascending order of intensity. Originally, *surprised* meant 'suddenly attacked, assailed without warning', then 'taken unawares', hence 'detected, suddenly discovered', of which the first survives only as a military term.

suspect; surmise; suppose. 'To *suspect*' can be employed as a synonym of 'to *surmise*', but it is better to reserve it for pejorative uses. To *surmise* is 'to form a notion that the thing in question may be so, on slight grounds or without proof; to infer conjecturally', as in 'Whatever you may surmise about a future life, it is your duty to do your best by this one', 'Is it too much to surmise that he made a fortune during those prosperous years'. To *suppose* is 'to posit, for argument's sake'; especially, 'to incline to think; to entertain as an idea', as in 'Do you suppose that she wished to remain unmarried?', 'The roads were no better than the old Squire had supposed' (Violet Jacob). 'He may

be supposed to have thought more than he said' (Jowett). (*The O.E.D.*)

SUSPENDED PARTICIPLE, THE. Also known as the Misrelated Participle, this is treated fully at CONFUSED PARTICIPLES. Here are two examples from reputable authors:—

'Informing a maidservant that I desired private speech with her master, she explained that Mr Mannering was still at breakfast', Eden Phillpotts, *Physician Heal Thyself*, 1935.

(Apropos of the author's deliberately rambling commencement . . .) 'Having said so much, you will expect me, I suppose, to begin talking about . . .', Hilaire Belloc, *The Hedge and the Horse*, 1936.

suspicion for 'to *suspect*' is to be avoided; it is dialectal.

sustain, in *to sustain a fracture*, is a bad, unnecessary word, and appears to be suggested only by an excessive sense of the gravity of the occasion or by a wish to imitate (bad) medical jargon. 'He fell from a ladder and broke his leg' says all that can be conveyed by 'sustained a fracture', and the use of *sustain* in this sense robs it of its true and fuller meaning of *to support, to uphold*. *Sustain injuries* is, by many newspaper editors in their style sheets, condemned as incorrect for *receive injuries*. Both are correct; *receive injuries* is rather less formal, less pretentious.

swang. See SWING.

sweat (n. and v.) is a better word than *perspiration* and *perspire*. Obviously, if you do not wish to offend a lady, you do not tell her that she seems to be sweating freely, but the euphemistic, mealymouthed days of 'Horses sweat, men perspire, and women glow' have gone; certainly, men at least prefer to sweat. *Sweat—sweated* (less usual, *sweat*)—*sweated* (rarely *sweat*); participial adjective, *sweated*.

swell—swelled—swollen, less commonly **swelled.** The usual participial adjective is *swollen*.

swim—swam—swum. ⟦*Webster's* lists the preterite *swum* as dialectic and archaic.⟧

swing—swung (rarely **swang**)—**swung.**

Sybil (or **s-**), **sybyllic** (=the next), **sybylline, sybyllism, sybyllist, sybyllistic:** inferior to the spellings in *si-* (*Sibyl*, etc.): for the old French is *Sibile* or *Sibylle*; Med. Latin, *Sibilla* or *Sibylla* or *Sibulla*; from Greek *Sibulla*.

syllabification (formation of syllables; a dividing into syllables) is preferable to *syllabication*.

synonym of and **synonym for; synonymous with** (not *of*, nor *for*). The correct use of these collocations may be exemplified in three short sentences, thus:—'A synonym of *quick* is *fast*'; 'Synonyms for *rapid* are hard to find'; '*Mankind* is not synonymous with generic *man*'.

SYNONYMS: AND THE HERESY OF VARIETY, especially in dialogue. See also AFFECTATION, last paragraph.

There are extremely few exact synonyms; but here, as usually, *The O.E.D.* puts the case so well that to attempt to vie with its definition is not merely ineptitude and self-conceit but a mild form (perhaps not so very mild, after all) of madness.

'Strictly, a word having the same sense as another (in the same language); but more usually, either or any of two or more words having the same general sense, but each of them possessing meanings which are not shared by the other or others, or having different shades of meaning or implications appropriate to different contexts: e.g., *serpent, snake; ship, vessel; compassion, fellow-feeling, sympathy; enormous, excessive, immense; glad, happy, joyful, joyous; to kill, slay, slaughter; to grieve, mourn, lament, sorrow.*'

The educated person does not need to be told that, in the desire for variety, to consult a dictionary of synonyms (so called) and take haphazard an apparent synonym is to expose himself to the risk —almost to the certainty—of making himself ridiculous.

But, as a stylistic device (for the sake of emphasis or euphony), synonyms—in the looser, more general sense—are frequently used. Some are embedded in idiom (*to have and to hold*) and cliché (*free, gratis and for nothing*); others are stylistic (*the inaudible and noiseless foot of time; a figure, type, symbol, or prefiguration*); and both sorts are tautological.

Sound advice is this:—If you are in doubt as to which of two (or more) synonyms to use, consult a good dictionary that gives abundant examples.

And this:—If you wish to use two or more synonyms as a stylistic device,

make sure that the choice fulfils your purpose.

It follows, therefore, that it is dangerous to achieve variety at the expense of the meaning. Do not hesitate to use the same word (or even the same phrase) twice in the one sentence, if the repetition removes an ambiguity. Such variety as is seen in 'The person did not know what to do. This individual asked someone what he should do. Indeed, the man asked several bystanders what they advised' is absurd. If you must have variety (an important but not the primary consideration), obtain it by using a wide vocabulary and a pliant, versatile style, for these will yield a profound, a structural variety as opposed to a superficial, merely verbal variety. We have passed beyond Stevenson's insistence on variety at almost any price.

systematic and **systemic.** The general word is *systematic* (much less commonly, *systematical*); *systemic* being confined to physiology, in which it now = 'belonging to, supplying, or affecting the system or body as a whole', as in 'The . . . systemic sensation of hunger', 'systemic effects', 'The Systemic Circulation . . . divisible into Arterial and Venous'; and to pathology in which it now = 'belonging to or affecting the nervous system or special parts of it', as in 'systemic sclerosis of a small but defined tract of the spinal cord'. (*The O.E.D.*)

systematize and **systemize.** The latter is an inferior form. The sense is 'to arrange according to a system, especially according to the best system known or available; to reduce to system'. (*The O.E.D.*)

T

TAGS. See CLICHÉ.

take leave, as in 'I take leave to argue the point', is inferior to *take the liberty* (of arguing the point).

take off. Witness at Highgate Police Court: 'After inquiring where the bus was bound for, I asked the conductor what time it was to take off' (*The Evening News*, Feb. 9, 1938). *The O.E.D. Supplement* admits the expression as applied in aeronautics: *to start from rest, attain flying speed and become air-borne.* True, an aeroplane is often called a 'bus', so why may not a 'bus' be said to 'take off'? But 'take off' has several meanings already, both active and passive, and, unless we are to allow anything to mean anything and everything to mean everything else, some precision is advisable.

take on, in the sense of *get excited, be 'upset'* about anything, is a harmless vulgarism belonging to the kitchen: 'There's Missis walking about the drawing-room, taking on awful', Whyte-Melville, 1868.

talent. See GENIUS.

talisman has plural *talismans*—not *talismen*, as, e.g., in Robert Eton, *Not in Our Stars*, 1937. Do not confuse *talisman*, amulet or charm, with *talesman* (pl. *talesmen*), one of the *tales* or persons added to a jury to make up a deficiency in number.

talk is infelicitous—too informal—for *speech* or *address* or *lecture* in such examples as the following:—'A talk on disarmament', 'Twelve talks on French Romantic Literature'.

talkies, the. See MOTION PICTURES.

tall is opposed to *short*, as *high* is to *low*. 'A tall hill, a tall house' should ordinarily be 'a high hill', 'a high house'; *tall timber* (woods with high trees) is an Americanism. But ships and trees are *tall* when they are high in proportion to their width, especially in such collocations as *a tall chimney* or *house*, *a tall mast* or *ship*, *a tall column* or *spire*. Also, *tall* is applied to things that are 'of more than average length measured from bottom to top'—e.g., *a tall hat*, *a tall copy* of a book. *A tall story* is a colloquialism, originally American.

tankard for *mug*. 'What pseudo-ancient inns miscall a tankard—but Mr Freeman and I still call a mug—of draught ale', R. H. Mottram, in Preface to H. W. Freeman's *Joseph and His Brethren*, 1928. Here Mr Mottram is not sufficiently explicit. A *tankard* is a drinking-mug made of metal, usually pewter, in olden times of wood (like a barrel), but an earthenware *mug* would certainly be 'miscalled' a tankard; he seems to imply that in certain inns they do not know the difference. Perhaps they don't.

tantamount. See PARAMOUNT.

tasteful(ly); **tasty, tastily.** The former pair (= in good taste) is admissible, the latter (in the same sense) is as vulgar as *natty* (e.g., *natty gent's suiting*) or *nattily*. Even *tasty* in the literal sense, 'pleasant to the taste', should be avoided in good writing: it is a colloquialism.

TAUTOLOGY. * Cf. and contrast VERBOSITY, *q.v.*

Tautology, as defined by *The O.E.D.*, is 'a repetition of the same statement' or 'the repetition (especially in the immediate context) of the same word or phrase, or the same idea or statement in other words: usually as a fault of style'.

Before passing to a set of examples, I give a short list of very common tautological expressions, based on Maurice H. Weseen's *Words Confused and Misused* (English edition), 1932.

adequate enough
and etc.
appear on the scene
ascend up
at about (e.g., 3 *p. m.*)
attach together
attached hereto
both alike (see 'BOTH for *alike*')
burn down and *burn up* (see separate entry)
classified into classes
colloborate together
connect together and *connect up*
consolidate together
continue on and *continue yet*
co-operate together
couple together
debate about (v.)
descend down
discuss about
divide off and *divide up*
drink up and *drink down*
early beginnings
eat up
enclosed herewith (or *herein*)
end up
endorse . . . .: see *indorse* . . .
equally as
file away (commercially)
final completion
final upshot
finish up (v.t. and v.i.)
first begin
flood over
follow after
forbear from
forbid from
free, gratis, and for nothing
fresh beginner
from hence
from thence
from whence
funeral obsequies

* For a brief account, suitable to beginners, see Harold Herd, *Watch Your English*, 1925, at the chapter entitled 'Wasted Words'.

gather together
have got (for 'have' or 'possess': see
  separate entry)
good benefit
hoist up
hurry up
important essentials
in between
indorse on the back
inside of
join together
joint co-operation
just exactly
just merely
just recently
lend out
link together
little birdling
meet together
mention about
merge together
mingle together
mix together
more inferior
more superior
more preferable
mutual co-operation
necessary requisite
new beginner
new creation
new departure and *entirely new departure*
new innovation
not a one
(it) *now remains*
open up (v.t.)
original source
outside of
over again
over with (done, ended, finished)
pair of twins
past history
peculiar freak
penetrate into
plan on (v.)
polish up
practical practice
(one's) *presence on the scene*
proceed on(ward)
protrude out
raze to the ground
really realize
recall back
reduce down
relax back
remember of
renew again
repay back
repeat again
repeat the same (e.g., *story*)
(to) *rest up*

retire back
return back
revert back
revive again
rise up
seldom ever
(to) *separate apart*
settle up
shrink down and *shrink up*
sink down
steady on!
still continue
still more yet
still remain
study up
sufficient enough
swallow down
taste of (for *taste*, v.)
termed as
than what
this next week
twice over
two halves (except when from different
  wholes)
two twins (of one pair)
uncommonly strange
unite together
used to (do something) *before*
we all and *you all*
where at
where to
whether or not
widow woman
young infant

The recurrence of *about, again, back,*
and *together,* is significant.

Now, certain examples; unclassified,
it is true; but all of them illustrative of
common tautologies.

'That should leave me with twenty
houses left' (Frank Tilsley, *I'd Hate to
Be Dead*, 1938). Read, 'That would leave
me twenty houses' or 'I should still have
twenty houses'.

'Count A. was made the recipient of a
national presentation' (*The Times Literary Supplement*: cited by A. P. Herbert).
Read, 'A national presentation was made
to Count A.'

'She [a canteen assistant] set herself
a standard of endurance and privation
approximately as nearly as possible to
that which she understood prevailed on
the Western Front' (Ian Hay, *The
Willing Horse*, 1921). Read, '. . . approximately that which she understood . . .'.

'The first layer of cloth was plain.
The second had a lovely border on'

(Violet O. Cressy-Marcks, *Up the Amazon and over the Andes*, 1932). Omit 'on'.

'It sounded quite natural enough' (Henry Holt, *Wanted for Murder*, 1938). Omit either 'quite' or 'enough', according as the other is intended.

'Treadgold gave orders that Ragusi was to be watched carefully. . . . For some half an hour afterwards he sat at his desk with his head in his hands' (Anthony Weymouth, *Tempt Me Not*, 1937). 'Afterwards' is unnecessary; 'about' would be preferable to 'some'.

'He [a German] was a surprising contrast to some of the military police I had met in our own army, whose conduct was not always particularly edifying on all occasions' (Bernard Newman, *Spy*, 1935), where 'on all occasions' is redundant.

'. . . The pilot circling round up above' (*ibid.*). Omit 'round'.

'Occasionally she made a sale, but very seldom' (E. R. Punshon, *The Dusky Hour*), 1937 = 'Rarely, she made a sale'.

'We never made more than eight knots an hour' (W. H. G. Kingston, *Lusitanian Sketches*, 1845). 'An hour' is unnecessary, for a knot is a sea-mile per hour.

'Rupert Bond laughed at his friend. They were both men in their early sixties, and both had similar interests', G. Davison, *Murder in a Muffler*, 1937. Read 'They were in their early sixties, and they had similar interests'.

'"A canting hypocrite named Arpendrake," he began again, "has just absconded from England with the funds from an institution which really was supposed to be in the light of a great philanthropic affair"' (John G. Brandon, *The Mail-Van Mystery*, ca. 1937). Read, '. . . with the funds from a great, supposedly philanthropic institution'.

'It was a piece of ruled note-paper. . . . The quality was of a very cheap, coarse nature, such as comes in thick tablets which can be bought for a trifle at any stationer's' (S. S. Van Dine, *The Kidnap Murder Case* [English ed.], 1936). Read '. . . It was of a very cheap, coarse quality, such as comes . . .'.

'He idled along from one street to another. . . . But never once, so far as we could ascertain, did he appear to glance back' (Stephen Maddock, *Doorway to Danger*, 1938): 'appear to' is unnecessary, and 'never' is enough. (And 'ascertain' should be 'see').

'He could form no estimate at all of with how much favour he was regarded at the Admiralty' (C. S. Forester, *A Ship of the Line*, 1938). This sentence would be improved if 'of', which rings oddly, were omitted; after 'no', 'at all' is superfluous. Rewrite thus, 'He could not estimate with what favour he was regarded at the Admiralty'—or, better still, 'He could not estimate (*or* judge) how he stood with the Admiralty'. This example merits careful consideration, for it has been taken from one of the most economical (and best) of English post-1920 novelists.

'"How I came to find the suit-case was because . . ."' (E. R. Punshon, *op. cit.*). Read, 'I found the suit-case in this way'.

'Dwarfs in all ages have ever been objects of interest' (*Tom Thumb's Diary and Proverb Book*, 1893). Omit either 'ever' or preferably—it being a phrase as opposed to a word—'in all ages'.

'Dr T., whose knowledge of the lake and its neighbourhood can be second to that of none, pointed out to me . . .' (Joseph Ll. Thomas, *Oxford to Palestine*, 1890). The cliché, *second to none*, has been enlarged with an unnecessary 'that of'.

'Further whimsicalities consist in . . . demanding . . . that all the books he finds in any guest-room be forthwith removed as insults to his intelligence and that the hostess see to it at once that the complete works of Maxwell Bodenheim be substituted in their stead' (G. J. Nathan, *Intimate Notebooks of George Jean Nathan*, 1932), where 'in their stead' is unnecessary after 'substituted'.

In 1852, J. H. Brodribb (a boy of 14) wrote, 'I have not been to see the Crystal Palace at Sydenham. . . . The site of the old one looks quite desolate, as there is nothing left but dirt', and *The Times* (some time late in 1937, or in 1938) comments thus, 'The paragraph on the Crystal Palace, which seems so topical to the present time, is of course a reference to the rebuilding of Paxton's monument', where 'to the present time' is barely necessary and where 'of course' is certainly unnecessary.

teach. See at LEARN.

technic, technics; technique; technology. As an adjective, *technic* is obsolescent for *technical*. As a noun, *technic* is a collective term for 'technical methods and details', especially 'the formal or mechanical part and aspect of an art or science', as in 'In the technic of this art, perfection can be reached only by long training' (Lowell), but *technique* is now more general. *Technics* (as either a plural or a singular) may be used in the same sense: but here again, *technique* is more common. *Technics* in the sense 'the science or study of art or arts, especially of the mechanical or industrial arts' is inferior to the more usual *technology*. In addition to the sense noted above, *technique* means skill or ability in the formal, practical, mechanical details of one's art, i.e., mechanical skill in an art, especially in one of the fine arts, and above all 'in reference to painting or musical performance'. Likewise, *technology* has the further meaning, 'practical arts collectively' and 'technical terminology or nomenclature'. (*The O.E.D.*)

TECHNICALITIES. See JARGON.

teeming with is incorrect for *rich in*. 'Salamanca . . . a glorious old city, teeming with history', Bernard Newman, *Death Under Gibraltar*, 1938.

tele- means '(from) afar; distant'; it is also that form of *teleo* ('perfect, complete') which is employed before a vowel.

teleometer is incorrect for *telemeter* and the less general *telometer*.

tempestive and **tempestuous.** The latter means 'stormy'; the former, 'timely' or 'seasonable'. It is odd that any person knowing the word *tempestive* should not also know its meaning.

temporal and **temporary** are sometimes confused; the former is 'of or belonging to this life', as opposed to *spiritual*, 'belonging to the eternal'; the latter, 'not meant to last long', 'not permanent'.

temporize and **extemporize.** In good use, *temporize* is always intransitive; as = 'to improvise or extemporize', it is incorrect. To *temporize* is to adapt oneself, to conform to time and circumstance; *temporize with* is so to act or negotiate or parley as to gain time, also to negotiate with (a person); *temporize between* is to effect a compromise between (persons). To *extemporize* (v.i.) is 'to speak extempore; in music, to improvise'; v.t., it is to compose off-hand; to compose and utter off-hand; hence, to produce on the spur of the moment, to invent for the occasion'. (*The O.E.D.*)

tend and **trend.** In the sense, 'to have a general tendency, to have a disposition to', *trend* is obsolescent; *tend* is

the right word. *Trend*, however, is correct for 'to turn off in a specified direction; to tend to take a direction expressed by or implied in the context', and, of rivers, currents, coast-lines, mountain ranges, strata, territories or regions, 'to run, stretch, incline, bend (in some direction', as in 'The coast trends to the northward', 'In its course to the north, the Gulf Stream trends more and more to the eastward'. (*The O.E.D.*)

tend for for *tend to cause*. 'Dainty underwear was certainly intriguing, but tended for delay', Cecil Freeman Gregg, *Tragedy at Wembley*, 1936: correctly, tended to cause or create delay.

tend to has become incorrect for *attend to*, in, e.g., 'I must *tend to* my business'. *Tend* is now used mostly in *tending herds* or *flocks*.

tendencious is inferior to *tendentious*, which, by the way, means, not 'prejudiced' nor 'quarrelsome', but 'having, or composed or written with, a purposed tendency'.

tennis for *lawn tennis* is a shortening. *Tennis* properly so called is that royal game which arose in the Middle Ages and from which, in the 1870's, sprang the game of lawn tennis.

TENSE-SEQUENCE. In 'Devas had struck from an angle he had not considered, though it may well have been expected' (John G. Brandon, *The Dragnet*), *may* should be *might*.—'He never has and never will mortgage the national patrimony' (*The Daily Express*, Nov. 13, 1937) should read: 'He has never mortgaged the national patrimony, and never will (do so)'.—'The threat of danger gave me a fierce, triumphant determination that, come what may, one little estate would stand inviolate' (R. C. Sheriff, *The Hopkins Manuscript*, 1939) should read '. . . come what might'; and a careful writer would prefer *should* to *would*.

These examples will serve to indicate how necessary it is to ensure a right tense-sequence; to depart from that sequence is to produce always an effect of inelegance and often an actual ambiguity.

'The *Sequence of Tenses*', writes Dr Onions in *An Advanced English Syntax*, 'is the principle in accordance with which the Tense in a subordinate clause "follows" or is adjusted to that of the principal clause'; thus, in general, when the governing clause has a Present [e.g., 'he says'], a Present Perfect [as in 'he *has said*'], or a Future [as in 'he *will say*'], the subordinate clause has a Present (*Primary Sequence*); when the governing clause has a Past [whether progressive, as in 'he *was saying*', or preterite, as in 'he said'] or a Plu-perfect [the past perfect, as in 'he *had* said'], the subordinate clause has a Past (*Secondary Sequence*). The Sequence of Tenses applies chiefly to Final and Noun Clauses.

'I *tell*
have told } you that you *may* know.'
shall tell

[Here I should like to interpolate an interesting example of an error in the Historic Present (the present used, throughout a passage or a book, for the past tense): 'That night he's kind of brought up to the mark—prepared to smell a rat wherever he'll find a chance to smell one' (a detective novel, 1937): where 'prepared to smell a rat wherever he *finds* a chance' would be correct, *prepared to smell* being a virtual future.]

'I *told*
was telling } you that you *might* know.'
had told

'He *has* no idea what twice two *is*', but (subject to a modification hereinafter set forth) 'He *had* no idea what twice two *was*'.

'The master *says* we *may* have a holiday', but in the past it is 'The master *said* we *might* have a holiday', the master's actual words being, 'You *may* have a holiday'.

'I *took* care that he *should* not hear me.'
'If it is desired to mark something as true universally or at the time of speaking', the tense is not adjusted:

'He *had* no idea what twice two *is*.'
'Columbus proved that the world *is* round.'
'I *asked* the guard what time the train usually *starts*.'

There is no such implication of universality, no such emphasis on the time of speaking, in the following sentence (taken from Ronald Knox's *Double Cross Purposes*, 1937):

'And even if he does, I argued to myself, he would hesitate to complain of the loss, because it would involve him in some decidedly awkward explanations':

which should be written either 'And even if he *did*, . . . he would hesitate to complain . . . because it would involve him . . .' or 'And even if he does, . . . he *will hesitate* to complain . . . , because it *will involve* him in some decidedly awkward questions'.

The tense-sequence most difficult for most persons is that which is necessitated in a long passage to be cast into indirect speech: see REPORTED SPEECH. In the matter of reported speech, there is one point of particular interest: 'There is a tendency to break through the old sequence when a more accurate expression suggests itself. Thus instead of ["He *said* he *was going* to-morrow"] we may with greater accuracy say: "He *said* he *is* going to-morrow"' (Curme, *A Grammar of the English Language*, 1931). Dr Curme does not discuss the distinction between 'He said he *was* (or *is*) going to-morrow', where it is implied that, at the time of the reporting, he had not yet gone, and 'He said he *was* (not *is*) going on the morrow', where it is implied that, at the time of the reporting, he had already gone.

Not (or at least, not wholly) sequence but mood is involved in the correct use of the subjunctive, but there is, of course, a tense-sequence in the subjunctive: see particularly SUBJUNCTIVE, but also CONCESSIVE CLAUSES and CONDITIONAL CLAUSES and FINAL CLAUSES.

terminal and **terminus.** In Britain, they are distinct, but in the United States they tend to overlap.

terminate for *end, close, finish.* 'The proceedings terminated with a vote of thanks to the Chairman.'—It is always worth considering whether the dignity aimed at in such formal records as the Minutes of a Meeting is not better maintained by the true English word, as 'The proceedings (or the business) *ended*, etc'. And sometimes *expire* would be preferable, as in 'His subscription terminated last month and he has not renewed it': *terminated* = ended, for good and all.

TERMS OF ADDRESS. See TITLES.

testament, for *testimony*, is an occasional error caused by a misunderstanding of the two words; the former is a *will*, the latter 'an attestation in support of a fact or statement' (*The O.E.D.*).

testimonial on is incorrect for *testimonial to*, as in 'I dislike testimonials, but . . . here is a testimonial on mathematics', Stuart Chase, *The Tyranny of Words*, 1936.

testimony. See EVIDENCE.

tetralogy. See TRIUMVIRATE.

than, misused for *as*. 'More than twice as many gliding flights had been made than in the year before' (B. B. C., July 11, 1938).

than, misused for *other than*. 'He disliked the clash of personality, regarding any personality than his own as an intolerable intrusion', *London Symphony*, 1934.—*But* or *differing from* might also be substituted here for *than*.—Cf. 'He had scarcely won . . . the place . . . than his health was found shattered' (Froude, 1864), where 'when' should be substituted for 'than'. *Than* is never correct except with *other*, *else*, *otherwise*, or the comparative of an adjective or adverb.

than, misused for *than that*. 'We have borne so much for the peace we pray for, that I think that I would rather see all humanity lying dead like this German boy, than it should blunder blindly into a war more terrible than this has been', Warwick Deeping, *No Hero—This*, 1936. To omit the second 'that' would not be a grave error, but a *that* is necessary after the first 'than'.

than, misused for *to*. 'Modern dictionaries are pusillanimous works, preferring feebly to record what has been done than to say'—read, *to saying*—'what ought to be done', is an error committed by Mr A. P. Herbert himself in *What a Word!* (But that admirable book is not a grammar.)

than, misused for *when*. See BARELY THAN and HARDLY THAN.

than, different . . . 'Here was quite a different kettle of fish than the one they had served up in the past', Samuel Putnam, *Marguerite of Navarre*, 1936. The impeccably correct construction is *different . . . from*, although *different to* (cf. French *différent à*) is permissible (see, for evidence, *The O.E.D.*); if one says that 'one thing differs *from*' (never *to*) 'another', why does one not, with equal naturalness, say 'is different from'? [[*Different . . . than* seems to occur more and more frequently in the New York daily and weekly press. Evidently the comparative sense of the word rather than the fact of its positive form may govern the syntax. Whether this is regrettable is a question of taste.]]

than, else, is incorrect. See ELSE THAN.

than, inferior and **superior.** See INFERIOR THAN.

than me or **than I** may occur in a sentence such as 'You are a much greater loser than *me* or *I*' (here Swift wrote *I* and was, I think, incorrect). The arguments are (1) that *than* is here a preposition and governs an object; and (2) that *than* is a conjunction introducing a clause, only the subject of which is expressed, the remainder being an ellipsis. I much prefer the use of the objective case (in this example, *me*); and all authorities agree that *than whom* (not *than who*) is correct in 'He is a king than whom there has never been a greater'. [[American grammarians, even the liberals Krapp and Perrin, insist upon the second argument—which seems a pity, especially because school teachers have so much trouble trying to overcome the student's disinclination to use the nominative case in the final position.]]

than what. The writer of a letter in *John o'London's Weekly*, Dec. 17, 1937, discussing Mr Donald Wolfit's enterprise in producing Shakespeare in the provinces, says, 'His productions certainly do not belong to Mr Prentis's £5 class (than what is more wretched?), nor to his £25,000 class (than what is more vulgar?), but are adequate, etc.' There is no grammatical sense in 'than what'; the writer means 'than which, what is more wretched/vulgar?', though the juxtaposition of *which*, *what* is clumsy, and might be avoided by saying 'and what more wretched than that?' Often *than what* is merely tautological for *than*, as in 'It was easier than what he thought'.

thanks! is not incorrect; it is, however, informal. *Thank you!* is the safest form, *I thank you* being extremely stiff, slightly archaic, and perhaps affected, except when something follows, as in 'I thank you, sir, for your interest in my family'.

Thanksgiving Day is preferable to *Thankgiving day*; *Thankgiving* is not bad English, but it is too familiar for formal occasions. This annual American festival is held on the last Thursday of November.

that (conj.), misplaced. 'There is just a chance where there is any ornamentation that a stain might creep under it', for 'There is just a chance that, where . . ., a stain might . . .', Vernon Loder, *Choose Your Weapon*, 1937.

that (conj.), omitted. The omission

of the conjunctive *that* sometimes causes a momentary confusion. In Milton Propper's *The Great Insurance Murders* (an American 'thriller'), 1937, we find: 'There were no marks or scratches that indicated the lock had been forced' and 'Rankin ushered her to a chair and learned her name was Mrs Emily Reilly'. 'Indicated the lock' and 'learned her name' might possibly have been independent, self-contained statements: but with something of a jar, one finds that the sentences continue.—This defect is much commoner in American than in English writers.

that (conj.), redundant. This occurs in such a sentence as 'The sooner that this is altered, the better', where *that* is entirely uncalled for; and by unnecessary repetition, as in 'He said that, as the mistake had been made and was irreparable, that it was useless to discuss the subject again'.

that and which; that and who. See 'WHICH and THAT; WHO and THAT'.

that, misused for *it* and *this* (and *those* for *these*), is common in the Essex and Suffolk dialects, as illustrated in the village stories of S. L. Bensusan. But the misuse is also found in the speech of Irishmen and Scotchmen, both educated and uneducated; Dean Alford, (*The Queen's English*, 1870), 'A barrister tells me that the confusion is common in the Irish law courts: "Those arguments I now use," etc. Another Irish correspondent is often greeted with, "That's a cauld day, yer riv'rence". I have a Scottish friend, who always designates the book which he has in his hand as *that book*; the portfolio of drawings which he is turning over as *those drawings*.'

The Dean also quotes the ambiguous use of *that* in the Prayer-book version of Ps. xc.4, 'A thousand years in Thy sight are but as yesterday, seeing that is past as a watch in the night', where 'that' is a demonstrative pronoun referring to 'yesterday' and requires a special emphasis to remove the ambiguity. (The correct translation is that of the Bible: 'as yesterday when it is passed, and as a watch in the night'.)

that, misused for *so far as* or *for all that*. 'He found that it was unlocked; indeed, that he could see, [it] seemed to have no means of locking' (John G. Brandon, *The Pawnshop Murder*, 1936).

that, misused for *thus* or *to that degree* or, loosely, *so very*. 'Oh, it's not that urgent', said the doctor on the telephone,—and, in so doing, he used a colloquialism that is in England considered an illiteracy; his remark would have sounded better if he had said 'It is not urgent to that degree', or, less stiffly, 'It's not so urgent as all that'.

that, at. *At that* is a colloquialism, and therefore it should be eschewed in formal, official, and other serious writing. Its most frequent senses are 'moreover', 'even so', and 'in any case'. (English writers often use it without a due regard to its niceties. See my *A Dictionary of Slang*.)

that same day (month, etc.) is not so much incorrect as unnecessarily emphatic for *that day* or the stronger *the same day*; e.g., 'On that same night, he went to London'.

that . . . that is clumsy or, at best, cacophonous for *that . . . which* or *that . . . who(m)*, as in 'That man that you saw yesterday is a swindler' and 'That box that the porter took was valuable'.

the for *this* or *that*, especially preceding a relative clause beginning with *who* (or *which*), is not so much wrong as careless and inadequate, as in 'The man who says such things is obviously unfit to occupy so important a position', where *that man* would be an improvement; *'the* man *that'*, however, is both admissible and usual. *The* is insufficiently emphatic in 'It is not the man' for 'It is not *that* man' (but some other man).

the and The in titles. See TITLES OF BOOKS AND PERIODICALS.

the author is to be used for *I* (or *me*) on formal occasions only.

the said. Inadmissible except in legal documents. 'The said playboy was a millionaire's son' is absurd. (Harold Herd.)

the which is obsolete and now incorrect for *which*, as in 'The which barn is for sale'.

there, them, they for singular *he* or *she*, *his* or *her*. 'It was rather like a jig-saw puzzle to which everyone contributed their own little bit of knowledge', Agatha Christie, *The Murder of Roger Ackroyd*, 1926. An error commonly found in both speech and writing, and arising from our lack of a relative pronoun meaning *his-or-her*.

'I wore the fillet of the Golden Cobra, which could only be worn by one who had overthrown the cobra of the seventh ordeal, and in so doing had added strength to their will' (Joan Grant, *Winged Pharaoh*, 1938). In such cases the right pronoun is 'his', unless a woman is clearly referred to.

their's is incorrect for *theirs*—and astonishingly common.

them is constantly used for *they* (as *me* is for 'I'), after *as* and after *is*, *are*, *were*; 'It was not them' is incorrect, but, 'It was not them we wanted', quoted by *The O.E.D.*, has some justification since *them* represents *they whom*.

themselves. See MYSELF.

then for *and then* is too abrupt for use in formal or impressive writing or speaking, unless a semicolon separates the two statements. But 'He slept for a while, then took a walk' is good familiar English.

then for *than* is an error that is much more widespread than highbrows seem to think: it is not merely the illiterate who fall into it. The reason is not that, several centuries ago, *than* and *then* were spellings and pronunciations frequently interchanged, but that, where *than* bears no stress and is spoken very rapidly and lightly, it tends to approximate to *then* in sound.

thenceforth. See 'THEREAFTER and THENCEFORTH'; also 'HENCEFORTH and THENCEFORTH'.

theory is occasionally used loosely for *idea* (or *notion*), *view* or *opinion* or *expectation*, as in 'My theory of the war is that the mechanically stronger side will win', where *expectation* or *opinion* would be preferable.

there, introductory, is apt to cause the verb to fail to agree with the subject in number, as in: 'There was at this time, within the horrid confines of that prison, several fellows who were very much respected by the others' (Preface to Anon., *Thieving Detected*, 1777). 'There was my wife and daughter to consider, and my whole career', W. S. Masterman, *The Perjured Alibi*, 1935.— Cf. 'There still remains a few wilderness areas on the continent', Stuart Chase, *The Tyranny of Words*,1938. It is difficult to avoid the impression that these, and other, authors subconsciously regard *there* as a noun (therefore singular), hence as the subject of the sentence. Perhaps there is presumed an analogy in French *il y a*: cf. following entry.

there is many is incorrect for *there are many*, the subject being *many*; contrast French *il y a*. 'There is many a . . .' is correct.

thereabout and **thereabouts.** The *O.E.D.*'s examples (and precept) show that the latter is the more usual form.

thereafter and **thenceforth.** The former = 'after that date or time or place in a sequence'; *thenceforth* = 'continually or continuously from that time; indefinitely from that time; from that time onward'. *Both are formal words*, not to be used indiscriminately. 'Thenceforth her back upon the world she turned' (Morris); 'This prerogative . . . was thereafter . . . discontinued' (H. Brooke). (*The O.E.D.*)

thereby making. See THUS MAKING.

therefore and **therefor.** 'The reason *therefor* (i.e., *for it* or *for this*) is *therefore* (i.e., *for that reason*) unsatisfactory' exemplifies the difference between the two words. Many quite good writers do not even know of the existence of *therefor*.

theretofore. See ARCHAISMS.

these kind or **sort of.** George Parker, *A View of Society*, 1781, 'Queer as this *rig*' or underworld dodge 'may appear, there is a larger shop in London where these kind of rings are sold, for the purpose of going on the *Fawney*', i.e., practising the trick of ring-dropping. See also KIND OF, ALL.

they, their, misused for *he, his* as in 'Anyone thinks twice, when their life is at stake': read 'his life'.

think as a noun is colloquial when it is not dialectal, whether for 'an act of thinking; meditation' ('An occasional think does one much good') or for 'an opinion' ('My think is that he's a pretentious fool'). (*The O.E.D.*)

this much is incorrect for *thus much*, as in 'This much is evident to everybody'.

thoroughbred and **pure-bred.** *Thoroughbred* is preferred to *pure-bred* for horses, dogs, bulls, rams, but the terms are synonymous. *Thoroughbred* may be applied to persons, and it is also a noun.

thoroughfare, meaning nothing but *a way through* (for the public) makes ridiculous the following notice, to be seen in Guilford St., W.C.1, on Dec. 18, 1937, in letters 6 inches high:— 'Queen Sq. House. Private. No through Thoroughfare.'

those that; those who. The latter is preferable.

though and **although.** *Although* is the

more formal; *though* is the usual form in speech and in writings couched in familiar English. But even in dignified writing, *though* is sometimes preferred to *although*; this preference obtains only where *though* is more euphonious than *although*, or where the metre renders *although* awkward.

though (or **although**) is sometimes used to introduce a subordinate clause in a highly irrelevant way; Dean Alford quotes from a Law report in *The Times*, February, 1869, 'He, though a gentleman of property, was unhappily paralysed in his lower limbs', and adds, 'What a delightful idea this writer had of the usual exemption of the rich from the ills of humanity!'

though and **however.** The former should no more be used for the latter than the latter for the former! *Though*, like *although*, comes at the beginning of a clause—not, as in 'I did not like him though', at the end; nor in the middle, as in 'I must, though, discuss the doctrine of associations', I. A. Richards, *The Philosophy of Rhetoric*, 1936.

thrash; thresh. The latter is retained in reference to corn; in all other references, *thrash* is preferred, and is obligatory in figurative senses.

through for *by means of*, *by* is allowed by *The O.E.D.*; nevertheless, the best writers—at their best—avoid it. E.g., 'Through an addition to his salary, he was enabled to purchase the house he wanted' is unsatisfactory.

thus for *therefore* is an error. 'Freedom to individuals means that they can do as they like; thus we should see what they like to do before we congratulate them', examination script, March, 1938.

thus (or **thereby**) **making** is often very loosely used, as in 'The conversation and food were good, thus making the dinner very pleasant'. Turn thus: 'As the conversation and food were good, the dinner was very pleasant' or 'The conversation and food were good; consequently the dinner was very pleasant'.

tidy. Such expressions as *a tidy step*, *a tidy few*, are lower-class colloquialisms, though perhaps with no more intrinsic reason than are *pretty good*, *pretty well*, which are standard speech.

till is inferior to *until* in formal prose or verse.

time for *by the time that* is illiterate, though common in both Cockney and rural speech; 'It'll be openin'-time, time I get down there', said a West Country villager on a Sunday morning; and Clarence Rook in *The Hooligan Nights*, 1899, has 'An' time I'd got a 'ansom an' put 'im inside, the job was worked'.

timid and **timorous; apprehensive.** *Apprehensive* is 'anticipative of something unfavourable; in dread of possible harm or evil', as in *apprehensive of danger* and *apprehensive for one's life*. *Timid* is 'feeling or evincing want of courage or self-confidence; easily frightened or over-awed', as in 'Poor is the triumph o'er the timid hare' (Thomson of *The Seasons*). *Timorous* is synonymous with *timid*, but with emphasis on 'shrinking (with fear, or from doing something that requires courage)'; but one tends also to use *timid* of temporary fear, and *timorous* of a person habitually lacking in courage. (*Webster's*.)

titanic. See GIGANTIC.

title is occasionally misused for *term*. See the quotation at FORENSIC MEDICINE.—*Title* (v.) is inferior to *entitle* in reference to a book.

TITLES OF BOOKS AND PERIODICALS. This is a question often neglected; I have discussed it before at the entry *the* in my *A Dictionary of Slang and Unconventional English* (1937; 2nd ed., revised and enlarged, 1938).

Had I chosen the title *Dictionary of Slang*, it would have been incorrect to refer to it either as *A Dictionary of Slang* or as *The Dictionary of Slang* (very pretentious this!, for there are other dictionaries of slang); had the title been *The Dictionary of Slang*, it would have been incorrect (though excusable) to refer to it as either *A Dictionary of Slang* or *Dictionary of Slang*; but as it is *A Dictionary*, why impute telegraphese by calling it *Dictionary*, or conceit by changing it to *The Dictionary*? Hence I write 'My *A Dictionary of Slang*'. If the title had been *The Dictionary . . .*, I should have referred to the book as 'my *The Dictionary of Slang*'.

And let us italicize the initial 'A' and 'The' or, if the inverted-commas mode is preferred, have inverted commas before them. 'A correspondent on the *Times*' or 'A correspondent on the "*Times*"' is, to put it mildly, a feeble substitute for 'a correspondent on *The Times*' or 'a correspondent on "The Times"'. Luckily, few writers fall into the ineptitude of omitting the capital letter in the properly italicized or inverted-comma mode, as in 'a correspondent on *the Times*' or 'a correspondent on "the Times"'.

Admittedly, the general practice is against 'my *A Dictionary of Slang*': but should not exactitude overrule a practice that can hardly be classified as idiom? In familiar speech, 'my *Dictionary of Slang*' is permissible: it is a colloquialism. But I do recommend that scholars and reputable, serious writers (or humorous writers desirous of a reputation for good English as well as for acceptable humour) and cataloguers should retain the *A* and *The* that form the first word in a title. Is it not better to speak of J. M. Barrie's delightful book as 'Barrie's *A Window in Thrums*' than to refer to it as 'Barrie's *Window in Thrums*'? Is not the latter both ambiguous and impertinent—and just a little cheap? After all, we do not speak of 'Michael Sadleir's *Foolish Things*', but of 'Michael Sadleir's *These Foolish Things*'; we speak, not of 'Michael Arlen's *Charming People*' but of 'Michael Arlen's *These Charming People*'. *A* and *The* have their rights no less than *These* and *Those*.

In the titles of periodicals, however, there is an exception, consecrated by usage and justified by convenience: when the title becomes an adjective, *The* is omitted. 'A *Times* correspondent' is more convenient than, and is idiomatic for, 'A correspondent of (generally, on) *The Times*'. I do not suggest that we should either say or write 'a *The Times* correspondent' or 'the *The Times* correspondent'. But, as far as I can see, there is no excuse for 'The editor of the New York Times snorts balefully on discovering this sorry stratagem' (Stuart Chase, *The Tyranny of Words*, 1938): either 'The editor of *The New York Times*' or 'The editor of *The* (New York) *Times*' is required.

There is no doubt concerning what is to be done with 'a' and 'the' *within* titles. They are always written *a* and *the*, as in '*The Lady in the Case* is a good book'; but where a book-title or a periodical-title is involved, the above-enunciated rule is to be observed, as in '*The Ghost at The Times* is an excellent book' or, for the sake of clarity, '*The Ghost at "The Times"* is an excellent book'.

Not only *a* (or *an*) and *the* require small initial letters ('lower case', as printers say). So do prepositions—*at*

and *from* and *in* and *of* and the rest of them.

There is no generally accepted rule concerning the other parts of speech. My own practice is to 'capital' every word that is neither an article (*a* or *the*) nor a preposition. I see little reason for writing 'be', 'is', 'are', 'was', 'were', 'will', 'shall', 'would', 'should', 'must', 'ought' in lower case when all other verbs are written in upper case: why *The Lady is Dead* but *The Lady Fell Dead*? Why not *The Lady Is Dead*?

In this matter of titles, I advise authors not to submit to 'the rules of the house'—those rules which printers have formulated in self-protection—when they are *sure* of the rightness of their own titling. (Unless, that is, the printers' rules are those rules which have been proposed in this article.)

⟦For the citing of titles the most generally available American authority is probably the University of Chicago Press *A Manual of Style.*—As first words the articles *a* and *the* are part of the titles of books and one would expect them to be so treated—i.e., capitalized and set within the quotation marks or in the italic type that distinguishes the title. However, titles that make for awkwardness or misunderstanding—as in 'his *A Dictionary of Slang*' and 'Dr. Vizetelly's *The Standard Dictionary*'—will inevitably be shortened, now and again, when they interfere with the English language. The American rule for capitalization of titles is that the first word and all important words are capitalized. Often, however, on a title page the title is set entirely in caps as is the case with Mr. Partridge's dictionary. American librarians have solved the problem in this fashion: Partridge, Eric. Dictionary of slang . . ., a. They capitalize the first word and no other, and treat an initial article as an addendum. Editors, less bold than librarians, muddle along according to publishing house precedents or their own taste. In fact, no one style solves all problems. Authors can help by quoting rather than italicizing special words in titles.

There is no easy way of finding the correct and complete titles—if they exist—of the thousands of American newspapers. The two complete lists are arranged by states, towns, and short titles, as Texas, El Paso, Herald, Post, Times. (Moreover the banner heading on the front page of a paper may not be exactly the same as the masthead above the first column of editorials.) If an editor wishes uniform citations of newspapers, his most practicable course is to italicize or quote only the short title, as in the El Paso *Times*, the New York *Times*, the *Times*. The alternative is to give the masthead titles of newspapers he is acquainted with and to set the others by an arbitrary rule. The *Literary Digest* used to have three ways of citing newspapers (as I remember): one in the text, another in the credit line following a quotation, and still another in the credit line below a cartoon.

Magazines are fonder of their articles than are newspapers. *The Atlantic Monthly* and *The Saturday Review of Literature* wish *The* (and so, by the way, does The Johns Hopkins University— known locally as The Hopkins). It may be difficult to remember whether the *American Mercury* or *The American Mercury* would be most flattering. *The* or *A Life, Time, Fortune* would be ruinous. Should it be *The Reader's Digest*? Some quite literate editors follow what our friend Mr. Partridge would call the illiterate practice of ignoring the article in common citations of the periodical press. If we were presenting a Pulitzer prize or a sheepskin suitably inscribed, then we should ask the editor what he liked best. If the reader thinks the problem simple, let him consider —— magazine: it is **Harpers** MAGAZINE on the cover, *Harper's Magazine* on the contents page, **Harpers** *Magazine* on the masthead above the first article, and HARPER'S MONTHLY MAGAZINE on the running heads. What should an editor do? Call it *Harpers* for short and *Harpers Magazine* for long, and quote it often—that is good practice.⟧

TITLES OF PERSONS. This is a subject that belongs less properly to a book on English usage than to a book on etiquette. For the curious, however, I list here, three books:—

'Armiger': *Titles and Forms of Address*, 1936: comprehensive and dependable.

R. W. Chapman: *Names, Designations and Appellations*, 1936: Tract No. 47 of the S.P.E.

W. Whitten & F. Whitaker: *Good and Bad English*, 1938: a short, popular and useful account.

to, omitted. 'For years it was disputed as to whom the word referred', E. R. Suffling, *Epitaphia*, 1909. *Whom* is correct, but the *to* of *refer to* has been omitted owing to the influence of *as to*. The sentence should read 'For years it was disputed as to whom the word referred to' or, by substituting *about* for *as to*, 'For years it was disputed about whom the word referred to': the former is preferable because it is more idiomatic.

to for *to* + infinitive is colloquial, not Standard English; it is avoided in good writing, except (of course) in dialogue. 'I shall go; he doesn't want *to*'.

to, in *other to* and *different to*. See OTHER.

to, misused for *as to* (or *in respect of*), is exemplified in 'Since the two of them had been at a loss to what else to do, they had made the journey to St. Johns', Kenneth Roberts, *A Rabble in Arms* (English edition), 1939. In this example, *to* could have been omitted.

to-morrow and **tomorrow.** *The O.E.D.* prefers *to-morrow* and *to-day* to the variants; *Webster's* prefers *tomorrow* and *today*.

to-morrow is and **to-morrow will be.** The latter is more logical, except when, in a vivid and graphic context, the morrow is pulled back into the present, as in the catch-phrase, 'to-morrow is another day'.

tolerant to is incorrect for *tolerant of*.

Tommy (Atkins). See JACK.

too for *very* is a trivial colloquialism, as in 'Isn't it just too sweet!'

too is occasionally misused for *either* in negative sentences and phrases. 'I don't mean that we should shut our eyes to it; but it shouldn't make us shut our eyes to other things too', C. Daly King, *Arrogant Alibi*, 1938. It is Dr Pons, the psychologist (Daly King himself in fictional shape) who is speaking, not some illiterate moron. A sense construction? Perhaps; but it jars.

toper and **drunkard; drinker.** *Toper* (mainly literary) is synonymous with *drunkard*, 'a hard drinker'; for *drunkard*, see also at DRUNK. The term *drinker* requires a qualifying word or phrase, as in 'a hard drinker', 'a moderate drinker', 'a drinker of nothing but water'.—For *dipsomaniac*, see DRUNK.

topic and **subject.** *Topic* is nowadays confined—or virtually confined—to a subject or theme that is *topical*, 'of or pertaining to the topics of the day—the subjects of the day's discussions, subjects that are, at best, a nine days' wonder'. (*The O.E.D.*)

tornado. See CYCLONE.

tortuous is sometimes misused for *torturous* and for *tortious* (a legal term).

tost for *tossed* is now poetical. Avoid it in prose.

totalitarian is so often misused or loosely used that *The O.E.D.*'s definition may serve to redress the balance. 'Of or pertaining to a polity which permits no rival loyalties or parties', as in 'A reaction . . . against parliamentarianism . . . in favour of a "totalitarian" or unitary state, whether Fascist or Communist' (*The Times*, 1929) or Nazi.

totally destroyed appears, as a tautology, on the style sheets of many newspaper editors. 'A house is destroyed' is usually sufficient. But suppose that one is describing a row of houses subjected to fire: one house is *half destroyed* i.,e., destroyed as to one-half; the next, however, is wholly destroyed—*totally destroyed*. (Frank Whitaker. in *The J.I.J.*, January, 1939.)

tough, 'a street ruffian', is good American; so is the corresponding adjective ('of criminal or potentially criminal proclivities'). But *tough*, 'very unfortunate; unjust', is an American colloquialism.

trade-union and **trades-union.** The plurals are *trade-unions* and *trades-unions*. In England, the preferred form of the singular is *trades-union*; in the U.S.A., *trade-union*.

tragedy. See DISASTER.

tragic; tragical. *Tragic* is the correct form (opposed to *comic*) in the sense 'of, pertaining to, belonging to, proper to tragedy (a branch of the drama)'; but 'resembling tragedy in respect of its matter; relating to or expressing fatal or dreadful events, hence sad, gloomy' requires *tragical*, as does the sense 'excited with, (of a mood) coloured with, tragic feeling' ('This tragical mood', Miss Braddon); *tragic* is the right term for 'fatal, disastrous, calamitous; terrible' ('His short life had a tragic close'). (*The O.E.D.*)

transcendent; transcendental. *Transcendent* = 'pre-eminent', as in 'A person of altogether transcendent greatness' (Seeley); as a synonym of '(merely) eminently great or good; excellent', it is loose English. In the sense 'extraordinary', both forms are correct; but for

'superhuman, supernatural' and for 'abstract, metaphysical' (a vague usage to be avoided), *transcendental* is correct. In Theology, the word is *transcendent*; in mathematics, *transcendental*. In Philosophy, *transcendental* is applied to the system of Emerson and to a tenet of Schilling's system; in Aristotelian philosophy, the word is *transcendent*. Kant distinguishes: for him, *transcendent* = 'outside (or transcending) experience; unrealizable in human experience)', whereas *transcendental* = 'not derived from experience; a priori', and hence it is applied to any philosophy resembling Kant's 'in being based upon the recognition of an a priori element in experience'. (*The O.E.D.*)

transfer is occasionally misused for *change* and for *transpose*. The former error occurs in '. . . Some pencilled figures. Ten thousand dollars. Rebecca found him a pen and watched him transfer dollars into pounds', Warwick Deeping, *Sackcloth and Silk*, 1935.

transitory and **transient.** Both are correct in the sense 'temporary; fleeting; momentary'. *Transitory action* is a legal technicality. In philosophy, *transient* (often, for distinction's sake, spelt *transeant*) is opposed to *immanent*. (*The O.E.D.*)

transpire is loosely used for *happen* or *occur*; its figurative meaning is properly *to become known, to come to light*, from its almost literal sense of *to leak out*.

travail is 'the labour and pangs of child-birth', also 'to suffer these'; *travel* is '(a) journeying', also 'to journey'.

treachery and **treason.** The former has the wider meaning, being both general (when it is synonymous with *treason*) and particular (= 'an act of treason or perfidy'). In the general sense, 'deceit, cheating, perfidy; violation of faith, betrayal of trust', *treachery* is preferred to *treason*, but in the special application, 'deception or desertion of one's sovereign' or of the government of the state to which one owes allegiance, *treason* is preferred, with the variant *high treason*; and *treason* is, in all references and contexts, the legal term. *Treacherousness* is much narrower than either, for it is only an abstract, 'the quality of being treacherous'. (*The O.E.D.*)

treasonable and **treasonous.** In the extended sense, 'perfidious', only the former is used. In the nuances, 'of the nature of treason, involving treason, characterized by, hence characteristic of treason', the terms are synonymous: both 'a treasonable conspiracy' and 'a treasonous conspiracy' are correct; 'a treasonous libel', 'a treasonable letter' might also be 'a treasonable libel', 'a treasonous letter': but *treasonable* is gradually superseding *treasonous*. (*The O.E.D.*)

treat; treat of; treat on. *Treat on* is incorrect for *treat of*. To *treat of* is 'to deal with (some matter, whether in speech or in writing); to discourse on', as in 'His book treats of a most abstruse subject'. To *treat* a subject is to discuss it (in speech or writing), now generally 'to deal with [it] in the way of literary art', the former nuance occurring in 'What subjects did he treat?', the latter in 'I wonder how he will treat the subject', 'The life of St Stephen . . . has been treated in mural frescoes'. (*The O.E.D.*)

treble and **triple.** In the sense 'three times as much or many; multiplied by three; of three times the measure or amount', *triple* is preferable to *treble*; thus, 'a triple scale' (*not* in music), 'The quantity should not be less than triple the weight of the solids consumed', 'If *A* is the third part of *B*, *B* is the triple (part) of *A*'. In the sense 'consisting of three things (or sets of things) or members; threefold', *treble* and *triple* are synonymous; thus, 'a treble enclosure', 'A kind of shirt of double or treble elk-hide', and 'A triple bank of oars', 'Triple rows of chairs': but *triple* is now the commoner. In the sense 'having three applications or relations; of three kinds', *treble* is preferred, as in 'Every part and episode [of a certain book] has its double and treble meaning'. In music: *triple*, adjective, does not occur,—except in the phrases *triple counterpoint, triple fugue, triple rhythm, triple time*; as a noun, *triple* does not occur at all. (*The O.E.D.*)

trek is 'a journey performed in an ox-waggon', 'an organized migration or expedition by ox-waggon'; hence, 'any migration or collective journeying'—but not properly of a holiday movement to the sea-side (etc.). It has, among journalists, become a 'rubber-stamp word' (see AMAZING). [[Among American journalists the once-popular *trek* has been replaced by *hegira*; thus is misuse compounded.]]

trend. See TEND.

triad. See TRIUMVIRATE.

trial for *attempt* is incorrect, as in 'Like a fussy old man who'—properly *that*—'is afraid of losing his dignity, and

in the very trial at keeping it, is seen without it', Paul Horgan, *A Lamp on the Plains* (English ed.), 1937.

trilithonic is incorrect for *trilithic*, 'of or pertaining to a trilith' (a prehistoric monument of three large stones, two upright, with the third resting on them as a lintel). (*The O.E.D.*)

trilogy, trio. See TRIUMVIRATE.

tri-monthly, 'occurring once every three months' or 'lasting for three months'; in the former sense, *quarterly* is preferable; in the latter, *of three months*. Yet the sense in which a term is needed is 'occurring three times a month': therefore, why not adopt *trimonthly* in that sense?

trip is a short voyage, a short journey. *Journey*, by the way, refers to the land, *voyage* to the sea; a *trip* may be made on either.

triple. See TREBLE.

triumvirate (etymologically, a set or combination of three men, especially three rulers) is never, *trio* rarely, applied to aught other than persons. To write of 'a triumvirate of test matches' (for three such matches), as I have seen done by one who should know better, is faintly ridiculous. A series of three novels or (long) poems or plays is a *trilogy*; of four, a *tetralogy*. *Triad* may be used of three heroes, three matricides, three film stars, and so on; and is obligatory in certain learned or technical connexions (e.g., in music, in Welsh literature).

troop; troops; trooper; troupe; trouper. A *troop* is that sub-division of cavalry which corresponds to a company of infantry and a battery of artillery; *troops* is 'armed forces collectively' without *the*, as in 'to raise troops'; *the troops* is a colloquialism for 'soldiers' or 'the soldiers', as in 'The spirit of the troops is excellent'; there is no singular to either *troops* or *the troops*. A *trooper* is a horse soldier, a cavalryman, hence a cavalry horse. A *troupe* is a company of actors, dancers, or performing animals; a member of a troupe is a *trouper*.

troubled; troublesome; troublous. *Troubled* is applied to a sea or other extent of water, or a sky, that is stormy; to wine or water that is turbid (coloured with sediment; made muddy or thick). Also to moods, thoughts, attitudes, minds, hearts, sleep, periods of time that are disturbed, disordered, disquieted, agitated, afflicted ('a troubled ghost'; 'these troubled times', 'troubled reign',

'goaded by his troubled thought . . .').
Troublesome is now used but rarely in any
sense other than that of 'giving trouble;
causing annoyance; vexatious or distressing', as in 'a troublesome cough',
'troublesome neighbours': *troublous* is
also used thus, but is now less usual and
rather literary. *Troublous* is a literary
synonym of *troubled* as applied to a
stormy sea; hence it is applied to a violent wind—another literary application;
to periods, reigns, lives, state (of an institution); but in its own right, and
without the competition of either *troubled*
or *troublesome*, it further means '(of persons or their attributes) turbulent,
disorderly; restless, unquiet', as in
'Troublous and adventurous spirits, men
of broken fortunes . . . and boundless
desires' (Motley), but even here it is
rather literary than general for 'turbulent; restless, unquiet'. (*The O.E.D.*)

trout; plural **trouts**, except in sporting use: 'He may guddle trouts in a
stream', 'Pike and trout are to be had
in the lochs'. When various species (or
more than one species) are concerned,
the plural is—or should be—*trouts*, as in
'There is a good book on the trouts of
the Catskills'. See also SPORTING PLU-
RALS.

truculent is catachrestic in the sense
'base, mercenary'. Nor does it mean
'surly'. It = fierce, cruel, barbarous; (of
things, writing, etc.) harsh, violent,
scathing.

trustworthy; trusty. The former =
'worthy of trust or confidence; reliable';
so does *trusty*, but *trusty* is ever so
slightly archaic in this sense, except in
the phrase *our trusty and well-beloved* (in
letters from sovereign to subject).
[[*Trusty* (n.) in American usage means a
convict trusted and allowed special
privileges.]]

truth. See at VERACITY.

try and do (something) is incorrect
for *try to do* (something). Perhaps the
error arose from such collocations as
'He tried—and hard, how hard!—to do
something'. An astonishingly frequent
error. [[This usage is approved by some
grammarians as a comfortable English
idiom; it is labeled *colloquial* by *Webster's*.]]

tubercular; tuberculous. The latter is now reserved for pathological and
medical contexts ('tuberculous tissue',
'tuberculous meningitis', 'tuberculous
pork, tuberculous cows', 'hospitals for

the tuberculous sick'), whereas *tubercular*
is, in discriminating usage, reserved for
natural-history contexts, where it = (*a*)
'of a tubercle, consisting of a tubercle,
of the form and/or nature of a tubercle'
(a *tubercle* being a small tuber), or (*b*),
'tuberculate', i.e., having tubercles, or
covered with tubercles. (*The O.E.D.*)
[[In popular American usage, *tubercular*
is often used for *tuberculous*.]]

tubfuls; tubsfull. See the remark at
BASKETFULS.

TURGIDITY is 'inflation of language;
grandiloquence, pomposity, bombast'
(*The O.E.D.*); a seeming, but windy,
grandeur of language; a grandeur that
rings insincere or unsuitable. It is the
hall-mark of pretentious and ambitious
minor poets—the Montgomerys, Robert
Pollok, and their like. (Not a common
fault in the 20th Century.)

two first. See at FIRST, TWO.

two halves, cut into, is verbose,
redundant, absurd for *to cut into halves*.
But *two halves make a whole* is, of course,
correct.

two twins is tautological for *twins*
when only one pair is understood;
properly used, however, *two twins* = four
persons.

type (of), like *case (of)*, is often used
unnecessarily or infelicitously; as in
'He's not that type of person'; 'Events
of that type generally arouse suspicion',
for 'Such events . . .' or 'Events of that
kind . . .'; 'The rose is not that type of
flower'. Keep *type* in its right place.—
Cf. TYPICAL.

typhoon. See CYCLONE.

typical should be modified only after
due consideration. Such a sentence as
the following strikes one as odd: 'Now
there I had Smith's début—a rather
typical performance which gave me
quite a good idea of his methods',
Cameron McCabe, *The Face on the
Cutting-Room Floor*, 1937: why *rather*?

typist is the person operating a *typewriter* (the machine); 'to *typewrite*' is
obsolescent for 'to *type*', which is not,
as Weseen states, colloquial, for it is
Standard English.

typographic is perhaps obsolescent;
typographical, current.

U

uglily sounds ugly in many contexts;
not all, for in the following two quotations from *The O.E.D.* it is not cacoph-

onous (and there are many other instances where it is either tolerable or even euphonious);—'In those representations man indeed was not more uglily than fearfully made' (Sayce); 'The town is . . . uglily picturesque'. And it is much more economical than *in an ugly manner*.

ultra (adj.) is both ugly and odd for *excessive* or *immoderate*, as in 'ultra reverence', 'ultra respect'; fortunately it is obsolescent.

umbrella. See at PARASOL.

unable. See INCAPABLE.

un- and **in-** in adjectives. See IN-. Here, however, is appended a short list of *im-* or *in-* and *un-* terms.

impecunious
impenetrable
impertinent
imperious
implacable
inadmissible
incapable
incomparable
inconsequent
inconsolable
incredible
incredulous
indecisive
indelible
indirect
inexact
infamous
infelicitous
inhuman
intransigent
unable (but *incapable*)
unbalanced
unbelievable (but *incredible*)
unblessed
unbounded
uncomparable
unconsoled (but *inconsolable*)
uncrowned
undecided (but *indecisive*)
unequal
unfaithful
unfavourable
ungrateful
unhappy (but *infelicitous*)
unhorsed
unimaginative
unimportant
unpenetrated (but *impenetrable*)
unpleasant
unpretentious
untenable
untruthful

unambiguous should not be used as an exact synonym of *perfectly clear*. Thus Dr L. Susan Stebbing, in *Logical Positivism and Analysis*, 1933, writes: 'An *unambiguous expression* is not equivalent to a *perfectly clear expression*, since we may understand more or less clearly'—i.e., more clearly or less clearly. 'It is important not to confuse *ambiguity, vagueness, unclearness*; these three are quite different, and mutually independent.' This footnote is increased in significance when we see that the passage it glosses is this:—'Moore'—Professor G. E. Moore—'holds that to *understand an expression* is not equivalent to being able *to give a correct analysis* of its meaning. He has pointed out that the failure to see that these are *not* equivalent has been responsible for a good many mistakes with regard to the nature of philosophical problems and with regard to their possible solution.'

unanimous. See COMPARATIVES, FALSE.

unapt. See INAPT.

UNATTACHED PARTICIPLES. See CONFUSED PARTICIPLES.

unavoidable, misused for *unchangeable* (or *unchanging*). 'As was his unavoidable custom, he observed the faces of the crowd around him', Carolyn Wells, *The Clue of the Eyelash*, 1933.

unaware is the adjective, **unawares** the adverb.

unbeknown is not, as stated by Weseen, dialectal; **unbeknownst** is dialectal and colloquial. As a variant of *unknown*, it is perhaps unusual, but certainly not rare, as in 'the land of the unbeknown'; its commonest role, however, is that which it plays in the phrase *unbeknown to* (= *unknown to*), 'without the knowledge of', as in 'The bottle had been opened, unbeknown to the purchaser'; the elliptical *unbeknown*, 'without anybody's knowledge; unnoticed, undetected', is becoming rare ('My love rose up so early And stole out unbeknown', Housman). (*The O.E.D.*)

unbelievable and **believable** for *incredible* (or *difficult to believe in*) and *credible*, although theoretically possible and indeed listed in the best dictionaries, are somewhat unusual now and almost catachrestic; certainly they are to be avoided in connexion with persons or their representation in books. Obviously 'It is unbelievable' is permissible and even idiomatic when it applies to a fact or a rumour; but *unbelievable* rings oddly in 'The first readers of Mr McCabe's book . . . rightly refused to believe that there could possibly be a detective as unconventional and unscrupulous as Smith. The critics, therefore, attacked McCabe, the author, for having invented such an unbelievable character' (Cameron McCabe, *The Face on the Cutting-Room Floor*, 1937).

unbeliever. See DISBELIEVER.

unbend. Under the heading *The "Unbend" Mystery*, Mr Wilfred Whitten (in *Good and Bad English*) gives an admirable example of the misuse of this word, supplied to him by a correspondent: 'He was a stern and unbending old man, but he could unbend on occasion', and quotes his correspondent's comment: 'This choice specimen of literary English I came across in the work of an author of repute, but he sinned in good company, for they all do it. Only, one would think that the very form of the complete sentence would have shown him, had he taken a moment's thought, that the verb in the second half should be "bend".'

uncomfortable and **discomfortable.** The latter is the stronger, for it connotes discomfort, whereas the former connotes mere absence of comfort. (For *discomfortable*, see also DISCOMFIT.)

uncomparable is not the same as *incomparable*; it is a hybrid word, but necessary to distinguish its meaning, 'that cannot be compared', from that of *incomparable*, 'above or beyond comparison' (in the sense of likeness).—Both words are among the uncomparable adjectives, *q.v.* at COMPARATIVES, FALSE.

unconscious and **subconscious.** *Subconscious*, in ordinary language, is 'partly or imperfectly aware', as in 'He was subconscious that he was trying a bold experiment' (Hawthorne, 1864): this sense is now rare and it should be avoided. In psychology, it = 'partially or imperfectly conscious; belonging to a class of phenomena resembling those of consciousness but not clearly perceived or recognized'; hence, 'belonging to that portion of the mental field the processes of which are outside the range of attention'.

Unconscious, in psychology, means 'performed, employed, etc., without conscious action', as in *unconscious cerebration*. In ordinary language, it = 'unaware, unregarding or regardless' (as in 'He was unconscious of the danger

although it was obvious to everyone else'); 'not characterized by—not endowed with—the faculty or presence of consciousness'; 'temporarily without consciousness' (*knocked unconscious*); 'not known to or thought of as possessed by or existing in oneself' ('The boxer had an unconscious grace'); 'not attended by, or present to, consciousness' ('It is wrong to punish an unconscious act' (J. Martineau, 1866). *Subconscious*, then, should be confined to psychological contexts. [With thanks to *The O.E.D.*]

uncourteous. See at DISCOURTEOUS.

uncreditable. See CREDIBLE.

unctious is a frequent misspelling and mispronunciation of *unctuous*.

undeceived, as a participial adjective, can be ambiguous, for there is a verb *undeceive*, to tell the truth to, to inform a person of a mistake, with a past participle *undeceived* employable as an adjective. 'But she shook her head, undeceived', Agatha Christie, *Dumb Witness*, 1937, where the meaning is 'not deceived', but where one is delayed by the possibility of the meaning 'informed' (of something).

under and **below** and **beneath.** See 'ABOVE and OVER'.

underhand; underhanded(ly). The only sense in which the latter word is necessary (or desirable) is 'short of "hands"; undermanned', as in 'The clergy are utterly underhanded' (Samuel Wilberforce, 1874). *Underhand* (with several senses, including *sly*[*ly*]) is both adjective and adverb. (*The O.E.D.*)

underlay and **underlie.** Apart from the former as a printing technicality and the latter as a geological as well as a mining one, the essential difference is this:—*Underlay* is 'to support (something) by placing something else underneath it; to furnish *with* something laid below', as in 'You ought not to stitch any wounded finger, . . . but underlay it with little splinters' and 'Their project of underlaying the sea with electric wires' (*The Athenaeum*, 1851).

To *underlie* is 'to form a basis to; to exist beneath the surface-aspect of', as in 'That germ of truth which underlies all falsity and every falsehood': this is the dominant sense. A sense once important but now slightly obsolescent is, 'to be subjected to, to have imposed on one; to submit to, to undergo or suffer', especially in reference to accusation, penalty, punishment, pain, as in 'He underlies also the graver charge of intentional misrepresentation' (Donaldson, 1857), 'Since my last visit to the Russian lines I had underlain a ban' (O'Donovan, 1882). (*The O.E.D.*)

undersigned, I (or **we**) **the.** Permissible in law; affected or tediously jocular elsewhere. In 1868 Dickens could write, 'The undersigned is in his usual brilliant condition'; that was a long time ago.

understandable. See COMPREHENSIBLE.

UNDERSTATEMENT or *Meiosis*; and *Litotes. Understatement* is the everyday synonym of the learned *meiosis*; understatement itself is the supreme virtue of the middle-class and upper-class Englishman. If an Englishman says, 'I dislike that woman', that woman should remove herself as expeditiously as possible; if he says that some contretemps is 'rather a nuisance', he means that it is utterly damnable or extremely unfortunate.* But whereas, in speech, understatement is, all in all, a virtue, it may easily, in writing, become very misleading: do not, therefore, overdo British reticence and English *meiosis*.

Litotes is that 'figure of speech, in which an affirmative is expressed by the negative of the contrary; an instance of this' (*The O.E.D.*), as in 'a citizen of *no mean city*', 'He is no coward'.

under the circumstances. This almost universal construction is strictly incorrect, for 'circumstances' are not *over* but *around* us. *The O.E.D.*, defining *circumstances* as 'the external conditions prevailing at the time', says: 'Mere situation is expressed by "in the circumstances," action affected is performed "under the circumstances"'; thus, e.g., '. . . who found himself in circumstances to which he was unequal' (Froude); 'The desire to obtain the money will, under certain circumstances, stimulate industry' (Ruskin). When in doubt use *in*, which is always correct. See also the entry at CIRCUMSTANCES . . .

undiscriminating and **indiscriminate.** Usage is tending to confine the former to persons, the latter to aim, purpose, motive, impulse, selection, plan, method, treatment, behaviour; a tendency that, if given effect, makes for clarity and for that distinctiveness which characterizes all sensitive or subtle writing. The senses of *indiscriminate*

*See O. Jespersen, *Growth and Structure of the English Language*, Sec. II.

are: 'not marked by discrimination or discernment; done without making distinctions', hence 'confused or promiscuous'. The person of discrimination or discernment is a *discriminating* (or *discerning*) person.

undying. See DEATHLESS.

unelastic and **inelastic.** Either is permissible, though the latter is preferable. In figurative contexts *inelastic* is much the commoner.

unendurable. See COMPARATIVES, FALSE.

UN-ENGLISH PLURALS. See PLURALS, UN-ENGLISH.

unfertilized is correct; but rather *infertile* than *unfertile*, rather *infertility* than *unfertility*, etymology demanding *in-* and usage not rejecting it.

unfrequent is inferior to *infrequent*, but *unfrequented* is correct, *infrequented* incorrect; *unfrequency*, however, is rare for *infrequency*.

unharmonious is inferior to *inharmonious*.

unheard of = 'not before heard of, hitherto unknown', hence 'new, strange', hence 'unprecedented': it is, therefore, to be used with care.

unhospitable is inferior to *inhospitable*.

unhuman is much weaker than—not an error for—*inhuman. Unhuman* should be reserved for the sense 'not pertaining to mankind'; for the sake of clarity, use it neither for *inhuman* nor for *superhuman*.

unique, most or **rather** or **very.** An object that is 'unique' is the only one of its kind in existence; there can be no qualification of the absolute without a contradiction of the quality which it asserts. The frequent use of *unique(ly)* to express mere rarity or excellence is incorrect. See COMPARATIVES, FALSE.

United Kingdom, the. See GREAT BRITAIN.

unity for *entity* is a quaint mistake, yet it occurs rather frequently. In a candidate's essay, read in 1937, I found this, 'The British Empire is a political unity'.

universal. See COMPARATIVES, FALSE.

universal(ly) for *general*(ly) is not only loose, but also the cause of deterioration in the former word; as in 'Mr George Bernard Shaw's theories may be more universally accepted by future generations than they are to-day' (an L.C.C. essay, 1938).

unless, misused for *except*. 'Unless when carried out on a set purpose, it [i.e., alliteration] offends the ear', Alexander Bain, *English Composition and Rhetoric*, enlarged edition, Part II, 1888.

unloosen is obsolescent for '*to unloose*'. It is not synonymous with *loosen*.

unmeasurable is preferable in the two literal senses 'incapable of being measured, on account of great size, extent, or amount, in reference to material things, to dimensions, to time', as in 'The tower . . . was of an unmeasurable height', and 'not admitting of—insusceptible of—measurement; immensurable', as in 'The Church is unmeasurable by foot-rule'. (*The O.E.D.*) But in transferred applications, in figurative uses, immeasurable is preferable, as in 'immeasurable ambition', 'the immeasurable grace of God', 'Religion is immeasurable'.

unmoral, amoral, non-moral, immoral. The last—opposed to *moral*—is positive ('evil; corrupt, depraved'); the first three are negative, and synonymous one with another. Purists prefer *non-moral* to *unmoral*. *Amoral*, however, is the best word for the sense 'not to be judged by a moral criterion; not connected with moral considerations', though Fowler condemns it.

unpayable is incorrect for *non-paying* and *improfitable*. 'That would be a most unpayable business' (John G. Brandon, *The Mail-Van Mystery*, ca. 1937).

unpracticable is (or should be) obsolete for *impracticable*; **unpractical** is obsolescent as a synonym of *impractical*, but good writers distinguish *unpractical* (merely not practical) from *impractical* (decidedly the opposite of *practical*).

unqualified is not, as some persons assume, synonymous with *unrestricted* or *entire*. This erroneous presumption vitiates the homely force of 'To have unqualified charge of a garden makes a vital difference in a person's outlook on gardening' (an essay script in the L.C.C. Major Establishment examination, 1938).

unreadable is subjective ('too dull or obscure to be read with patience'); *illegible* is objective ('indecipherable'). Thus, 'Many of the manuscripts of unreadable novels are illegible'.

unreligious is neutral, 'not religious', or pejorative, 'ungodly'; *irreligious* is pejorative, 'ungodly, impious'.

unresenting of is incorrect for *unresentful of* (or *not resenting*), as in 'Unresent-

ing of his old friend's raillery', Carolyn Wells, *The Clue of the Eyelash*, 1933.

unresponsible = 'not in a position of responsibility; not yet at the age at which responsibility sets in'; *irresponsible* may be used in the same sense ('You shouldn't have handed the question-paper to an irresponsible person'), but generally, in current usage, it = 'feckless, shiftless, undependable'.

unretentive. See IRRETENTIVE.

unsanitary should be reserved for 'not possessing sanitation'; *insanitary* = 'injurious to health; unhealthy'. 'An uninhabited desert is merely unsanitary, but a camp of nomads therein may be offensively insanitary.'

unscathed. See SCATHELESS.

unsuccess means, negatively, 'lack of success'; positively, 'failure'. As one generally opposes *failure* to *success*, *unsuccess*, if used at all, might well be reserved for the negative sense, 'lack of success'. Etymologically, *insuccess* would be preferable to *unsuccess*.

unsufferable is not incorrect for—but it is certainly less usual and etymologically less sound than—*insufferable*.

until. See at TILL.

untouchable. See COMPARATIVES, FALSE.

uphold. See HOLD UP.

upon and **on.** Of these synonyms, *upon* is stronger (more emphatic) and more formal and impressive than *on*; but it is slowly falling into disuse in speech (more's the pity!); in writing, *upon* is often preferred to *on* on the score of euphony.—To convey both elevation and contact, *up on* is required.

upstair, whether as adverb or adjective, is obsolescent for *upstairs*; as a noun, only *upstairs* is permissible.

upward and **upwards.** *Upward* only is adjective; both *upward* and *upwards* are adverbs, but, in general, *upward* is the more usual. *Upwards*, however, is the idiomatic form in the sense 'to a higher aggregate, figure, price, height, length, etc.', as in 'Accommodation for three guineas upwards'. (*The O.E.D.*)

upwards of is incorrect for *rather less than* or *nearly* or *not quite*, as in 'upwards of a hundred' (some number in the 90's). Properly, *upwards of* = 'slightly or rather more than'. (*The O.E.D.*)

urban is 'of or belonging to or characteristic of or resembling a city', whereas *urbane* is 'having the manners or culture regarded as characteristic of a city', hence 'civil, courteous', hence 'blandly polite', indeed 'suave', and is used in transferred senses ('urbane manners', 'urbane mind'; 'urbane epistle').

USAGE. See IDIOM.

us both and **us each.** See WE BOTH ...

use (v.). See CONSUME.

USELESS LATIN ADJECTIVES. There are, in English, numerous Latin and Greek-derived adjectives that are unnecessary, for they duplicate an excellent or, at the least, a satisfactory 'Saxon' adjective (or noun used adjectivly). To speak of the *hodiernal post* (or *mail*) for *to-day's post*, *avuncular* for *uncle's* is intolerable; but then, very few of us would! See Jespersen's *Growth and Structure of the English Language*, Sections 131–132.

usual to is infelicitous for *usual for*. 'Ward Syme at six-thirty in the evening was in the state of cheerful confusion usual to that time of day', Josephine Bell, *Murder in Hospital*, 1937. It would have been still better for the author to write 'usual at that time of day'.

utmost, utter, uttermost. See COMPARATIVES, FALSE.

Etymologically, *utter* is the comparative, and *utmost* the (double) superlative of Old English *ut*, 'out' ('external'); *uttermost* = *utter* + *most*, an etymological absurdity.

Utter now = 'extreme, absolute, complete, entire', as in 'utter darkness'; (of denials, refusals, recantations, etc.) 'unmodified' or 'decisive'; (of persons) 'complete', as in 'an utter fool', 'that utter stranger'.

Uttermost is obsolescent in the senses 'outermost' ('He flew to the uttermost island of the Hebridean group'), and 'extreme' or 'utmost', as in Ruskin's 'To speak with the uttermost truth of expression'; its only active sense is the very restricted one, 'last in a series', as in 'I shall pay to the uttermost farthing'. *Uttermost*, in short, is disappearing from general use; it is already rare except in cultured speech and good writing.

Utmost, physically, = 'outmost' (most remote; most external), as in 'Knights of utmost North and West' (Tennyson); hence, it = 'furthest extended', as in 'With my utmost sight I could only just discern it',—a sense now becoming rare; obsolescent, too, is the sense 'latest (in time)' or 'final', as in 'Adding the utmost oil as a lubricant'. The predominant sense is 'of the greatest or highest degree,

number, amount; extreme', as in 'The utmost profit of a cow', 'With the utmost cheerfulness'.

V

vacant. See EMPTY.

vagaries is an ill-chosen word in this sentence (from a school examination script, March, 1938), 'Primitive man realized that he must have some protection from the vagaries of Nature—from the biting wind, the cold wet rain, and even the blazing sun'. Here the writer might better have used 'the vicissitudes', or 'the cruel caprices (of Nature)'. *Vagary*, 'an aimless wandering', implies something indefinite, whereas these natural phenomena, though often unforeseen, are very definite.

VAGUENESS. See WOOLLINESS.

valuable is that which has intrinsic value; VALUED is (that which is) regarded as having value. A *valuable* thing is perhaps not properly *valued*; a *valued* one is not necessarily *valuable*.

valueless. See at INVALUABLE.

vantage. See ADVANTAGE.

vapid (pronounced *vappid*) and **insipid.** *Vapid* (L. *vapidus*, savourless) is (of liquors, beverages) 'flat', (of food) 'flavourless'; hence, fig., 'devoid of animation, zest, or interest' (esp., 'vapid talk', 'vapid amusements'). *Insipid* (L. *insipidus*, tasteless) is, lit., 'without taste, or with very little taste'; hence, fig., 'lifeless; dull or unexciting', as in 'insipid compliments' and 'kisses, though pleasant in private, are insipid in public' (Lytton). The nouns are *vapidity* and *insipidity*; *vapidness* and *insipidness* are inferior forms. (*The O.E.D.*)

vari-coloured and **variegated** are, the former obligatorily, the latter preferably, to be used of or in reference to colour. *Varied*, already falling into disuse, can safely be discarded by those who fear to confound it with *various*, for every sense of *varied* is shared by *various*, which, moreover, has senses lacked by *varied*. As for *various*; the discriminating writer refrains from using it in the weakened senses 'more than one; several; many'. That nuance, 'many', is perhaps inevitable, for the meaning of *various* often merges into that of *many different*. 'We met various times' is, at best, infuriatingly vague: say *several* or *many* as the context demands. (*The O.E.D.*)

variant, misused. In 'He has heard

very variant opinions of his book' (from a private letter, January, 1938), 'variant' means 'varying, diverse'. Not strictly incorrect in the adjectival sense, *variant* is almost obsolete and is met with chiefly in biological and technical connexions. The latest instance of its use is given by *The O.E.D.* from J. M. Whitton, 1897— 'These are definitions not too variant to stand indifferently for synonyms of spirit'.

varied. See at VARI-COLOURED.

VARIETY. See SYNONYMS, last paragraph.

various, misused for *certain*, as in 'There are various things that no decent man will do', read '. . . certain things.'— And see at VARI-COLOURED.

various, used for *several*, is downright feeble—and careless.

venal and **venial** are often confused, but have opposite meanings; the former being 'purchasable', 'subject to mercenary or corrupt influences', the latter 'pardonable, excusable'. (*The O.E.D.*)

vengeance and **revenge** (nn.). See AVENGE.

venom and **poison.** The former is the poison secreted by snakes and certain animals; also it is used figuratively for 'virulence; bitter spite or malice'.

venture. See ADVENTURE.

veracity and **truth.** *Veracity* = 'truthfulness; accuracy', or even 'a truth', but not 'truth' itself.

VERB + (PRO)NOUN + GOVERNED VERB ('I *saw it gain* on him'); and **VERB + (PRO)NOUN + ing FORM OF VERB** ('I *saw it gaining* on him'). In the former, the second or governed verb expresses a single, definite, time-precise, completed action, whereas in the latter the *-ing* form ('gaining') expresses a continuous, incomplete action. In the former, the sense is 'I saw that it gained on him', but in the latter the sense is 'I saw that it was gaining on him, but I did not see what eventually happened'. —Cf. 'I shall see it gain on him' and 'I shall see it gaining on him', likewise 'I see [the true, not the historic present] it gain on him' and 'I see it gaining on him': the same nuances hold good in those two tenses, except that in the present the limiting of the action in 'I see it gain on him' is less clear-cut than it is in 'I saw it gain on him'. This generalization may seem obvious, as indeed it is; yet the rule therein implicit is often flouted by careless writers.

VERB UNCOMPLETED. 'Political upheavals in Europe influence the Londoner's daily life in strange ways, and they always have' (*The Evening News*, March 18, 1938). In my opinion, such ungrammatical short cuts are bad English; the change of tense necessitates a correct completion of the verb; 'and have always done so' would be correct and would avoid the jolt caused by leaving the auxiliary in suspense, like a horse without the cart.

verbiage and **verbosity** are occasionally confused. Roughly, *verbiage* results in *verbiage*; nowadays, *verbosity* is applied mostly to speaking, *verbiage* mostly to writing; *verbosity* is both tendency and result, whereas *verbiage* is only result. *Verbiage*, by the way, has a further sense, now rare and, indeed almost obsolete: 'wording, diction, verbal expression'.

VERBOSITY.

'A plethora of words becomes the apoplexy of reason.'

C. A. Ward, *Oracles of Nostradamus*, 1891.

The O.E.D. defines verbosity as 'superfluity of words', with the alternatives 'wordiness; prolixity'.

Verbosity is a general tendency and the resulting practice. (It sometimes overlaps TAUTOLOGY, *q.v.*) Wilson Benington has amplified *The O.E.D.* definition in this clarifying way:—'Using more words than are necessary, as though talking for the sake of talking or of hearing the sound of one's own voice; preference of long words, high-sounding phrases, complicated sentences, to simple language and clear expression:—habits noticeable in speakers afflicted with logorrhoea and equally characteristic of grandiloquent writers.'

A few brief examples of a fault exemplified best by long passages:—

'Such are the vicissitudes of this our sublunary existence': for 'Such is life'.

'Lassitude seems to be a word unknown to the vocabulary of the swallows' (Morris, *British Birds*, 1852): an amusing instance of ponderous circumlocution, all the heavier because it was intended to lighten the dulness of direct statement.

'Modern Stockholmers, *irrespective of class*, are accustomed to fairly substantial midday meals in restaurants, and typists must have shared the indignation of their managing directors at *being forced this week within the confines of a packet of sandwiches'* (*The Daily Tele-graph,* Jan. 22, 1938): the italics are mine.

'Are we quite sure that newly emancipated woman has yet acquired a sound biological status, or secured for herself a harmonious psycho-physiological equilibrium?' (a letter to *The New Statesman:* cited by A. P. Herbert, *What a Word!,* 1935).

'Your eyes will scarcely believe that cameras could record its roaring climax of catastrophe and desolation' (advertisement, February, 1938, of *The Hurri-cane*—a film).

* * * * * * *

Verbosity, therefore, is almost the same thing as *pleonasm,* which is 'the use of more words in a sentence than are necessary to express the meaning; redundancy of expression' (generally *re-dundancy* alone),—except that *verbosity* has certain connotations that are absent from the most extended signification of *pleonasm.*

Vergil is inferior to *Virgil,* the Latin being *Virgilius.* Hence *Vergilian* is also to be avoided. [[*Vergil, Vergilian* are the spellings preferred by *Webster's* and by *Harpers' Latin Dictionary. The O.E.D.* prefers *Virgil, Virgilian.*]]

vernacular is often used loosely for *low language* and *jargon* (technicalities). Properly, the noun and adjective = '(the language) naturally spoken by the people of a particular country or district', i.e., 'native or indigenous (language)'; hence, 'written, spoken or translated into the native language'; 'belonging to or characteristic of the native language'. In the 16th–17th Centuries, English was the vernacular, Latin the learned language, and French the language of diplomacy.

verse and **stanza.** For the sake of the valuable distinction, reserve *verse* (popularly what is here a stanza) for 'one line of verse or poetry' and use *stanza* for 'a small number of metrical lines forming a unit in a longer composition'.

verso and **recto.** The *recto* is the front, the *verso* the back of a manuscript leaf or a printed leaf or sheet. As *The O.E.D.* remarks, 'The left-hand page of a book is the verso of that leaf, and faces the recto of the next'.

vertebra has plural *vertebrae.*

very modifies adjective (*very angry*) or adverb (*very foolishly*), but not a past participle (*It is very improved* being

wrong, *much improved* being right). Cf. VERY INTERESTING.

Véry or **Vérey; Verey; Verry:** all these are misspellings of *Very,* the name of the flare, light or pistol.

very interesting but **much interested** or,‖less commonly, **very much interested.** Purists object to *very interested, very pleased, very disappointed, very annoyed,* etc. They prefer *much interested, much* (or *very much*) *pleased, much disappointed*; for the last, however, both idiom and precision demand *acutely disappointed.*

Clearly, idiom forbids *much interesting, much pleasing, much disappointing.*

vest and **waistcoat.** A *waistcoat* is that part of a man's suit of clothes which he wears under his coat and which is of the same material as the coat and trousers, unless it is an *odd* waistcoat or a fancy one,—usually called a *vest* in the U.S.A. In English usage, *vest* is the more common non-commercial name for a man's undershirt. In both English and American usage, *vest* is, with reference to women's apparel, (a) an undershirt, (b) 'part of a woman's dress bodice'. *Singlet* (once a kind of waistcoat) is 'an unlined woollen garment . . . worn as a man's undershirt' (adapted from *The O.E.D.*).

vestigial, misused for *rudimentary* or *rough-and-ready.* This error occurs several times in John Gunther's *Inside Asia,* 1939.

via, 'by way of', refers to the direction of a journey, not to the means of travelling; therefore the following is wrong, very wrong, misleadingly wrong: 'Out at the end of the wharf a man sold tickets to'—'for' would be better—'"excursion" trips via a speed boat', Erle Stanley Gardner, *The Case of the Dangerous Dowager,* 1937 (English edition).

vicar. See 'RECTOR and VICAR'.

vicarial. See RECTORAL.

vicinage and **vicinity; neighbourhood.** *Vicinage* is less usual than *neighbourhood* in the collective sense, 'a number of places lying near, one to another'; in this sense it is preceded by *a* or *the, this* or *that,* and it possesses a plural; 'The agricultural and mineral treasures of its vicinage'; frequent in the phrase, *in the* (or *this* or *our* or . . .) *vicinage. In the vicinage of,* like *in the neighbourhood of,* = 'near to, contiguous to'. Moreover, both *vicinage* and *neighbourhood* bear the transferred sense, 'the people living in a certain district or locality; the people living near to a certain place or within a certain range', as in 'The vicinage applied . . . to the bishop for leave to dig up the body and burn it' and 'The neighbourhood had scandalized her'. Both *vicinage* and *vicinity* mean 'nearness, propinquity, proximity', as in 'The common white pottery . . . will not bear vicinage to a brisk kitchen fire for half-an-hour' and 'Under these conditions all vicinity of watercourses, unless bridged, should be avoided'. Also *in the vicinity* = *in the vicinage, in the neighbourhood*; and *in the vicinity of* = *in the vicinage* (or *neighbourhood*) *of* = 'near or close (to)', as in 'The . . . ship "Marseilles" capsized in the vicinity of Portpatrick'. In a transferred sense, *in the vicinity of*, like *in the neighbourhood of*, = 'something near to (a specified amount)', as in 'In the vicinity of a hundred dollars', 'in the neighbourhood of sixteen pence'. (*Vicinism* is a botanical technicality.) (*The O.E.D.*) [[*Vicinage* is not current in American speech.]]

vicious for '(weather that is) *inclement* or *severe*' is not, as Weseen asserts, incorrect; it is, however, rather unusual and quite unnecessary.

victrola is a special (American) make of phonograph, and the registered trade name therefor. Not to be used as co-extensive (or exactly synonymous) with *phonograph.*—See also the entry at PHONOGRAPH . . .

victuals is not a mere synonym of *food*, as the elegancy-lovers, the big-word-mongers render it, for it means 'articles of food; supplies, or various kinds, of provisions; in later use, especially articles of ordinary diet prepared for use' (*The O.E.D.*, 1928). [[In American usage, *victuals* is limited to dialect and comic stories.]]

vide = 'see!, consult!'; *viz.* = 'that is to say; namely; to wit'. 'This strange event (*vide* Motley) has never been satisfactorily explained'; 'Three of Plumer's men . . ., *viz.* Troopers Abrahamson, White and Parkin'. Both *vide* and *viz.* (short for *videlicet*) should be written in italics.

view (v.), misused for *look.* '"If 'e can git aht o' 'ere", 'Big Bill' said, viewing round the place in the light of a candle he had lit, "'e's a dam' sight cleverer'n what 'e looks"' (John G. Brandon, *The Mail-Van Mystery*, ca. 1937).

viewpoint. See STANDPOINT.

vigil, properly a prolonged night-watch, is often misused to mean any wait, even if trivial and extremely brief. 'Selecting the most comfortable seat, and placing his beer on the floor beside him, Dick settled down to wait. It was not a long vigil; for in less than a couple of minutes Mr Potter made his appearance' (Victor Bridges, *Blue Silver*, 1936).

vigour for *rigour.* Frank Shaw, *Atlantic Murder*, ca. 1932, 'Even the crew-quarters underwent a microscopic examination. . . . [The new hands], naturally, were the ones to be watched with extra vigour'.

vintage should be used only in reference to wine: to speak, as the jocularly careless occasionally speak, of 'a (motor) car of ancient vintage', has ceased to be original or amusing.

violin. See at FIDDLE.

violincello is an incorrect spelling and pronunciation of *violoncello*.

virility should not be used of sexual power in women.

visa has been adopted—both officially and generally—at the expense of *visé. Visa*, therefore, need not be italicized; indeed, it should not.

vitamins.

From *The Observer*, 6th Feb., 1938.

Sir.—The uncertainty as to the pronunciation of the word "vitamins" referred to in the letter from Mr Henry Fields, of Leeds, published in your issue of 30th ult. in "From the Post Bag", should, I think, be dispelled by bearing in mind that scientific authorities mainly adhere to the old Latin pronunciations.

The derivation of "vitamin" from *vis, vita* apparently governs the question referred to.

One does not pronounce the word "vitality" or "vital" as *vee*-tality or vittality; nor do any of the scientific, medical, advisory, or general staff, nor any of our numerous medical, nursing or scientific visitors at the laboratories and factory dealing with the treatment of vitamins ever pronounce the word other than as vitamins—with the long "i".—

Yours, etc. J. H. Wrentmore, (Vitamins, Ltd.) Hammersmith.

vivarium and **vivary.** *Webster's* gives the latter as a mere variant of the former; *The O.E.D.* regards *vivarium* as the superior form. The learned plural is *vivaria*, the general plural is *vivariums* (cf. *aquariums*). A *vivarium* is 'a place

where living animals [L. *vivus*, alive,
living], especially fish, are maintained or
preserved for food'; also, 'a stretch of
water, specially adapted or prepared for
the keeping of living animals under
their normal conditions, either as objects
of interest or the purpose of scientific
study'. It is best to distinguish it from
aquarium (used in reference to fish and
aquatic plants). (*The O.E.D.*)

viz. See at VIDE.

vocation. See AVOCATION.

voluptious is a misspelling and a
mispronunciation of *voluptuous*; cf. PRE-
SUMPTIOUS for *presumptuous*.

voyage. See TRIP.

**VULGARISMS AND LOW LAN-
GUAGE.** *Vulgarisms* and *low language*
(*vulgar language*) are often taken to be
exactly synonymous. But it is well to
differentiate. *Low* (or *vulgar*) *language* is
of two kinds: (1) words foisted on one
social class by a lower class; words
brought from trade into drawing-room.
And (2)—closely connected and often
merging with (1)—those which have
been originated in and are used mostly
by the *proletariat* (a word employed
here, as a necessary classification).

With (1) we need not concern ourselves further: (2), however, is important. Examples of (2) are *dotty* and *dippy*
for 'mad', *lolly* (a sweet), *codger* and
geezer, *old woman* (wife), *to cop*, *to bash*,
to do or *diddle* (the latter being no longer
considered low). Of these, some are
slangy, others merely lowly and familiar.
The connection between the slangy and
the lowly words is so intimate that, the
moment they cease to be slangy or
lowly, they tend to—often do, eventually
—become admitted to the class of ordinary colloquialism. Yet the distinction
between such lownesses and slang is as
desirable as it is legitimate. Low words
are those which, used by the poorest
and meanest of the poorer classes, are
yet neither cant nor 'good' colloquialisms (admitted into Society): some are
slang, some are idiom, the idiom being
so lowly that often it is ignored. Excellent examples are found in 'deep'
Cockney (see the novels and stories of,
e.g., Pett Ridge, Barry Pain, and Neil
Lyons), where we see that some low
language is an almost inextricable tangle
of slang and idiom; much of it so racy
and picturesque and expressive that it
may put some Standard English into

the shade. Take such a passage as this
from *Arthur's*, by Neil Lyons:—

'"So it's corfee fur everybody", Jerry
the Twister had explained upon his
arrival at Arthur's stall. "Give me a
quid, 'e did, as a start-off an' then
blighted well *fought* me fur it, the
blighter. Where am I? ses 'e. Kennington
Road, ses I. Lead me to the Strand,
ses 'e. It was a lead, I give you *my* word.
'E was a 'ot un. Climb down nigh every
airey we passed, stole the milkcans, an'
tied 'em up to the knockers. Pinched a
rozzer in the leg, give 'im a visitin' card,
an' stole his whistle. Put 'is dooks up
to a fireman, tossed 'im fur 'is chopper,
an' kissed 'is wife. Run fur 'is very life
into Covent Garden Market (me after
'im), bought a cabbidge, took it into a
resterong where all the nobs was dinin',
sends fur the boss an' ses: Cully, cook
this for my dinner. Boss say: You be
damned! Collidge genelman takes off 'is
'at. I call upon you . . . to cook this
cabbidge. It is the law. I'll be shot if I
do, ses the boss. You'll be endorsed if
you don't, ses the toff. Give it 'ere, ses
the boss; I'll cook it. Cabbidge comes
up on a silver dish: charge two thick
'uns. Genelman pays the money, an'
breaks a glass: charge ten shillings.
Grand lark, ses the toff. I seen cheaper,
ses I. Put 'em up, ses the toff. Where's
yer money? ses I. 'Ere's a quid, 'e ses;
an' afore I can start on 'im up comes a
swaddy in a red cap. Give you a bob for
that 'at, ses the toff. 'Old 'ard, I tells
'im. That's a policeman, military policeman. Don't you 'ave no larks wiv' 'im.
Rats to you, 'e ses. I'll 'ave that to make
a wescoat of, ses 'e. An' 'e up an' snatches
it. *Then* the trouble began. 'Im an' the
swaddy an' two constables an' a cab-tout
was mixed up proper fur nigh on ten
minutes. Put 'em up grand, 'e did, the
toff, I mean. An' they squashed 'is 'at
an' tore 'is wescoat, an' the cab-tout
bit 'is 'and. An' 'e broke a window, an'
lost 'is watch, an' they frogs-marched 'im
off to Vine Street. 'Ere's a lark, ses 'e,
when they started".'

In such language as that, there are
many faults: but it is ruddy with good
health, and bursting with life. As G. K.
Chesterton said in 'A Defence of Slang'
(*The Defendant*, 1901), 'The lower classes
live in a state of war, a war of words.
Their readiness is the product of the
same fiery individualism as the readiness
of the old fighting oligarchs. Any cabman

has to be ready with his tongue, as any gentleman [had once—] to be ready with his sword.' For vividness at a still lower level of language than that of the extract from *Arthur's*, see 'Epsom's Attic Salt' in my *Slang To-Day and Yesterday* (pp. 241–7).

Now we come to *vulgarisms* in the sense in which I have for some years tried to fix it, to stabilize it, to get it accepted by the pundits and the philologists.

Vulgarisms are words that belong to idiomatic English or denote such objects or processes or functions or tendencies or acts as are not usually mentioned by the polite in company and are never, under *those* names, mentioned in respectable circles. Doctors may speak of them by their medical names, and anyone may refer to them—though not usually before members of the opposite sex—by their technical and generally Latinized or Grecized designations, and persons secretly libidinous or coprological delight to drag such words into their talk in terms of Freud and his followers. *Arse*, an excellent Old English word, is no longer obscene; it occurred in Frederic Manning's great war novel, *The Middle Parts of Fortune*, in 1930, and has, since ca. 1932, appeared in print with increasing frequency. Ca. 1850–1920, the usual 'Saxon' word was *backside*, but since the early 1920's—thanks largely to such 'choice spirits' as A. P. Herbert—*behind* has taken its place.* *Bum*, now decidedly vulgar, has become mainly a schoolboys' word; as used by Shakespeare, Dekker, Jonson, it was much more dignified. And, by the way, it is echoic—not a telescoping of *bottom*. *Bottom*, in very general use since ca. 1830, has always been considered more genteel than *backside*, which is mainly a man's word, whereas *bottom* is a woman's word; since *behind* acceded to the throne, *bottom* has taken to itself a moral rectitude even greater than *behind's* and an air of primness happily absent from *behind*. *Posterior* is politer still, but if we use the plural we connote

* [In American usage *behind* has for a long time been the usual nursery and homely word, much commoner than *backside* and somewhat effeminate as contrasted with the masculine *arse* (always pronounced, and popularly spelled, *ass*). But the present slang is *fanny*, which has had a spectacular career in smart publications and stage-shows; and in the home and nursery, whence it may have come (cf. *doll*), challenges *behind* itself.]

buttocks, which, so much more precise and 'Saxon', is not quite so acceptable to the prudish. Euphemism, here as in all such words, is often employed, sometimes in some such childish form as *sit-me-down*. *Chest* need not be a euphemism: as a synonym for the breast, it is merely—a synonym. But as equivalent to the female breasts, it is a silly, inexact euphemism. The 'Saxon' words for the male member (*membrum virile* is the technical term) and the female pudend (*pudendum muliebre*) are excellently idiomatic and belong to the aristocracy of the language, but, because they denote these intimate parts, they are—by a mental twist that we may leave to the psychologists—regarded as vulgar and, though they are certainly not slang, even as slangy. (A useful collective noun is *genitals*, usable of either sex.) The 'Saxon' words for 'to urinate' and 'to defecate' are idiomatic and perfect English, but association and prudery put them into quarantine; for the latter function, however, there exists the estimable *stool*.

These are vulgarisms. The *slangy* synonyms, which are numerous, belong to low language.

W

wage; wages. In the figurative sense, 'a reward or recompense', use *wage* ('The gods give thee fair wage and dues of death', Swinburne); this sense, however, is obsolescent. *Wages*, construed as a singular ('The wages of sin is death'), is an archaism. In ordinary English, *wages* (construed as plural) = 'the amount paid periodically, especially by the day or week or month, for the labour or service of a workman or servant' (as opposed to a *salary*, which is paid for non-manual or non-mechanical work); but the singular, *wage*, 'has sometimes a special convenience with reference to a particular instance or amount', as in '[Masters] commonly enter into a private bond or agreement, not to give more than a certain wage' and 'a day's wage for a day's work' (though 'a day's wages for a day's work' would also be correct). Note *a wage-slave*, *wage-labour*, and, in Political Economy, *wage-fund* (or *wages-fund*).

wait is the intransitive ('Will you wait, or not?'); **await** (or **wait for**) is the transitive form ('Will you wait for me?'; 'He awaits our arrival'). There is now an awkwardness in 'Wait what she's going to say' (detective novel, 1937); but this transitive use of *wait* is still acceptable in some locutions, such as, e.g., 'Keeping her thoughts from the ordeal that waited her' (Alec Waugh, *Going Their Own Ways*, 1938).—See also AWAIT.

waive, 'to relinquish, refrain, forbear', is occasionally confused with *wave*, to make a certain motion with the hands.

wake; waken. See AWAKE.

want (wish, desire). *Want* (v.i.) is 'to be lacking'; archaic except as *to be wanting* (to be lacking). *To want for nothing* is 'not to lack the necessaries or comforts of life'. As v.t., *want* = to *desire*, to *wish for* (something); also with infinitive as in 'He wants to do it' (he desires or wishes to do it); also 'to *want* a person to do something'; also it = 'to wish to see, or to speak to, a person', as in 'You're wanted at the door', which is familiar, not literary English.

-ward is a suffix both adjectival and adverbial, whereas **-wards** is adverbial only.

warn, 'to give timely notice of impending danger or misfortune' (*The O.E.D.*), with other slightly varying senses all implying danger or penalties, is often misused for *to give preliminary notice or information* without the implication of unpleasant consequences if the *warning* be neglected; *The New Statesman and Nation*, under the heading *This England*, once quoted from a letter in *The Eastern Daily Press*: 'I wonder if it is at all possible to be warned if there is likely to be a return of the aurora borealis at any time?'

warn of is incorrect for *warn against*, in 'Against unwarranted identification Korzybski delivers his major attack. He constantly warns of the *subject-predicate* form', Stuart Chase, *The Tyranny of Words*, 1938.

warrant, warranty; guarantee, guaranty. For the last two, see GUARANTEE. *Warranty* is noun only; *warrant*, both noun and verb. *Warranty*, in Law, is 'an act of warranting'; in literary use, it = 'substantiating evidence (or witness)', as in 'By what warranty A deed so hateful say you I have wrought?' (Whitelaw's *Sophocles*), and also 'a justifying reason or ground' (*for* an action or a belief), as in 'The Pope was claiming powers . . . for which there was no war-

ranty in the history of the Church'; for the second literary sense, *warrant* is a synonym ('Have we any warrant for a belief in immortality?'). *Warrant* bears the senses, 'sanction or authorization; an act of authorization; a token or evidence of authorization', as in 'An assembly that is without warrant from the sovereign is unlawful', 'He produced an old rusty sword and cried, "See, my lords, here is my warrant"' (Stubbs); concretely, *warrant* is 'a document conveying authority or security' (*search warrant*), 'a writ or order issued by some executive body', and there are special senses in stockbroking (*share warrant*) and commerce (a form of receipt). The verb to *warrant* has a technical sense in Law. As a general term, it = 'to guarantee as true, to make oneself answerable for (a statement), especially in *I warrant* or *I will warrant*; 'to attest the truth or authenticity of; to authenticate', as in 'That [his confession] was genuine could not be doubted: for it was warranted by the signatures of some of the most distinguished military men living' (Macaulay); 'to authorize (a person to do something), to authorize or sanction (a course of action)', as in 'Who has warranted this step?'; hence (of things), 'to furnish adequate grounds for (a course of action), to justify', as in 'It is impossible to say whether this accusation was warranted by facts' (Washington Irving) and 'We are not warranted in assuming that he has been telling lies'; 'to guarantee (goods, articles) to be of the quality, quantity, make, etc., specified', as in *warranted free from adulteration* or *colours warranted fast*. (*The O.E.D.*)

was or **were** in conditionals. If there is no doubt, use *was*, as in 'He was instructed to determine whether this *was*'—not *were*—'practicable'. When there is doubt, use *were*, as in 'If it *were*'—not *was*—'justifiable, the headmaster would take the necessary steps'. Based on Harold Herd. See also SUBJUNCTIVE. [[Some American grammarians are now inclined to accept for informal usage *was* in place of *were* in conditions of 'doubt'. See Perrin, pp. 588–591.]]

was (or **were,** or **is** or **are,** or **shall** or **will be**) *to* + infinitive + preposition. See IS TO + infinitive + preposition.

washwoman—wrongly stated by Weseen to be 'not a recognized word'—is American (but not the best American) for *washerwoman*, as *washman* is similar American for *washerman*; *washerlady*, *washlady* are absurdities, illustrative of euphemism-cum-genteelism raised to the *n*th.

watch out for *watch* is not only colloquial but unnecessary, as in 'I knew that something was going to happen. . . . So I watched out, thinking that perhaps I might be able to prevent the worst' (a detective novel, 1937).

'way (adv.) is short for (*far*) *away*, in such phrases as 'sold, way below cost', 'way down South', 'to go way off' (afar), 'way down East', 'from way back' (from a rural, or a remote, district): all are Americanisms (dialectal and colloquial).

'way for *entirely* is low colloquialism, as in 'He wrote and wrote, 'way through the night'.

way of being, by. 'I am by way of being an artist' is permissible, except in literary English, when the speaker wishes to make his statement appear more modest; but 'He is by way of being an artist' is a senseless circumlocution when nothing more is meant than 'He is an artist'; as a piece of facetiousness it is bearable—but only just.

ways, in *come* (or *go*) *one's ways*, is now either dialectal or solecistic. So, too, for *a little ways* and *a good* (or *great* or *long*) *ways*—a short or a long distance.

we aren't and **we're not.** (Reversed: only *aren't we* is possible as a shortening of *are not we?*) Weseen says that *'we're not* is preferred'; but let us take *we're not ready* and *we aren't ready*. If the emphasis is on *ready*, at least as many people would say, 'We aren't *ready*, you know', as would say 'We're not *ready*, you know'; if on *not*, 'We're *not* ready' is preferable; if on *we*, '*We* aren't ready' is probably as common as '*We're* not ready'.

weave. See at WOVE.

we both and **we each; us both** and **us each.**—See GENITIVE, VAGARIES OF THE, the last paragraph but one.

we'd is generally understood to = *we would*; not *we should*, though there's no *a priori* reason why it shouldn't = *we should*, and there is some authority for saying it does. *We'd* is also used for *we had*: this is regarded as being even more colloquial than *we'd* = *we would*. Some careful writers put *we'd* for *we had*, *we'ld* for *we would*, if they wish to use the contractions.

we'll is allowed by *Webster's* to represent either *we shall* or *we will*.

wed for *marry* is overdone by journalists, especially in headlines, where the short word is *so* convenient. Mr Frank Whitaker has stigmatized it as a 'rubber-stamp word' (see AMAZING).—*Wed* is in ordinary English inflected thus: *wed*—*wedded* (*wed* being dialectal)—*wedded* (*wed* being dialectal or poetical).

wedding for *marriage* is to be used with care. The following example is from an answer in a Scottish Leaving Certificate examination paper, March, 1938:— 'Miss Margaret X. has much pleasure in accepting Miss Mary Smith's invitation to her wedding to Mr John Brown, in the Marlborough House, on Tuesday, the 22nd March at 2 p.m.' The invitation was presumably sent by Mary Smith's parents *for the wedding of their daughter and John Brown*, and would have been correctly accepted in those terms, but, as Margaret expressed her reply, *marriage* would have been the right word to use. Properly employed, *wedding* = 'the performance of the wedding-rite' or 'the ceremony of a marriage, with its attendant festivities', as in 'weddings, christenings, burials', 'Are you to be at the Milton wedding next week?', 'I am told the wedding went off very well'.

week-end. A *week-end* (or *short week-end*) is from Saturday noon until Monday morning; a *long week-end* is from Friday evening until Monday morning. If you're invited to week-end at someone's house, arrive in time for tea (or in good time for dinner) on Saturday: if you think that the invitation was for a long week-end, make quite sure.

weigh is incorrect for *way* in *underweigh*, 'in preparation'. 'Getting under weigh', W. H. G. Kingston, *Lusitanian Sketches*, 1845; Louis Bromfield, *It Had to Happen*, 1936, 'Now that he had a project under weigh his spirits rose'. (The metaphor is nautical.)

well nigh. See NIGH.

Welsh Rabbit. See RABBIT, WELSH.

we're not. See WE AREN'T . . .

were to + infinitive + preposition. See 'IS TO + infinitive + preposition'.

westerly and **western.** Cf. the remarks at 'EASTERLY and EASTERN'.

westernly, good English in the 17th Century, is in the 20th regarded as a solecism for *westerly* and *western*.

Westralians is not a blend that West

Australians like. And, by the way, it is *West* (not *Western*) *Australia*.

westward; westwards. As adjective, only *westward* ('a westward view', 'a westward journey'). As adverb, either is correct, but *westward*, besides being much the older, is preferred by current usage.

wet—wet or **wetted—wet** or **wetted.** With *have*, *wet* is the commoner participle; with *be*, *wetted* is as common as and less ambiguous than *wet*. Usage, I surmise, will finally consecrate *wetted* at the expense of *wet* in both preterite and past participle.

wharfs; wharves. Both are correct; *wharves* is the more euphonious, and the usual American form; in Great Britain, *wharfs* has become commoner. (*Webster's*.)

what, as subject, takes the singular verb, whether the complementary noun be singular or plural: thus, 'What I like is sprouts', not 'What I like are sprouts'; 'What the public wants are crime stories' (Anthony Weymouth, *Tempt Me Not*, 1937) should be 'What the public wants is crime stories'; for 'It was indeed doubtful if the old man had really been interested in books—what he collected were ideas, legends, beliefs' (John Gloag, *Sacred Edifice*, 1937), read '. . . . what he collected was . . .'.

what for *those which* is incorrect. '"The bullets . . . known to have been fired by young Mr Moffatt . . . are the same as what killed this Bennett bloke"', E. R. Punshon, *The Dusky Hour*, 1937.

what for *which*. Until the present century, only purists objected to *what* in, e.g., 'He told the truth and, *what* is more, people recognized his statement to be true'. Nowadays, it is pretty generally conceded that the sentence should read, 'He told the truth and—which is more—' [or commas] 'people recognized his statement to be true'. *What*, here, could be only a compound relative = *that which*, but 'He told the truth and, *that which* is more, people recognized his statement to be true' can be defended only with difficulty and dialectic. The correct form is, 'He told the truth and, which'—i.e., which fact—'is more', i.e., more important, 'people recognized his statement to be true'. A principal clause and a dependent relative clause constitute a hypotactic construction: but such a construction can always be changed into a paratactic one (two principal clauses).

Thus, 'And, which is more, people recognized the statement to be true; this is more important' (than that he told the truth).

A good example of the correct use occurs in Cameron McCabe's most unusual detective yarn, *The Face on the Cutting-Room Floor*, 1937,—a book that, despite my frequent citations of error, is fascinatingly written:—'Yet, these very few blunders excepted, McCabe understood his opponents amazingly well, and—which is more important—made no attempt to deceive himself about their superiority in many stages of the "fight".'

what, as. 'But that I did see, sir, as plain as what I see you now', E. C. Bentley and H. Warner Allen in *Trent's Own Case*, 1936. The speech of an uneducated person, who should have said '*as plainly as I see you now*'.

what a many for *how many* or *what a number of* is a slovenly colloquialism. [[Unknown in American usage.]]

what . . . for?, as an inverted form of *for what*, is sometimes ambiguous, as in the question (overheard), of mother to child: 'What did he change his bright new penny for?', which might mean '*Why* did he change it?'

what . . . is when. A not unusual form of grammatical clumsiness, as in 'What is really shocking is when an artist comes to a serious subject such as this', Anthony Blunt in *The Spectator*, 6th May, 1938. This sentence might be better expressed in other ways, e.g., 'It is really shocking to see an artist come, etc.', or 'What is shocking is to find that an artist can come, etc.'

what use is incorrect in 'What use is it to learn Greek?' 'Of what use is it . . .?' would be correct. One may not say 'Is there any use in learning Greek', but 'Is it of any use to learn Greek?'

when can be used for *in which*, after, e.g., *year*, as in 'The year when it happened' (for 'the year in which it happened'); but care must be exercised in extending this usage. Thus *in which* seems to be, and indeed is, preferable to *when* in the following: 'Cases sometimes occur when there is marked disagreement between the cancellation date on the envelope and the date on the sheet it contains' (Nigel Morland, *The Conquest of Crime*, 1937).

when, misused for *whereas*. 'When the old Rhetoric treated ambiguity as a fault in language . . ., the new Rhetoric sees it as an inevitable consequence of the powers of language', I. A. Richards, *The Philosophy of Rhetoric*, 1936.—Was this particular error the result of a conscientious desire to avoid *while = whereas*, and of a too hasty solution of that stylistic crux?

when . . . ever is often misused for *whenever.* '"And the next time, Mac, don't tell me that if I'd just buckle down to the job a little sooner I could finish it with time to spare." "When did I ever say that?" I demanded with some heat', Isabel Briggs Myers, *Give Me Death*, 1935.

whence, from. Though found in the work of good writers, the 'from' is redundant. Swinburne, *Studies in Prose and Poetry*, 'The quarter from whence the following lucubration is addressed': this would be more correctly written 'The quarter whence . . .' or 'The quarter from which'. *Whence* and *whither*, with *hence* and *hither*, are now only literary, but perfectly admissible in speech. *Whence* is correctly used in the following: Stevenson, *Kidnapped*, 'There was no question put of whence I came or whither I was going', and in these stanzas from Fitzgerald's *Omar*:

Into this universe, and why not knowing,
Nor whence, like water willy-nilly flowing:
And out of it, as wind along the waste
I know not whither, willy-nilly blowing'.

What, without asking, hither hurried
  whence?
And, without asking, whither hurried
  hence!
Another and another cup to drown
The memory of this impertinence!

Whence is clumsily used in 'Here Machiavelli's earth returned to whence it rose' (Byron), where *to whence = to that place whence*. W.B.

where for *that* is incorrect, as in 'I see where they had a heat wave'—i.e., 'I saw, in the newspaper, that they had a heat wave'.

where for *whither* is now usual, as in 'Where are you going?' ('Where are you going to?' is redundant.)

where; wherein; at (or **in**) **which:** omitted. Although syntactically and structurally on a par with the omission of the relative pronouns, *that, which, who*, the omission of *where* (*in*) and *at* (or *in*) *which* is not the same analytically or

verbally, for *where = at* (or *in*) *which*, and *wherein = in which; where* and *wherein =* combinations of preposition + pronoun, whereas *that, which, who* are simples or singles (pronoun only). The result of omitting *where, wherein, at* (or *in*) *which*, is subjectively one of momentary ambiguity, objectively one of abruptness, as in 'Neil was for storming Erchany like young Lochinvar and carrying her to some place they could be married in secret' (Michael Innes, *Lament for a Maker*, 1938), where one is, for a split second, apt or tempted to think that *in order that* should precede 'they could be married in secret'.

where from and **from where.** *Where* can = *to where* (or *where to*), as in 'Where are you going?', and thus it takes the place of *whither*; but *where* does not take the place of *whence*, for which either *where from* or preferably *from where* must be used. 'I took that passage from Thucydides.' 'From *where*?'' 'Where did that man come from' is more idiomatic though less neat than 'From where did that man come?'

whether, of. 'The whole question of whether we like it is ignored' is redundant for 'the . . . question whether' or 'the question of our liking it'.

whether or no; whether or not. *Whether or no*, as in 'Whether or no it is possible, I cannot say', is obsolescent for '*Whether or not* it is possible, I cannot say'. But *whether or not* is tautological for *whether*, except where the doubt is to be emphasized.

which and **that; who** and **that.** Of these relative pronouns, *which* refers to things only; *that* to things and persons; *who* to persons only. But *that* is not a syntactical synonym of either *which* or *who*. The discrimination between *which* and *that* and between *who* and *that* is one of the marks of a stylist.

With the caution that 'the tendency to appropriate *who* and *which* to persons and things respectively often outweighs other considerations; thus, "People *who* live in glass houses" is preferred to "people *that*"; this is particularly the case with *those, they*, and other pronouns of common gender. "Those *who* are in favour of this motion", is more usual than "those *that*" [but this may be partly because *they who* and *those who* are *formulas*]', it is to be noted that relative clauses are used for two purposes:—

(1) The more sharply to define or to

limit the antecedent, which without the ensuing relative clause would either make no sense or convey a sense different from the intended one. 'This is the book that G. K. Chesterton wrote'; 'Uneasy lies the head that wears a crown'. Here, the relative clause is ushered—in by *that*, except after a preposition ('He is a man for whom'—not 'for that'—'I have the deepest regard') or where *whose* is inevitable ('He is a man whose opinion means much to me'). No comma (or other stop) is to be used to separate this relative clause from its antecedent, a rule applying also when *who* and *which* are used with a preposition or when *whose* is obligatory, as in 'The man whose son is alive is not heirless'. (In 'His recovery was hastened by . . . games on the enchanted heath, near which he lived', *Harrap Book News*, November, 1938, the comma after 'heath' is necessary, for there was only one enchanted heath, whereas 'His recovery was hastened by games on an enchanted heath near which he lived' would restrict the connotation of 'heath' and imply that there was more than one such heath.) The comma-less form is restrictive; the comma'd form is non-restrictive, i.e., it falls into the next class.—The relative may be omitted, as in 'This is the book G. K. Chesterton wrote'. The *that* relative occurs especially where the antecedent is shown to belong to a class, a group, a kind, a species, etc., as in 'All that live must die', 'The greatest dramatist (that) we've ever had', 'Adrian the Fourth is the only Englishman that has been Pope'.

(2) The more fully to give information about something (the antecedent) that is already defined sufficiently to make sense; this class of relative has various names, such as 'non-restrictive', 'parenthetical', 'explicative'. Compare 'His brother is very rich' with 'His brother, who owns a brewery, is very rich'; 'This book is excellent' with 'This book, which was written by Chesterton, is excellent'. Here, the relative clause must be ushered-in by *who* (*whom*) or *which*; a comma separates—or should separate—the relative clause from the antecedent; and the relative pronoun cannot be omitted. Here, too, the relative clause can be supplanted by a conjunction + a noun or a pronoun (and, of course, the rest of a sentence), thus: 'This book is excellent, and Chesterton wrote it'.

A useful rule—at least, *I* have found

it useful—is this of mine: the restrictive or defining or limitative or necessary relative clause (relatives of Class 1) forms an integral, irremovable part of the sentence and cannot be put within parentheses, whereas the non-restrictive relatives (Class 2) can always be put within parentheses and their omission would not render the sentence senseless.

In speech, the use of *which* for *that* is less reprehensible, for intonation will convey the sense. 'But in the written language the need of discrimination between the two classes described is often felt, and the non-observance of the distinction is liable to lead to misunderstanding. Example: "All the members of the Council, who were also members of the Education Board, were to assemble in the Board-room". This would naturally imply that all members of the Council were members of the Education Board. "That", instead of "who", would clearly express the meaning intended, which is that "those who are members of the Education Board as well as of the Council were to assemble". . . . Observe the significance of the distinction in the following: "In two of the instances, *which* have come under my notice, the system has worked well"; "In two of the instances *that* have come under my notice, the system has worked well". The first means: "Two of the instances have come under my notice; in [all of] these instances the system has worked well". The second means: "Instances have come under my notice; in two of them the system has worked well".' (Quoted from Onions, *An Advanced English Syntax*: on which the preceding part of the article has, in the main, been based. For a more leisurely—yet very useful—examination of the *that* and the *who* (and *which*) modes, see Jespersen, *Notes on Relative Clauses*, 1926.)

But I wish to add several points that have occurred to me:—

A. *Which* can be used for *that* or *who* in such a sentence as 'He's not the man *which* he was', where '*who* he was' would be absurd and ambiguous. But the wise man evades the difficulty: he says, 'He's not the man *that* he was'. By so doing he observes also the distinction between *that* on the one hand and *which* or *who* on the other.

B. (a) 'It isn't only homicidal maniacs that are dangerous.'

(a^1) 'It isn't only homicida₁ maniacs who are dangerous.'

(b) 'It is not only pictures that are beautiful.'

(b^1) 'It is not only pictures which are beautiful.'

In each pair (a and a^1; b and b^1), are both forms correct? If not, which?

(Note that in a and a^1, the answer need not take into account the fact that 'all homicidal maniacs are dangerous', and that in b and b^1, the answer need not take into account the fact that 'not all pictures are beautiful': the following explanation will show why.)

Of a and a^1, the second is correct: quite apart from the fact that a ('It isn't only homicidal maniacs that are dangerous') implies that some are harmless, its sense is obviously incomplete; b, conforming to good sense, is complete, for it makes the self-contained statement, 'Homicidal maniacs are dangerous, but they are not the only dangerous persons'. The good writer would say, 'Not only homicidal maniacs are dangerous', and thus avoid both verbosity and ambiguity.

Similarly, of b and b^1, the second is correct; b is obviously incomplete, for nothing has been said about 'pictures that are beautiful' (= 'those pictures which are beautiful'), whereas b^1 makes a complete statement, 'Pictures [as a class] are beautiful, but they are not the only beautiful things'.

Thus we are led to:—

C. (a) 'It is not only pictures that are beautiful that are valuable.'

(b) 'It is not only pictures, which are beautiful, that are valuable.'

(c) 'It is not only pictures that are beautiful which are valuable.'

(d) 'It is not only pictures, which are beautiful, which are valuable.'

Are all of these sentences correct? If not, which? Note that, in accordance with the general classification into (1), Restrictive, and (2), Non-Restrictive, a classification established in the third and fourth paragraphs of this article, there are two obviously incorrect variations: b cannot take the form, 'It is not only pictures which are beautiful that are valuable' (i.e., the commas cannot logically be omitted); and d cannot take the form, 'It is not only pictures which are beautiful which are valuable' (i.e., the commas cannot here be omitted, any more than they could in the other example).

Let us be patient: let us examine C, a—C, b—C, c—C, d in turn.

C, a: 'It is not only pictures that are beautiful that are valuable': is clearly incorrect. The correct form is C, c: 'It is not only pictures that are beautiful which are valuable'. C, c = 'Pictures that are beautiful [i.e., those pictures which are beautiful] are valuable; but ugly pictures may be valuable'.

C, b: 'It is not only pictures, which are beautiful, that are valuable': is incorrect for the same reason that C, a is incorrect; 'that are beautiful' does not complete the sentence, and it does not make sense.

'Pictures, which are beautiful' is not equivalent to 'pictures that are beautiful': 'pictures, which are beautiful' = 'pictures, which are usually (or as a class) beautiful.' Therefore C, d: 'It is not only pictures, which are beautiful, which are valuable': is correct for the same grammatical reason that C, c: 'It is not only pictures that are beautiful which are valuable'; is correct. Both C, c and C, d form complete sentences and make sense. But C, d is cacophonous; a good writer would say, 'Pictures, usually beautiful, are valuable, but so are other things', or turn the sentence in some other way, e.g. 'It is not only pictures (beautiful though many of them are) which are valuable'.

which and **who**. *Which* and *who* lead frequently to lapses from good grammar (and good sense); Byron can write (*Childe Harold*, III, 28), 'The thunderclouds close o'er it, which when rent The earth is covered thick with other clay, Which her own clay shall cover'.

Gilbert White commits the error of writing *and which*, where either 'and' or 'which' is unnecessary,—'This is their due, and which ought to be rendered to them by all people' (*The O.E.D.*).

A more illiterate error is *which he*, as in Dorothy Sayers, *Unnatural Death*, 1927: 'Ironsides . . . a clerk on the Southern, which he always used to say joking like, "Slow but safe, like the Southern—that's me"'; and 'I believe the gentleman acted with the best intentions, 'avin' now seen 'im, which at first I thought he was a wrong 'un'.

which for *which fact* is clumsy and sometimes ambiguous, as in 'That rifle cost me fifteen pounds, which has left me short of cash'.

which, like. See LIKE WHICH.

which . . . were for *which . . . was* may, to the sceptical, appear to be an error unlikely to be committed by the educated person. It is an error more frequent than the sceptical realize. For instance, in so good a writer as Wilfranc Hubbard, there occurs this sentence, 'You ask me which of the two lives were least'—better, 'the less'—'worthy of record' (*Orvieto Dust*, 1925).

while and **whilst.** See at 'AMONG and AMONGST'.

while, whilst for *whereas* or *and* (or even *but*). A. P. Herbert gives a comic example of this: 'The Curate read the First Lesson while the Rector read the Second'. And here is a less amusing but no less instructive example from Stuart Chase, *The Tyranny of Words*, 1938:— 'The Greeks had no algebra, no graphical methods, while the geometry of Euclid which they did possess dealt only in spaces and made no allowance for times.'

while for *although* is a perverted use of the correct sense of *while*, which properly means 'at the same time as', 'during the same time that . . .'.

whiskers and **moustache.** *The O.E.D.* settles the frequent confusion, thus:— '[*whiskers.*] The hair that grows on an adult man's face; formerly commonly applied to that on the upper lip, now called *moustache*, and sometimes to (or including) that on the chin (*beard*); now restricted to that on the cheeks or sides of the face.'

who and **that** (relative pronouns). See 'WHICH and THAT'.

who and **whom.** Such phrases as 'the man who I saw there' are very common in speech, for people appear to think that *whom* sounds pedantic. *Whom* for *who*, however, is the more frequent error in literary use. Thus Sir Wm. Gell refers to a character 'whom it is possible may be at some future time introduced to my reader'; and *The Daily Mail*, Dec. 28, 1933, has 'Mr Cornelius told a *Daily Mail* reporter that at 2 a.m. yesterday he was aroused by calls for help from a woman, whom he learned later was Lady . . .', *he learned later*, a parenthetical phrase, causing all the trouble; and Mrs Beatrice Kean Seymour, in *The Happier Eden*, 1937, has '"We've met several people here, who remember him." She had not said whom they were.' Such a sentence as 'Men say who I am' becomes, as an interrogative, 'Who do men say

that I am?', not as in the Authorized Version of the Bible, 'Whom do men say that I am?' (cited by Onions).

who else's. See at WHOSE ELSE'S.

whoever for *who . . . ever*; and vice versa. In 'Whoever saw him do such a thing? I've known him for twenty years and have never known him to do it', *whoever* should obviously be 'Who ever (saw . . .)'. But 'Who ever says such a thing is a liar' is incorrect for 'Whoever says such a thing is a liar'.

whole (adj.). See COMPARATIVES, FALSE, also COMPLETE . . .

whole (adj.) and **the whole** (n.) are sometimes confused, as in 'The whole proceedings are in this book' for 'The whole of the proceedings *is* . . .' or, better, 'All the proceedings are'.—And see following entry.

whole, the. 'The whole three of them' is incorrect for 'all three' or 'all the three'. 'The whole lot', however, is correct, whereas the common 'all the lot' is illiterate, for *lot* is singular, though meaning a group or number of things. Nesfield quotes *The Daily Telegraph*, February, 1900, 'This was the cost for removing snow from the whole of the thoroughfares of the metropolis' ('all the streets of London'). The same error appears in 'The whole three were now grappling on the carpet', David Haggart (who was hanged in 1821), *Life*, 1821.

whom. See 'WHO and WHOM'.

whomever, whomsoever; whosever, whosesoever. These are the correct accusatives and genitives respectively of *whoever* and *whosoever*. But *whosever* (not *whoseever*) is rare and *whosoever* is archaic; for either of these genitives, modern usage prefers *whatever person's*. *Whomever* and *whomsoever* are subject to the same confusion with *whoever* and *whosoever* as *whom* is with *who*; e.g., 'They shall not be impeded by whomsoever it may be' (Ruskin).

Whoso, whomso: archaic for *whoever, whomever.*

whose for *which*. Strictly, *whose* refers to persons only. But *whose* for *of which* is permissible when employed to avoid the awkwardness of *the* [noun] *of which*, as in 'A large number of brass discs, *whose* workmanship [= the workmanship of which] shows that they belong to the later period of Celtic art, have been found in Ireland'. (Onions.)

whose, and, misused for *whose*. 'She who swore away the life of Kidden **the**

porter, and whose (Kidden's) blood still cries aloud for vengeance', Joseph Cox, *A faithful Narrative of Thief-Takers*, 1756.

whose else's. Agatha Christie, *The Mysterious Affair at Styles*, 1920, '"You are sure it was Mr Inglethorpe's voice you heard?" "Oh, yes, sir, whose else's could it be?"' The correct form for familiar Standard English is *who else's*; less common but permissible when the noun does not follow is *whose else*. See ELSE'S.

why for. See FOR WHY.

wideness for *width* is unidiomatic. Cf. 'BREADTH; BROADNESS'.

wiggle and **wriggle.** To *wiggle* is now colloquial when it is not dialectal, whether it is v.i. (to waggle; to wriggle) or v.t. (to wriggle something about, to cause something to wriggle): so avoid it in good writing or in formal speech.

will and **shall.** See 'SHALL and WILL'.

will be to + infinitive + preposition. See IS TO + infinitive + preposition.

windward and **windwards.** The latter is obsolescent; it occurs only in *to windwards*, for which *to windward* is much commoner. As an adjective, *windward* = 'moving against the wind', as in 'Windward Great Circle Sailing' (J. Greenwood, *The Sailor's Sea Book*, ca. 1850); 'weatherly', as in 'An excellent windward boat'; and 'facing the wind', as in *the Windward Islands* (opposed to *the Leeward Islands*). As an adverb, *windward* = 'to windward, facing the wind', as in 'Tacking about, and so getting to Windward of them, they . . . gain'd a great advantage' (James Tyrrell, *The General History of England*, IV, 1700). (*The O.E.D.*)

wing—winged—winged. *Winged*, as preterite and as true past participle, is pronounced as one syllable. The participial adjective is also pronounced as one syllable when it = 'shot on the wing; disabled in the air', as in 'A winged bird cannot fly far', 'A winged aeroplane must soon descend'; but if it = 'having wings, represented with wings' or, fig., 'capable of or performing some movement or action figured as flight; flying or passing swiftly', it is two-syllabled, as in 'winged thunder' (Dryden), 'winged words'. (*The O.E.D.*)

with. Except where ambiguity would result, I urge that *with* should be used of the instrument and *by* restricted to the

agent. 'He was killed with [not by] a spanner.'

with + plural verb. 'Michael, accompanied by his wife, is at the door' is clearly correct; so is 'Michael, with his wife, is at the door' where the stress is on Michael, but if Michael and his wife are equally important (or unimportant), then 'Michael, with his wife, are at the door' (in which case, it is better to omit the comma after 'Michael'). See Onions, *An Advanced English Syntax*, §22b.

withal is an archaism, except insofar as it has been preserved as an elegancy.

within. See 'IN for *within*'. N.B.: this is not an error but an infelicity. When it is so easy to avoid confusion, why not avoid it? A good example occurs in the legend to be seen (in 1937–38, at least) on the vans of a certain London firm: 'Goods delivered in 36 hours'.

without for *unless* is now considered illiterate, as in 'Without something unexpected happens, the murderer will be hanged to-morrow'.

without doubt should be used as an adjective only with sedulous care. In e.g., 'It is not only McCabe's objectivity—though that is without doubt—but also a natural equality between the two opponents' (C. McCabe, *The Face on the Cutting-Room Floor*, 1937), where 'indubitable' or, better still, 'indisputable' would have been preferable.

witness, debased to = 'to *see*'. To *witness* is not merely to *see*, but to *testify*, or by being a spectator to be in a position to testify.

womanish; womanly; womanlike; female; feminine. *Womanish* is now mainly pejorative; *womanly*, generally favourable. *Womanish* = 'resembling a woman in her weakness' (physical disabilities, mental disabilities), as in 'Her spitefulness is, in short, womanish'; but if applied to a (young or youngish) girl, it = 'like a grown woman (in figure or in her ways)'. *Womanish* is often (contrast *mannish*, *q.v.* at MANLIKE) applied to effeminate or effeminate-looking men, as in 'that womanish exquisite!' *Womanly* = 'of, belonging to, characteristic of a woman' (neutrally or favourably), whether of women or their qualities or their actions, as in 'Her womanly kindness and gentleness redeemed her from insipidity'; also 'having the character of —befitting—a woman as opposed to a girl', as in 'A womanly sort of bonnet'. *Womanlike* is the feminine of *manlike*.

Female is merely the adjective corresponding to *male* (*q.v.* at MANLIKE); *feminine* corresponds to *masculine* (see at MANLIKE). (*The O.E.D.*)

wonder for *wonderful* ('a wonder child') is an example of journalistic 'rubberstamp words' (*q.v.* at AMAZING).

wonderful—more wonderful—most wonderful. The forms *wonderfuller* and *wonderfullest* are not recommended.

wondrous (adj.) is literary; as adv., it is archaic for *wondrously* (itself literary).

wooded, wooden, woody. *Wooded* = 'covered with growing trees; abounding in woods and forests', usually with adverb, as in 'The neighbourhood was richly wooded'. *Wooden* = 'made of wood; consisting of wood' ('A waggon with wooden wheels'); hence, 'produced by means of wood; relating to wood; hard or stiff like wood', as in 'a wooden (now also *wood*) fire', 'The fingers have . . . become . . . pale and wooden'; figuratively, 'lifeless, spiritless, dull and inert, unintelligent, insensitive', as in 'A dryasdust antiquary of the most wooden type', 'He has a wooden head', 'a wooden notion'. *Woody* is a synonym of *wooded* (but without adverb), as in 'The rose-hung lanes of woody Kent' (Morris). Its other senses are 'of a wood, situated in a wood' ('a woody nook', 'They left the woody path for a field'); 'of the nature of, or consisting of, wood; ligneous' (as in 'the woody knobs of rosebush roots', 'Fibrous and woody elements . . . exist . . . in all vegetable foods'); (of plants) 'having stem and branches of wood'; 'resembling wood; having the consistence and/or the texture of wood' ('a large, woody apple'); 'characteristic of wood; having some quality (e.g., smell) of wood', as in 'clean woody odours'; 'having a dull sound, like that of wood when struck', as in 'A little cottage piano, woody and dull of tone'. (*The O.E.D.*)

WOOLLINESS.

. . . Many people, either from ignorance or from carelessness, are far from being precise in thought and expression—they Mean not, but blunder round about a meaning. . . . Jespersen, *Language*, 1922, p. 274.

Woolly. Lacking in definiteness or incisiveness; 'muzzy'; (of the mind [style], etc.) confused and hazy. (*The O.E.D.*)

Woolliness is that fault of style which consists in writing around a subject instead of on it; of making approximations serve as exactitudes; of resting content with intention as opposed to performance; of forgetting that whereas a haziness may mean something to the perpetrator, it usually means nothing (or an ambiguity) to the reader or the listener. The ideal at which a writer should aim,—admittedly it is impossible of attainment,—is that he write so clearly, so precisely, so unambiguously, that his words can bear only one meaning to all averagely intelligent readers that possess an average knowledge of the language used.

But to generalize further on woolliness would serve no useful purpose. I shall particularize by giving, first, a number of brief examples and, in most cases, commenting on them, and, secondly, some longer passages and leaving them to the reader's angry bewilderment.

'Not a ship, nor a gun, nor a man, were on the ground to prevent their landing' (Gladstone, *Gleanings*, 1870). Why *ground*? (If Gladstone means 'at this part of the coast', why does he not write 'at this place'?) Does *gun* mean literally 'a cannon', or does it mean *gun-crew* or, rather, a *gun and its crew*?

'These men would have preferred Halliday [the headmaster elect] to get smaller results by conventional methods than Sam's [the present headmaster's] triumphs by different ones' (R. Philmore, *Short List*, 1938). A confusion of past with future, and of two constructions. Perhaps recast in some such form as this:—'These men would have preferred Halliday's minor success, attained by conventional methods, to Sam's major success, attained by unconventional ones.'

'Living in an age of transition, the outlines of the people round us grow insubstantial, are modified, mentally and physically, day by day' (Osbert Sitwell, *Those Were the Days*, 1938). This might have been put at AGREEMENT, FALSE.

'After dinner, they drove on to London, and found Mr Pegley's address was on the top floor of a new and very smart block of flats' (E. R. Punshon, *The Dusky Hour*, 1937). Better, '. . . found that Mr Pegley lived on the top floor . . .'

'He supposed some information about them might probably be obtained from Norris' (*ibid.*). To begin with, 'He supposed that' would remove an unnecessary ambiguity; 'might probably' arises from a confusion between 'might well' and 'would probably'.

'As essayists, the writings of Addison and of Steele are familiar to all readers of eighteenth-century literature' (John Dennis, *The Age of Pope*, 1894). And all he needed to say was 'As essayists, Addison and Steele are familiar . . .'; the intrusive 'the writings of . . . of' has produced a ludicrous example of false agreement and put the reader out of his stride.

'The afternoon gatherings were fewer than the evening ones, and their composition, their man-power, differed considerably. Less definite and of one tint, they included more of compromise with the world' (Osbert Sitwell, *Those Were the Days*, 1938). Both of these sentences are so ambiguous, so obscure, as to require an exquisite excogitation.

'It will be for him to decide if we proceed further' (Vernon Loder, *The Button in the Plate*, 1938). The author—as the context shows—intends 'whether'; 'if' yields a very different sense.

'His point is, I think, evidently mistaken' (I. A. Richards, *The Philosophy of Rhetoric*, 1936). Read, either 'His point is, I think, mistaken' or 'His point is evidently mistaken'. If the error is *evident*, why 'I think'? And if it isn't, why 'evidently'?

'In most prose, and more than we ordinarily suppose, the opening words have to wait for those that follow to settle what they shall mean' (*ibid.*). It is not the opening words which have to wait, but we who read them: *we* must wait for the ensuing words before *we* can settle what the opening words mean in the sentence.

'"Billy the Dip's" job was, as usual, outside man; which most important duty he would perform in the company of another ferrety-eyed person not present, who owned to the name of Abe Snitzler, and in whom was combined the cunning of the rat with the swiftness of the eel. These two would station themselves, the first on the corner of Regent and Maddox Street, the second in the alley at the rear of the premises by which' route the loot and get-away would have to be made' (John G. Brandon, *The Regent Street Raid*, ca. 1938). Concerning this paragraph, a much longer paragraph might be written.

'They say you can't kill a newspaper man or even one who wants to become one' (Russell Birdwell, *I Ring Doorbells*, 1939). The first 'one' is the impersonal 'one' (a person); the second = 'a newspaper man'. Hence, confusion.

'Like many genteel people, their own education was nothing to brag about' (a usually precise, always worth-while author). Read, 'Like that of many other genteel people, their own education was nothing to brag about'.

'Money won at billiards cannot be recovered' (Hay & Son Ltd's *Diary*, 1939). Not *won* but *lost* is the right word.

'It was more as if he lived in the shadow of something that no man could remain quite sane while contemplating' (Michael Innes, *Lament for a Maker*, 1938). The sentence has not been worked out; or rather, the thought has not been worked out. Perhaps '. . . something that no man, while contemplating, could remain quite sane against (*or* in the face of)' or, more elegantly, '. . . something, in the face of which, no man could remain quite sane while he contemplated it' or '. . . something that, if he contemplated it, left no man quite sane while he contemplated it'. The original sentence is too condensed and too pregnant with meaning to be either clear or comfortable.

'A man may look over the countryside below him and see it in detail, not too far away to be an indistinguishable blur, sufficiently far to give the sense of breadth and effect' (Robert Eton, *The Journey*, 1938), where 'not so far away as to be indistinguishable' is needed.

'Put very simply, a causal law may be taken as saying that, under certain conditions, of two events if one happens the other does' (I. A. Richards, *op. cit.*). Should this not read, 'Put very simply, a causal law may be taken as saying that if, under certain conditions, one of two events happens, the other happens also'?

'These few examples . . . show how easy it is to write sentences which are literally nonsensical without seeing that they are nonsensical' (A. J. Ayer, *Language, Truth and Logic*, 1936). It is.

'P. Lebrun . . . may have owed something to Shakespeare, Pichot . . . perhaps drew on Glover's poem . . . but external evidence is silent on those two points' (Eric Partridge, *The French Romantics' Knowledge of English Literature*, 1924). Read, '. . . but there is no external evidence on those two points': *external evi-*

dence has, in the original, been too drastically personified.

'He doesn't go out much, but he gives a man's dinner now and then, which are the best in London' (John Buchan, *The Power-House*, 1916). Read, '. . . now and then, and these are the best dinners in London'.

'The handwriting was like a sick man of ninety' (John Buchan, *The Moon Endureth*, 1912); better, 'like a sick man of ninety's' or 'like that of a sick man of ninety'.

'But probably he did, as we still may, find much to interest us in the work of the Lancashire poets' (Eric Partridge, *A Critical Medley*, 1926). For 'us', read 'him'.

'Not only are the frontiers of science traced out, its specialist lines of development where they are most significant, but its social and philosophic meaning are set out in direct form' (a publisher's book-list, February, 1939). Either 'meaning is' or 'meanings are'; the latter is preferable.

'Mr McCabe's is by nature a provocative mind. He does not always want it, but he can never help it' (i.e., avoid it), writes Cameron McCabe, *The Face on the Cutting-Room Floor*, 1937. To what do these *it's* refer? *It* should refer to *a provocative mind*; but if it did, the second sentence would make less than sense. What the author intends is, I think, this:—'Mr McCabe's is a provocative mind. He does not always want *to be provocative*, but he cannot avoid being so (*or* provocative)'.

'Usually he had some clearly defined purpose behind all his actions' (Stephen Maddock, *Doorway to Danger*, 1938).

'I am one of these who cannot describe what I do not see' (Russell, *Diary during the Last Great War*). Read, 'I am one of those who cannot describe what they do not see'.

'Another mode of spending the leisure time is that of books' (Cobbett: cited by Nesfield).

'Of this, however, we may be sure that he has, like every capable general does, put himself in imagination in his enemy's place' (*The Daily Telegraph*, December, 1899: cited by Nesfield).

'The humblest citizen of all the land, when clad in the armor of a righteous cause is stronger than all the hosts of error' (William Jennings Bryan, at the National Democratic Convention, Chicago, 1896).

'You shall not press down upon the brow of labor this crown of thorn. You shall not crucify mankind upon a cross of gold' (*ibid.*).

'I have been a militant Communist and a constitutional Socialist and a Pacifist, and always there have been moments when I see all people . . . as frightened children' (article, 'Under Thirty', *The Spectator*, Dec. 17, 1937).

'The fifteenth century has been termed "the golden age" of the English labourer, and up to the middle of the nineteenth century this may have been so' ('Social and Economic History', by W. O. Massingberd, in vol. II, published in 1907, of *The Victoria County History* of Lincolnshire).

'A third public school man writes: "If one thinks a little, retailing is a very real, alive and gripping 'profession', and well it may be termed, perhaps never before a profession, it is highly specialised where one brings into play every faculty one has been given. To those men who have been fortunate to have a good education, there is nothing else I know where every subject he has been coached in has been brought into use at one time or another. With this being such he will always be an ever-awake and useful member of the community"' (*The New Statesman*, in 1938, quoting advertisements by members of the staff of a great London shop). That, I think, is the best example I have had the good fortune to find: it is perfect.

Now for a few examples from Mr Ramsay MacDonald, the Rt. Hon. David Lloyd George, Mr Elihu Root, and Herr Adolf Hitler. (I might have taken passages from the speeches of other politicians, e.g., the Rt. Hon. Mr X., and from the works or speeches of other dictators, e.g., Signor Mussolini: but I do not think that I should easily have bettered the ensuing infelicities.) They will evoke irreverent chortles from the critical: indeed from all who prefer clear to blurred, and definite to hazy writing.

'Relativity was written plainly across the pages of history long before Einstein applied it to the universe. Relatively, Capitalism has justified itself in relation to the absolute criterion of Capitalist aims; but in relation to the absolute criterion'—as though there were one!—'of social wealth, harmony and happiness, and individual welfare, Capitalism has not justified itself and has to be transformed into something that is higher' (James Ramsay MacDonald, 'Socialism for Business Men,' a speech delivered on Oct. 1, 1925, to the Liverpool Rotarians).

'No employer can appeal straight to the hearts of his people [his employees] to sacrifice themselves in the national interests, because the moment he does that he raises in their minds the problem of the relationship between employer and employed.—He raises in their minds that unfortunate conflict of the economic, industrial and social interests of the two sides to this economic problem. Until we can abolish the two sides, and unite them in a new form of social service, we shall not be able to appeal to the communal sense of both, in order to do sacrificial work for the benefit of the whole community. There lies the philosophical basis of the class conflict, and you cannot remove it except by re-organisation' (*ibid.*).

'Religion, as faith, can be professed under any circumstances' (*ibid.*). For 'any' read 'all'.

'You get a society which is like a pyramid standing on its apex. I would like to turn it round and then I would say, "That is now safe". You cannot do that in a day or a week. There must be a change of faith' (*ibid.*).

'Socialism is an idea. The growth of Socialism is shown by the continued application of sound ideas, modifying the form and structure of the society in which we live, and moulding it so that as time goes on the form becomes more and more like the absolute idea itself.— It is the same in architectural conception and the religious conception. It is the same as the ideas in a man's mind when he starts out to build up a business' (*ibid.*).

'Mr Chairman, I am one of those people who never hide the fact that I am a patriot. You get sometimes queer definitions of patriotism, and in accordance with those definitions I am ruled out. But I am one of those people indifferent to what "they say"' (Ramsay MacDonald, 'Patriotism True and False', a speech delivered in America on Oct. 11, 1929: in his *American Speeches*, 1930).

'I daresay I have not many years now here and certainly I am in the position of a man who feels that the remaining

sands in the upper part of the sandglass become more and more golden in their preciousness, and therefore I am not anxious to waste them. I am not interested, therefore, so much in looking back and trying to devise agreements such as might apply under circumstances which I believe, if you and I make up our minds, are now dead' (Ramsay MacDonald, 'Among Old Friends', Oct. 11, 1929: in *American Speeches*). The first sentence is a bewildering abomination, and the second sentence lacks a tail.

'We have been working as well as preaching in Europe and I think we have been working with a considerable amount of success. We have been seeing to this— and this is of fundamental importance —that public opinion is demanding that those responsible for governments should not only take the risk of war, which they take when they begin to build competitively their armaments, but they should take the risk of peace' (Ramsay MacDonald, 'The Risks of Peace', later the same day: *op. cit.*).

'The problem of leisure or how to use leisure is the problem of human life, and there is nothing that a university can do that you will bless it for in your later years' more than this—it will give you an opportunity of appreciating things for yourself' (*id.*, 'Education', Toronto, Oct. 16, 1929: *op. cit.*).

(On Oct. 21, 1929, to the assembled staff and students of McGill University, on the occasion of a Doctorate of Laws conferred on him by that university:) 'As Prime Minister of Great Britain, I take this as an evidence on your part of the abiding and enduring loyalty to the common Empire to which we both belong. As one who has come over in order to try and bring a little closer not in the form of an alliance, but in the form of a closer and more affectionate unity of spirit and understanding these two great nations I take it in conferring this degree you have also had in mind' (*op. cit.*).

But let us pass to that other politician, that more celebrated orator, the Right Honorable David Lloyd George. His is a different sort of woolliness—the woolliness that results from an excess of metaphor and from a surfeit of words; a woolliness much less woolly than Ramsay MacDonald's, for the general (as opposed to the particular) meaning is nearly always clear, as in 'The Curse of Feudalism' (published in *The People's Will*, 1910)—a speech that begins thus:—

'The progressive forces in this country [Great Britain] are bending their energies to the task of uprooting the mischievous power of feudalism. The reactionary elements in the country, on the other hand, are, with the same [i.e., an equal; or, a similar] energy, with the same zeal, but, perhaps, with different weapons, undertaking the task of nourishing and feeding these roots [*which* roots?], and deepening their hold on the soil, and by tariffs and by something they call reform of the House of Lords, real progress in this country is barred in every direction by the feudal power.' Here the luxuriant verbiage rather induces a sense of woolliness than produces sheer woolliness: the passage, indeed, is far from being sheerly woolly: and as it fell, unhalting, from the orator's silver tongue, it was, one cannot doubt, eloquent and perhaps even impressive.

'What business could ever be conducted under the conditions in which you conduct agriculture? Would you ever get a business man risking the whole of his capital on improvements on a year's tenancy? . . . No business man would invest and risk his capital without a certain measure of security that he will reap the reward of it' ('Labour the Road to Freedom', in *The People's Will*, 1910).

'Belgium, once comfortably well-to-do, is now waste and weeping, and her children are living on the bread of charity sent them by neighbours far and near. And France! The German army, like a wild beast, has fastened its claws deep into her soil, and every effort to drag them out rends and tears the living flesh of that beautiful land. The beast of prey has not leapt to our shores—not a hair of Britain's head has been touched by him' ('A Holy War', Feb. 28, 1915: *Through Terror to Triumph*, 1915). The accumulation of imperfect metaphor produces a sense of discomfort; the effect is—woolliness. Cf.:—

'This desolating war has been forced upon us by an arrogant military caste that sought to enslave Europe, who thought they had perfected a machine that would tear through her vitals and leave her crushed and bleeding at their feet. The Prussian means to dominate the world. That is a mania which has possessed the military castes in every century. Once or twice it has succeeded,

and that has upset the balance of many who thought they could follow. But although they will not succeed, nevertheless to overthrow that ambition will cost Europe a ghastly price in blood and in treasure' ('How Long Will the War Last?', May 7, 1915). The fecklessly rapid changes of the grammatical subject—changes made without due regard to consecutiveness—are indefensible: and the effect is woolliness.

'I am only concerned with the causes of the shortage in the equipment and material of war in so far as it is necessary to understand them with a view to making that shortage up. That the shortage is serious from the point of view of the standard which has been created by this war is undoubtedly well known' ('The Munitions Bill', June 23, 1915: *op. cit.*). Here the cause of woolliness is verbiage.

'The trenches are not all in Flanders. Every [coal-] pit is a trench in this war, a labyrinth of trenches; every workshop is a rampart, every yard which can turn out the munitions of war is a fortress' ('Coal and the War', July 29, 1915: *op. cit.*). Here it is the inaptitude and the inaccuracy of the metaphor which have caused the haziness and the muzziness.

'We have just emerged from a great peril. We have emerged triumphantly. The greatness of the peril we can hardly conceive at the present moment. It will take time for us fully to appreciate its vastness. The greatness of the triumph we cannot fully estimate now. I met a man the other day who came to me and said, "This victory is so vast that I can only take it in in parts". I think that that was one of the truest things said of our triumph. He said, "I see one phase of it to-day, and to-morrow I see another, and the third day I see another". That is true about the danger we have averted and about the victory we have achieved' ('Reconstruction', Nov. 24, 1918: *Slings and Arrows*, 1929).

'The story of Liberalism has not yet been told. Whether it will have the responsibility, the independent responsibility, for the destiny of this great people and this great Empire as it has in the past, or whether it will act in combination with others as it practically has done since 1886, and what combinations and associations there may be I am not going to predict, but I am quite sure that the central ideas that Liberalism stands for are vital to the life and the continued power and influence of this country and of the world' (April 20, 1927, at The 1920 Club: *ibid.*).

But let us take an American statesman. Elihu Root. He is less woolly than the two English statesmen from whom I have quoted; much less woolly, in fact, than Ramsay MacDonald. No one, however, will (I hope) deny that the following passages create a rather blurred impression.

'One accustomed to the administration of municipal law who turns his attention for the first time to the discussion of practical questions arising between nations and dependent upon the rules of international law, must be struck by a difference between the two systems which materially affects the intellectual processes involved in every discussion, and which is apparently fundamental.— The proofs and arguments adduced by the municipal lawyer are addressed to the object of setting in motion certain legal machinery which will result in a judicial judgment to be enforced by the entire power of the state over litigants subject to its jurisdiction and control' ('The Sanction of International Law', April 24, 1908: *Addresses on International Subjects*, 1916).

'The war [1914] began by a denial on the part of a very great power that treaties are obligatory when it is no longer for the interest of either of the parties to observe them. The denial was followed by action supported by approximately one half the military power of Europe and is apparently approved by a great number of learned students and teachers of international law, citizens of the countries supporting the view. This position is not an application of the doctrine *rebus sic stantibus* [affairs being at such a point (or, at such a pass) . . .] which justifies the termination of a treaty under circumstances not contemplated when the treaty was made so that it is no longer justly applicable to existing conditions. It is that under the very circumstances contemplated by the treaty and under the conditions for which the treaty was intended to provide the treaty is not obligatory as against the interest of the contracting party' ('The Outlook for International Law', Dec. 28, 1915: *ibid.*).

Elihu Root (1845–1937), however, was generally lucid and direct, despite his tendency to verbiage. Compared with Hitler, he was almost indecently lucid. The Führer (born April 20, 1889) generates so much heat and smoke that, far too often, one *feels* what he means but one cannot see clearly what it is he means; far too often, indeed, one has the impression that he is expressing, not a precise meaning but an emotion or an aspiration, or some grandiose ambition: if that is so, then one must, in fairness, admit that, for his purpose, he does not need to mean anything precise. But those who attempt to deduce a precise meaning from his fiery, vatidical speeches and writings are often baffled by the muzziness of his style and the woolliness of his oratory. One feels that he writes as he speaks: at top shriek.

The ensuing passages are taken from *My Struggle*, the abridged English translation (1933) of *Mein Kampf* (Part I, 1925; Part II, 1927).

'The *psyche* of the mass of the people is not receptive of anything savouring of half-measures and weakness.—Like a woman whose sensibilities are influenced less by abstract reasoning than by an indefinable longing governed by feeling, for the strength which completes what is to be done, and who would rather bow to the strong man than dominate the weakling, the people love a ruler more than a suppliant and feel more inwardly satisfied by doctrines which suffer no rival, than by an admission of liberal freedom; they have very little idea how to use it and easily feel forsaken. They are as little conscious of the shame of being spiritually terrorized as of an abuse of their freedom as human beings, calculated to drive them into revolt; nor are they aware of any intrinsic wrongness in the teaching' (I, ii).

'The Jewish doctrine of Marxism rejects the aristocratic principle in nature, and in place of the eternal privilege of force and strength sets up the mass and dead weight of numbers. It thus denies the value of the individual among men, combats the importance of nationality and race, thereby depriving humanity of the whole meaning of its existence and *Kultur*. It would, therefore, as a principle of the Universe, conduce to an end of all order conceivable to mankind. And as in that great discernible organism nothing but chaos could result from the application of such a law, so on this earth would ruin be the only result for its inhabitants' (I, ii).

'The ordinary attitude towards politics current with us to-day rests in general on the notion that creative and civilizing strength ought to be an attribute of the State, that the latter has no part in matters affecting race but is a product of economic necessity or, at the best, a natural outcome of political forces. Carried to its logical conclusion, this basic attitude leads not merely to misrepresentation of racial causes, but also to failure to assign to personality its proper value. For denial that there is a difference between races as regards their capacity for building up culture is bound to extend that great error to judgments formed concerning the personality of the individual. An assumption that all races are equal as regards character will be followed by a similar way of considering nations, and so on to individuals' (II, i). But enough of these.

WORDINESS. See VERBOSITY.

working-man and **working man; workman.** A *working man* is vague, for it = 'a man that is or happens to be engaged in work', whereas *a working-man* is 'a man employed to work for a wage, especially in a manual or industrial occupation'; *working-man* includes *artisan, mechanic, labourer*. (The corresponding female is a *working-woman*.) A *workman* is 'a man engaged, on a wage, to do manual labour', especially if he is 'employed upon some particular piece of work' (an *operative*); often, the context shows that 'a skilled worker' is meant; often too, it is opposed to *employer* or to *capitalist*, though *worker* (especially in the plural) is more usual in this opposition. *Workman* has the further, more general sense, 'one who works—or practises his craft or his art—in some specified manner', e.g., in painting; thus, 'My health makes me a very slow workman'. *Workwoman* is 'a female worker or operative'. (*The O.E.D.*)

world. See EARTH and SPHERE.

worse is misused in the following, quoted by *The D.N.B.* from Gough the antiquary as his opinion of his contemporary William Maitland (18th Century): 'He was self-conceited, knew little, and wrote worse.'

worst, misused for *most*, as in 'What I need worst is a haircut'. A thoroughly idiomatic usage of *worst* is that with verbs of liking or loving, allowing, pleasing, as in 'This pleased them worst of all', where *worst* = 'least'. (*The O.E.D.*)

worst two is incorrect for *two worst* in, e.g., 'The worst two pupils were sent down to the class below'. Cf. FIRST TWO (for *two first*).

would, misused for *were*. See SUBJUNCTIVE. Here is a particularly glaring example:—'"Would it not be better," Pyke said very slowly, "if you *would* be quite frank with me?"', W. S. Masterman, *The Perjured Alibi*, 1935.

would, misused for *will*. See PAST SUBJUNCTIVE.

would and **should.** *The O.E.D.* quotes Mrs S. Pennington, 1766, 'I choose rather that you would carry it yourself', as misusing *would* for *should*; cf. 'And as we walked together, I asked Ptah that if I could comfort this woman, she would tell me of her grief' (from a novel published in 1937).

From R. H. Mottram, *The Spanish Farm,* 'He made a gesture, and she accepted the fact that he was rather taken with her. He would be': this use of *would be* is a common colloquialism but verges on slang. It is a short cut; and for its effect, it depends very largely on the peculiar emphasis placed on 'would' by a speaker. It is hardly admissible in literature.—But these two paragraphs merely skim the question.

Apart from its subjunctival use, *should* is the past tense of that *shall* which = 'to be obliged (to do something)', and *would* is the past tense of that *will* which = 'to be resolved (to do something)'. Thus 'He *would* go (= he was determined to go), say what I might'; 'I would not (= was unwilling to, did not wish to, refused to) answer him when he spoke to me yesterday'; 'It seemed to him that he could nowhere find in his heart the chords that *should* answer directly to that music'; 'As I was walking along the High Street, whom *should* I meet but my cousin Tom', where 'should I' = 'I was fated to'.

In conditional sentences of Group II (sentences in which 'the principal clause speaks of what would be or would have been and in which the *if*-clause states, or implies, a negative'), *should* and *would* are used in what is virtually the same way: 'Even if I knew, I *would* not tell' (= *should* not *be willing* to tell, or should not wish to tell); 'Wert thou creation's lord, thou *shouldst* not taunt me thus' (= *wouldst* not *be permitted* to taunt me thus': here, *should* and *would* are subjunctives.

Properly subjunctive, too, is *should*

in 'You *should* do that', i.e., 'You *ought* to do that', i.e., 'You *would* be bound to do that', i.e., 'It *is* right for you to do that'; 'I know that I *should* do that, but I cannot bring myself to do it'. But what the practice amounts to is this: the past subjunctive *should* is not only used in all persons, but it is employed as, virtually, a present indicative synonymous with *ought*.

Would as a past indicative is occasionally used, synonymously with 'used to', for past habitual action: 'He paid little attention to what was being said: he *would* constantly be looking at the window': this usage is now literary, not general.

So far we have considered *should* and *would* as words having independent meaning. Now we come to their employment as mere indications and auxiliaries of time as expressed in tense—the past tense; *should* and *would* being used in dependence on verbs that are themselves in the past tense. 'I knew that if I stayed here, I *should* see him pass', 'I knew that if you stayed here, you *would* see him pass', and 'I feared that he *would* come to a bad end'.

Thence we pass to their employment as indications—and auxiliary verbs—of mood: as subjunctives and subjunctive-equivalents. In the principal clauses of conditional sentences of Group II (see CONDITIONAL CLAUSES), *should* is to be used for the 1st person, *would*, for the 2nd and 3rd persons, as in 'Though you said it a thousand times, I *should* not believe it—no one *would* believe it'. But in certain subordinate clauses, *should* is used in all three persons, thus:—

(a) In such clauses as have an action stated or implied to be under consideration (in prospect, or a subject of contemplation), as in 'He refused to budge until he should receive a thousand dollars'.

(b) In conditional clauses of Group III (i.e., in conditional sentences in which the principal clause does not state, nor imply, what would be or would have been, but in which the *if*-clause not only indicates an action that is contemplated or planned but also connotes some degree of reserve on the part of the speaker),—i.e., in such conditional clauses as 'If the king *should* fall, he will fall in fair fight'

and the disguised 'I am sorry that you should be so angry'.

(c) In certain dependent statements or commands, as in 'It is natural that I *should* visit my family', 'It was disgraceful that you *should* fail us in that way', 'I saw to it that he *should* not give me the slip', 'I feel that I *should* not be successful' (or 'I felt that I *should* not be successful'), 'Providence furnishes materials, but expects that we *should* work them up by ourselves', 'I grieved that you *should* take offence,' 'That he should have done this is surprising', 'It is right that you *should* be dismissed', 'He commanded that no one *should* leave the room'.

It is an odd fact that whereas *would* is colloquially shortened to *'d* (better *'ld*), *should* has no shortened form. In *The Observer*, 1938, Mr Conor O'Brien writes: 'Sir,—we think, and we say colloquially, "I'd like . . ." We are told that this can only be expanded to'—better, 'can be expanded only to'—"I would like," and as half of us don't recast our thoughts when writing, we write down "I would"', although the correct form is 'I should like (to do something)'. 'Why, in the name of common sense', Mr O'Brien continues, 'cannot this necessary abbreviation stand equally well for "I should"? If that were accepted we might get back the correct usage of "will" and "shall". Will some grammarian please summon up his courage?'

A pertinent query. The trouble is that *'d* already = *had* ('I'd done it already') and *would* (for which I prefer *'ld*). Yet *'ll* = *shall* or *will*, so why should not *'ld* represent *should* or *would*? [[*Webster's* and certain American grammarians give authority for *'d* and *'ld* to represent both *should* and *would*.]]

would best is unfortunate for *had best* in 'I think I would best rent a house', 'She would best avoid such a marriage'.

would better is incorrect for *had better* in 'I would better depart now'.

would have, in conditional sentences, is incorrect for *had*, as in 'If he would have wished, he could have spared you a troublesome journey'.

would rather and **had rather.** In the first person, *had rather* is almost obligatory ('I had rather die young than live to be a hundred'); in the third, *would* *rather* is perhaps the more usual ('He would rather sleep than eat'); in the second, 'You would perhaps rather wait here than at the house' is preferable to 'You had rather'.

wove and **woven.** *Wove* is the preterite of *weave*; *woven*, the usual past participle, *wove* being inferior except in such technicalities as *wove mould* and *wove paper*. (*The O.E.D.*)

wrack is misused for *rack* in at least three senses. It should be a *rack* of clouds; *rack*, an instrument of torture, even so good a scholar as Swinburne falling into 'She had no heart's pain, but mere body's wrack'; and the horse's gait should be *rack*. In the sense 'ruin', both forms are correct, as in go to (*w*)*rack and ruin*, but, except in that phrase and its variants (*bring to, put to, run to r. and r.*), *wrack*—a cognate of *wreck*—is the more general. (*The O.E.D.*)

wrapt and **rapt.** In 'He was absorbed in wrapt meditation', *wrapt* is incorrect for *rapt*. *Wrapt* or, more generally, *wrapped* is the past participle (and participial adjective) of *wrap*, 'to cover or swathe by enfolding in, e.g., a cloth', 'to cover or envelop (an object) by winding or folding something round or about it', etc. *Rapt* is the past participle (and participial adjective) of *rape*, 'to take and carry off by force', fig., 'to delight'. *Rapt* = 'taken and carried away', whether lit. or fig.; hence, 'transported with some emotion or thought', as in 'The book held me rapt', 'I stood gazing, rapt in admiration', 'Rapt in adoring contemplation', 'rapt by wonder'. (*The O.E.D.*)

wrath, 'anger', and **wroth,** 'angry' (a literarism), are sometimes confused.

wriggle. See at WIGGLE ...

wring—wrung—wrung are the inflections now current. The preterite *wrang* is now dialectal, therefore incorrect except in dialect. The past participle *wringed* is obsolete.

writ. The noun *writ* is obsolete except in the phrase *Holy* (or *Sacred*) *Writ*, the Bible or Holy Scriptures, and in Law (a *writ of certiorari, writ of venire facias*, etc.; 'a Parliamentary writ').—The past participle *writ* is archaic, as in 'The moving finger writes, and having writ, moves on'.

writer and **author.** See MAN OF LETTERS.

writer, the; the present writer. These are not wrong; *The O.E.D.* admits

them without comment. But they are to be used in moderation; in general, the honest *I* is preferable.

write upon impulse. See PREPOSITIONS WRONGLY USED.

wrong (adv.) is obsolescent for *wrongfully* (mistakenly, erroneously), as in 'You have been wrong informed *or* informed wrong'; for *wrongfully, wrongly*, in the sense 'unfairly, unjustly', as in 'to set right what one has done wrong' (morally); and for *amiss, unduly, improperly* (not in the proper way), as in 'Every guest's uneasiness lest he drink his coffee wrong' (Owen Wister), except in *to go wrong* (to turn out badly, to err, etc.). Note that *a word pronounced wrong* is now less common than *a word wrongly pronounced* (preferable to *a word pronounced wrongly*). (*The O.E.D.*)

WRONG TENSE. See TENSE-SEQUENCE.

wroth. See at WRATH ...

X

x and **ct** variants (*connection, connexion; reflection, reflexion*). See '-ECTION and -EXION'.

Xmas as a contraction of *Christmas*, barely allowable in its common use in writing and printing, has no excuse in the pronunciation, *Exmas*.

Y

Yankee, loosely applied (in England) to all Americans (i.e., of the U.S.A.), means only 'a citizen of the New England states (Massachusetts, Connecticut, etc.), or by extension a citizen of any Northern state as distinguished from a Southerner.

ye in such popular uses as 'Ye olde Englysshe Tea-Shoppe' is founded on a complete misconception of the old symbol þ, the letter 'thorn', which in Old English and Middle English represented the sound of *th*. In printing, the *y* was substituted for it and has come to be mispronounced.

yet cannot always, as an adverb, be used for *still* or *even*. 'Hilary's letter had been written on plain white paper, and the envelope was probably yet less distinctive' (Millward Kennedy, *I'll Be Judge, I'll Be Jury*, 1937), where 'still less' or 'even less' would be much better. See also ALTHOUGH ... YET.

Yiddish is so often misunderstood and misused that the editor feels it incumbent on him to mention that, although the language is written in Hebrew characters, it is not Hebrew nor yet a dialect of Hebrew. Yiddish is 'the language used by Jews in Europe and America, consisting mainly of German (orig. from the Middle Rhine area) with admixture (according to local or individual usage) of Baltic-Slavic or Hebrew words'. The word is simply the English form of German *jüdisch*, 'Jewish', short for *jüdisch-deutsch*, 'Jewish-German'. (*The O.E.D.*)

Note that *Yiddisher* is not any Jew, but a Jew that speaks *Yiddish*. And *Yid* is a vulgar shortening of *Yiddisher*.

you aren't and **you're not.** Cf. the entry at WE AREN'T.

you both. See BOTH OF US.

young and **youthful.** The former is literal, with the stress on the mere fact of age; the latter stresses the fact that one has, or is characterized by, youth, or that one is still young; *youthful* also = 'juvenile; characteristic of or suitable for the young'; and especially, 'having the freshness and vigour of youth'. 'Though he is a young man (only 21), one does not think of him as being youthful', 'youthful impatience', 'Here we have ... an unmistakable attack made by the youthful Socrates' (Jowett), 'The world was still at its youthful stage'. (*The O.E.D.*)

Cf. the entries at 'JUVENILE and PUERILE' and 'CHILDISH; CHILDLIKE'.

youth and **youthfulness.** *Youth* corresponds to *young*; *youthfulness* to *youthful*, as in the preceding entry. 'The youthfulness of the old man was astounding'; 'Even in youth, he was like an old man'.

yourself; yourselves for *you.* See MYSELF.

Date Due

APR 2 6 '56		
NOV 2 8 '62		
MAY 30 '6		
OCT 2 4 '67		
APR 2 9 '70		
AUG 20 '71		
JUL 26 '74		